Special Edition

USING BORLAND C++ 5

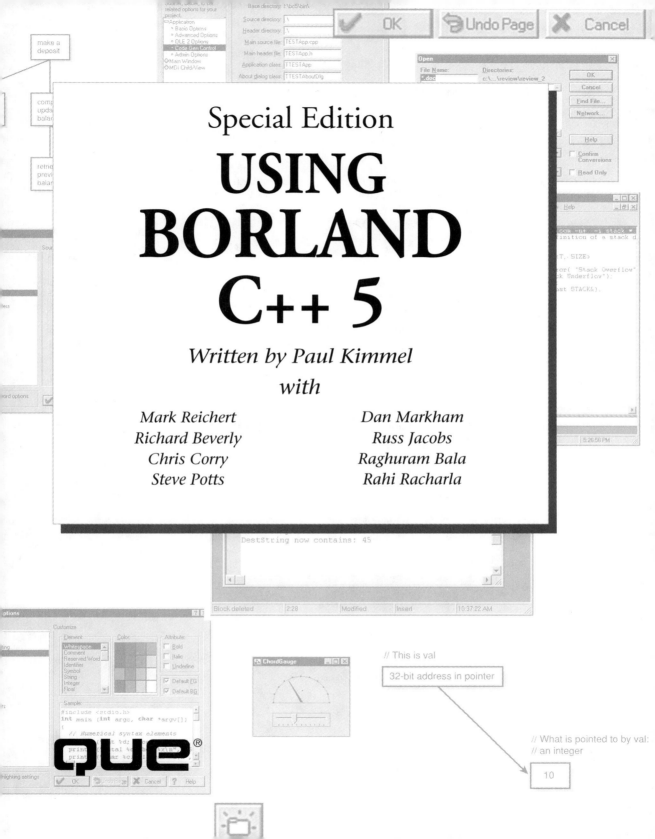

Special Edition

USING
BORLAND
C++ 5

Written by Paul Kimmel

with

Mark Reichert

Richard Beverly

Chris Corry

Steve Potts

Dan Markham

Russ Jacobs

Raghuram Bala

Rahi Racharla

Special Edition Using Borland C++ 5

Library of Congress Catalog No.: 95-71748

ISBN: 0-7897-0284-3

98 97 96   6 5 4 3 2 1

Interpretation of the printing code: the rightmost double-digit number is the year of the book's printing; the rightmost single-digit number, the number of the book's printing. For example, a printing code of 96-1 shows that the first printing of the book occurred in 1996.

All terms mentioned in this book that are known to be trademarks or service marks have been appropriately capitalized. Que cannot attest to the accuracy of this information. Use of a term in this book should not be regarded as affecting the validity of any trademark or service mark.

Screen reproductions in this book were created using Collage Plus from Inner Media, Inc., Hollis, NH.

Composed in *Stone Serif* and *MCPdigital* by Que Corporation

Credits

Publisher
Joseph B. Wikert

Editorial Services Director
Elizabeth Keaffaber

Managing Editor
Sandy Doell

Director of Marketing
Lynn E. Zingraf

Publishing Manager
Fred Slone

Product Directors
Kevin Kloss
Nancy D. Price

Production Editor
Caroline D. Roop

Editors
Elizabeth A. Bruns, Gillian Kent,
Susan Ross Moore, Anne Owen,
Nanci Sears Perry

Product Marketing Manager
Kim Margolius

Technical Editors
Karl Hilsmann, Steve Potts,
Dan Markham, Russ Jacobs

Technical Specialist
Nadeem Muhammed

Acquisitions Coordinator
Angela C. Kozlowski

Operations Coordinator
Patricia J. Brooks

Editorial Assistant
Andrea Duvall

Book Designers
Kim Scott
Ruth Harvey

Cover Designer
Dan Armstrong

Production Team
Anne Dickerson
DiMonique Ford
Jason Hand
George Hanlin
Sonja Hart
Damon Jordan
Daryl Kessler
Clint Lahnen
Julie Quinn
Kaylene Riemen
Laura Robbins
Bobbi Satterfield
Todd Wente
Jody York

Indexers
Sharon Hilgenberg
Craig Small

To Jack Nicholas Symons, the greatest man I have ever known.

—Paul Kimmel

About the Authors

Paul Kimmel is the president of the Okemos, Michigan-based Software Conceptions, Inc., which provides custom software development, software developer training, and technical writing services worldwide. He is the author of *Building Delphi 2 Database Applications* (also published by Que Corporation). Paul is married to Lori and father to Trevor, Douglas, Alex Marie, and Noah, all residing in Okemos, Michigan. He can be reached on CompuServe at **70353,2711** or via the Internet at **softcon@sojourn.com**.

Mark Reichert is a software engineer with SIRS, Inc., a publisher of multimedia reference materials for schools and libraries. His current project is a cross-platform, animated selection guide to popular children's books. Since 1987 he has applied object-oriented design and C++ internationally to such topic areas as world-wide software portability and reuse, compilers, computer-based instruction, real-time embedded systems, database design, and computer graphics. He lives in Boca Raton, Florida.

Richard Beverly graduated from Michigan State University with an MS in Computational Mathematics. While a student he became enthralled with software design and programming and hasn't looked back since. Richard has been programming with Borland C++ since 1990. He is currently a systems analyst at MSU and owns a software development firm called Sweetwater Software.

Chris Corry is a principal working in the Center for Advanced Technologies at American Management Systems of Fairfax, Virginia. Although his professional interests span a wide range of topics, he spends the majority of his time investigating object-oriented programming techniques, sofware component standards like OLE and OpenDoc, and distributed object technologies. He was a contributing author to *Killer Borland C++ 4* and *Using Visual C++ 2*, Special Edition, published by Que, and *OS/2 Unleashed*, published by Sams Publishing.

Steve Potts is a senior consultant for Osoft Development Corporation, an object-oriented software development firm based in Atlanta. Steve specializes in manufacturing and medical software systems on Windows platforms. He has authored numerous books on programming including *Killer Borland C++*, *Visual Basic 4 Expert Solutions*, *Visual Basic 4 By Example*, and *Using Visual C++ 4*.

Dan Markham is a computer consultant and freelance writer who has 15 years of experience in the computer industry. His recent work includes *Using MS Access*, published by Que Corporation and several articles for national magazines, including *Blue Ridge Country* and *Emergency*. He programs in 10 different languages and for the last five years has operated a consulting company, Kreative Kreations, from his home in Virginia. Dan specializes in object-oriented analysis and design and his clients include Fortune 500 companies from both the East and West coasts. He can be reached at 540-297-9187.

Russ Jacobs is a programmer/analyst for The Prudential. He is also the president of SoftWare Alchemy. He has been programming on the PC for 10 years using Pascal, BASIC, C, and C++ in the DOS, Windows, OS/2, and NT environments. Russ has contributed his expertise as technical editor for over 10 Que books, including *Visual Basic 3 By Example* and *Killer Borland C++*.

Raghuram Bala is a senior software engineer at Pencom Software in New York City with seven years of experience in developing client-server applications on Windows and UNIX using C++, Java, PowerBuilder, Delphi, Sybase, Oracle and DCE Tools. His current interests lie in the area of distributed application architectures utilizing Web technologies, communications protocols, and OOP. Mr. Bala formerly worked with Price Waterhouse as a senior consultant and served as an adjunct lecturer at Columbia University. He also frequently writes for various industry publications and serves as a contributing editor for several books.

Rahi Racharla is a senior software engineer at Pencom Software with over four years of experience in distributed client-server computing. He worked on various high-profile projects using C++, SmallTalk, X-windows, Delphi, AION, and Sybase. His present interests are distributed tier-less object-oriented technology, Internet Application development, and Java.

Acknowledgments

I would like to thank the many people who made this book possible: my wife Lori Kimmel, for being my best friend; my children Trevor, Douglas, Alex, and Noah, for the stolen moments; my mother Jacqueline, for each step; David Benavides, a giant among men; and my father Gerald, for inspiring a love of the written word.

I would also like to thank the many people who made this book from my manuscript. I would like to thank Caroline Roop at Que for keeping it all straight. Special thanks to Fred Slone and Lori Jordan (I hope you write a double-platinum song). I would like to thank everyone at Que Corporation who made this book possible. Special thanks to Mark Reichert, Chris Corry, Rich Beverly, and Brian Hildreth for pitching in.

My appreciation is extended to Dr. Robert Sedgewick at Princeton for letting me borrow ideas from his book *Algorithms in C++* (Addison-Wesley), and Addison-Wesley for their generous permission.

Contents at a Glance

Basic Features

Programming in C++

Advanced Programming

Using New C++ Features

Programming Tools

Appendixes

Contents

5 Commenting and Naming Conventions   77

6 Native Data Types and Operators   99

7 Pointers and References   125

8 Understanding Expressions through Expansion   145

27 Using the AppExpert 697

28 Using the ClassExpert 707

29 Using the Integrated Debugger 727

Introduction

Borland has long been committed to being the software developer's company. Borland C++ 5 again makes this eminently clear. Nowhere else are you likely to find such a complete implementation of C++. This book will give you an interpretation of this Windows 95, 32-bit development platform through the eyes of many people. As you read this book, you will see Borland's C++ implementation as we see it. It is impossible to tell you everything in one book because much of it hasn't been imagined yet. Some of what has not been done with Borland's C++ can be done by you. The latest features incorporated in the ANSI C++ specification of the language are found in this book.

Borland C++ Features

Some of the highlights of the language are the new ANSI String class, RTTI (Run-Time Type Identification), template classes, the new STL (Standard Template Library), and exception handling. Borland has coupled an exceptionally well-rounded implementation with a newer IDE, including an integrated Resource Workshop on top of a 32-bit operating system. That's power.

Special Edition Using Borland C++ 5 covers three aspects. The first is Borland's implementation of C++. This book provides extensive coverage of the C++ programming language; you will be hard-pressed to find this type of coverage anywhere else. The second is the user-friendly, fully integrated development environment, or IDE. Borland has incorporated changes to make the IDE more intuitive and functional. Third, is the extensive coverage of advanced topics, 32-bit language extensions, and the wide array of development tools that you get when you use Borland's C++.

This is not just a book on C++, nor is it just a book on a newer IDE or the assortment of tools provided to Borland developers. It is all three. If you are a novice and are at the first corner, fast approaching a speed bump, we'll help you learn C++. You get all of the information about a premier software developer's company and its product. (You may think Borland is giving me a product endorsement. I wish.)

Conventions Used in This Book

The following typographical conventions have been used throughout this book:

- A word or phrase that is used for the first time appears in *italic*.
- Text that you are asked to type appears in **boldface**.
- Screen displays, on-screen messages, and code appear in monospace. In code listings, if a line is too long, a code continuation character (➥) appears, indicating that the code continues on the second line.

What This Book Contains

In Part I, "Using C++'s Basic Features," you see what's new in Borland C++ 5, including an introduction to the new IDE and a chapter on object-oriented analysis and design. You also begin building the foundation that makes understanding more advanced topics easier.

In Part II, "Programming in C++," pointers and references are discussed; they afford C++ developers an expressiveness that allows developers to define their own memory-management systems. Chapter 8, "Understanding Expressions through Expansion," describes how to understand what some perceive to be the most advanced features of the language, including function and operator overloading. For the novice, there are topics on native data types and writing expressions, which provide the basis for aggregate types.

Part III, "Advanced C++ Programming," shows you how to use tried-and-true functions from the standard library and thoroughly explains and demonstrates some of the most advanced features of C++ programming. This section blows away the misconception that some of the most advanced idioms are difficult to learn. They are precise but not impossible. By the time you wind your way to Part IV, you'll have an intimate knowledge of C++, enabling you to use the most powerful and expressive features of this language.

Part IV, "Using New C++ Features," continues the language discussion with a chapter on inheritance and polymorphism. Other topics include the ANSI C++ String class, exception handling, Run-Time Type Information (RTTI), and namespaces.

Part V, "Borland C++ Programming Tools," contains the chapters "Using the Graphics Device Interface" and "Using the Multiple Document Interface." This part concludes with coverage of the suite of tools provided by Borland, including the AppExpert, Class Expert, Integrated Debugger, Winsight and WinSpector, and the new Integrated Resource Workshop.

> **Note**
>
> To a large extent, Parts III, IV, and V involve a discussion of the C++ language. While the developer will have to understand C++ to use the Object Windows Library (OWL), the chapters are not written from that perspective. OWL is an implementation built using C++, but is not the only way to write Windows programs with or without Borland C++. However, if the user understands the C++ language, OWL will be easier to use. The converse is not true.

Part VI, "Appendixes," provides you with an insight into the architecture, design, and inner workings of the Java language and its associated toolset. In addition, you learn how to build Java applications using the latest Borland C++ 5's Add-On Environment for Java, which includes tools such as AppExpert, AppAccelerator, and the Java Debugger. Borland also enables you to rebuild the Microsoft Foundation Classes (MFC) and use them with the Borland C++ 5 compiler.

In addition to all of that, topics have been added that make this book an easy-to-understand, extensive guide to the C++ language that we hope you'll refer to when you face some of your most interesting challenges. Find a cozy spot in the bookstore or maybe next to your computer and enjoy the sights and sounds of a fascinating language.

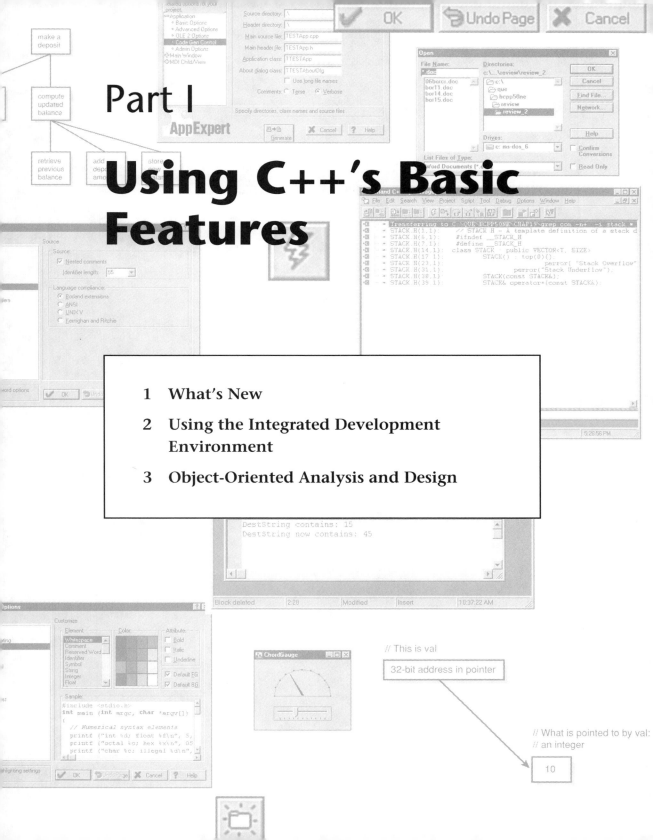

Part I

Using C++'s Basic Features

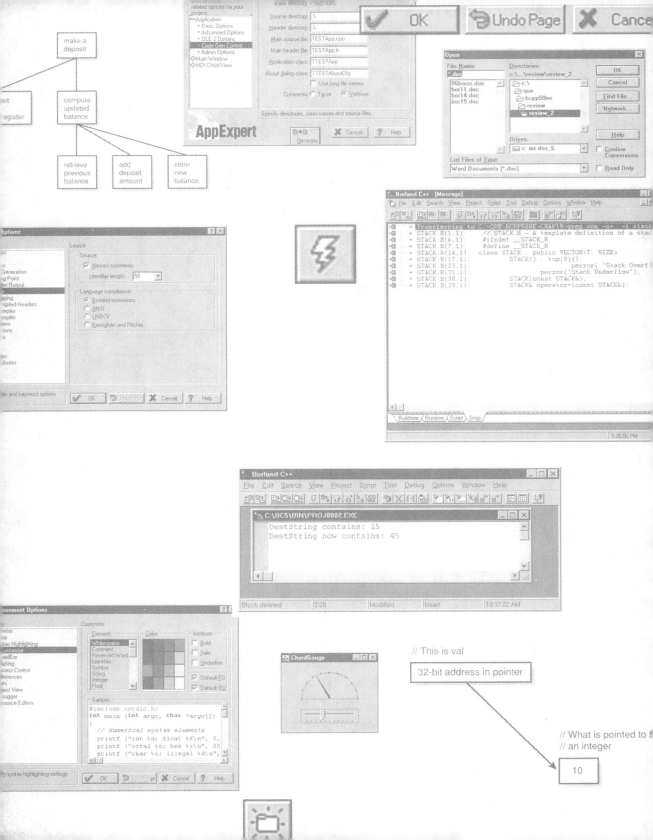

CHAPTER 1

What's New

Welcome to Windows 32-bit software development. This version of Borland C++ gives you asynchronous compiling and editing and faster executables. There are many new tools for building and distributing 32-bit applications. Borland C++ 5 enables you to build and debug Java applications in the integrated development environment (IDE). Borland C++ builds highly optimized executables with C++, the language pervading almost every other Windows language and uses one of the hottest new products, Java. This book explains advanced features of the C++ programming language, demonstrates Windows 95 32-bit advantages, and shows you how to take advantage of some hot new features from Borland.

To develop Windows 95 applications, you'll need this version of Borland C++ to do it. But, if you are like me, you are probably hoping for something more than compatibility. Once again, Borland has offered a lot of new and powerful features as well as new enhancements on existing features.

In this chapter, I will introduce you to the following features:

- The new 32-bit hosted IDE, which is a multithreaded application supporting asynchronous compiles and edits
- The new language tools that make implementing advanced features easier, including a Java debugger and compatibility
- Updated debugging tools that make 32-bit debugging a snap
- The inclusion of *InstallShield Express*, which makes distributing your applications easier and is one of my favorite add-ons

Introducing the New 32-Bit Hosted IDE

Some of the features discussed in this section can be implemented immediately. Other features might require some additional learning. The 32-bit integrated development environment is more than just a version upgrade. You get more power, faster applications, greater flexibility in managing the IDE itself, and an integrated Resource Workshop, all making your development process and the final product world-class.

New 32-Bit Multithreaded IDE

It has become cliché to say that any tool-building product must first be used to implement itself. Borland has done just that with C++ 5. Borland used this version of the compiler to build the IDE and the language extensions mentioned in this chapter.

The IDE uses the multithreading capabilities of the Windows 95 C++ compiler to implement multithreading in the IDE. Now you can edit your source code files while your application is building. (You still can't debug and compile at the same time.) The ability to simultaneously compile applications and edit the source code they are dependent on is referred to as *asynchronous compile and edit.*

Introducing the New 32-Bit Optimizing Compiler

You are using the Borland 32-bit optimizing compiler by default. The Bcc32.exe is the fast compiler you are used to. All you have to do to use the Bcc32i.exe compiler, which compiles more slowly but produces more highly optimized executables, is to select the Intel Optimizing Compiler from the Options, Project, 32-bit Compiler page.

The 32-bit compiler produces faster executable files. It takes advantage of the greater memory capacities and the Windows 95 operating system to optimize your code to a greater extent. While you may feel that the compilation process is slower, the compiler is actually doing much more work to produce faster code than ever.

Object Scripting

Object scripting offers you an object-oriented scripting language that allows you to customize the Borland IDE. The object scripting language is like C++ but like any other tool is still something you (the reader) will need to learn, to take full advantage of.

Borland offers many script file examples (*.spp) to help you learn how to use this feature. Remember, it is an object-oriented feature, so many of the implementation specifics are similar to C++ programming constructs. Chapter 2, "Using the Integrated Development Environment," demonstrates Borland C++ 5's new object scripting feature.

Integrated Resource Workshop

In earlier versions of Borland C++, you used the Resource Workshop to create, store, and reuse Windows resources such as icons, bitmaps, and cursors. The new integrated Resource Workshop can still be run as a separate application, but its ability to be incorporated into the IDE is seamless and easy to access.

If you already know how to use the Resource Workshop, you won't have any problems using it in Windows 95. Chapter 31, "Using the Resource Workshop," provides several detailed examples demonstrating how to use this feature.

Creating Add-On Interfaces

Borland has made features of the IDE available to developers, which facilitates the inclusion of custom add-on features. The text file \Bc5\Doc\Addon.txt describes which aspects of the IDE are available and the steps necessary for including custom add-ons.

The document Addon.txt lists the features of the IDE that are accessible for customization. These features are

- Commands and menus
- View management
- Editor buffers
- Virtual file system
- Make engine
- Add-on pages for option dialog boxes
- Project management
- Status bar
- Script engine
- Target options
- Tool management
- Custom target

The add-on capable IDE is (according to Borland) undergoing extensions. The last word on add-ons is provided in the Addon.txt document.

Language Tool Extensions

Borland has always taken the lead in providing development products for software developers. Their role includes providing a consistently high match to the ANSI/ISO C++ language and tools that enable developers to develop more robust applications quickly and easily.

In version 5, Borland has added features that enable you to develop a wider range of target applications. You can still build DOS-standard and DOS-overlay applications. You can build Windows 3.x, 16-bit applications, and, of course, 32-bit applications for Windows 95 and Windows NT.

Borland continues to provide backward-compatibility to earlier PC-based operating systems. In addition, Borland C++ 5 supports OCX container classes, Delphi integration, VBX controls, ObjectWindows' classes for WinSock, ObjectWindows for Windows 95 controls, and a Java debugger. Borland also provides examples that demonstrate how to use the Microsoft Foundation Class (MFC) library.

Introducing the Standard Template Library

Almost everyone agrees that the template idiom provides an extremely powerful and flexible way to maximize reusability. Templates, however, seem to be one of the more challenging aspects of C++ to master. Borland C++ version 5 includes a Standard Template Library (STL). Chapter 19, "Using Template Classes," covers some of the most powerful container classes and associated iterators already defined and ready for you to use and demonstrates how to use the BIDS and STL libraries in painstaking detail.

For online documentation, refer to the new Stl.hlp Help file. The STL libraries were provided by Rogue Wave. The Help file \Bc5\Help\STL.hlp and associated tutorial examples demonstrate how to use the template classes. The Standard Template Library itself includes classes such as Stacks, Queues, Vectors, Sets, Lists, and Maps, and a plethora of generic algorithms.

OCX Container Class Support

The ObjectComponents Framework has been extended to support building OLE controls (OCX containers). For an example of building OCXs, the tutorial in \Bc5\Examples\Owl\Tutorial\Step18 demonstrates how to use Borland C++ 5 to build powerful containers.

If you are keeping up with the changes in technology, be aware that VBXs (Visual Basic controls) only work in the 32-bit world if a thunking layer is used. In fact, VBX controls were never intended to be used with 32-bit programming languages. Alternatively, OLE controls (or OCXs) were designed for 32-bit operating systems and are intended to be more powerful and portable across different system configurations.

Delphi 2 and C++ Integration

Borland C++ offers greater integration with its new version of Delphi, version 2. The demo applications in \Bc5\Examples\Delphi demonstrate how to integrate Delphi .dlls and .obj files into C++ applications and vice versa. (You can specify that Delphi 2 units compile to .obj files now.)

You will need Delphi versions 2 and C++ 5 to try out the Borland C++ 5 Delphi examples. There are many supporters of the idea of truly language-independent reusable code. Borland, always a leader in developer technology, is moving closer to that ideal.

Support for the Microsoft Foundation Classes

If you want or need to use the Microsoft Foundation Classes for new or existing applications, Borland now provides support for the MFC libraries. The files \Setup\Mfc32\Readme.txt and \Setup\Mfc40\Readme.txt (on the Borland C++ 5 CD) were used as resources for appendix C, "Using the Microsoft Foundation Classes," which describes the process necessary for using MFC classes.

While using the MFC libraries does require a patch and a rebuild of those libraries, the Borland C++ 5 IDE does include integrated support for MFC. If you look at the TargetExpert in figure 1.1, you'll see that MFC support is provided in the IDE by selecting a check box.

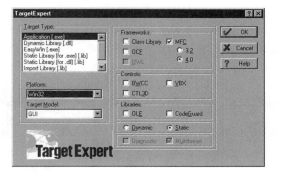

Fig. 1.1

The Borland C++ 5 TargetExpert has support for MFC integrated into the IDE.

Basic Features

ObjectWindows Classes for Winsock.dll

Classes were added to the ObjectWindows Library (OWL) to allow indirect support for .dlls unavailable on some platforms. The class TWinSock provides access to the Winsock.dll, TCommCtrl offers indirect support for CommCtrl.dll, and TWinG provides access to the WinG.dll.

The TCommCtrl class provides support indirectly for new Windows 95 custom controls, like the new Rich Text Format (RTF) editor tool. The RTF is commonly used to create Windows Help documentation. By indirect support, Borland is referring to the idea of using new Windows 95 controls for Window 3.*x*, 16-bit emulation, and Windows NT 3.51.

The TWinSock classes enable your applications to communicate over the Internet. The new Windows Socket classes are:

- TDatagramSocket
- THostInfoManager
- TINetSocketAddress
- TServiceManager
- TSocket
- TSocketAddress
- TSocketError
- TSocketManager
- TStreamSocket

The Socket classes offer support for both the Transmission Control Protocol (TCP) and User Datagram Protocol (UDP) data-transmission protocols.

ObjectWindows 5.0 Supports New Windows 95 Controls

The ObjectWindows Library (OWL) 5.0 has been extended to include support for new Windows 95 controls. Many of the OWL classes that support Windows 95 controls have been extended to offer 16-bit emulation of these controls, so you can get the Windows 95 look and feel in Windows 3.*x* applications. In addition to providing support for Windows 3.*x*, the ObjectWindows Library provides an implementation of Windows 95 controls that is compatible with Windows NT 3.51.

Figure 1.2 shows the output from the \Bc5\Examples\Win95\Comdlg32 project, which uses some of the new Windows 95 controls to produce the dialog box shown.

Fig. 1.2

An example of a Windows 95 look-and-feel dialog box, created with the new Windows 95 classes in the ObjectWindows Library.

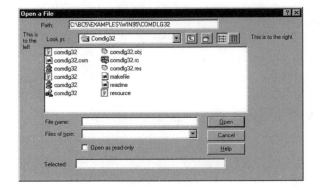

New Win32 Software Developer's Tools

Borland has extended and licensed tools from Microsoft's Win32 Software Developer Kit (SDK). Among these tools are the Help Compiler for Windows (HCW) and Help Workshop (HCRTF). The Win32 SDK tools are located in the \Bc5\Sdktools directory.

New 32-Bit Debugging Support

For 32-bit applications, you need 32-bit debuggers. Borland has extended CodeGuard, an integrated utility that adds debug code to your applications in development, to work with 32-bit applications as well as 16-bit applications. Turbo Debugger for Windows now also runs under Windows NT. The latest additions to the Borland C++ 5 suite are Java compatibility and debugging (see appendixes A and B for more information on Java). Figure 1.3 shows the ArcTest Java application included with Borland C++ 5, executing from the IDE.

As always, Borland is on the leading edge of language support and provides a complete set of tools to enable you to create robust, bug-free applications.

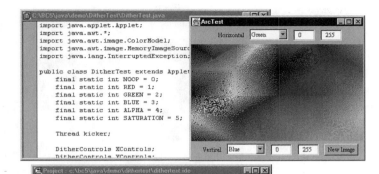

Basic Features

Fig. 1.3

A Java project window (lower-left), the code (upper-left) and the demo program ArcTest (upper-right) running from the Borland C++ 5 IDE.

CodeGuard

CodeGuard now works with Windows 95 32-bit applications. CodeGuard helps you to find errors in applications at runtime. By selecting CodeGuard protection in the TargetExpert (refer to fig. 1.1), it can help you detect errors caused by memory and resource misuse and validate function use.

CodeGuard detects errors associated with using faulty pointers, and problems that are indicative of lost references to memory (the slicing problem) in your applications. (Refer to chapter 17, "Constructors: Copy and Assignment," to learn some of the causes and how to avoid problems in C++ applications.)

C++ is a powerful, expressive language that lets you access memory directly. While pointers and references (see chapter 7, "Pointers and References") give C++ some of its power, they also provide an avenue for memory leaks in C++. Memory leaks are one of the most pervasive problems in C++ applications; they are due to improperly used resources, not shortcomings in the language. The techniques in this book and CodeGuard help seal memory leaks permanently.

Turbo Debugger for Windows NT

The award-winning Turbo Debugger for Windows (see fig. 1.4) can now be used with Windows NT. With Borland C++ 5, you can create applications with the Window 95 look and feel and debug them in Windows NT. The look, feel, and power of the new Turbo Debugger with Windows NT-compatibility is still as powerful and easy to use as ever.

Fig. 1.4

The Turbo Debugger for Windows 95 steps through the Commdlg demo program included with Borland C++ 5.

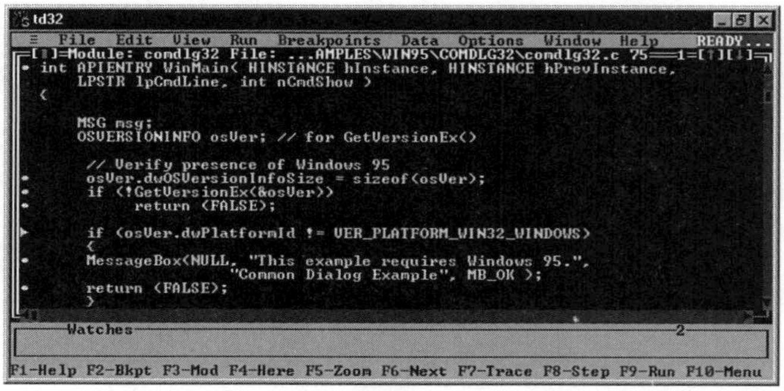

Additional resource material for Turbo Debugger (Td32.exe) for Windows 95 and Windows NT is found in \Bc5\Readme.txt and \Bc5\Doc\Td_rdme.txt. In these files, you'll find information about any last minute changes, as well as cool information about how you modify the Tdw.ini file video options section

```
[VideoOptions]
MONO=yes
```

to enable dual-monitor support. (You'll need a monochrome adapter and Crt, also.)

You can also use Td32 to debug multiple, simultaneous executables, which include Dynamic Link Libraries (DLLs). For many debugging chores—you'll learn how to employ some advanced techniques in chapter 4—the Integrated Debugger is an excellent tool, but when you need award-winning power, use Td32.exe.

InstallShield Express

InstallShield Express from Stirling Technologies and included with the Borland C++ 5 suite is a welcome addition. InstallShield is an intuitive and flexible application that enables you to create redistributable disks. InstallShield Express is BDE-aware, so it is fully capable of creating redistributable database applications.

Now you can easily design redistributable applications all from within the Borland C++ 5 suite of tools. Use object-oriented analysis and design, implement your DOS, Windows 3.*x*, Windows 95, or Windows NT applications, and when you are ready, you can create redistribution disks with InstallShield Express. It doesn't get any better than this.

From Here...

This chapter has introduced many of the new features of the Borland C++ 5. What I find most amazing about many of the new features is their seamless intregration into the IDE that is so familiar.

You won't have to look far to build and debug Java applications in the IDE, and using the Intel 32-bit optimizing compiler requires setting one button in the environment options, making highly optimized executables a snap.

As mentioned in this chapter, features like using Microsoft Foundation Classes (MFC), ansynchronous editing and compiling, and object scripting are a part of the IDE. To learn more about the new features of Borland C++ 5, check out the following chapters:

- Chapter 2, "Using the Integrated Development Environment," shows you how to access some of the features of the new 32-bit development environment.

- Chapter 4, "The Preprocessor," demonstrates some powerful debugging techniques that you can easily employ.

- Chapter 7, "Pointers and References," explains how and when to use pointers and addresses in function arguments and return types, and what kinds of performance benefits are provided by doing so.

- Chapter 17, "Constructors: Copy and Assignment," describes these two functions and how they can help you seal the most common source of memory leaks.

- Chapter 18, "Using Container Classes," demonstrates how to use the BIDS container classes and the new Standard Template Library.

- Chapter 19, "Using Template Classes," shows you how to select candidate functions and classes for templates.

- Chapter 31, "Using the Resource Workshop," teaches you how to incorporate reusable resources.

- Appendix C, "Using the Microsoft Foundation Classes," demonstrates how to recompile the Microsoft Foundation Classes so you can use them with Borland C++ 5.

CHAPTER 2

Using the Integrated Development Environment

In chapter 1, "What's New," you had your first taste of the Borland Integrated Development Environment (IDE). It is a complete workshop from which all of your creations can be built. The IDE contains everything that you will need to write, compile, run and debug your applications.

In this chapter, you learn:

- What the different interface elements of the IDE are
- How the IDE works
- How to configure the IDE to suit your own tastes
- What options you can set to personalize the IDE Editor
- What projects are and how to work with them

Introducing the IDE

The development environment that is provided with Borland C++ 5 is one of the finest in the industry. You can define all aspects of your projects from one interface. You can compile, test, run, and debug your programs from one easy, intuitive program. Figure 2.1 shows the default IDE after being started.

You notice a window with the path that you installed on your compiler, appended with the filename Noname00.cpp, which is the default state when the IDE opens. The IDE provides you with an editor window for typing in your own code. You can use this window to create a program, but you want to be able to customize and define your program before you begin writing the code.

The menu bar across the top of the main IDE window provides a wealth of functionality. Don't let the sheer number of options make you nervous; these options are explored slowly and methodically. The main interface elements are described in the next section.

Fig. 2.1

The default IDE screen.

IDE Interface Elements

The IDE allows you to maintain and compile all of your projects and programs. If you look at the menu bar, you will see eleven options. The easiest way to learn anything, of course, is to do it. So let's look at the different interface elements of the IDE.

The File Menu

The File menu (see fig. 2.2) in the IDE has features you've come to expect from a Windows application. You can use the File menu to create a new file; open, save, and print an existing file; or set up your printer.

Fig. 2.2

The IDE File menu.

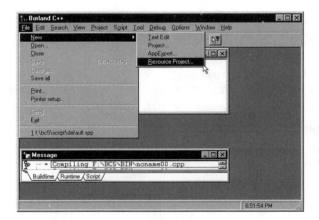

The Edit Menu

The menu bar also includes the Edit menu, which is a fairly common menu option for Windows applications. Choosing the Buffer List command allows you to see the currently active files and choose which one you want to work with. The buffer list is shown with the currently active files in the list (see fig. 2.3).

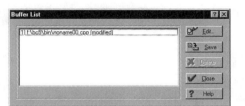

Fig. 2.3

The buffer list available from the Edit menu.

The Search Menu

Figure 2.4 shows the Search menu, which can be used to locate text phrases, or do a search and replace. There are several other commands the Search menu provides in Borland C++ 5 that are not common to other programs that just process text. The Locate Symbol command allows you to locate a function, member or constant symbol, enabling you to look for a particular function you have created. This can be especially helpful in larger projects when you don't remember exactly where a function exists.

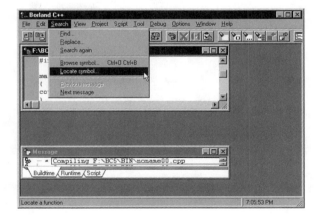

Fig. 2.4

The Search menu.

Another powerful feature available on the Search menu is the Browse Symbol command, which allows you to select text in your file and perform a lookup of the function, class, or operator. Figure 2.5 shows the browser window after highlighting the operator cout in the edit window. The browser allows you to look through your objects, functions, and variables. The scope of what you can browse does not have to include only your programs, but can include any classes, functions, or variables that are linked into your program.

Fig. 2.5

The Symbol Browser showing the cout *function.*

The View Menu

The View menu allows you to select different aspects of your program to view. If you look at figure 2.6, you will see the Project and Message options are grouped together. Both of these choices bring up different windows at the bottom of the IDE by default.

Fig. 2.6

The View menu.

Choosing View, Project shows all of the modules and files that are a part of a project. (shown is the Whello.ide project included with Borland C++ 5). You can double-click on any item in the Project window to view that item further. If you double-click on the Whello.rc, you reveal what that item is. Figure 2.7 shows the Whello.ico level of the project that is needed by the Whello.rc module. Notice the hierarchy of dependencies indicating which files are required, or dependent upon others.

The View menu offers you the ability to peer inside the inner workings and dependencies of your applications. Choosing the Classes and Globals options allows you to browse through your application's classes and global variables. Figure 2.8 shows the browser with all of the global variables within the sample application shown. Notice the Filters options below the Search text box. You can narrow the scope of data that is viewed by using the filters. For the Global browse in figure 2.8, the filters are Functions, Types, Variables, Constants, and Debuggable.

Fig. 2.7

The Project view showing nested dependencies.

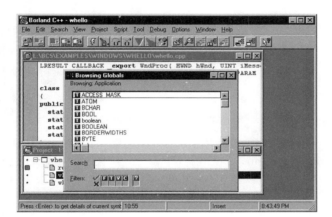

Fig. 2.8

Browsing globals from the View menu.

Using the filters in the browser enables you to see only the parts of your application you are interested in. For example, you can view only the functions or only the parts of the program that you can step into with the Debugger. There is a check mark and an "X" shown for the two rows of the filters. The default is for all filters to be used. To turn off a particular filter, simply click the mouse in the "X" row of that item. Figure 2.9 shows the Filters setup with only the variables that are debuggable selected.

Fig. 2.9

Using the filters in the browser.

The Script Menu

Borland C++ has included a new feature in version 5: the ability to create scripts and have them executed upon startup. These scripts can be used to automatically set up or configure your IDE. The scripting menu is shown in figure 2.10.

Fig. 2.10

The Script menu.

The script feature is similar to the macro feature in a word processor. The Script menu gives a listing of all of the "macro" commands that can be placed into a script to automate some of the processes that may take place in the development cycle on a regular basis. This can help to streamline some of the operations. It can activate the IDE as well as simulate keyboard input. Choosing Run brings up an edit box at the bottom of the IDE frame that asks for a script name. This script is then executed. The scripting feature is not limited to startup and can be used to perform common operations on the project.

The Project Menu

The Project menu shows all of the options related to creating and maintaining your projects (see fig. 2.11). You can specify a new target for your program. These menu commands allow you to create programs for different operating platforms. You can also compile, make, and perform a build on your projects. The final command allows you to have the IDE generate a makefile based on your current project. Projects themselves are covered in more detail later in this chapter in the section "Working with Projects."

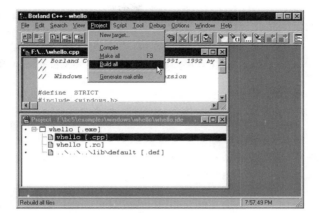

Fig. 2.11

The Project menu.

The Tool Menu

The Tool menu contains a variety of tools to assist you in creating your programs. The Turbo Debugger command is the offspring of the early DOS-based Turbo Debugger that came with Borland's Turbo C and Turbo Pascal. Re-written to run in Windows, this program allows you to debug your programs and see the results in Windows. When you start the program, you see a character-based GUI Debugger (see fig. 2.12).

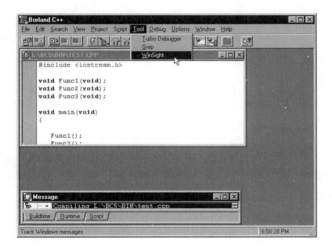

Fig. 2.12

The Tool menu.

You can use the Grep command to look for text. Grep was originally a UNIX-based test search tool that would search multiple files for the occurrence of a text string. This can be particularly helpful as the size of your project grows and you cannot remember just where you put a certain piece of code. Remember that the Grep command is case-sensitive. If you are looking for `MainDlgProc`, searching for `mainDlgproc` will not find the string that you are looking for. The last command on the Tool menu is WinSight. This is a programming aid that allows you to monitor application and system messages.

The Debug Menu

You can interactively run and debug your applications right from within the IDE. These options are available from the Debug menu. The Debug menu is shown in figure 2.13. The commands of the Debug menu will be covered in depth in chapter 29, "Using the Integrated Debugger."

Fig. 2.13

The Debug menu.

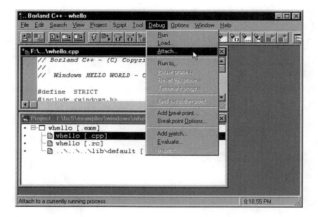

The Options Menu

The first two commands in the Options menu—Project and Environment—allow you to configure your projects and the IDE itself. The Options menu is shown in figure 2.14. Both of these commands are covered in detail later in this chapter in the section "Configuring the IDE."

Choosing the Tools option allows you to run a variety of external tools without leaving the IDE. You can even define your own if they are not already included. Figure 2.15 shows the Tools dialog box.

You also can choose the Style Sheets option to define your project's behavior. Style sheets define default compile and runtime options for your projects. Figure 2.16 shows the Style Sheets dialog box.

Fig. 2.14

The Options menu.

Fig. 2.15

The Tools dialog box.

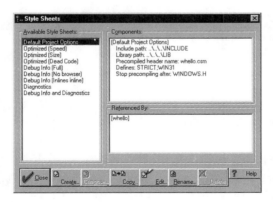

Fig. 2.16

The Style Sheets dialog box.

Choosing the Save command on the Options menu displays the Save Options dialog box (see fig. 2.17). In this dialog box, you can save your project settings. This can be useful if you have special requirements for different projects. You can have different colors and editor choices for different projects. Selecting the Environment option saves all of your custom settings. The Desktop option saves all of your desktop files, and the Project option saves all of your project-related files. All of these options are checked by default. This means that when you shut down the IDE, everything is saved. The next time you start up the IDE, everything is as you left it.

Fig. 2.17

The Save Options dialog box.

The Window Menu

The Window menu (see fig. 2.18) allows you to select how your windows will appear within the IDE. This is similar to the choices you make when customizing your groups in Program Manager. You can choose these options: Cascade, Tile Vertical, Tile Horizontal, or Arrange Icons. Additional options allow you to Close All, Restore All, or Minimize All windows to make your IDE easier to work with. The last section of the Window menu shows recently active files that you can reload just by clicking on the filename.

Fig. 2.18

The Window menu.

The Help Menu

The final element of the IDE's menu bar is the Help menu. This provides you with access to online Help for all aspects of Borland C++. You can look up information on any particular language element, or on the operations of the tools or the IDE itself.

The Speedbar

The last interface element that the IDE provides is the Speedbar, which is the toolbar located just below the menu. These icons provide a simple one-click method to execute virtually any action that the IDE can perform. The Speedbar can be customized to include more actions than are shown by default. Alternatively, you can eliminate some of the actions on the toolbar that are rarely used. Figure 2.19 shows the cursor pointing to the File Open icon in the Speedbar. If you notice at the bottom of the IDE, there is an informational line that tells you just what each icon is for as you pass the cursor over it.

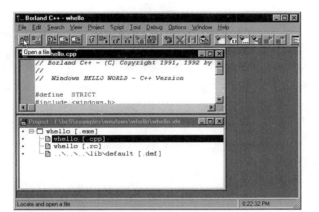

Fig. 2.19

The Speedbar.

Basic Features

Configuring the IDE

The IDE provides you with access to all tools and resources that are necessary when creating your programs without ever having to exit the IDE to perform another task. This type of seamless integration is what makes Borland C++ 5 such an easy package to use. The best way to show you how the IDE works is to use it to create a project. This section takes you through the steps of creating a project using the IDE.

The IDE can be customized to suit your individual tastes. You can choose how you want the Editor to behave, what colors you want to be used, and your personal preferences for how the IDE responds when you run or debug a program.

Editor Options

If you are familiar with the Brief Editor and the keystrokes it uses, you can tell the IDE to emulate Brief. This will avoid having to relearn a new set of keystrokes each time you want to perform an editing task. You can select the Editor options that you would like by choosing Options, Environment. You see the Environment Options dialog box (see fig. 2.20).

Figure 2.21 shows the Editor options that can be changed. These options enable you to change how editing features act during your IDE sessions. You can customize any of the options listed in the Topics box. This figure shows the main editor options in the Editor SpeedSettings group. You can choose what type of emulation you want the IDE's Editor to use: the default IDE settings, traditional Borland settings (if you are familiar with earlier Borland products), or Brief or Epsilon Editor key mappings.

Fig. 2.20

Setting Browser options in the Environment Options dialog box.

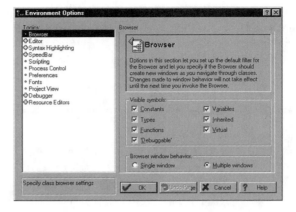

Fig. 2.21

Setting Editor options in the Environment Options dialog box.

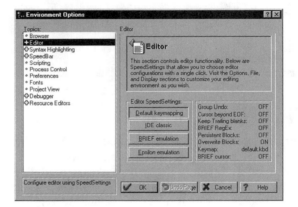

You can also choose different options for the Editor. These are shown in the Topics box as subheadings of the Editor (see fig. 2.22). To display any of these options, simply double-click on the option you want to view or change.

The File options of the Editor allow you to specify if you want to create backup files and where to put them. The Editor allows you to create a *mirror* of your files. A mirror is the latest version of the file you are working on. If you use this option, the mirror will be the file you are working on, while the original file remains untouched. This enables you to experiment with changes and not lose your original file.

There is one more item that you can customize with the Editor—the Display options (see fig. 2.23). These options allow you to choose what cursor types and fonts you want to use for your editing sessions. This is all a matter of personal preference; experiment with the settings to find the display style that you are most comfortable with.

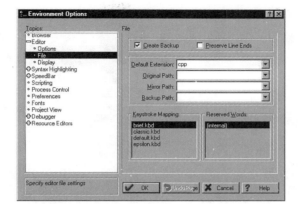

Fig. 2.22

You can choose File options from the Environment Options dialog box.

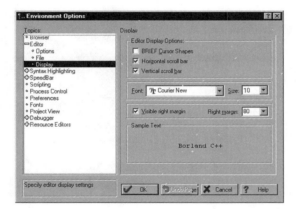

Fig. 2.23

Display options in the Environment Options dialog box.

Choosing Your Own Colors

The IDE allows you to completely customize how your sessions look. You can select from four predefined color combinations or you can customize the colors individually by choosing Options, Environment. If you choose Syntax Highlighting from the Topics box, you will see the screen shown in figure 2.24. This allows you to choose from four predefined color sets: Defaults, Classic, Twilight, and Ocean.

If you do not like any of the predefined color sets, you can always customize the colors any way you would like to. Figure 2.25 shows the Customize group of options when the Syntax Highlighting option is selected.

Fig. 2.24

Choosing from the four predefined color sets.

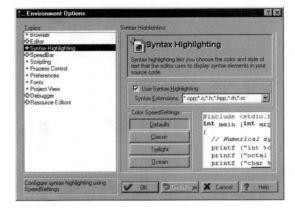

Fig. 2.25

Customizing the individual colors of the IDE.

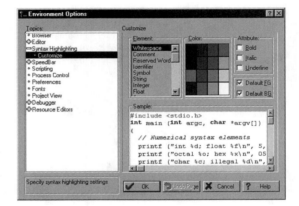

Setting Personal Preferences

You can also customize the IDE to save and autosave different parts of your project whenever you run or debug your project. It is always a good idea to save everything prior to running your program. (You could have a bug in your program that will lock up the system, and then you will lose any changes that you made since the last time you saved.) If you have the IDE automatically save your changes prior to attempting to execute your program, you will never lose any work. The preferences you can customize are shown in figure 2.26.

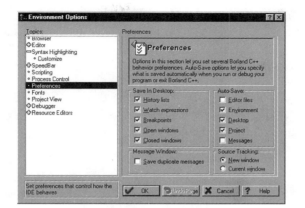

Fig. 2.26

The Preferences options.

Working with Projects

Projects are the heart of your efforts. You can create individual projects for each program you want to write. This allows you to customize each project to a particular platform using different libraries or tools. So let's create a project to see how it's done.

1. With the IDE open, choose File, New, Project. You are presented with the TargetExpert dialog box shown in figure 2.27.

This dialog box allows you to define the name of the project and executable that you are going to create. It also allows you to select what type of application you would like to create, and what platform it will be running on.

Fig. 2.27

The TargetExpert dialog box.

2. Select the project name entry field and change the name of the project to **CH02.IDE**. When you do this, you will notice that the target name changes to CH02 as well.

3. For this project, choose the application type to be EasyWin. This creates a text-based program that will run under Windows.

4. Click the Advanced button from the right-hand side of the TargetExpert. This allows you to select what type of node you want to create. Figure 2.28 shows the Advanced Options dialog box, which allows you to specify what types of files you want to include in your project.

Fig. 2.28

The Advanced Options dialog box.

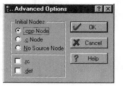

Note

A *node* is a file type within your application. Different nodes are Project, which contains information about project-specific details; Target, which contains information about the executable program or DLL that you are going to create; Source, which represents the files that are used to create the target program; and Run-Time, which contains information about startup code and libraries needed when your program is run. Run-time nodes do not normally appear in the listing for a project.

---

5. For this simple project, choose .cpp and turn off the .rc and .def options by clicking on the check boxes next to them. Your screen will look like figure 2.29. You can now click on the OK button in the Advanced Options dialog box and on the TargetExpert dialog box.

Fig. 2.29

The CH02 Advanced Options dialog box choices.

You have now created a project that has one .cpp node, indicating that it is a C++ program, and one executable that is called ch02.exe.

Of course, there is no code within this program to perform any tasks or provide any useful functions, but you have a shell that you can use to write a simple program. This is similar to what was done in chapter 1, but let's take this project a little bit further. Double-click on the Ch02.cpp document in the Project window at the bottom of the IDE. This will open up the Ch02.cpp file for editing. You will notice that the file is empty. Let's add a simple request for input and then an output statement to provide a little functionality to this program. Type in the following code:

```
#include <iostream.h>

void main()
{
char Name[40];
cout << "What is your name ? ";
cin >> Name;
cout << "Hello " << Name << endl;
}
```

Your screen will look like that shown in figure 2.30.

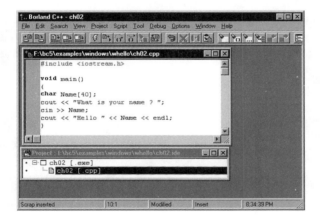

Fig. 2.30

The CH02 program.

Now choose Debug, Run to run your program. You see the IDE compile your program and then run it. If there are any errors, the compilation will stop and you will have to go back and correct them. If you do hit an error, make certain that you typed in the code exactly as shown.

If your program does not have any errors, you will see a screen similar to that shown in figure 2.31, prompting you to input your name. Type in your name and press Enter. The program will respond by saying hello to you.

Although this is a very simple project, it does illustrate how to create and run a project. You will use these techniques throughout this book to create the projects that illustrate the different features of Borland C++ 5.

Fig. 2.31

The CH02 program is running.

From Here...

In this chapter you learned about how to use and customize the Borland IDE. You were introduced to the different menus and Speedbar options that allow you to create your own projects and customize them to suit your needs, as well as the needs of your program's users. You saw how to create and save a project and how to customize the IDE to suit your own tastes for colors, fonts, and Editor operations.

- In chapter 3, "Object-Oriented Analysis and Design," you learn about the foundations of C++. These basic fundamentals will be used as the building blocks from which you can expand your knowledge and understanding of C++.

- In chapter 27, "Using the AppExpert," you learn about using this feature to help you tailor and create your applications.

- In chapter 29, "Using the Integrated Debugger," you learn about how to use and exploit the power of the Integrated Debugger to help you write bulletproof applications.

CHAPTER 3

Object-Oriented Analysis and Design

An e-mail recently circulated through the company where I work that read, "Due to popular demand we will be offering training sessions in using WordPerfect, DOS, the Internet, etc., more effectively. If you feel that you need instruction in other areas, feel free to suggest a course topic to us." A few days later a researcher/proofreader—whose experience with software packages is limited to word processing and e-mail—took the time to respond, "I'd like a course in C++."

C++—in addition to being a programming language—is a buzzword. In the past few years, lingo previously reserved for "computer nerds" has gone mainstream; it permeates the media. Today it's not uncommon for purchasers of software I work on to inquire, "What programming language do you use, C++?" As I code away on my current project, nontechnical coworkers casually query, "Are you using C++?" And any extended casual conversation on C++ cannot help but lead to that other buzzword—"object-oriented."

It's a common misconception that C++ programming is synonymous with object-oriented programming. As you probably already know, this is not the case. C++ is a language with constructs that supports the object-oriented programming paradigm, nothing more, nothing less. It's up to the individual programmer whether he takes advantage of them or not. See chapter 14, "Basic Class Concepts," for an in-depth look at class constructs like constructors, destructors, and member functions.

In this chapter, I examine objects and how to design software that exploits the object-oriented constructs of C++. You learn to

- Differentiate between procedural and object-oriented programming
- Understand the characteristics of an object and related terminology
- Apply object-oriented analysis and design techniques to your own programs
- Appreciate alternate uses of the object-oriented paradigm, like the concept of "resource acquisition is initialization"

Understanding Procedural versus Object-Oriented Programming

In the struggle against software complexity there have arisen various tactics for engineering solutions to programming problems. Historically, computer programming began on a very small scale, due to hardware limitations. The problem domain was limited primarily to mathematics, where the goal of the average program was to perform one task and perform it well (produce logarithmic tables, calculate the trajectory of a missile). As hardware became more powerful and inexpensive, the demands placed on software grew. Ever more complicated tasks required new programming tools; thus, the birth of high-level programming languages like FORTRAN, COBOL, Pascal, and C (as opposed to low-level machine or assembly-language programming). With more complicated tasks came more complexity. Soon programmers realized that problems became easier to solve when broken into smaller sub-problems, which were, in turn, well-suited to sub-programs (subroutines, procedures, and functions). These sub-programs are the hallmark of procedural programming.

Let's consider, for example, how you might solve the following problem—making a deposit to a savings account—by breaking it into smaller sub-problems.

If you consider making a deposit to a savings account, what types of activities take place in your account? First of all, your deposit must be stored somewhere. Secondly, your balance has to be updated (in a positive direction for a change). To do so, your previous balance must be available, to which you add your deposit amount to arrive at the new balance. If you draw your problem and sub-problems, it might resemble figure 3.1.

Fig. 3.1

The procedural approach: dividing the problem of depositing to a savings account into smaller sub-problems.

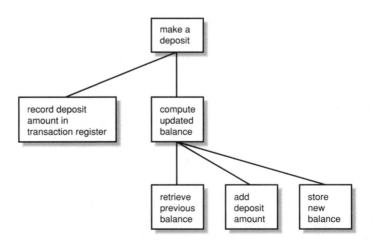

You notice that the diagram is tree-shaped. The problem with trees in computer science is those pesky branches. If you have too many of them, your problem becomes unmanageable. The main drawback of procedural programming and abstracting large problems into smaller sub-problems is that eventually, if the problem you're solving is large enough, the number of smaller sub-problems becomes enormous and difficult to manage; it's no longer easy for you or a team of programmers to grasp your own solution in any abstract sense.

> **Note**
>
> Regardless of whether there is a quantifiable point at which the complexity of procedural programming becomes unmanageable, it happens. Some computer scientists estimate this meltdown point at around 100,000 lines of code. I recently worked on a digital telephone switching system where the lines of code topped 8,000,000. Even when breaking the project down into more abstract modules (in the 1,000–2,000 range), there were very few departments, much less individuals, capable of understanding how everything fit together.

Out of procedural programming evolved a new tool for combating software complexity: object-oriented programming. In object-oriented programming you try to abstract beyond breaking a problem into smaller sub-problems. You attempt to view your software problems as consisting of interactions between abstractions of real-world objects. The goal, then, is to help understand programs by using common knowledge and expectations of behavior associated with everyday objects.

Going back to the deposit example, let's consider the objects involved in that problem. First of all, there is a savings account and there is a transaction register. How do they interact? In making a deposit to the savings account, a record of the deposit is made in the transaction register. To compute the updated balance, the new transaction needs to be added to the existing ones. But this addition is really inherent to the transaction register; all that it really needs to do is report the new balance back to you. Drawing your two objects out, it might look something like figure 3.2.

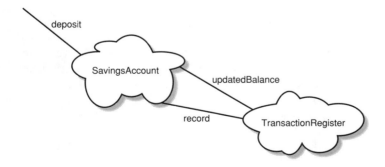

Fig. 3.2

The object-oriented approach: dividing the problem of deposit to a savings account into interacting objects.

You notice that our object-oriented solution is more graphlike than treelike; this is typical of object-oriented designs. Notice that in having two objects with which you associate certain functionality, your design becomes simpler and easier to understand.

Using Characteristics of an Object

Now that you have an idea of how object-oriented design differs from procedural programming, let's consider the "object." For the purposes of this chapter, let's define an *object* as something abstract or real from our problem domain with clearly defined properties or roles. Similar objects, then, have similar properties or roles, while dissimilar objects do not. In object-oriented programming, similar objects share the same or similar class, just as they do in the real world.

Consider the mammal class (you remember high school biology, don't you?). What are some "objects" belonging to the mammal class? Dolphins, cows, and humans are all mammals—very different objects in some sense, yet very similar. What types of properties or roles do dolphins, cows, and humans share? They are all warm-blooded, give live birth, and produce milk for their offspring. The sharing of roles and properties can also occur within computer programs—and it is the goal of object-oriented design to discover these relationships. In fact, in C++, objects are instances of a class, just like they are in other scientific classification methods. Before jumping into object-oriented design, though, let's consider some of the properties common to the "object" class.

Abstraction

In the previous section, I mentioned that the goal in object-oriented programming is to identify abstractions of real-world objects in your problem domain. What types of real-world objects am I referring to? Well, really anything that provides a concept of what your programs do or provide. These objects can be tangible—rockets, cookbooks, diapers. Or they might be roles—guard, father, painter. Events are fair game—out of memory, sale, house closing. You get the picture: Anything that gives you an idea of what the object provides.

Let's consider an example in C++. Assume that you need to provide the functionality for a savings account in a program. What types of roles or properties are associated with a savings account? Consider the roles or functionality first. A savings account can be opened with an initial balance. In addition, it should provide a mechanism for making deposits to and withdrawals from the account. Perhaps a mechanism for recording a varying rate of interest can be provided. Finally, you need a way to close out the account. In the way of properties, a savings account has a balance and a rate of interest. Of course, you can come up with more roles and properties, but for the example's purpose, this should suffice. In C++, you can represent your abstraction of a savings account with the following:

```
typedef float Balance;
typedef float Amount;
typedef float Rate;
```

```
class SavingsAccount {
public:
    SavingsAccount(Balance initialBalance);
    virtual ~SavingsAccount(void);

    void deposit(Amount depositAmount);
    void withdraw(Amount withdrawalAmount);
    void setInterestRate(Rate interestRate);

    Balance currentBalance(void);
    Rate currentInterestRate(void);

private:
    Balance currentBalance;
    Rate currentInterestRate;
};
```

If you haven't read through chapter 14, "Basic Class Concepts," some of the notation in this class may be unfamiliar to you. In essence, you have a class with a constructor `SavingsAccount` that must be called to create a `SavingsAccount` object with an initial balance, equivalent to opening an account. Likewise, you have a destructor `~SavingsAccount` that is called when a `SavingsAccount` object is destroyed (closing an account). The class also provides member functions like `deposit`, `withdraw`, and `setInterestRate` to carry out some action on the savings account, as well as other member functions (sometimes referred to as accessor functions). *Accessor functions* report back to the client of the `SavingsAccount` object the values of certain private data contained within the object.

In examining `SavingsAccount` class, an instance of which is a `SavingsAccount` object, you have abstracted an object with clear-cut functionality in the language of your problem domain—personal finance. There are no surprises and it is pretty much what you expect when considering a savings account. Your abstraction provides the necessary characteristics of a savings account.

As of yet, there is no functionality provided by the `SavingsAccount` class. How it keeps track of your current balance and makes deposits or withdrawals is really not important to a client object making use of the `SavingsAccount`'s services. However, this point leads us to the next characteristic of an object, encapsulation.

Encapsulation

Whereas abstraction concerns itself with the roles and properties provided by an object, *encapsulation* focuses on the implementation and structure of an object. How an object performs is of no concern to the client of an object, generally speaking (it may become a concern if the services provided are faulty or too slow); it only cares that the services advertised by an object are indeed provided. As such, in an object, implementation and structure are usually hidden from the client; a synonym for encapsulation that you'll come across is *information hiding*.

Looking back at the `SavingsAccount` class, you may have noticed the private data item `currentBalance`. It is highly unlikely that a `SavingsAccount` class simply stores the current balance of the account; more probable is some sort of transaction register associated with the account, where each and every deposit to and withdrawal from the account is recorded. To calculate the current balance might entail the transaction register adding up all the transactions and reporting the result as the current balance. Let's assume a class with this functionality exists, called TransactionRegister. What happens then when you change SavingsAccount to

```
class SavingsAccount {
public:
    ...
    Balance currentBalance(void);
    ...

private:
    TransactionRegister transactions;
    ...
};
```

In the first SavingsAccount class, the accessor function currentBalance's implementation might have been as trivial as the following:

```
Balance SavingsAccount::currentBalance(void)
{
    return currentBalance;
}
```

Assuming that TransactionRegister provided a member function computeBalance, currentBalance's implementation in the second SavingsAcccount class might have been:

```
Balance SavingsAccount::currentBalance(void)
{
    transactions.computeBalance();
}
```

The point is, regardless of how the accessor function currentBalance is implemented, to the class that makes use of the SavingsAccount's services, the end result is the same; it receives the current balance of the savings account. Encapsulation allows users of an object to ignore implementation details, which provides for less complex systems. This is particularly advantageous in large-scale programming projects or libraries, where end users of an object play no part in its implementation. The only party concerned with the implementation of SavingsAccount should be its author or authors.

Modularity

Encapsulation allows you to hide certain implementation details from end users, keeping your system less complex and easier to grasp. The concept of modularity goes one step further. Now that you have identified your objects and hidden any unnecessary detail, attempt to group your objects into logical modules that unite related classes and objects. Once you have your modules, make only those interfaces available to other modules that are absolutely necessary.

In C++, make these interfaces available in header files (convention dictates that these files usually end in .h or .hpp). Your implementation, then, which is of little importance between modules, is confined to files ending in suffixes like .c, .cc, .cp, or .cpp. What exactly are the advantages of such a practice?

First, consider a programming project where a number of programmers are involved. With your classes and objects separated into modules, each programmer can work independently of the others. What ties the modules together is the interfaces in the header files, which are usually defined before implementation. Modularity supports programming-in-the-large—large-scale software design—as opposed to small-scale design where the tendency is to lump all of your classes and objects together.

> **Tip**
>
> In object-oriented design—as in all design—try to identify the abstract and logical relations before the more physical implementation.

A second, related advantage of modularity is that the implementation in individual modules can change and be recompiled, without greatly affecting the rest of the system; the interfaces remain the same.

Going back to the 8,000,000-line digital switching system example I mentioned earlier, developers were responsible for one or more modules. As long as their interfaces did not change, they—for at least a portion of the development cycle—could tinker on their implementations at will. Weekly compilations of updated modules then brought the implementation changes into the system, without affecting those modules that made use of the interfaces in question. However, it was a very different story if a developer needed to change an interface between modules. Any change in interface, of course, required every module that made use of the interface to be correspondingly updated (yes, tempers often flared) and recompiled. Each and every owner of affected modules had to be notified and their signatures were required to change the interface. Only then could all of the affected modules be recompiled. As this recompilation took the better part of a 24-hour period, you can see where judiciously breaking your projects into modules can pay off.

> **Tip**
>
> When creating header files for interfaces, always try to bracket them with some variation of the #ifndef, #define, and #endif constructs demonstrated here. Defining _SAVINGS_HPP in listing 3.1 allows multiple modules to include the header file without causing the compiler to balk at multiple declarations of the SavingsAccount class. What the #ifndef _SAVINGS_HPP, #define SAVINGS_HPP, ..., #endif accomplishes is limiting the number of times that savings.hpp actually is included in your compilation. It is only included when _SAVINGS_HPP is not defined such as the first time. If you are unfamiliar with macros like #ifndef, #define, #endif, and #include, see chapter 4, "The Preprocessor."

Consider the SavingsAccount class again. If the first SavingsAccount class declaration had been in a header file called savings.hpp, what would have happened to another module that made use of the header file (via #include "savings.hpp"), when you changed the private data item currentBalance to transactions? As you see in listing 3.1, the interface is changed—well, not so much an interface but the definition of the object—causing the other module, as well as your own, to be recompiled. (The compiler needs to know in the module that includes savings.hpp just how much space to allocate for a SavingsAccount object.) This is exactly what you want to avoid through modularity. A good example of modularity (see the previous section, "Encapsulation") is when you changed the implementation of the accessor function currentBalance. If your change had been limited to the file containing your implementation, for example Savings.cpp, the benefits of modularity would have really paid off in your overall system.

Listing 3.1   Savings.hpp—The *SavingsAccount* Class Declaration

```
// savings.hpp

#ifndef _SAVINGS_HPP
#define _SAVINGS_HPP

typedef float Balance;
typedef float Amount;
typedef float Rate;

class SavingsAccount {
public:
    SavingsAccount(Balance initialBalance);
    virtual ~SavingsAccount(void);

    void deposit(Amount depositAmount);
    void withdraw(Amount withdrawalAmount);
    void setInterestRate(Rate interestRate);

    Balance currentBalance(void);
    Rate currentInterestRate(void);

private:
    Balance currentBalance;
    Rate currentInterestRate;
};

#endif
```

The third—and for this chapter—final advantage of modularity is the ease of reuse when objects and classes are separated into modules. Given a well-grouped set of objects that offers a clearly defined functionality and that can stand alone, you theoretically can reuse this module in other software projects, with few or no changes. For example, you can make use of the SavingsAccount class in any number of projects in the arena of personal finance. Software reuse is one of the highest goals of object-oriented design; what better way to simplify a system than reusing classes, objects, and modules with which you're already familiar!

Hierarchy

Even with abstraction, encapsulation, and modularity, you can still lose the big picture of your design—there are just too many abstract objects floating around that you can't keep track of. This is where hierarchy comes into play. *Hierarchy* is perhaps the single-most identifiable modus operandi of object-oriented design and object-oriented languages. Some sticklers go so far as to insist that if your object-oriented design does not make use of hierarchy (you soon come across the synonym *inheritance*), it's not object-oriented.

In looking at abstraction you observed how identifying objects with a clearly defined functionality was advantageous. In analyzing your problem domain, it often becomes apparent that certain objects share similar structure or functionality. When a class or object shares behavior with another class, you have an instance of *single inheritance*. If a class shares the structure or functionality of two or more classes, this is an example of *multiple inheritance*.

Inheritance is often defined as being able to express an "is-a" relationship between classes, objects, and data types. Going back to the mammal class, a dolphin "is a" mammal just as a human "is a" mammal. Dolphins and humans inherit certain traits from the mammal class such as live birth. As chickens do not give live birth, they are not mammals and as such should not inherit from the mammal class. Consider the platypus, however; it lays eggs but is warm-blooded and covered with hair. Here's an example of where multiple inheritance comes into play. A platypus inherits certain traits from the mammal class and other traits from the fowl class!

Without hierarchy or inheritance you're constantly reinventing the wheel. If you had to define a class for dolphin, it would include traits commonly associated with mammals as mentioned above. Without the benefit of hierarchy, defining another class for humans would force you to duplicate many of the properties already defined for the dolphin, adding unnecessary detail and overhead to your design and implementation.

Let's now take a look at how you can identify hierarchy in your personal finance problem domain—thus, simplifying your understanding of the domain and design—and put inheritance to use in C++.

Single Inheritance. In the problem domain used in this chapter, you know that you deal not only with savings accounts but also with checking accounts. But what can you do differently? In analyzing the problem, you may have come across the abstraction that savings and checking accounts are both types of bank accounts. All bank accounts have a balance and provide some means for making deposits and withdrawals. As such, you can start by defining a `BankAccount` class instead of jumping right to `SavingsAccount`:

```
class BankAccount {
public:
    BankAccount(Balance initialBalance);
    virtual ~BankAccount(void);

    void deposit(Amount depositAmount);
    void withdraw(Amount withdrawalAmount);

    Balance currentBalance(void);

private:
    TransactionRegister transactions;
};
```

You might realize that savings accounts usually earn interest whereas checking accounts sometimes do not. Checking accounts often have a set minimum balance
while savings accounts do not. If you accept these admittedly simple assumptions,
you can define SavingsAccount as

```
class SavingsAccount : public BankAccount {
public:
    SavingsAccount(Balance initialBalance);
    virtual ~SavingsAccount(void);

    void setInterestRate(Rate interestRate);

    Rate currentInterestRate(void);

private:
    Rate currentInterestRate;

};
```

and CheckingAccount as follows:

```
class CheckingAccount: public BankAccount {

    CheckingAccount(Balance initialBalance);
    virtual ~CheckingAccount(void);

    void setMinimumBalance(Balance minimumBalance);

    Balance minimumBalance(void);

private:
    Balance minimumBalance;
};
```

Notice that SavingsAccount and CheckingAccount both inherit from BankAccount
while adding their own properties and functionality. In the case of SavingsAccount,
handling of an interest rate was added to the class; for CheckingAccount, minimum
balance was added. Both of these new derived classes of BankAccount (BankAccount is
called a base class of SavingsAccount and CheckingAccount) inherit member functions
for depositing and withdrawing funds as well as a TransactionRegister. In all three

classes, you can deposit and withdraw funds in exactly the same way. When you can do something in the same way and share functionality, you have simplified the complexity of your problem considerably.

Multiple Inheritance. What if you needed to implement a `CreditCard` class? Credit cards are indeed bank accounts; you can deposit (or pay off) and withdraw (or spend)—more likely spend than pay off—but credit cards are also a type of loan. Loans, in general, have such properties as an interest rate, loan duration, monthly payment, and so on. As such, a `CreditCard` class may inherit from both the `BankAccount` class and a `Loan` class.

Loans, too, however, are bank accounts; consequently, a `Loan` class would probably inherit some functionality from the `BankAccount` class. Credit cards often offer insurance to pay off the minimum balance in times of need, most notably unemployment. As such, credit cards are an insurable item just like your home or your car. `InsurableItem` may qualify as a base class in your personal finance domain. If you assume that an `InsurableItem` has a monthly premium, you might define `InsurableItem` class as follows:

```
class InsurableItem
{
public:
    InsurableItem(Amount insuredAmount);
    virtual ~InsurableItem(void);

    void setMonthlyPremium(Amount premiumAmount);

    Amount monthlyPremium(void);

private:
    Amount monthlyPremium;
};
```

What if your credit card—which is an insurable item and a bank account—needs to offer a certain rebate percentage on purchases (something your home or car loan doesn't have the decency to provide!)? The `CreditCard` class, having properties of a `BankAccount`, `InsurableItem`, in addition to its own specific characteristics may be defined as follows:

```
class CreditCard: public BankAccount, public InsurableItem
{
public:
    CreditCard(Amount creditLimit);
    virtual ~CreditCard(void);

    void setRebatePercentage(Rate rebatePercentage);

    Rate rebatePercentage(void);

private:
    Rate rebatePercentage;
};
```

As you can see, hierarchy or inheritance has greatly simplified the `CreditCard` class. With little effort `CreditCard` can record a rebate percentage, monthly premium, handle deposits and withdrawals, and report a current balance, with only one member function specific to the `CreditCard` class—you inherit the rest of the functionality. This is another object characteristic that you should always try to locate in object-oriented analysis and design.

Now that you're familiar with the desired properties of objects and some related terminology, let's take a more in-depth look at how to discern the interactions between abstract objects in your problem domain.

Exploring Analysis and Design

Sometimes the terms object-oriented analysis, design, and programming are used interchangeably (you may have noticed this already in this chapter). They indeed are all very close cousins, but before going on, let's briefly differentiate among the three.

- In object-oriented analysis you most likely find yourself at the beginning of your development cycle; you begin to examine a problem from the perspective of classes and objects.

- In the design phase, you have a firm grasp on the entities and relationships at work in the problem and begin to break the task at hand into actual classes and objects.

- In object-oriented programming, it's time to implement your classes and objects (using C++ in this case).

This chapter concentrates on analysis and design; implementation issues are discussed throughout the rest of this book.

> **Note**
>
> Go to the technical section of your local bookstore and you're more than likely to find a number of texts on object-oriented design and analysis. While authors like Booch (the work of whom influences this chapter most), Rumbaugh, Coad, Yourdon, Jacobson, and many others—theoreticians and practitioners alike—offer great insight into, and variations on the theme of, object-oriented design, all readily agree on Bjarne Stroustrup's (the father of C++) comment that there are no perfect rules for identifying objects in a problem domain. Bearing this in mind, always remember that what works for you is as good as any method you might read about in a book. Experiment, learning from your successes as well as your failures. What follows are some general rules of thumb.

Analysis Tools

In object-oriented analysis, the goal is to discover the objects within your problem domain. You are attempting to classify various objects according to like properties and functionality. It is not an easy task, but just remember—there are sciences much older than computer science where classifying objects within their problem domains is still a popular pastime. Also, there is no wrong or right—if it works for your design, go with it!

Behavior Analysis. Most of the examples to this point have focused on identifying real-world objects in the problem domain. In personal finance, it's fairly obvious to pick out such items as a savings account and a credit card. Sometimes, however, you can center on the responsibilities inherent in your domain—who needs to provide what to whom. Once you have accomplished this, you can group common responsibilities, forming a hierarchy.

Domain Analysis. If you're developing a system for someone, it's very rare that it's the first system of its kind. Talk to those in the know, people familiar with the domain. If you're developing a new time-billing system for a law firm, talk to the lawyers and the legal secretaries. They've used similar systems in the past and possess a wealth of knowledge as to what a new system in their domain not only should provide but what it should avoid. They are also familiar with the types of "objects" that show up in such systems—logs, reports, and so on. Never underestimate the knowledge and valuable input of the end user.

Use-Case Analysis. Domain experts become indispensable when you approach a problem from the perspective of how it is used. In discussion with users, attempt to identify various scenarios of what your system must provide. Then in walking through the scenarios, try to identify objects, responsibilities, and behavior required to support the described functionality.

CRC Cards. Stack up on index cards! Class/Responsibilities/Collaborators cards are a brainstorming method for object-oriented analysis. Write in pencil on the top of the card the name of the class. Have various development personnel or analysts be responsible for one or a number of cards. In discussing the proposed system, jot down which classes it must collaborate with and the responsibilities of the class. If you find that cards can be combined, combine them. If some need to be broken up, rip them in half; index cards won't break your budget.

Informal Description. Write an informal summary of what your system needs to provide, and then carefully read through your description and underline meaningful nouns and verbs. Consider nouns as possible objects and verbs as potential member functions. As most verbs can be made nouns and vice-versa, however, always remember to look at your list from both directions. It is just brainstorming, after all.

Structured Analysis. Remember the example of procedural programming from the section "Understanding Procedural versus Object-Oriented Programming" where I analyzed the problem of making a deposit to a savings account? We are all very familiar with breaking a problem into sub-problems. Perhaps it's our educational background or perhaps it's in our nature, but it comes easy for most of us. Once you have the various steps and sub-steps, try to identify objects and their responsibilities. In our savings account example, it was fairly easy to pick out the savings account and transaction register, from our initial procedural approach as you may recall.

Whatever analytical approach you take to a problem (and it may be your unique way of doing things), just remember what you're looking for. Remember the key object characteristics: abstraction, encapsulation, modularity, and hierarchy. Once you've abstracted objects from behavior, domain analysis, brainstorming, or whatever, start zeroing in on what type of information is absolutely necessary for collaborator classes (encapsulation). Try to identify what types of classes belong together and which do not (modularity). Also be on the lookout for objects that share properties and functionality (hierarchy). Remember that you're free to combine objects, break up objects, and so on, as long as you're in the analysis/design phase. After you've started your implementation, you may be too far along to go back. Experiment while you still can!

The Design

As mentioned earlier, object-oriented analysis and design are very close cousins. Once you have analyzed your problem domain, all that really remains is to firm up details for implementation. It's time to concentrate on interfaces between objects and modules. Consider the types of inheritance between objects, what types of messages are needed, number of parameters, and so on. There are a number of notations, which are outside the scope of this chapter, for getting your design down on paper. Jot things down on paper: class names, messages between objects, public data, private data; all can be written down for posterity. A well-documented design can make your implementation relatively easy; a couple notes on a cocktail napkin usually can't swing it in your larger development efforts.

The Benefits

Now that the characteristics of objects and some related analysis/design techniques have been examined, let's briefly make note of the benefits of object-oriented development. Your design should

- *Put those object-oriented constructs of C++ to good use.* Use well-defined classes liberally and don't forget inheritance.
- *Create classes that can stand alone.* They're often good candidates for reuse.
- *Be understandable.* The greatest benefit of object-oriented design is expressing a problem in a way that's easy for all to comprehend.

Resource Acquisition Is Initialization

One benefit of object-oriented programming that is often overlooked is Bjarne Stroustrup's concept of "resource acquisition is initialization." You see references to this concept throughout the rest of the book. Because it is a benefit of object-oriented design, it is briefly mentioned here.

In C++, constructors are called when an object is created and destructors are called when objects are destroyed, such as when they go out scope and are no longer needed. Objects that require resources, however, such as a file, a transaction register, or memory, must successfully acquire those resources before the object can truly be considered created.

For instance, let's rewrite the `BankAccount` class from the earlier section, "Single Inheritance," changing the private data item transactions of `TransactionRegister` class to a pointer to `TransactionRegister` class that is allocated at runtime whenever a `BankAccount` object is created:

```
class BankAccount {
public:
     BankAccount(Balance initialBalance);
     virtual ~BankAccount(void);

     void deposit(Amount depositAmount);
     void withdraw(Amount withdrawalAmount);

     Balance currentBalance(void);

private:
     TransactionRegister *transactions;
};
```

When creating a `BankAccount` object, you need to allocate a `TransactionRegister` in the constructor:

```
BankAccount::BankAccount(Balance initialBalance)
{
     transactions  = new TransactionRegister;
     transactions.record(initialBalance);
}
```

What happens, if when allocating a new `TransactionRegister`, you're in a low-memory situation and transactions cannot be allocated (ignore the obvious consequence that transactions would be equal to zero, causing a certain protection fault when `transactions.record(initialBalance)` is invoked)? Concentrate on what happens later when you need to make use of `BankAccount`. What happens when you try to make deposits to or withdrawals from your bank account? Most likely a lot of runtime errors. The `BankAccount` object is for all intents and purposes useless without a `TransactionRegister` to store your banking transactions in.

As such, in object-oriented programming it should be another one of your goals to ensure that when an object is created, it is fully created and not left in some dangling halfway state. An object advertises certain services and this includes its creation.

From Here...

This concludes the discussion of objects and object-oriented analysis and design. As mentioned earlier, you meet up with lots of implementation details throughout this book, which is the next step in object-oriented programming. You also come across various techniques for dealing with failed resource acquisition including exception handling.

- Chapter 4, "The Preprocessor," introduces you to macros like `#include`—important tools for adding modularity to your programming.

- Chapter 14, "Basic Class Concepts," delves more deeply into the implementation details of C++ classes and objects, which have only been hinted at here in the analysis/design phase.

- Chapter 20, "Inheritance and Polymorphism," introduces you to the ins and outs of hierarchy.

- Chapter 22, "Exception Handling," details some strategies for identifying error situations in constructors and throughout your C++ programming.

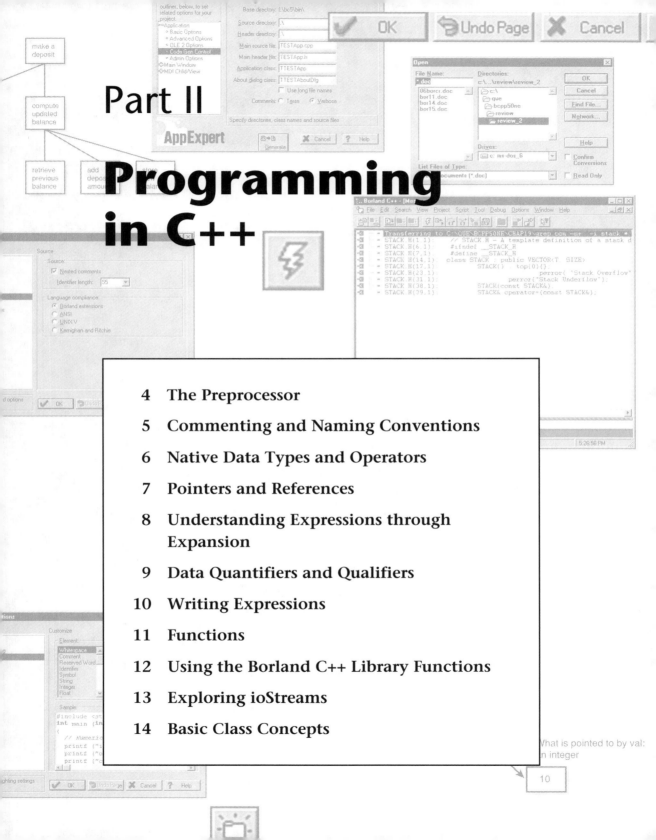

Part II

Programming in C++

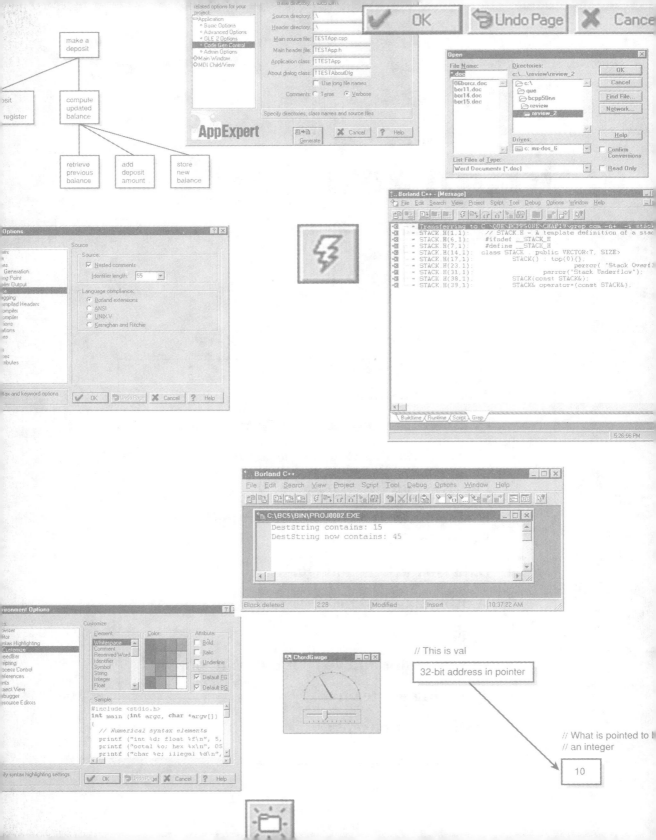

CHAPTER 4

The Preprocessor

The preprocessor has played several roles in the implementation of C++ and is still an integral part. C++ preprocessing *is* C preprocessing. This chapter examines some of the historical uses of the preprocessor—roles it has played in the past as well as current and future roles.

Surprisingly, the preprocessor played an integral role in the first implementation of C++, referred to as *C With Classes*. Templates can be exemplified and were first implemented with macro trickery. There are still some advantageous uses of the preprocessor, and some that are completely and absolutely necessary.

The goal of this chapter is to examine where the preprocessor fits into C++, and how you can take advantage of this viable tool. In this chapter, you learn about:

- The preprocessor's historical role as well as its current role in building applications
- Other preprocessor directives
- Advantageous uses of the preprocessor
- Techniques for writing clean debug code

Historical Role

The preprocessor is a tool that, for the most part, acts as a code substitute. The preprocessor does its job before the compiler and is not part of the compiler. It is part of the compilation process, however. The simplest understanding of how the preprocessor performs its magic is that wherever certain keywords occur, the preprocessor performs text substitution. I am wholly convinced that even the creator of the device did not comprehend the extent that the tool would be used.

In certain regard, the preprocessor is analogous to DOS commands, which were used in a manner other than their original intention, creating an opportunity for ingenuity to aggregate a whole greater than the sum of its parts. If my analogy is unclear, examples throughout this chapter may shed some light, even if you have never written a batch file.

Uses for the Preprocessor

The story goes that C (not C++) was written because the creators, Brian Kernighan and Dennis Ritchie, didn't want to program in Assembler. What was left out of the story was that they didn't despise the Assembler altogether. It is apparent that they appreciated Assembler's ability to program right down to the frame, and I would further surmise that someone in that group liked *macros* quite a bit too.

If you have ever written any assembly code, you will recognize that a macro definition such as

```
MACRO Trap
      int     3h      ;Debug Pause interrupt
END
```

is suspiciously like

```
define Trap() { asm int 0x03 }
```

Both techniques work identically. The first one is Assembler: Wherever `Trap` appears, it is replaced with `int 3h` by the Assembler. The same text-replacement is performed by the preprocessor using the C-style macro.

I am not advocating the use of either; rather, I am simply presenting a historical perspective. As a matter of fact, except for some required uses and a few modest exceptions, the macros as presented in the latter example are now replaced with inline functions. (You'll see why in future chapters.)

C programmers have (and some still do) use C to declare manifest constants:

```
#define MAX 10          /* a manifest constant */
#define NULL (void*)0    /* perhaps another */
```

Other uses have been for macros, as you have already seen, and still further uses exist today. For example, the `#include` compiler directive is used to include header (.h) files in both C and C++.

The Preprocessor's Role in the Big Picture

The preprocessor has an early role in the whole process of building an executable program, which includes dynamic-link libraries, executable programs, device drivers, or any other file that contains executable code.

The preprocessor is not invoked directly; instead, it runs before the compiler when compilation is specified. I am not going to pretend that I understand every aspect of its implementation; my goal is to highlight the general purpose. The simple explanation is that I was not involved in the implementation of the preprocessor, nor do I have access to the code.

The preprocessor is executed implicitly when you compile. The # symbol acts as a prefix that signals the preprocessor that a directive—read command—to the preprocessor follows. Generally, the # (pound) symbol prefixes a keyword that describes a directive that tells the compiler what to do with the token that follows it. For example,

```
#include <iostream.h>
```

tells the preprocessor to include the text contained in the file iostream.h. The <> wrapped around the filename indicates that the file iostream.h should be found in a directory defined in the system path or the project path. In other words, the file should be accessible. As demonstrated earlier, you saw how #define is used to indicate token replacement. In the example, wherever the token Trap() occurred in the code, { asm int 0x03 } was placed instead.

A second common usage of the #include preprocessor directive, or command, is to enclose the filename in double quotes.

```
#include "iostream.h"
```

Using double quotes around a filename with the #include directive instructs the preprocessor to look in the current directory (or working directory).

You'll see further uses throughout this chapter. I will indicate those that you may still find useful and refer you to future chapters where better alternatives have been implemented.

Following the text replacement, referred to as preprocessing, comes compilation. The compilation process builds intermediate files with an .obj extension from the header (.h or .hpp) and module files (.cpp). The definition file describes how much stack and heap space should be allocated to the program. (There is a default module definition file, \Bc5\Lib\Default.def, that the compiler will use if you fail to define one.) The resource (.rc) file contains the external, reusable resources comprising part of the visual makeup of your program.

An object file is created for every source module (.cpp) file that defines your program. Others are included when you include preexisting functionality. Once these intermediate binary files (not quite executable code) have been created, the linker is called to resolve things such as function calls and executable program results.

There are subtleties that require a moderate amount of explanation but are not difficult to understand. The first is that the compiler, which is not the linker, basically creates token names for items, such as functions, that are assigned addresses. The reason is that after the code is linked, it is addresses, not names, that are called. Object files containing code ending up in your application may exist in a collection referred to as a library (.lib) file. It is no more difficult for the addresses to be resolved in either state.

A second qualification of the explanation is that the resulting linked file does not have to have an .exe extension, but this is typically what you think of as a program.

You may also choose to build a dynamic link library (DLL) or some other type of output file. C++ can also be used to create device drivers, which enable you to designate a .sys or .bin extension. Device drivers require specialized knowledge of the operating system and are often loaded in the Config.sys file, for example

```
device=c:\mydriver.sys
```

Windows programs may compile code creating a Windows executable by declaring a WinMain function, or may create a dynamic link library by defining a LibMain function. There is a little more to it than that. The general idea is there are files that are compiled and linked, but the end result doesn't have to have an .exe extension. (Let's not forget the command (.com) files.)

Implementing C With Classes

The preprocessor was used to implement the first (or predecessor to) C++, referred to as C With Classes. Bjarne Stroustrop assures us, in both the *Annotated Reference Manual* and *The C++ Programming Language,* that C With Classes was not simply preprocessor trickery and included more than simple token replacement. However, the preprocessor's role was significant.

There are a few suggestive phrases in books that stir the imagination; therefore, it is not inconceivable to create a Pascal-like language with preprocessing. For example,

```
#define begin {
#define end }
```

I don't think it would be that far of a stretch to come up with alternatives that might mimic C++. I have not had the opportunity to completely research exactly how the preprocessor was used to implement C With Classes, and the details are of more a historical than practical significance. The preprocessor implementation of C With Classes was discarded—as quickly as possible—and the language was implemented, resulting in the preprocessor assuming its more traditional role.

C and C++ preprocessing are now identical; however, this was not the last time the preprocessor was used to implement some functionality that was inevitably slated to be a language feature. The preprocessor was used next to implement templates.

Implementing Template Classes and Functions

Template (or generic) classes and functions are those special functions whose implementation can be logically separated from the data type to which they are applied. An illustration of a generic function might be a bubble sort. Ask yourself if you can think of a bubble sort function independent of the data type being sorted. The answer is yes, because if you implement a sort for several data types, you will find that, upon subtracting the data being sorted, you are left with a nested for loop. The same might be said for a bound array class.

Applying the same test, can an array exist for more than one type, and does it vary only by the data type? Again if the answer is yes, then the array can be converted to a parameterized class. The objective of separating implementation from the data type is satisfied by templates. Templates have existed in the Borland implementation of C++ as far back as version 3.*x*.

While templates exist as a fully implemented feature of C++, they were first demonstrated as a viable language feature implemented via the preprocessor. Using a function that swaps two variables by assigning to a temporary third variable of the same data type can be used as an example. This simple type of swap might commonly be implemented any time data is being arranged in a sorted order. The pseudocode algorithm might be represented like this:

> Given two variables x and y, assign x to a temporary variable of the same data type, assign y to x, and complete the swap by assigning the temporary to y.

Using the char type to demonstrate, the Swap function might look like this:

```
inline void Swap( char& x, char& y )
{char t=x; x=y; y=t;}
```

> **Note**
>
> The inline keyword is not necessary here. The inline keyword is a hint to the compiler that you would prefer the code that comprises the function body to be used instead of a function call.

The solution shown is exactly the same one I would use to swap any two datum. The only difference between this version and a floating-point version, for example, is the data type. A little macro trickery demonstrates that the two can be separated (even before templates were implemented).

```
#define SWAP(T) \
inline void Swap( T& x, T& y )\
{ T t = x; x = y; y = t; }
```

Now, to instantiate a swap function for any data type, simply place a call to the SWAP macro in the space where a function definition would be valid. For example,

```
SWAP(double);
```

would cause the preprocessor to generate the function

```
inline void Swap( double& x, double& y )
{ double t = x; x = y; y = t; }
```

The same holds true for any data type. This code is used here only to represent a historical perspective; thankfully, templates are a fully implemented feature of C++. Their use is actually simpler than using macros and is fully described in chapter 19, "Using Template Classes."

Killing the Preprocessor

Stroustrop, the creator of C++, mentions that he would like to get rid of the preprocessor. This would not be done immediately because it would break a lot of code. (Transferring the capabilities of the preprocessor to those of a fully implemented C++ language may eliminate the preprocessor in the future.)

The process of dismissing things from a language follows a cycle that can take several years. The usual cycle entails implementing better alternatives and proffering warnings that the feature is "old." Successive implementations move the component in question to a full-fledged error, and then it is dropped. This takes a while because it may require several versions to get replacements in place, and changing the feature immediately would break existing code, which usually results in lots of rude e-mail to the language implementers.

Note

Does the discussion of phasing language features sound analogous to what is going on with DOS right now? Long filenames, which are incompatible with non-Windows 95 operating systems, are incomprehensible to older versions of Windows and DOS. Long filenames may be the proverbial straw that breaks DOS's back.

I am guessing that the preprocessor may be around for several more years because I have not seen any suggested solutions to preprocessor directives that replace the functionality of integral features #include. The C++ language grows and changes through the collective bargaining of members of the ANSI C++ committee—interested members whose ranks include members from Bell Labs, Microsoft, and Borland. If you have an opportunity to read the *The Annotated Reference C++ Manual* referred to as the ARM, Bjarne Stroustrop—the inventor of C++ and Chairman of the ANSI C++ committee—places great weight on the gradual phasing out of old features and the introduction of new ones. Gradual changes are necessary to avoid breaking existing code.

I mention all of these things because I am going to demonstrate current required uses of the preprocessor and a few advanced uses, and I do not want you to think that I am depicting oddities that will no longer exist tomorrow. Some coming applications of the preprocessor have probably existed in similar forms for about twenty years; they will help you write cleaner, more manageable code.

The Preprocessor's Current Role in Building Applications

The preprocessor maintains some of its historical uses. All new code still uses the #include directive to replace text from header files. And you will probably come across existing code that uses the preprocessor for manifest constants and macros. In sections that follow, I discuss those uses that are still the best approach, describe some additional applications, and look at replacements that have already been implemented.

As mentioned earlier, the preprocessor is the first step in building programs. In this role, the preprocessor is used to include text files, called header or .h files, containing an assortment of code. Header files are usually used to specify the interface to classes or functions referred to as the declarations.

C++ is a strongly typed language, which means the declaration of classes and functions, as well as data, must occur before first use. The declarations also act as the interface, or the "map" of how each element will be used throughout the application. Because the header can be included and the *declaration* must appear before the *definition*, headers have been assigned this role. This is not a role that the compiler enforces; rather, it is a convention that programmers have learned to employ through trial and error over the years.

Before I demonstrate the two forms used for including files, let's agree upon a general understanding of what the difference is between *declaring* and *defining*. To declare something means to specify what it is without allocating memory or indicating its state. To define means to indicate the content of a function or class or the state or value of data.

These two terms probably afford you the least harm from a loose interpretation. Here are some examples:

```
extern int a;          // declaration: in a second file or later
int a;                 // definition: a has been allocated memory
class FOO{};           // declaration: null class declaration
void Sort( int a[], unsigned int sz);
                       // declaration: Sort function
inline int Sum(int a, int b){ return a + b; }
                       // definition: inline function with body
```

Most idioms of C++ are unforgiving if misapplied. The difference between declaring and defining is one of the few that will tolerate some shades of gray. In general, header files are used to declare, and module (.cpp) files are used to provide a value or function body, or to define class member functions. Again, this is the common usage, which is not enforced by the compiler.

The two syntactically correct applications of the #include directive are, first

```
#include <filename.exe>
```

which suggests to the preprocessor that the file exists in a directory specified in some path—either the Options, Project, Directories path statements (see fig. 4.1) or the system path—usually set in the Autoexec.bat file. The second use is to wrap the header file in the double-quote pair, like this

```
#include "filename.ext"
```

where filename.ext is a header file in the current directory. These are usually header files that you create, but they don't have to be.

Fig. 4.1

At project inception, it is a good idea to specify the source and output directories in the Project Options dialog box.

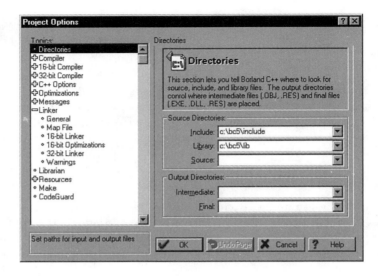

Once the preprocessor has made all such replacements, the compiler is free to do its job, followed by the linker, which results in your executable program. Learning and understanding each of the different files take some practice. A good place to start is by typing in some of the example programs in this book.

Note

Out of habit I still use the 8.3 filenames of yesteryear; Windows 95 and Borland C++ 5 both support long filenames. To maintain compatibility with older operating systems, the long filenames are also stored in the older 8.3 format using the tilde (~), which compresses longer names.

Other Preprocessor Directives

Your reference manuals are a good resource if you need to know all of the keywords or features of Borland C++ 5. I abhor rote memorization and almost always suggest abstinence. Reference manuals make ideal containers for facts. Thus, while I do not always include complete lists and tables of everything, I do make an attempt to present language elements in context.

There are several directives that the preprocessor recognizes. Some may appear intuitive to you, and others may not. In addition to the commonly used #include, there are the directives that make up conditional statements, much like writing C++ if...else statements. The goal of both is similar. With the code version, you are modifying program flow; with the preprocessor version, you want to determine which code is actually compiled and which is screened out before compilation.

Some of the if conditional directives are #ifdef, #ifndef, #else, #define, #undef, and #endif. You can think of #ifdef and #ifndef as the negation of each other, and the same holds true for #define and #undef.

Using *#define* and *#undef*

These two preprocessor directives are used to establish the identity or otherwise of user tokens. (The #define directive has been used in the past to create macros.) The #define directive is used to indicate to the preprocessor that the defined word is recognizable or has value. Once a token has been defined, it can be used in simple tests. For example,

```
#define DEBUG
```

creates a recognizable token DEBUG that can be used in a conditional test by the preprocessor. The #undef directive has the reverse effect. Whereas conditional tests using DEBUG would evaluate to true, applying the #undef directive to DEBUG would cause the same tests to evaluate to false. The next section demonstrates this technique.

Using *#ifdef*, *#else*, and *#endif*

The #ifdef, #else, #endif if directives are used in concert. You will always need to use the #endif when you use the #ifdef, but use of the #else is optional. Use it when an alternate set of conditions makes sense.

Referring back to the function (text insertion), the preprocessor performs in relation to the #include directive, you can apply the #ifdef, #define, and #endif in a constructive and necessary manner.

When you create a header (.h) file, the objective is to declare those functions, classes, or other items that may need to be included in more that one module (.cpp) file. If the code were included in several files containing program code, when the compiler executes, it places all of the tokens in a symbol table. What will occur if not done correctly is that name clashes will arise between symbols that are identical because they came from the same header file.

There is a consistent technique that can be employed to avoid this, and it is the same technique used by tool developers at Borland. The technique consists of wrapping the code in the header file in a preprocessor directive that acts like a gatekeeper. The gatekeeper stops redundancy from occurring in the symbol table.

Using the header file from the parameterized swap function, listing 4.1 shows how the technique is employed, followed by an explanation.

II

Programming in C++

> **Listing 4.1   parmswap.h—Generic Functions before They Were Adopted as Part of the Language**
>
> ```
> 1: // PARMSWAP.H - Demonstrates pre-template parameterized types.
> 2: #ifndef __PARMSWAP_H
> 3: #define __PARMSWAP_H
> 4: #define SWAP(T) \
> 5: inline void Swap( T& a, T& b )\
> 6: { T t = a; a = b; b = t; }
> 7: #endif
> ```

All that is required is a unique token. I use the filename, replacing the period by an underscore and prefixing two underscores to the filename. So, parmswap.h becomes __PARMSWAP_H. This is a simple way to come up with a guardian token. I apply an #ifndef directive to the token on line 2, which I haven't defined, evaluating to true, causing the code in the header to be included. In doing so, it also causes the token to be defined on line 3. Line 7 rounds off the #ifndef with an enclosing #endif.

The next source code file that tries to perform text replacement will be greeted by the gatekeeper, and the #ifndef will evaluate to false. This will force the compiler to resolve references to the names by searching in the symbol table, where in fact the names do reside. This technique needs to be applied consistently to every header file you create.

This is an example of the reworking of the compiler that would have to be done before the preprocessor could be retired.

Creating Strings

There are many little techniques employed by the preprocessor to achieve specific results. Another one you haven't looked at yet is the ability of the preprocessor to create strings from text. The # symbol before text indicates to the preprocessor that the text should be converted into a null-terminated (or ASCIIZ) string.

This is by no means earth-shattering, but it has been employed usefully in a few situations. To use this technique, simply prefix the text with the pound (#) sign, and the preprocessor will convert it to a printable string. You will see a use for this in coming sections.

#error

The #error directive throws an error to the compiler, halting compilation. You can use the #error directive to stop compilation when a semantic violation has occurred.

Listing 4.2 shows a simplified example demonstrating the syntactical application of the error directive.

Listing 4.2   Error.cpp—Demonstrates the Syntax for Using the
***#error* Directive**

```
// ERROR.CPP - Demonstrates #error preprocessor directive
#ifndef __ERROR_H
#error Use when a semantic error has occurred
#endif
void main(){}
```

This code demonstrates a trivial working application that throws an error during compilation because I forgot to include the module's header file. This is a less than practical use but does demonstrate the syntax of the directive.

Finding a suitable application for the technique, as with all other programming, is up to your discretion. Check some of the header files in the Bc5\Include directory to see how it has been used by Borland. One example in varargs.h uses the #error directive to avoid including header files with similar but incompatible declarations.

Advantageous Uses of the Preprocessor

The preprocessor inherited from C still has advantageous applications. Some of these have been demonstrated already. While teaching beginning to advanced programmers to use C++, I have found that coding techniques evolve as programmers become more skilled.

The newest programmers tend to be verbose and use text cutting and pasting when conditions in their programs require a change in the code used. While this is not uncommon in many endeavors, it is worth noting that books and other resource materials can accelerate the progression of the learning curve. The old adage applies: "Learn from the mistakes of others."

A Hypothetical Skill Progression

I have seen this kind of skill progression often enough to believe that it is not uncommon. Novice programmers encumbered with tracking down errors become diligent in placing debugging statements in their programs from the onset. Having tested the program and resolving any bugs, moderately skilled programmers may then cut debug code.

Realizing the extra work involved in cutting and reimplementing debug code if more testing is required later, the programmer may begin to comment out the code, making it readily reusable when further testing is required. The effort it takes to rewrite the code is greater than the effort required to uncomment. A natural tendency toward conservation of work—some call laziness—is followed.

Commenting is easier but it doesn't take too many programs shipped with debug code (because you forgot to comment something) to realize that a better way is needed.

After some experience, programmers may lean toward using preprocessor directives to effectively "comment out" code by changing the directive's status from defined to undefined. Simply wrapping the code in a compiler directive, like

```
#ifdef DEBUG
        // debug code here!
#endif
```

then modulating the token DEBUG will cause the preprocessor to include or not include the code inside the wrap. Whether this level of understanding is arrived at very early or much later depends on the individual. If you are self-taught, learning by trial and error, the technique may take quite a while to present itself. If you are reading this book, an even better way will be presented next, which means your progression will pace the rate at which you read.

The problem with the last technique, while better than the first two, is that it makes your code look as if it has been hit with an ugly stick. If you are conscientiously testing each code path, loop controls, and the like, you will have these DEBUG directives littered throughout your program. Debugging is necessary, but this makes your code very busy and adds many extra lines to read. The later section, "Techniques for Writing Clean Debug Code," demonstrates a much cleaner method.

Handling Header Files

The header file convention is used to contain the presentation of each module's interface. The interface then consists of those items that you decide need to be shared with other modules. These items may be comprised of functions, classes, or other items. Placing declarations in header files is only a convention, but as in life, if you want to be unconventional, the penalties can be severe.

While the declaration and definition can appear adjacent to each other, the declaration—as it pertains to functions, often referred to as the interface—must precede the definition, and both of these things have to be done before first use. This requirement is necessary to allow the compiler to perform type-checking. Failing to provide a declaration before using a type, function, or variable will cause a compilation error. By making declarations in the header file, you can be assured that they are all included where necessary by using the #include directive in the modules that refer to these items. The module that contains the definition is the first that comes to mind.

Sometimes the placement of elements reduces the work involved. Suppose, for example, that you want to include a header file foo.h in the module Foo.cpp. If you place the gatekeeper preprocessor directive (see the section "Using #ifdef, #else, and #endif") in the module file, like this

```
// FOO.CPP - Module file
#ifndef __FOO_H
#define __FOO_H
     #include "foo.h"
#endif
```

then you will have to place it in every .cpp file that needs some foo. Alternatively, by placing the preprocessor directive in foo.h around the declarations contained therein, you have to write the three lines only once. Both techniques work, but the last one reduces the number of times you have to use it to one, and it is less likely that you will forget to do it. Both applications will avoid the "multiple declaration" error, but the placement of the directives in the header is the more correct method.

Error Reporting

There is a somewhat philosophical approach to programming. Simply stated, by forcing errors as early as possible, the likelihood that they will be more easily detected and less problematic increases. A runtime error for an air traffic control system is likely to get someone killed, but the same is not true for an error that is detected by the preprocessor or the compiler.

A more significant consideration is that runtime errors reflect badly on you as a programmer, and may be annoying enough to have adverse effects on your future financial situation. As I am attempting to tie the philosophic considerations to your finances, here it is in a nutshell: The earlier the problem is detected, the more likely and less expensive the resolution will be.

Let us apply this to the syntactical preprocessing that occurs. You may have noticed that the color and font of the code changes, depending on the usage. In the default environment settings, comments become blue and italicized, keywords are black and bold, and preprocessor directives are green. If these changes do not occur for these kinds of constructs, then you are immediately made aware of a syntax error. (The notification is implicitly made due to a lack of the change in color and type.) There is no point in compiling when you know there is a syntax error, and the error should be easy to find because it is localized to that fragment of text.

Compiler errors are often easier to detect than runtime errors because of the good error reporting system built into the compiler. Linker errors often become a little more difficult to find, so effort should be made to push errors back to the compiler. In lieu of C++'s strong type-checking, many errors that might be due to improper function arguments are now caught by the compiler. Runtime errors are the least favorable and should be avoided at all costs—or be sure to update your passport!

I have not yet mentioned the #error directive. This is because I wanted to present background arguments beforehand. Assuming you agree upon the order of errors, such that syntax errors are the most favorable, followed by compiler errors, and then linker errors, and runtime/logic errors are the least favorable, then whatever measures you may employ to force errors as close to compile time as possible is the ideal.

One technique you can employ is to use the #error directive to indicate when something has broken your semantic vision of correctness. While this is not always easy to do, a little effort spent early on may save hours later. If a semantic relationship is identifiable, then using the #error directive can cause the compiler to stop when a violation occurs. It is up to you to detect the relationship and to define what a violation is; the #error macro can help you enforce it.

II

Programming in C++

None of the techniques are meant to satisfy or be used in every set of circumstances; rather, it is up to you, the craftsmen, to find adequate employment for each.

assert

The preprocessor has long been used to implement what is commonly know as assert. The exact specification of assert can be found in the file \Bc5\Include\assert.h. I have not included that code because emulating the functionality is easy enough.

The assertion macro—which means it is created by a #define statement—simply takes an argument that can be evaluated like a Boolean. This applies to any datum or conditional statement that can be evaluated to some integral result. So any zero value would evaluate to false and any non-zero would evaluate to true. If the condition evaluates to false, then the assertion terminates program execution, displaying the fact that an assertion failed, including which file and line numbers were involved.

How *assert* Works. assert is defined as a macro because it uses the __FILE__ and __LINE__ keywords. These exist internally for each file and line, and are available for use while debugging (which means you can use them, but you are not responsible for maintaining them). The specific reason a macro was used is in lieu of its text replacement properties. When a #define is used, it implies that wherever the defined name appears, it should be replaced with its value.

This text replacement is necessary because otherwise the __LINE__ and __FILE__ values would not contain the filename and line number where the assertion failed, but rather they would be the same: where the assertion function was defined.

An assertion function might easily be defined as a macro taking an argument that, on evaluating to non-zero, simply returns, or, on evaluating to zero, prints a simple message, line number, and filename, and then terminates the program execution.

The assertion function already exists. To use the assert macro, include the assert.h file and call assert with a Boolean evaluative argument. For example,

```
assert(1);
```

passes the assertion test, but

```
assert( 5==2 );
```

does not because 5==2 evaluates to false. The assert function is a macro because the preprocessor can use the __LINE__ and __FILE__ values maintained by the IDE to coincide with the location of the assertion test.

Why *assert* Anything? The assert macro is used for invariant testing. In other words, it is a debugging technique. Assertions are used when certain conditions, criteria, or range values must be met. These kinds of items are referred to as *invariants*.

When building software, one debugging technique that can be employed is to use the assert macro everywhere that certain minimum conditions must be maintained for proper performance of the code. The `assert` macro will inform you in a very abrupt manner when these assumptions are depended on but have been violated.

Suppose, for example, that you have defined a simple array as follows:

```
const int MAX = 10;
int a[MAX];
```

Any time the array is accessed, you can assert that the index is not out of bounds. For example,

```
assert( j>=0 && j<MAX );
a[j] = 5;
```

In this very simple example it is unlikely that, seeing a's maximum value, a user would access a with an invalid index. Unfortunately real programs are seldom this simple.

Assertion code should never replace runtime conditional checking. Thus, if you were using such native data type arrays in code, you should be checking the range of the index with runtime code. Thus, the fragment becomes:

```
assert( j>= 0 && j<MAX );
if( j>=0 && j<MAX )
     a[j] = 5;              // access a[j]
else
                           // some kind of run-time exception handling
```

The reason is simply this: When the mechanism enabling the assertion is turned off, you do not want to leave the direct access to the array unguarded. Asserting invariants—in this case, the range 0...9 is the invariant—is an added measure to force misuse to be redressed as early as possible.

Building these kinds of checks and balances into your code at design-time will have the effect of shortening the total time it takes to debug the rest of your program when it is complete. This is a debug-as-you-go technique as opposed to one monolithic testing phase.

Using *assert*. Using `assert` is a straightforward process. By including the assert.h header file invariant, violation detection is immediately available. Remember the `assert` function terminates a program, so leaving it in may scare the bejeesuz out of your user community. Fortunately, removing the assertion is very easy. Simply define `NDEBUG` on the line right before the included assert.h file, and the assert is invalidated by preprocessor replacement.

Whenever I include the assert.h file, I include the commented out `NDEBUG` so I remember to turn assertions off. Here is how it looks in my code:

```
// #define NDEBUG // uncomment this to turn assert off
#include <assert.h>
```

By using these two lines in concert, I am informing those who follow how to undo my invariant checks without removing the actual code from the module.

Uncommenting NDEBUG makes the compiler do the work, making it less likely that I will miss any calls to assertion. When I am ready to extend my program, or when a bug is discovered, commenting the #define NDEBUG and recompiling enables all of my assertions.

This notion of using the preprocessor to control how and when debug code is included can be emulated by copying the way that the designer of assert.h defines the assert macro based on a preprocessor directive. The result is cleaner debug code.

Techniques for Writing Clean Debug Code

Debug code seems to be an afterthought in many programs that I have seen, written by a wide variety of programmers from diverse backgrounds. This may be a perception or it may be that universities and trainers present it that way.

Using a hotel metaphorically to represent a program, inserting debug code after the program is built seems to me the same thing as ripping out the walls to put in sprinklers, alarms, and circuit breakers after the paper, paint, and carpet have been applied; it's much harder, it's expensive, and it would seem to waste a ton of resources.

Debug code serves its purpose more easily and probably more thoroughly if applied as conscientiously as the rest of the program and at the same time. The simple fact of the matter is that I can more readily come up with events or data that might break my code while defining each piece than I can a month later, when the testing green light goes on.

The preprocessor can be used to clean up test code and make it easier to control when or if the code actually exists in the compiled program. You saw in an earlier section that by wrapping debug code in a compiler directive, it could easily be stripped or included in the compilable code by whether or not the directive was defined or undefined. Taking this example one step further, the same result can be achieved with a lot less typing by altering the debug code a little, which results in cleaner code.

Debug Print

Borrowing the assert macro as an example, you can make a debug print macro that can be easily turned on or off and used to trace code execution. There is no absolute, correct way to perform this technique, but I will demonstrate one option from which I hope you can create others.

This specific implementation of the technique involves console output (outputs to the screen). I am the first to admit that you may need to establish an alternate way to perform the output based on your program's interface choice.

> **Note**
>
> Alternate output devices might consist of writing to a text file using fstreams, printing to a message box using a VBX or OWL control, or some other appropriate mode of recording the trace.
>
> You could easily define several in a single macro, using a compiler directive to determine which is applied. This would involve the use of the #elif directive.

Listing 4.3 shows one implementation of the technique, followed by its explanation.

> **Note**
>
> The line numbers in the following listing are used as a reference point but should not be placed in a program.

Listing 4.3 bugprint.h—Debugging a Statement around Code

```
1: #include <iostream.h>
2: #ifdef DEBUG_PRINT
3:     #define DebugPrint(arg) cout << "executing: " << #arg << endl; \
4:                 arg
5: #else
6:     #define DebugPrint(arg) arg
7: #endif
```

> **Note**
>
> The code in listing 4.3, which is borrowed from David Thielen's *No Bugs!* (Addison Wesley, 1992), requires a slightly different form of output based on the kind of user-interface your program uses. (As it appears here, this example works well only for console output.)

Placing this code in a header file, whenever I want a console code execution trace technique, I would simply need to include the header file and #define DEBUG_PRINT.

> **Tip**
>
> Declaring DEBUG_PRINT in all uppercase is simply a convention that I use. My convention also declares class names and consts of all uppercase. You don't have to follow any one person's convention, but be consistent within your own code.

Perhaps I would call this file bugprint.h. Once I have included the header and defined the preprocessor token, the macro can be used in the following manner:

```
DebugPrint( a=5 );      // sample arbitrary code
```

It looks just like a function call, but the preprocessor converts it to

```
cout << "executing: " << "a=5" << endl;
a=5;
```

The pound (#) symbol converts the code passed as arg to a string, and the second line simply executes the code. In this fashion, not only is the code executed, but the executing code is printed to the standard output device. Modifying it to print to a message box, file, printer, or something else simply requires you to change the code from cout... to code that calls a function to write to another device.

Adding the __LINE__ and __FILE__ values to the output statement enables you to make a down and dirty code tracer. Certainly a similar kind of thing is accomplished by a debugger, but this is a more passive version of the same thing. You can easily disable the DebugPrint by undefining DEBUG_PRINT with #undef.

When you use #undef DEBUG_PRINT and recompile, the macro is simply replaced with the code itself, without the output code. In this manner, you have localized the use of the #ifdef wrap to the macro instead of littering your program with it.

Code Trapping or Logging

A similar technique can be used to trap a program's flow or to log the flow of execution to a data file. Determining how to use this information is up to you, but there are many constructive ways to use the information.

Some experts suggest that it is a liability not to ensure that every code path has been tested. By using the filename and line number, you can ensure that every line of code has been traced and alternate paths have been adequately exercised. (I expect that in the not-too-distant future this will be an ingressive point for litigation.) Once the code has been adequately tested, the tracing or logging can be turned off.

Borland has brought back the Profiler, whose job it is to find bottlenecks. Using a variant of the DebugPrint may be useful in ascertaining where you might begin to look for bottlenecks in your code. By examining the log file, you will be able to determine which line numbers appear most often. The goal here is not to replace existing tools, but rather to make them easier to use.

Tip

When you are optimizing code, find the 20 percent of your code that consumes 80 percent of the execution time and optimize that code.

A Code Trap

When implementing a code trap, create a macro—remember you need the line and filename—that calls a function, passing it to the code that was executed, the filename, and the line number, and then writing this information to an arbitrary file.

Listing 4.4 shows an example that writes the information to a file named Deleteme.trp. This technique works passively in the background and the output file may be viewed after the program is finished. (I would not use this in a multithreaded program.)

Listing 4.4   trap.h—Traces the Line and Module of the Flow of Program Execution

```
1: // TRAP.H - Code trapping macro
2: #ifndef __TRAP_H
3: #define __TRAP_H
4: #include <fstream.h>
5: inline void Trap( const char* arg, char *file, int line,
6:     const char* fname = "DELETEME.TRP" )
7: {
8:     ofstream of(fname);
9:     of << "code: " << arg << endl
10:         << "file: " << file << endl
11:         << "line#: " << line << endl;
12: }
13: #ifdef TRAP_CODE
14:     #define TRAP(arg) \
15:         Trap( #arg, __FILE__, __LINE__ ); \
16:         arg
17: #else
18:     #define TRAP(arg) arg
19: #endif
20: #endif
```

Line 1 is a friendly reminder that when the file is printed, the filename does not appear unless you place it in a comment.

Lines 2, 3, and 20 are preprocessor directives that enable the compiler to avoid name collisions. Using these consistently in every header will save headaches later.

Line 4 includes the fstream.h file. This file includes the definition of the file stream classes. Derived from the iostream class hierarchy (see chapter 13, "iostreams"), this class contains functionality that enables you to manipulate files using the ostream operator << for output. (A complete understanding of how this works requires knowledge of the classes, the stream class, and operator overloading.)

Lines 5 through 12 define the workhorse function that is an inline function that writes the code fragment, line number, and filename to a text file. By using a default argument for the log file, I can elect to change the filename at a later date or modify how the log filename is derived.

Lines 13 to 19 comprise the macro. If the TRAP_CODE is undefined, then all the macro does is execute the code; on the other hand, when TRAP_CODE is defined, the code fragment is logged as well as executed. Remember a macro is used in this instance to coordinate the __LINE__ and __FILE__ values with those in the code.

The following test program demonstrates how to include the trap and an example of its use:

```
// TRAP.CPP - A simple test for code execution trapping and logging
// This code does not need to be included to use the logging macro.
// It exists to test the macro only.
#define TRAP_CODE
#include "trap.h"
void main( int argc, char* argv[] )
{
    // simple program that prints command line arguments
    // argv[0] is the qualified program name
    for( int i=0; i<argc; i++ )
    {
        TRAP( cout << argv[i] << endl );
    }
}
```

In this context, the program prints out the command-line arguments, while the Deleteme.trp file contains:

code: cout << argv[i] << endl

file: Trap.cpp

line#: 17

The Trap.cpp file was created to provide a simplified test of the trap; all you would need to do to use the trapping mechanism is to define the preprocessor name followed by an inclusion of the trap.h file.

Replacing the Preprocessor

The potential for preprocessor misuse exists. In cases where preprocessor misuse is the most problematic the most problematic, it has already been replaced. While a systematic replacement of functionality (once the domain of the preprocessor) is in effect, many items such as #include are still necessary, preventing it from being dropped from the language for the time being.

Undoubtedly almost all existing code would be broken simply by the lack of backwards support in any replacement device for the #include directive. However, some things do have C++ replacements, which are welcomed by many and spurned by some.

Replace *#define* Manifest Constants with *const*

Preprocessing is not the same as compiling. The C-style constants of days gone by should be replaced with C++ const data. The preprocessor does not check to ensure type-compatibility between a manifest constant defined like this:

```
#define MAX 10
```

and the context within which it is used. Therefore, if MAX were used in a context where it doesn't make sense, it may be difficult to detect. These kinds of constants must be replaced with the const keyword, making the previous statement

```
const int MAX = 10;
```

The latter version is handled by the compiler, so its use in context can be checked by the compiler, resulting in good error reporting if necessary.

Tip

There is one instance where neither method is appropriate or works correctly. This is the case of the old NULL definition. In C-style programs, programmers may have defined NULL as

```
#define NULL 0
```

but the use of #define to create manifest constants is not compatible with the new paradigm. The solution might be to apply const then. The problem is how to define NULL. Simply defining a const NULL as some specific data type won't do, because it will cause an error when assigned to any other data type. For example, defining NULL as

```
const int NULL = 0;
```

won't compile assigned to user-defined types. Defining multiple NULLs based on type is confusing and requires users to remember too many names. The solution, then, is to simply use 0 when you mean NULL, for every data type. Using 0 is the only thing that works correctly and consistently in every context.

Using *Inline* instead of Macros

The C-style macro definition, which is a carryover from Assembler days, has been replaced with a compiler version that is type safe, overloadable, and ultimately has the same effect.

I read somewhere that C was designed by Brian Kernighan and Dennis Ritchie because they didn't want to program in Assembler; then it becomes easy to trace the use of #define as an extension of Assembler's macro substitution mechanism. You have already seen a few remaining uses of macros in earlier sections, where one might argue that it is advantageous to use them still. In fact, the techniques shown would not work in quite the same way without them.

The difference is that, in general, it is appropriate for several reasons to use inline functions. Specifying a function as an inline function is accomplished implicitly by defining a function in a class, or by preceding its declaration or definition with the keyword inline. What the compiler does with inline functions then, is that everywhere a function call would have been made, the body of the inline function is placed instead.

The result is that for very simple functions, the overhead of a function call is avoided. On the flip-side, if a function was inlined no matter what, code-bloat could occur because multiple occurrences of the same, large code would cause more lines of code to be generated than would occur had a simple function call been made. This is why use of inlining, whether explicit or implicit, is suggestive at most.

As a general rule of thumb, good candidates for inline functions are those that are very small and do not contain loops. The syntax for an inline function can be found in the Swap example.

Inline Benefits. An immediate benefit of using inline functions instead of macros is that the compiler can check every occurrence of the function call and can ensure that the argument types match. Another benefit is that inline functions can be traced by debuggers, whereas macros cannot. This makes it easier to hunt down bugs. A third benefit is that the error-handling system will refer to an error in a #define at compile-time at the point in which the macro is used, as opposed to an inline function: The error system will typically refer to the line of code in the inline function. In almost all circumstances, use inline functions rather than #define macros.

The Faces of Inline Functions. Inline functions can appear in a couple of different forms. It is important that you recognize them. The most obvious form of an inline function is a function whose declaration

```
inline void Swap( char& a, car& b); // declare swap
```

or definition

```
inline void Swap( char& a, char& b ) // define swap

{ char t = a; a = b; b = t; }
```

is a prefix at the point of declaration or definition. A less obvious face of an inline function is when it is defined in a class.

C programmers should assume for now that a class is simply a better struct. (Non-C programmers may ignore the previous sentence.) Suppose there is a class F00, declared in the following manner:

```
class F00
{
    void FOOBAR(){};     // a null inline function
};
```

Because of the appearance of the function-body {} (regardless of the fact that it contains no code) next to FOOBAR, this function is considered to be an inline function. So when you see the {} (left and right brackets) within a class declaration, like the example, it means that this function is implicitly defined as an inline function.

In the *Annotated Reference Manual* (ARM), by Stroustrop and Ellis, it is stated that use of the keyword inline is redundant in this context. While it may be redundant, it is not an error and may make understanding the intent of the programmer a little clearer, so I would suggest that you consider using it.

From Here...

This chapter covers some of the historically important roles the preprocessor has played in the evolution of C++ as a language. In addition, it demonstrates some techniques that are still viable, including the use of assertions and creating other debug techniques. While demonstrating some of these facets of the preprocessor's previous and current roles, I may have introduced some topics that are unclear to you.

Further examples of those features can be found throughout this book. From here, you will find:

- Chapter 5, "Commenting and Naming Conventions," discusses topics related to commenting styles and naming conventions.
- Chapter 9, "Data Quantifiers and Qualifiers," examines the use of const and other qualifiers.
- Chapter 10, "Writing Expressions," covers writing the general expressions that comprise the building blocks of all code.
- Chapter 14, "Basic Class Concepts," covers basic class concepts.
- Chapter 19, "Using Templates Classes," covers templates in their fully functional form.

CHAPTER 5

Commenting and Naming Conventions

We all know deep down that comments are essential for documenting source code, and we know that naming conventions make source code more readable and understandable. But who among us has not—in a caffeine-fueled burst of keystrokes on the eve of a pressing deadline—fired off a great new member function (or a whole new class) peppered with variable declarations like int x and char *p without a single comment? Admit it. I have…and still do. And, no, it's not the end of the world. That brand new member function probably works like a charm and is bug-free to boot. It ships in your next product release and you forget all about it.

Six months later, it's crunch time on your next release and you happen across that same function. You look at it again and again, and ask yourself, "What the heck was I thinking of here?" Now you have to spend an hour tracing through that once stellar code just to figure out what is going on. Just imagine what choice words the programmer in the next cubicle will have for you if he has to deduce your twisted logic! To avoid these types of situations, we examine some common and fairly simple commenting and naming conventions in this chapter.

In this chapter, you become familiar with:

- Commenting C++ source code, including source and header files, member functions, variables, and so on
- Maintaining your comments
- Deciphering Hungarian notation and applying it as a naming convention
- Exploring some alternatives to Hungarian notation
- Self-documenting C++ source code through judicious naming choices

Using Comments for More Understandable Source Code

Comments in any programming language allow you to clearly document your source code. In fact, if you are undertaking a smaller project that lacks external documentation of some sort, program comments are often the sole means of documentation. In C and C++, programmers often pride themselves on very optimized solutions that can appear almost cryptic (commenting often has the added bonus of deciphering accompanying source code).

I recently inherited some source code from a prototype C++ application, the function of which was to convert some last name/first name pairings of the following form:

```
(last-1, first-1) (last-2, first-2) ... (last-n, first-n)
```

into

```
first-1 last-1, first-2 last-2, ... and first-n last-n
```

So, for example

```
(Washington, George) (Adams, John) (Jefferson, Thomas)
```

can be displayed as

```
George Washington, John Adams and Thomas Jefferson
```

For the purposes of our example, however, we simplify the function to just convert a single name pair.

Naturally, being a quick prototype, the function in question lacked any comments whatsoever. The C programmer responsible rarely made use of C's string library functions, electing rather to undertake all character searching using his own in-line pointer iterations. Let's take a look at the cryptic result (which appears just as often in C++ as it does in C):

```c
void ConvertInternlNameToFirstLast(char *string, char *result)
{
    char *p;

    *result = '\0';

    while (*string && *string != '(')
    {
        string++;
    }

    if (*string == '\0') return;

    p = ++string;

    while (*p && *p != ',' && *p != ')')
    {
        p++;
    }
```

```
if (*p == '\0') return;

if (*p == ')')
{
    while (*string && *string != ')')
    {
        *result++ = *string++;
    }

    *result = '\0';
}
else
{
    p++;

    while (*p && *p == ' ')
    {
        p++;
    }

    if (*p == '\0') return;

    while (*p && *p != ')')
    {
        *result++ = *p++;
    }

    if (*p == '\0')
    {
        *result = '\0';
        return;
    }

    *result++ = ' ';

    while (*string && *string != ',')
    {
        *result++ = *string++;
    }

    *result = '\0';
}

}
```

This piece of source code requires a great deal of thought to figure out exactly what its intent is. Beyond its stated requirements, it's obviously doing a lot of error checking and handling of special conditions, such as allowing padded spaces and single names (for example, Madonna) that lack commas. Adding comments to the code makes the code readily understandable. Before we do this, let's consider the commenting syntax of C++.

Types of Comments in C++

Two types of comments are available in C++. The first style of commenting begins with the token /* and ends with the token */, which is already familiar to those of you who have experience programming in C. Here are a few examples:

```
/* this is a one-line comment */

/* this is a comment that extends
   over multiple lines */
```

Comments using the tokens /* and */ cannot be nested.

For instance

```
/* Here's one comment, now /* let's start another */ */
```

is invalid. You often run into this situation if you use comments to debug your code. In a debugging situation, you might have a few lines of code as follows:

```
while (*string && /* *string != ')' */)
{
    ...
}
```

where you've commented out the condition *string != ')' temporarily. If you then decide to comment out the whole while-loop using /* and */ as follows:

```
/* while (*string && /* *string != ')' */)
{
    ...
} */
```

you'll receive an error message during compilation similar to the following in Borland C++ 5.0:

```
Expression syntax
```

The Borland compiler, however, does offer you the option to explicitly allow nested comments using compilation flags from within the IDE. To do so, follow these steps:

1. From the Option menu, choose Project. The Project Options dialog box appears (see fig. 5.1).
2. In the Topics list, double-click Compiler.
3. Click Source (one of the sub-topics under Compiler).
4. In the Source options on the right side of the Project Options dialog box, check the Nested Comments box to enable nested comments.
5. Click OK to save your changes.

Now any nested comments within your source code will compile error-free. If you use the Borland C++ compiler from the command line, simply include the -C flag for any source files that you compile:

```
BCC32 -C main.cpp
```

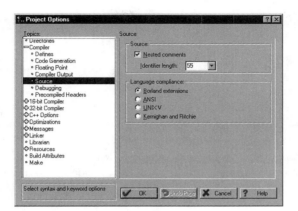

Fig. 5.1

Enabling nested comments in your projects.

The only drawback to allowing nested comments within your Borland C++ projects is if you move your source code to other compilers or other platforms that don't support nested comments, you'll have to change all of your comments accordingly to compile successfully. If you don't find yourself in such a cross-compiler/cross-platform environment, feel free to use the nested comments feature of Borland C++ 5.0.

Tip

An easy way to avoid the problem of nested comments across compilers is to rely on preprocessor macros to comment out large sections of source code that contain comments. For instance, we could comment out our while-loop—which contains a /* ... */ comment already—using #if and #endif:

```
#if 0
while (*string && /* *string != ')' */)
{
    ...
}
#endif
```

The #if macro checks if a condition is True—because 0 is never True, the code enclosed by #if and #endif is not compiled. Not relying on compiler implementation of a nested comments feature, the practice of using #if and #endif works across all C and C++ compilers.

The second style of comment in C++ begins with the token // and terminates at the end of the line where the token occurs. As such, the // comment can only be used on a single line. If you do have multiple lines of comments, simply start each line with //:

```
// this is a comment that extends
// over multiple lines
```

II

Programming in C++

Single-line comments can also follow code; they do not need to extend across the whole line of source code. For instance:

```
while (*string && *string != ')')   // Loop until a close paren is found
                                     // or until we've reached the end
                                     // of string.
{
    ...
}
```

Note also that the // comment can be included in a /* ... */ comment. Therefore, if you restrict yourself to // comments in your code, in a debugging situation you can use the /* ... */ comment to comment out large blocks of code without worrying about compiler errors resulting from nested comments:

```
/*
while (*string && *string != ')')   // Loop until a close paren is found
                                     // or until we've reached the end
                                     // of string.
{
    string++;
    ...
}
*/
```

Applying C++ Comments to Our Example

Now that we're familiar with the various types of comments provided by C++, let's add some to the previous example and see just how more readable and understandable the noncommented code becomes.

```
// The following function accepts a string (char *string) which represents
// a last name/first name pair of the form (last-name, first-name) and
// converts it to the form first-name last-name, returning the result in
// char *result.  It is the responsibility of the calling function to
// provide adequate storage for the result.

void ConvertInternalNameToFirstLast(char *string, char *result)
{
    char *p; // p iterates over the input string.

    // If our function encounters an error, we want to set result equal
    // to an empty string.
    *result = '\0';

    // Iterate until the first open paren is found; i.e., ignore
    // any erroneous leading characters.
    while (*string && *string != '(')
    {
        string++;
    }

    // If we don't find the first open paren, return an empty string.
    if (*string == '\0') return;
```

```
// Skip the open paren; it's not included in the result.
p = ++string;

// Iterate until the first comma or close paren.  We include the
// close paren to catch single names like Madonna.
while (*p && *p != ',' && *p != ')')
{
    p++;
}

// If we don't find a comma or close paren, return an empty string.
if (*p == '\0') return;

if (*p == ')')
{
    // In the case of a single name, copy from the first character
    // of the input string
    // to the character before the close paren.
    while (*string && *string != ')')
    {
        *result++ = *string++;
    }
}
else
{
    // In the case of a first and last name, skip the comma
    // and any spaces following the comma.
    p++;

    while (*p && *p == ' ')
    {
        p++;
    }

    // If we reach the end of the string (i.e., all spaces), return
    // an empty string.
    if (*p == '\0') return;

    // Copy all characters from the first character of the first
    // name to the character
    // before the close paren.
    while (*p && *p != ')')
    {
        *result++ = *p++;
    }

    // If we reach the end of the string without finding a
    // close paren, return an empty string.
    if (*p == '\0')
    {
        *result = '\0';
        return;
    }

    // Store the space which separates first name from last name.
    *result++ = ' ';
```

```
        // Copy all characters from the first character of the
        // last name to the separating comma.
        while (*string && *string != ',')
        {
            *result++ = *string++;
        }
    }

    // Terminate the resulting string.
    *result = '\0';
}
```

Although the comments shed some light on the example function, you'll see later in the section, "Naming Variables and Functions," how following a naming convention in the function also helps the code's readability. In that section, you will see that we have gone a little overboard on the comments in this function.

Commenting Conventions

There is one difficulty associated with commenting and naming conventions: sticking to them. If you are employed in a programming capacity and your company has published conventions, the problem becomes moot—it's your job. Some conventions, in large software organizations, actually overwhelm the source code. I recently worked for a large corporation where the comments preceding a function extended over the better half of a page, cross-referencing design and function specifications, test plans, and so on. The in-house compiler even checked the syntax of our comments! The majority of you, however, probably don't face such rigid standards—you're simply looking for a convention that's easy to implement and presents a uniform style for readable and understandable code.

A very simple standard that is fairly common among developers is associated with a popular cross-platform development library—the *Zinc Application Framework*. It is extremely easy to follow and lends a clean, crisp commenting structure for your code. The types of comments suggested by the convention are aimed at files, functions, variables, and blocks.

Before examining this commenting convention, bear in mind that you need to feel comfortable personally (or as a group, department, or company) with any commenting or naming conventions that you apply to your projects. Conventions can—and should—be customized to suit your particular needs. The convention proposed by the Zinc Application Framework is just one option.

Files

Source and header files should generally begin with a block of comments that states the application or library name, filename, and any associated copyright information. For instance, if our previous example function is part of an application entitled "Bibliographies-R-Us" and is contained in a source file entitled Convert.cpp, an appropriate block of comments at the beginning of our source file may be:

```
// Bibliographies-R-Us - CONVERT.CPP
// COPYRIGHT (C) 1995-1996.  All Rights Reserved.
// Macmillan Computer Publishing.  Indianapolis, Indiana  USA
```

A block of comments similar to this one lends every source and header file in a project a uniform block of information that clearly distinguishes where the file belongs. It also presents a nice header during printing (if your text editor doesn't provide the luxury of generating automatic headers). If you desire additional information, like the responsible programmer's name, for instance, just add an extra line or two. Remember to keep it consistent across all your files, though!

Functions

Functions and member functions in most commenting conventions require a block of comments that briefly states the purpose of the respective functions. It is also customary to describe any input and output parameters to the function. Try to keep it short and to the point, if possible—remember, it's code, not the great American novel!

```
// The following function accepts a string (char *string) that represents
// a last name/first name pair of the form (last-name, first-name) and
// converts it to the form first-name last-name, returning the result in
// char *result.  It is the responsibility of the calling function to
// provide adequate storage for the result.

void ConvertInternalNamesToFirstLast(char *string, char *result)
{
    ...
}
```

Other items, such as the programmer's name, a list of calling functions, side effects, and error conditions, are sometimes included in comments and describe a function. You can add such items if your project requires a higher level of detail. This brings us to commenting of variables.

> **Note**
>
> Classes can make use of this same type of commenting—a brief description of the functionality contained in the class. In addition, classes may also contain comments internal to them; for instance, a brief description of a private data item.

Variables

Any important variable declarations that merit description or clarification should be followed by a brief comment. The comments in general must adhere to a certain punctuation style; for example, starting the comment with a capital letter and ending with a period. Many programmers choose to align such comments with tabs as follows:

```
char *p;                // An iterator for characters in the input string.
char *q;                // An iterator for characters in the result string.
int numberOfNames = 0;  // The number of names processed.
```

II

Programming in C++

Maintaining such a clean tab alignment can become a hassle, therefore, it's just as likely to see:

```
char *p;      // An iterator for characters in the input string.
char *q;      // An iterator for characters in the result string.
int numberOfNames = 0; // The number of names processed.
```

Whichever style comes easier to you is fine.

Blocks

Finally, within functions, blocks of code often require explanation if their logic is not trivial or immediately obvious. Perhaps you're implementing an algorithm consisting of a number of distinct steps. You may need to describe one or more of the blocks (loops, conditional statements, collection of statements) with a brief comment. Some developers place their comments on the beginning line of a block of code as follows:

```
while (*string && *string != ')')  // Loop until a close paren is found
                                    // or until we've reached the end of
                                    // string.
{
    ...
}
```

while others choose to precede the block of code with a comment line, such as:

```
// Loop until a close paren is found or until we've reached the end of
// string.
    while (*string && *string != ')')
{
    ...
}
```

Preceding the block of code with a comment line has a couple of advantages. First, if you need to copy a block of code, you have the choice of copying just the code (leaving out the preceding comment) or copying both. Otherwise, you always need to copy the comment and then remove or alter it when pasting the code in its new location. Second, placing the comment before the block of code as opposed to the end of a line keeps line lengths fairly consistent. Often when you place comments at the end of a line, they tend to run off the edge of the display. Although your text editor might easily accommodate this, someone else who needs to read your code might not have a text editor that does.

As a general rule, individual lines of code probably don't need their own comments. The exception is when the single line of code is not clear from context. For example:

```
// The initial '(' of a pair is not included in the result.
p = ++string;
```

The question of when to comment and not to comment is a tricky one and brings us to our next topic.

Maintaining Your Comments

As we've already seen, comments are great at making source code more readable. However, as in most things, too much of a good thing often leads to undesirable results. Consider the programmer who comments practically every line of code he produces. This may be great for that individual programmer, but consider for a moment another programmer who needs to peruse that same source code. Instead of clearly documented code, he might see a lot of added text that simply clutters the source code—it's really quite difficult to see the code for the comments. As with commenting conventions, all programmers involved have to feel comfortable with the amount of comments—when to comment and when not to.

One major problem associated with using too many comments is maintenance. Suppose, for instance, some source code with a considerable amount of comments needs to be revised. You come in and change a few lines of code, ignoring the comments. You compile the code, it works and the revision is complete. Everything's fine, right? Wrong! If you have comments in your program, they—like the code—need to be maintained. Updating the code and not the comments leads to discrepancies between code and comments. A comment that previously added enlightenment to a section of code may become misleading, inappropriate, or downright wrong.

As stated, the quantity of comments is really up to the individual programmer. However, if you're looking for some guidelines, Bjarne Stroustrup, designer of C++, suggests a few tips that will help in making your comments concise and pertinent.

- *First, if a concept is clearly stated by the C++ source code, there is no need to add a comment (avoid redundant comments).* For example, if you have a counter variable entitled wordCount, a comment like the following is completely redundant:

  ```
  wordCount++;  // increment the current word count
  ```

  If you're a C++ —or a C—programmer, wordCount++ is comment enough. Reading wordCount++ automatically brings to mind "increment the current word count"— there is no need for a comment. A comment, in such a case, simply becomes a deterrent from the source code and a potential maintenance problem. This issue is discussed a little more toward the end of the chapter when we discuss self-documenting code.

- *Try to limit your comments to places where they do the most good.* Each source file probably needs a comment describing how the functions or the variables in the source file form a cohesive whole, such as what type of functionality does the source file provide as a unit. A comment for each class is often a good idea; a brief description of the purpose of a class goes a long way toward knowing when to use the class and, better yet, when the class might be reused.

  As for functions, if their names describe their purpose, you can probably leave out a descriptive comment. If not, add a brief description. Note any assumptions, special algorithms or side effects related to the function. Inside of functions, again, let the code do the talking. However, if a few lines are really obtuse and nontrivial, add a comment.

Finally, global variables often merit a brief comment. Too often it's easy to lose track of free-standing variables that get used throughout your code.

Again, these tips are just suggestions; experiment not only with the style of your comments but also with the quantity. Once you've reached a comfort zone with the quantity of your comments, you will also have quality comments.

Naming Variables and Functions

Aside from commenting, there is one other type of convention that is integral in making your source code more readable and understandable: naming conventions. Too often programmers quickly create variables and function names with little meaning. Take, for example, the variable:

```
int x;
```

x, in some instances carries a great deal of meaning. If you are plotting a two-dimensional graph in the x-y plane, x is a great variable name; it is clear, concise, and appropriate for the problem domain. If you're solving a linear equation for x, again x is a perfect variable name; it is the unknown variable in most of the equations you have encountered since grade school. However, x just doesn't cut it when it comes to the number of vacation days an employee can expect at the end of the month, or the interest rate on that employee's individual retirement account. For instance, if x is equal to 8, how appropriate is the following code for calculating the estimated yearly interest on a balance (granted, a very simplified formula):

```
float y = z * x / 100;
```

The calculation will certainly work, but it has little meaning to a programmer unfamiliar with the code. If you hate to type, these quick, one-letter variables may seem like lifesavers, but consider again someone else who needs to deal with this line of code. The following comment could help:

```
// yearly interest = beginning balance * interest rate / 100
float y = z * x / 100;
```

but then you really require comments whenever you refer to x, y, and z; they don't have any meaning apart from this comment. The following requires a bit more typing, but it improves the situation tremendously:

```
float yearlyInterest = beginningBalance * interestRate / 100;
```

Notice that carefully chosen variable names go a long way towards making code self-documenting, that is, not requiring comments. It may take a little more time to think of an appropriate variable name, but if your code has any type of longevity (that means you or someone else will look at it again), it's well worth it. From looking at this line of code, you can determine exactly what's happening.

Some programmers, however, still may feel something is missing in the carefully chosen variable names `yearlyInterest`, `beginningBalance` and `interestRate`—the data types of the variables. In the expression:

```
float yearlyInterest = beginningBalance * interestRate / 100;
```

the programmer can obviously determine that the type of `yearlyInterest` is `float`, but what are the types of `beginningBalance` and `interestRate`? The programmer could use the text editor to search for the first occurrence of these variables and find the types, but right now there's no quick way to determine the variables' types.

> **Note**
>
> If you use a commercial text editor or class browser that's C++ syntax-aware, it's usually fairly easy to click on a variable and instantly determine its type.

This brings us to Hungarian notation, which offers a solution to the very problem of identifying data types.

Deciphering Hungarian Notation

A naming convention that has risen to popularity hand-in-hand with Microsoft Windows is the so-called Hungarian notation, which is probably familiar to those of you who use the Windows API or libraries written for Windows. Hungarian notation was developed at Microsoft by Charles Simonyi, a native of Hungary. The name also refers to the somewhat cryptic nature of the convention to new (non-native) users. "It's Hungarian to me" replaces "It's Greek to me" in this instance—you'll see why in a moment.

Hungarian notation, for the most part, is language-independent; it's as at home in C++ as it is in C, PASCAL, Basic, assembly language or spreadsheet macros. The advantages of Hungarian notation are largely of a mnemonic nature. Glancing at a variable or function name written in Hungarian notation not only suggests a meaningful use like `beginningBalance`; it also indicates the type of the variable, `float`. This is particularly useful when new programmers deal with existing code. In addition to meaningful names, the data types of variables aid in understanding exactly what's happening in a given section of code. Also, as with most naming conventions, the rigid confines of Hungarian notation offer a uniform and, thus, readable structure to code. It doesn't take a lot of thought process to invent or understand variable names—they pretty much all look alike.

If you've read any books on the Windows API or if you make use of Help features of Borland C++, you've already been introduced to Hungarian notation. For instance, if you need to allocate a block of memory, you might consult some reference material, either in hard copy or online, for the function prototype of `GlobalAlloc`. In Borland C++'s Help files, it's given as the following:

II

Programming in C++

```
HGLOBAL GlobalAlloc(UINT fuAlloc, DWORD cbAlloc);
```

Let's consider the variable names listed here, for a moment: `fuAlloc` and `cbAlloc`. If you're not familiar with Hungarian notation, you may ask yourself, "What can `fu` and `cb` possibly mean?"

Identifiers in Hungarian notation consist of a series of prefixes, or base types, and a qualifier. In the case of `fuAlloc` and `cbAlloc`, you can dissect them as follows:

fuAlloc = f (flag) + u (unsigned int) + Alloc

cbAlloc = c (count) + b (bytes) + Alloc

`fuAlloc` is an unsigned integer flag specifying how to allocate memory, whereas `cbAlloc` is the count, or number, of bytes to allocate.

A typical usage of `GlobalAlloc` could be:

```
HGLOBAL hGlobal;
void *lpvBuffer;

hGlobal = GlobalAlloc(GPTR, 32 * 1024);
lpvBuffer = GlobalLock(hGlobal);
...
GlobalUnlock(hGlobal);
GlobalFree(hGlobal);
```

Here you have simply defined `hGlobal`, a handle to some global system memory, and `lpvBuffer`, a long `void` pointer to a buffer. Allocating 32K of dynamic memory using `GlobalAlloc` stores a handle into `hGlobal`; locking your handle returns a `void` pointer into `lpvBuffer`. After using the memory, you can unlock and release the memory handle using `GlobalUnlock` and `GlobalFree`. Notice by examining the two variables in this small block of code—`hGlobal` and `lpvBuffer`—you not only get meaningful names but data types as well (handle and a long pointer to void). This, again, is the predominant advantage of using a naming convention like Hungarian notation.

Now that you have a feel for Hungarian notation, let's examine some of the more popular prefixes, in alphabetic order, with a few examples.

Integers of Varying Byte Lengths

The following prefixes refer loosely to integers of varying byte lengths:

Prefix	Integer	Byte Length
b	byte	Typically 8 bits
w	word	Typically 16 bits
l	long	Usually 32 bits
u	unsigned int	
uw	unsigned word	
ul	unsigned long	

Assuming that `interestRate` from a previous example was a 16-bit word, you can add the prefix w:

```
short wInterestRate; // a 16-bit interest rate
```

You have already seen b in the example of `cbAlloc`:

```
DWORD cbAlloc; // cbAlloc is a count (the number) of bytes to allocate
```

Likewise you can substitute other integer prefixes. If you write your own timer function to track ticks since application startup, you can use a definition like the following:

```
unsigned long ulTicks; // the number of ticks since application startup
```

Variables Denoting a Count

A count of some type is commonly noted with the prefix c. If you have an array defined as follows:

```
long rglEmployeeNumbers[MAX_EMPLOYEES]; // an array (rg) of long (l)
                                        // employee numbers
```

you can keep track of the current number of employees with a variable:

```
long clCurrentEmployees; // the number of (a count of long)
                         // current employees
```

Likewise in a custom `strlen` function of some sort you can have the following variable defined:

```
int cchLength; // the number of (a count of) characters counted thus far
```

Character Variables

ch, as just mentioned, signifies a one-byte character:

```
char chInput; // an input character from the keyboard
```

Often times you deal with pointers to characters as iterators through strings. A character pointer can take on the following form:

```
char *pchCurrent; // a pointer to the current character
```

or

```
char *lpchCurrent; // a long pointer to the current character
```

Pointers, as we'll see, can be specified as p or lp (lp simply emphasizing the four-byte length of most pointers) and, for the most part, are used interchangeably.

Differences between Variables

The difference between two variables of a type can be preceded with a "d." If, for instance, you subtract two unsigned long variables, the expression can be written:

```
// the difference between two tick measurements
unsigned long dulElapsedTicks = ulTicks - ulPrevTicks;
```

If you specify x coordinates in an x-y plane, you can have

```
int dx;
```

where x is your own prefix. You will see later in section, "Deciding When to Use Hungarian Notation" that you can, of course, define your own Hungarian notation prefixes.

Flags

f, as you have already seen, indicates a flag of some sort—usually a Boolean or logical value. Examples include:

```
bool fError; // a flag indicating whether or not an error has occurred

bool fQuit; // a flag indicating whether or not it's time to quit

bool fPromptForPassword; // a flag indicating whether or not to prompt
                         // for a password
```

As you can see in these three examples, once you're familiar with f representing a flag in Hungarian notation, comments describing these variables are actually quite redundant; the variable names are self-commenting.

Function Pointers

fn denotes a variable that is a pointer to a function. In the declaration

```
int (*fnAdd)(int, int);
```

fnAdd is a pointer to a function that takes two integer parameters and returns an integer value.

Handles

As seen earlier in the GlobalAlloc example, h indicates a handle (typically a pointer to a pointer). To free a handle to some global dynamic memory, for instance, you can make the following call:

```
GlobalFree(hGlobal);
```

where hGlobal is the handle associated with some dynamic memory.

Array Indexes

An index into an array is denoted with an i. If you have an array of characters:

```
char rgchName[80]; // a character array that stores a name
```

you can change all characters in the array to uppercase using the following loop:

```
for (int ichCurrent = 0; ichCurrent < 80; ichCurrent++)
{
    rgchName[ichCurrent] = toupper(rgchName[ichCurrent]);
}
```

Pointers

Pointers, in Hungarian notation, are symbolized with p or lp (lp being a long pointer, emphasizing the length of a pointer). Very often in consulting Borland C++ Help files, you see variables declared starting with lp:

```
int lstrcmp(LPCSTR lpszString1, LPCSTR lpszString2);
```

lstrcmp compares two C strings (sz, stands for a zero-terminated string). Adding lp to sz simply signifies a pointer to a zero-terminated string; you may be more familiar with the old faithful type of such a variable: char *. lpszString1 is a long pointer to a zero-terminated String1 and lpszString2 is a long pointer to a zero-terminated String2.

Floating-Point Numbers

Floating-point numbers are denoted with r and d, where r indicates single-precision and d indicates double-precision. currentBalance (from a previous example), then, can be declared as follows:

```
float rCurrentBalance;
```

or

```
double dCurrentBalance;
```

if you need double-precision for the balance.

Arrays

rg, somewhat counter-intuitive at first, indicates an array in Hungarian notation, referring to an array as the range of a function (you may recall this from calculus). You have already seen a character array. If you have an array of memory handles, you can declare your array as:

```
HGLOBAL rghMemoryManager[32]; // we need handles for 32 distinct objects
```

A two-dimensional array can be indicated by simply tacking on a second rg:

```
int rgrgdxLengths[100][100]; // a 100x100 array of lengths (differences in
                             // x coordinates)
```

PASCAL and C Strings

st and sz both refer to strings. A Pascal-type string (the first character contains the length of the string) is referred to by st; a C-type, zero-terminated string is indicated by sz.

```
char rgchName[80]; // an array of characters that stores a name
char *lpszCurrentName = rgchName;
```

Programming in C++

Global Variables

A global variable in Hungarian notation can be specified by inserting a v at the beginning of a variable name. If a flag to quit your application is global, you can change its declaration to

```
bool vfQuit;
```

Likewise if your tick counter is global, you can represent this variable as

```
unsigned long vulTicks;
```

As seen before, v can also stand for void, which is used mostly in conjunction with pointers.

Deciding When to Use Hungarian Notation

Hungarian notation does take some getting used to, doesn't it? And I've spared you a discussion of what Hungarian notation functions look like (let's just say they incorporate prefixes for the return type and all parameters!), as they're rarely seen in practice. Although somewhat cryptic at first, Hungarian notation does achieve its goal: to add a mnemonic data type to all variable names. A quick glance at most variables gives you not only an idea of the variable's use, but also a nearly positive identification of the variable's data type.

The prefixes listed in this section are the most common; there are others, of course. Also, most users invent their own prefixes to suit the problem domain in which they're working. For instance, if in a graphics application you make use of many different color levels, you might invent the prefix co to stand for color. The value of the color red, then, might be stored in a variable coRed. If you decide to implement some form of Hungarian notation in your projects and invent your own prefixes, make sure they are documented somewhere—either in comments or external documentation, as future programmers on the project will probably run into some difficulties deciphering your abbreviations.

Many individuals and companies shy away from Hungarian notation due to the somewhat steep learning curve associated with it. In fact, aside from the Windows platform and some DOS libraries, I personally have not run across too many instances of Hungarian notation. If it suits your needs, it can be a great tool for understandable code. If not, let's consider a quick alternative.

Exploring an Alternative Naming Convention

An easy alternative to Hungarian notation can be found in the conventions suggested by the Zinc Application Framework, which have been adopted by many independent programmers. It abandons the idea of including a mnemonic data type in names, though, so if you feel the need for such a practice, you should probably go with some form of Hungarian notation. Like Hungarian notation and most C++ naming conventions, however, the naming convention proposed by Zinc also uses the uppercase letter to separate words in variables (`currentBalance`, for example), which you may have noticed earlier, as opposed to the more C-style underscores (`current_balance`), which are reserved in Zinc's naming convention for classes, structures, and constants.

To name a variable in Zinc's naming convention (which should be as self-explanatory as possible), start with a lowercase letter for the first word, then uppercase for all subsequent words:

```
float currentBalance = 0.00;

unsigned long daysSince1970;

char *firstName;
```

Whereas in Hungarian notation, a v preceded all global variables, Zinc and many C naming conventions place an underscore before a global variable:

```
unsigned long _ticks;

char *_recordBuffer;
```

Functions, on the other hand, begin with an uppercase letter and are equally descriptive:

```
char *ConvertStringToUpperCase(char *lowerCaseString);

void AddToList(Node *insertedNode);
```

Functions and variables, then, are differentiated by the first letter in the corresponding name.

Classes, structures, and constants are exclusively uppercase, with internal words separated by underscores:

```
class LINKED_LIST;

class STACK : public LINKED_LIST;

struct NODE;

const int TITLE_LENGTH = 80;

const bool TRUE = 1;
```

This naming convention is not quite as descriptive as Hungarian notation, lacking its mnemonic value, but it is easy to follow, remember, and stick with. It lends a uniform, readable, and understandable style to your source code. Again, feel free to tailor it to your individual needs, but give it a try.

II

Programming in C++

> **Note**
>
> Too often when purchasing third-party libraries for your source code, you find yourself running into conflicts between global function and variable names. For instance, if you purchase a GUI library for 32-bit protected-mode DOS applications and you're also making use of the standard Windows header files for DOS protected-mode memory allocation (`GlobalAlloc`, etc.). If the third-party library contains a call entitled `CreateBitmap`, it will conflict with the `CreateBitmap` included in `<Windows.h>`, even though you're not planning on using the Windows function. To combat this when creating your own libraries—or even in your own code—you can adopt a custom signature for your global function and variable names. If you implement your own `CreateBitmap` function, for example, and your library name is DOSGL for "DOS graphics library," you can add the signature DOSGL to your function names:
>
> ```
> DOSGLCreateBitmap(...);
> ```
>
> Such a practice can often save you from chasing down conflicts when using multiple libraries.

Making Your Way to Self-Documenting Code

As a conclusion, let's briefly consider the result of combining carefully chosen variable names (following a naming convention of some sort) with the judicious use of comments (as suggested by a commenting convention). When you're successful in combining these two camps, your source code really does start to do the talking for you. As Bjarne Stroustrup would say, it is the language itself that makes your source code more readable and understandable. The code becomes self-documenting without the aid of external documentation.

The following code shows the `ConvertInternalNameToFirstLast` function again and integrates Hungarian notation and the Zinc Application Framework commenting and naming conventions.

```
// The following function accepts an internal name which represents
// a last name/first name pair of the form (last-name, first-name) and
// converts it to the form first-name last-name, returning the result in
// lpszFirstLastResult.  It is the responsibility of the calling function
// to provide adequate storage for the result.  In an error condition,
// the function returns an empty string.

void ConvertInternalNameToFirstLast(char *lpszInternalName,
    char *lpszFirstLastResult)
{
    const char TERMINATING_NULL = '\0';
    char *pchCurrent;

    *lpszFirstLastResult = TERMINATING_NULL;

    // Ignore any erroneous leading characters.
    while (*lpszInternalName && *lpszInternalName != '(')
```

```
{
    lpszInternalName++;
}

if (*lpszInternalName == TERMINATING_NULL) return;

// Skip the open paren; it's not included in the result.
pchCurrent = ++lpszInternalName;

// Iterate until the first comma or close paren.
// We include the close paren to catch single names like Madonna.
while (*pchCurrent && *pchCurrent!= ',' && *pchCurrent != ')')
{
    pchCurrent++;
}

if (*pchCurrent == TERMINATING_NULL) return;

if (*pchCurrent == ')')
{
    // In the case of a single name, simply copy the name.
    while (*lpszInternalName && *lpszInternalName!= ')')
    {
        *lpszFirstLastResult++ = *lpszInternalName++;
    }
}
else
{
    // In the case of a first and last name, skip the
    // comma and any spaces following the comma.
    pchCurrent++;

    while (*pchCurrent && *pchCurrent == ' ')
    {
        pchCurrent++;
    }

    if (*pchCurrent == TERMINATING_NULL) return;

    // Copy the first name.
    while (*pchCurrent && *pchCurrent != ')')
    {
        *lpszFirstLastResult++ = *pchCurrent++;
    }

    if (*pchCurrent == TERMINATING_NULL)
    {
        *lpszFirstLastResult = TERMINATING_NULL;
        return;
    }

    // Separate first name from last name with a space.
    *lpszFirstLastResult++ = ' ';

    // Copy the last name.
    while (*lpszInternalName && *lpszInternalName != ',')
    {
```

```
                         *lpszFirstLastResult++ = *lpszInternalName++;
                    }
               }

               // Terminate the resulting string.
               *lpszFirstLastResult = TERMINATING_NULL;
          }
```

As you can see, the function remains a little heavy on the comment side (but for the purpose of this book, it adds to the clarity). However, mixing in Hungarian notation, you can quickly glance at any variable in the function and determine its data type. Notice also how the Zinc Application Framework convention of putting constants in all capital letters really makes them stand out from the code.

Whether this function is self-documenting really depends on your point of view. I personally feel the use of Hungarian notation takes away from the self-documenting nature of code because most identifiers appear mangled to my eye, which distracts me. To another programmer, however, identifiers that include type information add a bit of documentation and mnemonic value to each and every line in which they appear. Also, the low-level, pointer-based iteration of this example rarely looks self-documenting to a beginning C/C++ programmer. If you fall into this group, give yourself some time. No matter how much effort you put into naming your variables, identifiers, such as ++, *, ==, and !=, can really distract you, despite your best efforts.

My advice is to experiment and find the commenting and naming conventions that best suit your personal or company preferences. Always try to keep your code as clear and understandable as possible for yourself, and you'll be well on your way to the elusive self-documenting code!

From Here...

As you move on to the following chapters on C++ syntax—and even more advanced topics—and begin to work examples, remember that well-placed comments and carefully chosen names will really serve to make those examples more readable and understandable as you return to them. Whether you follow the commenting conventions described here or naming conventions like Hungarian notation—or invent your own conventions—consistency does pay off.

- Chapter 6, "Native Data Types and Operators," will offer you more in-depth coverage of the C/C++ data types that show up in Hungarian notation. You'll also become more familiar with operators that can also help your source code document itself.

- Chapter 9, "Data Quantifiers and Qualifiers," will introduce you to the different types of linkage in C++. You'll come to grips with some of the clashes that occur between function names when you link your code. You'll also become much more aware of different types of global variables.

- Chapter 10, "Writing Expressions," will offer you another tool for letting your source code speak for itself. Integrating carefully chosen variable names into expressions goes a great way toward self-documenting code.

CHAPTER 6

Native Data Types and Operators

Native types are the building blocks of C++ programs. Operators are the glue, cement, and sometimes rubberbands with which programmers assemble reusable components. With C++, you may realistically be building systems to model car engines, data-modeling for derivative investment products, or really cool reusable visual components for a variety of desktop tools.

Underneath it all though you'll find the few native data types and the many operators that enable C++ developers to express their ideas with code. Like everything in the universe, a few subset elements are the building blocks without which nothing else exists.

If C++ is brand new to you, don't forge ahead without reading this chapter. Even if you are an old C hat or have some experience with C++, read this chapter. I promise you that you'll learn something new and gain new a perspective of C++.

In this chapter, you learn about

- Native data types
- Native data types as functions
- new and delete operators
- iostream operators
- Operators as functions

Understanding Native Data Types

The native data types are your sand, stone, and water. From these basic items you can create the mud to mold the bricks to build the home. The key to building large software systems is to build advanced aggregate types from the language's built-in types. Keeping the building process from becoming overly complex is achieved by "training" your new types how to behave in a manner much like the built-in types.

Before examining the process of aggregation, let's take a look at each of the native data types and their various forms.

The Native Types

The native types, or built-in data types, are the char, int, long, float, and double. The maximum and minimum values for the integral types—char, int, and long— are defined in \Bc5\Include\limits.h. The maximum and minimum values for the floating-point types, sometimes referred to as real numbers, are defined in the header file \Bc5\Include\float.h.

> **Tip**
>
> You don't need to memorize these range values. These maximums and minimums are fairly straightforward to remember if you tie the maximum and minimum values to the amount of storage for each type.

The char type is considered to be a byte. A byte is comprised of 8 bits. (The term bit is derived from *bi*nary dig*it*.) Binary numbers are used to record the state because the memory used to record states is two-state switches that naturally map to the binary number system. (It wasn't done to torture you.) The values for these data types is based on binary number (base 2) numbers, therefore, the maximum values are derived from the equation

$$2^n - 1$$

where *n* is the number of bits used to store the number. Therefore if a char uses 8 bits, the maximum value is 255; the minimum, of course, being 0.

The general equation shown above applies to unsigned (positive) numbers. Signed numbers—numbers that are both positive and negative—range from about plus or minus half, or $\pm(2n-2)$ because one bit is used to store the sign. The number of bits provides a quick clue as to the maximum and minimum value of integral types. The int type's value is derived from integers as 16-bit numbers; applying the same equation to integers implies that the maximum value for unsigned integers is 65,535. A long integer can store values between 0 and about 4 billion.

> **Caution**
>
> Designing software with dependencies based on the size of the native data types may make your application unportable at best and incorrect under extreme circumstances.
>
> If you look in the Help file, you may note that the int type can have a maximum value equivalent to that of a long applied to the 32-bit language implementation, but only 64K if used in a 16-bit context.

The floating-point numbers, `float` and `double`, use 4 and 8 bytes respectively, but do not store the data in such a simplistic manner. Floating-point numbers use the bytes as packed bit arrays where some of the bits are for the sign, some for the mantissa (significant digits), and the exponential multiplier. The exact ranges for either of those types can be deferred to a later time if you determine that the exact values may be a problem. In general, the `float` type is capable of storing numbers from approximately

$$3.4 \times 10^{-38} \text{ to } 3.4 \times 10^{38}$$

The `double` type can store numbers ranging from approximately

$$1.7 \times 10^{-308} \text{ to } 1.7 \times 10^{308}$$

The exact values for all native data types can be referred to at anytime by accessing the Help file, using the key phrase "data types." I would suggest you access the Help file when these numbers' ranges of values come into question.

Note

It is worth noting that floating-point numbers take more instruction cycles because of their packed bit array nature. There is no substitute when you need floating-point precision, so there is no alternative to using them.

Quantifiers

The general syntax for defining variables is to state the data type followed by the variable name. To define a simple integer variable j, write:

```
int j;
```

Integers defined like this are *signed* by default. Thus, the above definition is identical to the more verbose

```
signed int j;
```

Signed integral types use the most significant bit (msb) to store the sign—positive or negative—of the integral type. Unsigned integral types use the msb as an additional storage bit for the value and not the sign. To define an unsigned integer, add the keyword `unsigned` to any variable integral definition. For example, defining an unsigned integer k with an initial value, looks like

```
unsigned int k = 13;
```

> **Note**
>
> The actual way that signed integral numbers—char, int, and long—are stored is referred to as 2s complement. The floating-point numbers use the IEEE standard for floating-point numbers, which is different from the 2s complement.
>
> For example, a signed integer assigned the value -1 can be defined like
>
> ```
> signed int k = -1;
> ```
>
> Internally the number is stored as 32-bits, all set to 1. Writing each bit
>
> ```
> -1 = 0x11111111111111111111111111111111 // 32-bits
> ```
>
> 1s complement means to toggle the state of each bit, Thus, 32-bits set to 1 become 32 0-bits
>
> ```
> 0x00000000000000000000000000000000   // 1s complement
> ```
>
> 2s complement is ones complement plus 1. So, finally the 2s complement of all one bits is
>
> ```
> 0x00000000000000000000000000000000 + 1 =
> ➡0x00000000000000000000000000000001
> ```
>
> which is 1.
>
> Floating-point numbers actually use a more complex internal representation, where some bits are used to store the sign, exponent, and a normalized mantissa (drop the most significant bit).
>
> The internal representation of integrals and floating-point numbers is maintained by the compiler. Mastery of how numbers are stored internally is unnecessary.

Bit Fields

Certain programming domains require the use of individual bits. Some values stored in the system are bit-packed arrays, where each bit, as opposed to the byte, is a value.

> **Tip**
>
> Hexadecimal, or base-16, numbers are written with a prefix of 0x to distinguish them from decimal numbers and variables. The hexadecimal number
>
> ```
> 0x400 // Read four-zero-zero
> ```
>
> is equal to 1024 decimal.

Several examples are readily identifiable. One example exists at the absolute address 0x0417. This byte contains the keyboard status bits for DOS-based systems. Each bit at this byte contains the current state of special keys like Num Lock and Caps Lock. Another example exists in the bit-packed fields of the time and date stamps in the directory entry table for each file.

Some system's programming problems, or other circumstances may require you to access individual bits. C++ was defined as a superset of C in part because of C's ability to get close to the architecture—access memory addresses, I/O ports, and other hardware-specific things. In addition to pointing to locations in memory, C++ variables can be defined as bit fields.

The smallest number of any native variable is 8-bits, which is the number of bits used to define the value of a character. The *bit field* notation allows you to specify some number of bits, storing the value assigned to these bits in a native type. The following definition defines a 4-bit variable:

```
int bits:4;    // 4-bit number
int bits:7;    // 7-bit number stored in an integer
```

A 4-bit number—applying the equation defined earlier—is capable of storing values from 0 to 15. The bitfield notation is beneficial to properly defining variables stored as a bit-array, like DOS-based system times and dates.

Building Blocks for Aggregation

The native data types are your basic building blocks. It is up to you to determine in which context they are used and their meaning. Oftentimes, representing the data in a well-crafted format makes all the difference in whether code is required to access the data or whether an accurate model of the data negates the need for code.

The C++ language paradigm suggests that many entities be represented as a class. As you see throughout this book, not every entity is a class and there are other kinds of structures besides classes. Before you begin writing code, consider the data model.

Exploring Operators

Operators, such as +, -, * (multiply), and \, are familiar to you from simple mathematical relationships you used throughout your many years of education. Operators are used to express relationships between data. There are many common operators that may already be familiar to you, many more may not be, and still more that you may not consider to be operators at all. Prefacing the rest of this chapter, I emphatically suggest that if the use of operators is unclear to you, indicate your meaning precisely with parenthetical grouping.

Note

With other subjects, I defer a complete list of operators to the help information provided by Borland. I will use the time and space in this chapter to clarify points that may be unclear. If you need to perform a particular operation, refer to the Help file to obtain the specific operator and its usage.

Operator Precedence

Operators have a parse order precedence that determines what operators are applied to which operands and in what order. While this order is by no means arbitrary, some operators have different meanings in a variety of contexts. An expedient example is the * (asterisk) operator. The * (asterisk) operator plays the role of the multiplication and a dereference operator used with pointer types. The context of the operator defines, in part, its precedence.

Some operators are familiar to you, and their parse order is the same as you might expect. For example, the code fragment

```
b + c * d
```

uses the arithmetic parse rule whereby the multiplication is performed first, followed by the addition of b.

If any use of operators has an unclear meaning, use the parentheses to clarify your intent. The previous fragment becomes

```
(b + (c * d))
```

While no ambiguity existed previously where the compiler was concerned, now the exact intent of the user is explicitly clear to the human reader.

Tip

If certain operators seem unclear, assume that every special character (that is not an alphabetic or numeric character) is an operator that has some meaning, precedence, and performs a particular function.

Operators are the cornerstone of writing expressions. Those that are unfamiliar to you should invite experimentation.

Unary Operators

The word *unary* itself implies a count of one. This means that if an operator is a unary operator, the number of operands (variables) that the operator performs its task on is one.

One useful, unary operator used for testing is the ! operator (referred to as the *not* operator), which evaluates the negation of a test. The negation of a test evaluating to True is False and the not of False is True. The same applies for any integral value or pointer, where zero values or pointers are read as `false` and any non-zero is `true`.

The general form of unary operators is

```
unary_operator operand
```

Thus, applying the general form to the `not` operator, you can contrive several examples:

```
char *p = 0;
if( !p )                // evaluates to true
```

Pointers can be used in conditional statements like the preceding. In C++, Boolean values, integrals, and statements can be evaluated in conditional tests. Logically, anything evaluating to 0 is treated as a False condition; anything not evaluating to 0 evaluates to True. Reading p as its Boolean equivalent of False, the statement above becomes "if(not *false*)." The negation of False is True.

```
int a = 5;
if( !a )                    // evaluates to false
```

Remembering that in conditional expressions, anything evaluating to a non-zero is True, therefore, the above expression "if(not *true*)" evaluates to False.

There are several unary operators that you see used throughout this book. Some of these include both prefix and postfix increment and decrement (++ and - -) used to increment or decrement integral types by 1. For example,

```
int num = 10;
num++;       // same as num = num + 1 or num += 1
--num;       // same as num = num - 1 or num -= 1
```

The difference between prefix and postfix is the position and timing of the operation, specifically when the operand is used in an expression. Placing the operator to the left invokes the prefix operation, which increments prior to any test or assignment and the postfix operation is invoked after any evaluation.

The unary complement operator, represented by the tilde (˜), performs the 1s complement operation (mentioned earlier). Taking the complement of -1:

```
int a = -1;
a = ˜a;
results in 0.
```

The + and - operators have both a unary and binary form. The unary form of the plus operator (+5) is redundant because unless you specify that an integral is negative (-5), then integrals are positive by default.

There are various forms of several of the operators, whose contextual use must be considered to understand their meaning. Both the reference (*) and address-of (&) operators have unary and binary forms. Applying the unary operator to a pointer is referred to as *dereferencing*. Preceding a pointer with the unary operator

```
char far * p = 0x00000417;
*p ¦= 1;
```

means you are referring to what is pointed at.

There are two special unary operators `new` and `delete` that are used to manage memory resources. You learn how to use these operators in other chapters throughout this book.

Binary Operators

The term *binary* indicates the operand count for these kinds of operators. Some of the most common binary operators are +, -, \, and *. Their usage and names are unchanged from the mechanics of calculator mathematics.

The general form of binary operators is

```
operand binary_operator operand
```

which means that *bi*nary operators require two operands.

The rules of associativity, distributivity, transitivity, and symmetry become very important when you begin to consider more advanced uses of these operators. Table 6.1 contains an operator summary describing operator-tokens, names, and syntax listed and grouped by precedence. Those having the highest precedence are at the top of the list.

Table 6.1 Summary of Operator Tokens, Names, and Syntaxes

Token	Name	Syntax
::	scope resolution	`class_name::member`
::	global	`::name`
.	member selection	`object.member`
->	member selection	`pointer->member`
[]	subscripting	`pointer[ expr ]`
( )	function call	`expr( args )`
( )	value construction	`type( args )`
sizeof	size of object	`sizeof expr`
sizeof	size of type	`sizeof( type )`
++	postincrement	`lvalue++`
++	preincrement	`++lvalue`
– –	postdecrement	`lvalue--`
– –	predecrement	`--lvalue`
~	complement	`~expr`
!	not	`!expr`
–	unary minus	`-expr`
+	unary plus	`+ expr`
&	address of	`&lvalue`
*	derefence	`*expr`
new	create (allocate)	`new type`
new [ ]	create array	`new type[]`
delete	destroy (de-allocate)	`delete pointer`
delete[ ]	destroy array	`delete [] pointer`
( )	cast (type conversion)	`(type) expr`
.*	member section	`object.pointer-to-member`
->*	member section	`pointer->pointer-to-member`
*	multiply	`expr * expr`
/	divide	`expr / expr`
%	modulo (remainder)	`expr % expr`

Token	Name	Syntax
+	add (plus)	`expr + expr`
–	subtract (minus)	`expr – expr`
<<	shift left	`expr << expr`
>>	shift right	`expr >> expr`
<	less than	`expr < expr`
<=	less than or equal	`expr <= expr`
>	greater than	`expr > expr`
>=	greater than or equal	`expr >= expr`
==	equal	`expr == expr`
!=	not equal	`expr != expr`
&	bitwise AND	`expr & expr`
^	bitwise exclusive OR	`expr ^ expr`
|	bitwise inclusive OR	`expr ¦ expr`
&&	logical AND	`expr && expr`
||	logical inclusive OR	`expr ¦¦ expr`
? :	conditional expression	`expr ? expr : expr`
=	simple assignment	`lvalue = expr`
*=	multiply and assign	`lvalue *= expr`
/=	divide and assign	`lvalue /= expr`
%=	modulo and assign	`lvalue %= expr`
+=	add and assign	`lvalue += expr`
-=	subtract and assign	`lvalue -= expr`
<<=	shift left and assign	`lvalue <<= expr`
>>=	shift right and assign	`lvalue >>= expr`
&=	AND and assign	`lvalue &= expr`
|=	inclusive OR and assign	`lvalue ¦= expr`
^=	exclusive OR and assign	`lvalue ^= expr`
,	comma (sequencing)	`expr, expr`

Summary of operators from The C++ Programming Language, *Second Edition, Addison-Wesley, 1991.*

The count of the operator—unary = 1; binary = 2; and ternary = 3—determines the number of operands, 1, 2, or 3, respectively. Applying the count to different binary operators, it is relatively easy to devise statements using binary operators. For example, declaring three integers variables

```
int a = 5, b = 3, c;
```

II

Programming in C++

expressions using plus, minus, division, or multiplication appear

```
c = a + b;      // assign a plus b to c
c = a - b;      // assign a minus b to c
c = b % a;      // assign b modulo a to c
c = b * a;      // assign b multiplied by a to c
```

The marvel of using statements with simple operators is that most people have 15 or 20 years experience writing expressions using binary operators, or typing entries into a calculator, and the syntax is only slightly, if at all, different. You more than likely have significant experience writing expressions with the arithmetic operators, and if you have had classes in logic or discrete mathematics, you have experience with the slightly more esoteric Boolean operators.

Combining prior knowledge of the operators and your past experience will enable you to write the most common expressions. The binary operators that include the assignment in their names are used for cumulative operations. Consider

```
a = a + 5;
```

This statement increments a by 5. Since only a and 5 are involved in the statement, you can replace the expression with

```
a += 5;
```

Each operator combined with an = token can be used in place of the two separate = operators if one of the operands is the recipient of the result. The language does not require you to make such substitutions; the choice is yours. In all likelihood, with the preceding information in mind, you already have the skills to write expressions using more than half of the total operands.

With this knowledge, you can implement many of the most common types of algorithms. New C++ programmers take a moment to make a tick mark next to operators you may already know how to use. The remaining list is the operators with which you should write a few short programs and experiment. Mastering the skills to use every operator is half the battle. In chapter 16, "Operator Overloading," I show you how to make operators behave when applied to new types.

Ternary Operators

There is only one *ternary* operator. The ternary operator is the ?: pair. This operator uses three operands and is just an abbreviated form of the if...else pair. Anywhere you would replace the ternary operator, you can replace it with if...else. The general format of the ternary operator is

```
test ? true_test : false_test;
```

The test is a condition that evaluates to an integral, like a==b, !p, or other forms of tests. If the test evaluates to True then the true_test code (between the ? and :) is executed. If the test evaluates to False, then the false_test code is executed.

The ternary operator works best when the code executed in an if...else is simple and when the return value of a function can be determined with a simplified test. The ternary operator statement is read *if test then execute the true_test code else execute the false_test code*

You see applications of this abbreviated ternary test operator in examples throughout this book.

Using Operators as Functions

The C++ language treats operators as special functions. Like functions—some of you may feel as though we have stepped into the twilight zone—*operator functions* have return types, function names, and arguments. To some extent, the return types and arguments are definable by you.

Set the particulars aside for a moment. If the concept of an operator as a function is completely new to you, accept it on faith. Some aspects of operator functions can be introduced at this juncture without understanding every detail of operator functions. Operator functions have a specialized syntax that is written much like every other function. The difference between a regular function and an operator function is primarily the function name. When naming regular functions, a goal is to choose a name that describes what the function does. With operator functions, the token does that nicely. Operator functions use the keyword operator followed by the specific token that represents a particular operation. In contrast, a function representing addition might be syntactically written:

```
type Sum( type leftOperand, type rightOperand );
```

An operator function performing the same addition operation might be implemented the same way except where the function name Sum appears, the keyword operator and the addition operator would appear. Thus,

```
type operator+( type leftOperand, type rightOperand );
```

Operator function calls are usually implicit but they can be called directly, as you will learn in chapter 16, "Operator Overloading."

Operator Functions

You have more than likely heard many references to the object-oriented paradigm. The view of operators as functions is not necessarily a direct aspect of the object-oriented paradigm, but it is necessary to the C++ view of object-oriented programming; it provides an expressiveness that is an added benefit to the new approach to software development.

If there is a typical use of operators, it can be expressed in the syntax of the operator and the operands it performs on. Using the binary addition (plus) operator as an example in a statement-fragment, it appears in this format:

```
a + b
```

where a and b are usually numbers. The result of this operation is the sum of a and b. The familiarity with the manual operation of writing expressions longhand or making entries in an adding machine is what makes native types and operators easy to use.

Regardless of the specific numeric type, whether `float`, `double`, `long`, or `int`, the C++ view of the expression a + b can be viewed implicitly as a function call with a highly specialized syntax, taking two arguments and returning a third all of the same type.

Supposing that the following function declaration

```
number operator+(number a, number b);
```

defines addition for an imaginary type number, then a function call can be resolved when the compiler encounters two variables of type number used in coordination with the addition (+) operator.

If I suggested that cost programmers write a function named `Add`, which accepts two variables returning the sum, you might reasonably expect something like

```
number Add( number a, number b );
```

which follows the general form of C++ functions. Except for the differences between the function names, `Add` and `operator+`, the two functions look identical.

There is more to writing operator functions than what has been presented so far. You do not need to write operator functions for native types, nor do you have to write operator functions at all. The benefit is that once you have mastered creating your own classes, writing operator functions for user-defined classes will make writing expressions for user-defined types as easy as writing them for native types.

The implication is that there is an implicit extended view of operators as functions. The reason for this is that most people have a vast pool of experience extending back to grade school in writing expressions using +, -, *, and \. In other words, you have this tokenized view of writing expressions. Thus, it is convenient to allow operators to play an integral part in writing programs for all types.

You can agree that using operators like plus, minus, subtraction, and division adds simplicity. However, operators with a similar syntax that perform new or unfamiliar functions can also be easy to use. The use of familiar operators makes it easy to learn to use native data types. Operators are integral in writing expressions, which are the cornerstones of programming, and a recurring theme in this book.

If you are just beginning to learn to use C++, don't fret, you will not need to write operator functions, nor will you need to learn a specialized syntax to use them. For now, you should know that in C++, there is an additional view of operators as functions.

A Few Guidelines

The idea that operators in C++ are functions is referred to as *operator overloading*, however, do not be concerned about overloading operators right now. What follows are a few brief guidelines that will enable you to write clear statements involving operators that will be easy to maintain and easy for other programmers to understand:

- Keep the number of operators and operands to a smaller number in compound expressions.

- Use intermediate results for complicated expressions involving more than one or two operators. The compiler may perform some automated optimizations and any minor savings you may have achieved in writing compound singular statements will be lost when maintaining the code.

- Make the meaning of operator expressions by applying parentheses.

Note

You may recall from simple mathematics that a + b * c means to multiply b and c, adding a to the result. But a + (b * c) leaves little room for misinterpretation as to your intended meaning.

As you become more adept at writing expressions, keep in mind the operators as functions. Remember from table 6.1 that there are operators whose meaning was better expressed in words, like new and delete.

Using *new* and *delete* Operators

The new and delete operators are used to allocate memory for variables. There are two places where variables exist. One place is called static, or *stack memory*; the other is called the *free store* or heap. Aside from the difference in how these concepts are represented, it is worth noting that variables "living" on the free store are the ones that are managed using the new and delete operators. Let's begin by comparing the two kinds of places where variable memory can be allocated.

Stack Memory

There are several levels of understanding where stack memory is concerned. We are going to look at it as a general entity. You can think of your program as a list of instructions; your computer's microprocessor tells the program to read and execute each instruction line-by-line until a signal to stop is received.

In your everyday busy life, you may be in the process of doing one thing and then set it aside to handle something else. When you are finished, you return to the previous task where you left off. A program works in much the same way. The program is a "to-do list" and sometimes the program is sidetracked (by a function call). Your computer has to have a convenient way to pick up where it left off when it's ready to return to the interrupted task.

During a program's normal execution, the program needs to perform an intermediate operation. To perform the intermediate step, the program needs to "remember" where it was and what it was to doing to enable it to return to the work in progress. "Remembering" is performed by the stack. When the program is ready to return to what it was previously doing, it retrieves the information from the stack.

Another use of the stack is to provide a convenient place to maintain storage space for variables defined in a function—called *local functions*. Variables defined within functions usually only require memory within the limits of the function. By using the stack for function variables, the computer has a reusable source of memory for variables with a short lifespan.

> **Tip**
>
> Think of a stack as a very neat pile of greenbacks. As you need to pay bills and buy groceries, you take money from the pile. When earnings come in, you rebuild the pile. This ebb and flow is much like how your program's stack manages RAM (*random-access memory*).

The program uses the stack to keep track of where it was interrupted, which enables the program to eventually return to the location. At the end of a function, the program no longer needs the local variables it put on the stack and can discard the information. This action returns the program to the information that indicates where it left off originally.

There is a very plausible reason to store a variety of information—which are bits representing different things—on the same pile. The explanation is simply that it would be too hard for the computer to have a lot of different little places for all of this stuff.

Why isn't everything stack-based, eliminating the need for programmers to manage some of the total resources? One of the reasons is that the stack does not represent an infinite pool of memory. A second is that the stack is a busy place. This "yo-yo" piling and peeling works simply, but sometimes variables may need to exist beyond the framework of a single function or accessibility needs to be more random. A stack works simply in that, generally, only items on the very top of the stack are accessible.

Others might argue then, why don't you just make those things global? An overabundance of global variables adds complexity issues, and they are stored in the data segment at compile time. Again, there is not an infinite pool of memory in the data segment. In fact, the free store is usually all of the memory left over to the program when the memory allocated to the stack segment, data segment, and the code segment is subtracted. The free store memory is also referred to as the *heap* and is usually the largest block of available memory resource.

> **Note**
>
> A general view of these individual clumps of memory is that the *data segment* is where identifiable variables at compile-time are stored, the *code segment* is where the program code is located, and the *stack* is where the program's bookmarks and temporary variables are stored.
>
> Variables inside functions, unless created with `new`, are stored on the stack. Variables outside of functions, referred to as `global` variables are stored in the data segment. Keep in mind these aspects of the program are managed by the computer for you.

Heap Memory

The free store is a resource available for you to create variables where you may need a higher degree of control over their lifetime or when you need larger chunks of memory that exceed what's available in the stack, or both.

Objects are allocated on the heap by declaring pointers and requesting memory with the new operator.

Caution

Many operators have shared responsibilities. For example, the * acts as both the reference operator and the multiplication operator. Another example is the << operator, which is both a left bit-shift and the ostream operator.

The meaning of operators is derived from their contextual use. When * is used like this:

```
2 * 3
```

it is interpreted as the binary multiplication operator. When the same character is used like this:

```
int *a
```

its meaning indicates that a is an integer pointer (reference).

Comparing the difference in appearance between a statically declared variable and one in which heap allocation is usually expected is the appearance of the pointer operator:

```
int var;        // statically allocated
int* pvar;      // expect a call to new
```

It is especially important not to get confused here. The variable var and pvar both exist statically; it is what pvar will point to that is allocated on the free store. The first definition is an integer that uses 32-bits or 4 bytes. The second variable is an *integer pointer* that also uses 32-bits (in Borland C++ 5), but instead of being assigned to a number, it will probably be used to point to the first element of an array of integers.

Using *new*. Yes, new is an operator. That explains, in part, why I spent a few lines introducing the idea earlier in the section. The actual implementation of the new operator is contained in an operator function, but the use of the operator looks syntactically similar to that of an operator, while its activity is actually more like a function.

There are two uses of the new operator. One is to allocate a single object, and the second is to allocate an array of objects. Either way, if the new operator call is successful, it returns a pointer to the first element. This is why you use pointer variables in conjunction with free-store allocation.

Allocating a Single Object Dynamically. Objects in this context refer to variables. (You can certainly think of variables of native data types as objects of the class of that type.) The general use of the new operator to return a pointer to a single object is

```
var_type * var_name = new var_type;
```

or

```
var_type * var_name;
var_name = new var_type;
```

where the `*`, `=`, new, and `;` (semicolon) are precise. The var_type and var_name are in the correct location but need to be placed with an actual variable type and name. An example applied to integers could be

```
int * pvar = new int;
```

or

```
int * pvar;
pvar = new int;
```

whereas the second example indicates that the definition and assignment to point to some memory can be separated.

Tip

There are few absolutes. A pointer variable may be used to point to an existing resource or an address and no coordinated use of new may exist.

The ability to point to memory locations is what makes C++ a language that can be used for an extremely wide variety of applications' domains, including systems programming.

When the resources pointed to are no longer needed, they should be released. See the section "Using *delete*," for more on this.

Allocating an Array of Objects Dynamically. The syntax for allocating an array of objects on the heap is slightly different. An *array* is a contiguous block of memory of the same data types. The location of the first object, the zero object, is the one pointed to by the pointer variable. This object can be accessed by dereferencing the pointer

```
int *p = new int[5];
*p = 1;                    // dereference pointer
p[0] = 1;                  // same thing
```

or indexing the array with an index of 0. Every other object resides at successive indexes, which is the same as dereferencing the pointer + index. So the second object in the first index is represented by either

```
*(p+1) = 2;
```

or

```
p[1] = 2;
```

For notational convenience, the array (`[ ]`) operator is preferable.

The example demonstrates how to allocate an array of integers. To allocate an array of anything, the only variation in the syntax is the specification of the alternate type and the specification of the size. To allocate an array of single-precision floating-point numbers, use

```
float *pfloat = new float[100];
```

Using *delete*. The most important rule pertaining to new and delete is that if you don't release the memory, the system will not likely regain the use of it. The delete operator is applied like an operator and translates to a function call.

When you allocate with new, there must be a matching call to delete or you will probably not like the results as you'll see in the next section.

Choosing the Form of delete. The form of the delete operator call must match the new call for each variable. What does this mean? It means simply that if you use the array operator [ ] in the call to new for a variable, then you must use it in the call to delete. If you allocate a single object—do not allocate an array of objects using [ ]—then you do not need to use the array operator in the call to delete.

For example, allocating a single int

```
int * p = new int;          // call to new
delete p;                   // correct call to delete
```

If you allocate an array then delete an array:

```
int * r = new int[10];      // array of ints
delete [] r;                // delete array of ints
```

While you have to specify the size when allocating an array, you do not have to specify the size when de-allocating the array. The size is actually stored and managed with the array. Think of new and delete as a smart, coordinative pair of operator functions.

In the second example, calling

```
delete r;
```

means exactly the same thing as

```
delete r[0];
```

Both tell the program to delete just the first element of the array. What you almost always want to do is delete the entire array.

Avoid Memory Leaks and Pitfalls. Remember, I said that the pointer, not the pointed to chunk of memory, is likely to be lost if the function exits, or the scope changes. Each scope is usually defined by an enclosing pair of brackets, like those found at the beginning and end of functions.

Consider this example:

```
void Foo()
{       // Start of Foos scope
        int * p = new int[10];
        // other code.
}       // end of foos scope.
        // oops we forgot to call delete
```

In this example, `delete` was not called. When the function ends, the pointer-to-integer p is lost when the stack is cleaned up. Once that variable p is lost, the reference to the array of `int`s is lost with it, but the array of `int`s is not de-allocated. When blocks of memory are orphaned, it is referred to as the *slicing problem*.

In fact, this function is so bad that you are going to lose ten integers every time the function is called. You will see several manifestations of the slicing problem. I will try to demonstrate throughout the course of this discussion all of the manifestations of this kind of error.

How Were *new* and *delete* Implemented?

Following the development of programming languages and programs, you will discover a recurring theme of aggregation and extensioning. Back in the days of binary programming, there was a progressive inclination towards constructs built on top of instructions to refer to instructions. Machine language became assembly language, where numeric instructions were replaced by symbolic instructions.

When recounting the development of C, several sources suggest that C was developed because Brian Kernighan and Dennis Ritchie—the creators of C—didn't want to program in assembler. The C programming language moved away from assembler in that it offered software developers English words, simpler constructs to represent what may take many lines of assembler code to write. In C, programmers could draw from the set of C instructions and create aggregate operations called functions.

A function allows programmers to refer to a set of instructions by a symbolic name. There is no limit—except imagination—to the extent to which smaller pieces can be used to create a larger piece. The result is a progressive departure from very terse, short pseudo-instructions to constructs that execute thousands of lines of code via a referral to one construct.

Your PC is provided instructions at the operating-system level to allow programs to request and release pools of memory. From a C perspective, there are two functions that were built on top of these operating system facilities to allow C programmers a constructive way to request and release memory. These functions are named `malloc` and `free`. The function `malloc` is used for memory allocation and `free` is used for a complementary effect.

The `malloc` function returns a pointer to a void type (`void*`). Specific data types were the recipient of the memory allocated by `malloc` then `not`. If the type a programmer was allocating memory for was not a `void` pointer, then you had to typecast the return type `void` to the specific type. Typecasting every allocation is messy and error-prone.

```
char * pchar = (char*)malloc( char );
```

There are more problems with `malloc`'s complement `free`. Deleting a null or zero pointer is undefined with the `free` function. The `new` and `delete` operators were implemented to resolve some of the deficits of C's `malloc` and `free`. For example, if a new fails, it returns a null-pointer. You do not need to typecast the return type of new; it works properly with any type. The delete operator behaves correctly if you call delete on a null pointer too. It is unnecessary to know every curative that was applied; simply use new and delete where you would have used malloc and free before.

It is interesting but not surprising to note that if you check implementations of new and delete, you will find that new and delete were implemented in terms of malloc and free. By creating the new operator (think function) on top of malloc, for example, the implementor of new could add the code necessary to ensure the return type is correct and that a null pointer was returned if malloc failed. The improvement of earlier implementations through aggregation continues in C++. Some C++ implementations are designed with C style functions performing the mechanics with the added checks to make them more robust, like the relationship between new and malloc. Still other C++ entities were first implemented in terms of C entities—for example, iostreams were wrappers for stdio.h functions—and later re-implemented completely without the C functions.

Note

The *Annotated Reference Manual,* by Bjarne Stroustrop and Margaret A. Ellis (Addison-Wesley) indicates that the classes istream and ostream, used to write to the console and read from the keyboard were built on top of the C functions printf and scanf. Stroustrop goes on to say that these were eventually re-implemented from scratch without using the C functions.

Using iostream Operators

The iostream class is not part of C++; however, the class was created from C++ constructs. The iostream class was created to replace C input and output functions. The major components from C libraries targeted for replacement were printf and scanf. The printf function was used to send formatted output to an output device, like the monitor. Its counterpart, scanf, was used to read formatted input.

In the next section, I emphasize several facets of the C++ paradigm along with the shortcomings of implementing printf and scanf.

printf and *scanf*

The printf and scanf functions were implemented for C programs. The functions can be used by including the header file stdio.h—standard input/output. The header file includes the declarations for printf and scanf, which look something like this:

```
int printf(const char*, ...);
int scanf(const char*, ...);
```

Examples of using these functions are in chapter 13, "Exploring iostreams." The const char * argument is used to pass a formatting string, which indicates how the other arguments are handled. (You ask, what other arguments?) The other arguments are represented by the ellipsis, which is referred to as a variadic argument specifier. The variadic argument (...) indicates that a varying number and type, from zero to many, of arguments may be passed where the ellipsis is used.

Herein lies the problem. Because a varying number and type of arguments can be passed, for example

```
const char* msg = "World!";
printf("Hello, %s", msg);
int birthday = 1974;
printf("You were born in %d\n", birthday);
```

all working uses of printf, traditional methods of matching variables and arguments, cannot be used.

Note

The const char* formatting string can contain string literals and parameters, like %d (decimal), and %s (string), which help the function figure out what arguments to expect.

See chapter 13, "Exploring iostreams," or your help for more parametric argument types.

The compiler uses the exact match of the argument types to determine how the variables are culled from the program's stack. (The variables are placed there when a function is called.) However, because the variadic argument type is used, it is the format string that figures out both the count and type of arguments passed. This is accomplished by counting the number of parametric arguments—like %d, %f, or %s—to establish the order, number, and type of arguments to pull from the stack. Then the arguments are taken from the stack by manipulating the stack pointer.

It is this capability of accepting variadic arguments, and the code necessary to parse the formatting string, that make printf and scanf slow. (Learning all of those cryptic formatting techniques was no cakewalk either.) As a result, a better technique for input and output was needed.

cin and *cout*

The iostream class was created in the early days of C++. Surprisingly enough, the ostream operator << and istream operator >> in this class were originally built on top of printf and scanf. This may seem odd, but as difficult as these functions were to use, they had been proven to work. By insulating the peculiarities of printf and scanf in classes, the need for understanding and employing the C formatting characters mentioned in the last section was insulated from the user.

> **Note**
>
> Refer to chapters 14, "Basic Class Concepts," 16, "Function Overloading," and 17, "Operator Overloading," for a better understanding of how functions can be wrapped in classes and tied to operators such as << and >>.

The tokens `cin` and `cout` are not functions; they are not operators. They are objects (or instances of classes). (Refer to chapter 13, "Exploring iostreams.") Their function is to replace the functionality of `printf` and `scanf`, and they afford a much simpler syntax.

To make `cin` and `cout` available, simply include the iostream.h file in your module, like this:

```
#include <iostream.h>
```

Having done that, you may use these objects, applying a simplistic and consistent syntax to achieve the exact same functionality as `printf` and `scanf`. The biggest difference is that the syntax appears very symmetric, offering a "kinder, gentler" learning curve.

> **Note**
>
> The two objects, `cin` and `cout`, are instantiated as static objects for you. See chapter 10, "Writing Expressions," for an explanation of static. For now just accept that by including the iostream header file these objects are available for input and output.

For writing to the out device use cout:

```
int birthday = 1974;
char *greetings = "Hello, World!";
cout << greetings << " I was born in " << birthday << endl;
```

Notice the consistency in the syntax regardless of the data type. I included an integer, and `char*` variable, a string literal, and that funny `endl`, all in exactly the same manner. As a matter of fact, every native type can be output the same way. The syntax for `cin` is almost identical:

```
int a = 0;
cout << "How old are you?" << endl;
cin >> a;
```

The only change is the direction of the `istream operator >>`. You may recognize that the << is the left-shift operator and the >> is the right-shift operator. They were *overloaded* (refer to chapter 16, "Operator Overloading") to have a new meaning dependent on the context. Used as the left-shift and right-shift, they are used for integral bit-shifting, which equates to multiplying and dividing, respectively. However, used in the context of iostream objects, they write to and read from output and input devices, like the keyboard and console. Don't worry about overloading for now, simply rely on the consistent syntax of the objects.

II

Programming in C++

> **Note**
>
> The token endl appearing in the code fragment above is a *stream manipulator*, which you'll learn how to write in chapter 16, "Operator Overloading." It performs the same function as the \n character in C programs. Both endl and \n, referred to as newline, insert a carriage return linefeed into the output.
>
> Believe it or not, endl is actually a function. The C++ language is expressive and powerful allowing very functionally complex ideas to be represented with a simplistic syntax.

The objects cin and cout used printf and scanf to actually perform input and output operations. printf and scanf were slow to begin with because they used variadic arguments. Clearly, if you take a slow function, like printf, and aggregate—use it within another function—you will end up with an even slower function. And, using cin and cout for console used to be depressingly slow. Now cin and cout no longer use printf and scanf, making them more efficient.

iostream Operators

When discussing iostream operators, I am referring to the << and >> operators. In addition to being used to write and read input from the keyboard and console for native data types, an identical syntax is used to allow the same kind of syntax and functionality for input and output to files (refer to chapter 13, "Exploring iostreams.")

The added benefit is that these operators can be re-implemented as your skill progresses, to make reading and writing to your aggregate types—classes—as easy as reading and writing the native types. All of this can be done without using complex formatting characters, or varying the syntax for different data types.

How is all of this achieved? As you will see, there are more advanced concepts that have to be grappled with before it becomes apparent. For now, use cin and cout to read and write native types. As you progress through the book, you will see how the following concepts support the other facets of iostreams:

- Name mangling is discussed in chapter 15, "Function Overloading."
- Operator and function overloading are discussed in chapters 15, "Function Overloading," and 16, "Operator Overloading."
- Stream manipulators are also discussed in chapter 16, "Operator Overloading."

Example Program

Here is an easy sample program that demonstrates the ease of use of the iostream objects. Remember cin and cout are objects of the istream and ostream classes, respectively. The objects cin and cout are global static objects instantiated automatically and available to any module that includes <iostream.h>.

```
#include <iostream.h>
// Compiled with Target Model = Console
void main()
{
    char buf[128];
    cout << "Hello. What is your name?" << endl;
    cin >> buf;
    cout << "Nice to meet you " << buf << endl;
}
```

Using Native Data Types as Functions

The notion of operators as functions has been discussed throughout this chapter. On the surface, operators are typically used as single tokens, and syntactically do *not* appear to be function calls. The same holds true for the native data types. The built-in types are not functions, but there exists solutions that employ data types in a manner consistent with the function notation.

- One aspect of this notation is when data types, both native and aggregate, are used for typecasting.
- The second notion is when data types are used as conversion operators.

You need to have an introductory understanding of both of these views of data types as they help you understand more advanced topics that support the object paradigm.

A goal of object-oriented programming is based on the assumption that the use of the built-in data types is inherently easy. Extrapolating from this assumption, if you make complex types work as simply as the native data types, programming is easier. Considering the elements of the language that makes programming with native types easy is the ability to write operations with predefined operators and types. If you can "train" new types to work with operands in previously understood ways, then even complex types should be easier to use.

The notion of built-in types as operator functions becomes fundamental because at some level you may need an easy way to convert between types. Defining a type as an n operator function, referred to s conversion functions, is explained in chapter 16, "Operator Overloading."

Typecasting

The native data types are at times used to convert from one type to another. Applying the syntax to do so is referred to as *typecasting*. C programmers employ this technique every time they use malloc. The malloc function returns the void* pointer to void. However, the type needed was often more specific, like char*, which was used for strings.

Keeping in mind that the return type of malloc is void*, the code might look something like this:

```
char *str = (char*)malloc(14);

strcpy( str, "Hello, World!");
```

The first line allocates 14 bytes, enough for a 13-character string plus the null (\0) byte. The typecast is after the equals operator: (char*). The cast casts the void* to a char*.

Note

The necessity for casting the return type every time malloc was used is one of the reasons that malloc has taken a back seat to new. Another reason is that if the type is larger than a single byte, you will have to multiply the number argument by the size of the data type. This is error-prone. You do not have to do either with the new operator.

There is another form of typecasting that you may see. It looks more akin to a function call or *constructor* call. The second form of a cast places the parentheses around the variable instead of the type. Thus, if you have an integer that you want to cast to a character, assuming it isn't greater than the maximum allowable value of a char, the notation can be

```
int A = 65;
char wasInt = char(A);
cout << wasInt;      // prints 'A' instead of 65
```

as opposed to the already seen typecast that looks like this:

```
int a = 5;
char wasInt = (char)a;
```

Typecasting is sometimes necessitated by the fact that there may be times when one type is offered but another is required. Try to avoid a lot of typecasting in new code, but expect to see some of it in existing programs.

Types as Functions

There are times when one type is expected and another is proffered. C++ is a strongly typed language. In this context, the implication is that if a particular data type is expected, the compiler will force you to provide it. Typecasting in a simple sense solves this problem. However, there is a better way.

If one type is, in fact, a kind of reinterpretation of another type, like an array of characters can be a string if the array is null-terminated, then it is natural to expect some kind of facility for converting between the two types to appease the compiler. We identify circumstances where these relationships exist by creating a conversion operator. In the simplest sense, a conversion operator is a function that takes an argument of one type and returns an argument whose underlying representation is similar but whose name is not.

The syntax of the conversion function is:

```
operator compatible_type( alter_ego );
```

The syntax of these kinds of functions appears unusual. Instead of a return type as the first token, the keyword operator is applied. The function call for this very specialized kind of function is implicit as opposed to looking like a function call. Therefore, the operator keyword is used to indicate that the compiler has to recognize this function call without the traditional signal (which is the use of the function name and parentheses).

From Here...

This chapter presented a straightforward examination of operators and built-in types. The outward appearance of native types and operators is as you might expect. In fact, the most common use of operators and variables is akin to that of writing calculator equations. In C++, however, things are not always what they seem.

If C++ were just another ordinary language, operators and native types would work as their outward appearance might suggest—c = a + b, but C++ is no ordinary language. To support some of the extraordinary idioms and design alternatives, there often needs to be more than meets the eye. The C++ language embodies the kind of programming it supports. Details are often encapsulated to hide the inner mechanics. As a C++ programmer, encapsulation makes your job easier because you don't have to know every detail to use an object. As a programmer learning C++, you must learn what it is that is being encapsulated and emulate the steps required to create the black boxes, like cin and cout, that appear very simple on the surface.

This chapter presents what is a first glimpse at new idioms. In coming chapters, you will learn to model the steps it took to create classes like cin and cout. For now, take solace in the knowledge that you do not have to understand the advanced idioms to begin using C++, but when you are ready they will be waiting for you. To learn more about the expressive side of operators and data types, refer to:

- Chapter 8, "Understanding Expressions through Expansion," demonstrates how to understand the underlying operations of objects.

- Chapter 10, "Writing Expressions," demonstrates how to use the built-in constructs, like for loops and conditional statements, which are the building blocks for all programs.

- Chapter 13, "Exploring iostreams," exemplifies the power of good C++ architecture. The chapter explains and demonstrates the breadth and depth of these well-built tools.

- Chapter 15, "Function Overloading," covers the powerful idiom that extends the range and expressiveness of C++.

- Chapter 16, "Operator Overloading," clearly shows you how to understand and use this powerful technique, which enables you to write code that makes your classes as easy to use as built-in data types.

CHAPTER 7

Pointers and References

If any operators can be attributed as having the most important status, it is probably the pointer and reference operators. Pointers and references enable C++ to get close to the hardware, making C++ capable of spanning the spectrum from low-level driver to mastering the esoteric and aggregate.

Because of low-level access to hardware through points and the ability to create aggregate entities, for instance, with the class idiom, C++ is used to implement everything from device drivers and library tools for other software development tools, real-time hardware control and simulation systems, operating systems and compilers, to animation and multimedia applications. The C++ language is an ideal tool in an amazingly wide variety of application domains.

This chapter shows you the ins and outs of pointers, references, and the array operator. In this chapter, you learn about:

- Using pointers and references
- Accessing dynamic objects through pointers
- Understanding pointers and references used with parameters
- Understanding pointers and references used with return arguments
- Avoiding problems with arrays and pointers

Using Reference Operators *, [], and &

The reference operators play many roles in the C++ language. The array operator ([ ]) is used to access contiguous blocks of memory. The reference operator (*) is used to designate pointers to objects as well as pass arguments through a reference. The address operator (&) plays an important role in the management of large objects passed as arguments.

Each of these operators plays several roles; C++ allows users to re-designate the specificity of the operators' functionality, enabling operators' exact role in all contexts to be defined by individual programmers. (I am referring to the topic of *operator overloading*, which is covered in chapter 16, "Operator Overloading." Because operators can have contextual meanings defined by other users, and pointers and references play an integral role in C++, it is necessary to understand the basics of pointers and references.

You may have read in other books that C++ is like C, but better, meaning that you can use the language much like C while you are still learning. The more advanced uses of language idioms can be postponed with no harmful effects. More advanced idiomatic uses, like operator overloading, will not propagate out of control automatically; rather, you must specifically and intentionally choose to use them or not. If you postpone the use of the more expressive, advanced features of C++, you will not be "accidentally" subverted by the language.

Understanding the Reference Operator(*)

The asterisk (*) is referred to as the *reference operator*. The word object is analogous to a variable. An object is the generic term for a variable instance, or an *instance* of a class. When you use the reference operator in a variable definition, you are designating the variable as a pointer to a specific instance of that data type.

It is imperative that you establish a visual concept of pointers in your mind's eye. This makes the intent of code using pointers more clear, such as defining a variable as an integer pointer:

```
char *p;
```

The pointer is not an object itself, rather it contains a 32-bit number that is equal to the block of data it points to (if the pointer is non-zero). The pointer itself has no storage space, except for the address of the object pointed to (see fig. 7.1).

Caution

Pointers are not initialized automatically in C++, which means that you should set the pointer to an initial value. There is an inherent danger in not doing so; the danger is that accessing an uninitialized pointer is undefined. (More than likely it will crash your program and Windows.)

Pointers are used for more than just accessing chunks of memory allocated with new. They are also used to represent elements that have a physical location. This location may be the address of the state of a hardware or firmware component, or the addresses of items created at runtime.

Initial Values for Pointers. Pointers should almost always be given an initial value by the programmers. There are two kinds of values that you can assign to a pointer. The first is the pointed-to block of memory, and the second is 0. (Notice I didn't say NULL.)

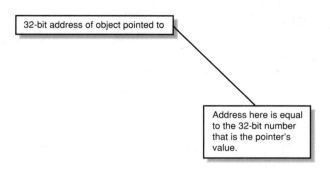

Fig. 7.1

Representation of pointer and pointed-to object if the value of the pointer is non-zero.

I will settle any potential dispute right now. The value of a pointer is undefined unless you assign it a value. If you forget to give a pointer an initial value, then you have no reliable way to compare it to an initial state. If you cannot determine the pointer's validity by checking it against some initial value, then you have no way of ascertaining a good pointer from a bad. Secondly, because pointers are often used with new, followed by a call to delete, it is inherently dangerous to call delete on a pointer pointing to some unknown address. The same doesn't hold true for 0; the delete operator compares the pointer to zero and can safely handle this occurrence.

Assigning an initial value to a pointer means at the point of definition, it must be given an address of an object or memory location, assigned to a call using the new operator or the number 0. Examples of each kind of initialization might appear like the following:

```
char *kybdBios = (char *)0x00000417;   // memory location
int *intArray = new int [10];          // 10 integers
char *p = 0;                           // initialized character pointer to 0.
```

Initializing Pointers to 0. Notice that you do not use a mnemonic token or manifest constant for NULL initialization. C++ is a strongly typed language. Therefore, the difficulty becomes to what data type would some NULL constant be assigned. The data types need to match exactly, so defining a NULL as a const is difficult at best because a single data type would not suffice.

Using a unique name for NULL for differing data types is out the question because it would require the use of too many names. NULL was defined in C as

```
#define NULL (void*)0
```

casting the integer 0 to a void* (void pointer). This won't work in C++ because you would need to cast the NULL for every pointer type, which results in ugly code. Here are some examples of ugly code using the old C-style NULL:

```
char *p = (char*)NULL;
int *pint = (int*)NULL;
```

An exception is the use of a constant integer value when you mean NULL. Typically, use mnemonics for constant values because it makes code more readable. The use of 0 is an exception.

The Array Operator (*[]*)

In some regards, the array operator and the reference operator are used interchangeably. In Borland C++, the relationship is that the first element of an array is the same as the element returned by dereferencing a pointer. Thus, defining a as a pointer to an array of integers, like

```
int *a = new int[5];
```

means that either *a or a[0] returns the first element of the array. Often, when passing static or dynamic arrays as arguments to a function, the reference operator is used.

> **Caution**
>
> The acceptance of * and [ ] as interchangeable operators is not guaranteed to be portable across operating system platforms. Refer to the current ANSI C++ definition or the *Annotated Reference Manual,* called the ARM, by Stroustrop and Ellis, if you are writing code that may need to be ported to other environments.

To demonstrate, suppose a Foo function accepts an array of integers. The function declaration might look like this:

```
void Foo( int *array, unsigned int size);
```

Then variables that meet the requirement for matching this declaration can be either of the form

```
int buffy[10]; // static allocation
Foo(buffy, 10);
```

or

```
int *jody = new int[10]; // free store allocation
Foo(jody);
```

Playing with buffy or jody, you can demonstrate a for loop initializing each element of the array. Consider

```
for( int j=0; j<10; j++)
  buffy[j] = 0;
```

or

```
for( int k=0; k<10; k++)
  *(jody + k) = 0;
```

As a matter of fact, both code fragments work: The first example uses the array ([ ]) operator; the second uses the index to perform arithmetic and the reference (*) operator to deference each element. For notational convenience, you use the array operator, but you may see code employing either method.

Being consistent with the previous section, I want to emphasize that each element of an array needs to be initialized immediately, too. Use an initial dummy value, like 0, if the values of each element are unknown.

The Address Of (&) Operator

The relationship between a pointer and an address of (&) operator is that the values of pointers are addresses. Every object has an address. This implies that aliases can be created for an actual object.

The address of operator plays an integral role in several aspects of C++. You will see examples and demonstrations of these throughout this chapter and the rest of the book.

Demonstrating the relationship between objects—read variable if it helps to clarify—and their addresses, you can define an integer statically:

```
int nut = 5;
```

If I write

```
cout << nut << endl;  // prints 5
```

the number 5 is written to the output device. If, however, I write

```
cout << &nut << endl;  // prints address of nut
```

some 32-bit number will be written to the standard output device. Illustrating the relationship to pointers, if I write

```
int * pnut = nut;
```

I have created a pointer, pointing to memory location 5. (Probably not a good idea.) However, if my intention is to create an alias for the variable, I would write

```
int * donut = &nut;
```

To modify nuts value through donut, I simply need to dereference donut. Here is the code:

```
*donut = 0;
```

There are several scenarios where alias relationships crop up (some are extremely useful). One advanced use for alias relationships is employed in making Windows 95 itself work. I am referring to *functors* (pointers to functions). Functors are used in several problem domains, one of which is to establish callback functions, like *interrupt handlers* and *event handlers*. (Functors are discussed in chapter 12, "Using the Borland C++ Library Functions.")

Accessing Dynamic Objects

The pointer operator (->) is used to access elements of dynamic, aggregate objects. This is designed to introduce the keyboard pair - and >, typed as **->**, which is used to access elements of objects allocated on the free store or heap. *Aggregate* objects refers to variables whose data type is some collection of data types, whether this collection is a class or struct; *dynamic* means that the variable is a pointer type and the new operator was probably used at some point; *element* means some variable within the aggregate variable.

II

Programming in C++

The `struct` keyword is used to define what might most closely be related to a record, where each field is a data type and variable name pair. The simplest use of the `struct` keyword is to collect data, allowing you to refer to all elements by the `struct` name or any individual element using the `struct` name as a prefix. For example,

```
struct INTS
{ int thingOne, thingTwo; };
```

In this example, the elements are `thingOne` and `thingTwo`.

If a variable of this type, referred to as an object, were defined as a pointer variable

```
struct INTS *ints = new INTS;
```

then accessing either element would be done by appending the pointer operator (`->`) to the variable name, followed by the element name. Thus

```
ints->thingOne = 1;
ints->thingTwo = 2;
```

Using the C++ vernacular elements is often referred to as *member data*. Remember the pointer operator is not used for pointers; it is used for elements of pointer objects that have sub-elements called members. These members are not limited to data alone but include functions as well. As I said in earlier chapters, the C++ paradigm is creating new types by binding data and functions together to create advanced types that are as easy to use as the native data types.

Note

As a matter of convention, I use the `struct` from C when I want to declare a variable as a simple data collection. This is a convention, so other programmers may not adhere to it.

Part of the obstacle to learning a language as expressive and complex as C++ is differentiating between conventions and requirements of the language. A second, often more convoluted obstacle, is acquiring the necessary understanding of new and synonymous terms. The effort required to overcome this obstacle is why programmers get the big bucks.

Accessing Static Objects

In addition to the pointer (`->`) operator, the second kind of allocation is static. Defining variables without using the reference operator `*` and `new`, implies a static allocation. Statically allocated variables are given space from the program's stack, which is managed by the program.

Using the same `struct` from the preceding section, the only difference in code is that no asterisk is used when the variable is defined. Thus, the code looks like this:

```
struct INTS ints;  // no * or call to new operator
ints.thingOne = 1; // use of . (read dot operator)
ints.thingTwo = 2; // instead of -> (pointer operator)
```

The dot operator (.) is used to access statically allocated objects. The second noteworthy change is that the `new` operator is not used. (This means you won't call `delete` either.)

Furthering your understanding of these additional operators, you need to examine how this applies to functions as well. Where functions are concerned, you must examine the function arguments to determine how the objects are used within the function itself.

The relationship is simple: If the * asterisk is used in the function interface, such as

```
void Foo( struct INTS* ints); // function interface
```

then the `->` operator will be used to access elements of the `struct` within the function body. This is irregardless of how the passed-in variable was defined. If the address of operator (&) is used in the function interface, then the dot operator (.) is used within the confines of the function itself, irregardless of how the original object was defined.

It is important to remember that I am referring to aggregate types here, as opposed to the built-in data types. An aggregate type can consist of a single built-in data type.

Argument Declarations Using Reference Operators

There is a significant difference between arguments that use either of the reference operators to pass functions, and those arguments that don't. To determine if you will use reference operators in a given example depends on what requirements the particular code fragment has. In the next section, I will demonstrate how to weigh the merits of using the reference operator, address of operator, or nothing at all by comparing the benefits in performance increases as opposed to the expenses in lines-of-code incurred. Understanding the implications of argument passing will help you make better design decisions. There are significant implications as well as minor syntactical changes in the code depending on which specifier is used when passing and returning arguments.

Terminology

Before beginning, let's agree on some basic terminology, such as the difference between declaration and definition. As far as functions are concerned, the *declaration* provides the interface only, which consists of the return argument, function name, the parentheses operator, the arguments, and a semicolon. A syntactical representation of this is:

```
return_type function_name(...);
```

Thus

```
void Foo( int num );   // declare Foo
```

is an example, where `void` is the return type, `Foo` is the function name, the (&) are the parenthetical operator pair, `int` is the data type and `num` is the variable, followed by the semicolon. The difference between the declaration of a function and the definition is that the semicolon is replaced with the body of the function (enclosed in the left and right brackets). Thus, Foo might be defined as

```
void Foo( int num )
{cout << num << endl; }
```

Interface refers to the way the function is declared. The reason you must declare functions—and the declaration must appear before the first use of the function—is that C++ uses the function declaration to enable the compiler to check if you are using the function correctly (passing the correct number and type of arguments).

Pass by Value

The phrase *pass by value* means that you are passing the value of one variable to another variable. What you are getting then is a copy. The interface of arguments passed by value consists of an argument, including the type and variable name, without the use of the *, [], or & operators (usually just the * or & are used by convention).

When you pass by value, whatever steps necessary to make a replica of the variable are used and you get a copy of the variable. This means that if the function changes the value of the variable within the function, there if no effect on the original.

This simple program illustrates:

```
void HeyNordge( int anInt )
{  anInt = 5; cout << anInt << endl; }
```

Calling HeyNordge—"Hey, Nordge."—causes the value of anInt to be 5, which will be written to the output device. From the outside view, no change is apparent:

```
int otherInt = 10;         // outside of HeyNordge
cout << otherInt << endl;  // prints 10
HeyNordge( otherInt );     // prints 5
cout << otherInt << endl;  // still 10
```

After the call to HeyNordge the otherInt is still equal to 10.

Tip

A convention employed in this book is to use NameCase function names. Using conventions, whether this one or your own, is better than being inconsistent. Refer to chapter 6, "Native Data Types and Operators," for examples of conventions you may come across, and the conventions used in this book.

It is not particularly expensive to pass the built-in types by value, especially if you do not need a modified return value. Unfortunately, things are not always as simple as they seem. Imagine complex aggregate types built from many built-in data types. The effort required to replicate objects with many smaller elements may incur expensive performance penalties. For more information on this, see chapter 17, "Constructors: Copy and Assignment."

Caution

I strongly recommend that you read and thoroughly understand the finer points of how objects are passed as arguments (read chapter 17) before you begin writing and using your own classes. I have come across a lot of code that has memory leaks induced because of a few missing elements.

Pass by Reference

When the * or & operators are used, you are indicating to users that it is possible for the particular function to modify the value of the variables.

Sometimes this is exactly what you intend, and other times it is more efficient to *pass by reference* (or pass an address.) (Refer to chapter 17 for complete discussions on object passing.) For now, you are concerned with the design decision to allow a function to modify some externally defined variable's state.

Note

What does it mean to call a function? Functions are assigned locations in memory, so they have an address. To access the code in a function, the compiler records the current execution point of the program, places the address of the function (assigned by the linker in some registers) and executes an *assembler call* instruction.

Arguments are sent to a function by a prearranged agreement that their values are also recorded in such a manner that the function can access the values by some preestablished means. The center of this activity is the *stack*. Most kinds of programming tasks do not require you to manipulate the stack; the compiler and language take care of it. However, some systems programming requires stack manipulation, and it is worth noting in general.

Address Of Arguments. The address of (&) operator used in a function's interface indicates that you are passing that argument by reference. When using the address of operator, it is the address of the object—remember, object can refer to an aggregate or built-in variable type—you are passing to the function.

Every variable has to reside in memory, which means that each has an address. However, there is a subtle distinction between the address of an object and the object's value. Suppose you went to any physical street address, like 1600 Pennsylvania, and knocked on the door. Would it make a sound? Of course, even though you referred to the physical location by address, it is the entity that resides there. If you were to paint the door calico (same address), would you be arrested? (This is only an illustration; don't get arrested folks!) Sure, because the door would be painted calico and that would look silly on the White House.

The relationship between an address and an object is that if you make changes to the value of an object through its physical location—the memory address—the changes are no less real. If you intend for your operator function or "plain old" function to have a lasting effect on an object, then you pass the object by reference. This is simply accomplished by inserting an ampersand between the data type and variable name. An example of both kinds of functions accepting reference arguments is

```
void SetValue( int &val );   // by reference
```

which is a plain function that accepts an integer reference.

The second example

```
ostream& operator<<(ostream& os,
    STRING& str);   // ostream by reference
```

might be a declaration of operator, << for STRING objects.

At this point, the only important aspect is the use of the by-reference argument passing notation. The SetValue function is simply a contrivance and has no special meaning, but this chapter does include an example program demonstrating the syntax and effect of each idiom.

When you use an object passed by reference, no special syntax is required to set its value. Reading or writing the value of an object passed by reference—using the & operator—requires exactly the same syntax as does an object passed by value. Thus, to change the value of val in SetValue, the following syntax works:

```
void SetValue( int &var ){ val = 10; } // a one-liner
```

I mention this specifically because the syntax of reference objects contrasts a bit with that for pointer objects.

If the passed-in argument is an aggregate type, then the dot (.) operator is used to access elements. (Refer to the previous section on "Accessing Static Objects," for details.)

Pointer Arguments. Pointers take the same position, between the data type and the variable name if they are used. Figure 7.2 shows the general format of a function declaration. The difference between the declaration and definition is that definitions include the function body between the left and right brackets { }. (We will look at the return types in just a minute.)

Fig. 7.2

Shows the general syntax of a function declaration. The absence of the {} (which contains the function body) and the use of a semicolon are what make the distinction. Both return types and arguments (or parameters) can be quite simple or complex.

// Function Declaration

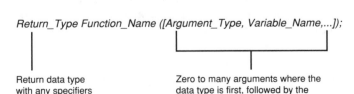

Return_Type Function_Name ([Argument_Type, Variable_Name,...]);

Return data type with any specifiers

Zero to many arguments where the data type is first, followed by the variable name including any specifiers

When a pointer is used in the argument list, you are informing the compiler that the appropriate use of the function requires a pointer argument. This has an effect on the notation used in the body of the function. While it is not wrong to pass pointers, they are less common in C++ than in C. Where a reference is required, it is more common to see the address of operator used. This is due to the requirement that a notational difference be used when pointer arguments are accepted.

Here is the SetValue function from the previous example, using pointer arguments instead of reference arguments:

```
// Function definition
void SetValue(int *val)
{ *val = 10; }
```

Notice that I have to dereference the pointer to access the value of pointed-to objects. Figure 7.3 illustrates the relationship between a pointer and what is pointed at. The data type indicates what lies at the other end of the pointer; the use of the reference operator (*) specifies the variable as a pointer; and the name is how it is referred to.

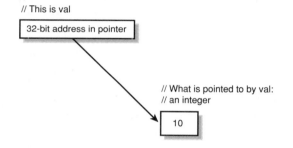

Fig. 7.3

Illustrates the relationship between pointer and pointee. This example refers to a contrived int pointer named val and what it points to: an integer equal to 10.

> **Note**
>
> In the SetValue function, the dereference is *val. By preceding the pointer with the reference operator, the code fragment is read as "assign the integer 10 to what val points to."

Why use pointers at all? Pointers are simply ways to refer to locations in memory. This is how function calls work, so they are used in the background anyway. By providing direct support for them, the language provides a notation that enables you to implement some very complex abstractions.

Returning by Reference

The focus of this section is return arguments and the use of references. There are several considerations when returning objects by reference, some of which are directly related and others indirectly so. This discussion is critical because it plays a later role in the fundamental design techniques you will need to consider when building your own functions and classes.

In this section, I introduce the term *scope* and the role scope plays in determining how values are returned. You see a couple of different ways that information can be returned from a function, and what considerations you must give the data.

Scope

You may be hard-pressed to find a single textbook definition of scope. The word itself may appear in discussions relating to many C++ language features. Conferring with the *Annotated Reference Manual* (ARM), it states that there are four kinds of scope: local, function, file, and class. If you refer to the index of the ARM, there are about 30 index entries related to scope.

The use of the term scope is relative to the context in which it is used. For now, you are only concerned about scope as it applies to variables declared in functions, or local scope. Specifically, you are concerned about the difference between variables declared within functions and those that are not.

Local Stack Allocated Objects. Objects allocated within a function, including all of the built-in native types and any aggregate types, are local to the function. This means that if you define a variable between the left and right brackets of the function definition, the variable is allocated on the stack memory space.

The result is that the variable has space allocated to it when the function is called, and the stack pointer is readjusted when the function exits, which, in effect, destroys the variable. This happens regardless of the particular data type, as long as the type and variable name were declared within the function body. All of this activity is controlled behind the scenes, so there is little you can do about it. You need to understand it, though.

To demonstrate, suppose I declared two simple variables within some function:

```
void SomeFunction()
{
 char *p = 0;
 int num = 32;
 // Some code...
}
```

The chunk of memory used to store these two variables is taken from the stack by adjusting the stack pointer, which allows the correct amount of storage. When the function exits, the stack is returned to its previous state—prior to this function call, gobbling up the space previously given to the char pointer p and the int num. (This is discussed in chapter 4, "The Preprocessor.")

Note

While discussing the way local variables are given space on the stack, I intentionally use words like "chunk" and "gobble" because the technical specifics are not as important as the general idea. My reasoning is that unless you do systems programming, where you need to manage the stack, the names are less important than the operations.

> To satisfy your curiosity, the stack segment is some block of memory; the size is specified in the .rc file given to your program. The stack pointer SP is manipulated to store information related to the last instruction location prior to a function call. Variables are passed on the stack and local variables are given their storage requirement needs from the stack space. This is all usually performed by instructions native to the computer and behind the scenes.

Variables, like the ones defined in SomeFunction, are usually intended for use with the function in the local scope. Problems arise when programmers try to use locally scoped variables as return arguments. Keep reading and you will see why.

Dynamic Objects Allocated with Local Pointers. The other half of this discussion refers to the blocks of memory that are pointed to by local variables, like char* p from the last section. While p is local to SomeFunction, pointers are often assigned to a block of memory with the new operator, and the pointed-to block is allocated on the heap.

This means that p is a logical "handle" that allows you to deallocate the memory pointed to by p. As stated in the last section, local variables like num and p are automatically cleaned up when a function goes out of scope (when the code reaches the right bracket). The same is not true for the dynamic data that is pointed to. As a general rule, you must have a matching call to delete for every new (as discussed in chapter 6, "Native Data Types and Operators").

For the purposes of this discussion, I am referring to scope as it applies to variables defined within the confines of a function.

Returning References to Local Objects

Specifying a data type only as the return type indicates that you are returning by value. In this chapter, you will see the circumstances where a return by reference might be improperly used.

During the discussion on scope, I discussed how variables defined in a function have local scope, the storage space is in stack memory, and the cleanup is automatic. While this is true for pointers too, it is not true for pointed-to data. (The distinction between a point and the data it points to is important!)

Returning the Address of an Object. The more you use C++, the more you see the use of functions that return the address of some object. This means the address of (&) operator is used with the type of the return argument, like this:

```
Return_Type & Function_Name( [Argument_List] );
```

Code written with the address of operator after the return type indicates that you are returning an address of an object of that data type. This is fine, if it is done correctly (in some circumstances is exactly what you want). However, if you are returning the address of a variable local to the function, then you are returning the address of something that is going to be cleaned up automatically when the stack is adjusted.

Here is what the incorrect code may look like, if applied to a simple function using integer arguments:

```
// Example of the slicing problem. Returning references to local
// objects at best will give you weird results, at worst, it will
// crash your program.
int & ReturnLocalInteger()
{
  int val = 5;
  return &val;
}
```

The result of this function is undefined. At times, it may appear to work, but this is really an example of the slicing problem. To visualize what the slicing problem is, first think of a pointer that points to some undefined block of memory, anything that causes this situation to incur is part of the slicing problem. More succinctly, when pointers and blocks of memory become disassociated abnormally, you have slicing.

As a general rule, don't return references to local objects. There are circumstances where returning a reference is exactly what you want (I will point those instances out when they arise). It should be defined several times throughout, but I will use it here, too.

Returning a Pointer to a Local Object. Using the reference operator(*) to return a pointer to a local block of memory is wrong most of the time. Suppose, for example, you want to allocate the array of integers within a function. In general, it is a good idea to delete the array before the function exits.

If you return a pointer to a block of memory allocated within a function, then it may be difficult to determine whose responsibility it is to deallocate the resources. Even worse, it may be difficult to ensure that the right form of delete is used. As I said in chapter 6, "Native Data Types and Operators," the call to new and delete must match; if you used [ ] (array operator) with new, then use it with delete (it may be hard to keep track once a pointer has been returned). Another problem is tracking the size of the array; losing track of the size invites indexing out of bounds.

Suppose you choose to use a dynamically allocated array of objects within a function because the number of elements required is not known at design-time. The approach your implementation takes is to accept the array size as a function argument, allocate the array with new, use the array (also based on the size), and then delete the array. If you postpone deallocation to some point outside of the function, maintaining information about the array size may be challenging and complex. This kind of programming invites errors.

Note

One noteworthy exception is the C strdup function, which allocates enough space for an array of characters used to store an ASCIIZ string. This is safely accomplished because the \0 at the end of the string can be used to detect the size of the array (or number of elements).

> The strdup function does include comments warning you that you must be responsible for calling free on the array of characters.
>
> The strdup function uses the function malloc, so if you use malloc, you must release the memory with the free function. It is undefined—which means you may be in deep poodoo—if you mix the use of new and delete with malloc and free.

Returning a pointer to data allocated locally to a function might take on this appearance when applied to characters:

```
// Don't do this unless you are sure of what you are doing.
char * ReturnCharPointer( unsigned int size )
{ return new char[size]; }
```

Or even worse, if you allocate memory using new, forget to deallocate and the pointer is not returned (this is demonstrated on an array of floating-point numbers):

```
// default argument for size used
void ArrayOfFloats( unsigned int size = 10 )
{
    float * farray = new float[size];
    // some code
}
```

Forgetting to call delete on the array of floats, farray, you lose the reference to it. This means that you cannot recover that memory because you have no way to refer to it after the pointer is lost. This is another example of code that causes the slicing problem. Again, unless you are exactly sure of what you are doing, try to avoid returning references to local variables.

An Exception to the Rule: *static.* If you have to depend on a variable retaining its value between function calls, the static keyword may be what the doctor ordered. Using the keyword static tells the compiler to maintain the variable even after the function exits.

This feat is accomplished in the background by allocating space for the local, static variable in the global space. While it acts like a local variable to the function, it is not stored on the stack. The result is that the language can maintain the value between function calls. Here is what the code may look like, if applied to an array of characters:

```
char * ReturnCharP()
{
 static char buf[128];
 cin.getline( buf, 128 ); // read until carriage return or 127
                          // the last byte is for the '\0'
 return buf;
}
```

It is probably a good idea to store or use the value because even though the local variable is used with static, the next call to the function is likely to overwrite the contents of the variable. This technique simply ensures that the contents are not sliced off before they can be used as a return value.

II

Programming in C++

Understanding Pointers

A *pointer* is a name used to refer to a memory location. This may be memory allocated by new, it may be an alias for a static block of memory, or it may be used to point to some address. The pointer itself has no storage space, except for the number that it contains. This number is an address.

The pointer's address value specifies what it points to and what it points to is what contains the storage space. Getting this relationship straight takes some getting used to, but is important because pointer misuse is a big source of errors. It is for this reason that many languages and desktop-development tools avoid pointers. While they may allow access to addresses, there is no simple notation, rather the addresses are gleaned from a function call.

Pointers facilitate the use of many programming idioms that make it easier to express all kinds of implementations with a brief, clear notation. Through the use of pointers, you can have aliases for objects, create function handlers and callback functions, and optimize the utilization of resources, like memory, through reference counting.

I am mentioning some of these concepts in an effort to allow you a sneak peak at some things to come. At this point, I prefer you to have at least been introduced to new concepts in context, even though you may not understand the meanings.

Exploring Problems with Arrays

Arrays are efficient and simple to use. An array is a contiguous block of like data types. Mechanically accessing any indexed element of an array can be accomplished by adding the size * index to the address of the array. Thankfully, we can use the array operator [ ] and the arithmetic is performed by the compiler. There are two ways to implement arrays using the base language. The first is to implement an array as a static array

```
type var_name[ size ];
```

and the other is dynamically, with a call to new:

```
type * var_name = new type[ size ];
```

Creating an array either way is easy to do, and using the array can be accomplished with a simple and clear notation: by using the array operator [ ]. Using the array operator, arrays can be accessed as either a right-hand-side or left-hand-side argument. Right-handedness or left-handedness refers to which side of an operator, like the assignment operator =, the array appears on. The following code demonstrates a simple character array used as both a right-hand argument (or rvalue) and as a left-hand argument (or lvalue):

```
const int MAX = 26;
char characters[MAX];
for( int j=0; j<MAX; j++ )
  characters[j] = j + (int)'A'; // fill the array 'A'..'Z'
                                // left-hand-side
```

```
                                        // write the alphabet
    for( j = MAX; j>=0; j-- )
      cout << characters[j] << endl;// right-hand-side
```

When arrays are used in such a simplistic manner, there is seldom a problem. However, when arrays are bounced around the program, the likelihood that an array will be accessed with an invalid index increases. It is because of the simplicity in the syntax, the general ease of use that arrays are so popular, and it is for this reason that you need to understand how arrays in C++ work in general.

Why the First Index Is 0

An array is a contiguous block of memory. This means that element 2 is at exactly the same distance from 1 in memory as 3 is from 2. By adding the index, multiplied by the size of the data type to the first element, you can find any element. The equation is

```
    (base_address + (index * sizeof(an_element))
```

This notation is clumsy and probably even more error-prone than the one usually used. For this equation to work, it must work for all indexes. If a pointer points to the base address (beginning address) of an array, then plugging an index of 1 into the equation yields a number equal to the base address plus the size of one element. This means that the space for the first element is wasted, or some kind of exceptions must be made in the code that supports this low-level operation. The more exceptions you have in your code, the more complex it is to write and maintain.

As a result, a base index of 0 is used. As a result, this simple kind of equation can be used to access contiguous elements. C++ will allow you to use arithmetic expressions to access elements of an array, but using the array operator represents a much simpler notation. Here it is:

```
    pointer[ index ];      // pointer is equal to the base address
```

Remember I said that you can think of operators as a specialized kind of function call where the name of the function is comprised of the keyword operator, followed by the operator symbol. Let's apply this conceptually to the array operator and see what it might look like:

```
    Return_Type & operator[]( Index );   // an array operator function
```

The function returns an address of one of those contiguous elements (Return_Type &). Use the special notation (operator[]), and the remaining part looks like a function call taking an index.

The body of the function can be written to perform the calculation that is required to get the element and you would need to return a pointer to it. This is just a hint at how a complex-looking function

```
    (base_address + (index * sizeof(an_element))
```

can be used to implement a simpler notation

```
    base_address[ Index ]
```

Indexing Out-of-Bounds

An *out-of-bounds* index is one that is greater than or equal to the size of the array. I say equal to because if you begin counting with zero, you have the number of elements when you reach a number one less than the size of the array.

Indexing beyond the last element of an array can crash your program or Windows. One of the most common errors is the off-by-one error where an array is indexed one index greater than the maximum number of elements.

If you can imagine that an array operator can be implemented as a function, then you might also be able to imagine code in the array operator function that performs out-of-bounds checking.

Bounded Arrays

C++ does not directly support pointers or arrays that have bounded indexes. Normally an array has indexes from 0 to the size of the array - 1. Referring to an array as bounded means that some other arbitrary indexes were used. However, some solutions may be more intuitively implemented with a bounded array. Again, if you can imagine that an array operator can be written as a function, then try to imagine a simple addition operation that adjusts an index to a number between zero and the size of the array.

One of the features that makes C++ so powerful is its ability to allow the developer to express complex ideas using the convenient and simple notational features. If data types—like a bounded array—can be designed using the notational conveniences that make using the built-in types so easy, then much of the programming will be as easy as using the native types. As you progress through the book, keep in mind that some of these concepts are building blocks to using more advanced C++ idioms.

From Here...

This chapter introduced some of the ways in which several operators might appear in the context of a program. The discussion was intentionally general because I expect some of the basic uses are familiar to many of you. I would prefer you think about the implications of the discussion rather than focus on any single use.

If any of the operators in this chapter is completely new to you, then wrapping most of them in the main function of a program will enable you to practice using them. On the surface, their use is almost exactly as it appears. Things, however, are not at all superficial in C++, so you will see the outward simple usage of each notation later in the book.

A good exercise for beginners is to create a static then dynamic array of integers, as-sign some values to each element, and write the array to the console using a `for` loop or `while` statement. Several complete working applications are included for this chap-ter on the companion disk to help you understand each of the operators presented.

Further discussions related to the topics of this chapter can be found in:

- Chapter 9, "Data Quantifiers and Qualifiers," demonstrates using the `static` keyword and others.
- Chapter 10, "Writing Expressions," shows the form of many kinds of expressions, including those that use references.
- Chapter 11, "Functions," demonstrates how to write functions, including using reference operators and a specialized use of pointers to functions.
- Chapter 17, "Constructors: Copy and Assignment," shows you the ins and outs of writing classes, and you see what a critical role references play in the C++ paradigm as pertains to the copy and assignment constructors.
- Chapter 19, "Using Template Classes," shows you how to implement functions and classes once and use them for any data type.

CHAPTER 8

Understanding Expressions through Expansion

The word "terse" has been applied to both the C and the C++ languages. In a conversation with a manager from the Milford Proving Grounds, the word "elegant" was also applied to C++. (But often the code they write is *not* elegant.) The implication of these statements is that some think C++ is a terse language; others feel that it is capable of expressing codified ideas elegantly, but you don't have to. In this chapter I am going to demonstrate techniques that will help you understand any code that you use or maintain whether it is elegant or terse.

What expense is paid for the price of elegance? Sometimes the price we pay to use the full range of expressiveness in C++ is the perception of clarity. Language features, such as templates, overloaded operators, and conversion operators, don't jump out and grab programmers; they take a little getting used to. With this chapter, I decided that I want to point out some of these things to you, and show you how to expand the subtle expression into its verbose form or meaning. Learning from others' code or maintaining existing code is a lot easier if you know how to find the root of the code.

In this chapter, you learn about

- Simplifying code with parenthetical grouping
- Understanding conditional statements
- Expanding operator functions
- Detecting and locating conversion operators

Synonyms

Alias declarations can pose a real problem for novice C++ programmers. Part of the magic of C++ is that the core language is so small. Like Lego or primary colors, what you create depends on what you see in your mind's eye. There are about a half dozen native data types. They are easy enough to learn because there are so few of them.

However, individual designers or entities perceive slightly different versions of the object-oriented paradigm. Top-notch designers, like Grady Booch, seem to see a language where domain experts—people who do the hands-on work in the areas of expertise—practically choose the verbiage used. Entities, such as Microsoft, create whole notations, like the Hungarian notation, where there seems to be a deluge of new names. I am not trying to make an assessment of the value or lack of it in their respective efforts. Instead, I am suggesting that the core language can appear almost to morph from one group of programmers to the next.

C++ is a strongly typed language. This means that declarations must match usage closely. Consider the possible representations of dates:

```
int day, month, year;
```

or:

```
struct DATE{ int day, month, year; };
typedef struct DATE date;
```

or even:

```
typedef unsigned char DAY;      // Smallest data type to hold 1-31
typeded unsigned char MONTH;
typedef unsigned int YEAR;
DAY day;
MONTH month;
YEAR year;
```

The first version uses native data types. If you know what values are satisfactory for those, you're all set. If you don't, these are defined in Limits.h. The second may be easier to pass, but you would have to learn a little about the alias date to know how to assign values to objects of this type. In a more object-oriented fashion, defining aliases for each of the types may be more appealing, because the language takes on a more self-commenting pose. Consider a function declaration declared with these argument types:

```
void PrintDate( DAY d, MONTH m, YEAR y );
```

This has its appeal. Herein lies the problem: You are sure to find these and other variations in existing code. While an appealing thought might be to maintain a consistent standard for such things—the norm seems to be that there is little consistency between coding styles, let alone conventions of this sort—many programs rely on code written by outside vendors; they are not going to use your standard.

How, then, can you cope with the problem? The first solution is to create and implement a standard internally. The second is to ensure that everyone is capable of expanding declarations that are not comprised of native data types. This means classes, structs, unions, enumerations, or typedefs.

What you really need to know is some of the places to look and tools to use. There are two or three places to look and ways to look. Use the Borland IDE's Search, Find command (see fig. 8.1). If what you want is not found in the current file, check other files in the current project. You can select from those available by selecting from the files list in the Window menu (see fig. 8.2).

Fig. 8.1

Fill in the dialog box, selecting the filters you want the Search command to use.

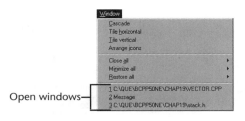

Open windows

Fig. 8.2

You can select different open Windows from the Window menu shown here.

II

Programming in C++

Still can't figure out what the declaration means? Check the context-sensitive online Help. Place the editor's cursor on the word, or type and press F1. Having exhausted these sources, my favorite standby program is *Grep.com*. Shell from Windows 95 to the DOS prompt (it's still there), and run Grep. By running grep ? with the question mark, a full syntax listing appears. This is Grep's Help. The easiest use of Grep is:

```
grep -i type *.h *.cpp
```

where the type is the token string whose meaning is unclear, the i switch causes Grep to perform a case-insensitive search, and the files searched will be files matching the two file masks. (You are not limited to an arbitrary number of file masks.) You can also run Grep from the Tool, Grep menu in the IDE. Figure 8.3 displays the Grep input dialog box. Add the arguments to Grep in the dialog box. Figure 8.4 displays the Grep page of the Message window notebook page.

Having traced to the source of the declaration, you now have the information necessary to provide the right arguments and values to the underlying data types. Synonyms present problems only if you do not know the underlying data types involved and don't know how to figure out what they are.

Fig. 8.3

Grep.com can be run from the old DOS command line, producing a text-based output, or from within the IDE, producing output in the Message window tabbed notebook.

Fig. 8.4

The output from running Grep on the Stack.h file included on the companion disk.

Conditional Statements and Loops

Conditional tests may seem unnecessarily complex. The result they provide and the method for providing a specific range of values may be required, but the confusion of conditional statements can make the test mollified.

There is a study of mathematics, *discrete mathematics,* which uses a symbolic calculus to enable developers to minimize logic equations (often used in tests). In most cases this is overkill; besides, if you need *predicate calculus,* you would probably be better off subdividing the problem.

Conditional tests in while loops, for statements, or if conditionals are more often used in a common sense manner. If the test is simple enough, most likely this technique will work. These kinds of tests, for example, may be:

```
if( a > 5 )
while( k-- > 0 )
for( int j = 0; j < MAX; j++ )
```

These are not really what concerns me here. I am more concerned with tests that perform work, use pointers, or contain more than a single clause. A good first step is likely to reduce the complexity of reading statements of this sort, but a busy for loop already is a hub of activity. Let's consider some ways to figure out what the code is supposed to say and make sure it says that.

One way to simplify complex conditional tests is to extract the unnecessarily complex test (or don't put it in there in the first place), and create an inline function, replacing the terse test code with a well-named function. The function name can provide a clearer idea of what functionality the code provides or what test is being performed.

The body of the function also offers more space in which to comment. This cleans up the locale around the loop, and using the *inline* specifier may soften any potential performance penalties. As an added benefit, if the loop performs a specific kind of functionality, making a function out of the entire loop, and not just the test, will make your code more readable, and will enhance the likelihood that the code will be reused.

The following statement converts an ASCIIZ string to an uppercase string. The macro `toupper` converts a single character at a time, and often it is really an entire word or phrase that is to be converted to uppercase.

```
char * msg = "Jumanji";
// Converts an ASCIIZ string to all uppercase
for( char *p = msg; *p; *p = (char)toupper(*p), p++);
// Produces "JUMANJI"
```

Placing this code right smack in the center of other code tends to make it unnecessarily hard to read. If you were to state what this code does, you might say something like: "It assigns the string to a pointer; while the pointer has not reached the null character '\0', call the macro `toupper` for each character and increment the temporary pointer."

I am not advocating writing this kind of code, but you will see it and have to cope with it. I tend to convert clever code of this sort to simpler functions, perhaps inline functions.

<table>
<tr><td>

Caution

</td></tr>
<tr><td>

Applying the inline specifier to functions containing `for` loops causes a warning. You shouldn't deliver programs with warnings in them. At a minimum, you can dispense with the warning by placing the preprocessor directive:

```
#pragma warn -inl
```

which turns inline warnings off. It may be a better tactic to remove the cause of the warning, rather than gag it.

</td></tr>
</table>

Listing 8.1 is a short sample program that illustrates how to clean up clever code. In effect, what I have done is to put a nice coat of varnish on the `for` loop and give it a more meaningful name.

Listing 8.1   Jumanji.cpp—Using Code through a Meaningful Construct Name

```
1: // JUMANJI.CPP - Demonstrates simplification of code
2: #include <ctype.h>
3: #include <iostream.h>
4: char* UpperCase(char* str)
```

(continues)

```
Listing 8.1    Continued

 5: {
 6:    // Assigns a pointer to the str
 7:    // argument. While what p points to
 8:    // (*p) does not equal '\0'
 9:    // convert each p[i] to uppercase;
10:    // This version does not require an
11:    // if statement because the test is in the for loop.
12:    for( char * p = str; *p ; *p =(char) toupper(*p), p++);
13:    return str;
14: }
15: #pragma argsused
16: void main( int argc, char* argv[])
17: {
18:    cout << "Program Name: " << UpperCase(argv[0] )
19:       <<    endl;
20: }
```

The benefits of this modification are

- If you place the declaration in a header, you have a reusable utility function.
- There is now a more convenient place to add clear comments.
- Using the functionality supplied is cleaner and easier (see line 19).

The function name makes the functionality, if not the implementation, clearer. It is not an either/or contest; both need to be clear and concise. If the name does not describe the functionality, that must be commented on as well. Moderate changes, in the way you code or changes in existing code of this sort, will have a cumulative effect on the lifetime cost and headache of maintaining your programs.

Clarifying Boolean Algebra with Parenthetical Grouping

If a logic statement seems unclear to you, it will definitely seem unclear to the next guy. Token operators are a blessing when used in common expressions, such as:

```
int a= 5 + b;
```

but when you start applying operators and operands in complex statements, or use uncommon Boolean, bitwise, or logical operators, things are not quite so clear.

Rather than go to the *ARM* or your Borland C++ documentation, use the tried-and-true method of applying parenthetical operators. A good rule of thumb is that if you use more than one or two operators and operands, place parentheses around the subexpressions to clarify your meaning.

You may find uncommented code, or code that relies upon the assumption that operator precedence is common knowledge (stuck in wet-ram for instant recollection). For many operators, rules apply that we have relied on since early childhood, but some operators (or even the operations they perform) may represent new ideas. When you come across statements containing a snarl of operators and operands, ensure that they are commented, and use parentheses to make the meaning clear.

Unfortunately, you may be in the unenviable position of deciphering statements of this sort because they often go hand in hand with errors. Table 8.1 shows the C++ operator precedence order taken from the *The C++ Programming Language*, Second Edition, by Bjarne Stroustrop. Those operators with the greatest precedence are listed first.

Table 8.1   Operator Precedence Table, Grouped by Precedence

Token	Name	Syntax Example
::	Scope resolution	class_name::member_name
::	Global	::name - has global scope
.	Member selection	object.member
->	Member selector	pointer->member
[ ]	Subscript	pointer[expr (or index)]
( )	Function call	func_name(argument_list)
( )	Value construction	type(argument_list)
sizeof	Size of object	sizeof(argument)
sizeof	Size of type	sizeof(type)
++	Postincrement	lvalue++
++	Preincrement	++lvalue
--	Postdecrement	lvalue--
--	Predecrement	--lvalue
~	Complement	~expr
!	Not	!expr
-	unary minus	-expr
+	unary plus	+expr
&	address of	&lvalue
*	dereference	*expr
new	create (allocate)	new type
new	create array	new type[ ]
delete	delete (deallocate)	delete pointer
delete[ ]	delete array	delete [ ] pointer
( )	cast (type conversion)	(type) expr or type(expr)
.*	member section	object.*pointer-to-member

(continues)

Programming in C++

Token	Name	Syntax Example
->*	member section	pointer->pointer-to-member
*	multiply	expr * expr
/	divide	expr / expr
%	modulo (remainder)	expr % expr
+	add (plus)	expr + expr
-	subtract (minus)	expr - expr
<<	left shift	expr << expr
>>	right shift	expr >> expr
<	less than	expr < expr
<=	less than or equal	expr <= expr
>	greater than	expr > expr
>=	greater than or equal	expr >= expr
==	equal	expr == expr
!=	not equal	expr != expr
&	bitwise AND	expr & expr
^	bitwise exclusive OR	expr ^ expr
|	bitwise inclusive OR	expr | expr
&&	logical AND	expr && expr
||	logical inclusive OR	expr || expr
? :	conditional expression	expr ? true_expr : false_expr
=	simple assignment	lvalue = expr
*=	multiply and assign	lvalue *= expr
/=	divide and assign	lvalue /= expr
%=	modulo and assign	lvalue %= expr
+=	add and assign	lvalue += expr
-=	subtract and assign	lvalue -= expr
<<=	shift left and assign	lvalue <<= expr
>>=	shift right and assign	lvalue >>= expr
&=	AND and assign	lvalue &= expr
|=	inclusive OR and assign	lvalue |= expr
^=	exclusive OR and assign	lvalue ^= expr
,	comma (sequencing)	expr, expr

Lists and groups operators by precedence. Those at the top of the list (and in the first group) have the highest precedence.

The syntax example in table 8.1 shows the number of operands and the locations relative to the operator of each operand. Use the table as a guide for applying parentheses. Ensure that you understand which form of the operator is being used.

> **Note**
>
> The Borland C++ compiler is an optimizing compiler. It is capable of optimizing statements and subexpressions. If a statement is too complex, it may be a good idea to break it up into many subexpressions, storing and using intermediate values.
>
> Remember, your greatest savings will come over the life of program maintenance, and the compiler can more than likely produce more optimal code. You aim for clarity; let the compiler worry about squeaking the most performance out of the code. Nice relationship!

Implicit Data Conversion

Extremely convoluted bit-shifting and masking can often be simplified by representing the data with an appropriately defined structure. Structures, and especially unions, can be applied to this end.

> **Tip**
>
> Unions can play a unique role in software development. A union combines all the enclosed types in one address space. The enclosed types do not have to be of similar types or sizes. Having similar types mapped to the same address is how we can implicitly convert between types (or perform bit-masking). Mapping dissimilar types to the same address space with unions, then using a flag field to describe which elements are in use, can be used as a space conservation technique. It is an interesting technique, but seldom needed.

An example of the kind of problem that may prompt you to write code that masks bits is when you are presented with packed values. For example, DOS-based computers used a packed date and time; *Binary Coded Decimal* numbers are packed, one integer to four bits. You may encounter BCD numbers, but packed numbers, more often than not, are found when you are writing systems programs, or writing code to interface with hardware.

As an exercise, let's examine a packed BCD number. Each *nibble* (4 bits) of a byte can represent the numbers from 0 to $2^4 - 1$, which is the same as 0 to 15. To convert the BCD number 99 to a decimal number, you might write the code:

```
// Converts 99 bcd to ninety-nine
char bcd = 0x99;   // equals 9 * 16 + 9
int num = ((bcd & 0xF0) >> 4) * 10 + (bcd & 0x0F);   // Boy is that ugly!
```

Instead, you could modify the representation of the BCD type to be a union of a `char` and two, 4-bit fields:

```
union BCD
{   char char_bcd;
    struct{ int lower: 4; int upper:4; } bcd;    // as bit fields
    operator int(){ return bcd.upper * 10 + bcd.lower; }
};
```

> **Note**
>
> Storing numbers as binary coded decimals was not intended as a space-saving device. One BCD byte stores the numbers 0 to 99, but a byte can normally hold 0 to 255. However, if you compare BCD numbers to character-string, the space spaced in favor of BCD numbers is 2-to-1. One character digit is held in one byte; you can get two in a BCD number.

Extracting the value is greatly simplified by assigning part of the BCD union to the character and using the bitfield components. Even better, write a conversion operator, so when an integer is expected in context, the conversion operator is called implicitly (see chapter 16, "Operator Overloading").

Listing 8.2   Bcd.cpp—Demonstrates a Technique for Implicitly Unpacking Binary-Coded Decimal Numbers

```
 1: // BCD.CPP - Demonstrates implict type conversion.
 2: #include <iostream.h>
 3: // Binary Coded Decimal
 4: typedef union BCD
 5: {   char packed_bcd;
 6:   struct {
 7:     unsigned int lower: 4;
 8:     unsigned int upper: 4;
 9:   } bcd;
10:   int BcdToInt(){ return bcd.upper * 10 + bcd.lower; }
11:   operator int(){ return BcdToInt(); }
12:   BCD( char c ) : packed_bcd( c ){}; // constructor
13: } BCD_NUMBER;
14: void main()
15: {
16:   char asBcd = 0x23;    // Treat as bcd number instead of 2 * 16 + 3 = 35
17:   int asNum = ((asBcd & 0xF0) >> 4) * 10 + (asBcd & 0x0F);
18:   cout << "Messy conversion: "<< asNum << endl;
19:   BCD_NUMBER bcd = asBcd;
20:   cout << "Implict conversion: " << bcd << endl;
21: }
```

The test `main` function has the messy function on line 17, which contains all of the messy bit-shifting and bit-masking. Although we have to provide a package to simplify the conversion, it isn't that hard to do. The BCD number has two views: the packed char view and the two nibbles containing each number.

Between lines 4 and 13, I've represented both views of BCDs and have added some features to simplify expressing BCD numbers further.

Lines 4 and 13 create an alias for the union with a typedef.

Lines 5 and 6 to 9 represent the data fields' portion of the union; both the packed_bcd char and the struct named bcd are capable of storing the same number of bits.

Line 10 contains an accessor function that returns the number as an integer. The conversion is much easier now; simply multiply the upper four bits by 10, and add the lower four bits.

Line 11 is an inline operator int conversion function. Chapter 16 will explain that a conversion function can be called explicitly, but is called when the type appears in the context where another is expected. In this case, where a BCD_NUMBER is used and an integer is expected, the operator int() function is invoked.

Note

Implementing an accessor function, like BcdToInt, and then implementing a conversion operator in terms of the accessor function can simplify the whole process. In short, you are dividing the tasks. You are separating the slightly more complex syntax of operator functions from their implementation.

This technique also makes it possible for moderately skilled users to access the functionality without understanding conversion functions. Then, later, it is easy to substitute the more subtle conversion function where the accessor appears. By following this kind of approach, you can make advanced features available without hampering program development.

Line 12 clearly demonstrates that classes aren't the only thing that can have constructors. You probably won't read much about it, but unions can have their own constructors and destructors. (Refer to the *ARM* or the ANSI C++ document for what is and isn't in the language.)

Mentally Parsing Functions

C++ is a subtle language, and things can happen to C++ code, so that what you see is not always exactly what you get. Chapter 17, "Constructors: Copy and Assignment," contains examples of how the C++ compiler can generate a default copy constructor and assignment operator. In this section, we will take a look at other things that the compiler does that are not always readily apparent to programmers on the up-sweep of the learning curve.

One Conversion Rule

The C++ programming language can make a single conversion to get argument types to match a function declaration. We'll refer to it as the *one conversion rule*. C++ requires that a function's declaration appear before its first use in code. The convention of declaring functions in header files, then including the header file in modules that need the declaration, has been adopted for this purpose.

What happens if no "exact" matching declaration exists? C++ is allowed to make a single conversion, if a definable route for such a conversion exists, in order to match a declaration to the code usage. Consider a function `Print`:

```
void Print( String );
```

which takes an argument of type `String`, an imaginary `String` class. The language now includes a definition of the `String` class (refer to chapter 21). What would happen if the function were called by a user this way:

```
Print( "Thank you, Dr. Sedgewick!" );
```

The answer can be determined in the form of a question: "Is there a way to convert a `char*` to a `String`?" If the answer is yes, compiler can create a *temporary* `String`, and the function call will match exactly.

Note

A single conversion from one type to another usually involves a constructor. Most likely, if there were a constructor defined as:

```
String( const char* );
```

or:

```
String( char* );
```

this would be the route through which the temporary, matching object would be called. Chapter 14, "Basic Class Concepts," explains constructors and destructors.

You could easily and explicitly indicate that the same result is desired; it would look like the following:

```
Print( String("Thank you, Dr. Sedgewick!" ));
// Explicit instruction to 'create a temporary'
```

There are several reasons why you need this information. One reason is that it's a good thing to know what your compiler is and is not capable of doing. A more important reason involves testing and debugging. You need to know which paths are being taken in order to trace and debug them.

Matching Function Calls to Interfaces

Now you know that one implicit conversion can occur to match declarations to code. There other kinds of activity that go on behind the scenes, and if you know about them they don't seem so foreign. C++ facilitates, even invites, operator and function overloading. Chapters 15 and 16 describe and provide exemplars of these things; here we're concerned with detecting when they are used in code, more than actually how to create them.

Functions can be overloaded based on the argument types. Combine function overloading with the *one conversion rule,* and you may find it challenging to match a function call to the function actually called. Using the Integrated Debugger, you can press the F7 key to trace into code, but you may wonder where this takes you.

A conversion may occur where you have argument types within the same family, for example, integrals. You can use the function name to find the likely candidate match. To get a picture of this, think of a function that accepts a *double* and is offered an integer; the conversion from integer to double can be made.

However, when you see a function name but the argument types are not remotely related, you must suspect that function overloading has occurred. If a conversion can't be resolved, you will receive an ambiguity error. If no function can be found, you will get an error indicating this sort of problem.

A third more subtle contextual expectation can make it slightly confusing to figure out what's going on. Suppose you see code of this nature:

```
SomeType var;
cout << var;
```

You may safely assume one of two things: Somewhere there is an operator<< function defined for objects of SomeType, or, there is a conversion operator somewhere. Either of these things must be true unless the code prints the address of the object, which is what the code looks as if it should do. Chapter 13, "Exploring iostreams," explains how the operator<< function can be overloaded for ostreams, and chapter 16, "Operator Overloading," explains conversion operators.

The key for locating the hub of activity is to match types and tokens. If, for example, you find a function operator<< that takes an object of SomeType, it is likely that this is the function (or method) employed. If a conversion operator is being used, it will be in the class definition for SomeType, and the keyword operator will be involved.

Locating the hub of activity is important because it may be here that you may need to test values, add debug code, or place breakpoints when designing and testing. If you are the implementor of the code in question, you'll know where and what it is, because you will have put it there. In general, things can be more problematic if you are using someone else's designs. Although you may not be able to directly modify the design of existing code, but having this knowledge may help you find and report a bug.

Expanding Operator Functions

Operators can and are overloaded in large quantities. Probably the first program you ever wrote involved overloaded operators. I would wager that writing expressions containing operators, like +, - /, and =, are common to almost everyone, including nonprogrammers. Further, it wouldn't be much of a leap to surmise that the greatest experience in writing expressions for any programmer involves using operators.

Whether intentional or not, operators have been exploited for these reasons: they are easy to use, and they are familiar. Operators have been exploited further now. C++ allows programmers to define new ways to use operators with new types. Generally, it is suggested that semantically similar uses are employed, but the variety of new types using operators grows daily.

When you read C++ code, begin to think of simple expressions, such as:

```
int a = b + c;
```

on two levels: first, as an expression and, second, as two operator functions, one for each operator. This is less true for operations involving native data types, but very true for user-defined types, whose number far surpasses the native types. I'll demonstrate with `int` for simplicity.

First, let's take a look at how we might write two functions to perform the same task. Here is my pseudocode for doing so:

```
int Assign( int val );
int Sum( int, int );
```

The first function accepts an argument, and simply returns it to be assigned to the left argument. The second `Sum` takes two arguments, and adds them together. Now imagine that you want to offer this functionality in a more natural way. How would you do it? The solution is to use the actual operator-token and, to make it less confusing:

```
int +(int, int );  // Looks weird
```

precede the token with the keyword `operator`. The result is

```
int operator=(int);
// Represents the idea but is not syntactically accurate
int operator+( int, int );
```

This functionality is defined for integers, so we don't worry about these. Generalizing the functions even more by assuming any data type results in:

```
type operator=( type );
```

and:

```
type operator+( type, type );
```

There is an implied rule here, too. Because the arguments in both lists will not be modified—you never modify the left or right operand `int` expressions like 5+3—we can specify this by adding the following:

```
type operator=( const type );
type operator+(const type, const type );
```

> **Tip**
>
> Such expressions usually involve the address of the operator for optimization. For the most part, it is more efficient to pass the address, but this does not give you carte blanche to add an address operator to arguments and return types.

When you read an expression involving operators and operands, remember that, if it is not a native type, and what you are reading is not pointer arithmetic, there probably exists an underlying operator function. Finding the function containing the functionality is easy enough. First, the number of arguments must match the count of the operator: one for unary operators, and two for binary operators. Second, you have to remember that the type of the object points to the class containing the definition of the operator function, and third, the keyword operator and the token must be involved.

What you may find is a *friend* declaration (see chapter 14, "Basic Class Concepts"), but you will find the declaration. Finding them is the first step in understanding, as you will be able to trace them through and get a feel for how they operate in programs.

> **Note**
>
> This is advanced subject matter. If you do not understand it immediately, it will be clearer as you work through the book and become more familiar with C++.
>
> As I have said, the count of the operator indicates the argument count. However, the number of objects can be satisfied in a couple of different ways. While chapters 14 and 16 explain this in detail, remember this rule: if the operator function is defined as a member of the class (not a `friend` or `global`), the argument count—variables between the function parentheses—will be `operator count -1`. If the function is `global` (`friend` or otherwise), the actual number of arguments passed will be the same as the argument count. The former rule results from the fact that the object itself will count as one of the operands.

Detecting Conversion Operators

I am fortunate enough to know a few people with a variety of C++ skill levels. And as an instructor, I meet those just starting out. I have found that the problem with understanding conversion operators is that they have still have not reached the mainstream of discussion and may be perceived to be too difficult to understand. The conversion operator idiom is a powerful mechanism that works, sometimes where no other may work.

A conversion operator is a function that returns an object of one type where another is used. There may be many reasons for using these kinds of functions; an example is the extensive C libraries that have existed for years. Developers writing new aggregate types may want to employ existing functionality. Who can blame them? The question is: How is this done?

First, let's look at what I call *contextual expectation*. An example might be:

```
String str("Example");
int len = strlen(str);
```

The `strlen` function has been around for a while. It takes a `const char*`, but clearly `str` is a `String` object. So, in this example, contextual expectation refers to the fact that `strlen` is expecting a `const char*`. Problems of this sort are sometimes solved in this way:

```
String str("Example");
char * rep = str.GetString();      // Accessor for my String class
int len = strlen( rep );
```

As you can see, I had to create a temporary of the correct type and use an accessor function, assuming one existed, to get at the underlying representation in order to use the existing function. (Even I used to think this was ridiculous.) When I wasn't using conversion operators, I was performing a lot of unnecessary work, the amount of which increased depending on the difficulty of getting at the underlying representation of the aggregate type.

Explaining the implementation of such functions is deferred until chapter 16. Right now, we are concerned with being able to detect these idioms. When you see an argument type that seems incongruous with the type you know should be used, assume that a conversion function may be involved. Find the class of the object in question. Look for a member function, which is probably very short—it may be only a return statement. The first word of the declaration is the operator, followed by the type of data the function in question should get.

Assuming my imaginary string class had an operator conversion function, converting from a `String` to a `char*`, this statement:

```
int len = strlen( str );    // str is an object of my String class
```

actually invokes the conversion function. Expanding the code, which you could do explicitly, but is ugly, causes the statement to look like the following:

```
int len = strlen( str.operator char*());    // Wowsers
```

Therefore the function

```
operator char*(){ return char_pointer; }
```

exists in the class. Otherwise, the argument type wouldn't match, resulting in an error.

From Here...

I tend to think of C++ as a spider web—it's interconnected, can hold several times its own weight, and it's marvelous to look at early in the morning with a bit of dew glistening on it. C++ is not a frivolous language, and things do not exist in a vacuum. Everything about the language is intentional and interconnected. While you cannot always find a linear or ordinal connection from one point to the next, the relationship to other language features exists.

It is the subtlety of such features, as discussed here, that enable C++ developers to write well-constructed, reusable, and even elegant code. Of course, the ability to write elegant code requires a degree of understanding beyond what it takes to program in BASIC; and management is seldom interested in elegance, it is the artistry of the language that makes it the programmer's language.

Learn the language well first, and it will then be easier to use tools libraries, design your own tools, and write Windows (or any other operating system) programs. Related topics can be found in these chapters:

- Chapter 4, "The Preprocessor," covers some of the historical uses of the preprocessor.

- Chapter 9, "Data Quantifiers and Qualifiers," teaches you about the language features in C++ that will add richness to your programming.

CHAPTER 9

Data Quantifiers and Qualifiers

You have heard the phrase "everything but the kitchen sink." The sink's in this chapter, too. Chapter 9 is not a chapter to be read as a last resort; rather, it was written and designed as a place for you to learn how to use the many special keywords, like `struct`, `union`, `static`, and `typedef`, that you will find in every C++ program.

These keywords, or *specifiers*, play an integral role in the C++ programming language. The good thing is that you don't have to memorize them. If you read the chapter, experiment with some of the examples, and refer to the chapter as you need to, that will suffice.

If you are completely new to C++, or consider yourself in an early learning phase, apply the language to classical programming problems and develop critical skills in steps. The language is too large—notice I didn't say too complex—to learn all at once. Many interesting small problems can be solved as you learn many of the different language features.

The material in this chapter is *not* advanced, although it does have an effect on the way the code is compiled and ultimately on the way the solution is accomplished. There are also some interesting topics in this chapter that suggest a quick read as well as a use as a reference.

In this chapter, you will learn:

- How solutions can be derived with code and through better data modeling
- To use various language features to add rich flavoring to C++
- How to use keywords to extend the depth of C++

Using *extern*

The `extern` specifier plays several roles in C++ programs. There are also roles that have been replaced by better conventions. This section discusses each so that you understand the contextual role that the keyword plays when it appears in existing code, or you need it.

The C++ programming language is a strongly typed language that requires functions, variables, and other entities to be declared before they appear in code statements. The specifier played a historical role in declarations, and you may see it in existing or legacy C code. Because C++ is often used in a capacity as a tools language for other programming tools, like creating *dynamic link libraries* (DLLs), *Visual Basic controls* (VBXs), or *OLE controls* (OCXs), the extern specifier plays a revived role as a linkage specifier. The following sections describe and explain these uses of the extern keyword.

External Linkage

Michigan State University began basing its computer science curriculum on C++ in 1992. Working in my capacity as an instructor for software developers, I am finally seeing corporations spend training dollars on C++ on a large scale. In the scheme of things, C++ is a relatively new language but is becoming the leading development language.

These companies will eventually have to convert legacy C programs to C++, object-oriented programs. Part of the conversion process will be knowing which old idioms or conventions have been replaced and with what.

The extern keyword has been used in the past to resolve external linkage between variables and functions. Preceding such a declaration with the extern keyword means that the declaration or definition exists elsewhere. This can be in another module or later in the same module.

Listing 9.1 is an example program containing the extern keyword as it appears in a variable and function declaration.

Listing 9.1   Externs.cpp—Demonstrates How to Use Extern-Defined Functions and Variables

```
1:   // EXTERNS.CPP- Makes a call to an external function and stores the
2:   // result in an externally defined value.
3:   #include <iostream.h>
4:   extern unsigned long factorial;
5:   extern unsigned long Factorial(unsigned long );
6:   void main()
7:   {
8:      factorial = Factorial( 7 );
9:      cout << "7! (factorial):" << factorial << endl;
10: }
```

The declarations on lines 4 and 5 define an unsigned long and a (recursive) factorial function as external to the module in listing 9.1. The actual variable and function are defined in a separate module (extern2.cpp) in listing 9.2.

Listing 9.2   Extern2.cpp—Definitions of Variable and Function Used in Listing 9.1

```
// EXTERN2.CPP - Contains definitions
unsigned long factorial;
unsigned long Factorial( unsigned long num )
{
    return num > 2 ? num * Factorial( num - 1 ) : num;
}
```

Note

A factorial function is a function that calculates the multiplicative value of all of the digits up to and including a particular number. To do so recursively means that the function calls itself as part of the solution. For example, 5 factorial written as 5!, is calculated by the equation 1 * 2 * 3 * 4 * 5 = 120.

This use of the `extern` keyword for functions has been replaced by writing the function in its own module, placing the declaration (or interface) in a header file, and including the header file in every module that uses the function. If possible, avoid using global variables altogether in C++.

There are a couple of reasons the header file has been adopted. One is that it is much easier to include a header containing the declaration rather than reentering the declaration. Another reason is that the declarations must match exactly. The header convention is less error prone.

Declaring External C Linkage

C++ is often used as a platform for implementing tools that make it easier to acquire advanced features in other Windows programming tools. As a by-product of this role, the `extern` keyword is used to define linkage for tools, like VBXs, DLLs, and OCXs, written in C++.

Windows development tools, like Borland's Delphi (which uses Object Pascal) and Visual Basic, pass parameters (also called *arguments*) differently than C++. (Remember I am talking about Windows programs here.)

Arguments are passed to functions by placing their values or addresses in the stack (memory) segment. Behind the scenes they are pulled off the stack to initialize the values of the parameters for functions. BASIC and Pascal accept arguments from the stack in the order they appear. C and C++ use a reverse order stack-storage. The convention used can be dictated by the developer and must also be used by the user of the compiled component.

By applying the `extern` C specifier to a function declaration, you are "telling" the compiler to do two things:

- Use the C method for parameter passing
- Use the C naming convention

The C naming convention means that function names will get an underscore (_) prefix, and they will not be mangled. Name *mangling* is something the compiler does that supports operator and function overloading. Mangling is performed by C++ compilers and is discussed in detail in chapters 15, "Function Overloading," and 16, "Operator Overloading."

The `extern` C linkage specifier is placed as a prefix or used with the brackets to define C linkage for more than one function. Here are two examples:

```
// A single function using C linkage and compiler-naming
extern "C" void Foo( int a );
// A couple of functions using the C naming convention and linkage
extern "C"
{
    void OneFunction( char a );


    int TwoFunctions( float f );
}
```

A sample program defining Foo as just shown with the Options, Project, Linker, Map File, Publics option set in the IDE produces the following excerpted map file:

Address	Publics by Value
0001:00000000	Idle __acrtused
0001:00000074	Idle __GetExceptDLLinfo
0001:0000007C	Idle _Foo

Indicated by the map file, the name has a prefixed underscore and is not mangled. (For examples of mangled names see chapter 15, "Function Overloading.")

Declaring Pascal Linkage

The logical opposite of C linkage is Pascal linkage. If you were to write a program or library module in C++ directly, using the Windows calling convention, you might see the Windows main function

```
int PASCAL WinMain( HINSTANCE hInstance,
            HINSTANCE hPrevInstance, LPSTR lpszCmdLine, int nCmdShow )
```

Microsoft—because it defines the Windows protocol—uses the Pascal calling convention, which tells the compiler not to prefix the underscore. No mangling occurs. This convention is exactly the same as that used for Visual Pascal and Object Pascal programs. Using either the `cdecl` or Pascal qualifier is fine; you just have to maintain consistency by using the same convention across compiled files. (See the section entitled "Using *cdecl*"; it demonstrates this technique using C-linkage.)

Neither method is right or wrong. Different languages require different implementation approaches, but it is these kinds of things that make cross-language programming somewhat "sticky."

Understanding *struct*

C structs were the standard for C aggregation. In C, structs were a lot like Pascal *records*. The struct is used to collect data under a single name. The new convention in C++ is the *class*. While the class idiom is preferred for many reasons (refer to chapter 14, "Basic Class Concepts"), struct is still used and can be found in a lot of existing code and books.

> **Note**
>
> In C++, the struct has gained a lot of added features. Structs may have constructors, destructors, operators, and other member functions. The class idiom is preferred when you need these features.

The data members in a struct are defined the same way they would be defined in any namespace: *type var_name*. The following is taken from dir.h and defines a structure named ffblk:

```
struct  ffblk   {
    char ff_reserved[21];
    char ff_attrib;
    unsigned ff_ftime;
    unsigned ff_fdate;
    long ff_fsize;
    char ff_name[13];
};
```

(This structure is used by many functions; it matches a DOS-based file system directory entry somewhat.) structs are *public* by default. (This terminology comes from C++. Refer to chapter 14, "Basic Class Concepts," for different *accessibility specifiers*.) Being public means that variable instances of structures allow all users of the structure to access the data members directly. (This is not true with C++ classes.)

Thus, by using an ffblk variable defined as

```
struct ffblk fileBlock;
```

you can directly copy a filename into the ff_name member, like this:

```
#include <string.h>
// ...
strcpy( fileBlock.ff_name, "COMMAND.COM" );
```

Structures used for grouping data to form a related entity are still used and exist in a good deal of functionality.

As you will see in the section "Using *union*," structures can be used to play a role in implicit data conversion, potentially saving you a lot of coding in some circumstances.

Using *static*

The keyword static has a context-based meaning. While the underlying meaning equates to global linkage, how it is perceived and employed depends on the context in which it is used. The first context should be easy enough to understand, but the second requires some understanding of the object-oriented paradigm. I have separated the explanations into two separate subheadings. Feel free to make a note—go ahead, write in the book—next to the second subheading. The note might read: "Read chapter 14, 'Basic Class Concepts,' before getting too wrapped up in the use of static."

Extending the Lifetime of a Variable

A common use of the static keyword is to extend the life of a variable beyond its scope. To understand this, you must acquire or have some knowledge of scope and why it affects the lifetime of a variable.

The *scope* of a variable is that region of code in which a variable has storage space allocated to it. This is most often between two braces { }. A common place for these braces is the beginning and end of a function. Thus, variables defined inside a function have function scope. A variable's *lifetime* is defined by its scope.

Caution

Notice I refer to the scope as the region in which space is allocated, *not* value. C++ does not guarantee that variables or objects will have an initial value unless you provide one. This is another reason why constructors are so important.

The same is not true for static variables. Static variables *are* automatically initialized to 0 if you do not specify an initial value.

Stack (sometimes referred to as statically allocated or static) variables are created in the stack space when their scope is entered. For example, an integer variable defined in a function is in scope when the function is entered. It is important to know the location in memory where space is allocated to the variable. The stack of a program is generally self-managed, except for programs written to manage the stacks themselves.

Think of the stack space as a pile of pancakes. Equate a function call as the cook piling up the flapjacks. Upon exiting the function, the same amount of flapjacks added to the pile when the function was entered is removed. Variables defined in a function, for instance, fall into this consumptive category. What this means to you, the programmer, is that the variable is located between the left and right braces and then it must be considered gone.

> **Caution**
>
> Unless you carefully make allowances for variables local to functions (within the function's scope), it is an error to return a reference to a `stack` variable. A reference is either a pointer or address; what you are returning is the location of something that won't be there when the scope is exited.
>
> The use of `static` variables can sometimes be used to resolve this kind of error. Returning a reference to a local variable is another form of the slicing problem.

This is where `static` variables can be employed. Applying the `static` keyword to a variable local to a particular scope extends its lifetime beyond its scope. In essence, its lifetime is similar to variables with global scope, although it is accessible within its defining scope.

Suppose you defined a function called `GetToken`, declared as

```
char * GetToken( const char* fileName, const char* token );
```

The function's role is to return the context of a token string in a file, like a concordance. The implication of the function declaration is that it will return a `char*`, and by the looks of things, that `char*` variable will be defined in the function.

If you are not careful, you may unwittingly introduce a memory leakage. Defining the `tokenStr` as

```
char tokenStr[128];
```

and returning

```
return tokenStr;     // ERROR: tokenStr undefined when out of scope
```

will cause the value of the returned `char*` to intermittently look like a valid value and garbage. This is because the *stack pointer* will have effectively consumed the space in which `tokenStr` is defined once the function exits, and some other variable may be using that space by the time the return value is used.

Because your design requires the found `tokenStr` to be returned, you have one of several choices:

- Redesign the function passing the `char*` as an argument
- Make `tokenStr` global
- Make `tokenStr` a static variable

II

Programming in C++

I don't care for global variables, and using the `static` keyword provides a perfectly good solution. Here is the redeclaration of `tokenStr`:

```
// Useful if we have to refer to tokenStr outside of its scope
static char tokenStr[128];
```

Now when the scope is exited, `tokenStr` is not automatically cleaned up—which is an error if we are returning a reference to it—by the stack.

The stack method for declaring variables is a great scheme: It allows a finite resource to be used over and over, and it does not need to be managed by the programmer. Because the STACKSIZE in 32-bit programs can be much larger, you can expect to see much larger statically allocated variables in future programs.

Slicing Problems

Dave Thielens' book *No Bugs!,* published by Addison-Wesley, 1994, discusses ways in which you can force sliced variables to manifest themselves. The example in listing 9.3 is slightly more advanced than the material in this chapter. While the example is complete, the topics related to the use of the class idiom are discussed in chapter 14, "Basic Class Concepts."

C++ does not guarantee a known value of state for variables, but exactly known states are testable. By initializing an object/variable to a known state upon construction (read in the constructor) and again in the destructor, you can easily ascertain whether a variable/object is valid or invalid.

The example demonstrates using what I refer to as a brief stream class. By applying it to the example above—returning a local string—it demonstrates how insidious this form of slicing is. Sometimes this approach may be the only way to get physical evidence that a variable is bad.

Listing 9.3 Sliceit.cpp—Demonstrates How to Assign a Testable Value to an Object's Internal Representation

```
// SLICEIT.CPP - Combines some advanced features.
/* I first wrote about brief classes in the January 1996
 * issue of Software Development, a Miller Freeman publication.
 * This example program combines information derived from
 * chapter 14, "Basic Class Concepts," chapter 16, "Operator
 * Overloading," and chapter 19, "Using Templates Classes."
 * While you do not necessarily need to understand all of
 * these things to understand the results, you will need them
 * to understand the code.
 */
#include <string.h>
#include <process.h>
#include <iostream.h>
template <unsigned int STRLEN>
class DUMMY_STRING
{
```

```
public:
    // Constructor with default null string initial value
    DUMMY_STRING(char * str = "\0")
    {      if( strlen(str) > STRLEN )
            abort();
        else
            strcpy( text, str );
    }
    operator char* () { return text; } // Conversion operator function
#pragma warn -inl
    // Blocks 'for statements no expanded inline' compiler warning
    // destructor used to initialize released members
    // to 'testable' garbage
    ~DUMMY_STRING()
    {      // This is where we catch problems.
        for( int i = 0; i<STRLEN; i++)
            text[i] = (char)0xFE;
        text[STRLEN] = '\0';
    }
    char text[STRLEN + 1];      // Add 1 for '\0'
};
// typedef used to simplify the code appearance.
typedef DUMMY_STRING<20> STR;
char * ReturnLocalString()
{
    STR str("Hello, World!");
    // Invokes str.operator char*() on DUMMY_STRING objects
    return str;
}
char * ReturnStaticString()
{
    static STR str("Still Here!");
    // Invokes str.operator char*()
    return str;
}
void main()
{
    cout << "Local String: " << ReturnLocalString() << endl;
    cout << "Static String: " << ReturnStaticString() << endl;
}
```

The first line of code in the main function demonstrates that the object was sliced by printing garbage. The second output statement in main merrily prints "Still Here" because it is. The object containing that string was defined as a static object. There are several language features in this code fragment alone. See if you can identify some of the many different idioms used.

The next section is the one I mentioned earlier that you can postpone reading until you have read chapter 14, "Basic Class Concepts." The keyword static has different meanings based on the context in which it is used. We discussed one meaning of static in this section. The next section uses static in a different context, related to classes, so you can postpone reading the next section until after you have read chapter 14. Specifically, you will need to understand classes, member functions, and data to fully understand the application of static in the context it is used in the next section.

Static Members

Data and function members of classes can be declared as static. A class definition acts like a map of what each variable instance—called object—of that class has. For practical purposes, let's apply this idea to integers. int is the class name and any variable defined as an integer is an object.

The members of the class define what information objects of the class are capable of "recording" (and the functions describe the activity the objects can perform). Every instance of the class, referred to as an object, has a complete copy of each member, both data and functions. This picture of things is accurate unless you expressly define any members as static.

The static keyword used in a class means that every object of that class type shares the same static member. Figure 9.1 portrays a class containing no static members. Contrast that with figure 9.2, which contains a static member.

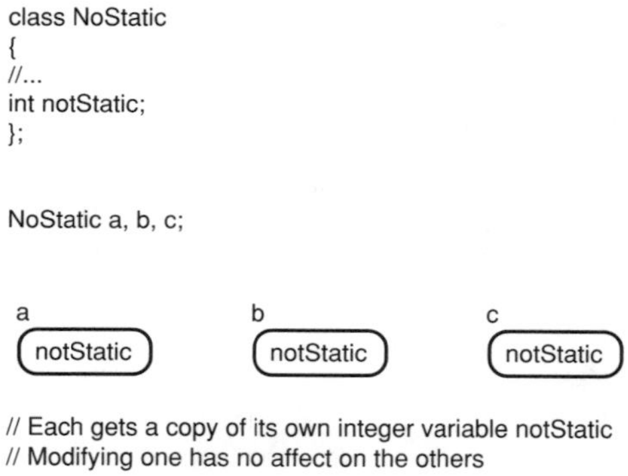

Fig. 9.1

This is an illustration of a class containing no static members (the only visible member is the integer). Each instance of the class, called an object, has its own copy of the integer member.

```
class NoStatic
{
//...
int notStatic;
};


NoStatic a, b, c;
```

```
// Each gets a copy of its own integer variable notStatic
// Modifying one has no affect on the others
```

Class members that are defined as static have exactly the same address in every object. They all share just one. Normally, for non-static members, every object gets a complete copy of every member of the class. Chapter 11, "Functions," describes a demo program that illustrates this concept.

There are several advanced programming techniques that use static members to achieve a desired result, plus some simpler ones. Suppose, for example, a *member function* performs exactly the same task regardless of the state of an object. Making that function static means that there are fewer copies (only one, instead of one for each object instance) of that function.

```
class HasStatic
{
//...
static int isStatic;
};

HasStatic a, b, c;
```

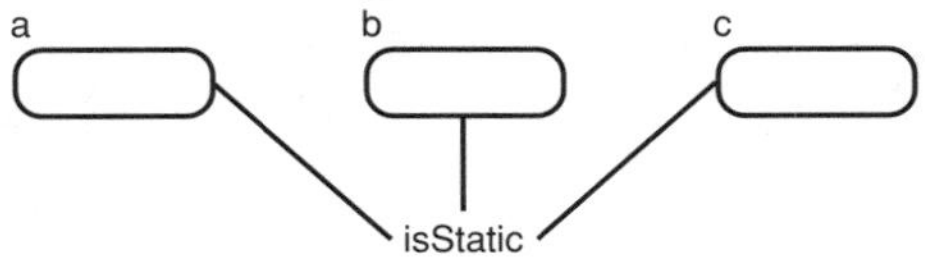

Fig. 9.2

The address of a static class member is the same for that member in every object.

```
// Every object shares the static member.
// If any object changes the value of the static member, all
// objects would share the change.
```

Using Bitfields

The C++ language has an amazing breadth. In the section, "Addressing Inline Assembler," you will see that the language even supports inline assembler. The discussion here pertains to a subject that is not so low-level—bitfields. C++ is often used as a systems programming language, where the vagaries of different architectures come into play.

One example is the way DOS- and Windows-based machines store dates and times as bit-packed fields. What is unusual about this is that the smallest data type is a character, or eight bits. A bitfield variable is defined in the normal way except for two additional considerations. The first is that the data type must be an integral large enough to hold the number of bits, and the second is that the variable name is followed by a colon and a number representing the quantity of bits required. This is exemplified by

```
unsigned int aBit:1;    // A 1-bit value can hold the numbers 0 or 1
unsigned int var:7;     // A 7-bit value can store numbers 0 to 127
```

Binary and Other Numbers

In case you may have forgotten, what follows is a quick discussion on bits. The word *bit* is derived from *binary digit*. Thus, a bitwise view is a binary, or base-2, number. All number systems can be represented by the same radix equation:

$$[ga]_0[gb]^0 + [ga]_1[gb]^1 + [ga]_2[gb]^2 + ... + [ga]_{n-1}[gb]^{n-1} + [ga]_n[gb]^n$$

where [ga] (alpha) is a valid digit in the system, [gb] (beta) is the base of the number system, and the exponent indicates the ordinal position. Mapping the decimal number system to this equation, valid values for [ga] are the digits 0 through 9, and the subscript to alpha represents the ordinal position in the radix; [gb] is the number 10, and the exponent is any number 0

(continues)

Programming in C++   **II**

(continued)

through [in] (infinity). Although we usually write numbers from left-highest to right-lowest, the equation is the other way around.

Let's look at a simple number, 123, mapped into this equation:

$$3_0 10^0 + 2_1 10^1 + 1_2 10^2 = (3 * 10^0) + (2 * 10^1) + (1 * 10^2) = (3*1) + (2 * 10) + (1 * 100) = 3 + 20 + 100$$

Adding the intermediate sums results in the number read as 123.

Applying the equation to binary numbers, valid values for alpha are 0 and 1 (the greatest digit is always one less than the base) and the beta value is 2 (thus base-2). If you encounter a binary number

1011

placing the value in the equation results in

$$1_0 2^0 + 1_1 2^1 + 0_2 2^2 + 1_3 2^3 = (1 * 2^0) + (1 * 2^1) + (0 * 2^2) + (1 * 2^3) = (1*1) + (1 * 2) + (0 * 4) + (1 * 8) = 1 + 2 + 0 + 8 = 11$$

read as 11 decimal and one-zero-one-one when read as a binary number.

Binary numbers were used in computers because at a hardware level it is much easier to make a two-state (digital) switch than a 10-state switch. Sometimes a problem arises when humans and computers interplay with numbers. This is one of the many reasons systems programming is considered slightly more complicated.

Although you certainly do not have to know how to convert between number systems to program in C++, you may find it helpful sometimes.

I mentioned that DOS-based architectures use packed data and time. If you needed to convert a directory entry from a packed bit array to a formatted string, you might have to do some bit-twiddling with these packed numbers.

A DOS-based (this means Windows 95, too) date entry is stored as a 16-bit integer. The map for this is:

```
struct DOS_DATE{
     unsigned int day:5;
             // 2⁵ = 32 - there are 1 to 31 days in most months
     unsigned int month:4;
             // 2⁴ = 16 - large enough to store 12 months
     unsigned int year:7;
             // 2⁷ = 128 - based date of 1980 (PCs introduction year)
};
```

You can assign to members of this bit-packed structure like any other integral data type. Declare the variable as

```
struct DOS_DATE date;
```

and assign a value to each member as you would any other variable:

```
date.day = 1;
date.month = 4;
date.year = 1996;
```

In your own programs it will probably be "cheaper" in terms of code and program size to *not* store values as bitfields. The reason involves the requirement of code to manage and convert between bitfields. The next section introduces a C++ keyword that provides an avenue around this sometimes, through implicit bit conversion.

Using *union*

The syntax of a union is much like that of a struct. The syntactical difference is the use of the keyword struct or syntax. The underlying meanings are quite different. Whereas a struct is used to group or aggregate several members, a union actually binds all *data* elements of the union to the exact same base address space. This is irregardless of the data members in the union.

> **Tip**
>
> Almost unbelievably, a union can have constructors and destructors. You will probably not hear much discussion on this subject, but it is true nonetheless. The job of a union's constructor and destructor is akin to that of a class's, and that is to ensure that proper initialization of the elements and the proper release of any resources allocated to the union.
>
> Although I haven't seen a lot of code containing union constructors, it is easy enough to implement and not especially difficult to find a use for them. Read chapter 14, "Basic Class Concepts," to learn about constructors and destructors. Although I only mention unions briefly in chapter 14, the notation for these special member functions is the same for unions as it is for classes.

Here is the external syntax of a struct:

```
struct struct_name
{
     // elements
};
```

followed by a union

```
union union_name
{
     // elements
};
```

Use a union when you determine that a single value may be represented by several different data types. I find unions to be most useful when I need to perform an implicit conversion between representations of data types.

The example program provided easily converts between the 16-bit, packed integers used in the file system's directory entries. The alternative would be to use bit-shifting (<<, >>) operators and binary operators to mask the bits out of the packed integer, which requires a lot of error-prone code. The program uses a bitfield structure, totaling 16 bits, and a union to combine the packed type with the bitfield type.

Listing 9.4   Union.cpp—Demonstrates Using *unions* to Perform Implicit Type Conversions

```
 1:  // UNION.CPP - Demonstrates implicit type conversion
     // with union bit-masking
 2:  #include <dir.h>
 3:  #include <dos.h>
 4:  #include <stdio.h>
 5:  #include <iostream.h>
 6:  // Uses a struct and a union to perform implicit type conversion
 7:  struct DOS_DATE
 8:  {
 9:      unsigned int day:5;         // a 5 bit field
10:      unsigned int month:4;       // a 4 bit field
11:      unsigned int year:7;        // a 7 bit field
12:  };
13:  // Uses a union to bind two types together
14:  union IMPLICIT_DATE_CONVERSION
15:  {
16:      unsigned int packed_date;
17:      struct DOS_DATE unpacked_date;
18:  };
19:  typedef union IMPLICIT_DATE_CONVERSION DATE;
20:  void main()
21:  {
22:      struct ffblk ffblk;
23:      int done = findfirst( "*.*", &ffblk, 0 );
24:      if( !done )
25:      {
26:          DATE d;
27:          // Performs the implict conversion
28:          d.packed_date = ffblk.ff_fdate;
29:          // Uses sprintf to format the date
30:          char buf[11];
31:          sprintf( buf, "%0.2d/%0.2d/%4d", d.unpacked_date.month,
32:              d.unpacked_date.day, d.unpacked_date.year + 1980 );
33:          cout << ffblk.ff_name << " was created on  " << buf << endl;
34:      }
35:  }
```

The struct DOS_DATE on lines 7 through 12 defines the date fields, totaling 16 bits. This part of the program is dictated by Microsoft. Lines 14 to 18 combine the unsigned int with the bit-packed structure. Now any assignment to either is an implicit assignment to the rest of the elements (because both the struct DOS_DATE variable unpacked_date and the unsigned integer packed_date share the same address).

Line 19 simplifies the union declaration by using typedef to create an alias.

Line 23 uses the DOS function findfirst, which is passed the requisite arguments. Lines 26 through 32 perform the implict conversion by assigning the packed integer array from the ffblk structure to the unsigned int packed_date element of the union.

Line 31 uses the sprintf declared in stdio.h to format the values from each of the unpacked_date elements of the union resulting in a formatted date string. The last line of code prints the filename and date.

This type of functionality is suited for a collection of utilities. I often create simple programs like this to test ideas. To make the implicit date conversion a reusable tool, add the struct and union to a header file, and maybe create a function that takes a packed date or ffblk and returns a formatted date string. Add the function's declaration to the same header, place the actual function in a module file, and add some comments or a scaffold demonstrating how to use the code.

Using *const*

The const declarator is often underused and can be misapplied or misunderstood. Using const when you intend something to be const actually plays a large role in building robust applications. When an object or function is constant, its immutability is a reliable aspect of the code.

When you declare a portion of your code, whether a variable or function, constant, you are saying, "The value of this constant thing is immutable and you can always depend on its value." When you can depend on such assertions, it goes a long way toward getting past that fragment of code during debugging and testing. That is, of course, if you are using the right form of constant.

If a variable or object is treated as a constant, then declare it so. Programming is one of those endeavors in life where explicitness pays off in large dividends. (This goes hand in hand with the rule: If the code is not self-commenting, then comment it.) By using the const declarator you are not only "commenting" the "constness" of the code, you are enforcing it.

In this section, you are going to look at the three combinations of "constness" when applied to variables (or objects, which is the C++ phraseology). Then you will wrap up this section by looking at constant functions. What you will see is, I hope, an easy method for determining which form of const you should use.

Constants Objects

There are three locations in a variable definition in which you can use the const keyword. A general variable definition looks like

```
type var_name [ = some_initial_value];
```

The keyword constant can be used to the left of the type, between the type and the variable name, or in both places. The meaning of each is somewhat distinct from the others. I often forget, so I thought of a way to explain it. I will define the type as a char* to illustrate the method.

Given a definition

```
char * COPYRIGHT = "by Automation Resource Corporation";
```

what does it mean to add the const keyword to the left of the char*, to the right between the type and the variable name COPYRIGHT, and in both places? If const is placed to the far left, as in

```
const char * COPYRIGHT = "by Automation Resource Corporation";
```

then each character in the string is immutable, but the pointer COPYRIGHT could be assigned to point to some other char* value. As pointers contain addresses, this means that COPYRIGHT could be assigned a new address. Thus

```
COPYRIGHT = "Software Conceptions, Inc";
```

when used to assign a new string is valid. However,

```
COPYRIGHT[0] = 'B';      // ERROR: each char is constant
```

would cause an error. In this example, almost deceptively the "constant" might not be what you think it is.

On the other hand, if I were to place the const specifier between the type and variable name, it is the pointer (the address of the string assigned to the pointer) which is constant, but the individual characters can be modified. Thus

```
char * const COPYRIGHT = "by Janice Szur";
```

means I can't do this

```
COPYRIGHT = "by Linda Koro";        // ERROR: Pointer is constant
```

but I can modify each character in

```
COPYRIGHT[11] = 'h' ;               // OK: Oops, misspelled Janice Shur
```

Again, the effect is not what you might have hoped for. If you want a pointer and what it points to to be constant, then you would apply the constant (the third form) in both places. Here you have

```
const char* const COPYRIGHT = "by Software Conceptions, Inc";
```

Now the value of the constant will always be exactly that of its initial value. How do you keep these three forms of constness straight? The answer is that you draw an imaginary line through the keyword const and whatever appears to the right of the line is what is constant (see fig. 9.3).

```
const char * COPYRIGHT = "QUE";

// Above, each character in the string is constant

char * const EDITOR = "Fred Slone";

// The pointer is constant, individual characters can be modified

const char * const PUBLISHER = "Macmillan Publishing";

// Both pointer and what's pointed to remain immutable
```

Fig. 9.3

Demonstrates a technique for applying const *and understanding what is and is not constant based on the placement of the keyword* const.

The sample program constant.cpp is included on the companion CD-ROM, but no code listing appears in the text. It may take you a little practice to get the hang of constant objects, but it is well worth the effort. Depending on a known state for an object is half the battle of debugging. Constants enforce this notion and reduce the number of unknowns.

Constant Member Functions

Again, I am talking about classes. When I refer to member functions, I am referring to members of classes. Member functions can be declared constant. This use of const requires the placement to occur after the function declaration and definition. To demonstrate, I will use a struct for simplicity (although a struct is not a class, it shares some of the same attributes).

```
struct B
{
     int a;
     int ReturnA() const { a; }      // Constant member function
}
```

The struct named B has two members: an integer and a function that returns the integer. The member function ReturnA is a constant member function. Defining a member function as constant means that the function itself will *not* change the value of the object. Constant functions can be invoked on both constant and nonconstant objects. The reverse is not true. A nonconstant function cannot be invoked on a non-constant object because it in no way ensures that it will not modify the value of the object.

Note

Member functions that provide users of classes (or structs) access to member data are often referred to as *accessor functions*.

Functions that return the value of a member are referred to as *read-only member functions*. If the function returned a reference to a member, for example

```
int& ReturnA(){ return &a; }
```

then it is referred to as a read/write accessor.

Provided in listing 9.5 for your edification is a short program. The lines of code containing const violations were intentionally commented as such and left in, so that you may experiment with constant functions and see the kinds of errors produced when a violation occurs.

Listing 9.5 Confunc.cpp—Demonstrates Constant Member Function Usage

```
 1:  // CONFUNC.CPP - Demonstrates constant member functions
 2:  #include <iostream.h>
 3:  struct CONSTANT_MEMBER
 4:  {
 5:      int val;
 6:      // Constructor with initialization list
 7:      CONSTANT_MEMBER( int v = 1 ) : val(v){};
 8:      int ConstRetVal() const;
 9:       int RetVal();
10:  };
11:  int CONSTANT_MEMBER::ConstRetVal() const
12:  {
13:      cout << "constant member called" << endl;
14:      return val;
15:  }
16:  int CONSTANT_MEMBER::RetVal()
17:  {
18:      cout << "nonconstant member called" << endl;
19:      return val;
20:  }
21:  void main()
22:  {
23:      const CONSTANT_MEMBER cm1(5);
24:      // WARNING: Nonconstant member called for constant object.
25:      cout << cm1.RetVal() << endl;
26:      // OK:Constant member function
27:      cout <<cm1.ConstRetVal() << endl;
28:      CONSTANT_MEMBER cm2(10);
29:      // OK: Can call constant member on nonconstant object
30:      cout << cm2.ConstRetVal() << endl;
31:      // OK: Can call nonconstant on nonconstant object.
32:      cout << cm2.RetVal() << endl;
33:  }
```

Line 25 produces a warning about calling a nonconstant member function for a constant object. The warning is placed into the Message window in the Borland C++ 5 IDE (see fig. 9.4).

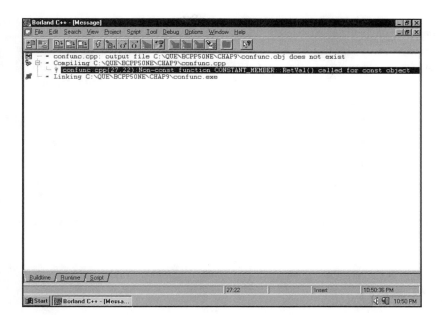

Fig. 9.4

This shows the warning received when you call nonconstant member functions on constant objects. You may call a constant member for both constant and nonconstant objects, but the reverse is not true.

Other *const* Stuff

The constant qualifier pops up in many circumstances. In the previous section, I demonstrated how member functions (see chapter 14, "Basic Class Concepts") can be declared constant. Chapter 15, "Function Overloading," and chapter 16, "Operator Overloading," discuss function and operator overloading. The const qualifier is an *overloadable qualifier*. This means that functions, operator and otherwise, can be overloaded on their constness (or lack thereof).

The keyword const can be used in casts as demonstrated in chapter 23, "Run-Time Type Identification (RTTI)." Classes can have constant members but must be initialized. All constants must be initialized at the point of definition unless they are references.

As I have said throughout this book, C++ is a challenging language. Certainly these challenges can be overcome, but it is not a trivial language. Like most spoken languages it is subtle in both its grammar and nuance. Learning and using C++ is both a pleasure and a challenge. I read a quote once referring to the notion that what we can think about is limited by our language. C++ is an expressive language. Part of its beauty is this aspect, and the other is that in its almost child-like simplicity you do not have to master the entire language to communicate. With practice and experience comes eloquence.

Using *enum*

C offers manifest constants by way of the #define preprocessor directive. In discussions on the subject most programmers agree that a constant name is easier to modify and relate to than constant values littered everywhere. A direct way to define a constant value is

```
const int BLACK = 0
const int BLUE = 1;
const int GREEN = 2;          // RGB color constants
```

or, alternatively

```
const int BLACK= 0;
const int BLUE = BLACK + 1;   // same thing, different technique
```

Two problems arise with this technique. The first is that it is tedious and requires a lot of typing, and the second is that you cannot initialize a constant in a class. (I will come back to the second example.)

When you have an ordered value of integral constants, using an enumeration (or enumerated list) often requires less work. An enumerated list is written

```
enum list_name { ITEM_1, ITEM_2, ITEM_3, [etc...] };
```

applied to the RGB (Red, Green, Blue) color values, you might define the enumeration as

```
enum RGB_COLORS { BLACK, BLUE, GREEN, CYAN, RED, MAGENTA,
BROWN, GRAY, DARK_GRAY, LT_BLUE, LT_GREEN,
LT_CYAN, LT_RED /* Maybe pink */ LT_MAGENTA, YELLOW, WHITE };
```

The enum keyword indicates a list. The list name plays the role of a type name, and the elements in the list are assigned the values 0 for the first element, 1 for the second, and so on. This ordinal assignment of values is used unless you explicitly assign a value for the enumeration items.

A second example, treating the addresses of video memory as an enumerated list, is as follows:

```
enum VIDEO_BASE_ADDRESS { VGA_EGA = 0xA000000, CGA = 0xB8000000,
➥MONO = 0xB0000000 };
```

> **Note**
>
> A convention I use is to make constants all uppercase with underscores separating words. Since enumerations and the values in the lists have constant values, I make them uppercase, too. As demonstrated by the second enumeration these values do not have to be sequential.
>
> Conventions should be employed to heighten consistency, but should be convenient.

I previously mentioned that there was a second consideration. Every name in the global namespace requires an entry into the symbol table. (The symbol table is used to resolve names to locations when the linker takes over from the compiler.) There is not an infinite supply of space in the symbol table. And, aside from this issue, semantically some things belong with classes or other aggregations. Among these other things are constants.

Often your design suggests that a constant identifier should exist in your class. Unfortunately, the solution that comes to mind—place a constant in the class—does not work. Variables or objects defined as constant require you to provide an initial value at the point of definition, but this is exactly what you cannot do when it comes to constants.

Consider a struct defined as containing a static-sized array of integers:

```
struct INT_ARRAY
{
    const int MAX = 100;      // ERROR: Cannot do this.
    int data[MAX];

    int& operator[]( unsigned int j );
    // See chapter 16, "Operator Overloading"
    // ... Other member functions
};
```

Since a const requires an initial value, but does not allow an initialization at this point, you cannot use const class members. However, a little enum trickery can be employed to achieve the desired result and avoid cluttering the global namespace. The technique simply involves adding an enumerated value, without the enumerated list name, to the class. Here's the struct with the change:

```
struct INT_ARRAY
{
    enum { MAX = 100 };
    int data[MAX];
    int& operator[]( unsigned int j );      // Ditto!
    // Other stuff
};
```

Note

While you may not use the explicit const in classes, as mentioned, you may get the desired result with an enum. Plus, you can use constant references, but these must be initialized and not assigned in classes.

Caution

The type INT_ARRAY shown is not a class; it is a struct. The differences between classes and structs are precise and usually the class idiom is the preferred method of defining types. I didn't use it here to minimize the use of "new" concepts.

(continues)

> (continued)
>
> While the general use of `class` or `struct` in discourse is probably all right because of similarities, I am using `class` to refer to an aggregate type. The differences between classes and structs is very distinct, and they are not so easily interchangeable in real programs.

Using *typedef*

The `typedef` specifier does not introduce a new type. It is used to create an alias for an existing type in general, or to simplify a complicated type that may be hard for the human reader to decipher all at once. On rare occasions, older versions of compilers had a moderate amount of difficulty parsing complicated types. In most cases, it is the human reader who benefits from a `typedef` alias.

Microsoft's code, which includes a lot of Windows SDK (Software Developer's Kit) and functions found in the API, use `typedefs` to designate an alias for commonly used Microsoft types. An example is the `lpStr` type. Plodding through some header files you will find this defined as

```
typedef char far * lpStr;
```

This is one syntactical presentation of the `typedef` command. The keyword is followed by the "real" type, and the last element is the alias. While aliasing types of this nominal complexity may seem questionable at first, it does provide an avenue for uniformity in code.

Note

Getting programmers to reuse code and maintain a similar coding standard seems to be a management challenge. Programmers seem to consider themselves rebels.

There is an intrinsic value in uniform code. Besides the fact that a large disparagement in the code in one program written by many programmers is unsightly, what measures do you apply to an engineered product? Without a standard in the style of programming it becomes difficult to train new programmers, maintenance is increasingly difficult and expensive, and creating standardized evaluative tests becomes more complicated.

Aside from offering suggestions for developing a "house standard," when I train programmers, I strongly suggest that creativity be saved for the solution, not the style.

Another form of `typedef` is not quite as clear as the first syntax. The form of aliasing I am about to demonstrate is a bit confusing. Chapter 11, "Functions," mentions the value and application of functors. In short, *functors* are function pointers that offer a flexibility in programming not found in many languages. They are fundamental to the Windows operating system.

> ▶▶ See chapter 11, "Functions," p. 228 for examples of employing functions.

The downside to functors is that their syntactical presentation looks complicated. A functor can have all of the components of a function, except they are pointers to functions. The syntax is

```
return_type (*functor_name)( [argument_list]);
```

A reference operator is bound (by parentheses) to the functor name. The appearance becomes even more confusing if the functor is used within an argument list, for example.

In an effort to simplify the syntax for using a functor, you can use `typedef` to assign a simpler alias. Based on your prior experience, you might expect the `typedef` for functors to model that of other typedefs. But they are slightly different. The alias name for a Functor `typedef` is embedded within the statement. If I defined a functor

```
void (*Functor)( int );
```

then the correct typedef is

```
typedef void (*Functor)( int );
```

Declaring a variable of this type then proceeds as if the alias were any type:

```
Functor fptr;
```

I introduced functors here because they require a slightly modified application of the `typedef` specifier. Focus on the two versions of the `typedef` command, and postpone excessive consideration for functors until you reach that section. The alternative would be to split up the discussion of the `typedef` command: half now and half after the discussion of functors in Chapter 11, "Functions." The key here is not to memorize the syntax. My goal is to instill an expectation for an alternative syntax so it won't seem too foreign and to briefly introduce a new subject.

Using Typecasting

A typecast is when you or I attempt to force a conversion between two similar but not identical types. One such substitution is when we attempt to convert between a family of types. The simplest example is the integral types.

Suppose an integer is provided, as is with `stdio.h` functions like

```
int get();
```

but what you want to get is a character. Using `get` with the `ostream` object `cout` results in an integer (number) being printed. For example, if the input stream has an "A," the code

```
cout << get() << endl;
```

Programming in C++

II

outputs the value 65. It is less likely that you will modify the function than it is that you will coerce the type to a character type. This "coercion" is referred to as typecasting: it takes on two forms with the same result. In the following code, I use the previous example, but assign the result of get to an integer:

```
int input = get();        // Input stream had 'A'
cout << (char)input;       // a typecast casts an integer
                           // to a character
```

or

```
cout << char(input);       // a typecast too, but looks like
                           // a function call
```

> ## Caution
>
> The latter form of typecasting can easily be confused with a function call. This is especially true if the type is not one of the native types. A native type will probably strike even the novice as odd, but applying the
>
> ```
> cast(  var )
> ```
>
> to a user-defined type is liable to be more error-prone than
>
> ```
> (cast) variable
> ```
>
> which looks nothing like a function call.
>
> A typecast is a good candidate for a comment. Explain why the typecast was performed and what, if any, assumptions or implications the cast has on the data.

The result of both forms of the typecast is that the integer type is cast as a character type. Depending on the conversion, some information may be lost.

Because C++ is a strongly typed language, you cannot just assume that the compiler will guess your intention. What this means to you is that the compiler won't make the cast; more than likely, it will squawk.

The idea that one type can be forced to appear as another must require a loss of information or the simple disregard of that data. A character is perceived to be a value within an eight-bit data set; an integer is 32-bit. In your example, the state of the other 24 bits is being ignored. If you know for sure, as with get() used with text input, that in your implementation it is okay to ignore these extra bits, then by all means apply the typecast.

Some existing functions may expect a pointer to void (void*) where it is convenient for you to use another type of pointer. Conversions of this sort seem to be pretty common; use them when your knowledge of the data is assured and your intention is clear. However, with aggregate types, like structs and classes, an often preferred method is to apply a conversion operator. Conversion operators are explained in chapter 14, "Basic Class Concepts." More type information is now available to C++ programmers, and some of the existing methods for converting between types have been supplanted. Check out chapter 23, "Run-Time Type Identification (RTTI)," for more details.

Using *cdecl*

The cdecl specifier is another keyword that is often applied to functions or tools that are used in cross-language programming. This distinction applies to functions that may be used both on C++ or C. C++ functions are mangled (to enable overloading); C functions are not. The cdecl keyword applied to a function is done to ensure that the C naming convention of prefixing a name with an underscore is used, the name is not mangled, and of course, the C calling convention is used. Both C and C++ share the same reverse-stack function calling convention (see the earlier section in this chapter, on "Using *extern*").

The keyword cdecl is still used in many of the library functions available to Borland C++ programmers. This is to ensure compatibility between different implementations of C and C++. (Borland has made several products over the years that have provided many of the same library functions.) If you go poking around in the header files, you may have some difficulty finding cdecl used directly; you may see a lot of RTLENTRY. Tracing this #define to its home file _defs.h, you will find a macro defining cdecl as RTLENTRY.

> **Note**
>
> If you examine the many target options offered in the TargetExpert, you will see that the Borland 5 compiler offers many target options. Among these are Win16, Win32, EasyWin, Console, and GUI. What appears to be a subterfuge—referring to the macro definition for cdecl—is probably necessary to maintain consistency and compatibility with all of the different target types.

Addressing Inline Assembler

Borland C++ allows programmers to intersperse inline assembler amongst C++ code. This is still a marvelous feature for DOS programmers because you could access all of the features of the operating system by filling the right registers and calling the right interrupt functions. You can still write assembler inline. And, you may even get away with calling some of those interrupt functions, too. In a lot of cases, however, this direct level of access has been closed off. Trying to use the video BIOS functions to write directly to the screen causes Windows to explode.

This section is not an introduction to assembler. While the facility still exists, the pool of people using assembler is diminishing. It is just too difficult to get the huge amounts of programming required done in assembler in a reasonable timeframe. I don't mean that it is not done; just that it is done less.

From Here...

The Annotated C++ Reference Manual, by Stroustrop and Ellis published by Addison-Wesley, and the ANSI C++ document are the definitive sources for what is and what isn't the C++ programming language. This book is neither of those things. Those documents may be difficult to read at best and are for reference. I wrote this book with the intention that it would be readable from front to back and act as a valuable reference.

I evaluated most aspects of the language and intentionally chose to include some and not others. This chapter was intended as a guide to assist you in understanding and employing some of the keywords that make C++ expressive. The keywords were included because they were most commonly found among the thousands of lines of code I have read over the years.

You will see these keywords littered throughout the text in many chapters. The key to understanding and using them creatively is to read and write many lines of code.

- See chapter 10, "Writing Expressions," for examples of common C++ expressions.

- Refer to chapter 15, "Function Overloading," to learn how to use this advanced feature and why you should use it.

- Chapter 16, "Operator Overloading," demonstrates how C++ facilitates making complex types as simple to use as native data types.

- See chapter 23, "Run-Time Type Identification (RTTI)," to learn how to take full advantage of this relatively new entry into the object-oriented paradigm.

CHAPTER 10

Writing Expressions

Earlier chapters have discussed the rudimentary components such as data types and operators for writing C++ programs. These components are pieced together to form an expression that performs computations. This chapter discusses the next level of putting pieces together to form a whole construct.

Statements are the smallest executable unit of code. They control the execution flow of a program. Statements in a block of code are executed in order, each completely executed before going to the next statement; that is, unless a decision or flow control statement causes the program to jump to another location. Statements can be divided into four categories: sequence, selection, iteration, and jump statements. Each category is covered in the following sections.

Using Sequence Statements

Sequence statements are simply statements that do not directly control execution of other statements. The majority of the statements in a program are sequence statements. There are five types of sequence statements: declaration, expression, null, compound, and label statements.

Declaration Statements

Declaration statements are the only type of C++ statement that can be placed outside a function. They consist of variable or function declarations ending with a semicolon (;). The semicolon acts as a statement terminator. Optionally, the declaration could be combined with the definition, as in the following example:

```
int i;
float a = 2.3, x, y = i;
```

Line two of the preceding code is a single statement even though there is more than one variable declared.

Expression Statements

Expression statements are expressions with a semicolon appended. These are the most common forms of statements. The following are examples of expression statements:

```
++i;
x * y;
x = tan(y) + z;
foo(x);
```

Note that though line two in the preceding code compiles without a complaint, it is useless. It doesn't have an effect.

Null Statements

A special form of the expression statement is the *null statement*, as in the following:

```
;
```

It consists of only a semicolon. While this may seem like a useless statement, it comes in handy when the language syntax requires a statement but one is not needed. This is sometimes the case with `while` and `for` statements:

```
while (foo(x));
```

Compound Statements

A *compound statement*, or *block*, is zero or more statements enclosed in braces ({}). Compound statements may appear anywhere in a program in which a single statement is legal. They provide a way of executing a sequence of statements where one statement is expected:

```
if (i >= 0) {
    int j = i + 1;
    n += j / m;
}
```

Variables declared within compound statements can be used only inside the block. Thus, the integer `j` in the preceding code is undefined outside the braces.

Function bodies must be enclosed in braces; therefore, a function body is a compound statement. An empty function body is one of the few instances where an empty block might make sense. When developing a program, you might create "stubs" of functions, functions with no body, and fill the body of the function in later.

A semicolon is not required after the ending brace of the compound statement, although it doesn't hurt anything if one is included.

Label Statements

A label statement contains an identifier followed by a semicolon. There are two types of *label statements*. The first is an *identifier label* that serves as a target for goto statements. It consists of an identifier followed by a colon and a statement:

```
goto FATAL_ERROR;
// Some statements.
FATAL_ERROR: abort();
```

The naming rules that apply to variables apply to label identifiers. The scope of the identifier is within the function in which it is declared. Labels have their own namespace, so it is possible to have a label and a variable using the same identifier within the same scope. Because goto statements are rare, identifier label statements are rare.

The second type of label statement is used in switch statements. These labels are covered in the section titled "switch."

Using Selection Statements

Selection statements execute other statements based on conditional values. This allows the flow of control to be based on testing criterion. There are two types of these decision-making statements: the if statement and the switch statement.

if

The if statement tests an expression. If the expression evaluates to a nonzero value, or true, the following statement is executed. If it evaluates to zero, or false, the following statement is not executed. The following code gives the form for the if statement:

```
if (i)
    ++i;
```

The parentheses around the expression i are required. The expression can be any type of expression that yields a scalar value that can be tested for equivalence to zero. The if statement in the preceding code can be written as:

```
if (i != 0)
    ++i;
```

Both of these forms are equivalent. The first if statement implies the test for zero, which is explicitly written in the second if statement. Most programmers prefer the first version: it requires less typing, and the intent is clear. When is a value zero? The answer is obvious for the types bool (false), short (0), int (0), long (0L), float (0.0), and double (0.0). What about char and pointer values? A char value of \0 is zero. Pointers are equivalent to zero if they have the value of NULL or 0:

```
char *str;
str = new char[10];
if (str)
    strcpy(str, "a string");
```

float and double values can be difficult to test for equivalence to zero. Errors can occur due to rounded errors in earlier calculations. It is generally not a good idea to use these values as equivalence test conditions. There are situations, however, where it is desirable to test the value of a float or double variable. Suppose that a float value was to be tested for equality (or near equality) with some value n. Also suppose that a value within 0.00000001 of n would effectively be n for this application. The value could be tested to be within this range of n. The following example illustrates this:

```
const float epsilon = 0.00000001;
if ((x > n-epsilon) && (x < n+epsilon))
    cout << "x is effectively equal to n \n";
```

Often the expression tested within an `if` statement is a relational or logical expression. In the preceding expression, it is a combination of both.

As stated earlier, a compound statement can be placed anywhere a single statement is expected. Thus, the statement following an `if` statement could be a compound statement:

```
if ((x < y) && !z) {
    x = y / 100;
    y += 100;
}
```

A common programming error is to forget the braces, so instead of the preceding, you get the following:

```
if ((x < y) && !z)
    x = y / 100;
    y += 100;
```

At first glance, both statements below the `if` statement are executed if the expression is `true`. But the compiler does not take indentation into account. `y` would be incremented by 100 even if the expression proved `false`.

Tip

Some programmers always use compound statements with selection and iteration statements, even if there is only one statement in the compound statement. If more statements are added later, forgetting the braces is not an issue. This, like the placement of braces, is a matter of style. Choose the style that suites you and stick to it.

The `if` statement has an optional companion statement, the `else` statement. It has the following form:

```
if (i)
    ++i;
else
    cout << "i = 0";
```

If the expression `i` in the `if` statement is `true`, the first statement, `++i`, executes. If the expression is `false`, then second statement, `cout << "i = 0"`, executes. This allows two exclusive courses of action to be taken based on the value of the expression. To allow more than a two-way selection, `if`-`else` statements can be placed together:

```
char menuCommand;
cin >> menuCommand;
if (menuCommand == 'a')
    foo1();
```

```
   else if (menuCommand == 'b')
      foo2();
   else if (menuCommand == 'c')
      foo3;
   else                                    // Default. This is optional.
      cout << "Error in input.\n";
```

Each `if` expression is tested in order. The statement following the first `if` expression that evaluates to `true` executes. All `if` statements below that are ignored, even if their expressions evaluate to `true`. If no test expression returns `true`, the default statement following `else` executes.

`if` statements may be nested to any depth. Care should be taken to ensure that the proper `else` is associated with the correct `if`. Listing 10.1 gives an example of what can go wrong.

Listing 10.1   If1.cpp—Sloppy *if-else* **Statements**

```
#include <iostream.h>

int main()
{
   char c;
   cout << "Enter a lower case alphabetic character.\n";
   cin >> c;
   if (c <= 'z')
      if (c < 'a')
         cout << "Invalid character (< a).\n";
   else
      cout << "Invalid character (> z).\n";
   return 0;
}
```

ASCII characters have a value. Lowercase characters have sequential integer values starting with the `'a'`=97 to `'z'`=122. The program should test input for valid characters. When the program in listing 10.1 is compiled and run, it flags all valid characters as bad (> `'z'`) and does not catch characters with values greater than `'z'`. The problem with the code comes from the fact that C++ matches an `else` (or `else if`) with the last unmatched `if` statement. Therefore, even though the indentation says otherwise, the last `else` statement is matched with the second `if` statement. Often, braces go a long way toward clarifying code. Listing 10.2 shows the program written with braces placed in appropriately.

Listing 10.2   If2.cpp—Correct *if-else* **Statements**

```
#include <iostream.h>

int main()
{
   char c;
   cout << "Enter a lower case alphabetic character.\n";
```

(continues)

II

Programming in C++

Listing 10.2   Continued

```
cin >> c;
if (c <= 'z') {
   if (c < 'a')
      cout << "Invalid character (< a).\n";
}
else {
   cout << "Invalid character (> z).\n";
}
return 0;
```

---

switch

A switch statement allows for multiple courses of action much like an if-else statement. In fact, any switch statement can be written as an if-else statement; however, it is sometimes more clear to use the switch. The following code illustrates the use of the switch:

```
switch (menuCommand) {
   case 'a':
      foo1();
      break;
   case 'b':
      foo2();
      break;
   case 'c':
      foo3();
      break;
   default:                            // Optional.
      cout << "Error in input.\n;
}
```

The value of the expression in parentheses following the switch statement in line one is compared to all the case values. case statements are label statements. Each case label must be an integer constant or convertible to an integer constant. Constants of type char, short, long, and enum are convertible to integer constants. An additional requirement for case labels is each value must be unique. Each case value is compared in turn to the value of the expression in the switch. When an equivalent case value is found, all statements following the matched case label value execute until a break statement is encountered or the end of the switch statement is reached. If menuCommand in the preceding code matches the first case, case 'a', the function foo1() is called. If there is no break statement after foo1(), foo2() is called even though menuCommand does not equal 'b'. This is usually undesirable behavior. The break statement causes execution flow to jump to the statement after the closing brace on the switch block.

There are times when this fall-through behavior is desired. In the preceding example, the user is required to enter lowercase a, b, or c. If an uppercase entry were okay, the following allows both cases:

```
    switch (menuCommand) {
        case 'A':
        case 'a':
            foo1();
            break;
        case 'B':
        case 'b':
            foo2();
            break;
        case 'C':
        case 'c':
            foo3();
            break;
        default:
            cout << "Error in input.\n;
    }
```

The function foo1() is called if menuCommand were either 'A' or 'a'. The default label is analogous to the else construct. As with the else, default is optional.

A problem can occur if an initialization is placed within a case sequence. Listing 10.3 gives an example of code that does not compile.

Listing 10.3   Switch1.cpp—Obscure *switch* Error

```
// ERROR: this will not compile!

#include <iostream.h>

int main()
{
    char menuCommand ;
    cout << "Area of a (C)ircle or (R)ectangle.\n";
    cin >> menuCommand;
    switch (menuCommand) {
        case 'C':
        case 'c':
            cout << "Enter the radius of the circle.\n";
            float radius;
            cin >> radius;
            const float pi = 3.1415926535;
            cout << "The area of the rectangle is " << pi*radius*radius << endl;
            break;
        case 'R':
        case 'r':
            cout << "Enter the length and width of the rectangle\n";
            float length, width;
            cin >> length >> width;
            cout << "The area of the rectangle is " << length*width << endl;
            break;
        default:
            cout << "Error in input.\n";
    }
    return 0;
}
```

The error given when the program in listing 10.3 is compiled is `Case bypasses initialization of a local variable`. The problem can be resolved by placing the body of the case statement sequence in braces. This makes the initialization local to the case sequence. Thus, the variable is not in the scope of the following case sequences. Listing 10.4 illustrates:

Listing 10.4 Switch2.cpp—*switch* Error Corrected

```cpp
#include <iostream.h>

int main()
{
    char menuCommand;
    cout << "Area of a (C)ircle or (R)ectangle.\n";
    cin >> menuCommand;
    switch (menuCommand) {
        case 'C':
        case 'c': {
            cout << "Enter the radius of the circle.\n";
            float radius;
            cin >> radius;
            const float pi = 3.1415926535;
            cout << "The area of the circle is " << pi*radius*radius << endl;
        }
        break;
        case 'R':
        case 'r': {
            cout << "Enter the length and width of the rectangle\n";
            float length, width;
            cin >> length >> width;
            cout << "The area of the rectangle is " << length*width << endl;
        }
        break;
        default:
            cout << "Error in input.\n";
    }
    return 0;
}
```

Using Iteration Statements

Iteration statements loop through a sequence of statements a fixed number of times or until a test condition is met. There are three types of loop statements: `while`, `do`, and `for`.

while

The `while` loop tests an expression and, if the expression evaluates to `true`, iterates through a single or compound statement:

```cpp
while (i < 100)
    str[i++] = ' ';
```

The expression is first tested. If i is less than 100, the following statement, str[i++] = ' ', executes. If i is greater than or equal to 100, the loop passes control to the statement following the while statement or block. An important characteristic of the while loop is that the loop statements never execute if the test expression is initially false.

> **Note**
>
> Note that i in the preceding statement is incremented for every iteration through the loop. A common problem occurs when the ending condition is never reached. This could be due to the loop control variables not changing in the body of the loop. The result is an infinite loop. In this instance, that error is easy to spot, but this is not always the case. Be sure that a terminating value for the expression is assured.

The rules for the test expression are the same as the rules for if statement test expressions. See the section on if statements for a discussion of test expressions.

The null statement is often used in conjunction with iteration loops. The following code copies one character string to another:

```
while (*str1++ = *str2++)
    ;
```

Listing 10.5 gives an example of using while loops.

Listing 10.5 While1.cpp—Using *while* Loops

```cpp
#include <iostream.h>

void main()
{
    const unsigned MAX_STR_LEN = 25;
    char s[MAX_STR_LEN];
    cout << "\nEnter strings separated by a new line (<Ctrl+C> to quit).\n";

    // getline will only read at most MAX_STR_LEN-1 characters into
    // s at one time. Therefore there is no danger of overwriting memory.
    while (cin.getline(s, MAX_STR_LEN-1)) {
        // Count the total number of characters in s, not counting the
        // terminating null.
        char *sp = s;
        int count = 0;
        while (*sp++)
            ++count;
        cout << "The string entered consist of " << count << " characters.\n";

        // Copy non-whitespace characters.
        sp = s;
        count = 0;
        char *sp2 = s;
        while (*sp) {
```

(continues)

Listing 10.5 Continued

```
            if ((*sp != ' ') && (*sp != '\t') && (*sp != '\n'))
                sp2[count++] = *sp;
            *sp++;
        }
        sp2[count] = '\0';
        cout << "The input string striped of white space: " << s << endl;
    }
}
```

A few things about the code in listing 10.5 are worth noting. First, is it possible for the outer while loop to enter an infinite loop? No. The user can terminate the program at any time by pressing Ctrl+C or Ctrl+Break. Can the getline() place more than MAX_STR_LEN-1 and thus cause problems for the inner while loops? Again, no. getline() copies input characters into s until MAX_STR_LEN-1 characters are copied or until a newline character is entered. getline() then places a null terminator in s. Thus, both inner while loops will always terminate.

Why not increment the pointer in the second inner while loop test expression as it is in the first inner while loop? Even though the increment operator is a postfix opera-tor, the expression is completely executed before the body of the while loop executes. If the pointer had been incremented in the while expression, the first character in the input string would have been skipped. What if a prefix increment operator had been used? The pointer would have been incremented, and then the value would have been tested. This is not the desired behavior.

Finally, note the value of count after each inner while loop. A common error is the *off-by-one* error. For example, count could have mistakenly been assumed to count the number of characters in s, *including* the null terminator.

do

The do statement is a looping statement much like the while statement. The only difference is that a do loop test expression is evaluated at the end of the loop, not at the beginning. This ensures that the body of the loop always executes at least once. The following example gives the form of the do loop:

```
int i, total = 0;
do {
    cout << "Enter a number (0 to quit).\n";
    cin >> i;
    total += i;
} while (i);
cout << "The total is " << total << endl;
```

The user needs to be prompted at least once for input. The do loop is the better choice here.

Listing 10.6 gives an example of two simple counting loops. The first is a while loop, and the second is a do loop.

Listing 10.6   Do1.cpp—*do* versus *while* Loops

```
#include <iostream.h>

void main()
{
   int count = 0;
   cout << "while loop count: ";
   while (count++ < 10)
      cout << count << " ";
   cout << endl;

   count = 0;
   cout << "do loop count: ";
   do
      cout << count << " ";
   while (count++ < 10);
    cout << endl;
}
```

The following is the output from the program in listing 10.1:

```
while loop count: 1 2 3 4 5 6 7 8 9 10
do loop count: 0 1 2 3 4 5 6 7 8 9 10
```

The do loop iterates 11 times, whereas the while loop iterates 10 times. In both instances, the final value of count is the same: 11.

for

When using while loops, the loop often has the following form:

```
init_expression;
while(test_expression) {
   // Sequence of statements.
   loop_control_expression;
}
```

This while loop usually occurs when the loop sequence needs to be executed a fixed number of times. C++ provides a construct to more compactly implement the preceding while loop. This type of looping statement, the for loop, is given in equivalent form to the preceding while loop by the following:

```
for (init_expression; test_expression; loop_control_expression) {
   // Sequence of statements.
}
```

As a for loop executes, the following sequence of events takes place:

1. The *init_expression* executes. This happens only once, when the loop is first entered.

2. The *test_expression* is tested. If it evaluates to true, control goes to step 3. If the value is false, the flow of control goes to the statement after the for loop block. An initial false value means the statements inside the loop never execute.

3. The sequence of statements in the loop executes.

4. The *loop_control_expression* executes.

5. Control returns to step 2.

There are few restrictions on *init_expression*, *test_expression*, and *loop_control_expression*. One or more can be omitted, though the semicolon cannot be omitted. Thus, the following is legal:

```
for (;;) {
    // Sequence of statements.
}
```

This is equivalent to the following while loop:

```
while(1) {
    // Sequence of statements.
}
```

Usually the *init_expression* is used to initialize and possibly declare a loop control variable. Other variables may also be declared and initialized here. The following code shows a typical use of for loops, initializing arrays:

```
int ia[10];
for (int i = 0, j = 100; i < 10; i++, j-=10)
    ia[i] = j;
```

Any variables declared in the *init_expression* have scope only within the for loop. Versions previous to this version of Borland C++ define the scope of the variable to be from the point of declaration to the end of the block enclosing the for statement. As a result, the following code compiles fine under Borland C++ 4.5 or earlier but returns an Undefined symbol 'i' error with Borland C++ 5.0:

```
int ia1[10], ia2[20];
for (int i = 0; i < 10; i++)
    ia1[i] = 0;
for (i = 0; i < 20; i++)
    ia2[i] = 0;
```

The change breaks some old code. That is, code that compiled without error in previous versions will sometimes not compile with the new version. Actually, this was a change in the language definition by the C++ standards committee. Frankly, it is more logical that variables declared here are used only within the for loop. The source of the error is easily identified and corrected. To correct the problem in the preceding code, add the declaration to the second for loop:

```
for (int i = 0; i < 20; i++)
    ia2[i] = 0;
```

The *test_expression*, as the name implies, is most often used to test for the ending condition. This is usually a relational expression like the preceding ones. As with the while and do loops, care should be taken that an ending condition is always reached.

The *loop_control_expression* is most often used to increment the loop counter. Does a prefix or postfix operator make a difference? Because the *loop_control_* *expression* executes in its entirety, it does not matter which increment operator is used.

Listing 10.7 implements a shell sort for sorting an array of randomly generated integers. This sorting algorithm compares elements that are far apart in the array and swaps them if necessary. The gap between compared elements is decreased to one. At this point, adjacent elements are compared and swapped if necessary. The array is then in sorted order. The C version of this shell sort was presented by Brian Kernighan and Dennis Ritchie.

Listing 10.7   For1.cpp—Using the *for* Loop

```cpp
#include <stdlib.h>
#include <iostream.h>

void main()
{
   const int ARRAY_SIZE = 10;
   int array[ARRAY_SIZE];
   for (int i = 0; i < ARRAY_SIZE; i++)
      array[i] = rand();

   cout << "The initial array is:\n";
   for (int i = 0; i < ARRAY_SIZE; i++)
      cout << " " << array[i];

   for (int gap = ARRAY_SIZE/2; gap > 0; gap /= 2)
      for (int i = gap; i < ARRAY_SIZE; i++)
         for (int j = i-gap; (j >= 0) && (array[j] > array[j+gap]); j -= gap)
{
            int temp = array[j];
            array[j] = array[j+gap];
            array[j+gap] = temp;
         }
   cout << "\nThe sorted array is:\n";
   for (int i = 0; i < ARRAY_SIZE; i++)
      cout << " " << array[i];
   cout << endl;
}
```

When compiled and run, the program produces the following output:

```
The initial array is:
 346 130 10982 1090 11656 7117 17595 6415 22948 31126
The sorted array is:
 130 346 1090 6415 7117 10982 11656 17595 22948 31126
```

Note that the random numbers generated on your machine may be different.

The array is first filled with computer-generated random numbers. The rand() function found in the stdlib.h is used to generate the random numbers. The sorting algorithm consists of three nested for loops. The outer loop sets the initial gap between compared elements to be half the size of the array. At each iteration, the gap is shrunk by half. The outer loop ends when the gap is zero. Is it possible for this test to fail, causing an infinite loop? Could gap get stuck at the value 1 or 2? No. gap eventually reaches 1, and the next division by 2 yields 0.5, which is truncated to 0 because gap is an integer.

The middle loop compares each element that is separated by gap elements. The loop variable i is initially set to gap. It is incremented by one on each iteration through the loop. The test condition will always be met.

The inner loop swaps any elements that are not in order. The loop variable j is initially set to zero for the first iteration through the middle loop, then set to 1 for the second iteration of the middle loop, and so on. j is decrement by gap amount at each iteration through the inner loop. The test condition consists of two expressions, both of which must be true for the loop to continue. It's easy to see that the first expression in the test causes the loop to eventually exit because the loop variable converges to zero.

Using Jump Statements

Jump statements unconditionally transfer program control to some target within the program. There are four jump statements: break, continue, return, and goto.

break

You have seen the break statement in the section on switch statements. When a break statement was encountered in the case sequence, program control passed to the statement after the switch block. In general, the break statement terminates the nearest enclosing while, do, for, and switch statements. Control is transferred to the statement following the terminated statement, if any.

Listing 10.8 gives an example of using a break statement in a while and for loop. The program is a simple game. The user is asked for character input until Ctrl+C is pressed or until a "secret" character is entered, thereby winning the game.

Listing 10.8   Break1.cpp—Using *break* Statements

```
#include <iostream.h>

void main()
{
   const unsigned MAX_STR_LEN = 100;
   const char c = '$';
   char s[MAX_STR_LEN];
   bool youWin = false;
   cout << "\nEnter a string with the secret character (<Ctrl+C> to quit).\n";
   while (cin.getline(s, MAX_STR_LEN-1)) {
      // Count the total number of characters in s, not counting the
      //  terminating null.
```

```
        char *sp = s;
        int len = 0;
        while (*sp++)
        ++len;
        for (int i = 0; i < len; i++)
            if (s[i] == c) {
                youWin = true;
                break;                          // Exits for loop.
            }
        if (youWin)
            break;
        cout << "\nSorry. Try again.\n";        // This will not be executed if
                                                //   break called.

    }
    if (youWin)
        cout << "\nCongratulations. You're one smart cookie!\n";
}
```

Okay, it's ugly. Most uses of jump statements, excluding the `return` statement and the use of `break` in `switch` statements, are ugly; they should be used sparingly.

continue

The `continue` statement terminates the current iteration through the nearest enclosing `while`, `do`, or `for` loop. Control is passed to the test expression for the `while` and `do` loops or the loop control expression for the `for` loop. Listing 10.9 provides an example.

Listing 10.9   Continu1.cpp—Using the *continue* Statement

```
#include <iostream.h>

void main()
{
    bool correctEntry = false;
    cout << "Enter the password (<Ctrl+C> to quit): ";
    char s[100];    // Allow for extra characters.
    while (!correctEntry) {
        cin >> s;
        // Check each character. Get another string when the first non-matching
        // character is found. Include terminating character in the check.
        if (s[0] != 'E') {
            cout << "\nCharacter 1 is wrong. Try again: ";
            continue;
        }
        if (s[1] != 'l') {
            cout << "\nCharacter 2 is wrong. Try again: ";
            continue;
        }
        if (s[2] != 'v') {
            cout << "\nCharacter 3 is wrong. Try again: ";
            continue;
        }
```

(continues)

Listing 10.9 Continued

```
    if (s[3] != 'i') {
        cout << "\nCharacter 4 is wrong. Try again: ";
        continue;
    }
    if (s[4] != 's') {
        cout << "\nCharacter 5 is wrong. Try again: ";
        continue;
    }
    if (s[5] != '\0') {
        cout << "\nAlmost. But character 6 is wrong. Try again: ";
        continue;
    }
    cout << "That is the correct password.";
    correctEntry = true;
    }
}
```

return

The return statement transfers program control to the calling function or exits the program if the return statement is in the main function. return statements usually return an expression. This returned value is the value of the function in which the return statement is executed. A void function is a function that returns no value. It requires that the return statement have no associated expression. The following lists a few examples:

```
return 1;          // Function returns a integer.
return x/y;        // Return type of x/y.
return;            // void function. No return value.
```

A return statement may be located anywhere in the function. Functions and return statements will be covered more fully in the next chapter.

goto

goto statements transfer program control to the specified label statement. The target label statement must be within the same function. goto statements may not cause a jump that bypasses a variable initialization within the same or higher scope. This is similar to the Case bypasses initialization of a local variable error encountered in the section on switch statements. Like the switch statement, the solution is to enclose the initialization of the local variable in braces, so the jump skips the entire block containing the initialization.

goto statements are usually a result of bad programming. Following the logic of a program that uses goto statements can be very difficult. There are very rare cases when the judicious use of a goto statement adds clarity.

Listing 10.10 illustrates a nonjudicious use of goto. Instead of using two break statements to exit the for and while loops, a goto statement is used.

Listing 10.10   Goto1.cpp—Using *goto* Statements

```
#include <iostream.h>

void main()
{
   const unsigned MAX_STR_LEN = 100;
   const char c = '$';
   char s[MAX_STR_LEN];
   cout << "\nEnter a string with the secret character (<Ctrl+C> to quit).\n";
   while (cin.getline(s, MAX_STR_LEN-1)) {
// Count the total number of characters in s, not counting the terminating null.
      char *sp = s;
      int len = 0;
      while (*sp++)
         ++len;
      for (int i = 0; i < len; i++)
      if (s[i] == c)
         goto YOU_WIN;
      cout << "\nSorry. Try again.\n";
   }
   cout << "\nBetter luck next time.\n";
   goto END;   // Don't give winner message.
YOU_WIN:
   cout << "\nCongratulations. You're one smart cookie!\n";
END: ;         // Ending brace cannot follow a label.
}
```

Using the *sizeof* Operator

The sizeof operator returns the number of bytes in memory used by the type or expression passed as a parameter. If an expression is passed, the expression is not evaluated. The sizeof operator is commonly used to determine the amount of memory needed when allocating a variable with the new operator. It is also used to determine the number of elements in an array for processing in an iteration loop.

The size of some types are dependent on the machine. It can also be dependent on which memory model is used.

List 10.11 applies the sizeof operator to various types. The program was compiled with Win32 as the target.

Listing 10.11   Sizeof1.cpp—Using the *sizeof* Operator

```
#include <iostream.h>

void main()
{
```

(continues)

Listing 10.11   Continued

```
cout << "The following are the result of various applications of the
➥sizeof operator.\n";
cout << " char: " << sizeof(char) << endl;
cout << " char&: " << sizeof(char&) << endl;
cout << " char*: " << sizeof(char*) << endl;
cout << " wchar_t: " << sizeof(wchar_t) << endl;
cout << " bool: " << sizeof(bool) << endl;
cout << " short: " << sizeof(short) << endl;
cout << " int: " << sizeof(int) << endl;
cout << " long: " << sizeof(long) << endl;
cout << " float: " << sizeof(float) << endl;
cout << " double: " << sizeof(double) << endl;
cout << " long double: " << sizeof(long double) << endl;

enum DIGIT { ZERO, ONE, TWO, THREE, FOUR, FIVE, SIX, SEVEN, EIGHT, NINE };
cout << " DIGIT: " << sizeof(DIGIT) << " Member: " << sizeof(ZERO) <<
➥endl;

char ca[10];
cout << " char[10]: " << sizeof(ca) << " # elements: " << sizeof(ca)/
➥sizeof(ca[0]) << endl;

double da[10];
cout << " double[10]: " << sizeof(da) << " # elements: " << sizeof(da)/
➥sizeof(da[0]) << endl;

struct cd {
    char c;
    double d;
} cda[10];
cout << " struct cd[10]: " << sizeof(cda) << " # elements: " <<
➥sizeof(cda)/sizeof(cda[0]) << endl;

char *cp = new char[10];
cout << " new char[10]: " << sizeof(cp) << " *cp: " << sizeof(*cp) <<
➥endl;
}
```

The following text is the result of running the program in listing 10.11:

```
The following are the result of various applications of the sizeof operator.
 char: 1
 char&: 1
 char*: 4
 wchar_t: 2
 bool: 1
 short: 2
 int: 4
 long: 4
 float: 4
 double: 8
 long double: 10
 DIGIT: 4 Member: 4
 char[10]: 10 # elements: 10
```

```
 double[10]: 80 # elements: 10
 struct cd[10]: 90 # elements: 10
new char[10]: 4 *cp: 1
```

Note that the amount of memory referenced by a pointer allocated with new cannot be determined with the sizeof operator.

From Here...

In this chapter, we have covered constructing statements from rudimentary components such as variables and operators. Program statement are of four types: sequence statements, selection statements, iteration statements, and jump statements.

Sequence statements are all statements that do not control flow of execution in the program. This is really a "catch-all" category for statements that do not fit in the other categories.

Selection statements execute other statements based on some testing criterion. if and switch statements are selection statements.

Iteration statements loop through other statements. while and do statements loop until a test condition is met. for statements loop a fixed number of times.

Jump statements transfer execution control unconditionally to some target. The break statement terminates the nearest enclosing iteration loop or switch statement. The continue statement terminates the *current* iteration of the nearest enclosing iteration loop. return statements transfer program control to the calling program, and goto statements transfer control to a specified label statement.

■ Chapter 11, "Functions," covers the next logical step: putting statements together to form functions. This is the next step up in building components that form a program.

II

Programming in C++

CHAPTER 11

Functions

Creating functions was one of the first big steps for programming languages. Functions are the first fundamental building blocks after symbolic instructions (keywords). They enable you to combine several instructions into a new mnemonic name, providing a handle for referring to the steps as an entity.

It's no great surprise that programming languages evolved to include functions (names) for groups of things. Can you imagine if we didn't use simple names to refer to complex things? I think a definition of "learning" is a recursive aggregation and simplification of knowledge, using shorter phrases to describe complex things. It is a natural process to aggregate ideas and devise descriptors. Humans are constantly putting things on shelves, in car trunks, in boxes, and in envelopes. In an effort to organize, we devise containers for items and containers for our containers. This describes the mechanism we have devised to contain code: functions. Functions contain code and/or functions, which contain other functions. The key then, is to learn how to employ the device. Because functions are created via C++, employing functions is accomplished using C++'s grammar.

For the novice, this is one of the most important chapters because it explains the obvious and not so obvious details of functions, including syntax and concepts apart from pure syntax. Functions are fascinating. They may have moved from the limelight because of the class idiom, but classes without (member) functions are just records. For more advanced programmers, you may be surprised at some of the language features presented. In this chapter, we cover:

- Function syntax
- Using functions
- Recursive functions
- Overloading
- Functors
- Adding debug code as you go
- Why C++ functions require fewer arguments

Birth of a Function

In the nineteenth century, computers were people. Specifically, they were probably bookkeepers or mathematicians. I think it was Charles Babbage who explored the idea of a mechanical computational device because human computation was slow, tedious, and error-prone.

In the 1940s, computing machines ran on vacuum tubes to calculate missile trajectories. (Ever notice how many college trigonometry, calculus, and differential equations texts have an inordinate number of exercises geared towards calculating trajectories?) The computers of this time used simple two-state tube-switches and were instructed by a punch card version of machine language. From here, a progression was made to binary numbers and paper printouts.

Early films depict programmers as beleaguered mathematicians pondering reams of paper containing long streams of binary numbers. It is little wonder that those early programmers created mnemonics for binary instructions. This is the form of the first aggregations: converting binary numbers into equivalent pseudo-words. Thus, assembler was derived from this machine language.

The process continues today. The next step from assembler was to collect commonly recurring groups of instructions into macros, which is simple code substitution. Macro substitution replaces the text of instructions where a macro name was placed. The macro was equated to some coupling of instructions and the name is used where the code is desired. The replacement is automatic. To give you an idea of our current state of progression, macros are still used with assemblers, and both C and C++ support macros through the #define preprocessor directive.

If progress had stopped at code substitution, we would have real problems. Since a macro's code is placed wherever the name of the macro occurs, every program would have multiple, maybe hundreds of occurrences of the same code fragment. In an effort to simplify the problem, instead of bringing the body of the code to the location that the name occurs, the code became stationary. Fixing the code to a location in memory meant that the flow of program control had to be re-routed to the memory location where the affixed code was. Thus a function was born.

Languages like C++ are considered both high-level and low-level languages. C++ is a somewhat low-level language because the programmer can get close to the architecture; alternatively, it can be thought of as a high-level language (and is certainly not assembler.)

C++ enables software developers to aggregate thousands of instructions into single entities. Much of what surrounds us suffers from an ever-growing aggregation of technology. C++ is a powerful language that lets us have an affect on the level of abstraction we want to employ. In addition to using the keywords that comprise the language, C++ enables you to build complex entities, and functions act as a bridge between keywords and entities.

Functions are wonderful. One trick in designing good functions is creating a name that is a good descriptor for what the code does. Grouping is common place. We may do this because of our limited short-term memory. More importantly is that it is a skill you could not have gotten this far without. (After all, words are groups of letters.) Not only will we progress from here with syntactical examples, I will also demonstrate coding techniques, and throw in some hints that will help you decide what to put in your functions and how much.

Understanding Function Syntax

C++ is referred to as a strongly-typed language. This designation means that you must exercise some care and consistency in the declaration and definition of functions. The exact name—spelling and case—of a function matters. This section is geared towards showing the general syntax of a function, not all of the available bells and whistles. (You will have to read the entire chapter to get a handle on those.)

Before we begin let's come to agreement on some common ways to refer to functions. A *function declaration* refers to the function's interface. The interface is everything about the function except for the function body containing the code. The function declaration is a statement, including all of the parts of a function, terminated by a semicolon. A *function definition* includes the interface, attached to its function body. (I will point out the difference between a declaration and definition when I demonstrate the syntax.)

Saying C++ is a strongly-typed language refers then, in part, to the fact that the declaration must occur before the definition or first use (see the next section). Further, it means that the declaration must match the definition (the part that includes the declaration), and any use of the function must match, too.

The most general form of the syntax of a function is

```
return_type func_name( [arg_type arg1 [, arg_type arg2
➥[, arg_type arg3, ...]]] );
```

therefore

```
void Foo();
```

will be the declaration of a function that returns a void (nothing), named Foo, accepting no arguments. Using the [ ] above is a common notation that indicates a function can have zero or more arguments. I used the italicized font, which is also used commonly, to suggest that the words or phrases are not those actually used.

You can replace *return_type* with any of the native or user-defined types. The function can be *func_name*, but that is not a very good one. (See "Using Function Names" in this chapter for more examples.) The syntax of each argument is

```
type variable_name
```

If there is more than one argument, the list of arguments between the parentheses is comma-delimited. Here is an example of a function that takes three integer arguments a, b, and c:

```
void TakesThree( int a, int b, int c );
```

The ellipses used in the general syntax above is a convention that means etc., etc.

> **Note**
>
> Do not confuse the ellipses in the syntactical example of a function with the ellipses that Borland C++ uses to mean variadic arguments. Refer to "Using Argument Types" to learn more about variadic arguments.

The examples presented in this chapter by no means represent anything remotely close to the kinds of syntactical examples you may see. They do, however, represent a general syntax. So far, what you have seen—referring now to the sample declarations, *Foo* and *TakesThree*—were function declarations. Notice the terminating semicolon. The difference between these declarations and their definitions is the function bodies. Here are the same two functions as definitions:

```
void Foo()
{
    // some code here
}
void TakesThree( int a, int b, int c)
{
    // some more code
}
```

Note the differences. The definition requires no terminating semicolon and uses the left and right braces {} around the body of code. (These functions have comments where code would normally appear.)

Declaring Functions before Their First Use

C++ requires that you declare a function before it is first used in your program. This is different from C; C makes no such requirement. The "before first use" requirement can be met several ways. One way is to simply enter the function declaration at the top of the module file. When you declare a function at the return type, function name and argument types are required. You are not required to specify the variable names.

Applying this distinction, the TakesThree function can be declared like this:

```
void TakesThree( int, int, int );
```

However, I would suggest using the variable names because it may make your intended use of the function clearer. A second way that functions can be declared and included in any module that requires them is to declare them in a header (.h) file in the module with the #include directive. The preprocessor performs a text replacement when you compile and it is just as if you typed the declarations in yourself. (For a few helpful guidelines to consider when using #include, refer to chapter 4 "The Preprocessor.")

Tip

If you think the function will only be used in a single module you can declare it in that module. If you intend for the function to be used in many modules, place the function declaration in a header file; it will be easier to "declare" it again and will be less error-prone.

There are several reasons C++ requires function declarations prior to a function's first use. One such reason is that undeclared functions are a source of errors in C programs. Another such reason is that C++ supports function overloading, which—you will learn about in chapter 16, and—is facilitated by the name and function arguments.

I will be the first to admit and agree that hacking is a lot of fun and is sometimes beneficial in prototyping a variety of solutions quickly, but if you intend to use a particular function in a controlled manner, there should be little objection to stating what its interface is. If you are moving to C++ from a weakly-typed language, it won't take long to acquire the habit of prototyping your functions. A direct benefit of prototyping is that the compiler can check to ensure that you are using the function correctly, catching errors of this kind as early as possible.

From here we will pull functions apart so that you understand the various components inside and out. Understanding the variety of ways functions work will afford you the greatest potential for solving programming problems.

Using Return Types

The native data types are the most obvious candidates as return types. This means that void, char, int, long, float, and double are commonly used return types. A function return type is one way a function communicates information back to the caller. To be a return type means that the function will use the return keyword along with a variable of that type.

Consider a function defined to return a double:

```
double Pi( int precision )
{
   double pi;
   // Calculate pi to precision decimal places.
   // Thus if precision = 10 then pi would be calculated to
   // 10 decimal places. (See Numerical Recipes in C for an
   // implementation.)
   return  pi;
}
```

Note that the return statement is followed by a variable whose data type matches that of the return type. In addition, any user-defined types and some native types not mentioned, like `long double`, can be returned in this manner.

When a data type is used in this unadorned manner, it is referred to as a *return by value*. For the `Pi` function, the return result is what you would expect, the value that had been assigned to `Pi`. Much more complicated types, including structs and classes, can be returned by value, but there is often a cost in doing so.

Note

Return by value means that you are returning the value of an object. When the return type is a built-in type—which usually fits in one or two microprocessor registers—there is little overhead involved. A problem may arise when the return type is a user-defined type like a class or struct.

User-defined types may involve significant overhead to "build"; meaning that they may be comprised of one or more data types that might each require allocation or acquisition of resources and some initial value.

Why does this matter? Glad you asked. Returning by value implies that you are getting the value of the object but not *the* object. In fact what you are getting is a copy of the object. Because it is a copy, a new object must have been built, and this is where the cost is incurred. The cost is silent, but the penalty in performance may be steep.

I have heard some folks refer to programs in C++ being too slow. Properly implemented, C++ should be as fast as C—which produces some of the fastest programs—if not faster. I often wonder how many of these programs are producing silent copies in the manner we just mentioned.

Besides returning built-in or user-defined objects by value, you can adorn them with the reference operator (*) or the address of (&) operator. Read on to see the syntax of return types using these two operators.

Tip

This section is about functions and less about the effects of returning and passing objects by value or reference. The implications of passing objects by reference or by value is discussed in detail in chapter 17, "Special Constructors: Copy and Assignment."

Using the Reference Operator with Return Types

The reference operator (*), used with the return argument of a function, means that you are returning a pointer to an object. The declaration of functions with such return types is:

```
type * func_name( args_list );
```

The location of the reference operator is between the return type and the function name. The asterisk binds with the return type. This means that functions declared in this manner must return a pointer type or an address. Surprise! Here is an example:

```
char* DayOfWeek( unsigned int julianDate )
{
    static char * weekday[] = { "Sunday", "Monday", "Tuesday",
                       "Wednesday", "Thursday", "Friday", "Saturday" };
    return weekday[ julianDate % 7];
}
```

The DayOfWeek function accepts a julianDate—a total number of days since some reference date—and returns the day of the week as a pointer to a char. The weekday variable is read as an array of character pointers. So each weekday[i] is a char*, satisfying the return type of the function.

> **Tip**
>
> The array of char*s was declared static for a reason. Variables inside functions normally exist within the scope of the function. By declaring the array as a static array, the values are maintained between successive calls to the function.

The address of operator, which is denoted by the ampersand (&), can also be used. Given a function requiring a pointer to a data type

```
type * FunctionName( arglist )
{
    static type variable;
    // some code
    return &variable;
}
```

Returning the address of non-pointer of the same data type—declared static for the same reason (see previous tip)—satisfies the requirement of a reference operator because the value of pointers are addresses.

Using the reference operator in a return type is one way to return a value by reference, but the preferred way is to use the ampersand when you want to return by reference. Read the next section to see the syntax and for an explanation of why taking the address is preferred over returning pointers.

Using the Address Of Operator with Return Types

When you want to return an object by reference use the address of (&) operator. The operator is located in the same place as the reference operator, between the return type and the function name, but the effect is different.

Objects returned using the reference operator require a special syntax to access the value. If the object is a simple data type, like an integer, then you have to dereference the object to get the value.

```
int a = 5;
int * b = &a;              // b is an alias for a
cout << *b << endl;        // to print the value of b (note the use
                           // of the asterisk).
```

(For our demonstration, how b's value was established is irrelevant. It is the way we access the value that is what I wish to emphasize. The value could have just as easily been set by assigning it to the return result of a function.) We do not acquire the same problem if b were converted to a reference:

```
int a = 5;
int & b = &a;
cout << b << endl;         // prints the value of b which is equal to 5,
                           // not the address.
```

The rule for using the address of operator is not written in stone.

Many of the functions we use to manipulate char* (C-style strings that many programs still use) require a char* or const char*, so in at least one instance it is more convenient to use the reference operator token, but these kinds of situations notwithstanding, use the address of operator to return objects by reference.

Using Function Names

The strongly-typed designation plays a role in many ways. A significant role, which differs from other popular languages like Visual Basic, Delphi, and COBOL, is that C++ is case-sensitive. Therefore

```
void Foo();
void FOO();
```

and

```
void foo();
```

all refer to different functions. This is only an obstacle when programmers code sloppily. Programming suffers irrefutably from lazy, sloppy coding habits, or perhaps it is just that no one agrees on a particular style.

Develop a consistent convention for naming your functions; use it all of the time, and then you will no longer even notice that C++ is case-sensitive (at least as far as your function names go). I consistently use namecase function names. Namecasing means that each first-letter of each word of the function name is uppercase. Therefore, a single word function will be named as

```
int Size();
```

I name the sizeof operator, which looks like a function

```
size_t SizeOf();
```

Notice that S in "Size" and O in "Of" are in capital letters. That is what namecasing refers to. Another convention I employ is that I do not use non-standard abbreviations in function names. The first letter of each word being capitalized makes the function name easier to read, and avoiding non-standardized abbreviations eliminates the need for guessing. (Remember `DayOfWeek`: please don't ask me to read code where such functions appear as `'dyofwk`; or some other such nonsense.)

Consistency pays off in the long run. You do not have to use my convention, but establish one and stick to it within your programming community. My suggestions are admittedly highly opinionated and only that, suggestions. Refer to chapter 5, "Commenting and Naming Conventions" for alternatives.

Using Argument Types

Thus far, we have pieced together the return types and function names. We have yet to talk about argument types before having covered the general aspects of function declarations. This section covers some of the things we can do to function arguments. Following this section we will look at function specifiers and several examples of functions.

The same rules that apply to return types as presented so far, apply to function arguments. The notable differences between the syntax for return types and arguments types is that there is always only one return type, but there may be zero, one, or many arguments. Additionally, you may still use the variadic argument type (...), although there are few reasons for doing so.

Argument Types and Declarations

Any data type, whether a built-in type or user-type may be used as an argument type. As a reminder, the syntax of each argument, except for variads, is

```
data_type variable_name
```

An example might be:

```
blood howMuch
```

Function arguments, often referred to as parameters, are located between the left and right parentheses after the function name. Thus, if `blood` is the type of an argument to the function `Draculas`, returning a data-type count, the function declaration will be

```
count Draculas(blood);          // a little too cute!
```

because the declaration does not require the variable name. Just like return types, arguments can include either the reference or the address of operators. The reasons for doing so are similar to the reasons for using these qualifiers with return types. (We'll get to that in a moment.)

For each argument after the first, the variable name is followed by a comma and a repetitive syntax for each successive argument. Refer to the function `TakesThree` for an example. More importantly is what it means when you pass arguments by value or by reference.

Passing Parameters by Value or Reference

It is impossible to present every scenario for passing arguments to a function a certain way. What follows is a reason for passing arguments by reference as opposed to by value. (There are others that have to do with the "cost" of instantiating arguments; an explanation for which can be found in chapter 17, "Constructors: Copy and Assignment.")

One obvious way for a function to return a value is to use the value as the return argument. However, what if a function needs to modify more than one variable's value? One way is to derive a simple data type, like a `struct`, and return the modified struct. For example,

```
struct TWO{
      int a, b;
} two;
TWO ModifyTwo( struct TWO t )
{
      t.a = 5;
      t.b = 6;
      return t;
}
```

This approach works. A copy of TWO is modified and returned by the function `ModifyTwo`. Sometimes this kind of simple aggregation might be what you want. However, you do not want to be confined to fabricating structures all of the time just to modify more than one value. Besides, what if you want to modify the actual object passed in and not a copy.

Where you want to modify more than one value and you want to modify the actual value passed in, pass the argument by reference. (We will use the ampersand mode of pass-by-reference for the reasons previously stated.) Supposing I preferred to modify two objects—I will use integers for simplicity—passed as arguments to a function, I can define the function like this:

```
void ModifyTwo( int & a, int & b )
{
      a = 5;
      b = 6;
}
void main()
{
      int j = 1;
      int k = 2;
      ModifyTwo( j, k);
      cout << j << " " << k;        // writes 5 and 6
}
```

If the `ModifyTwo` accepts arguments by value, the main function will have output 1 and 2, respectively because copies of a and b would have been modified instead.

Variadic Arguments

Variadic arguments were used historically in functions like printf and scanf. The ellipse used in place of a parameter indicates that the number and type of arguments are not known until runtime. Flexibility of this sort comes at a cost because the arguments must be determined by some conditional statements, which determine the types of arguments and then the actual values are culled by direct stack manipulation. (Chapter 6, "Native Data Types and Operators" explains the concept in detail using some of the functions from stdio.h.)

Variadic arguments may still play a limited role in some specialized programs that use the interrupt keyword to create interrupt service routines (ISRs). And, you may find some specialized uses, too. The original intent was to allow a single function to work with many argument types. For example, users only had to learn printf to be able to print the values of native data types. It is arguably demonstrable that reducing the number of functions programmers had to learn was desirable. The reason I suggest that variadics are much less beneficial in general circumstances is because you can overload functions with C++ (see chapter 15, "Function Overloading").

> **Note**
>
> Interrupt functions are loaded by the ROM BIOS chips, drivers like Io.sys and Msdos.sys, and the Windows operating system. They are system functions that are called when hardware or software events occur. An example of an event is a keypress. When you press a key, an interrupt is generated, so the operating system can temporarily suspend what it is doing and handle the keypress (in our example).
>
> Terms commonly related to this subject are ISR, event handler, interrupt handler, callbacks, and functors. Functors represent the bridge between a program and these other things. I will discuss functors at the end of this chapter.

Just so you know it when you see it, a variadic argument is used in printf. Here is the function declaration:

```
int printf( const char *, ... );
```

When used with interrupt handlers the keyword interrupt is used and the variadic argument implies that a variable number of registers are used with different interrupt functions. Here is an example of an interrupt function:

```
void interrupt new_int4A(...);     // The DOS Alarm clock interrupt is 0x4A
```

Writing your own interrupt service routines is usually employed for specialized applications and Windows 95 may not take too kindly to you writing just any old interrupt handler. I wanted you to recognize variadic arguments and the context within which they may be used.

Default Values

There are many aspects of C++ that make it a flexible and elegant language. Default values for arguments is one of those things. In addition to being able to overload functions (described in chapter 15, "Function Overloading"), you can also choose between providing default arguments. First, I will show you what a default argument looks like, then I will provide you with fodder for using it.

Providing a default argument is accomplished by assigning a value to the variable parameter. It looks like this:

```
void Foo( int a = 5);
```

Now Foo can be called with an integer

```
Foo(10);            // a will be 10
```

or without

```
Foo();                      // a will use the default argument 5
```

which means a will be 5. Both function calls refer to the same function; in the first example, we are not using the default value for a and in the second example we are. If you can decide upon an appropriate value for parameters, it may make sense to do so.

Arguments can only have default values from right to left. This means that an argument to the left of another argument cannot have a default value unless *all* of those to the right have them, too. Here are some examples:

```
int Function1( int a, char * p = 0);                    // OK
void Function2( float pi = 3.1459, int precision = 4);  // OK too!
Complex Make( double r = 0, double i );                 // ERROR
```

The reasons for the order of the arguments is to avoid the ludicrous

```
Complex c = Make( /* no argument */, -1.0 );            // ERROR
```

which would result in comma counting. Having to place commas with no arguments is error-prone and looks bad.

Understanding that I have neither explained function overloading nor demonstrated it, I will proffer a suggestion for determining when you should consider default arguments as opposed to overloaded functions.

If the difference between what you might consider two disparate functions is the value of a candidate parameter, then use a default value. For example, Foo( ) is a good candidate because an integer was needed and 5 was a good default value.

If the difference between two similar functions is the type of the data, then you will probably best benefit from function overloading. In a nutshell, the deciding factor is the arguments:

- Use default values when the value of the argument is different.
- Use function overloading when the type of the argument is different.

The benefit is that you will reduce the number of function names and number of similar functions. These ease the burden of maintaining (synchronizing changes), debugging, and coping with inordinately large programs.

Function Specifiers

We have covered the general aspects of functions. Now we are moving into the province of keyword specifiers that create additional benefits to our C++ programs. Many of these are covered in general in chapter 9, "Data Quantifiers and Qualifiers." Here they are taken and applied in the context of functions specifically. I will begin with the `inline` keyword that affords all of the benefits of full-fledged functions and some of the benefits of macros.

Inline Functions

The `inline` keyword tells the compiler to take the code of a function and place at the location where a function call would normally go. The word appears before the rest of the function, if used:

```
inline return_type func_name( args_list );
```

This is kind of what the preprocessor does with macros, but inline functions allow you to express the types of the arguments, so the compiler can check for errors.

Using the `inline` keyword is a hint to the compiler. The compiler—because the compiler writers probably know more about how code is built into machine readable form than you and I—can choose to ignore the suggestion.

A function call must push the arguments on the stack, call the function, the function pulls the arguments from the stack, the function processes the code, and then returns. Using the `inline` specifier circumvents this activity, but if a function is too large it can actually cause code-bloat. The reason for this is that the code is placed where each function call occurs. I suggest that you use the `inline` keyword for small functions.

An example borrowed from chapter 4, "The Preprocessor" inlines the `Swap` macro. Applying the `Swap` algorithm to integers, here is a complete `inline` function:

```
// Uses & operator so the effect of swapping a and b is recorded outside of
// the function
void Swap( int & a, int & b )
{ int t = a; a = b; b = t;  }
```

This is about the relative length and complexity that I would try to maintain with inline functions. Table 11.1 provides a comparison between C-style macros, regular, and inline functions.

Table 11.1 Comparing C Macros, C++ Functions, and C++ Inline Functions	
Applies To	**Feature**
Macro, Inline Function	Code is placed where name occurs.
Macro, Inline Function	No function call indirection.
Inline Function, Function	Arguments are type-checked.
Macro, Inline Function	Body of code may appear multiple times.
Inline Function, Function	Can be overloaded.
Inline Function, Function	Can have default arguments.

Table 11.1 compares macros, functions, and inline functions. Note that each place a macro appears, so does the inline function. Inline functions were intended as replacements of C-style macros.

Use inline functions where you may have considered using a macro; otherwise, use a regular function. Read on for further keywords that play a role in designing functions.

Static Member Functions

When teaching C++ to programmers, I am often asked for a linear presentation, like learning mathematics. When we learn math beginning in grammar school, we are first presented with numbers, then counting, followed by simple arithmetic and so on. The problem is that C++ cannot be so neatly packaged in a linear format. Many aspects of the language depend on context.

The reference to member function pertains to classes. It is often confusing to talk about one aspect prior to explaining a related topic. I haven't mentioned classes much yet because functions are an important part of classes. Unfortunately, static member functions are important to the discussion of functions. So the quandary is do I talk about functions without static functions, then proceed to explain classes, and then come back to functions. If I did, things would be scattered all over the place:

functions=>classes=>functions.

Instead I will tell you that not everything is simple, C++ has contextually critical features (things have different meanings in different contexts), and this is what people mean when they say that C++ is a complex language. Life is like that; many things in life depend on the context.

Earlier, I mentioned that static variables maintained their value beyond the scope of the functions that they were defined in. For variables to exist beyond the scope of a function, they must exist outside of the function and not on the stack. So, implicitly a static variable exists outside of the scope it is defined in. In this regard, static variables and static member functions are similar.

However, if the meaning of static variables is that they maintain their values outside of the function, then the meaning of static member functions is one of unity. Here is a static member function in a struct.

```
1: // static.cpp - Demonstrates static member (of struct) function.
2: #include <iostream.h>
3: #include <string.h>
4: struct HAS_STATIC
5: {
6:    static void ObjectAddress(); // static member function declaration
7:    char name[15];
8: };
9: void HAS_STATIC::ObjectAddress()
10: {                                    // Function is intentionally null
11: }
12: void main()
13: {
14:    struct HAS_STATIC a;
15:    strcpy( a.name, "a");
16:    struct HAS_STATIC b;
17:    strcpy( b.name, "b" );
18:    cout << "Object " << a.name << "'s address: " << &a << endl
19:          << "Address of static member function: " << a.ObjectAddress << endl;
20:    cout << "Object " << b.name << "'s address: " << &b << endl
21:          << "Address of static member function: " << b.ObjectAddress << endl;
22: }
```

> **Tip**
>
> There are many similarities between structs and classes in C++. While C++ classes are the pre-ferred idiom, structs were included in C++ and do allow users to define member functions, constructors, and destructors. Read chapter 14, "Basic Class Concepts," to learn the complete set of differences between classes and structs.

Line 6 contains the static member function declaration. (A member function is a member of a group: struct or class.) The output from the main function clearly shows that the address of two objects is different, but the address of the static member is the same. So the meaning of static in the context of a struct or class is one of unity, meaning there is one, and only one, function shared among all objects of that type.

> **Tip**
>
> Using static member functions provides a unique way to logically connect objects of the same class. The technique is used in advanced topics pertaining to reference counting and a self-contained linked list presented in Bruce Eckel's C++ *Inside and Out* (McGraw-Hill).

A guideline for using static function is when the function operates on members of the class regardless of the state of type of each individual object. For example, a Swap function would still swap two elements regardless of their value.

II

Programming in C++

> **Note**
>
> C++ requires discipline other languages don't require. Consider a function like Swap. It can be an inline function. You can also implement Swap as a template function (see chapter 19, "Using Template Classes"). In addition, Swap can be a global function or a member function.
>
> I have found that I often implement things one way and later discover a more elegant method. In this way, C++ invites an iterative approach to software development; unfortunately this is contrary to what folks in management consider a preemptive requirement, which is "get it done!"

extern Keyword

The extern keyword applied to a function means that the function is defined somewhere else. This "somewhere else" can appear later in the module or in another module. Using extern in this

```
extern void Foo();        // Foo is defined elsewhere, either later or in
                          // another file
```

manner is somewhat outmoded. Its use in this context is to solve the requirement of declaring a function before it is used in a module. The convention now is to write the function declaration in a header file and use #include in the header file at the top of each module, thus solving the declaration requirement.

The current employment of extern is to combine it with "C" string to keep the compiler from mangling the function name. (Chapter 15, "Function Overloading," describes how mangling is employed to enable overloading.) C++ is a language used to implement tools for other languages, like Visual Basic, Delphi, and write Dynamic Link Libraries (DLLs). Since the developer is only going to (usually) know the name he entered and not the mangled name, it is this name that is presented to users of the tools.

Suppose you were to implement a Visual Basic component in C++ named

```
PasswordDialog
```

If C++ mangled the name (which it does by default), the user of the code won't be able to call the function without using the mangled name. Applying the specifier

```
extern "C" int PasswordDialog( some_msg );
```

the function name will not be mangled.

The extern "C" specifier can be applied to groups of functions by wrapping all of the functions not to be mangled in brackets:

```
extern "C" {
type func_name1( arglist );
type func_name2( arglist );
// etc
}
```

The reasons why a special specifier has to be applied to functions will be more apparent after a discussion of classes and overloading.

Using *cdecl* with Functions

The Borland IDE Help refers to cdecl as a modifier. The cdecl modifier is used to declare a variable with the C-style naming conventions. C-style names are case-sensitive and have an underscore appended. You will see this used in many of the header files in the \Bc5\Include directory for backwards compatibility with Borland's C compilers.

When a function is called, the stack address is used to store the arguments. (We say "pushed on the stack.") Using the modifier affects the order that these arguments are pushed (or copied into the stack address space). C functions push the last argument first.

The whole story is most important to cross-language programmers. For example Visual Basic pushes the first argument first, so a cross-language programmer has to address these kinds of considerations.

Note

If you want to use functions written in C or C++ contained in drivers, like the Windows API (Kernel.exe, User.exe, or Gdi.exe), simply match the form of the function declaration. Thus if the function uses cdecl in C, use it in Visual Basic or Delphi.

An alternative exists. The Pascal modifier is sometimes also applied. The Pascal modifier tells the compiler to push the arguments first argument first, which is how Visual Basic and Delphi do it.

I mentioned these things, not because I expect you to start programming cross-language tools, rather, when you see declarations in header files like

```
void _Cdecl abort(void);    // A C-style function which can be used with C++
```

you will realize that this function is akin to

```
void abort();                    // Terminates an application
```

and not be afraid to use it. The abort function can be used by including process.h.

Recursive Functions

A one-megabyte stack space is a recursive function's dream. A recursive function in case you don't know is a function that calls itself as part of the solution. When a function is called, information goes on the stack. After the function returns, the stack is restored.

Recursive functions often require less code to implement than non-recursive functions. But, historically recursive functions have been known to blow the stack because they call themselves many—maybe hundreds or thousands of times—before returning a single time.

Note

"Blow the stack" means that more space than has been allocated was required by the system stack. Think of the stack as an order pile of information. By taking items of the stack in reverse order, the program can essentially backtrack.

The CPU stack is self-managed. While the stack space is assigned a physical memory location, it manages and uses memory just like a stack algorithm does for a program.

Borland C++ 5 offers programmers up to a one-megabyte stack space, where previously only 64 kilobytes (K) was available. This suggests that much more deeply nested recursive functions can be used without blowing the stack.

Note

A factorial is the multiplicative value of all of the digits to a number n. In mathematics, it is often written with the exclamation mark (!). Thus 5! (read 5 factorial) is calculated by multiplying 1 * 2 * 3 * 4 * 5 resulting in 120.

Here is an example of a simple recursive function that calculates n-factorials

```
1: void Factorial( unsigned long n )
2: {
3: return n > 2 ? n * Factorial( n - 1 ) : n;
4: }
```

The function uses the ternary operator ?: read just like an

```
if( condition )
   statement;
else
   statement;
```

if...else clause. To the left of the ? is the if-conditional; between the ? and the : (colon) is the result of the statement if the conditional evaluates to true, and between the : and the ; (semicolon) is the returned value if the statement is true.

Therefore the code in line 3 is read

```
if n is greater than 2
   return n times Factorial( n - 1 )              // here is the recursive
part
else
   return n;
```

The function unwinds completely when n is less than or equal to 2. For n = 5 the function is called 4 times before the stack begins to unwind. You can imagine if *n* were a large number how many times this function would be called before unwinding.

> **Caution**
>
> This function only works to about 12!. 13! is about 6 billion and an unsigned long is only good for about 4+ billion. Unfortunately, while the stack space might accommodate us, the long integer is limited in this case. (Programmers can cause errors in a myriad of ways, can't we?)

There are goods that focus on advanced algorithms and cover such esoteric topics as *recursion removal*. Usually recursion removal involves a loop of some sort in place of the recursive function call. I prefer to solve the problem recursively and later remove the recursion once the program works correctly.

As you can see in at least this example, the factorial solution is pretty short. I can remove the recursion in this instance with a `for` loop.

```
unsigned long Factorial( unsigned long n )
{
    assert( n <= 12 );                // 13! ≈ 6 x 10¹² too big!
    unsigned long result = 1;
    for( ; n > 2; n-- )
            result *= n;
    return result;
}
```

The stack plays no role in this calculation, and it is probably quite a bit quicker. (For fun, use a `Timer` object to accumulate some empirical data and see which is really faster. The result will probably be in the micro-seconds.)

Understanding Overloading

This section does not explain function overloading in detail. It is an involved enough subject to warrant its own chapter. In an effort to reduce the number of names, and thereby ease a programmer's burden of remembering those names, the variadic argument was developed. The functions that use variadic arguments have an added run-time expense.

Creating a lot of functions and devising several names for functions that are semantically similar is tedious and time-consuming. Anything tedious and time-consuming becomes a candidate for automation, so why should the tools automators use be any different?

What you will learn in chapters 15, "Function Overloading," and 16, "Operator Overloading," is that our relatively simple mechanism was incorporated into the C++ language to provide direct support for overloading based on a combination of the name and argument types. The result is that you do not have to use variadic arguments; you do not have to remember disparate names contrived simply for the purpose of distinguishing functions by data type. (Read chapter 15 to learn how to implement this powerful aspect of C++.)

II

Programming in C++

Functors

Functors are another tool that you should have in your box. Someone suggested that functors are too advanced, but I think you will probably like them. Even if you never find a reason to use functors, you should know what they are.

Functors are commonly used to implement Windows 95 and Windows programs. In Windows they are used to establish callbacks. A callback works by passing a function a pointer to another function (functor), then that function can use the callback function when it deems it appropriate. Functors are also used to create dynamic menuing systems in the same way. Interrupt service routines are functors; an interrupt handler is set by placing the address of the function in the interrupt vector table. Interrupt handlers and functors are what make TSR (Terminate and Stay Resident) programs, like Sidekick, work.

Terms

It is not necessary to understand all of these terms, but I will provide a brief explanation of some of them. The skill for using them can be acquired from books; there are many on these subjects.

Interrupt—Your computer's microprocessor parses and executes machine language (which all programs are when they are compiled). At the end of each cycle, it checks to see if the Interrupt flag in the flags register has been set—meaning something that needs immediate attention has occurred—during an instruction cycle. If it has, it determines the interrupt number and uses that number as an index into the interrupt vector table located at memory address 0:0 to 0:400 (hexadecimal). At that index is the address of the code loaded by the ROM BIOS or other drivers like Io.sys or Msdos.sys, which performs the necessary function.

Interrupt vector table—Array of functors loaded by hardware and software drivers that make up your operating system.

interrupt handler—A function that contains the code necessary for processing interrupts.

Terminate and Stay Resident—TSRs are programs that remain in memory after they have appeared to exit. A functor is used to create interrupt handlers (usually to trap hotkeys) that enable these programs to pop up while other programs are running. That's why they are referred to as pop-ups.

All of this functionality was obtained via functors. I am not suggesting that you will be able to write them after reading this section, but you should have a pretty good idea of what they are when we are finished.

What Does a Functor Look Like

A functor looks a lot like a function that returns a pointer to a variable. But, in almost every other regard they look like normal functions. They can have a variety of return types, any name really, and you can specify the same diverse variety of parameters.

The difference is that the reference operator (*) used with functors binds with the function name.

```
char * Function();
```

Function() appears to return a char*. If this is a functor, then the reference operator will bind with the function name, but the compiler will bind the reference operator with char. Therefore you have to use the parentheses to tell the compiler that the reference operator binds with the function name.

```
char (*Function)();
```

That's what gives a functor its weird appearance. And, if you want the functor to return a char*, include the additional asterisk for the char data type. Thus a functor that returns a char* named Function looks like this:

```
char* (*Function)();
```

Aside from the (*) and parentheses around the function name, everything else is like any other function. The result, however, is that you may treat the function sort of like both a variable and a function. By this I mean that you can assign functors like variables, and you can use functions just like other functions. Read on and I will show you how to employ them and an application of functors.

Employing Functors

There is no getting around functors. Whether you implement them or not, they will exist in relationship to your programs and Windows. C++ is a powerful language. You have already seen how to use default arguments; in coming chapters you will learn how to overload functions and operators. Then you will learn how to implement *template* functions, which allow you to write a single function and vary the data type. Right now I am going to demonstrate how to write a single algorithm and vary the entire activity that is performed from that single function.

Listing 11.1 is fairly small, as to be easy to follow and demonstrate the topic. The program uses the *findfirst* and *findnext* functions paired to travel a directory. We will use a functor to enable the user to determine what the code does with each function. Keep in mind as you read the function that the code could be changed to traverse an entire disk, span multiple disks, and allow several functions to be chosen at runtime.

Listing 11.1 Gendir.cpp—Demonstrates a Functor

```
1: // GENDIR.CPP - This program uses a functor to perform a variety of
   // operations on files in a directory.
2: #include <iostream.h>
3: #include <dos.h>
4: #include <dir.h>
5: // Refer to chapter 14 for a reusable way to implement a scan of all files
   // in a directory.
6: // Traversal algorithm that can be reused, simply by passing a different
   // functor
```

(continues)

Listing 11.1   Continued

```
 7: void TraverseDirectory( const char* path, void (*Functor)( struct ffblk&
    ➥ffblk))
 8: {
 9:   struct ffblk ffblk;
10:   int done;
11:   done = findfirst( path, &ffblk, 0 );
12:   while( !done )
13:   {
14:           Functor( ffblk );        // Here we can vary the operation
                                       // performed on each file.
15:           done = findnext( &ffblk );
16:   }
17: }
18: // This function outputs a formatted directory listing of the file names.
19: void ListFiles( struct ffblk & ffblk )
20: {
21:   cout << ffblk.ff_name << endl;
22: }
23: unsigned long fileSum = 0;
24: // This function totals the file sizes.
25: void SumAllFiles( struct ffblk & ffblk )
26: {
27:   fileSum += ffblk.ff_fsize;
28: }
29: void main()
30: {
31:   TraverseDirectory( "C:\\*.*", ListFiles );
32:   cout << "The total disk space used by C:\\*.* is: " ;
33:   TraverseDirectory( "C:\\*.*", SumAllFiles );
34:   cout << fileSum << endl;
35: }
```

Line 7 contains the function interface for the function that traverses the directory specified by the "path" argument. The function takes a functor (a pointer to a function) with the following declaration:

```
void FunctionName( struct ffblk & ffblk );
```

So any function of that form will do. (I wrote two of them for you.) The function TraverseDirectory checks each file matching the filemask in the path argument.

Line 14 calls the function pointed to by the Functor argument, passing the correct argument as it passes through each iteration of the while loop.

Lines 19 and 25 contain the function interface for the two functions I created to demonstrate functors. The first function simply writes the filenames found matching the mask to the output device, and the second function sums the total disk space consumed by these files.

Lines 31 and 33 show you how to pass the functor arguments. When you pass the argument it is used like any other variable argument, requiring no special syntax.

The output from this program is the list of files on the root directory of the C drive and the total space used by those files. The important thing to note is that I never had to modify the traversal part of the program. With some modifications, like adding a header file, this code can be used over and over in any other program.

> **Tip**
>
> There are several ways to enhance this program. One way is to overload the function to accept different functors (see chapter 15, "Function Overloading"). A second and even better way is to make the function a template function. In this way, you can specify the type of functor as the template argument (see chapter 19, "Using Template Classes").

Simplifying Complex Types

Chapter 9, "Data Quantifiers and Qualifiers," introduces the keyword `typedef`. The `typedef` keyword can be used to introduce an alias that enables you to simplify your code by replacing complex statements with a simpler looking alias; the compiler makes the substitution. Functors are one place where this is beneficial. I have seen code that is too difficult for the parser to decipher and, even worse, too difficult for other programmers to decipher.

You can simplify a functor parameter type by using `typedef`. The normal appearance of a `typedef` is

```
typedef old_type alias_name
```

For example

```
typedef char far * PChar;
```

defines an alias for `far` character pointers. When applied to a functor, you might think the same order applies; it doesn't. I originally assumed that an alias for our functor in the preceding example would be written

```
typedef void (*)(struct ffblk &) Functor;  // ERROR: This is an incorrect
                                            // functor typedef
```

where functor is the alias. This follows the same rhythm I demonstrated earlier typedef/old type/alias, but when applied to the functor syntax, the `typedef` is followed by the functor declaration as if it were any function declaration. Thus the correct `typedef` for Functor is:

```
typedef void (*Functor)(struct ffblk&);    // CORRECT: Functor is still the
                                           // alias
```

Applied to our `TraverseDirectory` function definition (and declaration) the code will now look like this:

```
typedef void (*Functor)(struct ffblk& );
void TraverseDirectory( const char* path, Functor ftor)
```

The variable ftor is now the action token used just like a function. The result here is that the appearance of the function interface has been simplified. Functors are very powerful but take some getting used to. They are worth learning.

Adding Debug Code as You Go

The mistake I found myself making in the past was applying debug code after I found an error. Now I take the HMO approach: preventive medicine. (Please feel free to take my analogy with a grain of non-fat, low cholesterol, salt-substitute.)

If you add debugging code to your code as you go, you will find that the testing phase is shorter and quicker. The reason is that the debug code will have eked out the mistakes of your program.

How many of you suffer from analysis/design/coding/testing/debugging/maintenance programming cycles? Programs now are large and complex. A single, monolithic debug and test phase is more than likely going to allow a lot of errors to get by simply because you will "forget" to test some pieces or assume they are correct.

I apply a scaffolding approach. Here is what I mean. I add my debugging and testing code as I program. Prior to adding a sub-program to my main program, I incorporate a scaffold—*a program for the purpose of testing just the new code*—and test the new sub-program. There are several benefits in doing so. The first such benefit is that if I am unable to simply test the code in this manner, then the design of the sub-program is more than likely incomplete or has too many external dependencies. The second benefit is that I have reduced the likelihood of introducing new bugs into the main program.

Later when I am ready to test the whole program together, I usually have a more reliable program to begin with and I don't have to spend hours adding test code to an entire program.

Added benefits come during maintenance. Suppose another programmer has to fix a bug or extend the existing program. The scaffold tells that programmer that indeed the code was tested. The scaffold also provides the enhancer code with which the sub-program can be tested, so they do not have to produce a unique set of new test code. in addition, the scaffold provides an example of how the code is supposed to be used.

These ideas were borrowed from experience and Dave Thielen's *No Bugs!* published by Addison-Wesley. There is no fool-proof approach to debugging and maintaining, but a concerted effort with applied guidelines makes a big difference. What follows are suggestions that will get you started.

Scaffolding Modules

Scaffolding each module simply means, if possible, add a simple main function and compile the module as a separate program. Applying the technique is easy enough.

Add a preprocessor directive around the main function and the code will be "dumped" by the preprocessor when the directive is undefined.

Consider a function that performs some task. In the .cpp file containing the function definitions add something like this:

```
#ifdef TASKNAME_SCAFFOLD
// where task name is word indicating the functionality
// include headers need for the scaffold only here!
void main()
{
// test the function, class or whatever
}
#endif
```

Create a new project in the IDE, define the scaffold name, and test the code. When the module is included in the main program, simply do not define the scaffold name.

Assert Invariants

Every time you define a new function, assert those things that are invariants. To be invariant means that you assume that these things must not vary each time the function is used. Invariants can be almost anything. You can test loops, pointers, parameters, or whatever. If your function depends on something for it to work correctly, assert it.

The `assert` macro defined in assert.h is provided to assist you in performing invariant testing. The macro assert requires a Boolean or integral evaluable argument: anything that can be tested for a true or false condition. True is a non-zero value; false is a zero value.

Suppose you have a function that copies a string

```
void CopyString( char * dst, const char * src )
{
   // The program will terminate if the string is null
   assert( src == 0 );
   dst = strdup( src );    // Uses malloc must use free to deallocate
}
```

The CopyString function fails if the source string points to 0. That is what the assertion macro does. If the test evaluates to false, then the macro call prints a message indicating the line, module, and terse message assertion failed then calls abort.

Assertions should not be left in with distributable code. Rather it is to be turned on for testing and off for shipping. You never have to remove the assertions, all that is required is to place the preprocessor statement at the top of and before the line that includes assert.h:

```
#define NDEBUG
```

> **Tip**
>
> Debug code should be read-only and should never replace normal error checking. Read-only code is code that does not modify the flow of program control. If the debug code modified the flow of control, then your program might exhibit odd behavior dependent on whether the debug code was included or not.
>
> Normal runtime error checking should be included as well as debugging code, otherwise your users will be unprotected when the debug code is turned off. A lot of runtime error-checking consists of code that tests for valid data, range values or the like. Modern error-checking also consists of *exception handling* (refer to chapter 22, "Exception Handling").

The most important thing is to add the error code while you are writing your functions. At this point in development you should have an awareness of both the functions intended use and expected results. These are all testable.

Why C++ Functions Require Fewer Arguments

This chapter is not just about the number of arguments a function requires. C++ is an object-oriented programming language. In chapter 15, "Function Overloading," you will see that, in part, this means that data and functions are bound together in classes.

Each class has a scope of its own. Data and functions defined in a class have class scope, which means the functions can access the data without having to pass them as arguments. It's a lot like functions and global data. A function can access global data without accepting it as an argument. The difference is that class data is not global, but are accessible to member functions as if they were. Thus if the data is accessible, there is no need to pass them, resulting in fewer arguments.

I have also found that my functions are generally smaller. There may be reasons for this, but smaller functions are generally easier to test. There may be several explanations (I hope one is that I am getting better), but one of them has to be that designing classes tends to limit your focus to smaller pieces. Additionally, you may find that begin to match a functions definition more closely to its stated purpose, as opposed to trying to solve every problem with one function. Consider a function named `OpenFile`. Should the functionality for checking for the existence of the file be inside the function, outside or both? While highly subjective, my answer is "both."

Here are some possible declarations followed by an algorithm using the functions:

```
bool FileExists( char * fname );    // Return true if file exists, otherwise
                                    // false
int OpenFile( char * fname );       // Return handle to file
if (FileExists( fname ) ) then
   OpenFile( fname );
```

With this solution I can add an assertion inside the function, during development to assert the existence of the file. When I ship the code, the `OpenFile` function attempts to open the file only, making the function smaller than if it contained the check, too.

A second reason functions shrink is that more of the work occurs inside of the object. This includes initialization code and the use of overloaded operators replace long-name operations with simple token equivalents (see chapter 16, "Operator Overloading").

You will need to acquire the skills necessary for these things to occur, but a good application of C++ idioms reaps many rewards.

From Here...

Functions are probably one of the oldest building blocks that programmers have. C++ affords you with a large number and variety of ways to solve problems. This chapter demonstrates some of those techniques and directs you towards resources in this book to learn others. There may be an old adage that applies and will probably make your managers happy: "Solve the problem and worry about size, speed, and elegance later."

If you love programming, you'll love Borland's C++. The implementation is complete and functions are one of the best parts. Read the following chapters to learn more about topics related to functions:

- Chapter 5, "Commenting and Naming Conventions," discusses the use of comments and naming conventions, which make your source code more readable and understandable.

- Chapter 9, "Data Quantifiers and Qualifiers," compares how problems can be solved using code as opposed to better data modeling.

- Chapter 10, "Writing Expressions," discusses the use of statements in your code.

- Chapter 15, "Function Overloading" covers function overloading, which provides the basis for understanding other aspects of the C++ programming language.

- Chapter 19, "Using Template Classes," shows you how to write a function or class regardless of the data type and how to use it for each data type you can think of.

II

Programming in C++

CHAPTER 12

Using the Borland C++ Library Functions

The C++ language is a descendant of the C programming language and shares its heritage of portability. A C++ compiler has been written for nearly every hardware platform in production. The designers of C facilitated this platform independence by omitting certain language features from the language specification. If a language feature could not be implemented in a generic way on all platforms, the capability was added as a function call rather than as language syntax. This greatly enhanced the popularity of C because it made the compiler itself quite portable by allowing the compiler programmer to provide machine specific code in a set of clearly defined function calls. Every C programmer was intimately familiar with the use of these calls.

The advanced features of C++, like function overloading, reduce, but do not eliminate, the frequency of library calls in a typical program. The Win32 API and the OWL class libraries also contribute much of the traditional C library functionality to C++. All of the graphics calls are now handled with API and library calls.

At times, these functions need to be invoked. At times, it may be inconvenient to invoke the `iostream` class to do I/O, especially when converting from C to C++. It may also be wise to avoid certain Windows-specific code if porting to UNIX is anticipated.

This chapter explores some of the more common functions that you may need to write your applications. It is not a complete reference but rather an example of how these functions are included in C++ programs.

In this chapter, you learn about

- File attributes
- File modes for opening, reading, and writing
- Random-access and sequential-access file input and output
- Various string manipulation functions
- How to query and set the system date and time
- How to program a variable length argument list

Working with Disk File Input/Output

The use of files for the storage of information, parameters, system information, modem initialization strings, and so on, is a prerequisite for any program written today. Consider the compiler that you have loaded on your system. There are several executables just for the compiling, linking, and resource compiling. If you use the Integrated Development Environment (IDE), you are using another set of programs that calls the compilers and linkers. The source code you write is saved to a file; your preferences for colors when in Windows 3.1, Windows 95, or Windows NT is saved in .ini files.

Without the ability to store and retrieve data to a permanent medium, computers are little more than large, expensive calculators.

Using File Attributes

All files on both FAT and NTFS share certain attributes, and these are the ones that this chapter covers. The common attributes are Archive, Read-Only, System, Hidden, and Normal. While disks, directories, and sub-directories are not files, both FAT and NTFS treat them as such for writing, deleting, and updating purposes. The attributes specific to directories or disks are Volume ID and Directory.

Archive Attribute. The archive attribute is set for a file when that file has been backed-up or archived. This attribute is set by the DOS BACKUP command or by other backup programs. When a change is made to a file with the Archive attribute set, the bit that represents the Archive attribute is reset. Archived files can be read from or written to.

This attribute is useful when performing an incremental backup. If you have 200 files on a drive and have only made changes to three files, an incremental backup sees that only three files do not have the Archive attribute set and only backs up those three files, setting their Attribute bit as it backed up each file.

Read-Only Attribute. If the Read-Only attribute is set on a file, any attempts to write to that file or copy another file by the same name onto the file fail. This attribute is used to protect files from accidental erasure.

If you have a batch file that you use for compiling that contains all your environment variables, include directories, and so on, for a particular compiler, you may want to mark this file as Read-Only to prevent someone from inadvertently making changes to the file. This is also useful for reminding yourself when you try to make a change to a file: that you had protected it for a reason and that maybe the best course of action is to copy the file to another name and make your changes to the new copy.

System Attribute. The System attribute is used by the operating system to prevent the location of a file from changing. Certain disk fragmentation programs relocate all clusters of files so that they are consecutively arranged on a disk. This speeds up the read and write times for files because the system can locate the first cluster of a file and read through to the end without having to jump to another cluster or section of clusters to retrieve the entire file.

The operating system, whether DOS, OS/2, or Windows NT, expects certain files to be at certain locations. These files are marked as system files so they cannot be moved. The System attribute is usually used in conjunction with the Hidden or Read-Only attribute to prevent users from seeing the files or overwriting them.

Hidden Attribute. The Hidden attribute is used to prevent a file from appearing in a normal directory search. This effect can be seen by running the DOS DIR command on the root directory where DOS is installed. By typing

```
DIR /A-D
```

you see a list of all files regardless of attributes. Write down the number of files shown. This listing does not show directories. Now type in the DOS DIR command with the following flags:

```
DIR /AD
```

This command lists all directories. Again write down the number of directories shown. Add the number of files shown by the first and second DIR commands and compare them with the results from the following command:

```
DIR
```

The sum of the first two directory searches shows all files and directories, regardless of their attributes. The last command only shows the files that are not marked as Hidden. Depending on the system configuration, the results are different from machine to machine. On my system, the DIR /A-D command yielded 13 files, the DIR /AD command showed 16. However when the DIR command was issued by itself, only 21 files, including directories, appeared. The difference of eight files can be attributed to the Hidden attribute. This is the purpose of the Hidden attribute, to keep users from seeing files and, therefore, from tampering with them.

Normal Attribute. The Normal attribute is simply stating that no other attributes are set for the file. If a document is saved to disk, the attribute for the file is Normal. If the same document is backed up, either by DOS, Windows, or a third-party package, the Archive attribute is set. But until something is done that changes the attribute, the attribute remains at the Normal state.

Volume ID Attribute. The Volume ID attribute is used for the actual drive, not for a particular file. The drive can be a floppy disk, CD-ROM, hard drive, or logical partition of a hard drive. If the drive has its own unique drive letter, such as C, D, and so on, it also contains one Volume ID attribute. This is useful in install programs for determining if the proper disk has been inserted into the floppy drive. While all drive IDs can be read, not all can be updated. If the Read-Only attribute is also associated with a Volume ID, the Volume ID attribute cannot be written to. This is also true of non-writable media, such as CD-ROMs. The Volume ID can be checked but cannot be updated.

Directory Attribute. The Directory attribute is set by the system for all directory entries as they are created. Directories can be protected just as files can by setting the Hidden, System, or Read-Only attributes of the directory.

Setting additional attributes of a directory entry can be done either through a program or by using the DOS ATTRIB command with the proper switches. The following are the available flags for the DOS ATTRIB command:

- ■ + preceding an attribute to set the attribute
- ■ - preceding an attribute to clear the attribute
- ■ A for the Archive attribute
- ■ R for the Read-Only attribute
- ■ S for the System attribute
- ■ H for the Hidden attribute
- ■ /s to recurse all subdirectories

Notice that the Volume ID and Directory attributes are not supported by the ATTRIB command. The Volume ID can be set programmatically but not from the command line. The Directory attribute cannot be set by a program, only additional attributes can be added or removed from it. This prevents the problem that could arise from telling the system that a file is a directory, which plays with the FAT or MFT structures of the drives.

Understanding File Modes

File modes are often confused with the attributes of a file. Although there are some similarities, and files with certain attributes must be accessed using certain file modes, they are distinctly different.

Files can be accessed using the C++ runtime library routines. The file modes apply to all of the functions that access the files but are specified in the call to open the file. Some of the APIs for opening files include open(), fopen(), freopen(), and sopen(). The most commonly used API for opening files is fopen(). The modes for fopen() are the following:

- ■ Read-Only—File is opened for Read-Only access. Any attempts to write to the file result in an access-denied error.

- ■ Write—File is opened for Write access. If the file exists, it is overwritten. Files opened with Write access also have read privileges.

- ■ Append—File is opened for writing at the end of the file. If the file does not exists, it is created.

- Open for Update—A file is opened for reading and writing updates.

- Create—Create a new file for update, both Read-Only and Write access. If a file already exists by the same name, it is overwritten by the newly created empty file.

- Text—The file is opened for text mode. This mode is used in conjunction with the other file modes (that is, a file mode of at specifies "append text" as the open mode).

- Binary—The file is being opened for binary mode access. This mode is used in conjunction with the other file modes (that is, a file mode of wt specifies "write binary" as the open mode).

By using these file modes, either alone or combined with other mode flags, you can begin to write programs that take advantage of file I/O.

Opening and Closing Files

Files can be opened or created with certain modes of access allowed to the calling procedure. Since there is a limit of file handles available to the system, a good practice is to close a file handle as soon as you're through using it. C and C++ close all opened file handles when exiting an application, but the best practice is to do this clean-up yourself. The fopen() API has a corresponding API called fclose() that is used to close a file handle when it is no longer needed. An example of using fopen() and fclose() to create a file with Read-Write access and then close the file is shown in listing 12.1.

Listing 12.1   Using *fopen()* to Create a File with Read-Write Access

```
#include <stdio.h>

void main()
{
FILE *fHandle;

// Open a text file called CHAPT1201.txt for
// read-write access
fHandle = fopen ( "CHAPT1201.TXT", "wt" );

// Close the file handle
fclose ( fHandle );

return;
}
```

The code in listing 12.1 is very simplistic, yet it demonstrates the basic procedure for opening and closing a file using fopen() and fclose(). When you execute this program, the Chapt1201.txt is created in the current directory; the size of the file is zero bytes because no data was written to the file prior to closing it.

II

Programming in C++

Listing 12.2 adds the error checking necessary to ensure that the call to fopen() succeeds.

Listing 12.2   Checking for Errors Using *fopen()*

```
#include <stdio.h>

int main()
{
FILE *fHandle;

// Open a text file called CHAPT301.txt for
// read-write access
if ((fHandle = fopen ( "CHAPT1202.TXT", "wt" )) == NULL)
    {
        // If Error on file open, display
        // message and exit with a return code of 1
        printf("%s\n","Error Opening File");
        return (1);
    }

fclose ( fHandle );

return (0);
}
```

The preceding two examples show how to open, close, and check for an error when opening a file. The only problem with these examples is that they almost never fail. Take a look at listing 12.3 to see a version of listing 12.2, which generates an error every time it's executed.

Listing 12.3   Generating Errors Using *fopen()*

```
#include <stdio.h>

int main()
{
FILE *fHandle;

// Open non-existent file for read only access
if ((fHandle = fopen ( "CHAPT1203.TXT", "rt" )) == NULL)
    {
        // If Error on file open, display
        // message and exit with a return code of 1
        printf("%s\n","Error Opening File");
        return (1);
    }

fclose ( fHandle );

return (0);
}
```

The example in listing 12.3 may not make much sense, until you take a closer look at the file modes available to the fopen() API and how they interrelate. Table 12.1 shows the parameters available when making a call to fopen(). The result of running the program shown in listing 12.3 is shown in figure 12.1.

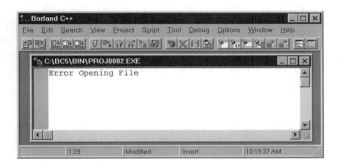

Fig. 12.1

Attempting to open a non-existent file.

Table 12.1 *fopen()* Mode Parameters	
Parameter	**Uses**
r	Marks access to the file as Read-Only. File must exist prior to the call to fopen().
w	Designates file access as Read/Write. If the file does not exist, it is created.
a	Marks access to a file as Append. Writing is allowed only at the end of the file. Creates the file if it does not exist.
r+	Opens an existing file for Read and Write Update access. Fails if the file does not exist.
w+	Creates a file for Update Write access. Overwrites the file if it already exists.
a+	Opens a file for appending. Creates the file if it does not exist.
t	Opens a file in text mode. This parameter is used in conjunction with the previous file open modes. For example, a file mode of rt opens a text file for Read-Only access.
b	Opens a file in binary mode. This parameter is used in conjunction with the previous file open modes. For example, a file mode of rb opens a binary file for Read-Only access.

By looking at table 12.1, you can see why listing 12.3 fails. The program is attempting to open a file as read-only and the file does not yet exist. Being able to create, open, and close files is very useful, but unless you can read from and write information to the files, they don't do you much good.

Reading and Writing Files

Now that you can open and close files, you can start to use them to store data. There are two basic types of data that can be stored in a file, text and binary. There are also two basic types of file access, *sequential* and *random*. This section covers sequential-access text files and random-access binary files.

Consider your Autoexec.bat or Config.sys files for a moment. These are both text files. There is no real rhyme or reason to the manner in which the information is contained within them. That is to say that the length of the PATH statement does not have to be exactly 80 bytes in length. For a program to process files of this type, each line has to be read in and then parsed to see if the string(s) of interest is in that particular line before reading in the next line and so on until the end of file marker is encountered. Changing the information contained inside a sequential-access file is also not very easy to accomplish (see listing 12.5 for an example of how to do this).

Take, for example, a program that holds information about your CD collection. The data structure used to create a record about each CD is of a fixed size. Creating a file with this type of fixed-length record is the perfect candidate for random-access programming. You can replace the fifth element of the file by overwriting a new record in its place without fear of running over and destroying part of the sixth record. This flexibility does not exist when dealing with sequential-access files.

Sequential-Access Files. Sequential-access files must be read from beginning to end, and the information required must be searched for line by line. Listing 12.4 creates a sequential- access file, listing 12.5 demonstrates reading the file, and listings 12.6 and 12.7 demonstrate the correct and incorrect ways to modify a sequential-access file.

When writing information to a text file, the fprintf() API can be used. This API is identical to printf() in all but one parameter. There is an extra parameter in front of the format string, which is the stream handle where the information is to be formatted and written.

Listing 12.4 Openfil1.cpp—Creating a Sequential-Access Text File

```cpp
#include <stdio.h>

int main()
{
FILE *fHandle;

// Open non-existent file for read only access
if ((fHandle = fopen ( "NAMES.TXT", "wt" )) == NULL)
    {
        // If Error on file open, display
        // message and exit with a return code of 1
        printf("%s\n","Error Opening File");
        return (1);
    }

// Using fprintf() to add lines to the file.
fprintf( fHandle, "%s\n", "Nanci");
fprintf( fHandle, "%s\n", "Jim");
```

```
fprintf( fHandle, "%s\n", "David");
fprintf( fHandle, "%s\n", "Chip");
fprintf( fHandle, "%s\n", "Cheryl");

fclose ( fHandle );

return (0);
}
```

When you run the program in listing 12.4, the program creates the Names.txt file. You can view the contents of the file by issuing the TYPE command from the DOS command prompt.

```
C:>TYPE NAMES.TXT
Nanci
Jim
David
Chip
Cheryl
```

There is really no way to determine the lengths of each line short of reading the line and then comparing the line to a string to see if you found a match.

Listing 12.5 shows how to read and display the contents of the newly created Names.txt file.

Listing 12.5   Readonly.cpp—Reading and Displaying a Sequential-Access Text File

```
#include <stdio.h>

int main()
{
FILE *fHandle;
char StrBuf[80];

// Open non-existent file for read only access
if ((fHandle = fopen ( "NAMES.TXT", "r+t" )) == NULL)
    {
        // If Error on file open, display
        // message and exit with a return code of 1
        printf("%s\n","Error Opening File");
        return (1);
    }

// Sequentially read and display the contents of
// the file, until the fgets() function returns
// a NULL to indicate the End of File has been reached
while ((fgets( StrBuf, 80, fHandle )) != NULL)
{
printf("%s\n",StrBuf);
}
```

(continues)

Listing 12.5   Continued

```
// Close the File Handle
fclose ( fHandle );

return (0);
}
```

Running the program shown in listing 12.5 produces the results shown in figure 12.2. You can change the names in the listing, and the results reflect the changes.

Fig. 12.2

Displaying a sequential-access text file.

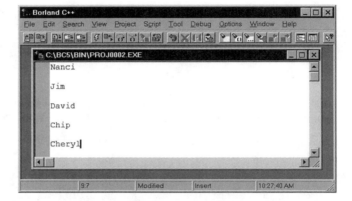

So how do you change the value of the fourth line of the file? By reading in the lines, searching for a known value, and replacing it is the normal response. To be able to write to a file in any manner other than appending, which up until now is how all writes have taken place, you must use the file pointer.

The file pointer keeps track of the current position of the next operation that takes place on a file, whether a read or write. Imagine writing to a file just like writing to the screen. The cursor position is where the next character is placed. The file pointer has very much the same responsibility.

The current position of the file pointer can be queried by making a call to ftell(). The return value from ftell() is a long int that marks the current position in the file that a call to any of the read or write APIs takes place at.

Simply being able to determine the position of the file pointer does not quite fulfill the need to move this pointer to the location that you want to write to or read from. Using the fseek() API allows programs to set the file pointer to any desired position within a file.

Listing 12.6 uses the ftell() and fseek() APIs to move the file pointer to the first character in Chip to be able to overwrite the string with another string.

Listing 12.6   Showerr1.cpp—Reading, Modifying, and Displaying a Sequential-Access Text File

```cpp
#include <stdio.h>
#include <string.h>


int main()
{
FILE *fHandle;
char StrBuf[80];
char NameCmp[] = "Chip\n";
long int  CurPos;

// Open non-existent file for read only access
if ((fHandle = fopen ( "NAMES.TXT", "r+t" )) == NULL)
    {
        // If Error on file open, display
        // message and exit with a return code of 1
        printf("%s\n","Error Opening File");
        return (1);
    }

while ((fgets( StrBuf, 80, fHandle )) != NULL)
{
// Get the current position of the file pointer
 CurPos = ftell( fHandle );

// Check to see if name read in matches
// the string being searched for.
 if (stricmp(StrBuf, NameCmp ) == 0)
 {
     // If a match is found, seek to the file position
     // at the start of the found string, and write
     // the new string in its place.
     fseek(fHandle,(CurPos - strlen(NameCmp)-1), SEEK_SET);
     fprintf(fHandle,"%s\n","Patty");
 }
}

// fseek to the beginning of the file
fseek(fHandle, 0, SEEK_SET);

// Sequentially read and display the contents of
// the file, until the fgets() function returns
// a NULL to indicate the End of File has been reached
while ((fgets( StrBuf, 80, fHandle )) != NULL)
{
printf("%s\n",StrBuf);
}

// Close the File Handle
fclose ( fHandle );

return (0);
}
```

Running the program shown in listing 12.6 gives the following results:

```
C:>CHAPT306
Nanci
Jim
David
Patty
heryl
```

As you can see, the insertion of text into a sequential-access text file is not as straight-forward as one might think. The program has no knowledge about what is in the file. It knows only that you have specified where and what you want to write into the file. This caused the loss of the C in Cheryl when the string Patty was used to overwrite the string Chip. The extra character in the string Patty caused the first character in Cheryl to be overwritten with the terminating NULL character.

By studying the code above, it is apparent that sequential-access files have their down-falls. They are good for small files that can be read from beginning to end in a short period of time and where the contents do not often require updating. Appending to a sequential-access file is simple. To update a value in the middle of the file requires opening a second file, writing all information up to the data needed to be changed to the new file writing the new data to the second file, and then continuing to process the first file by writing each piece of data to the second file. Once all processing is complete, the second file is copied over the original file, and the temporary second file is then deleted.

The restrictions and limitations imposed by sequential-access files make them rather awkward and difficult to use. Random-access files and their advantages are covered in the next section.

Random-Access Files. To understand and use random-access files, the first step is to understand C and C++ style structures. They are the basis for a record in a random-access file. A structure in C or C++ is a user-defined data type, containing any valid data types, including other user-defined data types.

Because a random-access file is made up of records that are of a given size, it is a rela-tively simple task to calculate the position of the fourth record in a file. If a data struc-ture called Names is 20 bytes long, the offset to the fourth record in a file can be calculated as the following shows:

```
OffSet = (4 * sizeof(Names);
```

To better illustrate this point, see listing 12.7. This program writes the same informa-tion that listing 12.4 did but in random-access format.

Listing 12.7   Randfil1.cpp—Creating and Writing to a Random-Access File

```cpp
#include <stdio.h>
#include <string.h>

// Define the record structure to use for the file
typedef struct _Names {
    char FirstName[20];
} NAMES;

int main()
{
FILE *fHandle;
NAMES NameRecord;        // Record Structure

// Open non-existent file for read only access
if ((fHandle = fopen ( "NAMES.BIN", "w+b" )) == NULL)
    {
        printf("%s\n","Error Opening File");
        return (1);
    }

// Copy the Names into the record, and write
// the records to the file.
strcpy(NameRecord.FirstName,"Nanci");
fwrite(&NameRecord, sizeof(NAMES), 1, fHandle);
strcpy(NameRecord.FirstName,"Jim");
fwrite(&NameRecord, sizeof(NAMES), 1, fHandle);
strcpy(NameRecord.FirstName,"David");
fwrite(&NameRecord, sizeof(NAMES), 1, fHandle);
strcpy(NameRecord.FirstName,"Chip");
fwrite(&NameRecord, sizeof(NAMES), 1, fHandle);
strcpy(NameRecord.FirstName,"Cheryl");
fwrite(&NameRecord, sizeof(NAMES), 1, fHandle);

// close the file handle
fclose ( fHandle );

return (0);
}
```

After executing this program, you have a file called Names.bin. This file cannot be displayed as easily as the text files in the previous examples. The program in listing 12.8 reads and displays the information stored in the Names.bin file.

Listing 12.8   Struct1.cpp—Reading and Displaying Information Stored in a Random-Access File

```cpp
#include <stdio.h>
#include <string.h>
```

(continues)

Listing 12.8   Continued

```
// Define the record structure to use for the file
typedef struct _Names {
     char FirstName[20];
} NAMES;

int main()
{
FILE *fHandle;
NAMES NameRecord;      // Record Structure
int     Err;           // Error Return Code

// Open non-existent file for read only access
if ((fHandle = fopen ( "NAMES.BIN", "rb" )) == NULL)
    {
         printf("%s\n","Error Opening File");
         return (1);
    }

// cycle through the file sequentially and print
// the values in the file
do {
Err = fread(&NameRecord, sizeof(NAMES), 1, fHandle);
  if (Err)
     // if Err is zero, the call to fread()
     // succeeded, so print the Name in the file
     printf("%s\n",NameRecord.FirstName);
} while (Err);

// Close the file handle
fclose ( fHandle );

return (0);

}
```

The output from listing 12.8 is

```
Nanci
Jim
David
Chip
Cheryl
```

The output from listing 12.8 is the same as that of listing 12.5. The main difference is the manner in which the data is stored on the disk. Regardless of size, each name stored now takes up 20 bytes of disk space. The Names.bin file size is 100 bytes, compared with the 33 bytes that the sequential-access version of the file required. This is probably the biggest drawback when using binary files. The space required to store a binary record is always a constant, even if the record is empty. This fact is also random-access files' biggest advantage over sequential-access files. Because the size of each record is known, any record can be accessed, without the need to read each record from the beginning of the file until you reach the desired record.

Listing 12.9 shows how to easily change the data within a file without damaging the other records.

```cpp
#include <stdio.h>
#include <string.h>


typedef struct _Names {
    char FirstName[20];
} NAMES;

int main()
{
FILE *fHandle;
NAMES NameRecord;
long int CurPos;
int     Err;

// Open non-existent file for read only access
if ((fHandle = fopen ( "NAMES.BIN", "r+b" )) == NULL)
    {
        printf("%s\n","Error Opening File");
        return (1);
    }

// cycle through the file sequentially and print
// the values in the file
do {
CurPos = ftell(fHandle);
Err = fread(&NameRecord, sizeof(NAMES), 1, fHandle);
  if (Err)
     {
     // if Err is zero, the call to fread()
     // succeeded, so test the name to see if
     // there is a match
     if (stricmp(NameRecord.FirstName,"Chip" ) == 0 )
     {
         // if a match is found reset the file
         // pointer, copy the new value to the
         // record, move the file pointer back
         // so the updated record will be read
         // next and continue processing
         fseek(fHandle, CurPos, SEEK_SET);
         strcpy(NameRecord.FirstName,"Patty");
         fwrite(&NameRecord, sizeof(NAMES), 1, fHandle);
         fseek(fHandle, CurPos, SEEK_SET);
         continue;
     }
     printf("%s\n",NameRecord.FirstName);
     }
} while (Err);
```

(continues)

Listing 12.9   Continued

```
fclose ( fHandle );

return (0);

}
```

Up to this point, you have merely seen how random file access can be performed much more efficiently, except for the disk space, than sequential file access.

Listing 12.10 shows the beginnings of a true random-access file. The record number of each entry in the file is calculated based on the size of the record to be written and the position of the file after the write has taken place. For example, if a record is 24 bytes in length, and the current file position is 0 (the beginning of the file), then the record number can be calculated as follows:

```
RECORD NUMBER = POSITION / RECORD SIZE
RECORD NUMBER = 0 / 24
RECORD NUMBER = 0
```

This logic works for all record sizes and relative positions within a file. The record number can be multiplied by the size of the individual record for the offset from the beginning of the file for the record position within the file. All record numbers to be used in this manner should start at 0 because 0 times any record size yields 0, which is the beginning of the file. See listing 12.10 for an example of random access into a file based on calculating the offset based on the structure size and record number.

Listing 12.10   Recnum.cpp—Calculating, Storing, and Retrieving Records from a Record Number

```
#include <stdio.h>
#include <stdlib.h>
#include <conio.h>
#include <string.h>

// Define the record structure to use for the file
typedef struct _Names {
    long int RecNo;
    char FirstName[20];
} NAMES;

int main()
{
FILE *fHandle;
NAMES NameRecord;
char    ch;
```

```
// Open non-existent file for read only access
if ((fHandle = fopen ( "NAMES2.BIN", "w+b" )) == NULL)
    {
        printf("%s\n","Error Opening File");
        return (1);
    }

// Copy the Names into the record, and write
// the records to the file, use the size of the
// record and the position of the file pointer to
// calculate the record number.

strcpy(NameRecord.FirstName,"Nanci");
NameRecord.RecNo = (ftell(fHandle)/sizeof(NAMES));
fwrite(&NameRecord, sizeof(NAMES), 1, fHandle);

strcpy(NameRecord.FirstName,"Jim");
NameRecord.RecNo = (ftell(fHandle)/sizeof(NAMES));
fwrite(&NameRecord, sizeof(NAMES), 1, fHandle);

strcpy(NameRecord.FirstName,"David");
NameRecord.RecNo = (ftell(fHandle)/sizeof(NAMES));
fwrite(&NameRecord, sizeof(NAMES), 1, fHandle);

strcpy(NameRecord.FirstName,"Chip");
NameRecord.RecNo = (ftell(fHandle)/sizeof(NAMES));
fwrite(&NameRecord, sizeof(NAMES), 1, fHandle);

strcpy(NameRecord.FirstName,"Cheryl");
NameRecord.RecNo = (ftell(fHandle)/sizeof(NAMES));
fwrite(&NameRecord, sizeof(NAMES), 1, fHandle);

/// Reset the file pointer to the beginning of the file
fseek(fHandle, 0, SEEK_SET);

// loop through the query, asking the user for a record
// number from 0 to 4 and displaying the information in
// the appropriate record
do
{
printf("\n%s\n", "Enter a number from 0 to 4");
printf("%s\n", "Any other key to exit");
ch = getch();
    if (ch >= '0' && ch <= '4')
        {
            fseek(fHandle, (ch-48) * sizeof(NAMES), SEEK_SET);
            fread(&NameRecord, sizeof(NAMES), 1, fHandle);
            printf("\n%s%d","Record Number ", NameRecord.RecNo);
            printf("\n%s%s\n","Name in Record ",NameRecord.FirstName);
        } else
            break;
} while (1);

printf("\nTerminating.....\n");
```

(continues)

Programming in C++

Listing 12.10   Continued

```
// Close the File Handle
fclose ( fHandle );

return (0);
}
```

Using random-access files can provide vast benefits in the speed for both retrieval and update of information over sequential-access files. When you run the program in listing 12.10, the results are those shown in figure 12.3.

Fig. 12.3

Accessing a random-access file by a record number.

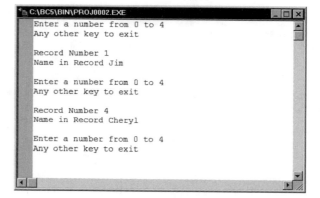

String Manipulation Functions

String handling is one area that all programmers need to deal with. Strings provide the ability to communicate with your users. Without the ability to use and manipulate strings, you would be reduced to using numbers to try and get your point across, and if that were the case, personal computers certainly would not be enjoying the massive popularity that they now do.

So what is a string? A string is a combination of characters that make up words or sentences. Using strings can pose a few problems given the nature of their implementation in both C and C++. A string is a NULL terminated character array. All of the functions designed to work with strings process all data until the NULL is encountered and assume that it is all part of the string. Combining strings and converting strings are two basic concepts that you need to understand to manipulate strings.

Combining Strings

At some point you need to combine two or more different strings to create a string that satisfies your program's needs. A simple example is prompting a user for his or her name and then using that name in another sentence. You can do this in several ways. If you use the cout operator of C++, you do not have to combine the strings, you simply tell cout which strings to print in which order. The following is an example of this:

```
cout << "Hello " << "World" << endl;
```

This is very simplistic and could easily be just one output string. The previous example is better suited for using a variable as one of the strings, as in the following:

```
cout << "Hello " << chName << endl;
```

What if you need to combine two strings and be able to treat them as a single entity? That is one place where the Borland C++ library string functions can come in handy.

The library function that allows you to combine, or *concatenate*, two different strings is strcat(). The syntax of this function is

```
#include <string.h>
char *strcat( char *DestString, const char *String2);
```

The strcat() function takes pointers to two strings as inputs. It concatenates String2 to the end of DestString and returns a pointer to the resultant combined string. You must include the string.h header file to use any of the library string functions.

Caution

It is your responsibility to ensure that the size of the destination string is large enough to hold the string created by strcat(). If the string is not large enough, strcat() truncates the string to fit in the available space.

Listing 12.11 shows how to use the strcat() function to combine two strings.

Listing 12.11   Using the *strcat()* Function

```
#include <string.h>
#include <iostream.h>

void main()
{
char DestString[100];
char *Str2 = "C++ 5.0";

strcpy(DestString, "Borland ");

cout << "DestString contains: " << DestString << endl;
cout << "Str2 contains: " << Str2 << endl;

strcat (DestString, Str2);
```

(continues)

Listing 12.11   Continued

```
cout << "DestString now contains: " << DestString << endl;

}
```

When you run the program in listing 12.11, you see the results shown in figure 12.4. The second string, Str2, is tacked on to the end of the first string to create a single string.

You also see another string function shown in the program, the strcpy() function.

Fig. 12.4

Using the strcat() *function.*

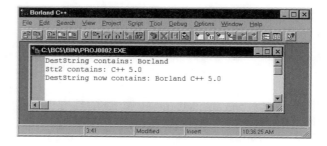

The strcpy() function copies one string to another. It is similar in syntax to strcat(). The syntax for the strcpy() function is

```
#include <string.h>
char *strcpy(char *DestString, const char *SourceString);
```

The strcpy() function can be used to load a value into a particular string. In listing 12.11, it is used to copy the string Borland into the DestString variable.

Converting Strings

When you are writing your programs, you inevitably find times when you have a string that contains numeric data that you need to use. You cannot multiply two strings together, even if they contain numbers, so you need to convert those strings to their numeric representation. Borland C++ provides several functions that allow for easy conversion of strings to numbers and numbers to strings.

There are three basic function pairs that can be used for the conversion of strings. Each of these functions acts in a similar manner, but they are intended for different types of numeric data. If you want to convert a string to an integer, use the atoi() (which stands for ASCII to integer) function. The syntax for atoi() is

```
#include <string.h>
int atoi(const char *Str);
```

The `atoi()` function has a counterpart function that takes an integer and turns it into a string. This function is `itoa()`. The syntax for the itoa function is

```
#include <string.h>
char *itoa(int Number, char *DestString, int Base);
```

The `atoi()` function takes only one parameter, the string to be converted. It then returns an integer provided that the string contains an integer. The `atoi()` function converts all numbers found in the string until it reaches the end of the string or until it encounters a non-numeric character.

To use the `itoa()` function, you must provide the function with three parameters. The first is the number that you want converted into a string. The second is the string that the number is converted into. The final parameter is the base of the number being converted. This can be anything from 2 to 36. If you are converting a hexidecimal number, the base is 16; the base is ten for all integers.

Listing 12.12 shows how to use the `atoi()` and `itoa()` functions to convert a string to a number, use it in a formula, and then take the result and turn it back into a string.

Listing 12.12   Atoi1.cpp—Using the *atoi()* and *itoa()* Functions

```
#include <string.h>
#include <stdlib.h>
#include <iostream.h>

void main()
{
char DestString[10];
int iNum;

strcpy(DestString, "15");

cout << "DestString contains: " << DestString << endl;

iNum = atoi(DestString);
iNum = iNum * 3;

itoa(iNum, DestString, 10);

cout << "DestString now contains: " << DestString << endl;

}
```

Running the program in listing 12.12 produces the results shown in figure 12.5.

II

Programming in C++

Fig. 12.5

Using the atoi() *and* itoa() *functions.*

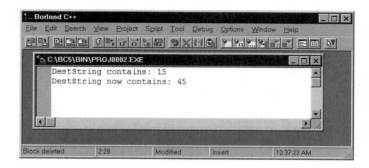

There are several other conversion function pairs. They are atol() and ltoa() for converting long integers and atof() and ultoa() for converting floating point and unsigned integers.

Accessing the Date and Time

When creating programs, you often find that you need to work with dates and times. You could be writing a program that does project scheduling or you may just want to know what time it is so that you can change a greeting within a program. The following sections illustrate how to get the system date and time and how to change them.

getdate() and setdate()

There are many date related routines built into Borland C++ 5. This section shows you how to use the getdate() and setdate() functions to get and set the system date.

The getdate() and setdate() routines both take a pointer to a date structure as the sole parameter. The syntax for these functions is

```
#include <dos.h>
void getdate(struct date *pDate);
void setdate(struct date *pDate);
```

The date structure is defined in the dos.h header file. The definition is

```
struct date{
    int da_year;   // current year
    char da_day;   // day of the month
    char da_mon;   // month (1 = Jan, 2 = Feb,...)
};
```

The use of these two functions is illustrated in listing 12.13.

Listing 12.13 Date1.cpp—Using *getdate()* and *setdate()*

```
#include <dos.h>
#include <stdio.h>
#include <iostream.h>
```

```
void PrintDate(struct date *CurDate);

void main()
{
    struct date CurDate, NewDate;

    getdate(&CurDate);
    PrintDate(&CurDate);

    NewDate.da_mon = 7;
    NewDate.da_day = 25;
    NewDate.da_year = 1999;

    setdate(&NewDate);
    PrintDate(&NewDate);
    setdate(&CurDate);

}

void PrintDate(struct date *CurDate)
{
    char DateString[15];

    sprintf( DateString,
                "%d,%d,%d",
                CurDate->da_mon,
                CurDate->da_day,
                CurDate->da_year);
    cout << "The system date is: " << DateString << endl << endl;

}
```

Running the code in listing 12.13 gives you the results in figure 12.6. The first date is the date your system clock is set to. This code saves the current date prior to changing it; therefore, the date can be reset prior to exiting the program. The time functions are very similar in nature; these are covered in the next section.

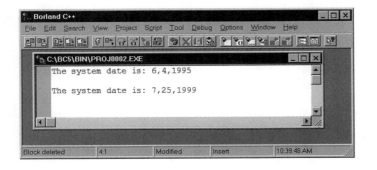

Fig. 12.6

Using the getdate() *and* setdate() *functions.*

Programming in C++

gettime() **and** *settime()*

The gettime() and settime() library functions are much like the getdate() and setdate() functions. They allow you to query the time of the system clock and to set it. The syntax for the gettime() and settime() functions is

```
#include <dos.h>
void gettime(struct time *pTime);
void settime(struct time *pTime);
```

The time structure is defined in the dos.h header file. The definition is

```
struct time {
    unsigned char ti_min;   // minutes
    unsigned char ti_hour;  // hours
    unsigned char ti_hund;  // hundredths of seconds
    unsigned char ti_sec;   // seconds
};
```

Listing 12.14 illustrates how to query and change the system time.

Listing 12.14   Time1.cpp—Using *gettime()* and *settime()*

```
#include <dos.h>
#include <stdio.h>
#include <iostream.h>

void PrintTime(struct time *CurTime);

void main()
{
    struct time CurTime, NewTime;

    gettime(&CurTime);
    PrintTime(&CurTime);

    NewTime.ti_hour = 5;
    NewTime.ti_min = 10;
    NewTime.ti_sec = 15;
    NewTime.ti_hund = 20;


    settime(&NewTime);
    PrintTime(&NewTime);
    settime(&CurTime);

}

void PrintTime(struct time *CurTime)
{
    char TimeString[15];

    sprintf( TimeString,
                "%2d:%02d:%02d.%02d",
                CurTime->ti_hour,
```

```
              CurTime->ti_min,
              CurTime->ti_sec,
              CurTime->ti_hund);
    cout << "The system time is now: " << TimeString << endl << endl;
}
```

Running the code in listing 12.14 gives you the results shown in figure 12.7. The first time is the time your system clock is set to. This code saves the current time prior to changing it so that it can be reset to its original value prior to exiting the program.

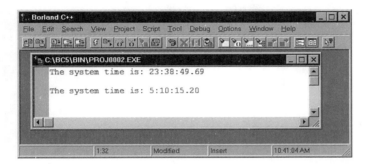

Fig. 12.7

Using the gettime() *and* settime() *functions.*

Working with Variable Length Argument Lists

One of the powers of C and C++ is the ability to write a function that can accept a variable number of arguments. You have already seen examples of several of these functions, printf() and sprintf(). These functions allow you to send them a virtually unlimited number of arguments, processing all arguments sent to them.

Borland C++ provides several functions that allow you to declare a function to accept a variable number of arguments and to retrieve them and process them within a function. C++ provides a data type, va_list, to access the variable argument list. There are three predefined macros for accessing the argument list. These are va_start, va_arg, and va_end. The va_start macro is called to initialize a pointer to the variable length argument list. The va_arg macro returns the next item in the list and increments the pointer to point at the next argument. The va_end macro needs to be called when all arguments in the list have been accessed; failure to do this can cause unpredictable behavior in your programs.

This sounds much more complicated than it really is. Listing 12.15 illustrates a function called AddThem() that can take any number of integers and return the result.

Listing 12.15   Vararg1.cpp—Using a Variable Length Argument List

```cpp
#include <stdio.h>
#include <stdarg.h>
#include <iostream.h>

int AddInts(int x,...);

void main()
{
    int Result;

    Result = AddInts(5,8,2,5,99,4,5);

    cout << "The returned value from AddInts is: " << Result << endl;

}

int AddInts(int x,...)
{
    int Sum = x;
    va_list ListPtr;
    int CurArg;

    va_start(ListPtr, x);

    while ((CurArg = va_arg(ListPtr, int)) != -1)
        {
            Sum += CurArg;
        }
    va_end(ap);
    return (Sum);
}
```

You can pass an unlimited number of arguments to the AddInts() function. The only caveat is that you have to have at least one fixed argument. This fixed argument serves as the anchor block for the va_list data type. You pass the last fixed argument to the va_start macro so that it knows where the variable list begins.

Using the va_ macros allows you to provide flexibility in the functions that you write. You no longer need to have functions that accept a fixed number of arguments.

From Here...

Now that you have learned about quite a few features of Borland C++ and how to write your own programs, you can experiment with different features of the language. If you are trying different functions and methods in Borland C++, you will inevitably run into problems with syntax, program execution, and many other items.

- For more information on input and output see chapter 13, "Exploring iostreams."

- For more information on the use of strings see chapter 21, "Understanding Strings in ANSI C and ANSI C++."

- Chapter 29, "Using the Integrated Debugger," demonstrates how to use the Integrated Debugger of Borland C++ 5 in your quest to track down and fix errors and problems within programs.

- For the detailed instructions on how to make a specific function call, consult the Borland C++ online Help.

CHAPTER 13

Exploring iostreams

The stream classes provide a consistent interface for writing to and reading from a variety of output and input devices. While the iostreams are not part of the C++ language proper, they do represent the power that can be achieved through a well-designed set of classes.

Think of streams as a resource for managing input and output in a well-defined way, regardless of the device from which the input is coming or where it is going. The iostream classes are easy to use because the interface and syntax is functionally similar, whether you are writing to the screen, to a printer, or to a file. The same also is true for input.

Input and output make up one of the most important aspects of most programs, of which the iostream library is an integral part. This chapter will show you how to use the existing functionality, and it will also demonstrate how input and output can be effortlessly added to the classes you design.

Prior to the stream libraries, we had `printf` and `scanf`. I do not want to knock these innovative functions, but they did require C programmers to learn very terse formatting characters, resulting in complicated input and output statements. In addition, the interface was inconsistent for different hardware devices, and in some circumstances was error-prone.

I must emphasize that C++ is not a language that can be introduced or learned in a perfectly linear manner. There are aspects of iostreams that are going to seem a little foreign, maybe even strange at first. If it were to only introduce those topics that are not dependent on other language features, this chapter would be short indeed. I recommend that when you get to the section "Writing Stream Manipulators," which begins the advanced material, you may want to read chapters 14, "Basic Class Concepts," 15, "Function Overloading," and 16, "Operator Overloading" before continuing with this chapter.

This chapter demonstrates a powerful tool set for C++ programmers, but it also allows new users a peek through the window at the power yet to be unleashed.

In this chapter, I am inviting you to skip around a little, but rest assured that I make every effort to explain what you need to know, including the following:

- Introduction to iostreams
- Basic uses of `cin` and `cout`
- Member functions
- Formatting output streams
- Writing stream manipulators
- File streams
- Buffered streams
- Overloading stream operators

Introduction to the iostream Class

This section will not look at class hierarchies; in fact, I won't say much about the stream classes from the hierarchical perspective in this chapter. That is not to say the relationships between the classes that define the stream libraries aren't important, but we have our work cut out for us learning how to use them. The design of object-oriented classes requires a discussion of its own.

First, let's look at what we do with streams, learn some of the general functionality, and learn how to extend and apply advanced features. Let's take a look at what streams are and how we use them.

Using Stream Classes

The stream classes were implemented as an object-oriented solution to reading and writing data. Because input and output is not a part of the C++ language, C++ at Bell Labs inherited input and output for files, monitors, and printers from C. If you know C—and probably love it—you might recognize the differences in the code required to write to the different devices mentioned.

> **Note**
>
> C++ is a superset of C. Bjarne Stroustrop, the "inventor" of C++, chose the C language as a base language for C++. I suspect there were several reasons. He mentions the accepted knowledge that C produces small, fast code and enables programmers to get close to the architecture or hardware. I suppose it is convenient to have a successful AT&T language—C, whose implementors, Brian Kernighan and Dennis Ritchie, still work at AT&T—as a starting point rather than starting from scratch.

The problem has been recognized that the greater the diversity of syntax, the more complicated and error-prone is the implementation of certain features of a language. Let's examine the differences between the C functions that perform input and output and the replacements we use in C++.

Comparing C and C++ Input/Output

C++ input/output does not have to be justified. I am presenting both the old and the new because I think you are likely to find both styles in existing and new C++ code. If I do my job correctly, though, you will choose the stream libraries for your new code.

I will start with console input/output and provide examples of ways of both writing to the console and reading from the keyboard. (I will clearly distinguish between the C and the C++ way.)

C and C++ Console Input and Output. The console consists of the keyboard and monitor. Writing to the monitor can be accomplished by including stdio.h and using the `printf` function. The `printf` function is declared:

```
int printf( const char*, ...);      // Uses variadic arguments
```

The appearance of the ... indicates that this function uses variable arguments, which must be culled from the stack; thus, `printf` is not going to be very fast. The const char* argument is often referred to as a format string. By using a very terse syntax, you actually have the job of assisting the `printf` function to determine what it is you are trying to print. Here is an example:

```
// This is not a working program!
#include <stdio.h>
char * doodleBug = "Pauly Wauly Doodle Bug";
printf( "%s\n", doodleBug );
// Outputs "Pauly Wauly Doodle Bug" followed by a carriage return.
```

Breaking apart the format string %s means that there is an argument (in the variadic position) that is a null-terminated string and \n is the newline escape character.

Here is the C++ equivalent:

```
#include <iostream.h>
char * doodleBug = "Pauly Wauly Doodle Bug";
cout << doodleBug << endl;
// Outputs exactly the same thing.
```

There is no benefit reaped in terms of lines of code, but compare the syntax. All we have to do is to include the right header file and use the argument with the << operator. There is no terse formatting syntax, and endl is a little easier to read than '\n' but both accomplish the same task.

Now let's look at what happens when we want to write an integer, for example. The C version is:

```
int num = 10;
printf("%d", num);      // A new formatting character: %d
```

The C++ equivalent is:

```
int num = 10;
cout << num;          // Exactly the same syntax as char*
```

Notice that you would be required to know a different formatting character to use the C function, but that the C++ style requires no new syntax. Formatting output with `printf` is almost an art form, but something as common as input and output should not require artistry. The C++ version is arguably the easier of the two to learn. (Formatting C-style output gets even more cryptic.)

What about input? Input has even more problems. Suppose you wanted to read integers from the keyboard. C++ uses a consistent input operator for all input types too, and C requires the same variadic pacification through a formatting string, but it's even worse than that.

Here is the C++ version of reading input:

```
int num;
cin >> num;          // Read an integer from an input device
```

You might think that the C version is equivalent to the C-style for printing:

```
int num;
scanf("%d", num);     // Error!
```

This causes an error. You must use the address of (&) operator, or you will most likely get an error that is Windows' fault (GPF). The code actually must be written:

```
int num;
scanf( "%d", &num );     // Oops! Don't forget the &
```

This is not C bashing. C provided state of the art programming, and is still widely used, but time has offered improvements. But, I want to convince you to waste little effort learning how to use `printf` and `scanf` unnecessarily.

As an added consideration, you will have to learn a new syntax and additional functions to read and write files. However, the exact same syntax—the << operator for output and the >> operator for input—is used with file stream objects. I will demonstrate these later in the chapter.

Interestingly enough, these C functions were originally used to implement the C++ stream classes.

The Original Implementation of Stream Classes. In the early 1980s, an object-oriented approach to input/output was implemented in terms of the existing C functions. This is not that uncommon. Many classes have functions that have been around for years, comprising their underlying functionality. Using a class to insulate the vagaries and complexities of functions proved beneficial, but it was a matter of adding an extra indirection to an already slow function.

What is difficult about the `stdio` functions? They require a knowledge of complex formatting characters and a funny syntax. The C++ language, through function and operator overloading, allowed the original implementor the ability to simplify this interface. Chapters 15 and 16 explain how this works, but the premise is that a symmetric interface could be used in spite of the underlying C functions. Keep that statement in mind when you read those two chapters.

Tip

If after reading Chapters 15 and 16, you do not see the connection between overloading functions and operators and how a function like `printf` could be used to implement the iostream classes, contact me on CIS @70353,2711.

Note

A complete explanation of operator and function overloading is contained in chapter 15, "Function Overloading," and chapter 16, "Operator Overloading." But imagine an algorithm that states: There exist several functions that accept a single native data type. Based on the type of data, call the appropriate function.

Now imagine that distinguishing between the data type is somehow automated by the compiler based on the type of the data. Underneath these functions exists a specific call to `printf`.

Using pseudocode for the function name, here is an example:

```
return_type function_name( char * str )
{
    printf( "%s", str );
}
```

Further imagine that the function name is actually an operator, and you have a perfect image of what operator functions look like.

The current iostream classes were given a new implementation removing the underlying slow `printf` and `scanf` functions. This was a natural evolutionary step that did not require a change in the outside interface.

Basic Use

Here we are going to learn how to use the most fundamental aspects of the objects `cin` (console in) and `cout` (console out). We'll begin by looking at what they are, where they are, and the easiest applications of these two objects.

The objects `cin` and `cout` are easily used with the native data types. The syntax is consistent for `cin` and `cout`, regardless of the (native) data type. The basic syntax requires that you separate each argument with the operator << for output and the operator for input >>.

> **Tip**
>
> Chapter 14, "Basic Class Concepts," introduces classes thoroughly. In the simplest sense they are collections of data and functions. Because cout and cin are instances of classes, we can make the assumption that there are available functions that can be used with these objects.

The objects cout and cin have member functions that define the behaviors of the operator << and the operator >> functions for iostreams. The result is that several different data types can be streamed in the same statement. (I could have used variables, but the distinctive point is the difference in the data types used with the same syntactical notation.) Look at the following:

```
cout << 10 << 'x' << 3.14159 << " is approximately " << (10 * 3.14) << endl;
```

The 10 is an integer, 'x' is a character, 3.14159 is a floating point number, " is approximately; " is a null-terminated (or ASCIIZ) string, 10 * 3.14 results a floatings point number, and endl is a *stream manipulator*.

On the input side, we could use the cin object, with its operator >>, to read any of these types. The type of the data doesn't matter.

> **Caution**
>
> Exercise some caution when reading character buffers and char* values—you don't want to read more characters than are allocated space. This potential pitfall is easily overcome, and should not be deemed a shortcoming of the implementation.

What Are *cin* and *cout*?

The two objects cin and cout are instances (or objects or variables) of the istream_withassign and ostream_withassign classes, respectively. This means that somewhere is a class specification for each and a statement that instantiates these two objects. The somewhere is the iostream.h header file. By including this file with a preprocessor directive, you make your program input/output-enabled. You will not have to instantiate either object because that has been done for you. The objects are in a global namespace, so they can be used within any scope in any of your modules that include the iostream header file.

> **Note**
>
> The istream_withassign and ostream_withassign are *derived* from the istream and ostream classes, respectively. The parent classes contain most of the functionality; the child classes add the ability to assign stream objects.

Read chapters 14, "Basic Class Concepts," 17, "Constructors: Copy and Assignment," and 20, "Inheritance and Polymorphism," to gain a complete understanding of *derived classes, child classes,* and the *assignment operator.* So far, they are not critical to our discussion.

Basic Examples

Listing 13.1 shows many syntactical examples of code fragments using `cin` and `cout` in common language statements. Draw on these if the topic is completely new to you.

Listing 13.1   Demonstrates the *cout* Object

```
// Example A: Use cout to write a single character of a string at a time
char buf[] = "Good morning Vietnam!";
for( int j=0; j<strlen(buf); j++ )
   cout << buf[j];
// Example B: Read an array of 128 integers
int * response = new int[128];
for( int k = 0; k<128; k++ )
   cin >> response[k];
delete [] response;
// Example C: Questions and answers
char buf[25];
cout << "What is your name: ";
cin >> buf;    // Read the next section for a better way to do this;
cout << endl << "Hello, " << buf << endl;
```

To try out any of these small fragments, include any of the code fragments from listing 13.1 in the main function of this code:

```
// DEMO.CPP - Plug and play the iostream examples.
#include <iostream.h>
void main()
   { // Place example A, B, or C here }
```

and compile the program as a Win32, *Console* program, or use the *EasyWin* target model.

Member Functions

Member functions, or *methods,* are functions declared in a class. Chapter 14, "Basic Class Concepts" presents a thorough discussion of classes. If you have experience with C, equate member functions to struct-member functions. If you are migrating from Visual Basic, think of a new and improved theoretical type that enables you to define functions as part of the type. The same is true for a theoretical Pascal record: you need one that can contain functions. Anything defined in a class is a member; whether it is a variable or function is the distinction we are talking about here.

> **Note**
>
> I am well aware that you cannot add functions to VB types or Pascal records, but maybe we will see them someday. Borland's Delphi, which is built on Object Pascal, does provide the class idiom and has done so for years.

The member functions discussed pertain to the `ostream` and `istream` classes. Other classes (in the hierarchy) will be discussed in sections that follow. This section is not meant to be inclusive; instead, I have chosen to demonstrate the more commonly used functions for input/output and avoid the functions relegated to stream housekeeping.

`cin` and `cout` both have a couple of functions provided to enhance input and output when the traditional operator function is not exactly what you want. That's right—the operator<< for `ostreams` and the operator>> for `istreams` are member functions.

> **Note**
>
> Both `istream` and `ostream` classes have several versions defined of the operator << and operator >>—at least one for each native data type, including the new *bool* type. This is discussed in detail in chapter 16.

As we have seen so far, the syntax for both objects is fairly straightforward. There are, however, other functions. Of those, we are going to look at ostream's `flush`, `put`, and `write` and istream's `get`, `getline`, `peek`, `read`, `ignore`, and `gcount`.

ostream **Member Functions**

The `ostream` members mentioned in this chapter pertain to writing data using a syntax varying from that already seen. I've already mentioned that you may easily write any of the native data types using the operator << with the object cout.

To use these member functions—or any member, for that matter—use the dot operator in the following manner:

```
cout.func_name( arglist );
```

Let's look at the calling syntax of each of the members listed, with a brief demonstration of how to use each.

Using *flush*. The `flush` member function takes no arguments. It is used to flush all of the data from the stream (holding place in memory) to the target output device. You don't often need to use this function directly, but you will quite often see it used in other member functions. The syntax for calling `flush` is:

```
cout << flush;     // stream manipulator
```

or you could use it so as to appear more like a function call, like this:

```
cout.flush();
```

The `flush` function clears the stream data. For instance, if you place the `endl` manipulator on the stream, it actually places the '\n' character on the stream, and then calls `flush`.

> **Note**
>
> The language still supports the terse newline, '\n', from C—after all it's a character, but you don't have to use it to get a newline into the output. And, `endl` is more meaningful than \n. The goal was to present a uniform interface, not reinvent the wheel.

Using *put*. The `put` member is actually used to put a single character into the stream. Calling

```
cout.put( '\t' );
```

inserts the tab character into the stream, or you could put that particular character on the stream this way, too:

```
cout << '\t';
```

The put function is actually defined in three different ways:

```
ostream& put(char ch);       // Read chapter 15, "Function Overloading" for
                             // an explanation
ostream& put(signed char ch);
ostream& put(unsigned char ch);
```

The crux of the definition is that it takes a character argument and returns a reference to an `ostream`.

Using *write*. The `write` method can be used to place *n*-number of characters, in one call, into the `ostream`. The declarations in the header file show that there are four forms of the `write` function that take an integer and either a const char*, const signed char*, or const unsigned char*. The result is that the number characters specified by the integer argument are printed, including any '\0' characters. This is somewhat different from:

```
cout << "Bubba said something I won't ever forget.";
```

which will write the ASCIIZ string but not the null (which you can't see).

istream Member Functions

The `istream` member functions complement the input stream `operator>>` function, and, for the most part, provide the converse functionality to the `ostream` members. The `get` and `getline` functions can both be used to read a line of text up to some arbitrary length or when a delimiter has been encountered. One form of the `get` function returns a single character at a time, one reads the characters into a character buffer, and a third reads the characters into a stream buffer.

If you have little or no knowledge of function overloading this may seem strange. Chapter 15, "Function Overloading," clarifies how overloaded functions work.

Using *get*. I am not going to show the variations based on a particular character type; rather, I want to demonstrate the bigger differences. Here are four different declarations for the get method:

```
// Form 1: Used with cin to return single integer sized characters
int get();
// Form 2: Reads len-1 characters into char or until the delimiter is
// reached
stream& get( char*, int len, char = '\n' );
// Form 3: Reads a single character into the char reference
istream& get(char&);
// Form 4: Reads the characters into the streambuf object
istream& get(streambuf&, char = '\n');
```

The version in Form 2 reads len-1 characters—always inserting the '\0' character to make a qualified string—or until the delimiter has been reached; notice that the default delimiter is the newline. Having a default argument means that you do not have to pass a value if the default suits your needs. Here is a code fragment demonstrating Form 2:

```
char buf[128];
cin.get( buf, 128 );   // Use '\n' by default for the third argument
```

> ### Tip
>
> Instead of using hard-coded values like 128, it is a commonly employed convention to use a const. The change might look like this:
>
> ```
> const int MAX = 128;
> char buf[ MAX ];
> cin.get( buf, MAX );
> ```
>
> You must usually assign a constant value to initialize constants. An alternative is to use the sizeof macro, which *does* work with constants. The first version enables you to change the value of MAX in one place only. The following version does not require the introduction of an additional name:
>
> ```
> char buf[128];
> cin.get(buf, sizeof(buf)/sizeof(buf[0]));
> ```

You can choose your own delimiter just as easily by providing the third argument; it depends on your implementation needs. The other versions of get can be applied as easily with a few minutes of experimentation.

The biggest difference between the Form 2 of get and the getline member function is that get does *not* remove the delimiter from the input stream, but getline does. If you want to read lines of text characters, use the getline function. The example fragment above works perfectly if you simply replace get with getline.

Using *gcount* and *read*. The gcount function will return the number of characters last read with the get, getline, and read member functions. The function takes two arguments: The first is a character array and the second is the number of characters to read. To check the number of characters actually read, use gcount.

Listing 13.2 Read.cpp—Demonstrates *istream* Member Functions

```
1:  // READ.CPP - Demonstrates the istream read and gcount member
2:  #include <iostream.h>
3:  void main()
4:  {
5:    char text[10];
6:    cout << "Enter some text" << endl;
7:    cin.read( text, 10 );
8:    int count = cin.gcount();
9:    cout << "Text: " << text << endl
10:       << "Character count: " << count << endl
11:       << "Next character: " << cin.peek();
12: }
```

This simple program demonstrates the read, gcount, and peek istream member functions. The program stops and waits for the user to input at least 10 characters, but doesn't return until Enter is pressed. Only 10 characters are read into *text*, illustrated by the value of count. The last line of code, line 11, uses peek to look at the next character in the input stream; it will be the eleventh character.

The peek function allows you to look at the next character in the input stream without removing it from the stream. The function takes no arguments and returns an integer. You could use the peek function to filter all input keystrokes until a key value within a range was entered. The ignore function has the following declaration:

```
istream& ignore(int n = 1, int delim = EOF);
```

Notice that its default arguments would cause the function to ignore one character at a time until the EOF delimiter was reached.

Formatting Output Streams

Output can be formatted by using members of the ostream class inherited through its base class. The semantics of the inheritance process are not critical to using these formatting values but do exist. So far, we have seen how to use the cout object and the operator<< to write native data types. Now we are going to look at how to apply the formatting flags of the class to modify the appearance of the output.

Both the istream and the ostream class inherit their formatting flags from the ios.h class. If you want to poke around in the iostream class, you can begin your search there. If you want to use the Help system in BC5 to find out more about the stream flags, look in the ios Help section.

Table 13.1 lists the formatting flags that can be set with the setf function. The setf function has two versions:

```
long setf(long _setbits, long _field);    // Form 1
long setf(long);                          // Form 2
```

Form 1 lets you specify the formatting flags to set, and the field argument clears the bits specified. Form 2 sets the flags corresponding to those passed in as the long argument. The enumerated values can be taken from the format flags (see table 13.1) defined in the ios class. You must precede the enumerated value with the class name, ios.

Table 13.1 Input and Output Formatting Flags	
Flag Name	**Function**
skipws	Skip input whitespace (e.g., spaces and tabs)
left	Left-justify output
right	Right-justify output
internal	Pad between the sign or number-base indicator
dec	Use base 10 for numeric output
oct	Use base 8 for numeric output
hex	Use base 16 for numeric output
showbase	Show the number base on output
showpoint	Show the decimal point for floating-point numbers
uppercase	Use uppercase A, B, C, D, E, and F for hexadecimal numbers
showpos	Show the + symbol for positive numbers
scientific	Use exponential or scientific notation for floating-point numbers
fixed	Use fixed decimal-point for floating-point numbers

Some formatting enumerates values that can be used as arguments to setf to modify the appearance of output. You can use Boolean operators to set multiple values (e.g., setf(ios::hex ¦ ios::uppercase)).

The first example program in listing 13.3 actually uses stream manipulators that set the basefield flags for either the hexadecimal, decimal, or octal number base.

Listing 13.3   Format.cpp—Demonstrates Formatting an *ostream*

```
// FORMAT.CPP - Demonstrates ostream formatting with cout.
#include <iostream.h>
void main()
{
    cout << hex << 15 << endl;      // f
    cout << oct << 15 << endl;      // 17
    cout << dec << 15 << endl;      // 15
}
```

This program outputs the number 15 as a hexadecimal (base-16), octal (base-8), and a decimal number. Read the next section to learn how to write your own stream manipulators. The other flag fields in table 13.1 require you to use the `setf` member function.

The next example program uses some more of the advanced stream formatting characters to get a nicely formatted hexadecimal number. All these examples are excerpted from Format2.cpp. The first fragment demonstrates additional formatting for number bases.

```
cout.setf( ios::showbase¦ios::hex¦ios::uppercase );
cout << 15 << endl;
```

The output is 0xF. The flags are defined as enumerations in the `ios` class, so we indicate this by using the class name and member of operator (::). The `showbase` flag adds '0x' to the output. The `hex` flag converts 15 decimal to 15 hex (f), and `uppercase` forces the f to F.

The next fragment from this module demonstrates the `width` command and the `right justify` flag. Setting the width to 80 and the adjust field to `ios::right` and writing "Hello, World!" displays the text on the extreme right-hand side of an 80-character-wide text screen.

```
cout.width(80);
cout.setf( ios::right );
cout << "Hello, World!" ;
```

The last fragment modifies the width to 40, so the text is displayed more toward the center of an 80-character text screen.

```
cout.width(40);
cout.setf(ios::right);
cout << "Width Based Justification" << endl;
```

In both examples, the last character of the string is written at the column passed as the value of `width`.

These examples should give you an idea of how to use the formatting flags in general. Getting the right look and feel in any application requires the developer to know what's available and to experiment a little. The next section, "Writing Stream Manipulators," demonstrates how to make your own manipulator tokens. These provide the simple token-insertion functionality that enables tokens like `hex` or `endl` to work.

Writing Stream Manipulators

You can write functions that can be inserted into streams like tokens. This is how manipulators like `hex` and `endl` work. They are not variables. The token `endl` is not the value '\n', although, in part, it does produce the same result as inserting the '\n' character into a stream. The purpose of a stream manipulator is to enable you to couple those aspects of advanced formatting that provide your input/output with exactly the result you are looking for, in a nice, tidy package.

Built-in Stream Manipulators

There are several built-in manipulators, like `endl`, that are extremely easy to use. This chapter gives you an idea of how some of these were implemented, to make it easier for you to understand how to write your own.

If you look in \Bc5\Include\iostream.h, the following declaration for `endl` is present:

```
ostream _FAR & _RTLENTRY _EXPFUNC endl(ostream _FAR &);
```

> **Note**
>
> Don't worry about some of the specifiers when looking at the Borland header files. The definitions for these can surely be found, but they are not as important as the general pieces. The general pieces from chapter 11 are the return type, function name, and arguments.
>
> If you look in iostream.h you will find __DEFS.H, which will help you decipher FAR, RTLENTRY, and EXPFUNC. These are preprocessor definitions that enable functions to work correctly based on the compiler target and model, whether you are making a DLL, a 16-bit application, or a 32-bit application.

Filtering off the extra stuff that tools implementors, such as Borland, have added to ensure different kinds of compatibility, we are left with:

```
ostream& endl( ostream& );
```

The declaration indicates that the function takes a reference to an `ostream` and returns one, thus allowing it to work in an output change without being a broken link. That's why you might see it in statements such as:

```
cout << "Line 1" << endl << "Line 2" << endl;
```

Again, this requires you to think of operators as a kind of function. In fact, where the `ostream` class is concerned, there are several operator << functions that return `ostream&` values.

The `endl` function is called implicitly by the operator << function, which returns an `ostream` reference. What does the function do? Well, it places a newline (`'\n'`) on the stream and calls the `flush()` member function.

> **Note**
>
> There are several important chapters that will help you understand how to use and detect stream manipulators. Refer to chapter 8, "Understanding Expressions through Expansion," which will help you detect when they are being used. Chapter 15, "Function Overloading," will ciearly explain how several functions having the same name can exist in the same module, and chapter 16, "Operator Overloading," describes how operators like the operator>> work with different data types and functions.

Writing Your Own Stream Manipulators

The endl manipulator is a member function. We do not necessarily want to create a new or derived stream class to enhance our formatting capabilities, so our stream manipulator functions will be global functions. This fact will have some effect on the actual number of arguments, but I will demonstrate the differences.

Let's begin with one we already know, the hex manipulator. As you may have guessed, there is already a hex manipulator that converts integral values to hexadecimal, but it doesn't add the base prefix and display the values in uppercase. We can quickly change all of that. Here's how. Write a header file (you may want to use this in any number of modules) and include a single inline function. Listing 13.4 shows the definition:

Listing 13.4   upperhex.h—An Inline Stream Manipulator Function

```
 1: // UPPERHEX.H - Contains inline stream manipulator.
 2: #ifndef __UPPERHEX_H
 3: #define __UPPERHEX_H
 4: #include <iostream.h>
 5: ostream& upperhex(ostream& os)
 6: {
 7:   os.setf( ios::hex ¦ ios::uppercase ¦ ios::showbase );
 8:   return os;
 9: }
10: #endif
```

Line 7 does all of the work. It calls the setf function, passing the enumerated arguments that provide the result we want. Applying this in an output statement

```
cout << uppercase << 35;
```

calls this function and produces

```
0x23
```

as the result. (The test scaffold is contained in Upperhex.cpp, but is not necessary to use this stream manipulator.)

File Streams

The file stream classes represent some of what is best about C++. The file stream classes allow you to easily instantiate a stream for files that uses an input and output syntax consistent with that of the console input and output streams. What that means to the C++ programmer is that once you have acquired the skills necessary to perform console input/output, you have also acquired the skills for file input/output.

An added feature is that the file stream classes demonstrate a concept referred to as *Resource Acquisition is Initialization* (RAI, pronounced *ray*). Typically in structured programming languages—for instance C, Delphi, and Visual Basic—there are several steps necessary to properly use resources like files. First, you must get a handle, then open the file, ensure the file was opened, use the file, and then close the file. If any one of these steps is left out, you have an error.

RAI means that if you can identify a proper set of steps for acquiring and then releasing a resource when you are finished, the class paradigm is a convenient vehicle for doing so.

In chapter 14, "Basic Class Concepts," you will learn about two special functions, the *constructor* and the *destructor*. All you need to know for now is that a constructor is called when an object (a variable instance of a class) is instantiated. When the object goes out of scope, the special function—the destructor—is called.

Conveniently, you can then bind the acquisition steps—get a handle, open a file, and check to see if the file was opened—to the constructor, and you can bind the release steps—closing a file—to the destructor call. Because you know both of these special functions are called and you know the relative time of the calls (beginning and end), you can ensure that resources are allocated and released correctly every time.

Think of it as creating an "init" and "done" for everything that has a definable series of initialization and de-initialization steps. I expect that you are somewhat unsure of what RAI is or how to implement it yet, but that's okay. All you need to know for now is that this technique was applied to the file stream classes (part of the iostream hierarchy), which provides you with a clean and consistent mechanism for using files in C++.

For the time being, put new terms like *constructor, destructor, object*, and *instantiate* on the back burner if they confuse you. Next, I am going to demonstrate how easy C++ file handling is by providing you with some easy-to-follow examples.

Using the *fstream* Class

You may incorporate file handling into your applications by including the fstream.h file. This will cause the proper class and function declarations to be made, and the linker will link in the matching functions.

Having included the fstream.h header file, you may now create both input file stream objects and output file stream objects. If it is easier, think of an object as a variable with initial values passed in instead of assigned. The input file stream class is called ifstream, and the corresponding output file stream class is called ofstream.

To read from a file, simply declare an ifstream variable with an initial value of a file-name. Probably all of us have an Autoexec.bat on our boot drive, so let's experiment with that file. Listing 13.5 is a short program that reads the entire Autoexec.bat file, echoing the contents to the screen.

Listing 13.5   Infile.cpp—Demonstrates a Simple Use of File Streams

```
 1: // INFILE.CPP - Echoes the autoexec.bat file to the console with ifstreams
 2: #include <iostream.h>
 3: #include <fstream.h>
 4: void main()
 5: {
 6:   ifstream in("C:\\AUTOEXEC.BAT");
 7:   char buf[256];
 8:   while( !in.eof() )
 9:   {
10:     in.getline( buf, 256 );    // Wow works just like with cin!
11:     cout << buf << endl;
12:   }
13: }
```

It's worth noting here that I used the getline command with an ifstream in exactly the same way that I used it with the cin (or istream) object. I could have just as easily written line 10 using the >>

```
10:     in >> ch;      // uses operator >> (ch is a character)
11:     cout << ch;
```

I didn't use >> for the simple fact that the while loop would have iterated many more times, treading character by character as opposed to a line at a time.

Output from Infile.exe was on my computer. (Your Autoexec.bat file will probably be different.)

```
@ECHO OFF
PROMPT $p$g
PATH C:\WINDOWS;C:\WINDOWS\COMMAND;C:\DOS;C:\MOUSE
REM PCM+ path added.
PATH C:\WINDOWS;C:\WINDOWS\COMMAND;PCMPLUS3;%PATH%
PATH=C:\ORAWIN\BIN;C:\IBLOCAL\BIN;C:\IDAPI;%PATH%;
SET LMOUSE=C:\MOUSE
SET TEMP=C:\DOS
IF EXIST TOSCD001 LH C:\DOS\MSCDEX /L:D /D:TOSCD001 /M:10
rem - By Windows Setup - C:\MOUSE\MOUSE
SET PATH=%PATH%;C:\Borland\Delphi32\Interbas\Bin
```

Making the following simple modifications to the infile program, I could easily create a text file backup program, as shown in listing 13.6:

Listing 13.6   Backup.cpp—A Simple Backup Program Using File Streams

```
 1: // BACKUP.CPP - A simple file backup utility.
 2: #include <iostream.h>
 3: #include <fstream.h>
 4: void main()
 5: {
 6:   ifstream in( "C:\\AUTOEXEC.BAT" );
 7:   ofstream out( "C:\\AUTOEXEC.BAK");
```

(continues)

Programming in C++

Listing 13.6   Continued
```
8:    char textline[256];
9:    while(!in.eof())
10:   {
11:     in.getline( textline, 256 );    // in is an ifstream object
12:     out << textline << endl;        // out is an ofstream object
13:   }
14: }
```

The biggest difference is that this program opens an output file (line 7) and sends the input to that file (line 12) instead of the console.

Other Features of File Streams

The last section illustrated that functions and features of the objects `cin` and `cout`, which are instances of the `istream` and `ostream` classes respectively, existed in the `fstream` classes. The reason for this is that these classes have a common origin. The technical jargon is that each is a child class derived from base classes in the same hierarchy.

While all of this does not mean simply that functionality found in one or the other was cut and pasted into the others, in a very simplistic sense you may think of it this way. There are distinctions, however; things that make sense for files do not necessarily make sense for the console.

So far I have demonstrated (see the last section) that the `operator<<`, `operator>>`, and the *getline* function work with both `iostreams` and `fstreams`. There are many other methods because of the common base classes in the stream hierarchy. The exact member functions shared can be culled from the iostream.h, fstream.h, ios.h files, and the context-sensitive Help system.

A distinction that must be made regarding files is the mode in which the files are opened. Files come in a couple of different flavors. One is text files, distinguished by strings and newlines; the `getline` function makes sense with these files. Another mode is binary files. These may contain bytes that fit some structure, referred to as records, or may be a single datum collectively, like bitmaps. It doesn't make sense to open a binary file and try to read lines of text.

Because of these differences, the user (any programmer who uses these classes) has been provided a facility for specifying the mode. This is accomplished by indicating the mode when you instantiate the object. There are actually four different constructors for the `ofstream` class; let's look at the one we used.

The `ofstream` constructor we used allows you to specify one to three arguments, though only one is required. The second two arguments have default values. We relied on the default values and passed a filename as the first parameter. The second argument is the open file mode (open_mode enumerated) values defined in the `ios` class. Looking at the declaration:

```
ofstream(const char *name, int mode = ios::out, int prot =
➡filebuf::openprot);
```

you can see that the ios class name and *member of operator* (::) are used to access these values. In addition to passing a single value for the open mode, you may use Boolean operators to set multiple values. For example, to open a file in binary mode, use Boolean algebra to *or* in the binary open_mode flag:

```
ofstream out( "SAMPLE.BIN", ios::out ¦ ios::binary );
// we didn't use the third argument
```

Note

There are many side discussions we could take in this section. One is the specifying of initial values when declaring a variable, and why this looks like a function call. Another is how we are able to specify different argument values for what is apparently the same object instantiation.

These discussions have been postponed, not arbitrarily, until later chapters. Refer to the "From Here..." section at the end of this chapter for the pertinent chapters.

You may also use the default file stream constructor for both ifstreams and ofstreams, postponing opening the file until a later time. Here is a code fragment demonstrating the technique:

```
ofstream out;
// ...Some code
out.open( "\AUTOEXEC.BAT" );
if( !out )    // Why does the operator! work here
              // The file open command failed
```

The same code works for an ifstream. This demonstrates that you are not required to open the file at the same point in the code at which you declare the fstream object.

Note

When you see operators used with user-defined objects, like fstream objects, there is probably something going on behind the scenes. I am speaking specifically of the

```
    if( !out )
```

test shown in the example code fragment preceding this sidebar. In part, operator tokens make programming much easier. Historically, new types were created without operator support, thus were arguably only partially complete. C++, however, enables programmers to specify the operator behaviors with new types. Chapter 16, "Operator Overloading," explains how this works and how to do it. The class designer of the fstream classes applied the operator! behavior for streams.

Buffered Streams

Objects instantiated from the `streambuf` class are used as members in the higher-level classes. The `streambuf` class provides byte array data management for the file stream and console classes.

The `ios` class is "contained" in the `iostream` and `fstream` classes through inheritance. Defined in the `ios` class is the `rdbuf()` function, which returns a pointer to `ios` data member `streambuf`. Listing 13.7 is an example program of a fragment excerpted from the `streambuf` Help example.

Listing 13.7   Demonstrates Using a Buffered Read

```
#include <iostream.h>
void main()
{
   int c;
   streambuf *input = cin.rdbuf();    // rdbuf returns a pointer to cin's
                                      // streambuf member
   clog << "Input some text. Use Control-Z to end." << endl;
   while ( (c = input->sbumpc() ) != EOF)
     cout << char(c);
}
```

The program demonstrates how the internal representation of streams can be connected by the `streambuf` component of streams. In the example above, a "hook" to the `cin` object is assigned to the console input stream object's `streambuf`, and then simply depleted until the user presses Ctrl+Z. The point is not the result of this simple program, rather it is the capability of the data contents to manipulate the streams through the `streambuf` object.

The program example includes the use of `rdbuf` and `sbumpc`. The `rdbuf` function returns a pointer to the stream's `streambuf` member, and `sbumpc` returns the current character from the stream. Rather than listing every member of every class, I would refer you to the Borland context-sensitive Help files when you sit down to write your code. Borland does a great job of documenting its product in the online Help system. Before you set out to write a new function, check the Help files exhaustively first to see if an existing function or aggregate of functions will provide the solution.

The next section discusses an advanced topic related to both iostreams and *operator overloading*. You may want to read chapters 14, 15, and 16, which provide the theory and examples supporting the topic in general.

Overloading Stream Operators

Assuming you skipped to chapters 14, 15, and 16 first, or you already have a pretty good idea about how operator overloading works and is supported, let's talk about overloaded stream operators. Newly created aggregate types would be disproportionately out of balance if they were unable to work with operators like native types. If this were the case, you might successfully argue that the aggregation idiom in C++ is incomplete. This is not the case.

C++ allows software developers to "train" our types—classes and structs—to work with tokens, just like the built-in types. Statements, such as 1+2, comprise the easiest aspects of programming and are among the first learned. It makes sense to provide this level of support to user-defined types.

What makes this possible is not especially hard to imagine. First, the language must be able to distinguish between vaguely disguised operator functions. Because it does this already, all we need to know is the grammar for employing the language feature. And you must match the number of arguments to the count of the operator. We are talking about the iostream operators, << and >>, which are both binary operators, so the number of arguments is two.

Finally, we must establish what the iostream operators should do, and the order and placement of the arguments.

What Should the *iostream* Operators Do?

The iostream operators read or write data to data streams. Their roles do not change simply because they are associated with a class. The question now becomes "But what is it they are writing"? The answer is "That's up to you"!

Most often the ostream and istream operators for functions are responsible for writing and reading some formatted output either to initialize an object or to display the contents of an object. This is most easily done by using the data members of the class.

Consider a class DATE. This class contains three unsigned integers, representing the day, month, and year. Ask the question, "How should the date be written to an ostream"? (The console, for example.) The answer might be to write the date in *dd/mm/yyyy* format using the day, month, and year to create a formatted string.

The result of applying << to some DATE might appear:

```
DATE d( 2, 12, 1996);    // Takes three unsigned integers
cout << d;               // Writes "02/12/1966"
```

There are no languages that I am aware of that would perform this behavior without some assistance from a programmer. C++ is no different. However, the code you write can be tied to <<, so that the code for writing dates uses the same syntax as the code for writing a simple native type.

In our example, I decided that "outputting dates" meant writing a formatted version of the three data elements representing the calendar date. This is reasonable. C++ does not decide for you what the ostream operator should do. Programming is subjective; therefore, you must still decide. C++ provides an idiom that enables you to make the grammar appear consistent between native and aggregate types, but it neither forces you to use it nor dictates the terms.

> **Note**
>
> Using the notion of DATE class, you could implement date printing functionality in a number of
> ways. For example, you could write a member function, Print, which would print the values of
> the day, month, and year member. For instance:
>
> ```
> DATE d(2, 12, 1996);
> d.Print();     // Outputs "02/12/1996"
> ```
>
> Underneath you might implement Print like this
>
> ```
> void DATE::Print()
> {
>     printf( "%0.2d/%0.2d/%0.2d", day, month, year );
> }
> ```
>
> which uses the %0.2d decimal-formatting command, which zero fills if the number is a single
> digit. Or, you could use:
>
> ```
> void Date::Print()
> {
>     // Alternative using the ios member functions width and fill
>     cout.fill( '0' );
>     cout.width( 2 );
>     cout << day << "/";
>     cout.fill( '0' );
>     cout.width( 2 );
>     cout << month << "/" << year;
> }
> ```
>
> The problem is that now you have more than one way to do what is really the same kind of
> thing. For native types you use cout, but for DATE types, users would call Print. When writing
> to a stream, it is much easier if all types are performed the same way:
>
> ```
> int a = 5;
> cout << a;     // No difference!
> DATE d(2, 12, 1996);
> cout << d;     // No difference!
> ```
>
> Grammar is easier to learn if it is consistent. If input and output functionality is required for
> your classes, write an ostream and istream operator function.

Writing iostream Operators

Both the istream and ostream operators require the same number of arguments and
have a distinct format for most classes you will write. The syntax for either the
operator<< or operator>> is typically:

```
class X
{
public:
    // ...
    friend ostream& operator<<( ostream&, X& );
    friend istream& operator>>(istream&, X& );
};
```

All you have to do is to write these down and keep them handy. There are reasons why the declaration is precise and why it is as it appears. Let's take it step by step.

Define Stream Operators as Friend Functions. The friend specifier provides access to the private members of a class. If a function is a member, it already has access, so the specifier is used with nonmembers (see chapter 14, "Basic Class Concepts"). We use the friend specifier with the iostream operators because they should be global functions and not members.

The reason for this is simple. If a function, like the operator<< function, is a member, invoking the function requires an object to be on the left-hand side of the function. Therefore, if operator<< (or operator>>) were a member function, writing an object x would look like this:

```
x >> cout;      // Error of semantics!
```

Borrowing the notion of understanding expressions through expansion (see chapter 8), this is an implicit call to the "member" operator<<:

```
ostream& x.operator<<( ostream& );   // Error of semantics!
```

This would probably cause a stir because the usually expected form of the call is

```
cout << x;            // What is usually expected
```

Expanding the declaration of this form results in

```
cout.operator<<( operator<<( ostream&, X& ) );
```

where the nested operator<< returns an ostream& argument and the outer operator<< takes a reference to an ostream.

To recap, the iostream functions are friends because

- They will probably require access to the data, which is likely to be *private*.
- The ostream object should be on the left-hand side to avoid a confusion caused by a semantic violation.
- The operator<< is an operator; therefore, there must be two objects. Because the function is global, both objects must be passed as arguments.

Define Stream Operators to Return a Reference to a Stream. The typical use of the stream operators is such that they may be used in a long chain of output statements. You have already seen several examples of output statements that combine a variety of data types. To violate this in your classes would be a semantic error. By returning a reference to a stream object, your stream operators will not break the chain.

Considering our (as yet undefined) DATE class, you could then write:

```
cout << "Today is: " << date << endl;   // Where date is an object of class
DATE
```

If the ostream operator for DATEs returned void, or something other than an ostream&, the "chain" would be broken, and the previous statement would not compile.

Define Stream Operators to Take Two Arguments. The iostream operators are binary operators. The count is two, meaning that the operator must have two operands (or objects). If they were member functions, one object would be satisfied by the calling argument, and the other would be passed in.

> **Note**
>
> If an operator function is a member function, one object is always the calling object. If that operator is a binary operator, the second one will be passed in as an argument. The count of the operands never changes, but the location of the objects does.
>
> The compiler will inform you with an error message if the counts are not correct. If the operator is a unary operator, member functions require no arguments between the parentheses. If the operator is global, the number of arguments is one (passed between the parentheses). The same logic applies to binary operators: For member functions, one operand is the calling object and the other is passed; for global functions, both are passed between the parentheses.

However, because we have established that the istream input operator and the ostream output operators are both global functions, both functions require both arguments to be passed between the left and right parentheses. The first argument is always of the same stream type and the second is a reference to the class type.

Stream Operator Arguments. The precedence for the stream operator functions is "stream reference" followed by an "object reference" of the class type. The order is dictated by the same semantic rule as mentioned above. The normal expected order is stream object on the left (or first) and operand on the right (or second).

Chapter 17, "Constructors: Copy and Assignment," describes how passing arguments by reference avoids an additional call to the copy constructor and the matching destructor call, instead manipulating the actual object through its address.

A Demonstration of Defining Stream Operators

The example class in this section focuses on a demonstration of defining both the input stream operator and the output stream operator for the hypothetical DATE class. The operator writes a formatted date to the console, and reads in a date in the form of the day, month, and year, creating a DATE object (see listing 13.8). (Error checking for valid dates is left as an exercise.)

Listing 13.8   date.h—Header File Containing a *DATE* Class Definition

```
// DATE.H - Defines a simple date class to demonstrate both operator<< and
// operator>>
#ifndef __DATE_H
#define _DATE_H
#include <iostream.h>
```

```
// Warning: This class provides no date validity checking.
class DATE
{
public:
   DATE( unsigned int day=12, unsigned int month=2, unsigned int year=1966);
   ~DATE();

   friend ostream& operator<<( ostream& , DATE& );
   friend istream& operator>>( istream& , DATE& );
private:
   unsigned int day;
   unsigned int month;
   unsigned int year;
};
#endif
```

As listing 13.9 shows, the header file defines the class as containing three unsigned integers, a constructor with default arguments for the date values, a destructor (which we do not really need), and the two stream operators.

Listing 13.9   Date.cpp—The Definition of Class Members

```
1: // DATE.CPP - Defines the DATE class members and provides a test scaffold.
2: #include <stdio.h>
3: #include "date.h"
4: // Constructor with three default arguments
5: DATE::DATE( unsigned int d, unsigned int m, unsigned int y )
6: {
7:    day = d;
8:    month = m;
9:    year = y;
10: }
11: // Destructor doesn't do anything
12: DATE::~DATE(){}
13: ostream& operator<<(ostream& os, DATE& date)
14: {
15:    // I didn't say I don't like the stdio functions from C
16:    static char dateStr[11];
17:    sprintf( dateStr, "%0.2d/%0.2d/%4d", date.month, date.day, date.year );
18:    return os << dateStr;
19: }
20: istream& operator>>( istream& is, DATE& date )
21: {
22:    return is >> date.day >> date.month >> date.year;
23: }
24: #ifdef DATE_SCAFFOLD
25: void main()
26: {
27:    DATE d;
28:    cout << d << endl;
29:    cout << "Enter day month year (separate with white space)" << endl;
30:    cin >> d;
31:    cout << "New Date is: " << d << endl;
32: }
33: #endif
```

Lines 13 through 19 define the operator<< (or ostream operator) and lines 20 through 23 define the istream operator. In the output stream operator we want to print the formatted date string. Surprise! I used the function sprintf, like printf from C, except this function prints to a character buffer instead of the output device. The dateStr variable is static because it is defined within the scope of the function, but I want its lifetime to exist beyond that scope. The function returns the passed in ostream& object (continuing the stream chain), now with the formatted date on it.

The istream operator function reads each of the data elements into the argument object. A prompt suggesting the order of the data and some error-checking would normally be in order. As a class for managing dates, DATE is incomplete, however it does demonstrate the way in which you might generally define input/output for a class. The actual interface to the two stream operator functions changes very little between classes.

Lines 24 to 33 define a scaffold. A scaffold is a small test program that you can include within your module. Scaffolding allows you to test your class separately from any particular use. This scaffold uses the default object line 27, writes it to the console, and then prompts the user for new date values. Notice the syntax for actually using the DATE class is very simple.

There is an added bonus here. Recall from an earlier section how the syntax, except for the left-most object, was the same for writing to or reading from different devices. For the same reasons that input and output devices can vary—between files, the console, or the keyboard—they can also vary with our DATE class. istreams and ostreams are in the same class family as iostreams and fstreams (file streams). This allows the device to vary regardless, but does not require the syntax to vary. Thus

```
DATE d;
cout << d;          // Writes the date to the console
works just as well as
ofstream out( "DATE.TXT");
out << d;           // Writes the date to the file stream
```

does not require you to change the class.

This has nothing to do with the class or its complexity; rather, it is a result of the design of the iostream classes. The file stream classes inherit this behavior from their base classes, which include the iostream classes.

From Here...

The iostream classes are not part of the C++ language proper. They do, however, play a big role in the language and demonstrate the power of many aspects of the C++ programming language. Some parts of this discussion may have been easy to follow; others may have been more difficult or will require additional investigation.

This chapter has demonstrated how to perform input and output. There are many interesting aspects of the language that have to be learned and skills that have to be acquired before you will be writing classes encompassing this level of design.

While C++ is not a simple linear subject, it is not a complex, indecipherable subject either. The language was designed and evolves with express intent, and nothing is left to guesswork. To read about how other language features support designing well-crafted and easy-to-use classes like those found in the iostream hierarchy, refer to:

- Chapter 3, "Object-Oriented Analysis and Design," examines objects and how to design software that exploits the object-oriented constructs of C++.
- Chapter 6, "Native Data Types and Operators," discusses native data types and operators that enable C++ developers to express their ideas.
- Chapter 14, "Basic Class Concepts," teaches you how to employ C++ and object-oriented programming to solve complex programming problems.
- Chapter 15, "Function Overloading," discusses how you can use function overloading to manage hundreds of function names and how it provides the bases for understanding language idioms in C++.
- Chapter 16, "Operator Overloading," demonstrates how to write operator functions through a discussion on operators as functions, overloadable operators, operator expansion, and unary operators.

CHAPTER 14

Basic Class Concepts

Basic class concepts introduce those elements of classes that are essential because they support the object-oriented paradigm. This does not necessarily mean that the topics in this chapter are easy or trivial.

Note

The word "Basic" is used to indicate that the class concepts are necessary but not necessarily simple.

I weighed two alternate perspectives: should I avoid the more advanced aspects of classes, in an effort to avoid confusion, or should I opt for thoroughness and hope that perspective, background information, and demonstrations will make the great quantity of information decipherable? I chose the latter, because you are completely free to ignore the object-oriented aspects, including classes of C++ and use Borland C++ 5 as a "better C" while you are learning. More importantly, there are inherent dangers involved in showing just some of the language features and not all.

If you want to postpone your understanding of classes and stick to a structured programming style for the time being, you might postpone the reading of this chapter. Or read it and mentally set aside the information for the time being. C++ is a fascinating language. The language supports the modeling of data after a fashion that most of us have been using for some time. C++ is the language that supports this kind of design, analysis, and programming. When you are ready to write object-oriented programs, this chapter is the first step towards understanding *how* to employ C++ and object-oriented programming to solve complex programming problems.

There is a lot of information about classes in this chapter, including:

- An introduction to classes
- Comparing classes and structs
- Classes viewed as types
- Access specifiers

■ `this`: pointer to self
■ Demo utility

An Introduction to Classes

I begin by showing you simple details and proceed by slowly pulling back the layers to reveal some implicit aspects of classes that are not readily detectable. Let's begin by looking at the syntax of a class.

The Syntax of a Class

The keyword `class` is used to specify that you are creating a conglomeration of information. Regardless of a class's intended purpose or use, the external syntax of a class does not change. Setting aside that you may not know what a class is, what it does, or when to use classes, you certainly can be shown the syntax.

The exterior view of the keyword `class` is

```
class CLASS_NAME
{
};
```

The word `class` is a keyword recognized by the compiler. The `CLASS_NAME` is a unique name. The convention I like to use is all uppercase letters, but that is a convention only. You will see as many other conventions for class names as you do for variable names. The body of the class—its definition—is indicated by the left and right brace followed by a semicolon.

> **Caution**
>
> If you forget the semicolon after the right brace, the compiler may report several errors, none of which indicate that the semicolon is missing. If you recognize the absence of a semicolon, you may want to create a simple class later and compile it, noting the errors.

There are very few absolutes in life, but the example shown pretty much presents the appearance of a simple class. The exceptions are that the line containing the keyword `class` may have some added information if the class denotes an inherited class, a template class, or is simply a forward declaration.

> **Note**
>
> You may also see a declaration in the code like the following:
>
> ```
> class CLASS_NAME;      // class declaration
> ```
>
> without the class body. This is a forward declaration. Don't be alarmed; using forward declarations is done sometimes to introduce the name into the namespace. You will find the definition of the class later. This technique is used to resolve inter-class dependencies.

Class Members

There are many ways to learn new things. Sometimes we get a shock and something completely new pops right up in front of us and then we seek understanding. Other times we learn about things in the abstract and then we actually see one. In college, for example, we tend to hear a lot of theory and then we see "one." I have simply chosen to show you first. (Maybe for shock value.) You will get some theory, too.

In the last section you saw the outside appearance of a class. Let's look now at what goes in the inside. Though full of little details on the inside, generally the class body consists of data and functions.

Data Reflects Knowledge. We refer to the data and functions of a class as *members*. The data of a class can be anything that can be thought of as a data type. This obviously includes the native data types, but it also includes aggregate data types, too, which means other classes, as well as structs, unions, and enumerations.

The simplest kinds of data members are those that are variables based on native data types. There is no prescribed order—mostly convention—in which the data members are placed in a class. The only requirement is that the definition, or placement, use the same syntax as you normally use to define variables anywhere else.

Demonstrating. The following code:

```
class INT
{
    int j;      // simple int data member
};
```

represents a class with a single integer data member. (The member shown is a *private* member. Read the "Using Access Specifiers" section later in the chapter for more information.)

For each data member the syntax follows the same order: data type followed by the variable name. Half of the view of classes is to record what the class knows. Member data is used to store this information.

> **Note**
>
> Philosophically integers can be thought of as a class of counting numbers. In fact, the same can be said of any native data types: it is a class of that type. This is why the terms type and class are somewhat interchangeable and so are the terms variable and object.
>
> A variable, as well as an object, is a name of something with a specific type. We need these symbolic names to refer to specific instances of a specific type.

Methods Reflect Capability. Member functions make up the other half of a class. Like real world entities, things are usually classified by description, which is defined by what they know about themselves and what they can do. We learn how to identify the world around us by appearance and functionality.

Modeling this kind of understanding in the digital world is accomplished by recording the descriptive details in variables and the functionality in functions. (How else would you do it?) The class then becomes the vessel for combining these aspects.

To maintain consistency, functions in classes are declared exactly as they are outside of the class. A return type is followed by a function name and an argument list and is completed by tacking a semicolon on the end. Thus

```
class INT
{
    int j;          // member data
    int GetJ();     // member function, sometimes called a method
};
```

defines a class INT, with one data member j, and one method GetJ(), which returns an integer.

When functions are part of classes, they are sometimes referred to as methods. A *method* means a member function. The primary goal when designing classes is to determine those data members and functions that express the concept you are trying to define.

Note

The abundance of synonyms for things may lead to some confusion in discourse. You may have forgotten the simple reason why this paradox occurs. Almost all of us glean understanding based on prior knowledge. This is achieved by equating new things to things we already understand.

This approach to learning is probably innate, definitely useful, and unlikely to be turned off. The term "method" is probably borrowed from another object-oriented language: SmallTalk. Everything is an object in SmallTalk and all functions are referred to as methods. Thus, the term was probably borrowed in someone's attempt to understand class functions as they pertain to C++.

Comparing Classes and Structs

There are several similarities between classes and structs. The class keyword represents the new aggregation feature supporting the object-oriented paradigm. The struct comes from the structured programming world of C. C++ is a superset of C—meaning C comprises a subset of C++'s make-up, so the keyword struct exists in the C++ language to maintain backward compatibility.

In general, you want to move to the object-oriented paradigm which means using classes, but you find structs in existing and new code compiled with a C++ compiler. In part, this probably occurs because some C programmers are using C++ compilers to write C-styled programs and some C++ proponents are using structs as a convention for classes that contain data without functions.

There are many similarities between the syntax and usage of structs and classes; we'll look at both similarities and differences here. The goal is to demonstrate them both so neither seems foreign, but I would emphasize that, in general, you use classes even to represent the class as a collection of data without functions.

Similarities between Classes and Structs

Both classes and structs use a very similar notation in defining the entity. The difference from the previous class example is the use of the keyword `struct` in place of the keyword `class`.

Thus the class `INT` defined takes on this appearance if it is defined as a struct:

```
struct INT
{
    INT j;      /* a struct containing an integer. (This is a C-style comment) */
};
```

The only readily apparent difference is the use of the keyword `struct`.

Knowing that you may not know what these terms mean, other similarities between structs and classes include: both can have member functions and data; both can have the special member functions referred to as constructors, a destructor, a copy constructor, and an assignment operator; and both structures and classes can be used in inheritance relationships.

However, structs are not classes. Some differences between the two are fundamental to the object-oriented paradigm.

Differences between Classes and Structs

One obvious difference between a class and a struct occurs when you instantiate an object. Instantiation of objects looks exactly like declaring a variable instance of a native type, except that more work goes on behind the scenes.

The syntactical difference between instantiating a struct object and a class object is the requirement that the keyword `struct` be used for structs. Consider the following two instances of a class and struct:

```
SOME_CLASS someInstance;          // define a SOME_CLASS object
struct SOME_STRUCT aStruct;       // uses the keyword struct
```

This is only a slight nuisance but does require a slightly more cumbersome notation for structures. There are less apparent differences, too.

Accessibility Differences. The term accessibility refers to the circumstances in which members are accessible. (A complete explanation of accessibility is provided in the later section "Using Access Specifiers.") There are three levels of accessibility: *private* being the least accessible, *public* being the most accessible, and *protected* in the middle.

These access specifiers are available for your use, so you can determine the right access for your design. However, structs and classes do have default accessibility built into them. The class is `private` by default. Structs are `public` by default. This means that if you do not specify an alternative accessibility, then data members of classes are private—inaccessible—and structs are public—highly accessible.

The reverse of what you think may be true: restricting access is actually a more desired attribute, thus making the class more appealing but the struct a bit simpler to use.

Differences in Inheritance. Structs can be inherited from; they cannot inherit. For now think of inheritance as the compiler doing the cutting and pasting from other classes or structs to create a new struct or class.

Suppose for example that you defined a class describing what characteristics you needed to express some kind of fruit digitally. Now suppose you wanted to use some of that code to create a specific kind of fruit, maybe a Macintosh apple. One way to do it is to copy the characteristic devices from fruit with your code editor into the new struct describing apples.

The relationship between the fruit and the apple then is one of manufactured derivation. The inheritance idiom is that the compiler supports this kind of relationship through code as opposed to cutting and pasting. It is this relationship that can be expressed with classes, not structs.

Class: The New Paradigm. I wonder a little whether or not the new keyword class was introduced, for the most part, to get programmers to think in new, object-oriented ways. It may have been possible after all to convert the old struct into a new and better struct. This is not what happened, however.

There are many new aspects in C++ found in C that are dependent on the use of classes as opposed to structs. Some of these by name are inheritance, polymorphism, virtual classes, and templates—also referred to as generic classes. These advanced idioms are supported best by using classes.

Exploring Classes Viewed as Data Types

The class idiom is a notation used to allow the programmer to express a relationship between some functions and data to create a new entity. The purpose of creating entities has many facets. Some of the reasons for doing so digitally are akin to the reasons we do so in the real world.

For example, a woman might say to her friend, "That's a beautiful diamond." As opposed to, "What a particularly elegant hunk of cut, crystallized, and compressed carbon." The word "diamond" says all of that. On the surface this equates to our goal when we are trying to express complex ideas. Not only is the name pretty important, but the information we provide to express it must be accurate in the context of need.

The outcome is that we can refer to the aggregate idea by a single mnemonic, which simplifies the appearance of the code we write. Having created an abstraction for a compound idea, we can then hope to contrive simple ways to express the manipulation of the new entity. Ultimately, if we can express intuitive ways to manipulate the class with operators and easy to understand functions then the new complex class should be almost as easy to use as the built in data types.

All of these goals, while not necessarily easy, are supported by the C++ programming language. C++ applied correctly can enable you to express complex ideas in relationships that seem intuitive and apparent. If it were not for our innate tendency to aggregate and create symbolic abstractions for complex ideas, we would all still be saying "ugh! bug!," living in caves, and chasing mice.

Is Everything a Class?

We have a natural tendency towards grouping things, aggregating. If we are inclined to aggregate, then the only obstacle to doing so in programming is learning the forms for expressing these relationships in our language of choice.

Don't go overboard. Everything is probably not expressed best as a class. Some things may resist being a class altogether, and still others may not really be suited to designation as classes. However, exploiting aspects of classes makes the idea easier to express. Determining whether the creation of a class makes the concept easier to express is a good measuring stick to use. The easier to express measurement is not nullified simply because you do not know how to write classes yet.

When to Use Classes. You can apply some general guidelines when trying to ascertain when to use the class idiom and when to avoid it. As with all guidelines these should be applied subjectively. Create a class when a concept has more than one or two members, whether data or functions. An exception to this guideline is to use classes when doing so supports the proper initialization and de-initialization of a resource. The latter applies to things like files, hardware devices, or processes that require a definable series of steps to initialize and release the resource.

When Not to Use Classes. Avoid using classes in general when the abstraction contains very few data members or functions. Single functions also do not usually constitute a class relationship. Examples of these are sorting or searching algorithms. (The only variant in a sort or search may be the data type. This solution is probably best expressed as a template function, not a class. See chapter 19 "Using Template Classes.")

Programming is difficult because designating a solution as good or poor is highly subjective. Assuming two disparate solutions provide the correct answer and relatively the same execution time, it is highly subjective whether one implementation is poorer and the other better. While you are learning, aim for correctness. Providing that you have mastered the language sufficiently to solve problems, work toward simplicity of expression and later be somewhat mindful of speed. Correct is better than wrong and fast; simple expressions are easier to maintain than long convolutions, and much of the speed is provided by the hardware.

Complexity Hiding

Large programs go astray when there are too many names that the programmer has to cope with. If every single variable and function is designated as a global function, without the benefit of aggregation, the programmer becomes overwhelmed. This is, in fact, what consistently happens in medium to large projects.

Complexity hiding, or information hiding, refers to that aspect of a class which alleviates the user from concerning himself with every variable and function. The class paradigm supports this notion, called *encapsulation*, which allows the class developer to implement the functions and data that consist of a complete idea.

By encapsulating the functions and data in a class, the developer is saying to the user (in this context users are programmers who use the class) that you do not have to concern yourself with every aspect of the class. Rather, simply consider those parts of the class that make up the public interface.

If the class represents a complete entity, then some of the details of the entity are not necessary at every level of understanding. Consider a car. There are many levels of understanding in the car user-community. Children use cars as passengers; adults use cars as operable modes of transportation; autoworkers perceive cars as a means of income, and mechanics do too but after something's gone wrong.

Each of these users must have a different level of understanding of cars. The model of the car doesn't change, just the perception depending on the perceiver. The same holds true for classes. The class designer must know all of the intimate details, like the folks at the UAW, but those who drive the class must only be familiar with those aspects related directly to driving.

When you are programming in C++, consider whether you are building a class or using the class as a complete entity. If the former is true, focus on the class somewhat independently of its intended resting place. If the latter is true, focus on those pieces of the class that help solve a larger problem and not the specific details of the class itself. (Autoworkers are aware that cars need to stop, that's why they add brakes. However they are not that concerned with the circumstances under which a driver stops while installing the brakes.)

The class idiom supports this separation of issues, which reduces the complexity; we refer to the encapsulation of the details of a class as information hiding or complexity hiding. It is not necessarily easy to do.

Managing Complexity

Encapsulating small pieces that together comprise a whole, constructive, new concept helps you as a programmer manage complexity. Properly defined entities can be taught to work with operators, like native data types, and they provide simple mnemonic representations of complex ideas. The class idiom supports this division of considerations. Divide and conquer most assuredly applies to programming.

We'll look at examples demonstrating how the class idiom can be used to divide programming issues after we have examined a few more parts of a class.

Using Access Specifiers

The access specifiers are used to determine what kinds of code have access to individual areas within a class. Remember that the members of a class are private by default. This is exactly the same as using the private access specifier. The other two levels of accessibility are public and protected.

The C++ has the language features for several reasons. The first is that computer scientists have identified complexity management as critical to developing complex software systems. Therefore, hiding complexity should be supported by the language. The public, protected, and private access specifiers are provided so that you may specify to users of your classes which parts they need to be concerned with. This is, as you shall see, dependent on what you intend to do with the class.

public

The public access specifier is used to indicate the highest level of accessibility. This means that any functions declared after the keyword public (followed by a colon), but before any other specifier, are available for use by code within and without.

Use of the public access specifier

```
class PUBLIC
{
public:
     void Function();
     int data;
};
```

uses exactly the same syntax as private and protected; the access specifer followed by a colon. In our example, Function() and data are accessible by all users of the class directly. Thus

```
PUBLIC p;
p.Function();
p.data = 5;
```

written outside of the class represents an appropriate usage of the class PUBLIC. We say that the functions and data in the public access region make up the public interface. The public data and functions are those that you make available to other programmers, including yourself when you use the class, to enable them to manipulate objects instantiated from your class.

There is little requirement as to the number of data or functions that should go in any section of a class, if any. The choice is entirely up to you. Because the public interface is accessible to all, one convention is to always place items that make up the public interface first in the class.

> **Caution**
>
> A class consisting of only private data and functions is of questionable use. How would you manipulate the class at all?

protected

The keyword protected is a lot like keyword private. Users of the class cannot access data or functions declared protected. However, protected members are accessible to child classes.

> **Note**
>
> If C++ is completely new to you, remember you can think of inheritance as borrowing existing code. Instead of using the code editor to cut and paste, the compiler can be directed to do so.
>
> The language has an express notation for creating derivative types. While the process is not so simple as automated cutting and pasting, it is sufficient to think of it in those terms for now.

One convention is to place the protected specifier, if used, second because it is slightly more accessible than private members. When you specify that members are protected, you are in effect suggesting that you expect others may want to create a new type inherited from the old type, and it will be convenient for them to have access to those members.

private

The private access specifier indicates that the members within comprise the implementation of the entity but are of little concern to those looking in. This is analogous to the driver of a car: the parts used to build a carburetor are generally of little concern to the average driver.

Whereas the public access specifier makes up the public interface, members declared after the keyword private make up the implementation. The implementation, like the carburetor, is necessary, but the details of it do not have to be understood to use the car.

When you place data and functions in the private access region, you are suggesting to the average user that the details contained within do not affect how or why you use this class, so don't concern yourself.

friend. For notational convenience and sometimes speed, the friend notation was created to allow other classes and functions to violate the private access region. The keyword friend is used in the function or class declaration to indicate that the particular function or class can access the private region.

The use of the `friend` idiom appears in the class extending the friendship. Therefore, if a class wanted to allow a particular function access to its private members, the following syntactical example demonstrates the use of the specifier:

```
class FRIEND_SYNTAX
{
friend return_type FunctionName();// friend function
friend class CLASS_NAME;// friend class
public:
private:
// friends of this class are declared in the class
// and are allowed access to the members in this region
};
```

The placement of the friends must be within the class definition (between { and }). As a convention, I place them first, in deference to their special relationship and so that they stand out. This is only a convention.

Friends of a class can access the private members of a class and, therefore, have the potential to violate the integrity of the class. It is probably a specifier used sparingly. There are alternatives to extending friendship. You will see these in chapter 16, "Operator Overloading."

Alternatives to Using *friend*. There is an alternative to using the `friend` specifier. While I am not going to go into specifics, I do want to prepare you for it. (You will see the alternative in chapter 16.)

Consider what I said the `friend` specifier is for: accessing private members of the class. Often it is used to specifically access private data members. Now consider what an accessor does: it provides you with a function that can be used to provide access to private members, specifically data.

The accessor provides restricted—through the accessor only—access, and the `friend` specifer provides notational convenience. What if restricted access could be provided allowing for notational convenience?

When presented this way, I hope that it seems like a natural, evolutionary step. There is such an animal. We refer to them as conversion operators. Remembering the notion of operators as functions from chapter 6, "Native Data Types and Operators," conversion operators are special functions that return a data of the type expected within the context of the sub-program it's used in. Often these contextual conversions are individual data members of a class.

Data Conventions

There are many conventions. There are probably nearly as many conventions as there are programmers. One convention is to make all data private.

```
class DEMO
{
public:
    // ... public functions
```

```
protected:
    // ... protected functions
private:
    // ... all of the data
    int d, e, f;
    float g;
};
```

Having done so, you must then provide functions to allow the user to access this data. (Remember if `private`, it is inaccessible to users of the class.) Functions for the sole purpose of accessing data are referred to as accessor functions.

There are plausible arguments for employing the data is private convention. To understand why, ask yourself where a big cause of errors is in programs. The answer is in the misuse, intentional or otherwise, of data. By placing class data in the private access region, you have explicit control over the circumstances surrounding the use of the component parts of your classes.

By using accessor functions to get the data, you have in effect created a digital toll booth. The users of your class must pay the toll (meet the criteria, established by you conveniently enough) to be allowed access to the class data.

Because it is understood that you would not intentionally misuse a class that you derived, enforcing the same standard for other users of your sub-programs can be accomplished with accessor functions. The previous `INT` class, containing an integer and the member function `GetJ()`, illustrates a simple accessor function: `GetJ()`.

The Big Four: Four Elements to Consider in Every Class

To this point, I have written in generalities mostly. The time has come for this to stop. This section addresses four class members that you must address, and we must be specific, including examples, at this point.

The big four are four very special members that must be considered when creating every class. They are: the default constructor, the destructor, the copy constructor, and the assignment operator. I did not say that you must write these four functions for every class; what I did say is that you must consider the disposition of these four members for every class that you write.

These four members are functions but are not typical. They look much like functions, but you will notice that some of them do not use a return argument. The functions have to do with the initialization, copying, and the de-initialization of objects of classes.

Constructors

Constructors are members used to create objects that are instances of classes. There are several kinds of constructors, including some twists, but the primary purpose of a constructor is the same. Its job is to provide a convenient way for you to construct an object—an instance of a class—made up of several elemental components.

The constructors we examine in this section include, the default constructor, the copy constructor, default constructor arguments, and other constructors.

As earlier stated, constructors are member functions that have no return arguments (not even void). Another peculiarity is that the function name must be exactly, including case, the same as the class name. Thus if a class is named F00, its constructor must also be named F00.

Default Constructor. The *Annotated Reference Manual* states that a default constructor is one that takes no arguments. This is significant because the *Annotated Reference Manual*, by Stroustrop the creator of C++, is usually the source from which the ANSI C++ document is in part founded.

Therefore, a default constructor for any class looks like the following:

```
class ANY_CLASS
{
public:
    _CLASS();       // default constructor
};
```

The default constructor's job is to build objects of the class when no arguments are specified. In general, constructors are declared in the public access region. Since the constructor's job is to create objects of the classes type, they are called from outside of the class. This call is implicit, but it does occur outside of the class dictating the location of its declaration.

A single object of type ANY_CLASS is created by

```
ANY_CLASS ac;      // ac is an ANY_CLASS object
```

Notice that no parentheses were used in this statement; construction is an implicit operation. An array of ANY_CLASS can be created like

```
ANY_CLASS aac[10];        // aac is an array of size 10
```

Again exactly the type of syntax used to declare a static array of native data types. I mentioned in an earlier chapter that one goal of the C++ language is to allow users to express complex types as much like the built-in types. The implicit nature of construction meets the first aspect of this goal: object creation looks like variable creation.

Copy Constructor. The copy constructor's job is to allow initialization of one object from an existing object. There are many implications that require more room than we have in this chapter, but I will introduce it here. The general syntax of the copy constructor is

II

Programming in C++

```
X(X&);      // where X is the name of the class
```

The body of the copy constructor is generally a series of assignments, whereby each element of the argument object is assigned to each of the matching elements in the calling object.

There are many considerations involved, all of which are extremely important to C++ classes. I am postponing further discussion of the copy constructor until chapter 17, "Constructors: Copy and Assignment." Fear not; we can tip-toe around the subject for now.

Default Constructor Arguments. Any function may have default arguments. This includes constructors, other members, and global functions. A default argument is the value that is assigned to an argument if none is provided by the user.

As we are concerned particularly with constructors here, I will demonstrate the idiom accordingly. Default arguments provide a notational convenience, whereby if a known particular value satisfies the argument but an alternative might at times be preferable, a default argument may be used

```
class DIR
{
public:
    DIR( char * fname = "*.*" ); // "*.*" is a default argument
    // ... other stuff
};
```

This class says to the trained observer, "If you do not pass a char* argument to DIR then I will use "*.*"." Either is acceptable. So instances of DIR objects may be created like the following:

```
DIR default;          // *.*
DIR root("C:\\");     // fname = "C:\\"
```

The rule for using default arguments is that if used they must be used from the right argument to the left argument, skipping no arguments.

Here are some examples of both valid and invalid default arguments for dummy constructors:

```
F( int a = 0, int b );      // error: F( , 5) looks silly
G( int a, int b = 10 );     // ok: G( 5 ); G( 3, 4 );
H( int a, int b );          // ok: H( 3, 4); only
```

The rule for default arguments was implemented to avoid the space-comma-argument (see constructor F) which is prone to error and doesn't look so hot either.

Constructors in General. A constructor's job is to provide an opportunity for the class designer to initialize each of the sub-parts of a class. There is no limit to the number or variety of arguments to a constructor. Usually, however, the argument types match the data members—it is these we intend to initialize after all—of the class.

The guidelines for constructors that do exist are: you *should* provide a default constructor, there is no return argument type, and the name of the constructor is exactly the same as that of its class. A technique I employ is to address the big four first to ensure that their disposition has been decided upon. Much of the details of the constructor declaration, including the name and the choice of return types, is out of your hands.

Destructors

The destructor has a complementary job to that of the constructor's. Where there may exist many constructors in a single class, there is only one destructor.

The syntax of a destructor is very close to that of a default constructor. The constructor name is the same as the class, and the destructor takes no arguments. The biggest difference is that the destructor, being the complement of construct, is prefixed by the complement operator (~). Thus, for any class

```
class ANY
{
public:
     ANY();      // default constructor
     ~ANY();     // the destructor. there can be only one
};
```

the destructor is of the form shown.

The call to the destructor is almost always implicit. The call is made either when the static variable goes out of scope, or the delete operator is called on a dynamic object.

Virtual Destructor. A virtual destructor is used when the class may be inherited from. The syntax of a virtual destructor is the same as that of any other destructor, except for the use of the keyword `virtual`, as the first word of the destructor declaration.

The only difference in the previous class is

```
class ANY
{
public:
     ANY();             // default constructor
     virtual ~ANY();    // now a virtual destructor
};
```

There is no performance penalty for designating a destructor as virtual, so a suggested convention is to always make destructors virtual unless you have a very specific reason for not doing so. Inheriting from base classes without virtual destructors can introduce the slicing problem. (Read chapter 20, "Inheritance and Polymorphism" for more details.)

Demonstrating Implicit Constructor and Destructor Calls. The following example program was created to demonstrate the implicit calls to the constructor and destructor when a class is instantiated. Listing 14.1 simply prints a message when either the constructor or destructor is called.

Listing 14.1 Chap14.cpp—Demonstrates Examples of Static and Dynamic Allocation

```
1:  #include <iostream.h>
2:  // This class simply demonstrates the implicit call to the
3:  // constructor and destructor
4:  class DEMO
5:  {
6:  public:
7:      DEMO(){ cout << "constructor"  << endl; }
8:      virtual ~DEMO(){cout << "destructor" << endl; }
9:  };
10:
11: void main()
12: {
13:     DEMO staticDemo;                    // static allocation, destructor
                                            // called at end-of-scope
14:     DEMO *dynamicDemo = new DEMO;       // dynamic allocation, destructor
                                            // called when deleted
15:     delete dynamicDemo;
16: }
```

This program was compiled using a Win32 Console target.

Lines 4 to 9 define a simple class containing only a public destructor and constructor. These two functions are also declared and defined in the class. The constructor prints the word "constructor" when it is invoked, and the destructor prints "destructor."

Lines 12 to 15 of the main function create two objects, one on the stack and one on the heap. The output from this example file is

```
constructor
constructor
destructor
destructor
```

where the last word—destructor—reflects that the destructor for the static object was called last as it went out of scope: at the point the line containing the enclosing closing brace for main was reached.

The Assignment Operator

A class assignment operator has the task of allowing you to make one existing object equivalent to another. The operator itself is the equal (=) sign. Assignment is so important that if you do not create one, the compiler does it for you.

Earlier in the chapter, recall that I said you must consider the default constructor, copy constructor, assignment operator, and the destructor for every class you create. In some circumstances, the course of action you may decide upon is to allow the default—that is, the compiler's version—copy constructor and assignment operator to be used.

Unfortunately, this is not the case. Sometimes you may decide that initializing or copying objects from other objects should not even be allowed. There are specific ways to indicate this in your code. Refer to chapter 17, "Constructors: Copy and Assignment." The examples we use between now and then will not introduce errors due to faulty copy and assignment functions.

Understanding an Object's Pointer to Self: *this*

Every object has a location. We call locations in programming addresses. In general, pointers are used to store addresses. When we refer to a pointer pointing to something, what we are really referring to is that the value of the pointer is the address of an object.

Every class like every person is aware of its physical location. Just like we sometimes refer to ourselves as being somewhere, it can be notational convenience to use the address of an object. The address of every object can be obtained from the pointer referred to as this.

Each class has an internal this pointer, which simply points to self. In fact, anytime you refer to members within the scope of the class member functions, you are making use of the this pointer. Here is an example:

Listing 14.2 Verbose Use of the *this* Pointer

```
class THIS_DEMO
{
public:
    THIS_DEMO(){ this->a = 5; }
private:
    int a;
};
```

The fragment in the constructor for THIS_DEMO assigns the value 5 to the integer member. The code usually is written without the explicit use of this. Thus appearing as a = 5;.

While it is easy to refer to members of an object from within a class, the problem is how else would you refer to the whole object from within. The keyword this was provided as a notational convenience because sometimes that is exactly what you want to do.

Using a Demo Utility

To demonstrate some of the language idioms presented in this chapter, I will demonstrate a small utility sub-program that you may find useful. The utility demonstrates the use of a pair of functions that enable you to list files in a directory that match a given file mask. As presented here, they produce a demonstration program that looks a little like the old DOS DIR command.

II

Programming in C++

Instead of just listing the code and explaining the most important features, I have chosen to present the solution in an iterative series of steps. The result, I hope, is a more easily reusable class that exploits the special class functions, making the resultant sub-program easier to use.

First Iteration

The first example solves the problem using the function pair, `findfirst` and `findnext` in a small, structured program. Both functions are available by including the dos.h and dir.h header file.

For simplicity, I compiled the code as a Win32 Console application. It does not have to be. Listing 14.3 is the first stab:

Listing 14.3   Dir1.cpp—Shows Code to List All of the Directories in a Single Directory

```
 1: // DIR1.CPP - Demonstrates a program that returns a directory listing.
 2: // Copyright (c) 1995. All Rights Reserved.
 3: // By Paul Kimmel
 4: #include <dir.h>
 5: #include <dos.h>
 6: #include <iostream.h>
 7: void main()
 8: {
 9:         // ffblk defined in dos.h
10:          struct ffblk ffblk;
11:         // findfirst( filemask, ffblk, attribute_byte)
12:         int done = findfirst("*.*", &ffblk, 0 );
13:         while( !done )
14:         {
15:             cout << ffblk.ff_name << endl;
16:             // use the filename return in ffblk to get the next file
17:             done = findnext( &ffblk);
18:         }
19: }
```

The code as actually used simply demonstrates the ease with which the two functions can be used in a structured program manner. Line 10 defines a `struct ffblk`. This is defined in the dos.h header file. It has information in it that closely matches a directory entry on a disk drive.

Line 12 defines an integer used as a test in the next line and its initial value is the return value of the `findfirst` function. `findfirst` takes a `filemask`, a reference to an `ffblk`, and a number which completes the match criteria.

In line 13, while `done` is equal to 0, the current filename in the `ffblk` is output to the console and `findnext` uses that file block to find the next match. The resultant list is a list of all files in the directory where the program is executed.

What we can identify in this example of the code is that `findfirst` and `findnext` are used in concert, with some kind of loop test. We could naturally cut and paste this code anytime we needed this particular kind of functionality.

However, it is the manual cutting and pasting that is error prone. I stated earlier that one view of the class paradigm is to create aggregate entities; another is to bind processes together that are used in coordination to acquire a resource or accomplish a task. Let's try to simplify the use of these two functions.

Second Iteration

After a second look, I have established that the key functionality resides in the coordination between the two functions and a loop control mechanism. My next goal is to simplify the use of the functionality, so it is consistently and easily used every time I need it. I achieved something a little easier to use by combining the component parts into a class.

> **Note**
>
> A simple way to test your classes is to add the code to test the class right into the .cpp file containing the method definitions. This is referred to as *scaffolding.*
>
> By scaffolding—wrapping the test code in a preprocessor compiler directive—you accomplish several tasks. The first is that you provide an easy and convenient way to test each class; the testing code can easily be included or left out by defining or undefining the preprocessor directive. In addition, you clearly indicate to other programmers that not only have you tested your class but you demonstrated how others might instantiate your class.

Listing 14.4 is a sample program, called a scaffold, that demonstrates how easily the new class can be used, achieving the same result.

Listing 14.4   Dir2.cpp—Demonstrates Converting the Utility Code into a Reusable Class

```
1:  // DIR2.CPP - Class methods and testing scaffold
2:  #include "dir2.h"
3:  // constructor definition
4:  DIR_LIST::DIR_LIST(char * fname, int attrib )
5:  {
6:      done = findfirst( fname, &ffblk, attrib );
7:  }
8:  // return whether or not a next file matching the mask exists
9:  int DIR_LIST::Next()
10: {
11:     return (done = findnext( &ffblk ));
12: }
13:  // Allow printing of the file name
14: char * DIR_LIST::Cur()
```

(continues)

Listing 14.4   Continued

```
15: {
16:     return done ? 0 : ffblk.ff_name;
17: }
18: // #undef __DIR2_SCAFFOLD  // excludes testing code
19: #define __DIR2_SCAFFOLD
20: #ifdef __DIR2_SCAFFOLD
21: #include <iostream.h>
22: void main()
23: {
24: // The example program shrinks!
25:     for( DIR_LIST list("*.*"); list.Cur(); list.Next()  )
26:         cout << list.Cur() << endl;
27: }
28: #endif
```

Look closely at lines 25 and 26. These two lines are all it takes to display a directory listing.

Lines 4 to 17 define methods of the new class which contain basically the same code as in Listing 14.3. There are several important differences here though: an important one is that most of the details of findfirst and findnext are encapsulated in the class DIR_LIST. In our example, this only alleviates a modest amount of complexity but consider that this one task may be part of a utility program that performs hundreds of such tasks.

Fig. 14.1

Code shown in listing 14.4 is probably very similar to the underlying implementations of many programs containing file management facilities, like the Windows 95 Explorer shown here.

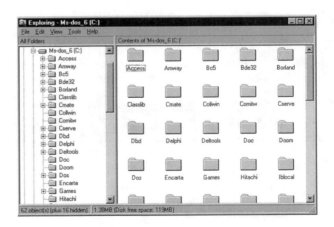

Line 2 contains the header file that contains the class definition (see Listing 14.5).

Listing 14.5   dir2.h—The Class Definition Using Functions to Iterate Through the Directory

```
1:  // DIR2.H - Simple Directory Listing Class
2:  #ifndef __DIR2_H
3:  #define __DIR2_H
```

```
4:  #include <dir.h>
5:  #include <dos.h>
6:  class DIR_LIST
7:  {
8:  public:
9:      DIR_LIST( char* fname = "*.*", int attrib = 0);      // default
constructor arguments
10::      virtual ~DIR_LIST(){}; // destructor not really required
11:      int Next();                 // return 0 if done, otherwise return the
                                     // next string
12:      char * Cur();               // return 0 if done, otherwise return the
                                     // next string
13: private:
14:      struct ffblk ffblk;
15:      int done;
16: };
17: #endif
```

In the second listing, lines 6 to 16 define the class. The class contains a constructor, a destructor with nothing to do, a Next function, and a Cur() function that returns the current filename. The data members, lines 4 and 15, are the same done and ffblk that we saw in the first listing.

This is where subjectivity plays an important role. I like this better than the first example, but I still don't like it. The for loop in lines 25 and 26 of the Dir2.cpp listing don't seem natural. Let's see if one more iteration provides any improvement.

Third Iteration

There is no rule that says you have to re-design your classes a certain number of times. Our example is fairly easy to use; all we need to walk a directory listing is a single for loop. As a subjective measurement (and for demonstrative reasons), I would prefer some refinements. The most obvious one is that I would prefer a more natural appearing syntax when used with a for loop.

Caution

The example in this section demonstrates idioms that we have not seen yet. It is not necessary that you understand everything, especially what we haven't discussed.

I will clearly point these items out with comments and tell you where you will encounter further details on these advanced idioms later in the book.

The great thing about classes is that once the class works, you do not have to rewrite that functionality again. Keeping this in mind, I have spent a little more time on it and came up with Listing 14.6.

Listing 14.6 Dirlist.cpp—The Scaffold Demonstrates the Simplicity of Using the Final Iteration of the _DIRLIST_ Class

```
1:  // DIRLIST.CPP - I prefer this example
2:  #include "dirlist.h"
3:  void main()
4:  {
5:      for( DIRLIST list; list; list++ )
6:          cout << list << endl;
7:  }
```

Not only is the final product short and easy to implement, it looks like code that belongs in a for loop. The class is quite a bit more esoteric, and notice that I did not define any member functions here, so they must be defined inline (in the class). They are in listing 14.7.

Fig. 14.2

The Open dialog box is common in many programs. A simple reusable class, like the one in listing 14.7, makes it much easier to produce such tools.

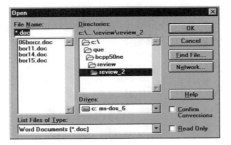

Listing 14.7 dirlist.h—The Last Implementation of the Directory Listing Replaces the _Cur_ and _Next_ Functions with a Conversion Operator and Both Prefix and Postfix Increment Operators to Traverse the Directory

```
1:  // DIRLIST.H - Contains a derived directory listing class.
2:  #ifndef __DIRLIST_H
3:  #define __DIRLIST_H
4:  #include <dir.h>
5:  #include <dos.h>
6:  // DIRLIST is derived from struct ffblk
7:  class DIRLIST : public ffblk
8:  {
9:  public:
10:     // constructor with default arguments, no destructor required
11:     DIRLIST( const char * fname = "*.*", unsigned int attrib = 0 )
12:     { done = findfirst( fname, this, attrib ); }
13:
14:      // new stuff - conversion operator (See chapter 16)
15:     operator const char*(){ return done ? 0 : ff_name; };
16:      // postfix operator++ (See chapter 16)
17:     int operator++(int){ return (done = findnext(this)); }
18:     // prefix operator++ calls postfix++ (See Chapter 16)
19:     int operator++(){ return operator++(0); }
20: private:
```

```
21:     int done;
22: };
23: #endif
```

I decided that I would like to express this class as a kind of `ffblk`, so I inherited from the struct `ffblk` in line 7. (See chapter 20, "Inheritance and Polymorphism.") The constructor defined in lines 11 and 12 is almost identical, except I defined the constructor inline, too.

The new stuff is defined in lines 15, 17, and 19. However, if you ignore the startling syntax and look at the function bodies in lines 15 and 17, you will note that the definition of these functions is exactly the same as `Cur()` and `Next()` from the prior attempt.

The new notation allows me to express the same functionality with a more notationally convenient idiom. Writing functions using the keyword `operator` is referred to as operator overloading. Which, in a nutshell, means specifying behaviors for operators as they pertain to specific classes.

II
Programming in C++

Tip

A good way to begin understanding functions like those in the example class in dirlist.h is to step through the code using the Trace feature of integrated debugger. (Figures 14.4 and 14.5 show a single Trace step into the conversion operator `char*()` function for the `DIRLIST` class.)

Caution

Member functions defined as inline functions cannot be traced unless you enable Options, Project, Compiler, Out-Of-Line Inline Functions (refer to figure 14.3).

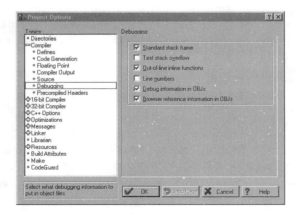

Fig. 14.3

Use the Project Options dialog box to enable inline function tracing.

Fig. 14.4

Executing the main function in the Dirlist.cpp module, shows that the simple-looking code cout << list << endl; *actually makes an implicit call to the conversion operator* char*( ) *(see fig. 14.5).*

```
// DIRLIST.CPP - I prefer this example

#include "dirlist.h"

void main()
{
    for( DIRLIST list; list; list++ )
        cout << list << endl;
}
```

Fig. 14.5

Pressing F7 once from the statement in the for *loop traces into the conversion operator function shown in the window for dirlist.h.*

```
// new stuff - conversion operator
operator const char*(){ return done

// postfix operator++ (See chapter
int operator++(int){ return done
```

Operator (and function) overloading is a complex subject. I do not expect you to digest it all at once, that's why chapters 15 and 16 discuss this powerful language convention in much greater detail. Keep in mind one of the features of C++ is that it allows us to train new data types to work with old operators, making the code and syntax much like that of the native data types: easier to use.

From Here...

Chapter 14, "Basic Class Concepts," is a turning point. Many C++ pundits say that you can use C++ as a better C, avoiding the class paradigm altogether. It is true, but if that is all you do with C++ you are missing many of the features that make it a powerful and expressive language. This chapter demonstrates information from the basic syntax to subtle aspects that may not jump up and grab you, but they come in handy. To continue the learning process, step through the last example program. After you have traced it once or twice the following chapters provide more details:

- Chapter 6, "Native Data Types and Operators," discusses native data types and many operators that enable C++ developers to express their ideas with code.

- Chapter 11, "Functions," covers functions, which are the fundamental building blocks of code.

- Chapter 15, "Function Overloading," teaches you about overloading functions, name mangling, and overloading function versus default arguments.

- Chapter 17, "Constructors: Copy and Assignment," covers the copy constructor, which creates new objects from existing objects, and the assignment operator, which makes an existing object equivalent to another object.

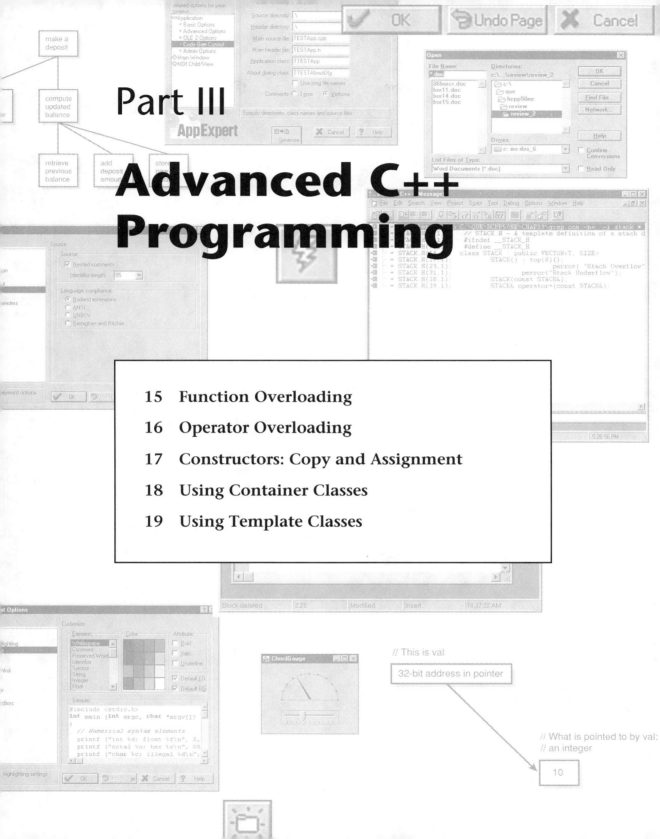

Part III

Advanced C++ Programming

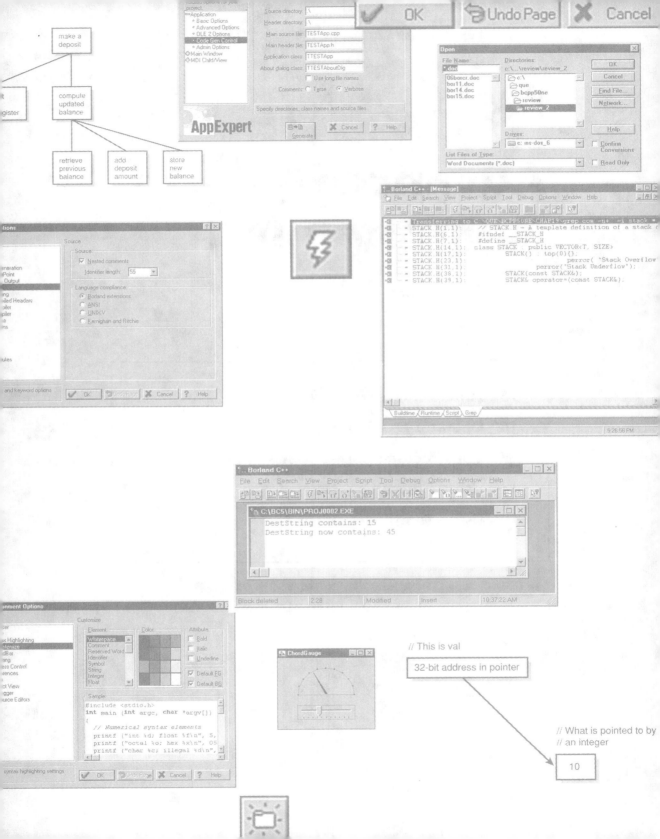

CHAPTER 15
Function Overloading

Developing software is complex. C++ was designed and evolves with complexity reduction as a primary focus. Where identifiable obstacles exist, language idioms have been implemented to overcome them. A common problem occurring in large software systems is the sheer number of names.

Function overloading not only reduces the juggling act used to manage dozens or hundreds of function names, but it is also necessary to support other idioms that are essential to the language. In addition to showing you how to use overloaded functions, this chapter provides the functions background information to make functions easier to understand and use.

In this chapter, we will unveil function overloading, which provides the groundwork for understanding other idioms, by discussing:

- Overloaded functions
- Name mangling
- Overloading versus default arguments
- What is not overloadable

Understanding Overloaded Functions

Overloading functions simply refers to using the same function name for different functions. Traditional structured languages require you to derive unique names for every function, regardless of similarities between the functions.

C++ enables you to use the same name for functions that perform similar actions, like printing, but the specificity of the action is not identical. Suppose, for example, that you need a print function for every native data type. Using a traditional language, you might choose to use the data type as part of the function name, resulting in

```
PrintInt( int var );        // pseudo-code functions

PrintChar( char var );

PrintFloat( float var );
```

To add to the complexity, suppose you have to discern to which device to print—file, printer, or screen. You might solve the problem by placing a `switch` statement or `if...else` clause and passing the device as some kind of constant. Alternatively, you may choose to create a function for each type and each device. (Don't laugh; I've seen other programmers do each of these!)

The problem you would soon encounter is that there would be a huge list of names for this one kind of functionality—printing. (What happens when we add aggregate types to our list of print functions?) Function overloading on the surface helps avoid this kind of problem. Function overloading facilitates a reduction in the number of contrived function names and is necessary for other things, but we'll start with this one aspect.

Unfortunately, support for overloading functions adds to the list of things the programmer must learn to do, but overloading solves the pernicious problem of contriving and remembering a multitude of function names and can be learned if you know a little bit about how overloading is supported in C++. Let's start with examples of overloaded functions.

Examples of Overloaded Functions

The C++ language support for function overloading reduces the number of unique names that we must contrive for our programs—this is good. Functions, like printing, are created to print some data to a device. The function `printf` from C was created for this purpose.

The solution the designers of this function came up with in an effort to reduce the number of names was to use variadic arguments. (Refer to chapter 6, the section "*printf* and *scanf*" for more details.) A variadic argument, denoted by the ellipsis (…), indicates that you may be using a number and variety of arguments at runtime. This is why `printf` takes a format string—the formatting symbols in the first argument help the `printf` function to get the arguments from the stack. In essence, what the implementors of `printf` and `scanf` did was to create an implementation based on intimate knowledge of how arguments are passed on the stack, to determine what data is there, and then to cull it from the stack in an effort to avoid cluttering the `stdio` functions with excessive names. Believe me, there is quite a bit of work involved, and the results are very slow. The only reason to do this would be to avoid something much more problematic.

C++'s support of function overloading enables you to vary the argument types without using microprocessor-intensive variadic arguments. Applying overloadability to the print functions in the last section, this is what the function declarations might look like:

```
int Print( int );      // Function names are identical, arguments differ
int Print( char );
int Print( float );
int Print( double );
```

Notice that the function names are all the same. The difference is the argument types. As a matter of fact, it is the arguments that overloading functions are based on. Overloading is passive; you do not have to do anything other than to have functions with the same name but sufficiently different argument types. If the *sufficiency* criteria is not met, the compiler warns you with an ambiguity error.

The previous four function declarations allow us to call the function Print with one of the defined argument types, and the actual function called is determined by the compiler at compile-time rather than by manipulating the stack at runtime (which is how printf works).

Benefits of Overloading

A direct benefit of function overloading is the reduction of unique names the programmer has to derive and remember. Comparing the declaration of the (imaginary) Print function and the (stdio) printf function, ours are easier to use because no formatting string is required to print the data. Before function overloading, the programmer was required to choose a specific function with a unique name.

Supporting function overloading becomes critical in the context of the class idiom. As you saw in the last chapter, constructors appear in many forms. These included a default constructor and a constructor with arguments, as well as others. This is important. Suppose you wanted an array of objects; allocating an array of any type, statically or dynamically, looks like this:

```
CLASS_NAME arrayOf[ size ];                        // a static array of
                                                   // size objects.
CLASS_NAME *dynamicArray = new CLASS_NAME[ size ]; // dynamic array of
                                                   // size objects
```

Notice that there is no place for constructor arguments. One of these two examples must call the default constructor. (In C++ this is a constructor taking no arguments; in Borland C++ the same is true, or the default constructor can accept arguments as long as they have default values.) As an alternative, you may want to construct objects passing specific argument values, like our DIR_LIST class from chapter 14, "Basic Class Concepts." Then you would need a constructor that accepts arguments specifiable by the user of your class.

Function overloading places the onus of calling the exact constructor—a special function—on the compiler, which it can easily determine from a combination of the name and argument types. Remember, a constructor must use the name of the class as the constructor name because the class name takes on the part of data type when objects are constructed. Without overloading, you would have to choose between a default constructor, meaning you can allocate arrays, or constructors with arguments, meaning you cannot allocate an array of objects. All of the native types support both arrays and single objects; not providing the same support for classes would be asymmetric and ungainly.

There are other language idioms that require overloading. How do you suppose objects of the iostream class, `cin` and `cout`, use identical syntaxes for all of the built-in types? Chapter 16, "Operator Overloading," explains this perspective.

When Does Overloading Occur?

Function overloading is automatic. If you specify functions with identical names, including case, differing in the argument types, the compiler takes care of it.

The compiler uses the same functions behind the scenes whether you use identical function names or not. The reason for this is the fewer the keywords and the more consistent the rules for compiling are, the easier it is to implement the language. Thus, if overloading required some keyword like overloaded, the compiler would have another keyword to look out for.

Instead of creating special rules for overloaded functions, all functions are handled the same, reducing the number of exceptions that implementors of the language have to code. (Compiler writers are programmers too.) Let's take a look at how this unique language feature was implemented. Understanding the way overloading was implemented makes it a lot easier to learn the idiom and to exploit it.

Name Mangling

I came across a magazine article a while back that was intended to instruct managers on questions to ask potential C++ candidates when interviewing for a job. One of the questions was to explain name mangling.

Name mangling presents a problem to cross-language programmers. When you declare a C++ function in other languages, like Visual Basic, you must remember that the name is not the one you defined. Rather, it has been mangled.

If you are writing C++ functions to be used in DLLs, in addition to requiring other subjects related to DLLs, you will probably need to use the *extern "C"* specifier. This tells the C++ compiler not to mangle the name of the function preceded by extern "C."

Many of the functions in the Borland C++ libraries—check the header files—were intended to be used with C compilers too. These function declarations and the Help files demonstrate the proper use of this idiom.

The C++ compiler has a mangle rule that it follows for every function name. It has to have a unique name because the names are how the function calls are resolved. The function names are mangled then assigned an address and placed in the symbol table.

It is from the addresses assigned to the function names that the compiler resolves function calls. It's not really so hard.

Understanding the Symbol Table

The symbol table is a logical place where names used in your programs are stored. Referring to chapter 4, "The Preprocessor," the preprocessor runs, followed by compilation. The compiler takes each unique function name, mangles it, places the mangled name in the symbol table, and assigns a relative address to the name.

The functions are assigned an address because machine-readable code is based on simple instructions, like *Call*, which work with addresses not names. When the compiler comes across a function call in C++ code, it can resolve that call based on a match and address found in the symbol table. Take a look at a fragment of a .map file showing the mangled names as they go into the symbol table (see listing 15.1).

Listing 15.1   Symbols.cpp—An Example of Borland Name Mangling

```
 1:  // SYMBOLS.CPP - A look at the symbol
 2:  #include <stdio.h>
 3:  // Program demonstrates function overloading.
 4:  // Take a look at the SYMBOLS.MAP file for
 5:  // the mangled names.
 6:  // printf was used for implementational convenience.
 7:  int Print( int num )
 8:  {      // use printf for easier implementation
 9:        return printf( "%d", num );
10:  }
11:  int Print( char ch )
12:  {
13:        return printf("%c", ch );
14:  }
15:  int Print( float fl )
16:  {
17:        return printf("%f", fl );
18:  }
19:  void main()
20:  {
21:        Print( 'A' );  Print( '\n');
22:        Print( 10 );   Print( '\n' );
23:        float PI = 3.14519;
24:        Print( PI );   Print( '\n' );
25:  }
```

The previous sample program contains three functions, all named `Print`, differing by the argument type only. The program itself is not the focus. We are concerned with what the compiler does with the names when placed in the symbol table, as viewed through a .map file.

Fig. 15.1

The Project Options dialog box allows you to generate a map file with or without mangled names.

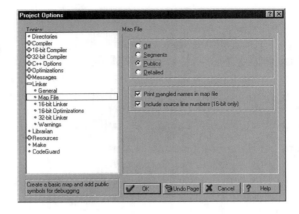

Here are the unmangled function names as they appeared in the map file that was generated:

    0001:00000074 Idle Print(int)
    0001:00000089 Idle Print(char)
    0001:000000A0 Idle Print(float)

The symbols in the previous map-file fragment look a lot like plain old function declarations. Below are the same functions with the mangled names printed to the map file.

    0001:00000089 Idle @Print$qc
    0001:000000A0 Idle @Print$qf
    0001:00000074 Idle @Print$qi

The symbol table contains the names used in programs. The address associated with the names is how C++ calls the correct function, and it is the unique names generated by mangling that the linker uses to find the correct function.

Note

C++ uses mangled names to resolve the problem a unique function name to a specific address. The Linker Options dialog box allows you to decide which version you want to be printed in a map file. Typically, printing the map file is unnecessary. However, it is insightful, and comparing the differences between the two map files does indicate how the unique names are generated.

Resolving Function Calls

When you declare a function, an entry into the symbol table is made by the compiler. The compiler mangles the name, assigns an address, and stores the information. When the linker runs, it resolves occurrences of function calls to those addresses by matching the name found to that stored in the symbol table.

Because the token name is used to match the function to a location at which it will reside in memory, the string names must be matched. Think of the symbol table as a dictionary and the definition as an address. If the names were not unique, finding a match would be impossible.

To allow programmers to use identical function names for similar activities, the compiler mangles the name, which resolves name conflicts by using the argument types as part of the name. If you look closely at the names in the mangled version of the map file, you may note that the scheme used by Borland concatenates the function name to a $q followed by the first letter of the data type.

Note

The Annotated Reference Manual (ARM) describes a slightly different mangle-formula for function overloading. But it is the result that is important, not the implementation—the way things are mangled.

Name mangling is important to the extent that it alleviates the burden of creating and remembering an excessive number of unique names. The compiler and linker mangle and resolve the use of names automatically. If neither of these can resolve the problem, you are likely to get an ambiguity error at compile-time.

The ARM describes a slightly different mangle-formula, but the result is the same; the burden of remembering and contriving unique names is placed on the compiler.

Overloading Functions

Overloading occurs automatically. On your part, you have to decide when to use comparatively similar names. Function overloading must be used where constructors are concerned because constructors require the same name for every constructor of a single class. The name of operator functions may differ by return type and argument type, but the function name must be the same for each operator.

The last category of functions to be overloaded is global functions. There are a few more subjective rules that apply to global functions. We'll look at the different categories of functions that are candidates for overloading and some guidelines as to when overloading is necessary and when it is optional.

Global Functions

Global functions refer to functions that is defined in the global namespace. In other words, they are not member functions of a class. Global-function overloading, including operator-function overloading, refers to functions with the same name but differing arguments (see chapter 16, "Operator Overloading").

As mentioned earlier, function overloading occurs when two functions with exactly the same name are defined in the same namespace. As this pertains to nonclass functions, I am referring to functions declared in the same module. This means if you declare a function in a header file and include that header file in a module (.cpp file), two functions with the same name are in the same namespace. For this to be acceptable, they must have different argument types. In the general case, this means that the data types used are different, but overloading can also occur based on *constness*. (The last section of this chapter identifies specifically what can and cannot be overloaded.)

Here are some general guidelines to aid you in determining when to overload, or when to use other conventions. The return argument type plays no role in the overloading process, so overload global functions when:

- It is notationally convenient to use the same function name, including case.
- There are alternative algorithms based on differing types of arguments passed.

However, if you feel the function name should be the same and the data types differ, but the algorithm differs only by the data type, then what you want is a generic function—meaning the code in the function body. Generic functions are explained in chapter 19, "Using Template Classes."

You have already seen some simple examples of global function overloading in earlier sections. The rules for overloading member functions that are not constructors is pretty much the same—do so when the data and code required to manipulate the data is different, but the use of the same name is convenient. Now let's look at some guidelines for overloading constructors.

Constructor Overloading

Constructors must use exactly the same name as the class. Constructors have no return types, so even though overloading is not based on the return type, it is less applicable here. Overloading on constructors, which are special class functions, is also dependent on the argument types and count, just like global functions.

Default Constructor. Constructors represent one aspect of C++ where function overloading is not just convenient but is necessary. We looked at a couple of different kinds of constructors in the last chapter. One was the default constructor, requiring no arguments. The default constructor is used to build a default object. As a reminder, one instance of default construction occurs when arrays of objects are allocated.

In Borland's implementation of C++, a default constructor is also one that has a default value for each argument of the constructor. If you examine the class definition, a constructor of this type will have an equal sign (=) followed by an initial value for each argument in the constructor list.

Constructor with Arguments. Classes may have several constructors. Another kind of constructor we looked at was a constructor taking varying types and quantities of arguments. This kind of constructor is used when the class designer intends that the user be allowed to specify the value for the data members, determining the specific properties of an individual object.

Copy Constructor. The copy constructor is so important that if you fail to define one, the compiler does it for you. The copy constructor is of the form X(X&) where X is the class name. Copy constructors are used to ensure proper object initialization from existing objects.

Because the copy constructor has the same name as the other, it is an overloaded function. Copy construction is a singularly important topic. A detailed explanation, including examples, can be found in chapter 17, "Constructors: Copy and Assignment."

Example of Overloaded Constructors. Listing 15.2 provides an example of a trivial class X containing three constructors. It also introduces the initialization list.

Listing 15.2   Construc.cpp—Compiling to See How Constructor Names Are Mangled

```
1:  // CONSTRUC.CPP - Demonstrates constructor name mangling
2:  // Don't worry about the implementation of each constructor
3:  // It's not important. Look at the map file
4:  // as an indicator of how constructors are overloaded.
5:  class X
6:  {
7:  public:
8:      X() : n(0) {}               // default constructor, with
                                    // initialization list.
9:      X( int a ) : n(a) {}        // integer argument, initialization
                                    // and null function.
10:     X(X& rhs){ n = rhs.n; }     // copy constructor
11:     ~X(){};                     // destructor
12: private:
13:     int n;
14: };
15: void main()
16: {   X x;
17:     X y = y;                    // calls the copy constructor
18: }
```

Lines 8, 9, and 10 define three constructors inline. The first is the default constructor; the second is a constructor, taking one argument matching the internal data type; and the third is one implementation of a copy constructor.

Note

The use of rhs in the copy constructor is a convention some assembler language programmers use meaning *right-hand-side* argument. While I use assembler in some instances, rhs is not a conventional notation I use. More importantly, it is just a variable.

This class clearly demonstrates that no special notation is required to take advantage of overloading. What this code does not clearly demonstrate is that in addition to containing an assignment operator that the compiler defined for us, this class introduces a few new conventions.

Part of our objective in this chapter is to learn the language and its idioms. More information about the assignment operator can be found in chapter 17, "Constructors: Copy and Assignment." The two conventional devices employed in this class are inline functions and initialization lists.

Inlining Class Functions. In chapter 9, "Data Quantifiers and Qualifiers," you learned about inline functions. Using the word inline is a way for you to explicitly suggest to the compiler to place a function body inline, directly in the program, as opposed to making a function call.

Defining constructors and other member functions within the class is also referred to as inlining. Defining a member function in the class is the same as using the word inline. Bjarne Stroustrop, the inventor of C++, says that it is redundant to use the keyword inline under these circumstances. However, if it clarifies the meaning of the code to the reader, use the keyword. Refer to chapter 9 for more on inlining.

Initialization List. A constructor's job is to ensure the proper initialization of each object. Part of this equation is to initialize the data members of the class. The usual appearance of this initialization is the assignment of some value to each data member of a class. Recalling class data of any type, here is an example of some possible initial value assignments of a class containing a few simple data types (see listing 15.3).

Listing 15.3 Demonstrating Default Constructor Arguments Using a Class

```
1:   class SNAFU
2:   {
3:   public:
4:       SNAFU( int n = 0, char* str = "Hello");       // constructor
5:       // ... other stuff
6:   private:
7:       int num;
8:       char * name;
9:   };
10:      // Constructor not defined inline, demonstrating assignment to members
11:  SNAFU::SNAFU( int n, char * str )
12:  {      num = n;
13:         int l = strlen(str) + 1;       // get string length plus room for '\0'
14:         name = new char[l];            // allocate space for string
15:         if( name != 0 )                // new returns 0 if allocation failed
16:             strcpy(name, str );
17:         // Alternatively, it may be implemented as
18:         // strcpy( name = new[strlen(str) + 1], str );
19:  }
```

Line 4 declares a constructor accepting two arguments: an integer and a char pointer with initial values. Lines 11 to 19 define the class constructor. Line 18 contains a single replacement line of code for lines 13 to 16. C++, like C, allows you to write such terse code if you desire; this is both a boon and anathema to programmers.

What is demonstrated in this example is how data members are typically perceived to be assignable. You may be accustomed to making member-by-member assignments in other languages, but this is not the only way to assign arguments to class data members.

C++ enables you to use member initialization too. Adding a global function to duplicate strings, the SNAFU class may be rewritten using an initialization list (see listing 15.4):

Listing 15.4   Emulating the *strdup* Function to Use *new*

```
char * Strdup( const char* str )
{      // Don't forget the caller becomes responsible
       // for releasing s' memory.
       char * s;
       s = new char[strlen(str) + 1];
       if(s) strcpy( s, str );
       return s;
}
// A much shorter constructor, which uses member initialization
SNAFU::SNAFU( int n, char* str ) : num(n), name(Strdup(str)){}
```

The constructor is simpler and greater savings are obtained in a more subtle way. Often by using initialization, the compiler can optimize away additional work that is required when the arguments are more complex. (The constructor call in listing 15.4 employs a member initialization list.) Plus, initialization is required when the class has const data members. Chapter 17, "Constructors: Copy and Assignment," discusses further examples of behind-the-scenes operations that are performed without any obvious signs. Chapter 9, "Data Quantifiers and Qualifiers," covers constants in greater detail.

Overloading versus Default Arguments

Overloading occurs automatically. The signal to the compiler is, when functions have the same name but differing arguments, to create a unique token from a combination of the name and data. Default arguments are initial values that the programmer provides when some initial value is known.

A hurdle to jump is the syntax of C++. A much more challenging hurdle is the one that enables you to decide when to employ a particular idiom. Some things must be done, like addressing the disposition of the copy constructor and assignment operator, or your programs will come apart at the seams. Still other idioms are more for convenience and less disastrous if poor choices are made.

Studies have been done to estimate how much software maintenance costs companies each year. One such figure I heard was $1.50 to $3.00 per line of code per year. Whether these amounts are accurate for every company, one thing is certain: maintaining existing systems is expensive. Therefore, to some extent less is better.

If you choose poorly your program is less likely to die, but the programs may be more expensive to service. As an added factor, synchronizing code requires more work.

Provide default arguments when you are writing functions or constructors that perform exactly the same operations. If one version of the (function's) interface can be specified without arguments because default values work, and if one version requires users to specify the values, use default arguments.

> **Note**
>
> The use of the keyword `this` is a pointer to self that every object has. The `DIR_LIST` class (referring to chapter 14, "Basic Class Concepts") is derived from the `struct ffblk` defined in the dir.h header file. The `findfirst` function takes a pointer to an `ffblk` structure. Due to the relationship between a `DIR_LIST` and an `ffblk`—a `DIR_LIST` that is a kind of `ffblk`—the `this` pointer is an acceptable value for the `findfirst` function.

Suppose you are writing code and you identify one version of constructor that works because a default value can be applied. For example

```
// constructor, uses default *.*
DIR_LIST(){ done = findfirst("*.*", this, 0); }
```

The `DIR_LIST` utility class is defined completely in chapter 14. You have decided that the default arguments to `findfirst` should be *.*, and the attribute 0. Next, define a second constructor, accepting arguments for the filename and the attribute byte as follows:

```
DIR_LIST( char* fname, unsigned int attrib )
{ done = findfirst( fname, this, attrib ); }
```

In listing above, the constructor performs exactly the same operation as the first. It uses the `findfirst` function, but uses a variable instead of hard-coded values for the filename and attribute byte.

This scenario requires that both functions be debugged and tested. Certainly, this example is trivial enough that you could trust your eyesight, but not testing and debugging code because it appears simple is reinforcing a bad habit. More often than not, the code will not be this simple. Another problem is that you have unnecessarily added to the complexity of maintaining this program because you must keep each function synchronized whenever changes are made. Both of these problems are not the best we can do.

When you have a scenario similar to the one shown above, what you want is one function with default values:

```
DIR_LIST( char * fname = "*.*", unsigned int attrib = 0 )
{    done = findfirst( fname, this, attrib ); }
```

In our contrived example, the amount of code has been reduced to half. We no longer have a synchronization problem, and we only have to test one function while maintaining exactly the same functionality.

Identifying What Is Not Overloadable

Thus far you have seen how function overloading works and some examples of overloaded functions. To recap, the Borland C++ compiler mangles function names, using the name and the arguments to create a unique name. From this automated process, function calls can be resolved, taking into account the name and arguments types, matching the resultant mangled-name to an address associated with the name in the symbol table. This process occurs automatically when the conditions in the preceding section are met.

What we haven't discussed specifically are additional items that are overloadable, and a few that should not be overloaded. For a complete source, read ANSI C++ documentation or the *Annotated Reference Manual* by Stroustrop and Ellis. I provide some of the more difficult examples here. In doing so, I will point out what to avoid and additional qualifiers that you can use to overload functions.

The Borland compiler is pretty crafty. It is capable of catching all manner of ambiguities. Suppose that you have overloaded two functions; one takes an integer, the other a char *. For example:

```
void Foo( int n );
void Foo( char * p );
```

When you call

```
Foo(0);
```

the version of Foo requiring an integer is always called; 0 is an integer after all. This may not always be what you want, though. It is acceptable and reasonable to call

```
Foo( char * p );
```

with a value of 0. This, however, does not report an error; the version of the function taking a char * may never be called for 0 values.

Functions differing only by the address operator cannot be overloaded. For example:

```
int Foo( int & r );
int Foo( int r );
```

are not sufficiently different to overload.

Member functions differing in the respect that one is a *static* member and the other is not:

```
class X
{
public:
    static void F();     // error: not overloadable
```

```
    void F();              // error:
};
```

Functions differing by return-type only are not overloadable. Thus

```
void LuLu();              // error: cannot overload on return type
int LuLu();
```

are not overloadable. While the return-type may vary, it is the function name, argument count, and types that the overloaded function depends on.

From Here...

Function overloading is a practical matter implemented by a practical solution. For the linker to resolve function calls, it must look up the function name in the symbol table. To avoid name collisions during the lookup, the names must be unique. This has not changed in C++. The technique employed allows the compiler to create unique names based upon the function name and the argument types—referred to as name mangling.

Mangling the names with the first letter of the data type ensures that the symbol table still contains unique names so the function calls can be resolved. Function overloading is a nicety and a necessity. Without function overloading, multiple constructors and operator functions would not be possible.

Function overloading removes the tedium of contriving several function names for similar functions using different data and implementations, enables you to define multiple class constructors, and supports operator overloading.

- Chapter 4, "The Preprocessor," describes the role the preprocessor plays in C++.
- Chapter 9, "Data Quantifiers and Qualifiers," describes and demonstrates how to use special keywords that affect data types and functions.
- Chapter 11, "Functions," discusses how to declare and define functions and use special techniques like recursion.
- Chapter 13, "Exploring iostreams," explains key aspects of well-crafted stream classes, which exemplify good C++ programming.
- Chapter 14, "Basic Class Concepts," addresses the topics you need to use and write classes.
- Chapter 16, "Operator Overloading," covers one of the most powerful topics of C++ programming.
- Chapter 17, "Constructors: Copy and Assignment," discusses two special member functions that can make the difference between well-designed classes.
- Chapter 20, "Inheritance and Polymorphism," discusses the topic of reuse through aggregation and how polymorphism is implemented.

Operator Overloading

C++ is an expressive language. Part of that expressiveness is based on the language's ability to allow the developer to define relationships between operators and operands for new, aggregate types.

Since grade school most of us began an education that introduced us to simple operations based on values and tokens, like +, -, *, and /. Equations like 1 + 2 or 6/3 are instantly recognizable, easily understood, and provide an almost-shorthand notation, making them quick to reproduce. Most of us used these common operators in increasingly more complex relationships on in to high school and even through college.

Because of this vast pool of experience, operator tokens are like old friends. The brevity of expressions makes it easier to express elaborate relationships between operands (or variables). C++ takes this comfortable notion a step further. C++ allows you to define the relationships between operators—like addition, subtraction, logical, new, and subscript—and operands, usually objects.

The facility for doing this is already in place; it's just something you have to learn how to do. Operator overloading is not something you have to do to use C++, but it is something that will enhance the expressiveness and simplicity with which your classes are used. This chapter thoroughly demonstrates how to write your own operator functions, by describing:

- Operators as functions
- Overloadable operators
- Operator expansion
- Unary operators
- Binary operators
- Conversion operators
- Friend operator
- Subscripting operator[ ]

Understanding Operators as Functions

Familiar operators used in high-level language expressions are not really what is used by the computer itself. Tokens, such as + or -, are replaced with instructions like add and sub, and the parentheses used in functions are resolved to an address (of the function) and a call instruction. If you have ever programmed in assembler or seen assembler code, you will more than likely have used some of these instructions.

The point of the discussion is that operators are symbolic tokens that the compiler replaces with instructions. At the assembly code level, these are abbreviated names; at the machine level, they are numbers. When we are programming in C++ we refer to them by one- or two-character operators. Now I want you to think of operators as functions.

Operator Function Syntax

You do not have to overload operators to use C++. The notion of operators as functions is what supports operator overloading. Defining operator functions to work with your classes, which are aggregates of other data, affords instances of your classes the same kind of simplistic notation as other data types.

To acquire this ability, you will first need to learn the syntax of operator functions. The general syntax of an operator function is

```
return_type operator operator_token( [arg1, [arg2]] );
```

The return type is definable by you. The keyword operator must be used. The operator_token is a specific token that you are overloading, and you may define operator functions with zero, one, or two arguments. Except for the use of the token and the keyword operator, this looks just like a function:

```
return_type function_name( [argument_list] );
```

The biggest difference is the use of the operator keyword and operator functions, which generally require two or fewer arguments. The reason operators require fewer arguments is because the operator functions in general require the same argument count as they would when used for native data types.

How It Works

C++ was designed to allow operator overloading. Borland, following AT&T's lead, intentionally designed the language to support operator overloading. This means there must be precise rules; all you have to do is learn them.

From the aspect of the user of overloaded operators, you probably have already used a couple. (cout and cin are instances of stream classes, which have overloaded operators for the output stream <<operator and the input stream >>operator. The goal when overloading operators is not to controvert their meaning; rather, it is to define a similar meaning for a new class. In the simplest terms, you write an operator function describing (in code) how to manipulate objects when used with specific operators.

Unique Names. The use of operator functions you define and those used for the native types don't differ in the way they are used. However, the compiler's view of the overloaded operator functions is the one as a function that was defined by the class designer (you or whoever wrote the class).

Because the compiler views the operator as a function it must resolve the use of operators to the address of the operator function. Thus, operator functions must have unique names, otherwise the linker would be unable to resolve the use of operator functions. If the function name must always be operator token_symbol, like operator+, then the compiler must have some device to create unique names based on something else.

Mangled Operator Names. Operator functions are overloaded in much the same way as on-operator functions. The name is mangled with the name of the function plus the argument types. It is the combination of these two things that must be unique. Again, the return type is not involved in the mangling process, so you cannot overload on the return type alone.

Chapter 15, "Function Overloading," describes overloading and name mangling in greater detail. The gist is that either you or the compiler must come up with a unique name to resolve which function is actually being called. Because this is tedious and cumbersome, it was automated.

Suppose for argument's sake we overloaded the operator + for a class X. We would invoke the operator function + for X the same way we would use the + operator with operands of any native data type:

```
X x, y, z;  // x, y, z are X objects
x = y + z;  // syntactically the same if X where an integer for example
```

The syntax would have to be the same, otherwise using operator functions would require a different syntax. Whether X is an int or char, for example, or X is of some other type, the syntax is identical. This means the compiler must use a device to distinguish between specific uses of +. The problem is resolved because the compiler creates unique names—mangles the names—based on the function name *and* the argument types and count.

No Restriction in Return Types

Operator functions have no restriction on the return type. Because many of the operator functions you will define will be used in conjunction with as yet undefined classes, any return type can be used. Some of the time what you want to return may be an instance of the class the operator was designed for.

Some operators are not overloadable. Besides learning which of these can and cannot be overloaded, I will demonstrate how to overload many kinds of functions, provide you with constructive aids for determining when to use the operators, and how to determine the argument count and return type.

Exploring Overloadable Operators

Most operators are overloadable. Some are not. This is the intention of the language implementors. After I have shown you the two sets of overloadable and non-overloadable operators, I will also show you other uses for the *operator* notation.

It is probably unwise to expect to be able to implement a proper operator function for any type you can imagine, immediately. I will, however, demonstrate variations of several kinds, along with some guidelines enabling you to progress from here.

These Operators Are Overloadable

Table 16.1 lists all of the operators that can be overloaded. These are the tokens whose behaviors you may redefine for new entities, but it doesn't include everything that uses the keyword operator.

Table 16.1 Overloadable Operators	
Operator	**Comments**
new	If you define a new operator, define delete too
delete	
+	Addition
-	Subtraction
*	Multiplication
/	Division
%	Modulo—Returns remainder: 1 % 2 = 1
^	Xor—Bitwise exclusive or true when bits are different
&	And—Bitwise and true when bits are matching 1s
|	Or—Bitwise or true when either bit is 1
~	1s complement—Flip all bits
!	Logical negation true/non-zero evaluates to false/zero and false evaluates to true
=	Assignment
<	Less than
>	Greater than
+=	Addition with assignment a += b $\approx$ a = a + b
-=	Subtraction with assignment
*=	Multiplication with assignment
/=	Division with assignment
%=	Modulo with assignment
^=	Xor with assignment
&=	Bitwise and with assignment

Operator	Comments
!=	Bitwise or with assignment
<<	Left-shift operator (You have already seen this overloaded as the `ostream` operator.)
>>	Right-shift operator (`istream` class uses it as the input operator.)
>>=	Right-shift with assignment
<<=	Left-shift with assignment
==	Logical equivalence—for equality testing as opposed to assignment
!=	Negation with assignment
<=	Less than or equal to
>=	Greater than or equal to
&&	Logical and
||	Logical or
++	Either postfix or prefix plus operator (a++ ≈ a = a + 1)
—	Either postfix or prefix minus operator
->*	Pointer operator to a reference
->	Pointer operator
()	Function call operator
[]	Subscripting operator

Table 16.1 lists the current use of operators that you can overload. Classes do not require you to overload operators, but sometimes it makes the use of the class more intuitive. These are not the only things that use the operator keyword.

> **Tip**
>
> The assignment operator = must be a member function. Refer to chapter 17, "Constructors: Copy and Assignment," for an explanation of this important operator function. An improperly defined assignment operator function can introduce memory loss, known as the slicing problem, into your programs.

You should thoroughly comprehend an operator's intrinsic use before attempting to overload the operator. This includes the number of arguments, data types used, and the results. (A good exercise is to write a short program using each operator and examine the results.)

The basic meaning of an operator should not be controverted when you redefine it. What you are trying to do is pick the operators that have a similar contextual meaning in relation to your new class. For example, a Date class might overload the ++ and—operators to increment and decrement calendar dates.

Example 1. This section demonstrates a simple example of operator overloading. I will overload the plus operator to demonstrate an example of the syntax and provide you with a convenient way to *trace* through a C++ program. The example is intended to demonstrate the implicit nature of operator function calls. If you approach it from this perspective it makes sense.

The class presented in listing 16.1 has little value other than as a learning aid.

Listing 16.1   Int.cpp—Demonstrates Operator Overloading

```
1: // INT.CPP - Demonstrates an easy use of an overloaded operator
2: #include <iostream.h>
3: class INT
4: {
5: public:
6:      INT( int a = 0 ): data(a) {};
7:      friend INT operator+( const INT& lhs, const INT& rhs );
8:      friend ostream& operator<<( ostream& os, INT&rhs );
9:
10: private:
11:      int data;
12: };
13: // This is not a member function of INT
14: INT operator+( const INT& lhs, const INT& rhs )
15: {
16:      INT t = lhs.data + rhs.data;
17:      return t;
18: }
19: // This is not a member function of INT
20: ostream& operator<<( ostream& os, INT& rhs )
21: {
22:      return os << rhs.data;
23: }
24: void main()
25: {
26:      INT a(5), b(6);
27:      INT c = a + b;
28:      cout << "a = " << a << " b = " << b << " c = " << c << endl;
29: }
```

Line 1 indicates the file name and a general statement of the module's functionality.

Line 2 includes the iostream header file that provides access to the cout object within this module (.cpp file).

Lines 3 through 12 define the INT class. The class has a constructor that takes an integer or uses the default value 0. The constructor function is an empty function, and uses an initialization list: data(a). The integer data is the only data member. The INT class specifies that there are two friend functions: operator+ and operator<<. Preceding the function declarations with the keyword friend indicates that a function can access the private data (or functions) of a class. The addition operator and the output stream operator are *not* member functions.

Lines 14 through 18 define the global operator+ function and how it manipulates INT objects. The + operator is a binary operator, so there needs to be two arguments. (This does not mean that the arguments must be passed in the argument list. More on this later.)

Lines 19 through 23 define what the operator<< means when applied to INT objects.

The main function (lines 24 through 29) creates two objects, initializes a third with the sum of the prior two, and then all objects are written. Notice that the syntax of printing objects is exactly the same for constant strings, like a=, and INTs.

Tracing the Program. We can trace the program in the IDE with the F7 key. The output of the code in the main functions:

```
a = 5 b = 6 c = 11
```

The program starts at the line containing the function main. INT a(5), b(6); causes the program to make two separate trips up to the constructor. The code INT c = a + b; makes an implicit call to the operator+ function returning an INT object that is used to initialize c via a call to the compiler-generated copy constructor (refer to chapter 17, "Constructors: Copy and Assignment").

This simple program demonstrates the general appearance of overloading the operator<< for classes. It demonstrates one appearance of an overloaded operator+ in addition to alluding to the implicit nature of operator function calls. This may not be clear unless you trace through the program.

Things You Should Know. The operator+ and the operator<< could have been made member operator functions. Unfortunately, this presents some serious problems. First, the operator+ function needs access to the elements of INT objects. Making the operator function a member provides this access.

If operator functions are members then they only require one argument. So, operator+ would be declared like this

```
INT operator+(const INT& rhs);
```

and defined something like this

```
INT INT::operator+(const INT& rhs)
{
    INT t = data + rhs.data;
    // equivalently: INT = this->data + rhs.data;
    return t;
}
```

The reason for the reduction in the argument count is that the left-hand operand is the calling object itself. Referring back to our main function,

```
INT c = a + b;          // where a and b are INTs
```

a is the calling object (the one this refers to), and b is the passed argument (the one rhs refers to). The problem occurs when you look at slight modifications in the class.

Consider

```
INT c = a + b;
```

Expanding the operator+ function call to its verbose equivalent, the code looks like this

```
INT c = a.operator+(b);
```

When resolving the function call, the compiler and linker can match the arguments. There is a member function operator+ that takes an INT. The compiler and linker can also resolve

```
INT c = a + 5;
```

There is no operator+(int) function for INT objects. The language can make a temporary INT from 5, so the code is resolved to

```
INT c = a.operator( INT(5) );
```

where 5 is temporarily used to create an INT object. The code can then be resolved.

Note

The C++ language can make one conversion in an attempt to resolve function calls. This is similar to typecasting. If it makes sense in the context of the code to interpret data in a type-compatible way and there is a constructor that can create objects of the required type with the data provided, then the compiler will make a temporary object out the data to resolve its use.

When functions like operator+ are member functions, the problem arises when you attempt to use the same evaluation symmetrically. The same code with a and 5 transposed looks like this

```
INT c = 5 + a;
```

Expanding the function results in the ludicrous

```
INT c = 5.operator+(a);    // This obviously won't work.
```

The constant 5 is not an object, therefore, it cannot have member functions. The code fragment demonstrates that making the operator+ function a member function violates the principle of symmetry for addition, which is a breach of semantics. Therefore, operator+ should not be a member function unless you specifically intend for it to be used asymmetrically and, usually this is never the case with numbers.

Note

Reaching as far back as grade school or junior high, symmetry in mathematics dictates that a + b = b + a. (You thought you would never need that tidbit of information.)

If you design code that violates assumptions about symmetry, for example, your code will be harder to use.

Tip

There are number systems in mathematics that are not symmetric. I have also seen implementations of linked-lists (data connected by pointers) that use the + operator to replace the Insert function. The context meant append the node to the list.

There are few absolutes. However, if you are overloading operators to perform operations where assumptions about symmetry or transitivity, or whatever, can be made, you must consider the implications your definitions have.

More Things to Note. The previous section implicitly explains why the operator+ and operator<< functions must be friends. I will explain it clearly in case you missed it.

Here is what we know:

- Operator functions manipulate member data.

- Only members and friends can access private data. Thus, if an operator must access private data and is not a member, it almost always has to be a friend.

- Addition is a symmetric operation (a + b = b + a). Because its users are likely to depend upon the "symmetric property of addition," you do not want to violate the property.

- The result is that both the left and right operand must be passed as arguments, therefore the operator+ (in this context) should be a global function.

Note

The second assumption made about operators, private data, and their friend or member status is not absolutely true either. Read the section entitled "Conversion Operators" to see why.

The result of what we know is that the operator+ will have to be a friend, otherwise it is unable to operate on the data. This does not quite explain why the operator<< is a non-member, friend function. The reason for this is slightly different. (Chapter 13, "Exploring iostreams," provides an explanation as well as a thorough discussion of iostreams.)

Example 2. The example presented in this section is slightly more complex. It demonstrates an approach to solving a particular class of problems: indexing arrays out of bounds. There are programs, like Bounds Checker, that will help you find bugs of this nature, but the approach presented in this section uses the class paradigm to bind a solution to the origin of the problem.

Demonstrating the problem, using an integer array to illustrate, the problem takes this form:

```
int array[100];
array[100] = 0;          // Index 100 is out of bounds
```

This is the nature of the problem, though it is less likely that such an obvious violation would be committed. An obvious solution would be to remember to range check each index before indexing the array.

Caution

C++, as well as C, uses the zero'th element. Thus, the maximum element is max-*1*. A 100 element array has indices 0 to 99. Indexing the max'th element trounces all over something else's memory.

One example would be to use an `if` conditional statement:

```
if( j>=0 && j< size(array)/sizeof(array[0]))
    array[j] = 1944;
```

Additionally, we could use the `assert` macro defined in assert.h to ensure that we were informed when a bad index was attempted. Here is the code fragment with an assertion:

```
// #define NDEBUG // uncomment to turn off macro assertions
#include <assert.h>
assert( j>= 0 && j < sizeof(array)/sizeof(array[0]) );
if( j>=0 && j< size(array)/sizeof(array[0]))
    array[j] = 1944;
```

Besides runtime bounds checking performed by the if test, the assertion will halt the program allowing us to track down the source of the problem.

Note

The window dressing is used to provide a contextually plausible reason to employ an overloaded subscript operator. The assert macro, indices out of bounds, and range checking are important techniques, but are secondary in nature to operator overloading.

If everybody were doing this, a lot of bugs would be eliminated. "To err is human," so it might be better for all concerned if we derive some way to ensure this is done (at least during development) for every array used. An index out of bounds is a problem. Let's take a look at some possible solutions.

A Bounds-Checking Array. The identified problem is arrays out of bounds. We can bind the bounds checking to the point of access. A first course of action might be to bind range checking to each access of the array.

To bind the range checking to an array, we could overload the subscript operator for each class containing an array of whatever data type we need. Listing 16.2 shows the class declaration in a separate header file.

Listing 16.2   smaray1.h—Class Definition for an Array that Performs Bounds Checking

```
1: // SMARRAY1.H - Class definition for smart integer array.
2: // Copyright (c)1995. All Rights Reserved.
3: // By Paul Kimmel
4: #ifndef __SMARRAY1_H
5: #define __SMARRAY1_H
6: class INT_ARRAY
7: {
8: public:
9:     INT_ARRAY( unsigned int sz = 100 );
10:    ~INT_ARRAY();
11:    // Using an unsigned integer negates the necessity
12:    // for checking for an index < 0; it can't be
13:    int& operator[]( unsigned int index );
14: private:
15:     unsigned int max;
16:    unsigned int dummy;
17:    int * data;
18:    // Declaring these here makes them inaccessible.
19:    // Further, if I do not define them, then the compiler is blocked
20:    // from doing so, and effectively, block array copying
21:    // or assigning. Cool Huh?
22:    INT_ARRAY(const INT_ARRAY&);
23:    INT_ARRAY& operator=(const INT_ARRAY&);
24: };
25: #endif
```

Line 13 declares the subscript operator. When the return type is defined as a reference, it means that you are returning the address of the element. The result is, the subscript operation can be as an lvalue or an rvalue: on the left side of the evaluation or right side, respectively.

Tip

Class declarations are commonly used in header files because C++ requires declaration before use. By defining the class in the header, the declaration requirement can be resolved by using the #include directive.

The definition of the class plus a scaffold is shown in listing 16.3:

Listing 16.3 Smarray1.cpp—The Smart Array Class Methods and a Scaffold

```
 1: // SMARRAY1.CPP - The smart array definition with a scaffold.
 2: // Copyright (c) 1995. All Rights Reserved.
 3: // By Paul Kimmel.
 4: #include <mem.h>
 5: // #define NDEBUG // uncomment to turn off assertions
 6: #include <assert.h>
 7: #include "smarray1.h"
 8: // constructor - Adds one to the size of the array
 9: // to store a dummy value if a bad index is used
10: INT_ARRAY::INT_ARRAY( unsigned int sz )
11:     : max(sz), dummy( sz + 1), data( new int[sz + 1] )
12: {
13:     // If new returns a valid block of memory
14:     // then data is non-zero. The memset function
15:     // initializes the block to 0.
16:     if(data)
17:         memset( data, 0, dummy );
18:     else
19:         max = -1;
20: }
21: // destructor
22: INT_ARRAY::~INT_ARRAY()
23: {
24:     // de-allocate the array
25:     delete [] data;
26:     // setting the pointer to 0 provides a reference
27:     // point for testing for an invalid pointer
28:     data = 0;
29: }
30: // Pretty terse but it does check the validity
31: // of the index. This kind of problem is an ideal
32: // candidate for exception handling (see chapter 22).
33: int& INT_ARRAY::operator[]( unsigned int index )
34: {
35:     // Assert is 'disabled' if NDEBUG is defined
36:     assert( index < max );
37:     return index < max ? data[index] : data[ dummy ] ;
38: }
39: // Scaffolding your code shows that it was tested,
40: // provides easily accessible test code if modifications
41: // are made, is easily removed or included automatically by
42: // the preprocessor, and demonstrates how to use your
43: // class.
44: #ifdef SMARRAY1_SCAFFOLD
45: // The preprocessor directive is defined in the
46: // Options¦Project¦Compiler¦Defines
47: void main()
48: {
49:     INT_ARRAY startMeUp( 10 );
```

```
50:    for( unsigned int k = 0; k<10; k++)
51:        // operator[] accessed here
52:        startMeUp[k] = k;
53:
54: }
55: #endif
```

Line 11 initializes the data members of the class. The dummy member is used to store and retrieve a dummy value, when a bad index is used. In the code shown, the dummy value will be zero. Using this example, you may want to define a testable dummy value.

Lines 33 through 38 define the subscript operator for INT_ARRAY. The ternary ?: operator is used to test the index value. This class binds the range checking with the array access, but it does not handle a bad index well. While a bad index will not overwrite memory in our example, it is also likely that a user may never know a bad index was used. The original problem was a runtime error; now we have a logic error. The former crashes the program; the latter may produce the wrong results.

General Considerations. There are several improvements that we can make. The first is to consider whether or not this array can grow. If it can, we might redefine the subscript operator to allocate more space when an out-of-bounds index is used. Another consideration is the data types the array is capable of storing. This is one of those data structures that can be implemented type-independently. By type-independence, I am referring to the fact that regardless of the data type of the array, the code used to create it could be the same. When such a situation exists, you may want to define the class as a generic class. Type generic classes are called *template* classes. (See chapter 19, "Using Template Classes," for more details.)

The smart array is a marginal improvement on using an integer array directly. The smart array simplifies memory management—constructor allocates, destructor deallocates, binds the error checking to the array—but it also lends itself to improvement. The invitation for improvement illustrates the subtle nature of C++. C++ invites you to refine your classes iteratively, improving on previous designs through several iterations (or reexaminations) of the implementation.

This class invites us to consider template classes. It also suggests that we consider bad indices a little further, determining whether to increase the array size or find an ideal dummy value. Regardless of any of the decisions we make regarding any of these possible enhancements, this class will also benefit from an *exception handling*, which could provide for memory allocation failure, as well as a bad index. (For information on exception handling, see chapter 22, "Exception Handling.")

Operators that Aren't Overloadable
Table 16.2 defines the few operators that are not overloadable. These decisions are ultimately out of your hands.

Table 16.2 Operators that Cannot Be Overloaded	
Operator Token	**Purpose**
.	Class member access operator
.*	Pointer to member operator
::	Scope resolution operator
?:	Ternary if…else operator
sizeof	sizeof an object (`sizeof(x)/sizeof(x[0])` returns number of elements in an array x)
#	Preprocessing string conversion, also precedes preprocessor directives like `include`, `define`, and `endif` (sometimes referred to as stringizing)
##	Preprocessor operator to concatenate strings

Conversion Operators

You have seen tables indicating which operators can and cannot be overloaded. There are other kinds of functions that use the operator keyword. These are referred to as conversion operators. A conversion works on expectation. Where an object of one type is used, a conversion operator can be used to return an object of another type.

Consider the trivial INT class from an earlier example. Suppose instead of overloading the operator+ you defined an int conversion operator based on the following algorithm:

> where an int is expected and an INT is used return an int part of the class INT.

Thus

```
INT a(5), b(6);
INT c = a + b;
```

would be similar to

```
INT c;
c.data = a.data + b.data;
```

If I caught you sleeping, you might be nodding your head in acquiescence. For those of you not reading in bed, you might be saying, "Hey, I could do that if I made the data part public too." I am glad you are paying attention, but no.

What actually occurs (assuming we have defined a conversion from INT to int) is

```
INT c = a.operator int() + b.operator int();
```

The big difference is that by making the data public, you have lost control of it. Any user can access the data, which violates information hiding and encapsulation. The example shown allows read-only access of the integer part of the INT class.

Defining a conversion function is relatively easy. The syntax is

```
operator data_type (){ return variable_of_data type; }
```

which is a little strange. It looks like an operator function without a return type. Where conversion operators are concerned, the conversion type is in effect the type of the data returned, therefore the return type.

Applying the syntax to the INT class, the conversion operator appears as follows:

```
operator int() { return data; }
```

With this modification, where an INT object is used and an integer is expected, this function will be called.

Again, the INT class is for demonstrative purposes. Part of your job is to make a stretch and find out where these idioms are useful. There are several good ways to do this. One is to look at lots of code. Another is to experiment.

Consider a STRING class. There are a lot of good functions that work with char * (C style strings), but a STRING is not a char*. A string, however, can contain a char* data element to store the string. It would be a shame if all of these C functions in string.h, like strcmp (string compare) and strlen (string length) were to go to waste. Because of conversion operators, they do not have to. You could easily define

```
class STRING
{
public:
    // ...
    operator const char*() { return rep; }
private:
    char * rep;
};
```

to return the char* part of a string object. Like other operator functions, conversion functions are generally called implicitly.

Using Operator Expansion

Operator functions are usually called implicitly. We know this already. Operator functions that you define are used syntactically the same as operators when applied to native types. If they were not, they would be cumbersome to use, and the code would be hideous to look at.

The information contained herein is provided as an aid to assist you in understanding how to use operator functions. The topic of discussion in this section relates to expanding operators as a means to understanding them. With time and practice you will probably be able to do this in your head.

Expanding an Operator in Context

Expanding an overloaded operator function helps identify what the code really means. By expanding a code fragment like a = b + c, where a, b, and c are objects of some type and an operator+ function exists (on a chalkboard or in your head), a visual aid is provided that will help you understand the code fragment.

There are some simple aids you can use to match up the elements of a code fragment containing operators. The type of the operands identify the class, which in turn indicates where to look. Looking in the class definition—probably in a header file with a similar name—you can quickly reduce the number of possible functions. First, it must be an operator function, so only those member functions with the operator keyword are suspect. Second, the operator must match the operator used in the code fragment. Finally, if the keyword `friend` is used, the operator is a global function; if the keyword `friend` does not precede the function declaration, then the function is likely a member function.

If the declaration is not found, then you likely have a global function that is getting the data through some kind of conversion operator. Look outside of the class—in the header or module—for the operator keyword, the correct token, and argument types matching the type used in the original code fragment.

Choosing the Number of Arguments

There are a couple of factors that determine the number and location of the operands used in operator functions. The first is the argument count of the operator. Unary operators will have one object somewhere, and binary operators will have two.

Where the operand is found, whether as a passed argument or not, depends on the declaration of the operator function. If the operator function is a `global` and/or `friend` function, then the number of passed arguments will match the count of the operator. On the other hand, if the overloaded operator function is a member, then one operand will be the calling object (the `this` object), and if a second argument is required, it will be passed in between the left and right parentheses as an argument.

Here are some examples illustrating the location of the operand arguments:

```
class X
{
public: // ...
friend int operator>( const X&, const X& );
};
```

`class X` declares that the `operator>` is a `friend` function. Thus, the function is a non-member, binary function, so the two arguments are passed between the parentheses.

```
class Y
{
public: // ...
      Y& operator+=(const Y&);
};
```

`class X` declares the `operator+=` as a member function. The `operator+=` is a binary operator, so there must be two objects. One is obviously passed as an argument; the second object requirement is met by the `this` (reference to self) that will exist when this function is called. The declaration of `operator+=` as a member requires that a `Y` object be on the left side

```
    Y y += z;              // where z is or can be an object of type Y
```

Expanding the example above, the call is logically equivalent to

```
Y y.operator+=(z);
```

The compiler will remind you if you use the wrong number of arguments for operator functions. Some tips to remember:

- The number of objects must match the operator count.
- One object is satisfied by the `this` pointer for members.
- For non-member functions, the number of *arguments* must match the operator count: unary = 1, binary = 2.
- Overloaded operator functions can be member functions, global friend functions, or non-member, non-friend, global functions. In the latter case, the operator function must have access to the data manipulated because either the data is public or the class defines a conversion operator function.

Tip

You are not required to use overloaded operators. Many programmers are probably still using C++ as a better C. And as an alternative, you may still write regular functions to manipulate new types. For example, suppose you defined a class DATE. Further suppose you wanted to define a function that adds a number of days to a DATE object, you could define

```
void DATE::IncrementDate( unsigned int days );
```

or as

```
DATE& DATE::IncrementDate( unsigned int days );
```

IncrementDate as a member function and add the number of days to the Date object. The syntax of such a function is

```
DATE d;
d.IncrementDate( 5 );
```

This function would get the job done, and requires no special operator syntax. Then when you are more proficient at operator functions, you may realize that the IncrementDate function could be implemented using the operator+= like this:

```
DATE& DATE::operator+=( unsigned int days );
```

and used like this:

```
DATE d;
d += 5;
```

which is a little easier syntactically, but either is correct. Having done so, you would not need to rewrite the code that still uses IncrementDate. All that would be required is to redefine the member function in terms of the operator+= function.

```
DATE& DATE::IncrementDate(unsigned int days)
{ return operator+=(days); }
```

Changing the code that goes in a member function, as opposed to changing the arguments, requires no change in any code using the class: the DATE class in this example.

Using Unary Operators

Unary operators operate on one object. Thus, overloading a unary operator implies that there must be a single object to operate on. If the unary object is a member of a class, then the object will be accessed through the pointer to self, `this`. If the unary operator is global, `friend` or otherwise, then the object operated on will be passed in the argument list.

The syntactical use of the (overloaded) operator does not change, but the logical equivalent expansion changes. Given an object x for any unary operator α (alpha, representing any valid unary operator), if the operator function is a member, then the equivalent call expands to

```
x.operator α ();
```

However, for non-members the use of the operator expands to

```
operator α ( x );
```

Here is a demonstration using α, which represents any unary operator, as it would appear in context:

```
x = αx;    // perhaps alpha is !, -, or ~ for example
```

Two such operators bear additional attention. These are the unary ++ (increment) and -- (decrement) operator. The increment and decrement operators have both a prefix (before the object) and a postfix (after the object definition). Besides demonstrating examples of unary operator overloading, these two operators require a little additional attention.

The Increment and Decrement Operators: ++ and --

The `operator++` and `operator--` are used to increment and decrement ordinal native data types by one. Applying ++ to characters, integers, long integers, or pointers increments the variable by one. It is equivalent to x = x + 1 where x is one of the mentioned types. The decrement operator works the same way but subtracts one from the value.

Postfix and Prefix Increment and Decrement

The ++ and -- operators are applied in both a prefix (before the object) and postfix (after the object manner). Using the prefix operator (either increment or decrement) means that the object should be modified before evaluating the object. Using the postfix notation, for example x++, means that the object should be modified after evaluating.

Consider an integer used as the termination condition for a `while` loop. For example,

```
int num = 0;
// prints numbers 1 - 9
while( ++num < 10 )
    cout << num << endl;
```

num would be incremented to 1 then compared to < 10 in the first iteration of this loop. Using the postfix variation

```
// prints numbers 1-10
while( num++ < 10 )
    cout << num << endl;
```

num would be incremented after it was compared to less than 10.

When we write the code we can visually inspect the location of the ++ or -- operator to determine prefix or postfix. A minor problem arises when we want to overload the operators. The general appearance of operator increment and decrement respectively is

```
T& operator++();      // where T is a reference to the object type
```

and

```
T& operator--();      // ditto
```

with no visibly distinctive way to indicate whether you mean prefix or postfix. The mechanism devised was to require an (unused) integer argument when you mean postfix. Thus, the postfix operators would be declared like

```
T& operator++(int);     // postfix, returns reference to T and int remains
                        // unused
```

and

```
T& operator--(int);
```

The usage of either overloaded operator, as postfix or prefix, does not change in your code. The integer argument is never used; it just helps the compiler resolve the function declarations in the class.

It is probably unwise to overload postfix without prefix, and the reverse is also true. Here is an example of a class X with an overloaded increment operator pair:

```
class X
{
public:
    // ...
    X& operator++();        // prefix operator increment
    X& operator++(int)      // postfix implemented in terms of prefix
    { return operator++(); }
};
```

It is not uncommon to implement one of the pair in terms of the other. In class X, when the postfix operator is called, it passes responsibility to the prefix operator. The implicit nature of the declaration in class X is that prefix and postfix ++ perform the same action, which is also true for native types, the timing is just different. Defining one in terms of the other saves time, and you will only have to debug the function defining what operator++ means in the context of an X object.

III

Advanced Programming

Returning a reference to an object enables users of `class` X to chain the objects like this:

```
X x = ++y;      // calls prefix increment then creates x by a call to the //
                // copy constructor
```

Example of Overloading *Operator++*

Chapter 14, "Basic Class Concepts," defined a class DIRLIST, which uses the postfix and prefix operator++ to iterate through a directory listing. While this use of increment does not add one to an integral type, it is logically similar: It gets the next file name in the directory.

In chapter 14, DIRLIST was defined as a kind of ffblk. The ffblk structure is defined in dir.h as a structure that contains the kind of information found in a DOS-based directory entry structure. The functions findfirst and findnext require an ffblk pointer—DIRLIST IsA kind of ffblk—so this satisfies the requirement.

```
17:     int operator++(int){ return (done = findnext(this)); }
19:     int operator++(){ return operator++(0); }
```

Line 19 defines the prefix operator++ in terms of—meaning it calls—the postfix operator++. Line 17 defines the postfix operator to call the findnext function, both storing and returning the value of the member done. In listing 16.4, you see how the class makes iterating through an entire branch of a directory tree simple.

Listing 16.4 Dirlist.cpp—Testing the Completely Inlined DIRLIST Class

```
1: // DIRLIST.CPP - Listing from chapter 14
2: #include "dirlist.h"      // contains the DIRLIST class definition
3: void main()
4: {
5:     // default constructor uses "*.*"
6:     // the loop test ;list; uses a conversion operator which returns the
        // value of 'done'
7:     // list++ calls the postfix operator++ for the DIRLIST object list
8:      for( DIRLIST list; list; list++ )
9:          cout << list << endl;
10: }
```

Any program that needs to collect a list of file names from a directory listing can include dirlist.h and iterate through the list with the two lines of code on 8 and 9.

Using Binary Operators

Binary overloaded operators will require two objects. One object will be the left operand and the second will be the right operand. If a binary operator function is defined as a member function, then the left-hand operand will be the object referred to by this and the right will be passed as an argument. If the operator function is global, like operator<< for ostream, then both objects will be passed into the operator function by reference. The first argument will be the left operand and the second will be the right.

Using Conversion Operators

Conversion operators are the most unusual in appearance. Because of their strikingly odd appearance they are among the last discovered. I am making a specific point of bringing them to your attention here because sometimes they are exactly what is needed to complete a concept. (More on this in a moment.)

The syntax of a conversion operator is

```
operator data_type();
```

where data_type is the type of object, including native data types, that you want to return from an object of another class.

Consider, for example, a string class named STRING. There is an abundance of C functions that operate on char* (C-style strings). Unfortunately, these functions would not accept objects instantiated from the STRING class. However, an

```
operator const char*();    // returns const char*
```

conversion operator can be defined returning the char* part of a STRING object in the context where a char* is expected.

Without the conversion operator

```
STRING s("Hello, World!");
int len = strlen( s );          // s is a STRING
```

this code fragment would not work because strlen is defined roughly as

```
size_t strlen( const char * );
```

However, defining the conversion operator const char*() would cause

```
int len = strlen( s );
```

to implicitly call the conversion operator, making the code equivalent to

```
int len = strlen( s.operator const char*());
```

which satisfies the requirement for the strlen function defined in string.h.

III

Advanced Programming

Applying the notion to our DIRLIST class from chapter 14, the class needed something that could act as a loop termination value. An integral works just fine; we happened to have the int done, so a conversion

```
operator int();
```

works just fine, thus completing the pieces necessary to use DIRLISTs with simple loop structures like for.

> **Tip**
>
> Define conversion operators as member functions. The role of a conversion operator is to return an object of type Y where an object of type Y is expected but an object of type X is used. Usually what is returned by object is a data member of the object.

Using Friend Operators

An operator function is a friend if its declaration in a class is preceded by the keyword friend. From chapter 14, a friend of a class can access the private members of a class. Members of classes can already do that, so defining friend as a member that can access the private parts of a class would be redundant. The friend specifier was used to indicate non-members had access to the private parts of the class.

The members declared in the private part of the class are not accessible by non-members, so the friend specifier controverts the private specifier. This was done for those rare occasions when a member should be private, but convenience or necessity required some non-member to access the private members of another class.

When the keyword friend is used in conjunction with an operator function, you can assume certain things:

- The count of arguments is the same as the operator count.
- The function is not a member of the class it is a friend of.

When you are defining operator functions, define them as friends if you

- Determine or choose that it is more convenient or less-expensive to access the private data directly.

However, if a conversion operator exists, and it returns the relevant private data member, then extending friendship to the global operator function is not necessary.

Subscripting *Operator[]*

The subscript operator [ ] can be overloaded. Overloading [ ] enables you to use the array notation for aggregate types. This is extremely useful because the array is probably the simplest and most frequently used simple data structure.

The key to defining an array operator appropriately is to remember that arrays can be used on either side of an assignment.

```
int a[10];
for( int j = 0; j< 10; j++ )
{
    a[j] = j;                   // array on the left side
    cout << a[j] << endl;       // array on the right side
}
```

To maintain the symmetry of arrays in the context of your classes, you must define arrays to return objects that are lvalues: references to the individual object. Consider the following

```
class Y
{
public:
    // ...
    T operator[]( unsigned int j ) // wrong: should be a reference
    { return data ? data[j] : 0; }
private:
    unsigned int size;
    T * data;                   // T is a some data type
};
```

class Y returns a copy of a Y object from data[j]. This is fine when a Y object is a right-hand-side argument

```
Y y;
T t = y[0];        // ok: gets a copy of y.data[0]
```

but when Y is used as a left-hand-side argument

```
T t;
y[0] = t;                   // error: lvalue required
```

the compiler will give you an error because the notation indicates assignment to an *lvalue* (a reference, pointer, or array), but what it is getting is a single object of type T. Line 13 of the example program in the section entitled "A Bounds-Checking Array" defines the subscripting operator correctly: return a reference to the data type you are returning. Because you want the object in the actual array to be modified, you must return its address.

From Here...

Determining when and how to overload operators requires some extra work on your part. But, the idiom adds a rich flavor to C++ and is easily worth the effort. One of the first aspects of programming readily picked up in most languages is the use of native data types and operators. Most of us have much formal education supporting our understanding of them. By defining the use of operators in the context of more complex types, you will make using your classes easier to understand those who use your programs.

You still must decide and define those operators important to the implementation of your classes, but from then on using them becomes fundamentally as easy as using operators with native types. There is no single way to learn how to use operators. The theme of this chapter suggests that you can acquire the skill by mimicking the overloaded operators declared in the Borland C++ headers. A second way is to use functions to define class operations, then select the verb functions, like insert, add, append, or whatever, and implement those functions using an appropriate operator equivalent.

Starting with the knowledge learned thus far, extend your skills to the next level of comprehension by checking out:

- Chapter 6, "Native Data Types and Operators," presents a straightforward examination of operators and built-in native types.

- Chapter 8, "Understanding Expressions through Expansion," demonstrates techniques for simplifying code with parenthetical grouping, conditional statements, operator functions, and conversion operators.

- Chapter 14, "Basic Class Concepts," teaches you how to write object-oriented programs with C++.

- Chapter 17, "Constructors: Copy and Assignment," covers the copy and assignment operators, which are the functions that cause the most memory leaks in C++ classes.

- Chapter 21, "Understanding Strings in ANSI C and ANSI C++," shows you how string class instances can be seamlessly intermixed with C functions.

Constructors: Copy and Assignment

This chapter is about the copy constructor and the assignment operator. These two subjects deserve a chapter of their own. Creating C++ programs without intimate knowledge of these two member functions is akin to running a marathon without kidneys. (Well, I don't know if that is really the best analogy; let's just say that they are important.)

This chapter follows the chapters on function and operator overloading because without overloading, you would not be able to define these two functions. The copy constructor is an overloaded constructor, and the assignment operator (=) is overloaded, too.

The copy constructor is used to create new objects from existing objects. The assignment operator is used to make an existing object equivalent to a second, existing object. C++ makes few assumptions about how you want to develop applications. C++ is also a language that lets you define how almost everything should be done.

Ask the question: "What does it mean to make a copy?" The answer might be to assign the values of one object to that of another. But do not assume that is the only answer. C++ is a language that makes few assumptions about the way developers want to develop. How objects are copied is no exception.

If your classes only need to copy objects by duplicating the state of other objects, fine. That's easy enough and I will show you a recipe for doing so. However, if your application requires alternative ways to make duplicates, C++ will not get in your way. In this chapter, the ins and outs of this subject matter are covered in sections entitled:

- Understanding Copies
- Understanding the Four Most Important Member Functions
- Shallow Copy versus Deep Copy
- When Are Copies Made?
- Differentiating Copy from Assignment

- Location in Classes
- Blocking Copy and Assignment
- Tricks: Implementing Copy in Terms of Assignment
- Using Copy and Assignment in Child Classes

Understanding Copies

This chapter is about something that occurs all of the time in C++ programs. Directly or indirectly, C++ can make copies of the objects whirling about in your programs. So, in a sci-fi sort of way, duplicating objects from existing objects is like cloning.

As acknowledged in previous chapters, there are many places that can be considered starting points with new subjects. In this chapter, we begin by looking at the syntax of our subject matter and from there attempt to grasp a deeper significant understanding. How objects are, or can be, duplicated is an essential cog; poor engineering results in clunks and grinds that we would rather do without.

Define a Copy Constructor

A copy constructor is used to create new objects from existing ones. This means that like other constructors, the object built does not exist at the time of the call, but unique to the copy constructor, it takes a reference to an object as its argument. Therefore, the syntax of the copy constructor is easily defined. For any class X, the syntax of X's copy constructor is

```
X( const X& ):      // A copy constructor where X is the class name
```

Because the copy constructor is a constructor, it must have a name identical to that of the class, including a matching case. The purpose of the copy constructor is to duplicate a new object copying the state of the argument object. One guideline is that when an argument is not changed by the function, make it constant. Besides, if you did not make the argument const then you cannot copy const objects. And a constant argument can be passed a non-constant, but the reverse is not true.

The second part of the argument declaration, X, is easy: you are duplicating an object of the same type. The entire argument is read as a "constant reference to X." The reference part is significant for several reasons. The first is that by passing the address of the object, a copy does not have to be made of the caller's object. If it sounds like I am talking in circles, that should be a warning to you.

If the copy constructor's job is to make a previously nonexistent object from an existing object and passing by value—not using the address-of operator—causes a copy to be made, then the result is infinite recursion. Simply stated, if you pass an object by value, a copy is made; if you do so in the copy constructor, the copy constructor calls itself in an infinite loop until the resources expire.

Here are some simple rules to follow when declaring—coding the interface as opposed to writing the function body of—a copy constructor:

- The function name is exactly identical to the class name.
- The argument type is constant, so it will accept constant and non-constant objects.
- The argument type is identical to the class name.
- You must pass by reference: use the address-of operator.

When you begin to define a new class, immediately write the copy constructor declaration in the class so you don't forget.

Define an Assignment Operator

The assignment operator's functionality is similar to that of a copy constructor. The difference is timing. Whereas the copy constructor is invoked for new (or temporary) objects, the assignment operator is invoked for existing objects. The calling object is the left operand and the argument object is the right operand.

The assignment operator has a consistent syntax, too. The assignment operator is a member function and a binary operator. Therefore, (see chapter 16, "Operator Overloading") there must be two objects involved. The first is the calling object, referred to by this, and the second is the argument object.

For the same reasons that the copy constructor's argument is a constant reference, so is that of the assignment operator. For any class X, the syntax of the assignment operator is

```
X& operator=(const X&); // The syntax of an assignment operator for any class X.
```

Because assignment is an operator, we must use the operator keyword and the operator token. Since C++ allows a linear succession of assignments

```
a = b = c = d;   // C++ allows linear assignment; therefore, you should too.
```

we must return a reference to the object; otherwise, the chain is broken by our assignment operator. The function is declared as an assignment operator function, returning a reference to an object, and accepting a const reference to an object.

When you define a new class, immediately declare the assignment operator following these guidelines:

- The assignment operator must be a member function.
- It returns a reference to the object of the same class type.
- The function name is operator=.
- It accepts a constant reference to an object of the same class type. Using a const object reference enables the operator to handle both constant and non-constant objects.

Check for Assignment to Self. There is one additional aspect that must be present in every class's assignment operator. The assignment operator must always check for assignment to self.

Assignment to self occurs when one object invokes the assignment operator on itself, either through an alias or directly. It looks like the following:

```
X x;
x = x;              // assignment to self
```

when it occurs directly. While this is obvious, it is important to note that when it occurs it is less likely to occur this obviously. Assignment to self introduces the *slicing problem* into your program. In a nutshell, the slicing problem occurs when two objects, which includes aliases, refer to the same resource and one of them de-allocates the resource. The result is that the second object now refers to a resource in an undefined state.

There are many ways that slicing can occur, but to avoid slicing in your assignment operators, always check for assignment to self. It is easy to do and looks exactly the same for every assignment operator. To check for assignment to self, place the following code in every assignment operator:

```
X& X::operator=(const X& rhs )
{
       if( this == &rhs) return *this;    // check for assignment to self
                                          //... the rest goes here
       return *this;                      // return a reference to an object
}
```

Understanding the Code. The previous section shows you the syntax of the "check for assignment to self." This section provides an explanation of the code. The check itself is exactly the same for every assignment operator and so is the meaning.

The code

```
if( this == &rhs )
```

comprises the check itself. The pointer `this` contains the address of the calling object. That's what pointers do, contain addresses. The `&rhs` is read as "the address of `rhs`." So we are comparing two addresses. If they are equivalent (`==`) then the objects are the same object. If this is the case, `return *this;` causes the function to exit, satisfying the requirement of the function to return a reference to an object. (Notice we use the same code at the end of the function, too.)

Remember `this` is a pointer. The value of a pointer is the address of something. To get the value of a pointer, we dereference it. Dereferencing a pointer looks like

```
*ptr
```

The pointer `this` is dereferenced the same way

```
*this
```

Wrapping the body of the assignment operator with these two lines of code reduces the likelihood that your assignment operator causes memory leaks. If you remember the syntactical rules for copy and assignment presented here and declare them immediately when you define new classes, you will be best off.

The syntactical examples presented in this and the preceding section demonstrate the general syntax for both copy and assignment. Table 17.1 presents a table view of additional information regarding copy and assignment. Use the rules in the table when considering design alternatives.

Table 17.1 Language Rules for the Copy Constructor and Assignment Operator					
Function	**Inherited**	**Virtual**	**Return Type**	**Is Member**	**Default**
Copy	No	No	No	Yes	Yes
Assignment	No	Yes	Yes	Yes	Yes

Defines rules for the copy constructor and assignment operator. You may refer to this table when you are defining these functions.

Why Does C++ Require Me to Define These Member Functions?

C++ makes few assumptions about the way programmers want to develop software. Included among the items it doesn't assume is how you might want to define copy and assignment. You may be surprised at the number and variety of circumstances in which an object is copied. For very simple objects that contain one or two simple data members, the cost of making copies is small, but the more complex the object, like graphical user interfaces or complex data types containing dynamic memory, copying objects becomes more expensive.

First, you must be aware that C++ does create the copy constructors for every class if you do not define them (refer to table 17.1). The reason for this is that the compiler can choose to create copies itself, so these two functions must exist. Second, for complicated data structures, you may want to block copies from being made, you may want to employ reference counting, or you may contrive another way altogether. C++ does not assume what is right for every class, but it makes default versions of these member functions if you fail to address them.

The version of either function created by the compiler may not be what you want though. The compiler's version performs a shallow, or bit-wise, copy. In some circumstances, this is wrong. Take the time to learn how to address the problem for each of the several sets of circumstances that will arise in your programs.

The circumstances I am referring to are all of the myriad ways that copies can be made. Among these are:

```
X x; X y(x);              // Direct call of Copy Constructor
X x = y;                  // Looks like assignment but calls
                          // the copy constructor. Why? See
                          // the section Note
X x, y; x = y;            // Calls the assignment operator
X Foo();                  // Return by value, calls copy
void Foo( X );            // Pass argument by value, makes copy
```

Copies are made all of these ways and still others may be done because of compiler optimizations. This is an area where knowledge truly is power and everything else is the slicing problem.

Note

A statement like X x = y; does not call an assignment operator function for class X, though it may appear to do so. The reason is is that the assignment operator is actually a member function and, therefore, can only be called for an existing object. The code fragment is clearly instantiating an object, specifically x.

If the left-hand argument is being created on the same line of code, then a constructor is involved. The code

```
X x = y;      // calls copy constructor
```

is equivalent to

```
X x(y);       // calls copy constructor
```

and is not the same as

```
X x,y;
x = y;        // calls the assignment operator.
```

You need to know what is actually being called and when and why. This is definitely one of those things that makes C++ more challenging than C.

Understanding the Four Most Important Member Functions

The "Four" refers to the four (the Big Four) member functions you must address in every class that you define. Notice I did not say declare for every class, nor did I say define for every class; I said "address." This means that you must decide the disposition of these four functions, the default constructor, the destructor, the copy constructor, and the assignment operator, for every class you define.

The consideration of each is not arbitrary or random; rather, there are guidelines you can follow that will hold you in good stead for each class. In this section, we will define these rules for the copy constructor and assignment operator only (refer to chapter 14, "Basic Class Concepts," for the rules as they apply to the destructor and default constructor).

Addressing the Copy Constructor

This section provides you with some general guidelines that enable you to decide what to do with the copy constructor and when. (Keep in mind that I have intentionally not defined what goes in the copy constructor yet!)

The copy constructor's job is to replicate a new object from an existing object. If you do not define a copy constructor, the compiler creates one for you. The constructor it makes performs a bit-wise copy of the object. A bit-wise copy means it exactly reproduces the state of the bits of the data members in the source object—the object it is copying. Supposing the class contains pointers, then what is pointed to—the address-value of the pointer—would be identical. This means that two objects point to the same memory location, usually not a good situation. (The next section explains why.)

As a general rule, under the following circumstances the compiler's copy constructor is sufficient:

- There are no pointer (*) members in the class.
- There are no reference (&) members in the class.

In this context, addressing the copy constructor consists of deciding to use the one built by the compiler automatically. You may include a comment in the class indicating this decision.

Note

If you have programmers at many different levels using C++ where you work, you may want to use a comment in the class to indicate that a copy constructor was intentionally left out. In general, comments addressing the disposition of the Big Four might be appropriate in every class. Since you only have to write the class once, it is natural to assume the same is true for the comments.

Here is an example:

```
class X
{
public:
     X();          // default
     virtual ~X();     // virtual destructor
     // A copy constructor and assignment operator were intentionally left
     // undefined. This class contains only stack data, so the default copy
     // and assignment will suffice.
private:
     int data;
     char moreData;
     float noPointers;
};
```

If one or both of the items previously mentioned is not true, then you need to define both a copy constructor and an assignment operator. (You will probably never define just one of these.)

Addressing the Assignment Operator

The last section states that you will probably never define a copy constructor without an assignment operator or vice versa. Therefore, you can and may draw the conclusion that the same general guidelines exist for assignments as they do for copies.

If a class contains pointers or reference members, then you will more than likely need to define your own assignment operator. If none of the members in your class use * or &, then it is safe to use the compiler-generated assignment and copy, and it is probably a good idea to mention the disposition with a comment. While brevity is the soul of wit, software development is no place to be witty. This is especially true if your software lands planes or controls heavy equipment, trains, x-ray machines, or anything else that can be lethal. Developing good habits and having a modicum of conscientiousness doesn't hurt either.

Shallow Copy versus Deep Copy

The word "copy" used in this section pertains to the duplication of objects by either the copy constructor or the assignment operator. There are two types of copies that can be made. The first, which is the kind of copy you get from the compiler, is a *shallow copy*. The other kind of copy is a *deep copy*.

Shallow Copy

A shallow copy is also referred to as a bit-wise copy. A bit-wise copy means that the number and state of the data-bits in one object are exactly reproduced in a second object. For example, the 32 bits of an integer are exactly replicated; it also means that the 32 bits of a char* are exactly duplicated, too.

Recall that a pointer of any type has the number of bits for the pointer variable. The value of that pointer is an address (a location in memory). Usually at that address is some other resource, often a chunk of memory. The problem is that that chunk of memory is pointed to but is not a member of the class. Therefore, a shallow copy duplicates the value of the pointer, not what is pointed at.

Supposing the pointer points to a port or address that contains some relevant data maintained by the operating system. For example, at 0x00000417, the state of the Shift, Caps Lock, Num Lock, and Scroll Lock keys among other things, is maintained by the operating system. Bit-wise copying of a pointer of this type is not a problem because the class neither allocates nor maintains this memory location; the BIOS does.

Unfortunately, pointers are more often than not pointing at memory allocated by the program with a call to new. When this is the case, the shallow copy causes the slicing problem. As I mentioned earlier, the slicing problem occurs when two or more objects refer to the same memory resource and one of them releases the resource without informing the others. (Sorry, but you have to be the one to contrive an "informant" mechanism. If you were to contrive such a mechanism, it is less likely that you would introduce the error in the first place.)

Figure 17.1 illustrates the slicing problem. Assume that object 1 and object 2 are instances of the same class type, which contains a pointer to a block of memory. Further assume that object 2 represents a copy of object 1.

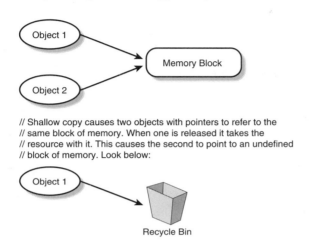

// Shallow copy causes two objects with pointers to refer to the
// same block of memory. When one is released it takes the
// resource with it. This causes the second to point to an undefined
// block of memory. Look below:

Fig. 17.1

This illustrates how a shallow copy can introduce slicing when pointers are involved.

If you haven't guessed, slicing is not good. When one object releases the resources pointed to by other objects, those other objects still have non-zero pointer values. When the program gets around to deleting those secondary objects, `delete` is called on the pointers contained in those objects. Calling `delete` on a pointer with a number other then zero is undefined but usually disastrous.

A primary objective of a class is to define it in such a way that every instance is self-contained and does not interfere with other objects of the same class. You can devise a class that counts the number of references to an object—each instance refers to the same resource block and de-allocation is intentionally managed, but it doesn't happen by accident.

Borrowing the `INT_ARRAY` class from chapter 16, "Operator Overloading," listing 17.1 emulates a shallow copy. This naturally results in errors because the class has a pointer member, which points to a chunk of memory allocated with `new`.

Listing 17.1   smarray2.h—Definition of an Integer Array that Performs Bounds Checking

```
1: // SMARRAY2.H - Class definition for smart integer array with copy.
2: #ifndef __SMARRAY2_H
3: #define __SMARRAY2_H
4: class INT_ARRAY
5: {
6: public:
```

(continues)

Listing 17.1 Continued

```
 7:    INT_ARRAY( unsigned int sz = 100 );
 8:    ~INT_ARRAY();
 9:    // Copy Constructor declaration
10:    INT_ARRAY(const INT_ARRAY&);
11:    // Assignment operator declaration
12:    INT_ARRAY& operator=(const INT_ARRAY&);
13:    // Using an unsigned integer negates the necessity
14:    // for checking for an index < 0; it can't be
15:    int& operator[]( unsigned int index );
16: private:
17:    unsigned int max;
18:    unsigned int dummy;
19:    int * data;
20: };
21: #endif
```

Line 10 demonstrates a properly declared copy constructor, and line 12 demonstrates a properly declared assignment operator for the INT_ARRAY class. The declarations are correct, but as you will see, the definitions are incorrectly defined for this class. (The definition consists of the function body containing the code.)

In fact, I intentionally defined the copy constructor and assignment operator to perform a shallow copy to demonstrate what you get from the compiler (see listing 17.2).

Listing 17.2 Smarray2.cpp—The Implementation of the Smart Array Class with an Incorrectly Defined Copy Constructor

```
 1: // SMARRAY2.CPP - The smart array definition with a scaffold.
 2: // Copyright (c) 1995. All Rights Reserved.
 3: // By Paul Kimmel.
 4: #include <mem.h>
 5: // #define NDEBUG // uncomment to turn of assertions
 6: #include <assert.h>
 7: #include "smarray2.h"
 8: // constructor - Adds one to the size of the array
 9: // to store a dummy value if a bad index is used
10: INT_ARRAY::INT_ARRAY( unsigned int sz )      : max(sz), dummy( sz + 1 ),
    ↪data( new int[sz + 1] )
11: {
12:    // If new returns a valid block of memory
13:    // then data is non-zero. The memset function
14:    // initializes the block to 0.
15:    if(data)
16:        memset( data, 0, dummy );
17:    else
18:        max = -1;
19: }
20: // destructor
21: INT_ARRAY::~INT_ARRAY()
22: {
```

```
23:    // de-allocate the array
24:    delete [] data;
25:    // setting the pointer to 0 provides a reference
26:    // point for testing for an invalid pointer
27:    data = 0;
28: }
29: // --Warning-- This class uses a shallow copy.
30: // Do not use this in a program.
31: // This copy constructor demonstrates the kind of
32: // 'shallow copy' constructor the compiler would
33: // generate. Not only do you have two pointers
34: // pointing to the same memory block, but the old one was
35: // never deleted.
36: INT_ARRAY::INT_ARRAY(const INT_ARRAY& rhs )
37: { // Use of this is redundant but clearly demonstrates this's role
38:    this->max = rhs.max;
39:    this->dummy = rhs.dummy;
40:    this->data = rhs.data;        // ERROR: Shallow copy
41: }
42: // --Warning-- This monkey is bug ridden.
43: INT_ARRAY& INT_ARRAY::operator=( const INT_ARRAY&rhs )
44: {
45:    if( this == &rhs ) return *this;
46:    this->max = rhs.max;
47:    this->dummy = rhs.dummy;
48:    this->data = rhs.data;
49:    return *this;
50: }
51: // Pretty terse but it does check the validity
52: // of the index. This kind of problem is an ideal
53: // candidate for exception handling (see Chapter 22).
54: int& INT_ARRAY::operator[]( unsigned int index )
55: {
56:    // Assert is 'disabled' if NDEBUG is defined
57:    assert( index < max );
58:    return index < max ? data[index] : data[ dummy ] ;
59: }
60: // Scaffolding your code shows that it was tested,
61: // provides easily accessible test code if modifications
62: // are made, is easily removed or included automatically by
63: // the preprocessor, and demonstrates how to use your
64: // class.
65: #ifdef SMARRAY2_SCAFFOLD
66: // The preprocessor directive is defined in the
67: // Options|Project|Compiler|Defines
68: #include <iostream.h>
69: void main()
70: {
71:         INT_ARRAY ouch;
72:         // Create an artificial scope so
73:         // startMeUp's destructor is called first
74:         {
75:             INT_ARRAY startMeUp( 10 );
76:             for( unsigned int k = 0; k<10; k++)
77:                 // operator[] accessed here
78:                 startMeUp[k] = k;
```

(continues)

Advanced Programming

```
        Listing 17.2   Continued
79:                      // Call the 'BAD' assignment operator
80:                      ouch = startMeUp;
81:              }
82:              // Demonstrates that 'ouch' and
83:              // 'startMeUp' point to the same memory block
84:              for( unsigned int k = 0; k < 10; k++)
85:                      cout << ouch[k] << endl;
86: }
87: #endif
```

Lines 35 to 41 define a copy constructor that performs a shallow copy. This is the same kind of copy you get by default from the compiler, unless you blocked copies (see the "Blocking Copy and Assignment" section later in this chapter) or defined a correctly implemented copy constructor.

Lines 43 to 50 define an equally bad assignment operator. Like the copy constructor, it does not release the memory allocated to the calling object's data member, and it does not re-allocate memory and copy each item from the array. All it does is assign the pointer values to the same memory.

Unless you implement some kind of reference counting mechanism, a class like INT_ARRAY performs a deep copy. The following are some general guidelines you can follow when implementing copy and assignment:

- If the class contains pointers or references or uses new and delete, then define a deep copy.

- If the previous statement is true, then you may, as an alternative, block copies altogether or employ some reference counting mechanism.

- The copy constructor should be equally blocked, equally reference counted, and use both shallow copy, or both deep copy. In other words, the type of mechanism employed should be the same for each. (The section entitled "Tricks: Implementing Copy in Terms of Assignment" demonstrates how easy it is to coordinate the efforts of both.)

Finally, the main function wraps the startMeUp object in an fabricated scope so its destructor is called at line 81 (before the destructor for ouch). Lines 76 to 78 assign the values 0 through 9 to the startMeUp object. Line 80 invokes a call to the assignment operator, which means the values in both objects should be equal to 0 through 9.

When line 81 is reached, startmeUp's destructor is called, releasing the int * data pointer memory. In a correctly defined class, this should not affect on another object of the same type. This class, however, uses a shallow copy where a deep copy is required. The result is that ouch points to the same block of data, resulting in ouch containing a pointer to garbage.

Remember when a shallow copy suffices, it is sufficient to use the copy and assignment created by the compiler. Let's take a look now at what a deep copy is and how to define it.

Deep Copy

A deep copy has to be defined by the class designer. A deep copy does everything a shallow copy does, plus it maintains resource blocks required by pointer members. The additional step requires that you release resources allocated by the target object, allocate new resources adequate enough to store a copy of the source data (data to be duplicated) and then define the steps necessary to duplicate the source block.

Note

The notion of deep copy presented here refers to the proper reproduction of memory blocks. With a little experience and variety it becomes apparent that manipulating memory is not the only operation performed in copy constructors and assignment operators. C++ is a broad spectrum language used for a wide variety of applications. In addition to the proper re-allocation of resources, copy and assignment may be required to initialize physical state hardware devices or processes external to the computer the code is running on.

Do not limit yourself to the descriptions here. This chapter is geared toward helping you avoid one of the most common errors: memory leaks.

Figure 17.2 illustrates the logical effect we are trying to achieve with deep copy. An appropriately defined deep copy, in addition to duplicating stack members, manages the re-allocation of resources for dynamic members.

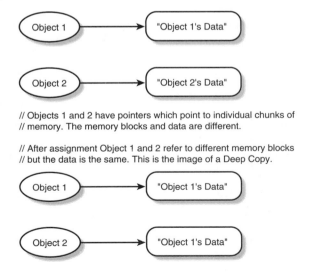

```
// Objects 1 and 2 have pointers which point to individual chunks of
// memory. The memory blocks and data are different.

// After assignment Object 1 and 2 refer to different memory blocks
// but the data is the same. This is the image of a Deep Copy.
```

Fig. 17.2

Illustrated is the logical effect that a deep copy produces. Each object maintains its own data, as well as resources referred to by those data.

III

Advanced Programming

Listing 17.3 modifies the definitions of the copy constructor and assignment operator from the INT_ARRAY class to demonstrate an example of a deep copy (the modified program Smarray3, as well as the incorrect program are included on the companion disk).

Listing 17.3   Smarray3.cpp—The Smart Array with Deep Copy

```
35: // Copy Constructor - Uses Deep Copy
36: INT_ARRAY::INT_ARRAY(const INT_ARRAY& rhs )
37: {
38:   delete [] data;
39:   max = rhs.max;
40:   dummy = rhs.dummy;
41:   data = new int [dummy];
42:   for( unsigned int j = 0; j<dummy; j++)
43:       data[j] = rhs.data[j];
44: }
45: // Assignment Operator:Uses Deep Copy
46: INT_ARRAY& INT_ARRAY::operator=( const INT_ARRAY&rhs )
47: {
48:   if( this == &rhs ) return *this;
49:   // Notice this code is identical to the Copy Constructor's code
50:   delete [] data;
51:   max = rhs.max;
52:   dummy = rhs.dummy;
53:   data = new int [dummy];
54:   for( unsigned int j = 0; j<dummy; j++)
55:       data[j] = rhs.data[j];
56:   return *this;
57: }
```

> **Note**
>
> The integer array class is only useful to the extent that it demonstrates language idioms appropriately. It was written with the intent that you use it to learn to implement classes correctly, but it is not for practical use.

Notice that lines 38 through 43 of the copy constructor and 50 through 55 of the assignment operator are identically defined to release the calling object's memory pointed to by data and then properly allocate and duplicate the same amounts and values from the argument object's data member.

The re-implementation—in its entirety in Smarray3.cpp—properly defines an integer array which performs a no-memory-loss copy constructor and assignment operator. For general guidelines indicating when to use which versions, refer to the previous section, "Shallow Copy." To see an easier way to implement the copy constructor, refer to the following section, "Tricks: Implementing Copy in Terms of Assignment."

"Blocking Copy and Assignment" shows you how to prohibit copies, and the last two sections demonstrate how to define copies in inheritance relationships and how to employ reference counting.

When Are Copies Made?

The cost of copying complex objects can be quite steep. If you consider the complexity of classes responsible for creating graphics, managing complex data structures, or reproducing single or multiple inheritance hierarchies, it is easy to imagine a heavy penalty indeed. For this reason, it behooves you to understand under what circumstances the copy constructor or assignment operator is invoked. As both are similar in responsibility, I will not distinguish between the functions but refer to copy in general.

A copy is made when you pass an object by value. To pass by value means that you do not use a & or * in the type-argument declaration of the function syntax. A copy is also made when you return an object by value. Here is an example of each:

```
void Foo( X arg );      // where X is any class X
X Foo();          // ditto
```

When objects are passed by value the changes you make to the object affect the copy. When an object originates inside of a function you want to return by value; you do not want to return an object originated in the function by reference. Consider the following:

```
X& Foo()
{
    X * x = new X;     // allocated locally
    return *x;
}
```

In this example, code outside of the function Foo would have to be responsible for deleting the object x allocated on the free store. This is error-prone. The next example allocates an object on the local function stack

```
X& Foo()
{
    X x;
    return &x;
}
```

The problem with this function is that when Foo exits, the destructor for x is called automatically (as local stack objects are cleaned up when they go out of scope). So when an object originates inside a function, you want to return a copy, and you need to know what it looks like.

Copies can also be made at the discretion of the compiler. The Borland C++ compiler is capable of optimizing code, and one of the rules supporting optimization is the ability of the compiler to make temporary objects.

Differentiating Copy from Assignment

This chapter quickly demonstrates and explains when the copy constructor is invoked and when the assignment operator is used. This is in addition to objects that are made by calls to the default or other constructors. Either the copy constructor or assignment operator is called when objects are made or copied from existing objects or data that can be used to create temporary objects.

For demonstrative purposes, we will use two objects y and z of class X (where X is any class) when each type of call is made. Consider calls of the form

```
X y(z);
```

This is a direct call to X's copy constructor. y is the calling object, and z plays the role of the argument object. Using the usual syntax for a copy constructor

```
X::X(const X& rhs );
```

within the copy constructor, the pointer this refers to y and the reference rhs is an alias for (the address of) z. The example must clearly use the copy constructor because the code is constructing a new object y.

The following example, not so obviously, also calls the copy constructor:

```
X y = z;
```

The appearance of the equal sign in the statement suggests that assignment is occurring. However, the statement is also creating a new object, X. If this code used the assignment operator, the expansion is

```
y.operator=(z);      // Wrong!
```

However, y does not exist yet, so the call must resolve to a constructor call. Because this code again is constructing using the values of an existing object, the copy constructor is called here, too.

The last example demonstrates code that invokes the assignment operator; both y and z exist already, and z is being assigned to y:

```
X y, z;
y = z;      // calls the assignment operator
```

These examples illustrate direct examples of the kinds of statements that call either member function. Listing 17.4 was contrived for no other reason then to illustrate each example. Here is the code which contains output strings indicating when each function is called.

Listing 17.4 Copies.cpp—Demonstrates the Kinds of Statements that Use the Copy Constructor and Assignment Operator

```
1: // COPIES.CPP - Demonstrates the forms of statements which invoke
2: // calls to the copy constructor and assignment operator.
3: #include <iostream.h>
4: #include <fstream.h>
```

```
5: ofstream of( "output.dat" );
6: class X
7: {
8: public:
9:     X();
10:    ~X();
11:    X(const X&);
12:    X& operator=(const X&);
13:    operator int(){return num; }
14: private:
15:    int num;
16: };
17: // Default Constructor
18: X::X()
19: {
20:    of <<"constructor" << endl;
21:    num = 5;
22: }
23: // Destructor
24: X::~X()
25: {
26:    of << "destructor" << endl;
27: }
28: // Copy Constructor
29: X::X( const X& rhs )
30: {
31:    of << "copy constructor" << endl;
32:    num = rhs.num;
33: }
34: // Assignment Operator
35: X& X::operator=(const X& rhs )
36: {
37:    if( this == &rhs ) return *this;
38:    of << "assignment operator" << endl;
39:    num = rhs.num;
40:    return *this;
41: }
42: // Return by value
43: X Foo()
44: {
45:   return X();
46: }
47: void Foo( X x )
48: {
49:    x = x;
50: }
51: void main()
52: {
53:    {
54:        X z;                // constructor
55:        X y = z;            // copy constructor
56:    }                       // two destructor calls
57:    {
58:        X z;                // constructor
59:        X y(z);             // copy constructor
60:    }                       // two destructor calls
```

(continues)

Advanced Programming

```
Listing 17.4   Continued
61:   {
62:         X z, y;                    // constructor
63:         y = z;                     // assignment operator
64:   }                                // two constructor calls
65:   {
66:         X y = Foo();               // constructor
67:   }                                // destructor
68:   {
69:         X y;                       // constructor
70:         Foo( y );                  // copy constructor
71:   }                                // two destructor calls
72: }
```

I used the {} bracket pair to force the destructor for each object to be called in an ordered manner. This is unusual and done here to pair constructor calls and destructor calls. The output from this program is contained in Output.dat and was inserted as comments into the code listing.

Location in Classes

The placement of the copy constructor and assignment operator in a class is important. The job of each of these member functions is to duplicate objects external to the class. Meaning that, in their normal capacity, they are invoked externally to the class. If member functions are to be called, implicitly or otherwise from outside the class, and the callers are not child classes or friends, then the functions must be in the public interface.

While this is the usual placement of copy and assignment, it is not the only option. In some circumstances you may want only child classes or friends to duplicate objects. This can be accomplished by declaring them protected or private.

A third alternative is to block copies from occurring at all. Some implementations invite this alternative approach (see the next section for the blocking technique). Table 17.2 describes general guidelines to assist you in implementing the copy constructor and assignment operator when defining classes.

Table 17.2   Acts as a General Guideline for the Placement of the Copy Constructor and Assignment Operator and Whether You Want to Allow Copies or Not

Class Description	Enable Copies	Location of Copy and Assignment
Contains References	Yes	Public interface
Contains References	No	Private declaration, do not define

Class Description	Enable Copies	Location of Copy and Assignment
No References	Yes	Default, compiler generated versions
No References	No	Private declaration, do not define

Blocking Copy and Assignment

Simple data types require little effort on the part of the language to allocate and reproduce. The more complex the data type the more time it takes to copy objects of that type. The kinds of classes that fall in the category of our discussion might contain chunks of memory managed with new or delete; they may require complex graphics calculations; they might be comprised of complex data structures, like linked lists, binary trees, or bags; they may be responsible for initializing external devices, or be part of deep inheritance hierarchy. Like most aspects of programming, *you* will have to decide what constitutes an expense or circumstance that necessitates the blocking of copies.

The technique for blocking the compiler from automatically creating the copy constructor and assignment operator is for you to declare it in the class but not define them. And the declaration must be private. So for any class X, the following declaration

```
class X
{
public:
      // public stuff
protected:
      // protected stuff
private:
      // private stuff
      // Block Copies
      X(const X&);
      X& operator=(const X&);
};
```

without a definition—no function body—causes the compiler to generate an error if any code creates a call to either member function. This technique does not allow copies of individual objects, but you can still have aliases. (As a reminder, an alias can consist of an argument name where an object was passed by reference for example.)

The technique may not be used often but adds a nice flavor to your repertoire when something extra is required. In most cases, you want to enable copies, either the default for simple classes without dynamic data or deep copies for classes with dynamic data.

Tricks: Implementing Copy in Terms of Assignment

I made a point to mention in earlier sections the similarity in responsibility and implementation of the copy constructor and assignment operator. The only real difference is that the assignment operator checks for assignment to self whereas the copy constructor is called for new objects, so there is no chance of self-assignment.

As the definition of each member is almost identical, we can exploit the closeness by implementing one in terms of the other. Not only does this make writing them quicker and easier, it also makes it easier to ensure that changes to one are uniform to the other. The trick then is to have one of the pair call the other for every class.

I have often seen it implemented in the following way:

```
class X
{
public:
        // .. constructor, destructor, and other class stuff

        // Copy constructor is implemented in terms of (implicitly calls)
        // the assignment operator
        X(const X& rhs )
        { *this = rhs; }

        // Assignment operator
        X& operator=(const X& rhs )
        {     if (this == &rhs ) return *this;
              // perform assignments, deep copy or whatever
              return *this;
        }
private:
        // data members
};
```

where the code `*this = rhs;` implicitly calls the assignment operator. I don't care for this form of pass the buck; it's too vague and may be error-prone. Where I have generally stated that the use of overloaded operator functions is generally implicit, here I voluntarily break the rule. I do so for clarity and because the class designer only needs to see this code statement anyway.

Listing 17.5 shows how to implement copy in terms of assignment:

Listing 17.5 Shows You How to Implement Copy, Using the Assignment Operator to Do the Work

```
// Copy Constructor explicitly calls the assignment operator like any other
// function.
X(const X& rhs )
{ operator=(rhs); }
```

```
// Assignment operator
X& operator=(const X& rhs)
{     if( this == &rhs ) return *this;
      // Assign/copy stuff here
      return *this;
}
```

I make an explicit call to the class's assignment operator just like the function it is. (What is not shown is that the this->operator=(rhs) prefixes the call; it is redundant but not incorrect to prefix the function call with the pointer.) Implementing copy in terms of assignment ensures that you only have to write the actual statements in one location—the assignment operator—regardless of the changes your class may endure through successive iterations.

> **Note**
>
> You should note that an added function-call indirection occurs by implementing copy this way. I have never found the added function call to cause a bottleneck or reduction in performance, but you should at least understand the considerations involved for thoroughness.

Using Copy and Assignment in Child Classes

Table 17.1 clearly indicates that the copy constructor is not inherited. Chapter 20, "Inheritance and Polymorphism," explains inheritance, but in a nutshell, it is the compiler's way of automating the cutting and pasting of functionality from existing types to create new types.

There is a syntactical approach that specifies this relationship. While the process is more involved then simple cutting and pasting, the result is an aggregation of existing and new functionality.

The same considerations have to be given a class that is in part comprised from other classes as given single class structures. You must determine which kind of copy— none, shallow, or deep—is appropriate and apply it. You typically perform the same type of copy in the child class (the new one created in part from the old one) as you do the parent class (the one inherited from). However, you are not prohibited from blocking in the class.

The focus of our discussion is the method and syntax employed to ensure that the entire object is copied. If I am losing you, you may want to place a bookmark here and read chapter 20 before proceeding. Assuming the parent class already has copy and assignment defined, then the trick is to invoke those operations as necessary.

III

Advanced Programming

Having read the previous section, "Tricks: Implementing Copy in Terms of Assignment," you can easily get the parent part copied, too. Consider the following class B which inherits from A:

```
// Read as B publicly inherits from A
class B : public A
{
public:
        B();                            // Constructor
        ~B();                           // Destructor
        X(const X&);              // Copy
        X& operator=(const X&);   // Assignment
private:
        // blah! blah! blah!
};
```

The class A has all of its affairs in order; it is a completely defined, tested, and function class. B is a class which is defined as a kind of A. Assuming B's copy constructor is implemented in terms of B's assignment operator, the result is

```
// The copy constructor
B::B(const B& rhs)
{ operator=(rhs); }       // let the assignment operator do the work

// The assignment operator
B& B::operator=(const B& rhs )
{
        if( this == &rhs ) return *this;
        A::operator=(rhs);        // Gets the A part copied
        // assign those data members in B only
        return *this;
}
```

The single line of code uses the class name and the scope resolution operator (A::) to call A's assignment operator explicitly, and the deed is done. If you do not want to implement copy in terms of assignment then you have to construct the base class in the copy constructor, too. The code for the assignment operator still does not change, but the code for the copy construct reverts to

```
// The first line uses an initialization list to call the
// copy constructor for the A part of B and the rest of the constructor
// is implemented by duplicating the data members.
B::B(const B& rhs ) : A(rhs)
{
        // Instead of calling operator=
        // Assign all of the B data members here!
}
```

The only noticeable change is that the A part of B must be duplicated, too.

From Here...

The subject of the copy constructor and assignment operator are of paramount importance. I would venture to guess that these two functions are the biggest source of memory leaks in C++ classes. These two functions are largely responsible for code that is crashing DOS- and Windows-based systems. While not the only source of the slicing problem, these two functions must be fully understood before C++ class designers can implement other than the most trivial of classes.

There are other chapters that support the material presented in this chapter. To gain insight into one of the most common C++ programming problems—memory leaks—and read about related material, read the following:

- Chapter 6, "Native Data Types and Operators," will give you a new perspective of C++ with discussions on native data types, the new and delete operators, iostream operators, and operators as functions.

- Chapter 14, "Basic Class Concepts," introduces you to the elements of classes that you need to learn to write object-oriented programs.

- Chapter 15, "Function Overloading," shows you how to use overloaded functions.

- Chapter 16, "Operator Overloading," demonstrates how to write your own operator functions.

- Chapter 20, "Inheritance and Polymorphism," covers the hierarchy of classes that are so important when defining relationships between classes and objects.

CHAPTER 18

Using Container Classes

Container classes are classes that provide structures for storing and maintaining virtually any sort of data, including user-defined data types. These containers implement common data structures such as *arrays*, *sets*, and *stacks*. Borland C++ 5 comes with two container class libraries: Borland's own class library called *Borland International Data Structures (BIDS)* and the *Standard Template Library (STL) containers*, which are part of the latest C++ language standard.

These libraries present somewhat different approaches. Borland's container class library, BIDS, models containers in a more traditional object-oriented fashion with heavy use of inheritance and encapsulation of all functionality within the container class. In contrast, the STL separates much of the functionality of the containers into global template functions.

BIDS

BIDS provide several common data structures including *array*, *bag*, *deque*, *dictionary*, *queue*, *set*, and *stack*. Each class provides member functions that are consistent with that type of container. For example, an array object will allow random access to its data members by the [ ] operator, whereas a stack object allows access to its members by the use of push and pop member functions. Several member functions are found in all the container classes. These common member functions include IsEmpty and IsFull.

To use the container class library, the appropriate library file must be included in the project. The naming convention used for the library files is BIDS*x*.LIB, where *x* is the memory model: S=small, C=compact, M=medium, L=large, H=huge, and F=flat (32 bit). Of course, the appropriate header file must be included for a container class to be used. To use the array class, the arrays.h file must be included:

```
#include <classlib\arrays.h>
```

The default location of the directory Classlib is:

```
\BC5\INCLUDE\CLASSLIB
```

Because the Include directory is listed in the Borland IDE Include directories by default, there is no need to explicitly add the Classlib directory to the projects list of include directories.

Template Implementation

BIDS are implemented as template classes, which will be covered in depth in chapter 19, "Using Template Classes." Templates allow the container class to be easily used for any data type. To declare an integer array, use the following:

```
TArrayAsVector<int> intArray(10);
```

intArray can hold 11 integers (the parameter 10 is the maximum array index: 0..10). The size of an array may grow as elements are added or an index greater than 10 is referenced if it is declared as:

```
TArrayAsVector<float> floatArray(100, 0, 5);
```

floatArray has an initial size of 101 elements with a starting index of 0 (the second parameter), and when floats are added at an index greater than 100, the array grows by multiples of 5 (the third parameter) until the index desired is within bounds.

Tip

Your code is much more readable and more easily maintained if you use typedef to define container class types. In the preceding example, use

```
typedef TArrayAsVector<int> INT_CONTAINER;
```

to define a type of array of integers. To declare a variable of this type, use

```
INT_CONTAINER intList(10, 0, 5);
```

A more interesting example is an array of user-defined class objects. To define a class that will be used throughout the chapter, see listing 18.1, which defines a class STUDENT.

Listing 18.1   student1.h—Example Class

```
// All member functions are inline for brevity.
#include <cstring.h>

class STUDENT
{
public:
    STUDENT()
        : id(""), grade(-1.0)
        {}
    STUDENT(const string &id_, float grade_=-1.0)
        : id(id_), grade(grade_)
        {}
    STUDENT(const STUDENT &student)
```

```
        { *this = student; }
    ~STUDENT()
        {}
    STUDENT& operator=(const STUDENT &rhs)
    {
        if (this != &rhs) {                          // Don't copy self.
           id = rhs.id;
           grade = rhs.grade;
        }
        return *this;
    }
    int operator==(const STUDENT &rhs)
    {
        return (id == rhs.id);
    }
    const string& GetId() const
        { return id; }
    float GetGrade() const
        { return grade; }
    void SetId(string &id_)
        { id = id_; }
    void SetGrade(float grade_)
        { grade = grade_; }
private:
    string id;
    float grade;
};
```

The STUDENT class includes a default constructor, a copy constructor, assignment operator, and a == operator. These constructors and operators must be well-defined to be stored in many of the container classes. Fundamental data types, such as integers and floats, meet this criterion. Pointers to objects also meet this criterion. User-defined classes must provide the necessary functionality.

Listing 18.2 demonstrates using an array container of STUDENT objects.

Listing 18.2 Arrays1.cpp—Using Array Class

```
#include <iostream.h>
#include <iomanip.h>
#include <classlib\arrays.h>
#include "student1.h"

typedef TArrayAsVector<STUDENT> STUDENT_CONTAINER;

int main()
{
    STUDENT_CONTAINER students(5, 0, 5);
    string id;
    cout << "Enter each student id and grade (enter stop to quit):"
    ➥<< endl;
    do {
        cin >> id;
        if (id != "stop") {
```

III

Advanced Programming

(continues)

Listing 18.2   Continued

```
                    float grade;
                    cin >> grade;
                    STUDENT student(id, grade);
                    students.Add(student);
        }
    } while (id != "stop");

    cout << endl << "The list of entered students is as follows:"
➥<< endl
        << setiosflags(ios::fixed) << setprecision(1);

    for (int i = 0; i < students.GetItemsInContainer(); i++)
        cout << "   [" << i << "] "
            << students[i].GetId() << "    "
            << students[i].GetGrade() << endl;

    return 0;
```

A new global type called STUDENT_LIST is declared using a typedef statement. A STUDENT_LIST variable is declared with an initial size of 5 elements, and the array will grow in increments of 5 as needed. User-entered STUDENTs are added to the array until the user exits the loop by entering "stop" for a student name. The array is then printed to screen.

A sample run of the Arrays1 program when compiled to an EasyWin target is shown in figure 18.1.

Fig. 18.1

Sample run of Arrays1 program.

```
Enter each student id and grade (enter stop to quit):
Student1 1.0 Student2 2.0 Student3 3.0 Student4 4.0
Student5 1.5 Student6 2.6 Student7 3.7 stop

The list of entered students is as follows:
    [0] Student1 1.0
    [1] Studnet2 2.0
    [2] Student3 3.0
    [3] Student4 4.0
    [4] Student5 1.5
    [5] Student6 2.6
    [6] Student7 3.7
```

Note

Early versions of BIDS implemented container classes through the use of common classes rather than templates. This implementation is not as straightforward as the current template-based version. For compatibility with programs written using the older style classes, the header files for the older classes are provided in Include\Classlib\Obsolete. Also, the Obsolete.lib must be included in the project.

Container Categories

There are two main categories of classes found in BIDS. The first category is made up of low-level container classes that are used to implement higher-level classes. These container classes, called *Fundamental Data Structures (FDS)*, include *binary tree* (binimp.h), *hashtable* (hashimp.h), *linked list* (listimp.h), *double-linked list* (dlistimp.h), and *vector* (vecimp.h). The FDS classes are used in the implementation of the second category of container classes: *Abstract Data Types (ADT)*. ADT containers are more commonly used instead of using FDS classes directly.

ADT classes include *array* (array.h), *bag* (bag.h), *deque* (deques.h), *dictionary* (dict.h), *queue* (queues.h), *set* (sets.h), and *stack* (stack.h). Each ADT is based on one or more FDS. The array class is implemented as a vector. Thus, the name of the class is `TArrayAsVector`. A stack may be implemented as a vector (`TStackAsVector`) or a list (`TStackAsList`). Table 18.1 lists each ADT and the FDS classes that are used to implement it.

Table 18.1 ADT Implementations Using FDS Classes

ADT	BinaryTree	Hashtable	Linked List	Double List	Vector
Array					X
Bag					X
Deque				X	X
Dictionary			X		
Queue					X
Set					X
Stack			X		X

Each ADT uses the FDS classes that are applicable for that type of container. It would make no sense to implement an array as a hashtable. Choosing FDS implementation is usually a trade-off of speed versus flexibility. A deque may be implemented as a double-linked list or as a vector. The double-linked list will give more flexibility in the number of elements but will be slower in access operations.

Direct and Indirect Containers

Container classes can store objects in one of two ways: *direct* or *indirect*. A direct container stores a copy of the object. The `studentList` object in listing 18.2 stores student objects by copying the objects into the container.

Indirect containers store pointers to objects. Listing 18.3 changes the code to store pointers to the objects.

III

Advanced Programming

Listing 18.3   Arrays2.cpp—Storing Pointers in Arrays

```cpp
#include <iostream.h>
#include <iomanip.h>
#include <classlib\arrays.h>
#include "student1.h"

typedef TIArrayAsVector<STUDENT> STUDENT_LIST;

int main()
{
    STUDENT_LIST studentList(5, 0, 5);
    string id;
    cout << "Enter each student id and grade (enter stop to quit):" << endl;
    do {
        cin >> id;
        if (id != "stop") {
            float grade;
            cin >> grade;
            studentList.Add(new STUDENT(id, grade));
        }
    } while (id != "stop");

    cout << endl << "The list of entered students is as follows:"  << endl
        << setiosflags(ios::fixed) << setprecision(1);
    for (int i = 0; i < studentList.GetItemsInContainer(); i++)
        cout << "   [" << i << "] " << studentList[i]->GetId() << "    "
        << studentList[i]->GetGrade() << endl;
    return 0;
}
```

The name of the array template class indicates what type of storage it uses. The initial T is followed by an I if the container stores pointers to objects:

```cpp
typedef TIArrayAsVector<STUDENT> STUDENT_LIST;
```

To use the direct containers, the objects being stored must have a well-defined default constructor, copy constructor, assignment operator, and == operator. Sometimes it is difficult or impossible to define the == operator. For example, suppose that the code for the class to be stored is not available, and the == operator is not defined. The only way to use a direct container in this situation would be to define a class that inherits from the original class and defines a == operator in the new class. Then objects of the new class type could be stored in a direct container. Indirect containers store pointers, for which all the needed functionality is well-defined.

Another factor in choosing a storage method is efficiency. The direct containers store objects by copying them, which could be costly for user-defined classes with a lot of member data.

Container Object Ownership

When storing pointers to objects in a container, responsibility for the destruction of the object must be decided. Assume that the user of the container is any part of the program that uses the container, directly or indirectly. Should the user of the container be responsible, or should the container destroy the objects when they are removed from the container? Who should "own" the objects? If the container is being used as temporary storage and the life of the objects being stored is longer than the life of the container, ownership should not belong to the container. On the other hand, if the objects being stored should exist only during the life of the container, it might be simpler to allow the container ownership.

Each indirect container has as a base class TShouldDelete, which is found in the header file shddel.h. This allows ownership of objects by the container to be retrieved and set through the member function OwnsElements. OwnsElements is an overloaded member function with two forms. The first form allows the user to query for the ownership status. It is declared in the TShouldDelete by:

```
bool OwnsElements();
```

The preceding function will return true if the container owns the stored objects or false if it does not. The studentList container in listing 18.3 can query ownership with the following:

```
if (studentList.OwnsElements() == true)
    cout << "studentList owns its students." << endl;
else
    cout << "studentList does not own its students." << endl;
```

By default, all indirect containers own their stored objects; therefore, if the ownership studentList has not been set otherwise, the studentList() will return true.

The second overloaded function allows the user to set the ownership status:

```
void OwnsElements(bool del);
```

To set ownership, simply call OwnsElements with true or false. To set studentList ownership to false:

```
studentList.OwnsElements(false);
```

To toggle the ownership status of studentList:

```
studentList.OwnsElements(!studentList.OwnsElements());
```

Listing 18.4 shows how to set and use ownership.

Listing 18.4 Arrays3.cpp—Illustrates Object Ownership

```
#include <iostream.h>
#include <iomanip.h>
#include <classlib\arrays.h>
#include "student1.h"

typedef TIArrayAsVector<STUDENT> STUDENT_LIST;

// Function to output ownership status.
void WriteOwnership(STUDENT_LIST&);
```

(continues)

Listing 18.4 Continued

```cpp
int main()
{
    STUDENT_LIST studentList(5, 0, 5);
    studentList.Add(new STUDENT("STUDENT1", 1.0));
    studentList.Add(new STUDENT("STUDENT2", 2.0));
    studentList.Add(new STUDENT("STUDENT3", 3.0));

    cout << "Default ownership:  ";
    WriteOwnership(studentList);                              // Owns objects.
    studentList.OwnsElements(false);
    cout << "After studentList.OwnsElements(false):  ";
    WriteOwnership(studentList);                              // Does not own objects.

    STUDENT *s;
    s = studentList[0];
    studentList.Detach(0);                                    // Element not destroyed.
                                                              // s valid.
    studentList.AddAt(s, 0);                                  // Put s it back.
    studentList.Detach(0, TShouldDelete::NoDelete);           // Equivalent to above
                                                              // Detach.
    studentList.AddAt(s, 0);                                  // Put s it back.
    studentList.Detach(0, TShouldDelete::DefDelete);          // s still valid since
                                                              // does not own elements.
    studentList.AddAt(s, 0);                                  // Put s it back.
    studentList.Detach(0, TShouldDelete::Delete);             // Element destroyed.
                                                              // s NOT valid.
    s = new STUDENT("NEWSTU1", 1.0);
    studentList.AddAt(s, 0);
    studentList.OwnsElements(true);                           // Change ownership back
                                                              // to the default.
    studentList.Detach(0, TShouldDelete::DefDelete);          // Element destroyed.
                                                              // s NOT valid.
    studentList.Destroy(0);                                   // Element destroyed
                                                              // regardless of ownership.
    studentList.Flush();                                      // Elements destroyed
                                                              // since owns elements.
    return 0;
}

void WriteOwnership(STUDENT_LIST &studentList)
{
    if (studentList.OwnsElements())
        cout << "Student list owns its objects." << endl;
    else
        cout << "Student list does not own its objects." << endl;
}
```

Direct arrays always own their objects. The objects added to the container are copied. When an element is removed from a direct container, the object in the container is destroyed. TShouldDelete is not a base class of direct containers, so OwnsElements is not a member of direct containers.

Special Memory Management

Each container has a version that allows the user to supply memory management for the container's objects. The user-supplied memory manager is in the form of a class. Suppose that STUDENT_MEMORY_MANAGER is a class that defines new, new[], delete, and delete[] for the STUDENT class. Then STUDENT_LIST can be declared as:

```
typedef TMArrayAsVector<STUDENT, STUDENT_MEMORY_MANAGER> STUDENT_LIST;
```

The M in the template name indicates this template requires a user-defined memory manager.

All container classes are derived from the "M" versions. The "non-M" versions use a standard memory-management class TStandardAllocator in alloctr.h. TStandardAllocator uses the globally defined new, new[], delete, and delete[] operators.

Defining your own memory management is usually very rare. If you are writing an application where speed is critical, allocating a pool of memory from which to draw for container objects will require writing your own new and delete for the class.

Sorted and Counted Containers

Some containers provide a version that automatically sorts elements as they are added to the container. To declare a sorted array type of STUDENTs, use the following:

```
#typedef TSArrayAsVector<STUDENT> SORTED_STUDENT_LIST;
```

Indirect containers can also be sorted:

```
#typedef TISArrayAsVector<STUDENT> SORTED_STUDENT_LIST;
```

Sorted indirect containers will sort on the object, not on the pointer.

How are the STUDENT objects sorted, by ID or grade? The STUDENT class defined in listing 18.1 does not have a sorting criterion. Comparing STUDENT objects is not defined:

```
STUDENT s1("John Newton", 4.0);
STUDENT s2("Scott Courey", 3.5);
if (s1 < s2)                                    // ERROR.
    ...
```

All data types stored in sorted containers must have well-defined comparison semantics. In other words, the < operator must be defined. Fundamental data types, such as int or float, meet this criterion. For classes, this means the < operator must be overloaded. The < operator is not defined for STUDENT class, so one must be added. Listing 18.5 gives the < operator definition portion of a modified STUDENT class.

Listing 18.5   student2.h—< Operator Defined

```
class STUDENT
{
public:
    ...
```

(continues)

III

Advanced Programming

Listing 18.5   Continued

```
int operator<(const STUDENT &rhs) // Sort students by grade.
   { return (grade < rhs.grade); }
   ...
};
```

Only the array container provides an S version of the ADTs. The FDS containers list, double list, and vector provide a sorted version.

Counted versions of some containers are also defined. These counted containers keep track of the number of elements in the container. These counted container names contain a C. Only the vector is provided in counted version.

Container Naming Conventions

The number of classes and long class names may seem complicated and unwieldy at first. The BIDS section of the table of contents in the *Borland Library Reference* gives a good overview of classes available. When studying the list of class names, it is apparent there is a pattern to the naming of classes. BIDS class names follow certain naming conventions that aid in finding a desired class or understanding the characteristics of a class. In general, the format of ADT container class names is

    T[M][I][S][ADT]As[FDS]

All class names begin with the letter T. The T is followed by zero or more modifiers. Each of these modifiers has been discussed in detail in previous sections in this chapter. M specifies that a user-defined memory manager must be supplied. I indicates the container stores pointers to objects rather than the objects themselves. S specifies a sorted container. TMISArrayAsVector is an example of a class name containing all modifiers.

FDS container class names have a slightly different format:

    T[M][I][S][C][FDS]Imp

The modifier C specifies a counted container, and the suffix Imp stands for implementation. TMICVectorImp and TMISVectorImp are examples of class names that use these modifiers.

Not all class names follow these conventions. For example, TArray and TSArray are provided as class names and are nothing more than synonyms for TArrayAsVector and TSArrayAsVector.

Container Iterators

All containers have member functions that allow access to its objects (*access* functions) that are consistent with the type of container. Arrays have a [] operator to allow access to its elements. A stack has push and pop member functions. At times, it is desirable to iterate over all the elements in a container. The basic functionality of a container like a stack does not offer this kind of access. The BIDS containers provide two solutions: the ForEach member function and an iterator class.

Most of the container classes provide a member function, ForEach, which allows the user to iterate over every element in the container and apply a user-supplied function:

```
void ForEach(InterFunc, void *args);
```

Suppose that you have a STUDENT container, and all grades are to be increased by 0.25 points. For a change of pace, use a stack.

A more versatile method of iterating over a container is to use an *iterator class*. Each container class has a corresponding companion class that allows the user to iterate over the contents of the container. The naming convention for this iterator is

```
[Container class name]Iterator
```

The ADT or FDS class name is followed by the suffix Iterator. Listing 18.6 demonstrates the use of an iterator class and the ForEach member function.

Listing 18.6   Stacks1.cpp—Using Iterators

```cpp
#include <iostream.h>
#include <iomanip.h>
#include <classlib\stacks.h>
#include "student2.h"

typedef TIStackAsVector<STUDENT> STUDENT_CONTAINER;

// BIDS suppiled iterator.
typedef TIStackAsVectorIterator<STUDENT> STUDENT_CONTAINER_ITERATOR;

// Function to be applied to each element by ForEach member function.
static void ChangeGrade(STUDENT &s, void *arg);

// Output students in the container.
void WriteStudents(STUDENT_CONTAINER&);

int main()
{
    STUDENT_CONTAINER students;
    students.Push(new STUDENT("STUDENT1", 1.0));
    students.Push(new STUDENT("STUDENT2", 2.0));
    students.Push(new STUDENT("STUDENT3", 3.0));
    students.Push(new STUDENT("STUDENT4", 4.0));
    float gradeChange = 0.2;
    cout << "Before grade change:" << endl;
    WriteStudents(students);
    students.ForEach(ChangeGrade, &gradeChange);
    cout << "After grade change:" << endl;
    WriteStudents(students);
    students.Flush();                          // Destroys elements.
    return 0;
}

void ChangeGrade(STUDENT &s, void *change)
{
    s.SetGrade(s.GetGrade() + *(float*)change);
```

(continues)

```
Listing 18.6   Continued
      // Keep grades valid.
      if (s.GetGrade() < 0.0)
         s.SetGrade(0.0);
      else if (s.GetGrade() > 4.0)                   // 4 point system.
         s.SetGrade(4.0);
   }

   void WriteStudents(STUDENT_CONTAINER &students)
   {
      STUDENT_CONTAINER_ITERATOR iterator(students);
      STUDENT *s;
      cout << setiosflags(ios::fixed) << setprecision(1);
      while (s = iterator++)
         cout << "    " << s->GetId() << "    " << s->GetGrade() << endl;
   }
```

Special BIDS Classes

In addition to the ADT and FDS container classes and iterator classes, there are a few other classes worth mentioning. `TShouldDelete` is discussed in the "Container Object Ownership" section. It provides ownership control for indirect classes through its member function `OwnsElements`.

Another special group of classes is used to implement dictionary containers. These classes, called *association classes*, have class names of the form `T[suffix]Association`. The suffix specifies the characteristics of the association class in much the same way as the `M` and `I` specifiers do for the ADT and FDS container class names. Using associations will be covered in greater detail in the section on using dictionaries.

The BIDS container classes use a lower-level class from which they inherit and that implements basic functions for that type of container. These classes have names that end with the `Imp` suffix, such as `TArrayAsVectorImp`. These classes are meant for internal use only, but studying the code for these classes can help in understanding the containers. Note that all FDS class containers (and header filenames) end with `Imp`.

The list and double-list containers use a class that provides a way of storing any type of object in the list. There is an element-container class for each type of list— `TMListElement` and `TMDoubleListElement`. These classes add pointer fields to the objects being stored in the list. The user never has to deal directly with these element classes.

Using BIDS Containers

The following sections explain the use of each ATD container and a couple of the more commonly used FDS containers, binary tree and double-linked list. Each section briefly explores the type of container, commonly used functions and operators, and gives an example of its use.

Array

Arrays are containers that allow arbitrary access to its elements through the use of the [ ] operator. The concept is very much like C arrays. Unlike C arrays, BIDS arrays can dynamically resize, and its elements are not necessarily stored in contiguous memory.

Using the STUDENT class defined in listing 18.5 (student2.h), common classes are:

```
typedef TArrayAsVector<STUDENT> STUDENT_ARRAY;

typedef TSArrayAsVector<STUDENT> SORTED_STUDENT_ARRAY;

typedef TIArrayAsVector<STUDENT> STUDENT_POINTER_ARRAY;

typedef TISArrayAsVector<STUDENT> SORTED_STUDENT_POINTER_ARRAY;
```

The constructors can take up to three parameters. The first parameter is required. It specifies the greatest index that is currently allocated. To declare a sorted array of 100 STUDENTs, use the following:

```
STUDENT_ARRAY studentArray1(99);
```

The array has a lower index of 0 and an upper index of 99. If the user attempts to add an element above index 99 or below 0, the array will not be resized, and the attempt will fail. The second parameter is the lower index. To declare a sorted array of up to 11 STUDENTs with indices from 10 to 20, use:

```
SORTED_STUDENT_ARRAY studentArray2(20, 10);
```

The default value of the lower index is 0. The third and last parameter indicates the number of additional elements that will be allocated at a time when additional elements are needed. By default, this value is 0, meaning no additional elements will be allocated and the size of the array is static. Thus, to declare a dynamic array, a third parameter greater than 0 must be specified. Declare an array of 100 STUDENT pointers that is resized in multiples of 5:

```
STUDENT_POINTER_ARRAY studentArray3(99, 0, 5);
```

There are two functions to insert elements into the array. The Add function will insert an element in the first available position:

```
studentArray3.Add(new STUDENT("JohnNewton", 3.5));
```

To insert an element in a particular position in the array, use AddAt. To add a student in the 9th position, use:

```
studentArray3.AddAt(new STUDENT("DeanBrown", 2.3), 10 );
```

The AddAt function is not available for the sorted containers. The order of elements in a sorted container is determined by the ordering operator.

Removing objects from an array is accomplished with the Destroy and Detach member function. When an element is removed, all objects in the array at higher indices are moved down one position in the array. Destroy will remove and delete the object. To remove and delete the student at index 10 in the array, use the following:

```
studentArray3.Destroy(10);
```

Element 10 is removed and deleted. The element at index 11 is moved to index 10, 12 to 11, and so on. To remove and delete student DeanBrown:

```
STUDENT s("DeanBrown");
studentArray3.Destory(&s);
```

Remember that equality operator (==) for the STUDENT class is defined by student ID equality.

Note

Direct container member functions that require an object of the container's element type expect a reference. Indirect containers expect pointers. Because studentArray3 is an indirect array of STUDENT objects, the parameter passed to Destroy must be an address of a STUDENT object (&s). If instead of studentArray3 the container variable studentArray1 defined above had been used, then a reference to s would have been passed:

```
studentArray1.Destroy(s);
```

This difference in member function parameters applies not only to arrays, but also to the other containers.

Detach will remove an object without destroying it:

```
studentArray3.Detach(10); // Detach element 10 without deleting it.
STUDENT s("DeanBrown");
studentArray3.Detach(&s); // Detach the specified student without deleting it.
```

For indirect arrays, Detach optionally takes a second parameter of type TShouldDelete::DeleteType, which specifies whether or not the element is deleted:

```
studentArray3.Detach(10, TShouldDelete::NoDelete);  // Default.
studentArray3.Detach(10, TShouldDelete::Delete);    // Delete object.
studentArray3.Detach(10, TShouldDelete::DefDelete); // Deletion dependent
                                                    // on ownership.
```

The last statement will delete the object if the container owns its objects. If container ownership for studentArray has been set to false, the last statement in the preceding will not delete the object. See the section, "Direct and Indirect Containers," for a discussion of ownership.

The Flush function will remove all elements in the array. If the array is an indirect array, an optional TShouldDelete::DeleteType parameter can specify deletion of objects:

```
studentArray3.Flush();          // Delete object if owned by container.
```

The preceding statement is equivalent to

```
studentArray3.Flush(TShouldDelete::DefDelete);
```

A `TShouldDelete::NoDelete` will not delete objects, and `TShouldDelete::Delete` will always delete objects regardless of ownership.

`ArraySize` returns the number of elements allocated, or current size of the array, and `GetItemsInContainer` returns the number of objects in the array.

`ForEach` is an iterator function that applies a user-defined function to each element in the array. Refer to listing 18.6 for an example of using this function.

There are three search functions that allow you to search the array. `HasMember` will search for a given element and return true if found. To query the existence of student John Newton in the array of STUDENTs, use the following:

```
STUDENT s("JohnNewton");
if (studentArray3.HasMember(&s))
    ...
```

Two similar functions, `FirstThat` and `LastThat`, will search the array according to a user-defined function and return a pointer to the element if it is found. `FirstThat` will return a pointer to the first element in the array that satisfies the condition. `LastThat` returns a pointer to the last element in the array that satisfies the condition.

Refer to listings 18.2, 18.3, and 18.4 for examples of using array containers.

Bag

Bags and sets are exactly the same with one exception: Bags can contain duplicate objects. *Bags* are unordered collections of elements that can be retrieved only by specifying the object.

Using the STUDENT class in listing 18.5 (student2.h), the commonly used classes are:

```
typedef TBagAsVector<STUDENT> STUDENT_BAG;
typedef TIBagAsVector<STUDENT> STUDENT_POINTER_BAG;
```

Each constructor optionally takes a parameter that specifies the size of the bag. If a parameter is not passed to the constructor, a bag of default size is constructed (see `DEFAULT_BAG_SIZE` in the resource.h file supplied by Borland in the \Bc5\Include\Classlib directory). The size of the bag is static and may not be changed. To declare a bag of 100 STUDENT objects:

```
STUDENT_BAG studentBag1(100);
```

To declare a bag of default size containing STUDENT pointers:

```
STUDENT_POINTER_BAG studentBag2;
```

Inserting objects into the bag is accomplished with the `Add` member function:

```
studentBag2.Add(new STUDENT("LisaCourey", 3.6));
```

The member functions `Add`, `Detach`, `Flush`, `GetItemsInContainer`, `ForEach`, `HasMember`, `FirstThat`, and `LastThat` behave the same as with the array versions. See the preceding section, "Array," for a full discussion.

III

Advanced Programming

Listing 18.7 demonstrates the use of bag containers using the STUDENT class defined in listing 18.1 (student1.h).

Listing 18.7 Bags1.cpp—Using Bag Containers

```cpp
#include <iostream.h>
#include <iomanip.h>
#include <classlib\bags.h>
#include "student1.h"

typedef TIBagAsVector<STUDENT> STUDENT_BAG;

// BIDS supplied iterator.
typedef TIBagAsVectorIterator<STUDENT> STUDENT_BAG_ITERATOR;

// Output students in the container.
void WriteStudents(STUDENT_BAG&);

int main()
{
   STUDENT_BAG students(10);
   students.Add(new STUDENT("JohnNewton", 1.0));
   students.Add(new STUDENT("DeanBrown", 2.0));
   students.Add(new STUDENT("CarlBishop", 3.0));
   students.Add(new STUDENT("GaryCook", 4.0));
   cout << "Inital bag of " << students.GetItemsInContainer() << " students:"
   ➥<< endl;
   WriteStudents(students);

   STUDENT *sp, s("DeanBrown");
   if (students.HasMember(&s)) {
      sp = students.Find(&s);
      students.Detach(sp);            // Element deleted. sp no longer valid.
      cout << "After removing " << s.GetId() << " :" << endl;
      WriteStudents(students);
   }
   else
      cout << s.GetId() << " not found." << endl;
   students.Flush();                  // Destroys elements.
   return 0;
}

void WriteStudents(STUDENT_BAG &students)
{
   STUDENT_BAG_ITERATOR iterator(students);
   STUDENT *s;
   cout << setiosflags(ios::fixed | ios::left) << setprecision(1);
   while (s = iterator++)
      cout << "    " << setw(20) << s->GetId()
         << "    " <<  s->GetGrade() << endl;
}
```

Deque

Deque (pronounced *deck* and short for *double-entry queue*) is a double-ended queue. Unlike a single-ended queue, elements may be inserted and removed on either end of the double-ended queue. The deque container is implemented with either a vector or double-linked list FDS container. Using the STUDENT class in listing 18.1, student1.h, the commonly used classes are:

```
typedef TDequeAsVector<STUDENT> STUDENT_VDEQUE;
typedef TIDequeAsVector<STUDENT> STUDENT_POINTER_VDEQUE;
typedef TDequeAsDoubleList<STUDENT> STUDENT_DDEQUE;
typedef TIDequeAsDoubleList<STUDENT> STUDENT_POINTER_DDEQUE;
```

The constructors for deques implemented as vectors optionally take a parameter that specifies the size of the deque. If a parameter is not passed to the constructor, a deque of the default size is constructed (see DEFAULT_DEQUE_SIZE in the resource.h file in the Include\Classlib directory). The size of the deque is static and may not be changed. To declare a deque of 100 STUDENT objects, use:

```
STUDENT_VDEQUE studentDeque1(100);
```

Deques implemented as double-list will automatically change size to accommodate any number of elements. Due to this flexibility, double-list deques are most often the better choice. The constructors take no arguments:

```
STUDENT_POINTER_DDEQUE studentDeque2;
```

The member functions Flush, GetItemsInContainer, ForEach, FirstThat, and LastThat behave the same as with the array versions.

Inserting elements into the deque is accomplished by the PutLeft and PutRight member functions:

```
studentDeque2.PutLeft(new STUDENT("ColetCook", 3.9));
studentDeque2.PutRight(new STUDENT("JamesBartley", 2.4));
```

The left side of the deque is called the *head,* and the right side is called the *tail.*

Elements are removed from either end with GetLeft and GetRight. The elements are not deleted when removed, but a pointer to the object is returned in the case of indirect deques and copied (passed by value) in the case of direct deques:

```
STUDENT *s1, *s2;
s1 = &studentDeque1.GetLeft();
s2 = studentDeque2.GetRight();
```

Two member functions allow access to the left (PeekLeft) and right (PeekRight) elements without removing these elements. These functions return a constant reference if the deque is a direct container and a pointer if it is an indirect deque:

```
const STUDENT  s1 = studentDeque1.GetLeft();  // const STUDENT& returned.
STUDENT *s2 = studentDeque2.PeekRight();       // STUDENT* returned.
```

Listing 18.8 demonstrates the use of a deque implemented as a double-linked list.

Listing 18.8   Deques1.cpp—Using Deques

```cpp
#include <iostream.h>
#include <iomanip.h>
#include <classlib\deques.h>
#include "student1.h"

// Deque holds pointers to STUDENTs.
typedef TIDequeAsDoubleList<STUDENT> STUDENT_DEQUE;
// BIDS supplied iterator.
typedef TIDequeAsDoubleListIterator<STUDENT> STUDENT_DEQUE_ITERATOR;

// Output students in the container.
void WriteStudents(STUDENT_DEQUE&);

int main()
{
    STUDENT_DEQUE students;

    // Insert at head.
    students.PutLeft(new STUDENT("JohnNewton", 1.0));
    students.PutLeft(new STUDENT("DeanBrown", 2.0));

    // Insert at tail.
    students.PutRight(new STUDENT("CarlBishop", 3.0));
    students.PutRight(new STUDENT("GaryCook", 4.0));

    cout << "Inital deque of " << students.GetItemsInContainer()
    << " students:" << endl;
    WriteStudents(students);

    cout << "The student on the left end (head) is:
    " << students.PeekLeft()->GetId() << endl;
    cout << "The student on the right end (tail) is:
    " << students.PeekRight()->GetId() << endl;

    STUDENT *sp;
    delete students.GetLeft();      // Remove left-most element and delete it.
    sp = students.GetRight();       // Remove right-most element.
    students.PutLeft(sp);           // Put at head.
    cout << "After removing left element and placing head at tail:" << endl;
    WriteStudents(students);
    students.Flush();               // Destroys elements.
    return 0;
}

void WriteStudents(STUDENT_DEQUE &students)
{
    STUDENT_DEQUE_ITERATOR iterator(students);
    STUDENT *s;
    cout    << setiosflags(ios::fixed | ios::left) << setprecision(1);
```

```
    while (s = iterator++)
        cout << "    " << setw(20) << s->GetId()
             << "    " <<  s->GetGrade() << endl;
}
```

Dictionary

A *dictionary* stores each object with an associated search value, or key, in a hash table.
The advantage of this container is fast retrieval of elements. The dictionary requires
that its elements be a special BIDS container called an *association*. Associations tie the
objects to be stored with an associated search key. The key object must either provide
a member function of the form

```
unsigned HashValue()
```

or a global function of the form

```
unsigned HashValue(KEY&)
```

where KEY to search key type. Using the STUDENT class in listing 18.1, student1.h, a
search key can be generated from the STUDENT::id using the C++ string's hash()
member function. A class could be defined that would "wrap" the C++ string class in a
new type that provides a HashValue member function. Listing 18.9 demonstrates this
class.

Listing 18.9   stu_key.h—Designing an Association Search Key

```
// All member functions are inline for brevity.
#include <iostream.h>
#include <iomanip.h>
#include <cstring.h>
#include <classlib\assoc.h>

// Need a search key for STUDENT which has a member function:
//          unsigned HashValue()
// or a global fucntion:
//          unsigned HashValue(KEY&)
// where KEY is the type used for a search key of the dictionary.
// The search key is derived from the STUDENT::id, which is type string.
// Put a "wrapper" on the string class to provide this hash member function.
class STUDENT_KEY
{
public:
   STUDENT_KEY() : id("") {}
   STUDENT_KEY(const string &id_) : id(id_) {}
   STUDENT_KEY(const char *id_) : id(id_) {}
   STUDENT_KEY(const STUDENT_KEY &key)        { *this = key; }
   ~STUDENT_KEY() {}
   STUDENT_KEY& operator=(const STUDENT_KEY &rhs)
   {
      if (this != &rhs)                       // Don't copy self.
      id = rhs.id;
      return *this;
```

III

Advanced Programming

(continues)

Listing 18.9   Continued

```
    }
    // Valid comparison semantics MUST be defined.
    int operator==(const STUDENT_KEY &rhs) const { return id == rhs.id; }
    int operator<(const STUDENT_KEY &rhs) const { return id < rhs.id; }
    const string& GetId() const { return id; }
    // Required function:
    unsigned HashValue() const { return id.hash(); }
private:
    string id;
};
```

Association template class constructors take two parameters: the *key* and the *value to be stored*. Either one may be direct or indirect. (See the section, "Direct and Indirect Containers," for a discussion on direct and indirect.) Using STUDENT objects as the value and STUDENT_KEY objects as the key, common association classes will be:

```
typedef TDDAssociation<STUDENT_KEY, STUDENT> STUDENT_DDASSOC;
// Direct key, direct value.
typedef TDIAssociation<STUDENT_KEY, STUDENT> STUDENT_DIASSOC;
// Direct key, indirect value.
typedef TIDAssociation<STUDENT_KEY, STUDENT> STUDENT_IDASSOC;
// Indirect key, direct value.
typedef TIIAssociation<STUDENT_KEY, STUDENT> STUDENT_IIASSOC;
// Indirect key, indirect value.
```

Defining an association variable can be written as:

```
STUDENT s("SamJohnson", 3.4);
STUDENT_KEY skey(s.GetId());
STUDENT_DDASSOC sAssoc(skey, s);
// Both parameters are passed by value.
```

HashValue is a member function that returns the HashValue result of its key object.

The Key and Value member functions return the key and value objects, respectively. For direct objects, the object is returned by value:

```
if (s == sAssoc.Value())
// Is true given above definitions.
    cout << "This is true." << endl;
```

If the key or value object is indirect, the return value of the Key and Value functions will be a pointer:

```
STUDENT *sp;
sp = new STUDENT("SamJohnson", 3.4);
STUDENT_KEY skey(sp->GetId());
STUDENT_DIASSOC spAssoc(skey, sp);
// Note the value is passed as a pointer.
if (*sp == *spAssoc.Value())
    cout << "This is true." << endl;
```

Association classes also define the == operator by using the == operator of the key data type. Thus, the key data type in the preceding case STUDENT_KEY must have well-defined comparison semantics.

As mentioned earlier, dictionary containers are implemented using association containers. Other than this requirement, dictionary containers are very similar in function to sets and bats. Using the STUDENT_DDASSOC type defined earlier, the common dictionary classes are:

```
typedef TDictionaryAsHashTable<STUDENT_DDASSOC> STUDENT_DICT1;
// Direct container.
typedef TIDictionaryAsHashTable<Student_DDASSOC> STUDENT_DICT2;
// Indirect container.
```

Dictionary constructors take an optional parameter specifying the size of the container. A default size of DEFAULT_HASH_TABLE_SIZE (see resource.h in the \Bc5\Include\Classlib directory) is used if no parameter is passed. To construct a container of 100 elements, use:

```
STUDENT_DICT2 studentDict(100);
```

To add elements, use the Add member function, and to remove elements, use the Detach member function:

```
studentDict.Add(spAssoc);
        // Add the association object defined above.
STUDENT_DIASSOC *sp2 = studentDict.Detach(sp);
        // Pointer parameter is returned.
```

Because the container is an indirect container, objects are passed as pointers, and return values are pointers to the association object, as well.

The Flush, ForEach, and GetItemsInContainer behave in the same way as the versions on other containers. See the section, "Arrays," for a discussion.

When locating an association element from the dictionary container, the member function Find is used. The parameter accepted by Find is dependent on the container being a direct or indirect container.

Listing 18.10 demonstrates the use of association and dictionary containers.

Listing 18.10 Dicts1.cpp—Using Associations and Dictionaries

```
#include <iostream.h>
#include <iomanip.h>
#include <classlib\dict.h>
#include "stu_key.h"

// STUDENT_KEY stored directly and STUDENT stored indirectly in association.
typedef TDIAssociation<STUDENT_KEY, STUDENT> STUDENT_ASSOC;
// Dictionary holds pointers to STUDENT_ASSOC objects.
typedef TIDictionaryAsHashTable<STUDENT_ASSOC> STUDENT_DICT;
// BIDS suppiled iterator.
typedef TIDictionaryAsHashTableIterator<STUDENT_ASSOC> STUDENT_DICT_ITERATOR;

// Output students in the container.
void WriteStudents(STUDENT_DICT&);
```

(continues)

Listing 18.10 Continued

```
int main()
{
    // Create some STUDENT data.
    STUDENT *s[4];
    s[0] = new STUDENT("JohnNewton", 1.0);
    s[1] = new STUDENT("DeanBrown", 2.0);
    s[2] = new STUDENT("CarolBishop", 3.0);
    s[3] = new STUDENT("GaryCook", 4.0);

    // Put the STUDENTs in the dictionary.
    STUDENT_DICT students(10);
    for (int i = 0; i < 4; i++)
        students.Add(new STUDENT_ASSOC(STUDENT_KEY(s[i]->GetId()), s[i]));
    cout << "Initial  dictionary of " << students.GetItemsInContainer() << "
➥students:" << endl;
    WriteStudents(students);

    // Create a search object. The value part of the association is not
    // needed.
    STUDENT_ASSOC *foundSAP;
    STUDENT_ASSOC searchSA("CarolBishop", 0);
    foundSAP = students.Find(&searchSA);
    if (foundSAP) {
        const STUDENT *sp = foundSAP->Value(); // Association value is a
                                               // pointer to student.
        cout << "Student " << sp->GetId() << " was found." << endl;
        students.Detach(foundSAP);                // Remove and delete (owns objects).
        cout << "After deletion " << students.GetItemsInContainer()
        ➥<< " students:" << endl;
        WriteStudents(students);
    }
    else
        cout << searchSA.Key().GetId() << " not found in dictionary." << endl;
    students.Flush();                              // Destroys elements.
    return 0;
}

void WriteStudents(STUDENT_DICT &students)
{
    STUDENT_DICT_ITERATOR iterator(students);
    cout << setiosflags(ios::fixed | ios::left) << setprecision(1);
    while (iterator) {
        const STUDENT_ASSOC *sap = iterator.Current();
        cout << "    " << setw(20) << sap->Value()->GetId()
            << "  " <<  sap->Value()->GetGrade()
            << "    Hash value = " << sap->Key().HashValue() << endl;
        ++iterator;
    }
}
```

Queue

A *queue* is analogous to a line at the supermarket. The first person in line is serviced first, the second next, and so on. People go in one end and exit at the other with no breaking in line (usually). The queue container is the same. The elements are accessed on a First In, First Out basis (FIFO). Common queue classes implemented as STUDENT containers are:

```
typedef TQueueAsVector<STUDENT> STUDENT_VQUEUE;
typedef TIQueueAsVector<STUDENT> STUDENT_POINTER_VQUEUE;
typedef TQueueAsDoubleList<STUDENT> STUDENT_DLQUEUE;
typedef TIQueueAsDoubleList<STUDENT> STUDENT_POINTER_DLQUEUE;
```

Constructors for queues implemented as vectors have an optional parameter specifying the size of the container. If no parameter is passed, a default value of DEFAULT_QUEUE_SIZE defined in the resource.h file, which is found in \Bc5\Include\Classlib directory, is used. To declare a queue containing up to 100 elements, use:

```
STUDENT_VQUEUE studentQueue1(100);
```

Queues implemented by using double-list are more versatile in that the container grows and shrinks in size as needed. The constructor takes no arguments:

```
STUDENT_DLQUEUE studentQueue2;
```

Member functions Flush, ForEach, LastThat, FirstThat, IsEmpty, and IsFull behave in the same way as the deque versions. See the section entitled "Deques" for a discussion of these functions.

Get and Put retrieve and insert elements from the container. Get retrieves the "oldest" element in the queue. Parameters passed to Put and objects returned by Get are pointers or references depending on the container type, indirect or direct.

Listing 18.11 demonstrates the use of the BIDS queue container.

Listing 18.11 Queues1.cpp—Using Queues

```
#include <iostream.h>
#include <iomanip.h>
#include <classlib\queues.h>
#include "student1.h"

// Deque holds pointers to STUDENTs.
typedef TIQueueAsVector<STUDENT> STUDENT_QUEUE;
// BIDS supplied iterator.
typedef TIQueueAsVectorIterator<STUDENT> STUDENT_QUEUE_ITERATOR;
// Output students in the container.
void WriteStudents(STUDENT_QUEUE&);

int main()
{
    STUDENT_QUEUE students(10);
    // Insert at head.
```

III

Advanced Programming

(continues)

Listing 18.11 Continued

```
   students.Put(new STUDENT("JohnNewton", 1.0));
   students.Put(new STUDENT("DeanBrown", 2.0));
   students.Put(new STUDENT("CarlBishop", 3.0));
   students.Put(new STUDENT("GaryCook", 4.0));
   cout << "Inital queue of " << students.GetItemsInContainer()
   ➡<< " students:" << endl;
   WriteStudents(students);

   delete students.Get();                    // Remove and delete element.
   cout << "After removing a student:" << endl;
   WriteStudents(students);
   students.Flush();                         // Destroys elements.
   return 0;
}

void WriteStudents(STUDENT_QUEUE &students)
{
   STUDENT_QUEUE_ITERATOR iterator(students);
   STUDENT *s;
   cout       << setiosflags(ios::fixed ¦ ios::left) << setprecision(1);
   while (s = iterator++)
      cout << "    " << setw(20) << s->GetId()
         << "    " << s->GetGrade() << endl;
}
```

Set

A *set* contains an unordered collection of elements with the following restriction: If object A and object B are in the set, A != B. Set and bag containers are the same except for this restriction. Using the STUDENT class, the following gives the most common set classes:

```
typedef TSetAsVector<STUDENT> STUDENT_SET;
// Direct container.
typedef TISetAsVector<STUDENT> STUDENT_POINTER_SET;
// Indirect container.
```

The constructors and member functions for the set behave the same as the bag container counterparts, with the exception of the Add member function. If the Add function is passed an object (for example, A) for which A = B for some object B in the set, Add will have no effect. Listing 18.12 illustrates the use of set containers.

Listing 18.12 Sets1.cpp—Using Sets

```
#include <iostream.h>
#include <iomanip.h>
#include <classlib\sets.h>
#include "student1.h"

// Direct set.
typedef TSetAsVector<STUDENT> STUDENT_SET;
```

```
// BIDS supplied iterator.
typedef TSetAsVectorIterator<STUDENT> STUDENT_SET_ITERATOR;

// Output students in the container.
void WriteStudents(STUDENT_SET&);

int main()
{
        STUDENT_SET students(10);
        students.Add(STUDENT("JohnNewton", 1.0));
        students.Add(STUDENT("DeanBrown", 2.0));
        students.Add(STUDENT("CarlBishop", 3.0));
        students.Add(STUDENT("GaryCook", 4.0));
```

Stacks

Whereas queues are First In, First Out data structures, stacks are Last In, First Out (LIFO) data structures. The last element inserted into the container is the first one retrieved. Elements are "pushed" to the top of the stack and "popped" off the top, as well. Commonly used stack constructors are:

```
typedef TStackAsVector<STUDENT> STUDENT_VSTACK;
typedef TIStackAsVector<STUDENT> STUDENT_POINTER_VSTACK;
typedef TStackAsList<STUDENT> STUDENT_LSTACK;
typedef TIStackAsList<STUDENT> STUDENT_POINTER_LSTACK;
```

Constructors vector-implemented classes take an optional parameter specifying the maximum size of the stack:

```
STUDENT_VSTACK studentStack1(100);       // 100 possible elements on stack.
```

If no parameter is passed, a default of DEFAULT_STACK_SIZE defined in \Bc5\Include\Classlib\resource.h is used.

The list implementation of stacks is dynamic. The size of the container will grow and shrink to accommodate elements. The constructor takes no arguments:

```
STUDENT_LSTACK studentStack2;
```

Most of the member functions are the same as in other containers. They include Flush, GetItemsInContainer, ForEach, FirstThat, LastThat, IsEmpty, and IsFull. See the section, "Array," for a full discussion of these functions.

Elements are inserted on the stack with the Push member function. Push accepts a container element object if it is a direct container and accepts a pointer to an element object if the container is an indirect container. See the section, "Direct and Indirect Containers," for a full discussion.

Stack elements can be accessed through the functions Pop and Top. Pop removes the object from the top stack. Top returns the object at the top of the stack without removing it.

Listing 18.13 demonstrates the use of a stack container implemented as a list.

Listing 18.13   Stacks2.cpp—Using Stacks

```cpp
#include <iostream.h>
#include <iomanip.h>
#include <classlib\stacks.h>
#include "student1.h"

// Direct stack.
typedef TStackAsVector<STUDENT> STUDENT_STACK;
// BIDS supplied iterator.
typedef TStackAsVectorIterator<STUDENT> STUDENT_STACK_ITERATOR;

// Output students in the container.
void WriteStudents(STUDENT_STACK&);

int main()
{
    STUDENT_STACK students;
    students.Push(STUDENT("JohnBown", 1.0));
    students.Push(STUDENT("BubbaJones", 2.0));
    students.Push(STUDENT("SallyRide", 3.0));
    students.Push(STUDENT("JoeLamb", 4.0));

    cout << "Initial stack of students:" << endl;
    WriteStudents(students);

    // Pop a one off.
    STUDENT s1(students.Pop());
    cout << "Student " << s1.GetId() << " has been taken off the stack."
    ➥<< endl;
    const STUDENT s2(students.Top());
    cout << "Student " << s2.GetId() << " is at the top of the stack now."
    ➥<< endl;
```

Binary Tree

Binary trees consist of nodes containing the data item to be stored and pointers to as many as two descendants: a left descendant and a right descendant. If a node has no descendant, it is called a *terminal node*. The first node to be added to the tree is called the *root node*. When an element is added to the binary tree, it is compared to the root node with the < operator. If the element is less than the root node, the comparison is repeated with the left descendant; otherwise, it is compared with the right descendant. This process is repeated until there is no descendant node. A node is then added containing the new data element.

The advantage of using binary trees is efficiency of element retrieval. This efficiency of retrieval is dependent on how *balanced* the tree is. An extreme example of an unbalanced tree would occur by adding a sorted list of items to a tree. Each node would have only one type of descendant: left if the list was sorted in ascending order, or right if sorted in descending order. The result is essentially a single-linked list. A well-balanced tree has roughly the same number of left and right descendants. Searching the tree and adding nodes are optimized when the tree is well-balanced. Inserting elements with a random ordering will usually result in a well-balanced tree.

The STUDENT class defined in listing 18.5 (student2.h) has well-defined equality and comparison operators. Thus, objects of this class type can be used in a binary tree:

```
typedef TBinarySearchTreeImp<STUDENT> STUDENT_TREE;
typedef TIBinarySearchTreeImp<STUDENT> STUDENT_POINTER_TREE;
```

Each constructor takes no arguments. The Add, Detach, Find, Flush, ForEach, GetItemsInContainer, and IsEmpty member function behave the same as the array container versions. See the section entitled "Arrays" for a full discussion of these member functions.

Listing 18.14 gives an example of using an indirect binary tree container.

Listing 18.14 Bintree1.cpp—Using Binary Tree Containers

```cpp
#include <iostream.h>
#include <iomanip.h>
#include <classlib\binimp.h>
#include "student2.h"

// Indirect binary tree.
typedef TIBinarySearchTreeImp<STUDENT> STUDENT_TREE;
// BIDS supplied iterator.
typedef TIBinarySearchTreeIteratorImp<STUDENT> STUDENT_TREE_ITERATOR;
// Output students in the container.
void WriteStudents(STUDENT_TREE&);

int main()
{
    STUDENT_TREE students;
    students.Add(new STUDENT("Cindy Smith", 3.0));
    students.Add(new STUDENT("Edith VandeHaar", 2.0));
    students.Add(new STUDENT("Andy Brown", 4.0));
    students.Add(new STUDENT("Barry Jones", 3.5));
    students.Add(new STUDENT("Dina Carlson", 2.5));
    students.Add(new STUDENT("Frank Slide", 2.0));
    cout << "Binary tree of " << students.GetItemsInContainer() << " stu-
dents:" << endl;
    WriteStudents(students);
    students.Flush();                             // Destroys elements.
    return 0;
}

void WriteStudents(STUDENT_TREE &students)
{
    STUDENT_TREE_ITERATOR iterator(students);
    STUDENT *s;
    cout << setiosflags(ios::fixed | ios::left) << setprecision(1);
    while (iterator) {
        s = iterator.Current();
            cout << "   " << setw(17) << s->GetId()
                << "   " << s->GetGrade() << endl;
        ++iterator;
    }
}
```

III

Advanced Programming

The output after running the program in listing 18.14 is

```
Binary tree of 5 students:
    Edith VandeHaar      0.0
    Cindy Smith          1.5
    Andy Brown           2.0
    Barry Jones          3.0
    Dina Carlson         3.5
```

Note that the iterator traverses the tree from left to right (ascending order). Remember that STUDENT objects use grade member variables for comparison purposes.

Double-Linked List

A *double-linked list* consists of nodes containing a data element and two pointers: a pointer to the next node in the list and a pointer to the previous node in the list. The ending node's "next" pointer is null. This node is known as the *tail*. The node at the beginning, or *head*, of the list has a null previous pointer. Because of these two pointers, a double-linked list can be traversed in either direction: head-to-tail or tail-to-head. Single-linked lists are very similar. The difference is that single-linked lists have only a next pointer. Thus it can only be iterated in one direction: from head-to-tail.

Unmanaged double-linked list of STUDENT containers are

```
typedef TDoubleListImp<STUDENT> STUDENT_LIST;
typedef TSDoubleListImp<STUDENT> SORTED_STUDENT_LIST;
typedef TIDoubleListImp<STUDENT> STUDENT_POINTER_LIST;
typedef TISDoubleListImp<STUDENT> SORTED_STUDENT_POINTER_LIST;
```

Most of the member functions are very similar to the other containers. Add adds a data element (encapsulated within a list node) to the head of the list. AddAtHead also adds an element to the head of the list. AddAtTail adds an element to the end of the list. Detach, which takes a list element object as a parameter, removes a node from the list if a match is found. DetachAtHead and DetachAtTail remove the head and tail nodes, respectively. All of the Detach member functions for indirect classes will delete the object, depending on the optional TShouldDelete::DeleteType parameter. See the section, "Container Object Ownership," for a full discussion.

FirstThat, LastThat, Flush, ForEach, GetItemsInContainer, and IsEmpty member functions behave in a similar fashion to the other containers. See the section, "Arrays," for more complete coverage. PeekHead and PeekTail member functions return the head and tail nodes, respectively, without removing them.

The iterator for double-linked lists provides an increment and a decrement operator. This provides the capability to traverse the list in either direction.

Single-linked lists contain the same functions except for the capability to directly access the tail; therefore, AddAtTail, DetachAtTail, PeekTail, and the iterator decrement operator are not available.

Listing 18.15 demonstrates a direct double-linking list, again using the STUDENT class defined in listing 18.5 (student2.h).

Listing 18.15   Dlist1.cpp—Using Double-List Containers

```cpp
#include <iostream.h>
#include <iomanip.h>
#include <classlib\dlistimp.h>
#include "student2.h"

// Direct double list.
typedef TDoubleListImp<STUDENT> STUDENT_LIST;
// BIDS supplied iterator.
typedef TDoubleListIteratorImp<STUDENT> STUDENT_LIST_ITERATOR;
// Output students in the container.
void WriteStudents(STUDENT_LIST&);

int main()
{
   STUDENT_LIST students;
   students.Add(STUDENT("Cindy Smith", 1.5));
   students.AddAtHead(STUDENT("Andy Brown", 4.0));
   students.Add(STUDENT("Barry Jones", 3.0));
   students.AddAtTail(STUDENT("Dina Carlson", 3.5));

   cout << "Student at head of list " << students.PeekHead().GetId() << endl;
   cout << "Student at tail of list " << students.PeekTail().GetId() << endl;
   cout << "Double linked list of " << students.GetItemsInContainer()
   ➥<< " students:" << endl;
   WriteStudents(students);
   students.Flush();                    // Destroys elements.
   return 0;
}

void WriteStudents(STUDENT_LIST &students)
{
   STUDENT_LIST_ITERATOR iterator(students);
   cout << setiosflags(ios::fixed ¦ ios::left) << setprecision(1);
   cout << "  Traversing the list from head to tail:" << endl;
   while (iterator) {
      cout << "   " << iterator.Current().GetId()
         << "   " << iterator.Current().GetGrade() << endl;
      ++iterator;
   }
   --iterator;                   // Put iterator on a valid element.
   cout << "  Traversing the list from tail to head:" << endl;
   while (iterator) {
      cout << "   " << iterator.Current().GetId()
         << "   " << iterator.Current().GetGrade() << endl;
      --iterator;
   }
}
```

STL

The design of the Standard Template Library (STL) is quite different than BIDS. In
BIDS, the functionality of container classes is encapsulated within the class in the

form of member functions. The STL separates much of the functionality of containers from the container classes and places it in algorithms. While BIDS makes heavy use of inheritance, the STL uses almost no inheritance.

Because much of the common functionality is located in global functions that work with all the containers, there is less source code than if functions had been implemented in the different container classes. Another advantage of the STL is flexibility. The STL algorithms can be used with C arrays and pointers, and not just with STL containers.

To use STL containers or algorithms, the header files from the \BC5\INCLUDE directory are included in the source files. For example, to use the vector container in a source file, the following #include statement is added to the source file:

```
#include <vector.h>
```

The STL consists of five main types of components:

- *Container:* A data repository.
- *Algorithm:* A function that acts on stored data.
- *Iterator:* A means to access stored data.
- *Function Object:* Encapsulates a function for use by other components.
- *Adaptor:* Modifies an existing component to provide different functionality.

Algorithms act on *containers* through *iterators*. Iterators allow the algorithm to sequentially access elements of the container.

Function objects are instances of a class that wrap around a function definition by defining the () operator. An object of that class can then be passed to another component. This method of passing functions is more type-safe and efficient than using function pointers.

Adaptors change the interface of an existing component. Adaptors come in three flavors: *container adaptors*, *iterator adaptors*, and *function adaptors*. An example of a container adaptor is stack. To create a stack, an existing container is used as a parameter. Using the definitions of STUDENT in listing 18.1, the following creates a stack of STUDENT objects:

```
typedef stack<vector<STUDENT> > STUDENT_STACK;
STUDENT_STACK studentStack;
```

Iterator adaptors and function adaptors work in a similar fashion.

Containers

There are two types of containers: *sequence containers* and *associative containers*. Sequence containers store objects in sequential order. Associative containers store objects based on a user-supplied key value, much as the BIDS dictionary container.

There are three sequence containers:

- vector
- deque
- list

Vectors are much like C arrays. Elements may be accessed in random order, usually with the subscript operator; however, the STL vector has advantages over a C array. A vector keeps track of information about itself, such as its size and the current number of elements in the container. A vector can resize as needed. The following creates a STUDENT vector:

```
typedef vector<STUDENT> STUDENT_VECTOR;
STUDENT_VECTOR studentVector;
```

A deque container is very similar to a vector with the exception that a deque efficiently adds elements to either the beginning or the end of the container. To be sure, a data element can be inserted to the beginning of a vector, but this requires a block move of all elements. The vector grows in size in only one direction, whereas the deque grows at both ends. This makes a deque container a good choice for FIFO (First In, First Out) data structure. The following creates a STUDENT deque object and copies 5 identical STUDENT objects into it:

```
typedef deque<STUDENT> STUDENT_DEQUE;
STUDENT_DEQUE studentDeque(5, STUDENT("StudentX", 0.0));
```

The *list* container is a double-linked list, meaning each node contains a pointer to the next and previous nodes; therefore, it may be traversed in either direction. Lists are more efficient at inserting or deleting data elements in the middle of the container but much less efficient in randomly accessing elements. A list does not provide the random access operator []. Instead, the list must be traversed one element at a time until the desired element is found. The following code segment creates a list of STUDENTs and copies all the data elements from the deque studentDeque above except the first one:

```
typedef list<STUDENT> STUDENT_LIST;
STUDENT_LIST studentList(++studentDeque.begin(), studentDeque.end());
```

As explained in the preceding section, container adaptors wrap around an existing container and use that underlying container to provide the adaptor's functionality. There are three container adaptors:

- Stack
- Queue
- Priority Queue

The underlying containers used by the container adaptors must be one of the sequence containers. Vector, deque, and list can be used to implement a stack. Deque and list can be used to implement a queue. Vector and deque can be used for a priority queue.

III

Advanced Programming

For all practical purposes, the container adaptors are treated the same as normal containers except for how they are instantiated.

Associative containers maintain an ordering of elements based on a key. Objects in the container are referenced via this key value. This makes for very fast retrieval of data.

There are four associative containers:

- Set
- Multiset
- Map
- Multimap

Sets store keys. In other words, the stored object is the key value. Maps, on the other hand, store data objects and associated *keys* separately. Both set and map require that keys in the container be unique. *Multiset* and *multimap* containers are versions of set and map that allow duplicate keys. Keys are compared to using a user-supplied compare function or, if none is provided, the less than operator < defined for the key objects. Thus, a set container can use the set<Key, Compare>, or set<Key> template classes. Similarly, a map container can use the map<Key, T, Compare>, or map<Key, T> template classes, where T is the object type being stored.

Before getting into an example, let's change the STUDENT class found in listing 18.5 (student2.h). Note that the equivalence operator and the less than operator are inconsistent. The equivalence operator is based on the STUDENT::id member variable whereas the comparison operator is based on the STUDENT::grade member variable. To make equivalence and comparison of STUDENT objects consistent, listing 18.15 redefines comparison on the basis of lexicographical order. Also it is sometimes useful to define an output operator (<<) for the class. Listing 18.16 demonstrates how this can be done.

Listing 18.16   student3.h—< Operator Redefined

```
class STUDENT
{
public:
...
    int operator==(const STUDENT &rhs) const
       { return (id == rhs.id); }
    int operator<(const STUDENT &rhs) const // Sort students by ID.
       { return (id < rhs.id); }
    int CompareGrade(const STUDENT &rhs) const
       { return (grade < rhs.grade); }
...
    // Define simple output.
    friend ostream& operator<<(ostream &os, const STUDENT &s)
    {
      os << setiosflags(ios::fixed | ios::left) << setprecision(1)
         << "    " << setw(17) << s.GetId()
         << "    " <<   s.GetGrade() << endl;
      return os;
    }
```

```
...
};
#endif
```

Now based on the new STUDENT class, listing 18.17 illustrates a simple use of a set and a multiset object.

```
#define RWSTD_NO_NAMESPACE
#include <iostream.h>
#include <set.h>
#include "student3.h"

// This set keyed on the < operator applied to student ID.
// Thus the ordering in the container will be lexicographical
// order of student names.
typedef set<STUDENT, less<STUDENT> > STUDENT_SET;

// Define a class in which to wrap the grade compare function.
struct GRADE_COMPARE
{
   bool operator()(const STUDENT &s1, const STUDENT &s2) const
   { return s1.GetGrade() < s2.GetGrade(); }
};

// Now define a set type that uses grades for ordering.
// Students can have the same grade, so a multiset is used.
// Remember multiset allows duplicate keys.
typedef multiset<STUDENT, GRADE_COMPARE> STUDENT_SET2;

int main()
{
   // This set will be ordered by STUDENT::id.
   STUDENT_SET studentSet;
   studentSet.insert(STUDENT("John Newton", 1.0));
   studentSet.insert(STUDENT("Dean Brown", 3.0));
   studentSet.insert(STUDENT("Carl Bishop", 2.0));
   studentSet.insert(STUDENT("Gary Cook", 1.0));

   STUDENT_SET2 studentSet2;
   cout << "First set " << studentSet.size() << " students (sorted by name):"
   ➥<< endl;
   for (STUDENT_SET::iterator i = studentSet.begin();i != studentSet.end();
   ➥i++) {
      cout << *i;
      studentSet2.insert(*i);          // Copy contents of StudentSet.
   }
   cout << "Second set " << studentSet2.size() << " students (sorted by
   ➥grade):" << endl;
   for (STUDENT_SET2::iterator i = studentSet2.begin(); i !=
   ➥studentSet2.end(); i++)
      cout << *i;
   return 0;
}
```

III

Advanced Programming

Iterators

Iterators are the key that algorithms use to work with containers. They are pointer-like objects that point to objects in the container. In fact, standard C++ pointers can be used as iterators. The operator * in an iterator always returns a value of a container element *if* the iterator points to a valid container element. A special iterator value is a *past-the-end* value that points past the last element in the container. In this case, the iterator is not *dereferenceable*: The operator * does not return a variable of the type stored in the container. An often used member function for all STL containers is the end() member function. end() returns an iterator pointing to one element past the last one in the container.

There are five types of iterators:

- Input
- Output
- Forward
- Bidirectional
- Random Access

The *input* iterator is read-only and can move in a forward direction only (the decrement operator is not defined). *Output* iterators are write-only and forward moving. These I/O iterators are the most restricted iterators. Each location in the container can be dereferenced only one time by an I/O iterator and for the purpose of accessing and storing container objects only.

The STL defines special input iterator and output iterator classes that work specifically with C++ input streams and output streams: istream_iterator and ostream_iterator. When an object of type istream_iterator or ostream_iterator is declared, two template arguments are passed: container element type and a distance type. A distance type measures the distance between two elements in a container. A standard type, ptrdiff_t, is almost always used. The constructor argument for the istream_iterator is the input stream to be accessed. For an ostream_iterator object, it is the output stream and an optional second argument. This second argument to the ostream_iterator constructor is a separator between each value being read in. Listing 18.18 provides an example of using these iterators with streams.

Listing 18.18   Streamit.cpp—Using *istream_iterator* and *ostream_iterator*

```
#define RWSTD_NO_NAMESPACE
#include <cstring.h>
#include <iostream.h>
#include <fstream.h>
#include <iterator.h>
#include <algorith.h>
#include <list.h>
#include "student3.h"

int main()
{
```

```
// Write text to a created file. Then open the file for reading.
ofstream outFile("streamit.txt");
outFile << "This is a test of istream_iterator and ostream_iterator."
➥<< endl;
outFile.close();
ifstream inFile("streamit.txt");

// Create an input iterator for file input and a special
// input iterator for testing end-of-file condition.
istream_iterator<string, ptrdiff_t> in(inFile), eof;

// Create an ouput iterator attached to the console.
// Separate each ouput value with a new line.
ostream_iterator<string> out(cout, "\n");

// Put STL copy to work: copy file to the console.
copy(in, eof, out);
inFile.close();

return 0;
```

Forward iterators contain all the functionality of I/O iterators plus there are no restrictions on dereferencing objects in the container.

Bidirectional iterators contain all the functionality of forward iterators plus they can move in a backward direction. The decrement operator, operator - -, is provided for this purpose.

Random access iterators are the most unrestricted iterators. They contain all the functionality of the bidirectional iterator and add the capability of accessing container elements with the [] operator.

Forward, bidirectional, and random access iterators can be constant iterators. This means the value returned by the iterator *operator* is a constant reference rather than a reference. Thus, a constant iterator cannot be used to modify the contents of the container. Output iterators are never constant, and input iterators always are.

STL algorithms access container elements via iterators. Usually the algorithm requires a starting iterator and an ending iterator. The algorithm will access elements between the element pointed to by the beginning iterator, inclusive, and the ending iterator, exclusive; therefore, it is important that the ending iterator be *reachable* from the starting iterator. Commonly used iterators are return values from the container member function begin(), which points to the first element in the container, and end(), which points to one past the last element in the container. The begin and end member functions return a bidirectional iterator or random-access iterator, depending on the containers. Only vector and deque support random-access iterators. All other containers support only bidirectional iterators. Listing 18.17 illustrates the use of the begin and end member functions. The iterator type given by STUDENT_SET::iterator is a bidirectional iterator because SET only supports bidirectional iterators.

Each STL algorithm expects a specific type of iterator as a parameter. It doesn't matter what type of container it is operating on or the type of container objects it is working with, except that certain operators for elements in the container are defined. It cares only about the type of iterator. Following is the declaration for the copy template function (see \Bc5\Include\algorith.h):

```
template <class InputIterator, class OutputIterator>
OutputIterator copy (InputIterator first, InputIterator last,
                     OutputIterator result)
{
    while (first != last) *result++ = *first++;
    return result;
}
```

The copy function is parameterized on two types of iterators. The names used in the template parameters indicate what types of iterator it expects: an input iterator and an output iterator. Throughout the STL, this naming convention is used to specify the *minimum* requirements for an expected iterator parameter. The names used for the other iterators are ForwardIterator, BidirectionalIterator, and RadomAccessIterator.

Note

As stated earlier, iterator types form a hierarchy with input and output iterators on the bottom (most restricted in function). Forward iterators, then bidirectional, and finally random access iterators get progressively less restricted. Each type contains all the functionality of the type below it. Thus, if an input or output iterator is expected, a forward, bidirectional, or random access iterator will do fine.

Just as there are container adaptors, there are also *iterator adaptors*. As with container adaptors, iterator adaptors work by encapsulating the existing iterator to provide different behavior. There are three types of iterator adaptors:

- Reverse iterators
- Insert iterators
- Raw Storage iterators

Reverse iterators do what their name implies: reverse the direction the iterator moves through the container. Thus the ++ operator moves in a backward direction in the container. Reverse iterators will work only with bidirectional and random-access iterators. Each container defines reverse and constant reverse iterator classes for use with its classes. These reverse iterators are based on the forward iterators found in the container class. Declaring a reverse iterator variable for use with a container is very similar to declaring a forward iterator:

```
list::iterator i;           // A forward list iterator.
list::reverse_iterator ri;  // A reverse list iterator.
```

Two container member functions analogous to begin() and end() are defined to work specifically with reverse iterators: rbegin() and rend():

```
for (list::reverse_iterator ri = rbegin(); ri != rend(); ri++)
    cout << *ri << endl;
```

Insert iterators are special forms of output iterators. When copy operations are performed on the container, the previous contents of the container are overwritten. Insert iterators insert the new elements into the container, moving the previous contents as necessary. There are three insert operators:

- `back_insert_iterator`
- `front_insert_iterator`
- `insert_iterator`

The `back_insert_iterator` adds new elements to the back of a container. This iterator can be used only with list, deque, and vector containers. The template parameter for this class is a container type such as `vector<string>`. The constructor for the `back_insert_iterator` takes a container object. The following code illustrates creation of a `back_insert_iterator` for a vector of strings:

```
vector<string> stringVector;
back_insert_iterator<vector<string> > backInserter(stringVector);
```

The most common use of all the insert adaptors is use in a copy function. Special STL functions are defined that give a simpler way to create the iterator for use as a function parameter. These functions are `back_inserter`, `front_inserter`, and `inserter`. To use `back_inserter` with copy, use

```
copy(sourceContainer.begin(), sourceContainer.end(),
back_inserter(targetContainer));
```

The `front_insert_iterator` inserts new elements into the front of the container and can be used only with list and deque containers. The template and constructor parameters are the same as `back_insert_iterator`.

Note

When `front_insert_iterator` objects or the function `front_inserter` are used to copy elements from one container to another, the order is reversed. For example, in the following code, the resulting deque contains the sequence 3, 2, 1:

```
int intArray[3] = { 1, 2, 3};
// Use a standard C array as a container.
deque<int> intDeque;
copy(intArray, intArray+3, front_inserter(deque));
// Use C pointers for begin and end inserter.
```

The `insert_iterator` inserts new elements at a location in the container pointed to by an iterator passed to the constructor for the `insert_iterator` object. Only the list container supports an `insert_iterator`. There are two template parameters required: a `container` type and an `iterator` type. The constructor and the function `insert_iterator()` also take two arguments: a container and an iterator.

Finally, the `raw_storage_iterator` is an output iterator that enables STL algorithms to store results in uninitialized memory. Thus, STL algorithms like copy can use blocks of memory allocated by `new` or `malloc` to store results.

Function Objects

Many of the algorithms in the STL require a user-supplied function to do their jobs. The ForEach member function of the BIDS container is an example of this mechanism. The BIDS ForEach function uses function pointers as a parameter. There is an analogous STL algorithm called for_each. Following is the definition of for_each:

```
template <class InputIterator, class Function>
Function for_each(InputIterator first, InputIterator last, Function f);
```

The for_each algorithm applies the function f to every element between first (including first) and last. f can be a function pointer or an instance of a class that defines the () operator. Listing 18.19 illustrates the use of both with for_each.

Listing 18.19 Illustrates Function Pointer and Function Objects

```
#define   RWSTD_NO_NAMESPACE
#include <cstring.h>
#include <iostream.h>
#include <algorith.h>
#include <vector.h>

// Function to use as a function pointer.
void WriteStr(string &s)
{
    cout << s << " ";
}

// Class for use as a function object.
// Note it only works with string elements.
class WRITE_STR
{
public:
    void operator()(string &s)
        { cout << s << " "; }
};

// A template function for use as a function object.
// A more general approach than "hard wiring" string output.
template <class T>
class WRITE_OBJECT
{
public:
    void operator()(T &t)
        { cout << t << " "; }
};

int main()
{
    vector<string> strVector;
    strVector.push_back("All");
    strVector.push_back("good");
    strVector.push_back("things");
    strVector.push_back("must");
    strVector.push_back("come");
```

```
    strVector.push_back("to");
    strVector.push_back("an");
    strVector.push_back("end.");
    cout << "Output using function pointer (WriteStr): ";
    for_each(strVector.begin(), strVector.end(), WriteStr);
    cout << endl;

    cout << "Output using function object (WRITE_STR): ";
    for_each(strVector.begin(), strVector.end(), WRITE_STR());
    cout << endl;

    cout << "Output using function object (WRITE_OBJECT): ";
    for_each(strVector.begin(), strVector.end(), WRITE_OBJECT<string>());
    cout << endl;
    return 0;
}
```

The code for the function is less complicated than the function object classes. So why use function objects? If the functionality is needed with only one class, then the WriteStr is fine. But if the functionality is needed for more than one type of object, the more general WRITE_OBJECT would be better.

The for_each algorithm expects a function that has a single argument. This is called a *unary* function. A *binary* function takes two arguments. The STL algorithm transform applies the user-supplied function to one or two input sequences. The difference between for_each and transform is that an output iterator is passed to the transform function for output of the results. If two input sequences are required, then a binary function is used. Listing 18.20 demonstrates defining and using a binary function for use with transform.

Listing 18.20   Binfunc.cpp—Defining and Using a Binary Function

```
#define   RWSTD_NO_NAMESPACE
#include <cstring.h>
#include <iostream.h>
#include <algorith.h>
#include <vector.h>
#include "student3.h"

string LetterGrade(STUDENT &s, float f)
{
    string result = s.GetId();
    result += " has an ";
    // Change the student's grade.
    s.SetGrade(s.GetGrade()+f);
    if (s.GetGrade() < 1.0)
        result += "F.\n";
    else if (s.GetGrade() < 2.0)
        result += "D.\n";
    else if (s.GetGrade() < 3.0)
        result += "C.\n";
    else if (s.GetGrade() < 3.5)
        result += "B.\n";
```

III

Advanced Programming

(continues)

Listing 18.20   Continued

```
    else
        result += "A. Good job!\n";
    return result;
}

int main()
{
    vector<STUDENT> studentVector;
    studentVector.push_back(STUDENT("John Smith", 1.0));
    studentVector.push_back(STUDENT("Donald Brown", 2.4));
    studentVector.push_back(STUDENT("Connie Enid", 3.3));
    studentVector.push_back(STUDENT("Alex Peterson", 0.5));
    float gradeChange[4] = { 0.5, 0.2, 0.2, 1.0 };
    transform(studentVector.begin(), studentVector.end(),
      gradeChange, ostream_iterator<string>(cout, "\n"),
        LetterGrade);
    return 0;
}
```

As shown in listing 18.20, defining your own function objects is simple. The STL provides several useful function objects. These are divided into three categories:

- Arithmetic operations
- Comparisons
- Logical operations

Tables 18.2, 18.3, and 18.4 list the STL function objects by category and the operation that each performs. The first argument to the function object is listed as x, and the second, if a binary function object, is indicated by y. Both x and y are of the type parameterized when the template class is declared. All these classes are defined in \Bc5\Include\function.h.

Table 18.2   Arithmetic Function Objects

Name	Operation Performed
plus	x + y
minus	x - y
times	x * y
divides	x / y
modulus	x % y
negate	-x

Table 18.3 **Comparison Function Objects**	
Name	**Operation Performed**
equal_to	x == y
not_equal_to	x != y
greater	x > y
less	x < y
greater_equal	x >= y
less_equal	x <= y

Table 18.4 **Logical Function Objects**	
Name	**Operation Performed**
logical_and	x && y
logical_or	x ¦¦ y
logical_not	!x

All of the classes in the preceding tables are subclasses of one of two base classes defined in the STL—which one is dependent on whether the function object is unary or binary. These base template classes are given here:

```
template <class Arg, class Result>
struct unary_function
{
    typedef Arg argument_type;
    typedef Result result_type;
};

template <class Arg1, class Arg2, class Result>
struct binary_function
{
    typedef Arg1 first_argument_type;
    typedef Arg2 second_argument_type;
    typedef Result result_type;
};
```

Just as containers and iterators have adaptors, so do function objects. These function object adaptors are of three basic types: *negators*, *binders*, and *adaptors* for pointers to functions. The *negators*, not1 and not2, negate the output of a predicate function. A *predicate* function is a function with a return value of true or false (either a bool or int value). not1 takes a unary function object (a subclass of unary_function) as its argument. not2 takes a binary function object (a subclass of binary_object).

A *binder* takes a binary function and a specific value as its arguments and binds the value to either the first or second argument to the binary function. bind1st binds the first argument, and `bind2nd` binds the second argument. The following example uses `not1` and `bind2nd` to remove all integers less than or equal to 10 from a vector of integers:

```
vector<int>::iterator I = remove_if(intVector.begin(), intVector.end(),
    not1(bind2nd(greater<int>(), 10)));
```

Another function object adaptor is `ptr_fun`. `ptr_fun` takes either a pointer to a unary function or a pointer to a binary function and converts it to a function object.

Algorithms

STL algorithms are template functions parameterized by iterator types. The type of iterator expected is indicated in the declaration of the template function, as discussed in the previous section. The compiler cannot check to see if the passed iterator meets the minimum functionality required. What would happen if a bidirectional iterator were passed to the `sort` algorithm? Following is the declaration for one of the `sort` functions:

```
template <class RandomAccessIterator>
void sort(RandomAccessIterator first, RandomAccessIterator last);
```

As indicated by the name of the template parameter, `sort` expects a random-access iterator. Member functions provided by the iterator are used in the `sort` function. Bidirectional iterators don't provide these member functions. Of course, the iterators lower in the hierarchy don't either. If a bidirectional iterator were passed, the compiler would give somewhat obscure error messages citing illegal structure operation in Bc5\Include\algorith.h. The moral of the story is to know the iterator type expected by an algorithm and supply that iterator or one higher in the hierarchy.

Many of the algorithms in the STL have copy and/or if versions. The copy version of an algorithm will place the results of the operation in a different container instead of replacing the contents of the container. The copy version of an algorithm is denoted by the suffix _copy. The if version of an algorithm uses a `predicate` function to determine whether an operation will be performed on an element. A `predicate` function is defined as a function that returns a `true`/`false` value. These predicate versions of a container are denoted by the suffix _if. If an algorithm has both a copy plus `predicate` version, it is denoted with the _copy_if suffix. For example, the `replace` algorithm has `replace`, `replace_if`, `replace_copy`, and `replace_copy_if` versions.

Another variation of STL algorithms determines how objects are compared. Many algorithms have a version that uses the objects' defined < and == operators. The other version takes a predicate function (or function object) as an additional parameter and uses it to make comparisons between objects. The comparison functions may be unary or binary functions.

The STL divides algorithms into four categories:

- Non-mutating sequence operations
- Mutating sequence operations

- Sorting and related operations
- Generalized numeric operations

In the sections that follow, each category's algorithms are listed, and the declarations for all the variants are given. The operations performed are briefly discussed.

Non-Mutating Sequence Algorithms. *Non-mutating sequence algorithms* do not change the contents of the containers on which they are operating. As the name implies, these algorithms work with sequence containers such as vector, deque, and list. These algorithms operate on a range defined by a first, inclusive, and last iterator.

for_each. for_each applies the function f to every element in the input sequence. The input sequence consists of the container elements between first and last including the element pointed to by first and one less than the element pointed to by last. This is denoted by [first,last). First and last must be input iterators or other types of iterators higher in the iterator hierarchy. See the section entitled "Iterators" for details. The function f is a unary function (or function object) with an argument of the container type T, the type stored in the container. Either a pointer to the function f or a copy of the function object f is returned by for_each.

```
template <class InputIterator, class Function>
Function for_each (InputIterator first, InputIterator last, Function f);
```

find. find searches the elements in the input range [first, last) for the first element that is equal to the value argument; or if the predicate version find_if is used, the first element for which pred(element) returns true. In either case, an iterator pointing to this element is returned. If the element cannot be found, last is returned.

```
template <class InputIterator, class T>
InputIterator find (InputIterator first, InputIterator last,
                    const T& value);

template <class InputIterator, class Predicate>
InputIterator find_if (InputIterator first, InputIterator last,
                       Predicate pred);
```

find_end. find_end searches the input sequence [first1, last1) for a match to a test sequence given the input sequence [first2, last2). The standard version of find_end uses the == operator to compare elements in the two sequences. The predicate version uses a binary predicate function that takes elements of the first sequence as the first argument and elements of the second sequence as the second argument. If more than one sequence matches, the last one is found—an iterator pointing to the last element in the match (not one past the last element). If no match is found, last1 is returned.

```
template <class ForwardIterator1, class ForwardIterator2>
ForwardIterator1 find_end (ForwardIterator1 first1, ForwardIterator1 last1,
                           ForwardIterator2 first2, ForwardIterator2
                           last2);

template <class ForwardIterator1, class ForwardIterator2, class
BinaryPredicate>
```

III

Advanced Programming

```
ForwardIterator1 find_end (ForwardIterator1 first1, ForwardIterator1 last1,
                           ForwardIterator2 first2, ForwardIterator2 last2,
                           BinaryPredicate pred);
```

find_first_of. find_first_of performs the same operation as find_end except the
first matching sequence is sought and returned, not the last matching sequence. See
the previous section on find_end for more discussion.

```
template <class ForwardIterator1, class ForwardIterator2>
ForwardIterator1 find_first_of (ForwardIterator1 first1,
                                ForwardIterator1 last1,
                                ForwardIterator2 first2,
                                ForwardIterator2 last2);

template <class ForwardIterator1, class ForwardIterator2, class
BinaryPredicate>
ForwardIterator1 find_first_of (ForwardIterator1 first1,
                                ForwardIterator1 last1,
                                ForwardIterator2 first2,
                                ForwardIterator2 last2,
                                BinaryPredicate pred);
```

adjacent_find. adjacent_find searches the input sequence [first, last) for two
adjacent elements that are equal or, if the predicate version is used, two adjacent elements for which binary_pred(element_i, element_i+1) returns true. If a match is
found, an iterator pointing to the first of the matching pair is returned. If it is not
found, last is returned.

```
template <class ForwardIterator>
ForwardIterator adjacent_find (ForwardIterator first,
                               ForwardIterator last);

template <class ForwardIterator, class BinaryPredicate>
ForwardIterator adjacent_find (ForwardIterator first, ForwardIterator last,
                               BinaryPredicate binary_pred);
```

count. count searches the input sequence defined by [first, last) for all elements
that are equal to value or, if the predicate version count_if is used, for which
pred(element) returns true. For every element found that meets this criteria, the
increment operator is applied to n.

```
template <class InputIterator, class T, class Size>
void count (InputIterator first, InputIterator last, const T& value,
            Size& n);

template <class InputIterator, class Predicate, class Size>
void count_if (InputIterator first, InputIterator last, Predicate pred,
               Size& n);
```

mismatch. mismatch iterates through the two input sequences comparing elements
with equal offsets: first1+i and first2+i, 0<=i<last1-first1-1. If a pair of elements is found that is not equal or for which binary_pred(first1+i,first2+i) is
true, then iterators pointing to the two elements are returned in a pair object. The
pair class is just an STL mechanism for returning two objects of possibly dissimilar
types in a function. The definition of pair template class is given here:

```
template <class InputIterator1, class InputIterator2>
pair<InputIterator1, InputIterator2> mismatch(InputIterator1 first1,
                                               InputIterator1 last1,
                                               InputIterator2 first2);

template <class InputIterator1, class InputIterator2,
class BinaryPredicate>
pair<InputIterator1, InputIterator2> mismatch (InputIterator1 first1,
                                               InputIterator1 last1,
                                               InputIterator2 first2,
                                               BinaryPredicate
                                               binary_pred);

template <class T1, class T2>
struct pair
{
    T1 first;
    T2 second;
    pair (const T1& a, const T2& b) : first(a), second(b) {}
};
```

An example of using `mismatch` and `pair` is given here:

```
pair<char*, char*> result = mismatch(str1, str1+10, str2);
if (result.first == str1+10)
    cout << "Mismatch found: " << *result.first != *result.second.\n";
else
    cout << "The first 9 characters of the two strings are equal.\n";
```

If a mismatch is not found, then the iterator `pair(last1, first2+(last1-first1))` is
returned.

equal. The `equal` algorithm compares two input sequences for equality. Equality is
defined by the `==` operator or a return value of true for the `binary_pred` function. It is
opposite of mismatch except it returns a `bool` value. If no mismatches are found, it
returns true; otherwise, the return value of `equal` is false.

```
template <class InputIterator1, class InputIterator2>
bool equal (InputIterator1 first1, InputIterator1 last1,
            InputIterator2 first2);

template <class InputIterator1, class InputIterator2,
          class BinaryPredicate>
bool equal (InputIterator1 first1, InputIterator1 last1,
            InputIterator2 first2,
            BinaryPredicate binary_pred);
```

search. search tries to find a subsequence defined by [first2, last2) in the sequence [firs1, last1). If a match is found, an iterator pointing to the beginning
element of the subsequence in the first sequence is returned. A match in the standard
version of the algorithm is defined by the `==` operator for the elements. For the predicate version, it is defined by a `true` return value from the binary predicate function
`binary_pred`. If no match is found, `last1` is returned.

```
template <class ForwardIterator1, class ForwardIterator2>
ForwardIterator1 search (ForwardIterator1 first1,ForwardIterator1 last1,
                         ForwardIterator2 first2,ForwardIterator2 last2);
```

III

Advanced Programming

```
template <class ForwardIterator1, class ForwardIterator2,
➥class BinaryPredicate>
ForwardIterator1 search (ForwardIterator1 first1,ForwardIterator1 last1,
                         ForwardIterator2 first2,ForwardIterator2 last2,
                         BinaryPredicate binary_pred);
```

Mutating Sequence Algorithms. *Mutating sequence algorithms*, like non-mutating sequence algorithms, perform operations on sequence containers such as vector, deque, and list. Unlike non-mutating sequence algorithms, they do modify the elements of the containers. These algorithms perform their operations over a range of elements defined by a pair of iterators: first and last. This sequence of elements, called the *input range*, is denoted by [first, last). It includes all elements in the container between first and last, including the element pointed to by first and excluding last.

copy. The copy function places elements in the input range [first, last) into the container pointed to by result. copy uses the assignment operator (=) to copy elements. The return value is an iterator pointing to one past the last element copied.

```
template <class InputIterator, class OutputIterator>
OutputIterator copy (InputIterator first, InputIterator last,
                     OutputIterator result);
```

copy_backward. copy_backward is very similar to copy. It copies elements from the range [first, last); however, copy_backward starts copying the element pointed to by last-1 to result-1 and proceeds to first. Thus, the destination range is [result-(last-first), result). The iterator returned points to the last element copied, not one past the last element.

```
template <class BidirectionalIterator1, class BidirectionalIterator2>
BidirectionalIterator2 copy_backward (BidirectionalIterator1 first,
                                      BidirectionalIterator1 last,
                                      BidirectionalIterator2 result);
```

swap. As the name implies, swap exchanges the contents of a and b. It uses the = operator defined for T.

```
template <class T>
void swap (T& a, T& b);
```

inter_swap. inter_swap performs the same operation as swap but takes two iterators as arguments. The contents of the object pointed to by a are swapped with the contents of the object pointed to by b.

```
template <class ForwardIterator1, class ForwardIterator2>
void iter_swap (ForwardIterator1 a, ForwardIterator2 b);
```

swap_ranges. swap_ranges swaps the elements in the range [first1, last1) with the elements in the range [first2, first2+(last1-first1)]. swap_ranges use inter_swap to do its work. The return value of the function is the iterator first2+(last1-first1) (for example, one past the last element swapped in the second sequence).

```
template <class ForwardIterator1, class ForwardIterator2>
ForwardIterator2 swap_ranges (ForwardIterator1 first1,
                              ForwardIterator1 last1,
                              ForwardIterator2 first2);
```

transform. In the first version of transform, the unary function op is called for every element in the range [first, last), and the result is put in the range [result, result+(last-first)). The single argument of the unary function op is of the type pointed to by first and last. The second version of transform uses two input sequences with ranges [first1, last1) and [first2, last2) as arguments to the binary function binary_op, and the result is placed in the range [result, result+(last1-first1)).

```
template <class InputIterator, class OutputIterator, class UnaryOperation>
OutputIterator transform (InputIterator first, InputIterator last,
                          OutputIterator result, UnaryOperation op);

template <class InputIterator1, class InputIterator2, class OutputIterator,
          class BinaryOperation>
OutputIterator transform (InputIterator1 first1, InputIterator1 last1,
                          InputIterator2 first2, OutputIterator result,
                          BinaryOperation binary_op);
```

replace. The replace function will replace each element that is equal to old_value in the sequence referred to by [first, last) with new_value. replace_if will replace elements for which pred(element) is true. The replace_copy and replace_copy_if copy the input sequence [first, last) to the destination range [result, result+(last-first)) substituting new_value when the element being copied is equal to old_value (replace_copy) or when pred(element) is true. replace_copy and replace_copy_if return an iterator pointing to one past the last element copied.

```
template <class ForwardIterator, class T>
void replace (ForwardIterator first, ForwardIterator last,
              const T& old_value,
              const T& new_value);

template <class ForwardIterator, class Predicate, class T>
void replace_if (ForwardIterator first, ForwardIterator last,
                 Predicate pred,
                 const T& new_value);

template <class InputIterator, class OutputIterator, class T>
OutputIterator replace_copy (InputIterator first, InputIterator last,
                             OutputIterator result, const T& old_value,
                             const T& new_value);

template <class Iterator, class OutputIterator, class Predicate, class T>
OutputIterator replace_copy_if (Iterator first, Iterator last,
                                OutputIterator result, Predicate pred,
                                const T& new_value);
```

fill. fill assigns value to every element in the range [first, last). fill_n sets every element in the range [first, first+n) to value. The return value for fill_n is an iterator pointing to one past the last element assigned a value (first+n).

```
template <class ForwardIterator, class T>
void fill (ForwardIterator first, ForwardIterator last, const T& value);

template <class OutputIterator, class Size, class T>
OutputIterator fill_n (OutputIterator first, Size n, const T& value);
```

generate. generate and generate_n perform the same operation as fill and fill_n except that instead of assigning value to each element, the result of the function, or function object, gen is assigned to every element. The function gen has no arguments.

```
template <class ForwardIterator, class Generator>
void generate (ForwardIterator first, ForwardIterator last, Generator gen);

template <class OutputIterator, class Size, class Generator>
OutputIterator generate_n (OutputIterator first, Size n, Generator gen);
```

remove. remove and remove_if eliminate all elements in the input sequence [first, last) that are equal to the supplied value (remove) or pred(element) returns true (remove_if). The elimination is accomplished by copying every element above the one being eliminated to a position one less in the sequence. The very last element in the sequence is NOT deleted. The return value of replace and replace_if is an iterator pointing to one past the last element in the input sequence. Thus, the unused elements on the end of the container are in the sequence [the return value of remove/remove_if, container.end()).

```
template <class ForwardIterator, class T>
ForwardIterator remove (ForwardIterator first, ForwardIterator last,
                        const T& value);

template <class ForwardIterator, class Predicate>
ForwardIterator remove_if (ForwardIterator first,
                           ForwardIterator last,Predicate pred);

template <class InputIterator, class OutputIterator, class T>
OutputIterator remove_copy (InputIterator first, InputIterator last,
                            OutputIterator result, const T& value);

template <class InputIterator, class OutputIterator, class Predicate>
OutputIterator remove_copy_if (InputIterator first, InputIterator last,
                               OutputIterator result, Predicate pred);
```

The copy version remove copy all elements to a new output sequence except those elements that meet the test conditions. The original sequence is left undisturbed. The return value points to one past the last element copied.

unique. unique removes all but the first element in a consecutive sequence of elements that meet an equality condition or for which binary_op(element, element+1) returns true. The test for equality uses the = operator defined for the stored objects. Just like the remove algorithm, the input sequence is compacted but no elements are deleted. The unused elements on the end of the input sequence are left for the user of the function to delete. The return value of unique can be used for this purpose.

```
template <class ForwardIterator>
ForwardIterator unique (ForwardIterator first, ForwardIterator last);
```

```
template <class ForwardIterator, class BinaryPredicate>
ForwardIterator unique (ForwardIterator first,
                   ForwardIterator last, BinaryPredicate binary_pred);

template <class InputIterator, class OutputIterator>
OutputIterator unique_copy (InputIterator first, InputIterator last,
                   OutputIterator result);

template <class InputIterator, class OutputIterator, class BinaryPredicate>
OutputIterator unique_copy (InputIterator first, InputIterator last,
                   OutputIterator result, BinaryPredicate
                   binary_pred);
```

The unique_copy versions vary from the unique versions in that they copy the output
to an output sequence. The return value points to one past the last element copied
into the output sequence.

reverse. reverse uses iter_swap to swap to reverse elements in the input sequence
[first, last]. reverse_copy places the results of the operator in the sequence
[result, result+(last-first)).

```
template <class BidirectionalIterator>
void reverse (BidirectionalIterator first, BidirectionalIterator last);

template <class BidirectionalIterator, class OutputIterator>
OutputIterator reverse_copy (BidirectionalIterator first,
                   BidirectionalIterator last,
                   OutputIterator result);
```

rotate. rotate takes an input sequence defined by [first, middle-1]+[middle,
last-1] and swaps the order of the sections to produce the sequence [middle, last-
1]+[first, middle-1]. rotate_copy puts the result in an output sequence rather
than modifying the input sequence. The copy version returns a pointer to one past
the last element in the output sequence.

```
template <class ForwardIterator>
void rotate (ForwardIterator first, ForwardIterator middle,
             ForwardIterator last)

template <class ForwardIterator, class OutputIterator>
OutputIterator rotate_copy (ForwardIterator first, ForwardIterator middle,
                   ForwardIterator last,  OutputIterator result)
```

random_shuffle. random_shuffle randomly shuffles the elements in the input sequence. The second version accepts a user-supplied random-number generator. The
requirements for this random number function are that it takes an integer n and returns a number between 0 and n-1.

```
template <class RandomAccessIterator>
void random_shuffle (RandomAccessIterator first,
                   RandomAccessIterator last)


template <class RandomAccessIterator, class RandomNumberGenerator>
void random_shuffle (RandomAccessIterator first, RandomAccessIterator last,
                   RandomNumberGenerator& rand)
```

partition. partition separates the elements in the input sequence [first, last) into two groups. The first group meet the criteria that pred(element) returns true. This group is placed in the first part sequence. The second group of those elements that do not meet the criteria are placed in the second part of the sequence. Stable partition version does the same operation and also maintains the relative order of the elements within a group. The return value of both functions points to the first element in the second group.

```
template <class BidirectionalIterator, class Predicate>
BidirectionalIterator partition (BidirectionalIterator first,
                                 BidirectionalIterator last,
                                 Predicate pred);

template <class BidirectionalIterator, class Predicate>
BidirectionalIterator stable_partition (BidirectionalIterator first,
                                        BidirectionalIterator last,
                                        Predicate pred);
```

Sorting and Related Algorithms. The STL algorithms in this category perform searching, sorting, merging, set operations on sorted containers, heap operations, and some miscellaneous algorithms. It is sort of a catch-all category. One thing these algorithms do have in common is that each has two versions. The first version uses the < operator defined by the type being stored in the container to make comparisons. The second version applies a user-defined comparison function that takes two arguments and returns a Boolean value. Other than the way comparisons are made, there is no difference in the two versions. All algorithms in this category don't use the == operator to test for equivalence. If a and b are two elements to be compared, a is equal to b if (!(a<b)&&!(b<a)) == true.

Unlike the two previous categories, algorithms in this category can work with associative containers.

> **Caution**
>
> Many of the algorithms in this category require random-access iterators. Only the vectors, deques, and C arrays provide these iterators. The rest provide for only bidirectional iterators. Using a bidirectional iterator can result in obscure error messages. Pay close attention to template parameter names to avoid the headache.

sort. sort arranges the elements in the sequence in ascending order. sort does not guarantee that equal elements will retain their original order.

```
template <class RandomAccessIterator>
void sort (RandomAccessIterator first, RandomAccessIterator last);

template <class RandomAccessIterator, class Compare>
void sort (RandomAccessIterator first, RandomAccessIterator last,
           Compare comp);
```

stable_sort. stable_sort performs the same operation as sort except that the relative order of equal elements is preserved.

```
template <class RandomAccessIterator>
void stable_sort (RandomAccessIterator first, RandomAccessIterator last);

template <class RandomAccessIterator, class Compare>
void stable_sort (RandomAccessIterator first, RandomAccessIterator last,
                  Compare comp);
```

partial_sort. partial_sort does a partial sort of the input sequence [first, last). The first middle-first elements in the resulting sequence are sorted elements from the entire input range. In the copy versions, the first result_last-result_first sorted elements from the range [first, last) are copied to the destination range [result_first, result_last). If last-first is less than result_last-result_first, the only last-first sorted elements are copied to [result_first, result_first+(last-first)). The return value of the copy version points to one past the last element in the destination range.

```
template <class RandomAccessIterator>
void partial_sort (RandomAccessIterator first,
                   RandomAccessIterator middle,
                   RandomAccessIterator last);

template <class RandomAccessIterator, class Compare>
void partial_sort (RandomAccessIterator first,
                   RandomAccessIterator middle,
                   RandomAccessIterator last,
                   Compare comp);

template <class InputIterator, class RandomAccessIterator>
RandomAccessIterator partial_sort_copy (InputIterator first,
                                        InputIterator last,
                                        RandomAccessIterator result_first,
                                        RandomAccessIterator result_last);

template <class InputIterator, class RandomAccessIterator, class Compare>
RandomAccessIterator partial_sort_copy (InputIterator first,
                                        InputIterator last,
                                        RandomAccessIterator result_first,
                                        RandomAccessIterator result_last,
                                        Compare comp);
```

nth_element. The nth_element functions place in the nth position of the input sequence the element with which it would be filled if all the elements were sorted. In addition, the resulting sequence is partitioned around the nth element. That is, all the elements below nth element in the sequence are less than it, and all elements above the nth element are not less than it. This function gives an easy way to locate the median of a sequence.

```
template <class RandomAccessIterator>
void nth_element (RandomAccessIterator first, RandomAccessIterator nth,
                 RandomAccessIterator last);
```

III

Advanced Programming

```
template <class RandomAccessIterator, class Compare>
void nth_element (RandomAccessIterator first, RandomAccessIterator nth,
                  RandomAccessIterator last, Compare comp);
```

lower_bound. lower_bound finds the first position in the input sequence [first, last) in which value could be inserted, and the sequence still remains sorted. Thus, these functions are for sorted containers. The return value points to a position in the sequence where value could be inserted.

```
template <class ForwardIterator, class T>
ForwardIterator lower_bound (ForwardIterator first,ForwardIterator last,
                             const T& value);

template <class ForwardIterator, class T, class Compare>
ForwardIterator lower_bound (ForwardIterator first,ForwardIterator last,
                             const T& value, Compare comp);
```

upper_bound. Like lower_bound, upper_bound is designed for containers with sorted elements. It returns the last position in which a value could be inserted and still maintain ordering.

```
template <class ForwardIterator, class T>
ForwardIterator upper_bound (ForwardIterator first,ForwardIterator last,
                             const T& value);

template <class ForwardIterator, class T, class Compare>
ForwardIterator upper_bound (ForwardIterator first,ForwardIterator last,
                             const T& value, Compare comp);
```

equal_range. equal_range is a combination of lower_bound and upper_bound. It finds the range in the input sequence in which value can be inserted and ordering can still be maintained. The return value is an instance of the pair template class. The first parameter is the result of lower_bound, and the second parameter is the result of upper_bound.

```
template <class ForwardIterator, class T>
pair<ForwardIterator, ForwardIterator> equal_range (ForwardIterator first,
                                                    ForwardIterator last,
                                                    const T& value);

template <class ForwardIterator, class T, class Compare>
pair<ForwardIterator, ForwardIterator> equal_range (ForwardIterator first,
                                                    ForwardIterator last,
                                                    const T& value,
                                                    Compare comp);
```

binary_search. binary_search searches a sorted input sequence for value and returns true if found; otherwise, it returns false.

```
template <class ForwardIterator, class T>
bool binary_search (ForwardIterator first, ForwardIterator last,
                    const T& value);

template <class ForwardIterator, class T, class Compare>
bool binary_search (ForwardIterator first, ForwardIterator last,
```

```
                          const T& value,
                          Compare comp);
```

merge. merge combines two sorted input sequences, [first1, last1) and [first2, last2), into a destination sorted sequence [result, result+(last1-first1)+(last2-first2)). The return value points to one past the last element in the merged sequence.

```
template <class InputIterator1, class InputIterator2, class OutputIterator>
OutputIterator merge (InputIterator1 first1, InputIterator1 last1,
                      InputIterator2 first2, InputIterator2 last2,
                      OutputIterator result);

template <class InputIterator1, class InputIterator2, class OutputIterator,
          class Compare>
OutputIterator merge (InputIterator1 first1, InputIterator1 last1,
                      InputIterator2 first2, InputIterator2 last2,
                      OutputIterator result, Compare comp);
```

inplace_merge. inplace_merge merges two sorted input sequences: [first, middle) and [middle, last). This means the two sequences must be adjacent containers in memory or two adjacent subsequences in the same container.

```
template <class BidirectionalIterator>
void inplace_merge (BidirectionalIterator first,
                    BidirectionalIterator middle,
                    BidirectionalIterator last);

template <class BidirectionalIterator, class Compare>
void inplace_merge (BidirectionalIterator first,
                    BidirectionalIterator middle,
                    BidirectionalIterator last, Compare comp);
```

includes. includes returns true if every element in the second range [first2, last2) of ordered elements is also in the first range [first1, last1) of ordered elements; otherwise, it returns false.

```
template <class InputIterator1, class InputIterator2>
bool includes (InputIterator1 first1, InputIterator1 last1,
               InputIterator2 first2, InputIterator2 last2);

template <class InputIterator1, class InputIterator2, class Compare>
bool includes (InputIterator1 first1, InputIterator1 last1,
               InputIterator2 first2, InputIterator2 last2, Compare comp);
```

set_union. set_union combines two sorted input sequences defined by [first1, last1) and [first2, last2) into a single sequence starting at result. If elements are duplicated between the two sequences, the sequence with the greatest number of equivalent elements is copied. The return value points to one past the end of the output sequence.

```
template <class InputIterator1, class InputIterator2, class OutputIterator>
OutputIterator set_union (InputIterator1 first1, InputIterator1 last1,
                          InputIterator2 first2, InputIterator2 last2,
                          OutputIterator result);
```

```
template <class InputIterator1, class InputIterator2, class OutputIterator,
         class Compare>
OutputIterator set_union (InputIterator1 first1, InputIterator1 last1,
                          InputIterator2 first2, InputIterator2 last2,
                          OutputIterator result, Compare comp);
```

set_intersection. set_intersection builds a sequence of sorted elements that consists of elements that are in two sorted input sequences. If [first1, last1) contains n1 elements equivalent to some value and [first2, last2) contains n2 elements also equivalent to that same value, then the resulting sequence will contain min(n1, n2). This is the opposite behavior of set_union. The return value points to one past the last element in the output sequence.

```
template <class InputIterator1, class InputIterator2, class OutputIterator>
OutputIterator set_intersection (InputIterator1 first1,
                                 InputIterator1 last1,
                                 InputIterator2 first2,
                                 InputIterator2 last2,
                                 OutputIterator result);

template <class InputIterator1, class InputIterator2, class OutputIterator,
         class Compare>
OutputIterator set_intersection (InputIterator1 first1,
                                 InputIterator1 last1,
                                 InputIterator2 first2,
                                 InputIterator2 last2,
                                 OutputIterator result, Compare comp);
```

set_difference. set_difference constructs a sorted output sequence from two sorted input sequences that consist of elements found in the first sequence but not found in the second sequence. The returned value points to the end of the output sequence.

```
template <class InputIterator1, class InputIterator2, class OutputIterator>
OutputIterator set_difference (InputIterator1 first1, InputIterator1 last1,
                               InputIterator2 first2, InputIterator2 last2,
                               OutputIterator result);

template <class InputIterator1, class InputIterator2, class OutputIterator,
         class Compare>
OutputIterator set_difference (InputIterator1 first1, InputIterator1 last1,
                               InputIterator2 first2, InputIterator2 last2,
                               OutputIterator result, Compare comp);
```

set_symmetric_difference. set_symmetric_difference builds a sorted output sequence of elements found in both sorted input sequences. The return value is the end of the output sequence.

```
template <class InputIterator1, class InputIterator2, class OutputIterator>
OutputIterator set_symmetric_difference (InputIterator1 first1,
                                         InputIterator1 last1,
                                         InputIterator2 first2,
                                         InputIterator2 last2,
                                         OutputIterator result);

template <class InputIterator1, class InputIterator2, class OutputIterator,
         class Compare>
```

```
OutputIterator set_symmetric_difference (InputIterator1 first1,
                                         InputIterator1 last1,
                                         InputIterator2 first2,
                                         InputIterator2 last2,
                                         OutputIterator result,
                                         Compare comp);
```

push_heap. The heap algorithms push_heap, pop_heap, make_heap, and sort_heap work with a specifically sorted organization of elements called a *binary tree*. Elements can be efficiently added and removed. A heap is defined over a range of random-access pointers [first, last) where *first is the largest element in the heap. Due to the random-access iterator restriction, heaps will work only with vectors and deques. Because of their structure, the heap is especially efficient for implementing a priority queue.

```
template <class RandomAccessIterator>
void push_heap (RandomAccessIterator first, RandomAccessIterator last);

template <class RandomAccessIterator, class Compare>
void push_heap (RandomAccessIterator first, RandomAccessIterator last,
                Compare comp);
```

push_heap adds a new value pointed to by last to a heap pointed to by [first, last-1).

pop_heap. pop_heap removes the greatest new value, *first, in the heap defined by [first, last). This is accomplished by swapping *first and *(last-1). Thus, in the return sequence, the new heap will be defined by [first, last-1), and the iterator last-1 will point to the desired element.

```
template <class RandomAccessIterator>
void pop_heap (RandomAccessIterator first, RandomAccessIterator last);

template <class RandomAccessIterator, class Compare>
void pop_heap (RandomAccessIterator first, RandomAccessIterator last,
               Compare comp);
```

make_heap. make_heap builds a heap out of an unordered input sequence.

```
template <class RandomAccessIterator>
inline void make_heap (RandomAccessIterator first,
                       RandomAccessIterator last);

template <class RandomAccessIterator, class Compare>
void make_heap (RandomAccessIterator first, RandomAccessIterator last,
                Compare comp);
```

sort_heap. sort_heap builds a sequence of sort elements from an input heap defined by [first, last).

```
template <class RandomAccessIterator>
void sort_heap (RandomAccessIterator first, RandomAccessIterator last);

template <class RandomAccessIterator, class Compare>
void sort_heap (RandomAccessIterator first, RandomAccessIterator last,
                Compare comp);
```

III

Advanced Programming

min. min returns the minimum of two objects. Both min and max are very generic functions and can be used with any object for which the < operator is defined or a compare function is provided.

```
template <class T>
const T& min (const T& a, const T& b);

template <class T, class Compare>
const T& min (const T& a, const T& b, Compare comp);
```

max. max returns the maximum of objects.

```
template <class T>
inline const T& max (const T& a, const T& b);

template <class T, class Compare>
const T& max (const T& a, const T& b, Compare comp);
```

min_element. min_element returns a value pointing to the minimum element in the input sequence [first, last). If the sequence is empty, the return value is last.

```
template <class ForwardIterator>
ForwardIterator min_element (ForwardIterator first, ForwardIterator last);

template <class ForwardIterator, class Compare>
ForwardIterator min_element (ForwardIterator first, ForwardIterator last,
                             Compare comp);
```

max_element. max_element returns the maximum element in the sequence [first, last). last is returned if the sequence is empty.

```
template <class ForwardIterator>
ForwardIterator max_element (ForwardIterator first, ForwardIterator last);

template <class ForwardIterator, class Compare>
ForwardIterator max_element (ForwardIterator first, ForwardIterator last,
                             Compare comp);
```

lexicographical_compare. lexicographical_compare iterates through two input sequences comparing corresponding elements. If the element in the first sequence [first1, last1) is less, the function returns true. If the element in the second sequence [first2, last2) is less, false is returned.

```
template <class InputIterator1, class InputIterator2>
bool lexicographical_compare (InputIterator1 first1, InputIterator1 last1,
                              InputIterator2 first2, InputIterator2 last2);

template <class InputIterator1, class InputIterator2, class Compare>
bool lexicographical_compare(InputIterator1 first1, InputIterator1 last1,
                             InputIterator2 first2, InputIterator2 last2,
                             Compare comp);
```

next_permutation. next_permutation creates all permutations of a sequence. This function is designed to be called repeatedly starting with a sorted sequence. Each call to the function generates the next permutation until all permutations have been generated. One more call to `next_permutation` will return a sorted sequence again, and the return value of the function is false.

```
template <class BidirectionalIterator>
bool next_permutation (BidirectionalIterator first,
                       BidirectionalIterator last);

template <class BidirectionalIterator, class Compare>
bool next_permutation (BidirectionalIterator first,
                       BidirectionalIterator last,
                       Compare comp);
```

prev_ permutation. `prev_permutation` undoes the `next_permutation` result. It reverses the permutation that occurred when `next_permutation` was called.

```
template <class BidirectionalIterator>
bool prev_permutation (BidirectionalIterator first,
                       BidirectionalIterator last);

template <class BidirectionalIterator, class Compare>
bool prev_permutation (BidirectionalIterator first,
                       BidirectionalIterator last,
                       Compare comp);
```

Numeric Algorithms. As the name implies, this category contains numeric operations. The `include` file for these functions is numeric.h.

accumulate. accumulate adds all elements in the sequence to `init` using the + operator and returns the result. The second version applies `binary_op(init, element)` for every element in the sequence and assigns the result to `init`:

```
template <class InputIterator, class T>
T accumulate (InputIterator first, InputIterator last, T init);

template <class InputIterator, class T, class BinaryOperation>
T accumulate (InputIterator first, InputIterator last, T init,
              BinaryOperation binary_op);

while (fist != last)
    init = binary_op(init, *first++);
```

inner_product. inner_product adds the sum of the product of elements from two input sequences with an accumulating total and returns the result. The second version of inner_product uses binary_op1 in the place of addition and binary_op2 in the place of multiplication:

```
template <class InputIterator1, class InputIterator2, class T>
T inner_product (InputIterator1 first1, InputIterator1 last1,
                 InputIterator2 first2, T init);

template <class InputIterator1, class InputIterator2, class T,
          class BinaryOperation1, class BinaryOperation2>
T inner_product (InputIterator1 first1, InputIterator1 last1,
                 InputIterator2 first2, T init,
                 BinaryOperation1 binary_op1,
                 BinaryOperation2 binary_op2);
```

III

Advanced Programming

```
    while (first1 != last1)
        init = binary_op1(init, binary_op2(*first1++, *first2++));
```

partial_sum. partial_sum produces an output sequence that is a running total of the elements in the input sequence. The resulting sequence contains the elements *first, *first+*(first+1), and so on. The second version of the algorithm applies the user-supplied binary_op function instead to the plus operator. The return value points to one past the last element written to the output sequence.

```
    template <class InputIterator, class OutputIterator>
    OutputIterator partial_sum (InputIterator first, InputIterator last,
                                OutputIterator result);

    template <class InputIterator, class OutputIterator, class BinaryOperation>
    OutputIterator partial_sum (InputIterator first, InputIterator last,
                                OutputIterator result,
                                BinaryOperation binary_op);
```

adjacent_difference. adjacent_difference produces a sequence of differences between adjacent elements in the input sequence [first, last). The resulting sequence contains *first, *first-*(first+1), and so on. The second version applies the binary_op function rather than the minus operator. A pointer to one past the last element in the output sequence is returned.

```
    template <class InputIterator, class OutputIterator>
    OutputIterator adjacent_difference (InputIterator first,
                                        InputIterator last,
                                        OutputIterator result);

    template <class InputIterator, class OutputIterator, class BinaryOperation>
    OutputIterator adjacent_difference (InputIterator first,
                                        InputIterator last,
                                        OutputIterator result,
                                        BinaryOperation binary_op);
```

Using STL Containers

The following sections explore the use of each STL container. Methods of construction, commonly used member functions and operators, and their usage with some of the algorithms are discussed and sample code is given.

Vector

A *vector* is an array of indexed elements much like a C array. Elements may be randomly accessed with the [] operator. Unlike a C array, the STL vector can dynamically resize to accommodate new elements. Elements deleted from a position in the vector other than the end cause automatic compassion. Elements inserted in the vector cause elements to be moved up in the array if needed. Also, the vector can be queried for information about itself such as the end of the vector and the size.

All types stored in a vector must provide a default constructor (a constructor with no arguments), a copy constructor, and a destructor. Note that the STUDENT class in the examples meets all these conditions.

Vectors are a good choice when a sequential data structure is needed and elements are usually added to the end and deleted from the end of the container. Deques are more efficient if elements are commonly added and deleted from both ends. Lists are most efficient in inserting and deleting elements from the interior of the container.

To use vectors, the include file vector.h, must be included. All STL header files are located in the \Bc5\Include directory.

Using the STUDENT class in listing 18.16 as a template parameter, a vector of STUDENT type, is written as:

```
typedef vector<STUDENT> STUDENT_VECTOR;
```

There are five vector constructors, which are listed in the following:

```
STUDENT_VECTOR studentVector1;                    // Default constructor.
STUDENT_VECTOR studentVector2(10);                // Vector of 10 students.
STUDENT_VECTOR studentVector3(10, STUDENT("Sam Adams", 0.0));
                                                  // Vector of 10 students.
STUDENT_VECTOR studentVector4(studentVector2);    // Copy constructor.
STUDENT_VECTOR studentVector5(studentVector3.begin(),
    studentVector3.begin()+5);                    // Copies first 5 elements.
```

studentVector1 is an empty vector. All the above vectors can be resized as needed. studentVector2 initially contains 10 STUDENT objects constructed with the STUDENT default constructor. studentVector3 also contains 10 STUDENT objects, but each is a copy of the STUDENT object passed to the constructor rather than created with the default constructor. studentVector4 is a copy of studentVector2. studentVector5 contains five elements consisting of copies of the first five elements in student Vector3. The iterators passed to this constructor need only be input iterators. The container used does not have to be a vector.

An assignment operator is provided. The following replaces the content of studentVector5 with the element of studentVector4:

```
studentVector5 = studentVector4;
```

Also an assign member function replaces the contents of the container. There are three forms of this function illustrated by the following:

```
studentVector2.assign(studentVector3.begin()+5, studentVector.end());
studentVector1.assign(15);
studentVector3.assign(25, STUDENT("Jack Breslin", 4.0));
```

The first form accepts two input iterators, first and last, and copies the contents of the input sequence [first, last) to the vector. The preceding statement assigns the last five values of studentVector3 to studentVector2. The second form replaces the contents of the container with the size argument number of default objects. Thus, studentVector1 would contain 15 default STUDENT objects. The last form replaces the contents with the number of copies of the supplied object specified in the first parameter. After the preceding statement, studentVector3 will contain 25 identical STUDENT objects with the ID Jack Breslin.

There are several type definitions. The more useful types are listed here:

III

Advanced Programming

- `reference`: A reference to a container element.
- `const_reference`: A reference to a container element that will not allow the element to be modified.
- `iterator`: An iterator of the type for this type of container. This iterator can be used as a random-access iterator.
- `const_iterator`: An iterator that will not allow elements to be modified.
- `reverse_iterator`: A reverse iterator adaptor.
- `const_reverse_iterator`: A backward-moving iterator that does not allow elements to be modified.
- `size_type`: An unsigned integer used for number of elements or amount of memory.
- `difference_type`: A signed integer used for distances between elements that can be described as the difference between two iterators.

Examples of using these type declarations with the preceding STUDENT vectors follow:

```
STUDENT_VECTOR::reference student = studentVector3[2];
STUDENT_VECTOR::iterator I = studentVector5.begin();
STUDNET_VECTOR::difference_type d = studentVector3.end() -
➥studentVector3.begin();
```

Four member functions return iterators:

- `begin()`: Returns an iterator pointing to the first element in the container.
- `end()`: Returns an iterator pointing to one past the last element in the container.
- `rbegin()`: Returns a reverse iterator pointing to one past the last element in the sequence.
- `rend()`: Returns a reverse iterator pointing to first element in the sequence.

Each of the preceding functions has a corresponding constant version.

`size()` returns the number of elements in the container. `capacity()` returns the maximum size of the container before additional memory must be allocated. `max_size()` returns the maximum size the container can reach. This is dependent on the amount of available free memory on the machine or possibly the upper limit of the `size_type` type.

`resize()` changes the size of the containers, adding or deleting elements from the end as necessary. This function has two forms. The first specifies the new size of the vector and, if additional elements are needed, uses the default `value_type` constructor. The second form of `resize()` takes two arguments: `new size` and an object of type `value_type` to copy if additional elements are needed.

`empty()` returns a Boolean value indicating if the container has no elements. `reserve()` allocates enough memory to hold the number of elements given by the `size_type` argument. Numerous allocations of memory can be very inefficient. It is often more efficient to allocate a large enough block to contain the expected number of elements.

Another problem with frequent allocations is that pointers, references, and iterators pointing to elements could become invalid after an allocation. If the `size_type` argument passed to `reserve()` is less than the current capacity, no action is taken.

The subscript operator `[ ]` works the same as with a C array. As with C arrays, the index passed to the subscript operator is a value representing the offset from the first element. The nonconstant version can be used as an `lvalue` because the return value is a reference.

Caution

As with C arrays, the index value passed is not verified. Unpredictable results will occur if the index is out of range. Care should be taken to keep the index in the range defined by the `begin` and `end` member functions.

The `at()` member function performs the same function as the subscript operator. The following code illustrates both:

```
if (!(studentVector3[2] == studentVector3.at(2)))
    cout << "This should not be possible!\n";
```

`front()` returns a reference to the first element in the vector, and `back()` returns a reference to the last element.

`push_back()` adds an element to the end of the vector, and `pop_back()` removes the last element:

```
studentVector2.push_back(STUDENT("John Newton", 3.4));
// Adds Mr. Newton to the end.
studentVector2.pop_back();
// Remove Mr. Newton.
```

`insert()` inserts one or more elements at a position in the vector described by an iterator passed to the function. The three forms of `insert()` are illustrated by the following:

```
// Insert a default element at offset 2. Elements in the range[2, end())
// move up one.
studentVector2.insert(studentVector.begin()+2);
// Insert a copy of the STUDENT object to offset 2. Elements are shifted up
// as needed.
studentVector2.insert(studentVector.begin()+2,
➥STUDENT("John Newton", 4.0));
// Insert a copy of all the elements of another vector at offset 5.
studentVector2.insert(studentVector.begin()+5, studentVector3.begin(),
➥studentVector3.end());
```

`erase()` removes elements from the position or range of positions specified:

```
// Remove the element at offset 15. Sift all element above offset
// 15 down one.
studentVector2.erase(studentVector.begin()+15);
// Remove the last 5 elements from the vector.
studentVector2.erase(studentVector.end()-5, studentVector2.end());
```

III

Advanced Programming

Finally, the member function swap() swaps the contents of two vectors:

```
// Swap contents of studentVector1 and studentVector2.
studentVector1.swap(studentVector2);
```

Listing 18.21 demonstrates the use of vector with various algorithms.

Listing 18.21   Vector1.cpp—Using Vectors

```
#define   RWSTD_NO_NAMESPACE
#include <cstring.h>
#include <iostream.h>
#include <algorith.h>
#include <vector.h>

// For use as a function pointer.
void WriteStr(string &s)
{
    cout << s << " ";
}

typedef vector<string> STRING_VECTOR;

int main()
{
    STRING_VECTOR sv1(8);
    sv1.push_back("All");
    sv1.push_back("good");
    sv1.push_back("things");
    sv1.push_back("must");
    sv1.push_back("come");
    sv1.push_back("to");
    sv1.push_back("an");
    sv1.push_back("end");

    cout << "Output in reverse order: ";
    for (STRING_VECTOR::reverse_iterator ri = sv1.rbegin();
    ➥ri != sv1.rend(); ri++)
        WriteStr(*ri);
    cout << endl;

    // Sort the vector.
    sort(sv1.begin(), sv1.end());
    cout << "Sorted vector: ";
    for (STRING_VECTOR::iterator i = sv1.begin(); i != sv1.end(); i++)
        cout << *i << " ";
    cout << endl;
    return 0;
}
```

The STL provides a special vector to work with sequences of Boolean values called vector<bool>. The Boolean values are stored as bit, so the space requirement is small. vector<bool> has all the member functions of vector with some additions. flip() inverts the bits for the whole vector or for a specified position:

```
vector<bool> bitVector(20, 0);      // Create a bit vector of 20 elements,
                                    // all set to false.
```

```
      bitVector.flip();              // Invert all 20 elements. All are now
                                     // true.
      bitVector[5].flip();           // Invert the element at offset 5, which
                                     // is now false again.
```

Deque

As stated earlier in the chapter, *deque*, pronounce *deck*, is short for "double-ended queue." The STL deque, like the BIDS deque, is somewhat more flexible. The deque container is very similar to the vector. Both are indexed containers where elements can be randomly accessed and efficiently added to the end of the sequence. Unlike vectors, deques can also efficiently add elements to the beginning of the container.

Deque handles memory differently than vector. Whereas vectors allocate a contiguous block of memory for all its elements, deques allocate blocks of memory as needed. This model for memory management will be slightly more efficient at inserting elements than a vector.

As with vectors, objects stored in a deque must have a default constructor, copy constructor, and destructor defined. In addition, many algorithms require that the object have the < and == operators defined.

To use an STL deque, the following line of code must be included in the source file:

```
      #include <deque.h>
```

The deque is declared the same way as a vector. All member functions, operators, and type definitions found in vector are also in deque with the exception of `capacity()` and `reserve()`. Deque also add two new functions: `push_front()` and `pop_front()`. `push_front()` adds an element to the beginning of the deque, and `pop_front()` removes the element from the beginning of the sequence:

```
      deque<string> strDeque;
      string str("front of the line");
      strDeque.push_front(str);      // *strDeque.begin() == str.
      strDeque.pop_front();          // Remove str.
```

For a discussion of common functions, refer to the previous section entitled "Vectors." Listing 18.22 demonstrates the use of the deque container.

Listing 18.22   Deques2.cpp—Using Deques

```
#define   RWSTD_NO_NAMESPACE
#include <iostream.h>
#include <algorith.h>
#include <deque.h>
#include "student3.h"

typedef deque<STUDENT> STUDENT_DEQUE;

int main()
{
   STUDENT_DEQUE students;
   students.push_back(STUDENT("Abe Line", 3.2));
   students.push_back(STUDENT("John Brown", 2.0));
```

III

Advanced Programming

(continues)

```
Listing 18.22   Continued
      students.push_back(STUDENT("Frank Coke", 2.5));
      students.push_back(STUDENT("Sam Adit", 0.6));
      students.push_back(STUDENT("Samual Cart", 4.0));
      students.push_back(STUDENT("Ida Smith", 1.4));
      students.push_back(STUDENT("Tom Johnson", 3.9));
      students.push_back(STUDENT("Carl West", 2.6));
      sort(students.begin(), students.end());

      cout << "Students sorted by name: \n";
      for (STUDENT_DEQUE::iterator i = students.begin(); i != students.end();
➡i++)
         cout << *i << " ";
      cout << endl;

      cout << "A middle student is "
         << students[students.size()/2] << endl;
      return 0;
   }
```

List

The STL list container is a doubly linked list. Each *node* in the list encapsulates a data element and two pointers, one pointing to the previous node and one pointing to the next node. This structure is different than the vector or deque. A vector container is a good choice when the size of the container is somewhat stable and elements are added and removed from the end of the sequence. Adding and deleting elements in the interior is costly. Deques can efficiently add and remove elements from either end of the sequence but are inefficient when inserted in the middle. The list container is best used when the number of elements is unknown and when elements are added and removed from the interior of the sequence. Other than adding and deleting from the interior of the sequence, the vector and the deque are more efficient.

The list container provides for bidirectional iterators, not random-access iterators like vector and deque. Elements cannot be randomly accessed with the [ ] operator.

Objects stored in a list must define a default constructor, a copy constructor, and a destructor. Fundamental data types meet this criteria. User-defined classes must use the compiler-generated constructors and destructors or ones provided explicitly by the maker of the class. If the class contains dynamically allocated variables, then these functions should be explicitly defined.

To use list, the list.h header file in the \Bc5\Include must be included in the source file. A list of STUDENT (see listing 18.16) can be declared in one of the following ways:

```
// Empty list.
list<STUDENT> studentList1;
// List of 10 default STUDENT objects.
list<STUDENT> studentList2(10);
// 10 copies of STUDENT Abel Stone in list.
list<STUDENT> studentList3(10, STUDENT("Abel Stone", 2.9));
// Copy constructor.
```

```
list<STUDENT> studentList4(studentList3);
// A vector of 100 copies the STUDENT Mr. Newton.
vector<STUDENT> studentVector(100, STUDENT("John Newton", 3.6));
// Now copy first 50 STUDENT element from studentVector to studentList5.
list<STUDENT> studentList5(studentVector.begin(),
studentVector.begin()+50);
```

Note

Because the random-access iterator returned from the `begin()` function supports the plus operator (`begin()+50`), the preceding will work. If another list were used to initialize `studentList5`, the `operator+(int)` is not available because list supports bidirectional iterators.

These constructors are analogous to the vector and deque constructors. Most of the member functions, operators, and type definitions in list are essentially the same as their vector counterparts.

The assignment operator replaces one list with another:

```
studentList2 = studentList4;
```

`assign()`, `begin()`, `end()`, `rbegin()`, `rend()`, `push_back()`, `pop_back()`, `insert()`, `empty()`, `front()`, `back()`, `erase()`, `max_size()`, `size()`, and `swap()` perform identical operations as vector member functions of the same name. The only difference is that the functions that return iterators return bidirectional iterators rather than random-access iterators. Also, there are several type definitions in list that correspond to the vector type definitions. See the section entitled "Vector" for a discussion. Two additional functions found in deque and list are `push_front()` and `pop_front()`. See the section entitled "Deque" for a discussion.

When insertions are made in vector and deque containers, references and pointers to elements could become invalid. This is not true of insertions into list. Because the location in memory of each element in not necessarily contiguous, elements do not have to be moved to keep a sequential order.

The `splice()` member function splices one list into another. The three forms of `splice()` are illustrated here:

```
// Insert all of studentList2 into studentList3 starting at the first
// element in studentList3. studentList2 is left empty.
studentList3.splice(studentList3.begin(), studentList2);
// Insert the from STUDENT John Newton to end of studentList4 into end of
// studentList3.
list<STUDENT>::iterator i = find(studentList4.begin, studentList4.end(),
STUDENT("John Newton", 0.0));
if (!(i == studentVector4.end())
   studentList3.splice(studentList3.end(), studentList4, i,
studentList4.end());
else
   cout << "John Newton not found in forth student list.\n";
```

The merge() member function merges two sorted lists. This function is much like the algorithm merge() except the member function is implemented efficiently for list. Like the global function, the member function has two forms. The first uses the < operator defined for the elements, and the second uses a binary function to make comparisons.

```
// Sort the list first.
studentList3.sort();
studentList5.sort();
// studentList5 will be empty.
student3.merge(studentList5);
```

unique() is also a member function that works with sorted list. It removes all but one of the consecutive equal elements. A binary predicate function can be provided to the function to test for equality.

```
// Assume studentList3 is sorted. Removes all duplicates.
studentList3.unique();
```

The sort() member function sorts the list. The member function is more efficient than using the global template function sort().

remove() removes all occurrences of the supplied object from the list. remove_if() removes all elements in the list for which the predicate function supplied as an argument returns true.

```
// The following is a predicate function to be used with remove_if.
bool Passing(STUDENT &s)
{
    if (s.GetGrade() < 1.0)
        return false;
    return true;
}
...
// Remove all STUDENT objects with ID "John Newton".
studentList3.remove(STUDENT("John Newton", 0.0));
// Remove all STUDENT objects which have a failing grade.
studentList3.remove_if(Passing);
```

Listing 18.23 demonstrates the use of list.

Listing 18.23 Lists1.cpp—Using List

```
#define   RWSTD_NO_NAMESPACE
#include <stdlib.h>
#include <iostream.h>
#include <algorith.h>
#include <list.h>

typedef list<int> INT_LIST;

int main()
{
    // Create 2 integer list.
    INT_LIST intList1, intList2;
```

```
    // Generate a list of random integers.
    generate_n(inserter(intList1, intList1.begin()),10, rand);
    generate_n(inserter(intList2, intList2.begin()),5, rand);

    cout << "intList1: ";
    copy(intList1.begin(), intList1.end(), ostream_iterator<int>(cout, " "));
    cout << endl;

    cout << "intList2: ";
    copy(intList2.begin(), intList2.end(), ostream_iterator<int>(cout, " "));
    cout << endl;

    intList1.sort();
    cout << "intList1 sorted: ";
    copy(intList1.begin(), intList1.end(), ostream_iterator<int>(cout, " "));
    cout << endl;

    intList2.sort();
    cout << "intList2 sorted: ";
    copy(intList2.begin(), intList2.end(), ostream_iterator<int>(cout, " "));
    cout << endl;

    intList2.reverse();
    cout << "intList2 reversed: ";
    copy(intList2.begin(), intList2.end(), ostream_iterator<int>(cout, " "));
    cout << endl;

    intList2.reverse();
    intList1.merge(intList2);
    intList1.sort();
    cout << "intList1 with intList2 merged: ";
    copy(intList1.begin(), intList1.end(), ostream_iterator<int>(cout, " "));
    cout << endl;

    cout << "intList2.empty() = " << intList2.empty() << endl;
    return 0;
}
```

Stack

A *stack* is a LIFO (Last In, First Out) data structure. Elements may be placed on top of the stack and taken off the top, but not the middle or bottom. The STL version of a stack is a container adaptor. Another container class is required to declare a variable of type stack. This container can be a vector, deque, or list. The stack container uses the functions of the encapsulated container to perform its functions.

Objects stored in a stack must define the < and == operators.

To use the STL stack, both the stack.h header file and the header file for the container, vector.h, deque.h, or list.h, must be included in the source file.

The declaration of a stack requires two template parameters: The type of object being stored and the container class to be used in the implementation of the stack.

```
    typedef stack<STUDENT, vector<STUDENT> > STUDENT_STACK;
```

```
STUDENT_STACK studentStack1;
stack<STUDENT, list<STUDENT> > studentStack2;
```

The stack container has few member functions. `empty()` returns a Boolean value indicating if the stack has no elements. `size()` returns the number of elements in the stack. `top()` returns a reference to the top element on the stack. `pop()` removes the top element. `push()` places the supplied object on the top of the stack.

Queue

The *queue* is designed to be a FIFO (First In, First Out) data structure. Elements are removed from the queue in the order they were placed into the queue. Elements are placed in the back of the queue and removed from the front. As with stack, the STL queue is a container adaptor. A deque or list class is required to declare a queue type.

To use a queue, both the queue header file, queue.h, and the container used in the implementation, deque.h or list.h, must be included in the source file.

The declaration of queue objects is very similar to stack.

```
typedef queue<STUDENT, deque<STUDENT> > STUDENT_QUEUE;
STUDENT_QUEUE studentQueue1;
queue<STUDENT, list<STUDENT> > studentQueue2;
```

There are six member functions. `empty()` returns true if the queue has no elements. `size()` returns the number of elements in the queue. `front()` returns a reference to the element at the front of the queue. `back()` returns a reference to the element at the back of the queue. `push()` places the supplied object at the back of the queue. Finally, `pop()` removes the element at the front of the queue.

Listing 18.24 demonstrates the use of the queue container.

Listing 18.24   Queues2.cpp—Using Queue

```
#define   RWSTD_NO_NAMESPACE
#include <iostream.h>
#include <deque.h>
#include <queue.h>
#include "student3.h"

typedef queue<STUDENT, deque<STUDENT> > STUDENT_QUEUE;

int main()
{
    STUDENT_QUEUE line;
    // Get'em in line.
    line.push(STUDENT("Abe Line", 3.2));
    line.push(STUDENT("John Brown", 2.0));
    line.push(STUDENT("Frank Coke", 2.5));
    line.push(STUDENT("Sam Adit", 0.6));
    line.push(STUDENT("Samual Cart", 4.0));

    cout << line.front().GetId() << " is in the front of the line.\n";
    cout << line.back().GetId() << " is in the back of the line.\n";
```

```
   cout << "Queue consist of " << line.size() << " students.\n";
   while(!line.empty()) {
      cout << line.front();
      line.pop();
   }
   return 0;
}
```

Priority Queue

A *priority queue* is a data structure that removes elements in the container not based on when the element was added like a stack and queue, but based on which element has the greatest priority.

Like stack and queue, the STL priority queue is a container adaptor. To declare a priority queue, a vector or deque class must be used. The include file for priority queues is queue.h, the same as for the queue container.

There are two means by which each element's priority is determined. The container can use the < operator defined by the type of object being stored, or a comparison function can be supplied:

```
// Use the < operator defined in STUDENT.
priority_queue<STUDENT, deque<STUDENT> > studentPQ1;
// Initialize new priority queue from existing container.
priority_queue<STUDENT, deque<STUDENT> >
   studentPQ2(studentVector1.begin(), studentVector2.end());
// Use a comparison function object COMPARE_GRADE.
priority_queue<STUDENT, vector<STUDENT>, COMPARE_GRADE > studentPQ3;
// Pass comparison function through constructor.
priority_queue<STUDENT, vector<STUDENT> > studentPQ4(GradeCompare);
// Initialize priority queue with studentDeque3 and pass compare function.
priority_queue<STUDENT, vector<STUDENT> >
   studentPQ5(studentDeque3.begin(), studentDeque3.end(), GradeCompare);
```

Five member functions are provided. push() adds the user-supplied object to the container. pop() removes the greatest element from the container. top() returns a reference to the greatest element in the container. size() returns the number of elements in the container, and end() returns true if the container is empty.

Listing 18.25 illustrates the use of priority queue.

Listing 18.25 Pqueues1.cpp—Using Priority Queue

```
#define RWSTD_NO_NAMESPACE
#include <iostream.h>
#include <deque.h>
#include <queue.h>
#include "student3.h"

// Define a class in which to wrap the grade compare function.
struct GRADE_COMPARE
{
    bool operator()(const STUDENT &s1, const STUDENT &s2) const
```

(continues)

Listing 18.25 Continued

```
                { return s1.GetGrade() < s2.GetGrade(); }
};

typedef priority_queue<STUDENT, deque<STUDENT>, GRADE_COMPARE > STUDENT_PQ;

int main()
{
   STUDENT_PQ studentPQ;
   studentPQ.push(STUDENT("Abe Line", 3.2));
   studentPQ.push(STUDENT("John Brown", 2.0));
   studentPQ.push(STUDENT("Frank Coke", 2.5));
   studentPQ.push(STUDENT("Sam Adit", 0.6));
   studentPQ.push(STUDENT("Samual Cart", 4.0));

   cout << "Student priority queue consist of " << studentPQ.size() <<
   ➥" students.\n";
   while(!studentPQ.empty()) {
      cout << studentPQ.top();
      studentPQ.pop();
   }
   return 0;
}
```

Set and Multiset

Set and *multiset* belong to the associative category of STL containers. Associative containers maintain an ordering of elements based on a key. For set and multiset, this key is provided by the stored object. This underlying ordering of elements makes adding, removing, and searching for elements very efficient. The difference between set and multiset is that set does not allow duplicate keys, and multiset does.

Objects stored in a set must define equivalence operator == and a comparison operator <.

To use set or multiset, the set.h header file must be included in the source file.

The operators, member functions, and type definitions are identical for set and multiset. The constructor for these containers comes in three forms:

```
// Default constructor. The integer set is empty.
set<int> intSet;
// A function object is passed for determining order in the set.
multiset<STUDENT> floatMSet(GRADE_COMPARE);
// studentSet is formed coping elements from a vector
set<STUDENT> studentSet(studentVector1.begin(), studentVector1.end());
// A multiset of integers is created and the content of a list copied.
// The ordering function
// used is the STL function object greater thus reversing the normal
// ordering.
multiset<int>intMS (intList.begin(), intlist.end(), greater<int>);
```

The `begin()`, `end()`, `rbegin()`, `rend()`, `empty()`, `max_size()`, `size()`, and `swap()` member functions behave as they do in the vector container. The iterators returned from function like `begin()` in vector are random-access iterators. In set and multiset, the iterators are bidirectional. Also set and multiset contain similar useful type definitions such as `iterator` that are similar to those found in vector containers. See the section entitled "Vector" for a discussion.

The `erase()` member function operates as it does in vector except `erase()` has an extra form in set and multiset. The extra form will take an object and search the container for it. If it is found, it will be removed. `insert()` will do nothing if used to insert an object with a key duplicated in the current set. This does not apply to multiset.

`count()` returns the number of elements that match the supplied object. For set, this will be one or zero. `find()` searches the container for an object and returns an iterator pointing to it if found or the end of the container if not found. `lower_bound()` returns an iterator pointing to the first element matching an object. `upper_bound()` returns an iterator pointing to one past the last element matching a supplied object. Both functions return an iterator pointing to the end of the set if no matching element is found. `equal_range()` returns a pair of objects containing the result of `lower_bound()` in the first argument and the result of `upper_bound()` in the second argument.

For an example of using set and multiset, see listing 18.17.

Map and Multimap

Map and *multimap* are much like set and multiset. All belong to the associative category of containers. The associative containers maintain an ordering of elements based on a key. With set and multiset, that key is the object being stored. Map and multimap separate the key from the object being stored. Map does not allow duplicate keys, while multimap does allow keys in the container to be duplicated. The concept of map is like the BIDS dictionary container.

Like set and multiset, the map and multimap containers provide for very fast insertion, removal, and searching of elements.

Objects used for keys must define a comparison operator, or a comparison operator must be supplied. To determine equivalence between stored objects a and b with keys aKey and bKey, the keys are compared in both directions: `Compare(aKey, bKey) && Compare(bKey, aKey)`.

To use map or multimap, the header file map.h must be included in the source file.

The commonly used member functions and operators in map and multimap are identical. They are also very similar to set and multiset. Only the differences will be covered in this section.

To declare a map or multimap, the type of key and the type of object to be stored must be supplied as template parameters. An optional parameter is the function object to be used for comparing keys.

```
// A map keyed on integers containing strings.
map<int, string> strMap;
// A multimap of strings indexed by integers.
multimap<int, string, greater<int> > strMMap1;
// A multimap of strings containing the copied elements of a vector.
multimap<float, string> strMMap2(strVector.begin(), strVector.end());
```

Set and multiset define a type called value_type that is the type of object being stored. Map and multimap also define a value_type, but it is a pair of values. The first value in the pair is the key. The second value is the stored object. Map and multimap define an extra type called key_type. To do searches of the container, map and multimap functions such as find() use key_type.

```
strMap.insert(map<int, string>::value_type(3, "three"));
strMap.find(3);
```

Dereference iterator returns a pair object.

```
typedef map<int, string, less<int> > STR_MAP;

STR_MAP::iterator ii = strMap.find(3);
if (ii != strMap.end())  // end returns an iterator and thus a pair object.
   cout << "Key: " << ii.first << "  Value: " << ii.second << endl;
```

Map provides the subscript operator []. A key is used as a subscript, and the return value is a reference to the type of object being stored.

```
cout << "The index value of 3 gives: " << strMap[3];
strMap[3] = string("THREE");
cout << "Now it gives: " << strMap[3];
```

Listing 18.26 demonstrates the use of map and multimap containers.

Listing 18.26 Maps1.cpp—Using Map and Multimap

```
#define  RWSTD_NO_NAMESPACE
#include <iostream.h>
#include <map.h>
#include "student3.h"

// This multimap keyed on the < operator applied to a string representing
// college courses. The container will contain STUDENT objects.
typedef multimap<string, STUDENT, less<string> > ENROLLMENT;
typedef ENROLLMENT::value_type ENROLL_TYPE;

void PrintStudent(const ENROLL_TYPE &s, bool printCourse = true)
{
   if (printCourse)
      cout << s.first;
   cout << s.second << endl;
}

int main()
{
   ENROLLMENT msu;
   msu.insert(ENROLLMENT::value_type("CS101", STUDENT("John Newton", 1.)));
   msu.insert(ENROLLMENT::value_type("CS101", STUDENT("Dean Brown", 3.0)));
```

```
msu.insert(ENROLLMENT::value_type("CS102", STUDENT("Carl Bishop", 2.0)));
msu.insert(ENROLLMENT::value_type("CS102", STUDENT("Gary Cook", 1.0)));

cout << "Map " << msu.size() << " students (sorted by name):" << endl;
for (ENROLLMENT::iterator i = msu.begin(); i != msu.end(); i++)
    PrintStudent(*i);

cout << "Students enrolled in CS101:\n";
for (ENROLLMENT::iterator i = msu.lower_bound("CS101");
    ((i != msu.upper_bound("CS101")) && (i != msu.end())); i++)
    PrintStudent(*i, false);
return 0;
}
```

From Here...

In this chapter we have discussed two C++ container class libraries provided by Borland. BIDS, Borland's own library, provides a traditional object-oriented approach using inheritance and encapsulating most of the functionality of the conatiners within the container classes. There are two categories of BIDS containers: The FDS (Fundamental Data Structures) containers are rudimentary containers that are used to implement the second category of containers, ADT (Abstract Data Types) containers.

The new C++ standard library, STL (Standard Template Library), takes a much different approach. Much of the functionality of the library is found not in the container classes, but in global functions. The scope of the functionality provided by the STL is much broader than the BIDS library.

- Both BIDS and the STL make heavy use of templates. See the next chapter, "Using Template Classes," for a detailed look at templates.
- Chapter 20, "Inheritance and Polymorphism" discusses many of the features we've seen of both BIDS and the STL.
- If you had a problem understanding the operator overloading discussed in this chapter, review chapter 16, "Operator Overloading."
- Usually user-defined class objects are stored in containers. BIDS and the STL require certain functionality be defined for these objects. Chapter 16, "Operator Overloading," and chapter 17, "Constructors: Copy and Assignment," will cover many of these requirements.

III

Advanced Programming

CHAPTER 19

Using Template Classes

Having acquired a taste for templates myself, I wonder why everyone isn't trying them. The only way you can refer to them is "cool." Parameterized types were introduced in a paper by Bjarne Stroustrop in 1988 and accepted in the ANSI document in 1990. The implementation, however, didn't seem quite baked until about 1992, which, by the way, seems to have been the year C++ really picked up some steam.

If you have read a couple of books on C++, you may have noticed that templates are often near the back of the book. The reason for this, I expect, is that parameterized types seem somewhat difficult to grasp. I am going to try to make them easier for you.

The template specification is exactly a separation between the type of data and an implementation of an algorithm. Notice I did not say what kind of algorithm or implementation. It doesn't matter. Generic functions and classes provide direct, type-safe, full-fledged support for writing type-independent implementations. This is reusability to the hilt, folks.

In this chapter, I am going to show you how to write a function or class regardless of the data type, write it just once, and use it for every data type you can think of. You will see just how easy it is to learn generic functions and classes and how to write generic sorts, data structures, and classes that can be mapped to hardware. In this chapter, we'll cover:

- An introduction to generic programming, in particular, templates
- Understanding generic functions
- Using generic-sorting algorithms
- Exploring generic classes

Introduction to Generic Programming: Templates

Parameterized types may have evolved in great part because of the extremely high cost of software development. Businesses are continually paying millions of dollars for custom and commercial software every year, and the quest continues for ever-cheaper methods for developing software faster. One way that software development costs are driven down is to abide by an almost rigid enforcement of code reuse. Templates provide an extremely high level of code reuse: Ideally there is only one implementation of any single algorithm for all data types.

Chapter 4, "The Preprocessor" describes how parameterized types may first have been implemented as macros and how the preprocessor was responsible for the insertion of the data type before the compiler kicked in. Now templates are (and have been for five years) a fully implemented language feature having their own syntax.

To proceed successfully with our discussion on templates, you will have to have acquired knowledge of the native data types, the class idiom, and the special class member functions, the *copy constructor* and *assignment operator*. If you are lacking knowledge of these fundamental language features, templates are going to seem unnecessarily difficult if not impossible to comprehend. If you need to fill in any of these gaps, chapter 6, "Native Data Types and Operators," covers the first requirement, chapter 14, "Basic Class Concepts," covers the second requirement, and the copy constructor and assignment operator are covered in detail in chapter 17, "Constructors: Copy and Assignment." I would suggest you read and understand these topics before venturing further.

Note

If you are having any problems understanding some of the concepts presented in this book, feel free to contact me on CompuServe at 70353,2711.

What Data Types Can Be Used?

As I will demonstrate, all of the built-in data types and just about any other contrivance you or I may think of can end up being a template parameter. Because the template specifier is used in conjunction with both classes and functions, I intentionally have not specified the syntax of the idiom yet.

What we know so far is that parameterized types enable software developers to implement an algorithm independently of the data type. Further, as I have just stated, the type of data supplied in the template argument is flexible. C++ is not a rigid language. It is a strongly typed language, but implementations of individual language features allow a lot of room for creativity and ingenuity.

Copy and Assignment

A problem area for generic functions is using them for data types that do not have proper type assignment or copy functions. Most of the native data types are assignable automatically, but aggregate types defined by users must have the right "kind" of copy and assignment defined for them; otherwise, a template sort, for example, may introduce errors into your programs.

Chapter 17 explains the kinds of problems improperly defined assignment operators and copy constructors can introduce. Even if the generic class or function is correct, if the data type is poorly defined, you will have problems.

Implementation Tricks

C++ does not require you ever to write or use parameterized types. In fact, having read thousands of lines of code, I still rarely come across tons of templates. The reason for this is lack of training, and not the value or lack of it in the template idiom. As universities turn out more and more computer science graduates trained in C++ (and as the professors learn it), and as C++ software developers make it into middle management positions, you'll see this language feature used more frequently.

A great way to learn how to implement and write templates is to write functions and classes in the usual way. That is, to implement an algorithm based on a particular data type and smooth out all of the bugs first. As your confidence in the robustness of a particular implementation grows, you will be less likely to second-guess the algorithm and will work on understanding the template idiom.

Those functions or classes that you identify as being data-independent are good candidates for experimentation. Convert the definition to a template and test the template using the original data type. Your experience and knowledge of that particular solution should be great enough that you can identify those inconsistencies that might point to a possible error. If good fortune shines on you and the code fragment works as usual, congratulations.

Don't Reinvent the Wheel: Check the STL Definitions First

Chapter 18, "Using Container Classes" introduced the new STL (*Standard Template Library*). Unless you are in a learning environment, don't reinvent the wheel. Check the STL tools first for existing template definitions before venturing forth and writing a new one. I remind you of this not because I don't think you can do it, but for the simple reason that library tools are usually developed and tested by some of the best programmers in the world. The likelihood is that the templates in the STL have been written, tested, debugged, and refined many times before you ever see them. Software development is time-consuming and expensive; take your savings wherever you find them.

Comparing Templates to Other Idioms

The template specification is not an alternative to other language features. The relationship is complimentary. There are many language features to help you eke the most out of your programming hour. To recap, I will remind you of those we have seen so far and those yet to come. Table 19.1 lists many of the different techniques you can employ; they are directly supported by the Borland C++ implementation.

III

Advanced Programming

Table 19.1 Time-Saving Language Features	
Technique	**Use It When**
Default Arguments	Just the value of an argument differs.
Function Overloading	The function is semantically similar (i.e., printing), but the data type differs.
Templates	This feature is flexible enough to provide for when only the data type differs, the implementation differs, or both.
Polymorphism	In Chapter 20, "Inheritance and Polymorphism" you will see that this aspect of C++ provides run-time type flexibility.

Understanding Generic Functions

The template specification applies to both functions and classes. Here we'll focus on the syntax and implementation of generic functions. The parameterized type can be either a class or a built-in data type. The syntax of a template function is like regular functions, except for the template prefix and the use of the parameterized argument.

I will begin by defining a function that swaps two arguments. (A swapping function is commonly employed in a data-ordering algorithm.) Because the function is small, I will use the `inline` specifier and will begin by making the function swap two integers, to get the implementation right.

```
inline void Swap( int& a, int& b ) { int t = a; a = b; b = t; }
```

Note that the function accepted two arguments by reference. This means that the function is exchanging the actual arguments and not copies (see Chapter 17). As you can see, the implementation of a swapping function is easy enough.

Now find the data in the implementation that is the focus of the function, and make that your parameterized argument. In this case, it is the integers passed by reference. The syntax of a template function is

```
template <class T>
[specifier] return_type function_name( [args_list ] );
```

thus our swapping function becomes

```
template <class T>
inline void Swap( T& a, T& b ){ T t = a; a = b; b = t; }
```

The parameter type is placed between < > and after the keyword `template`. (The parameter information is conventionally placed on the preceding line, but doesn't have to be.) To complete the definition of the template function `Swap`, replace all occurrences of the `int` type (which will change with the parameter type) with the parametric name, `T`. Again I use `T` (as in *T*emplate) as a convention, but you may use any name you like.

The template feature can best be used when the distinction between a particular implementation is the data. In our example, the data type was the distinctive factor.

Declaring a Template Function Instance

You can explicitly or implicitly declare an instance of the template function. Applying this idea to the Swap function, an implicit declaration of the template function would be to call the function with the Swap function like any other function. The compiler would derive the parameter type from the argument types. Thus

```
char * msg1 = "Cootchie Cootchie Coo";
char * msg2 = "Look out we're going to crash!";
Swap( msg1, msg2 );
```

would cause a template function with char* as the parameter type. The result is the same whether you use an implicit declaration or an explicit declaration the parameter type, like

```
Swap<char*>( msg1, msg2 );
```

Listing 19.1 provides you with an opportunity to experiment with a simple template function. The larger or more complex the implementation, obviously the greater the savings. Here the function is relatively small, but you still only have to write the one function.

Listing 19.1   Swap.cpp—Demonstrates a Simple Template Function Commonly Required for Sorting Algorithms

```
// SWAP.CPP- Demonstrates Swap Template function.
#include <iostream.h>
template <class T>
inline void Swap( T& a, T& b )
{ T t = a; a = b; b = t; }
void main()
{
    char * msg1 = "Cootchie Cootchie Coo";
    char * msg2 = "Look out we're going to crash!";
    // Implicit template function declaration
    Swap( msg1, msg2 );
    cout << "msg1: " << msg1 << endl;
    cout << "msg2: " << msg2 << endl;
    int c = 5, d = 6;
    // Explicit template function declaration
    Swap<int>( c, d );
    cout << "c: " << c << " d: " << d << endl;
}
```

It is important that you can choose to make the distinction between an implicit and an explicit declaration of the template instance. The reason is that by way of an explicit declaration you can create an alias for a template function or class if the syntax appears too confusing.

Creating a Synonym

On occasion, a particular template class or function may appear too confusing or syntactically unattractive. (Suppose, for example, some members of your programming team are syntactically challenged.) If you want to simplify the syntax of a template declaration, create an alias (or synonym) for the template function.

Again, using our Swap function as an example, I could create an alias for a floating-point version of the function

```
typedef Swap<float> FSwap;
```

After the typedef, where I might have used

```
float w = 1.0, x = 3.45;
Swap<float>( w, x );
```

I could replace the code with

```
FSwap( w, x );
```

hiding the aliasing declaration in a header file or among other declarations. Sometimes this technique makes the code appear to be simpler than it otherwise would be.

Another reason for creating a synonym is if the implementation details of a particular type can be hidden from the users of the code. In the last section of this chapter we talk about mapping template classes to hardware. It may be unnecessary to reveal the address or port of the resource to other programmers who may be using the class.

Other Considerations

Template functions require some additional considerations. When you use a particular template function with a data type for the first time, examine the function and ascertain whether or not the implementation is valid for that data type. Some types may have resources, such as memory, associated with them, and you may introduce errors into your programs if the operations aren't performed carefully.

Also exercise some consideration when the template function performs operations like assignment (=), tests for equivalence (==), or other comparative tests. Ask the questions, "Does the operation make sense?" and "Is it testing or assigning the right values?"

For example, using Swap with the char* data type, it is helpful to know that you are changing the address contained in the pointers. This is a shallow copy. Make sure, if you mean to test for equivalence of data values, for example, that you are *not* testing address equivalency. This is especially true for aggregate types. User-defined types do not automatically have such testing capability built in.

Defining Specific Implementations

The implementation of a specific template function can be modified to suit the needs of a particular data type. Therefore, if a particular type of data is not supported by your general implementation, then you can write a specific version for that data type.

Consider a function that tests whether the left argument is the greater of two arguments. Implement an inline template function called `IsGreater()`, as a function that takes a reference to two arguments and uses the comparison `operator>` to test the arguments:

```
// Prefix test functions with verbs
template <class T>
inline int IsGreater( T& a, T& b ){ return a > b ? 1 : 0; }
```

Unfortunately, if you attempt to test two null-terminated strings with this algorithm, the string with the greater memory address will be perceived as the greater string.

To provide a correct algorithm for ASCIIZ strings, I will implement a `char*` specific version of the function using the `strcmp` function. This function has the peculiarity that if the left string is greater than the right, a number greater than 0 is returned. Here is the ASCIIZ-specific version:

```
#include <string.h>            // Contains the declaration for strcmp (string
                               // compare)
// inline int IsGreater( char* a, char* b ) works too!
inline int IsGreater<char*>( char* & a, char* & b )
{ return strcmp(a, b) > 0 ? 1 : 0 ; }
```

From chapter 15, "Function Overloading," you know that C++ allows function overloading. Function overloading applies to template functions, too. The excerpt from our example program demonstrates that we can write specific implementations for those types that won't work with the general version. Listing 19.2 contains a complete listing that you can use to test templates and overloading templates

Listing 19.2   Igreat.cpp—Overload Template Functions for Data that Requires Special Handling

```
 1:  // IGREAT.CPP - Template overloading
 2:  #include <string.h>
 3:  #include <iostream.h>
 4:  // Remove the inline specification to trace into the functions.
 5:  template <class T>
 6:  inline int IsGreater(T &a, T& b)
 7:  { return a > b ? 1 : 0; }
 8:  // A specific version for char* (ASCIIZ) strings
 9:  inline int IsGreater( char* a, char* b)
10: { return strcmp( a, b ) > 0 ? 1 : 0; }
11: void main()
12: {
13:     char *str1 = "STRING1";
14:     char *str2 = "STRING2";
15:     int a = 1, b = 2;
16:     cout << "IsGreater( 1, 2 ) " << IsGreater( a, b ) << endl;
17:     cout << "IsGreater( str2, str1 ) " << IsGreater( str2, str1 ) <<
        ➥endl;
18: }
```

III

Advanced Programming

The template function beginning on line 5 and the overloaded version for char*s on line 9 illustrate that both generic and specific type functions can coexist in the same namespace. (Notice I used the simpler version for the function declaration beginning on line 9.) Even though templates facilitate writing generic functions, the correctly working implementation must be provided for each type used.

Using Generic-Sorting Algorithms

Often the more complex the algorithm, the more difficult and error-prone its implementation. Compression algorithms for bitmaps, data structure traversal algorithms, and sorting algorithms fall easily into this category.

In this section, I have provided a few implementations of some common sorting algorithms that you may plug and play into your programs if you like. The three sorts demonstrate an easy-to-implement sort to a fast sort for random data. The sorts are: the bubble sort, the selection sort, and the quick sort. They are all implemented as templates. I have included the declarations in header files, the code in .cpp files, along with some variations on swapping functions, and a couple of scaffolds that demonstrate how to use the sorts.

> **Note**
>
> Amazingly enough the bubble sort is a really simple sort that has as good or better performance than many others on data sets of about 1,000.
>
> As a refresher, for data sets of around 100 elements, the bubble sort is as good as any. For sets up to 1,000 elements, the selection sort, a modified bubble sort, has top-notch performance. One of the fastest sorts is the quick sort, which uses a divide and conquer method. The performance of a quick sort partially depends on the randomness of the data set; the quick sort performs poorly for data sets that are partially sorted.

Template Bubble Sort

The bubble sort gets its name because it swaps at every point in the data set in which a comparison test passes. In this manner the data bubbles its way to the top. The sort is surprisingly spunky for relatively small data sets. The theory referred to as *order of magnitude* is a function that describes the relative sort time of different algorithms. The bubble sort has an order of magnitude of n-squared (written as $O(N^2)$). For larger data sets, the sort time increases exponentially, resulting in extremely poor performance. Thus, the bad rap. However, for data sets less than 1,000, it does pretty well.

Interestingly enough, the order of magnitude also suggests the implementation of the algorithm—a nested for loop works—but now we're getting into a little too much theory. Using integers as our catalyst, sorting an array of integers looks something like this:

```
int a[] = { 10, 9, 8, 7, 6, 5, 4, 3, 2, 1};
const unsigned int MAX = sizeof( a ) / sizeof( a[0] );
for( int j = 0; j < MAX - 1; j ++ )
    for( int k = j + 1; k < MAX; k++ )
        if( a[j] > a[k] ) Swap( a[j], a[k] );
```

It is short and sweet and, as can you see, easy to implement. (The Swap function comes in handy, too.) Using the integer version of the sort, we can modify it to get the template version by ascertaining which element points to the candidate parameter. The answer is the data type of the array. There is another hitch here, too; we must consider that the comparison operator> may not work for every data type. The solution is to document the requirement of the data type, having an operator> function defined for it, or we need to find an alternative way to compare the data. The code fragment below demonstrates both an example of documenting the operator> requirement and an alternative way to overcome the necessity of the function, by implementing an IsGreater function.

```
#define SIZEOF( array ) sizeof( array ) / sizeof( array[0] )
template <class T>
void Swap( T& a, T& b ) { T t = a; a = b; b = a; }
template <class T>
inline int IsGreater( T & a, T& b ) { return a > b : 1 : 0; }
inline int IsGreater( char* a, char * b ){ return strcmp( a, b ) > 0 : 1 :
➥0; }
// If you want you could change the operator> test to IsGreater.
// If you use operator> ensure that there is one defined for user-defined
// types too.
template <class T>
void GumSort( T data[] )
{
    // Must call a macro because we are using a constant - value must be
    // known at compile time
    const unsigned int MAX = SIZEOF( t );
    for( int j = 0; j < MAX - 1; j++ )
        for( int k = 0; k < MAX; k++ )
            if( data[j] > data[k] ) Swap( data[j], data[k] );
}
```

Template Selection Sort

The big-O for the selection sort is the same as the bubble sort. The reason this sort has a slightly better performance is that the swap is made only at the ideal location and only once per iteration. You are still comparing n-squared elements, but you are swapping only less than or equal to n-times.

The previous section showed only the implementation of the sort listing. This section shows the entire listing of the header files and the module file containing the test scaffold, with some timing functions in there for fun.

Because the magnitude of the sort is the same, the implementation is similar—a nested for loop. The difference is that we record the optimal swap location and perform the swap at the end. Listing 19.3 shows the header file containing the different function declarations.

Listing 19.3 sort.h—A Header File Containing the Declaration of Some Useful Functions for Sorting

```
 1:  // SORTS.H - Some generic sorting functions.
 2:  #ifndef __SORTS_H
 3:  #define __SORTS_H
 4:  #include <string.h>
 5:  #define SIZEOF( array ) sizeof( array ) / sizeof( array[0])
 6:  template <class T>
 7:  inline void Swap( T& a, T& b ){ T t = a; a = b; b = t; }
 8:  template <class T>
 9:  inline int IsGreater( T & a, T & b ){ return a > b ? 1:0; }
10:  // Overloaded test for char*s
11:  inline int IsGreater( char* a, char* b )
12:  { return strcmp( a, b ) > 0 ? 1 : 0; }
13:  template <class T>
14:  void GumSort( T data[], unsigned long elem );
15:  template <class T>
16:  void SelectionSort( T data[], unsigned long elem );
17:  // This booger may blow the stack if the data set is huge.
18:  // template <class T>
19:  // void RecursiveQuickSort(T data[], unsigned long lo, unsigned long hi );
20:  #endif
```

Notice that on lines 14 and 16, I modified the function declarations (from the prior section) to take an unsigned long argument, which is used to pass the number of elements in the array. The reason for this is simple. When I implemented the code, I had not considered how my SIZEOF macro might handle ASCII strings. It doesn't calculate the size correctly. (This illustrates the point that there is a difference between theory and practice.)

As you will see in Lising 19.4, I left out the RecursiveQuickSort function (it is shown in the next section), I chose to use the IsGreater template function, and I implemented a really simple TIMER class within the scaffold.

Listing 19.4 Sort.cpp—The Implementation of the Sorting Functions Declared in Listing 19.3 (sort.h)

```
 1:  // SORTS.CPP - Contains the definitions and some test scaffolds
 2:  #include "sorts.h"
 3:  template <class T>
 4:  void GumSort( T data[], unsigned long elem )
 5:  {
 6:     for(unsigned long j=0; j < elem - 1; j++ )
 7:         for( unsigned long k=j+1; k < elem; k++ )
 8:             if(IsGreater( data[j], data[k] ) )
 9:                 Swap( data[j], data[k] );
10:  }
11:  template <class T>
12:  void SelectionSort( T data[], unsigned long elem )
13:  {
14:      unsigned long swapAt;
```

```
15:        for( unsigned long j=0; j<elem-1; j++)
16:        {
17:            swapAt = j;
18:            for( unsigned long k=j+1; k<elem; k++ )
19:                if(IsGreater( data[swapAt], data[k] ))
20:                    swapAt = k;         // Store the swap point
21:
22:            Swap( data[j], data[swapAt] );     // Swap after all have been /
                                                   // checked
23:        }
24: }
25: #ifdef SORTS_SCAFFOLD
26: #include <iostream.h>
27: #include <dos.h>
28: #include <stdio.h>
29: class TIMER : public time
30: {
31: public:
32:        TIMER(){ gettime( this ); }
33:        #pragma warn -inl
34:        friend ostream& operator<<( ostream& os, TIMER& t )
35:        {
36:            static char buf[9];
37:            sprintf( buf, "%0.2d:%0.2d:%0.2d",
38:                t.ti_hour, t.ti_min, t.ti_sec );
39:            return os << buf;
40:        }
41: };
42: void main()
43: {
44:        int d[100];
45:        for( int j = 99; j >= 0; j--)
46:            d[j] = j;
47:        TIMER start;
48:        GumSort( d, SIZEOF( d ) );
49:        TIMER stop;
50:        cout << "start - "<< start << endl
51:            << "stop - "<< stop << endl;
52:        for( int j = 0; j<100; j++)
53:            cout << d[j] << ", ";
54:        char * words[] = { "Winkie", "Willy" , "Wee" };
55:        SelectionSort( words, 3 );
56:        cout << endl << words[0] << endl
57:            << words[1] << endl
58:            << words[2] << endl;
59: }
60: #endif
```

This ditty is full of goodies. Lines 4 through 24 define the template sort functions discussed so far. Lines 25 to 60 contain the scaffold.

The scaffold contains a simplified TIMER class (lines 29 to 41). This class publicly inherits from the time struct (chapter 20), which enables TIMER to work nicely with library functions, like `gettime`, which require a time struct. The `TIMER` class gets the system time when an object is instantiated and provides a formatted output function, an overloaded `operator<<` function (see chapters 13 and 16).

Lines 42 to 59 provide a main function that *is* the scaffold. It demonstrates sample uses of the different sorts.

The focus of this section, the selection sort, is defined between lines 11 and 24. As you may have noticed, it is similar to the bubble sort (`GumSort`) except that the current swap position (`swapAt`) is updated and used in the comparison. The swap is deferred until line 22 when the inner `for` loop has examined all possibilities.

A Recursive Template Quick Sort

The quick sort is a speed demon for large random data sets. The order of magnitude is $O(\log_2 n)m$, which means for even large n (number of elements) the speed degrades slowly. There is a minor drawback to this sort. If the data set is partially sorted, the quick sort degrades to an $O(n^2)$. The reason is that the quick sort splits the data by halves. In an ordered set, the spacing between the low and high indexes is one.

Most of the time the quick sort is perfect for data sets approaching a thousand or more elements. If you are not sure whether a quick sort is suitable, try a random sampling of data and count the number of swaps. If the swap count is low, you may want to use another sort.

Note

This is not an algorithms book. There are many good books on the subject of data management and sorting. And there are arguably sorts better suited than these for many different data sets. If you find yourself in difficulties, get online or try a book like *Numerical Recipes in C* (Cambridge University Press, 1992).

Here are the two functions that comprise the quick sort. The partitioning function (in the following code fragment) ensures that the median index value is in its sorted position, and that all values below the median index are less than those above.

```
1:   template <class T>
2:   unsigned long Partition( T data[], unsigned long left, unsigned long
     ↪right )
3:   {
4:       unsigned long j, k;
5:       T v = data[right];              // Store the right element
6:       j = left - 1;
7:       k = right;
8:       do{
9:           while(data[++j] < v )       ;
10:          while( data[--k] > v )        ;
11:          if( j >= k ) break;
12:          Swap(data[j], data[k]);
13:       }while(1);
```

```
14:      Swap(data[j], data[right] );
15:      return j;
16: }
```

The `RecursiveQuickSort` function calls the `partition` function in the preceding code, which returns the median index, and then calls itself recursively for the relative lower and upper halves:

```
1:   // QuickSort
2:   template <class T>
3:   void RecursiveQuickSort( T data[], unsigned long left, unsigned long
     ➥right)
4:   {
5:      unsigned long j;
6:      if( right > left )
7:      {
8:            j = Partition(data, left, right );
9:            RecursiveQuickSort(data, left, j-1);
10:            RecursiveQuickSort(data, j+1, right );
11:      }
12: }
```

The template quick sort is modeled after the implementation in Robert Sedgewick's, *Algorithms in C++* (Addison-Wesley, 1992: pages 115–119). The template variation is my own, and in addition, I have modified the code using an unsigned index, which acts as a 0-value sentinel in line 10 of the `Partition` function.

This section demonstrates how advanced algorithms can be converted to generic implementations. The purpose of this chapter is to focus on the use of the template idiom, not on algorithms in general.

Exploring Generic Classes

Template classes afford the programmer the same opportunity to entertain a data-independent algorithm on a large scale. Whereas the template function affords us an opportunity for maximizing code reuse on a function-by-function basis, the class idiom does so on a much larger scale.

> **Tip**
>
> The term *generic* used throughout this text is something I chose to use because I like the imagery better. In discourse the keyword `template` is the preferred terminology. The term generic (or parameterized), as in generic class or parameterized class, is not wrong, simply outmoded.

I will provide several examples throughout this section, as opposed to trying to establish a definition of the general syntax. I will point out the usage of the idiom throughout the examples.

Template Vector Class

A template vector is a great class to have in your repertoire. Commonly referred to as an array, the vector class can be used as a base class for several interesting data structures, including queues, stacks, and lists. In addition, arrays are common enough so that they will be comparatively easy to follow.

Defining an array with a native data type is straightforward. Write the definition, stating the type, variable name, and the size between the array operator [ ]. Thus

```
int intArray[10];
```

defines an integer array. As shown in earlier chapters, arrays can be left-hand or right-hand arguments in a statement. You will want to provide similar functionality in your vector class.

Simply by writing an integer vector as a class, we can add bounds checking to the integer arrays in general. Using the same technique as before, I will define the class with a simple data type and then make the parameterized substitution (to show you how you can do it).

```
class INT_VECTOR
{
public:
      INT_VECTOR( unsigned long sz = 10 ) : size(sz), data( new int[sz + 1] ){};
      virtual ~INT_VECTOR(){ delete [] data; }
      int& operator[]( unsigned long index j )
      { return j < size ? data[j] : data[sz] /* dummy value */; }
private:
      unsigned int size;
      int * data;
      // Block copy and assignment - copying data structures is expensive
      INT_VECTOR( const INT_VECTOR&);
      INT_VECTOR& operator=(const INT_VECTOR&);
};
```

Declaring an INT_VECTOR is accomplished through the constructor. From that point on, it works much like any other array.

```
INT_VECTOR v( 100 );
v[0] = 3;
//...
int t = v[0];
```

Having implemented the integer vector, converting it to a template class is accomplished by establishing which items can be easily parameterized.

Because we are working in a 32-bit operating system, we can have much larger static objects. For this reason, I chose to parameterize both the data type, which is the common practice, and the size of the internal representation. In doing so, I have reduced the cost of instantiating vector objects. (Memory allocation and de-allocation are expensive operations.) The resultant class is as follows:

```
template <class T, unsigned long SIZE>
class VECTOR
{
public:
    // Constructor but no destructor is required
    VECTOR(){};
    T& operator[]( unsigned long j )
    { return j < SIZE ? data[j] : data[SIZE] /* can be used to store a
    ➥dummy value */ }
private:
    T data[SIZE + 1];
    // Can block copies too!
};
```

Implementing instances of this vector using any data type is just as easy as the INT_VECTOR. As with template functions, you can implement specific versions of the template VECTOR class, or any template class, for data types that may require special attention.

Notice that fewer operations are needed to instantiate objects of this type. Here is a sample definition of an integer vector having the same boundaries as the INT_VECTOR example:

```
VECTOR<int, 100> iv;
for( unsigned long j=0; j < 100; j++ )
    iv[j] = j;
```

Here are some other example types:

```
VECTOR<char*, 50> sv;
sv[0] = "This might lead to errors because assignment for char* copies the
➥value of the pointer.";
```

By providing a default value for the parameterized size of the vector class

```
template <class T, unsigned long SIZE = 100>
```

you can use the default value for the class and only specify the class type for the first parameter, or you can specify both arguments. Default values for parameterized types work much like default argument values for functions. The entire listing (plus scaffold) can be found in vector.h and Vector.cpp. (I intentionally modified the class so that the member functions were not inlined, thus demonstrating the "real" notation.)

Template Stack Class

Implementing a *LIFO (Last-In First-Out)* stack based on the template vector in the last example is relatively straightforward. A stack can be implemented with either pointers or an array; there are benefits and disadvantages to either method. Generally an array is easier to sort, and accessing data is quick because you can use an index, whereas an implementation using pointers makes it easier to maintain a sorted data structure and to add and remove elements.

Stacks are useful as tracking devices for an ordered series of events. Just as the system stack is used to store register states prior to a function call, a user-defined stack can be used to store the state of some values by pushing elements onto the stack, and to restore some states by popping elements from the stack. The stack grows when elements are pushed onto the stack and shrinks as elements are popped.

Listing 19.5 is a template implementation of a stack derived (see chapter 20, "Inheritance and Polymorphism") from the vector class of the last section.

Listing 19.5   vector.h—The Class Declaration of a Template Vector (or Array) Class

```
1:  // VECTOR.H - Defines a template vector (or array) class.
2:  #ifndef __VECTOR_H
3:  #define __VECTOR_H
4:  template <class T, unsigned long SIZE = 100>
5:  class VECTOR
6:  {
7:  public:
8:     // Constructor
9:     VECTOR();
10:      T& operator[]( unsigned long j );
11: private:
12:      T data[SIZE +1];
13: };
14: // I am disappointed that you still need to do this!
15: // The typedef dummyVector is never used; it is defined here
16: // to ensure that an instance of the proper parametric types is defined.
17: typedef VECTOR<int, 10> dummyVector;
18: #endif
```

Note

You have to go to the fringes of the language to find evidence of a kludge, but alas, one exists. Combining template classes and inheritance seems to present a problem. (Borland is not the only C++ company with this problem. It exists in several C++ implementations supporting both idioms.)

The problem arises when you try to inherit from a template class. The compiler doesn't seem to be able to create base class portion. The solution: use a typedef after the base class declaration, as I did on line 17 of the vector.h file. This causes the compiler to generate that version of the parameterized class.

Although the solution is easy enough if you know it, it is distressingly frustrating if you do not. Unfortunately, it looks as though you will need to do this for every variation. (Notice I named the synonym dummyVector. I don't use the alias; it is even more restrictive if you do.)

Listing 19.6   stack.h—Used Single Inheritance to Inherit the *VECTOR* Template Class, which Simplifies the Creation of a *STACK* Class

```
1:  // STACK.H - A template definition of a stack derived from a vector
2:  #ifndef __STACK_H
3:  #define __STACK_H
4:  #include <stdio.h>
5:  #include "vector.h"
6:  template <class T, unsigned long SIZE = 100>
7:  class STACK : public VECTOR<T, SIZE>
8:  {
9:  public:
10:     STACK() : top(0){};
11:     void Push( T elem )
12:     { if( top < SIZE )
13:             operator[]( top++ ) = elem;
14:         else
15:             perror( "Stack Overflow" );
16:     }
17:     T Pop()
18:     {
19:         if( top > 0  )
20:             return operator[]( --top );
21:         perror("Stack Underflow");
22:         return operator[]( SIZE );
23:     }
24: private:
25:     unsigned long top;
26:     STACK(const STACK&);
27:     STACK& operator=(const STACK&);
28: };
29: #endif
```

The stack.h header listed above derives the stack class in terms of a vector class. Line 7 is the syntax of public inheritance (an *IsA* relationship—the topic is discussed in chapter 20). Semantically the operations for a stack are Push and Pop, just like the assembler commands of the same name. These member functions are defined inline. Lines 13 and 20 demonstrate how base class member functions may be invoked, in this case used as accessor functions, to access the data of the base class.

Lines 26 and 27 make up a technique you can use to block the copying of objects. By declaring the copy constructor and assignment as private and not defining them, no copies are allowed. This is sometimes applied when duplicates are not desired or a performance penalty may result.

The implementation would probably prosper by including an IsEmpty algorithm. The implementation of this algorithm is left as an exercise. (*Hint:* Testing the value of top provides the desired result.)

III

Advanced Programming

> **Tip**
>
> Adding the *inline* specifier to the Push and Pop member functions would be redundant. If the functions are defined within the class definition, they are implicitly inlined. For clarity you may add the specifier if you desire.

In Listing 19.7, the module file is needed only to provide a scaffold (main function for testing the stack). Line 9 defines an integer stack capable of holding five elements. I picked numbers at random, pushing and popping the stack to test it. I Intentionally popped the stack one too many times to test the error-handling mechanism. The output from the scaffold should print the numbers in reverse order.

Listing 19.7   Stack.cpp—This Module Simply Provides a Console Mode Test Program for the Stack

```
 1:  // STACK.CPP - Contains a scaffold only. You do not need this
 2:  // to use the template STACK class.
 3:  #ifdef STACK_SCAFFOLD
 4:  #include <iostream.h>
 5:  #include "stack.h"
 6:  #define DebugPrint( arg ) cout << #arg << " " << arg << endl
 7:  void main()
 8:  {
 9:      STACK<int, 10> stk;
10:      stk.Push( 5 );
11:      stk.Push( 3 );
12:      DebugPrint( stk.Pop() );
13:      stk.Push( 10 );
14:      stk.Push( -13 );
15:      DebugPrint( stk.Pop() );
16:      DebugPrint( stk.Pop() );
17:      DebugPrint( stk.Pop() );
18:      DebugPrint( stk.Pop() );
19:  }
20:  #endif
```

From Here...

Template classes provide one of the most powerful features for writing data-independent implementations. In chapter 4, I demonstrated a C-technique that may have been used to demonstrate the feasibility of parametric data types. The template idiom has been in the language for several years now.

As I mention throughout the book and recap in this chapter, there are three or four specific language features that provide a breadth of design choices found in no other language. Templates seem to find themselves near the end of many books. For the most part, this is necessitated by a need for you to understand several other aspects of C++ programming.

Designing template functions and classes is not especially hard but, like other design choices, it requires consideration, effort, and experimentation. Learn how to use and practice using templates just as soon as you can find the time.

- To learn about the preprocessor's current role in building applications, see chapter 4, "The Preprocessor."

- To learn more about native data types as functions, refer to chapter 6, "Native Data Types and Operators."

- For an introduction to classes as well as a comparison between classes and structs, see chapter 14, "Basic Class Concepts."

- For an explanation of Borland's two new container class libraries, Borland International Data Structures (BIDS) and the Standard Template Library (STL), see chapter 18, "Using Container Classes."

Part IV

Using New C++ Features

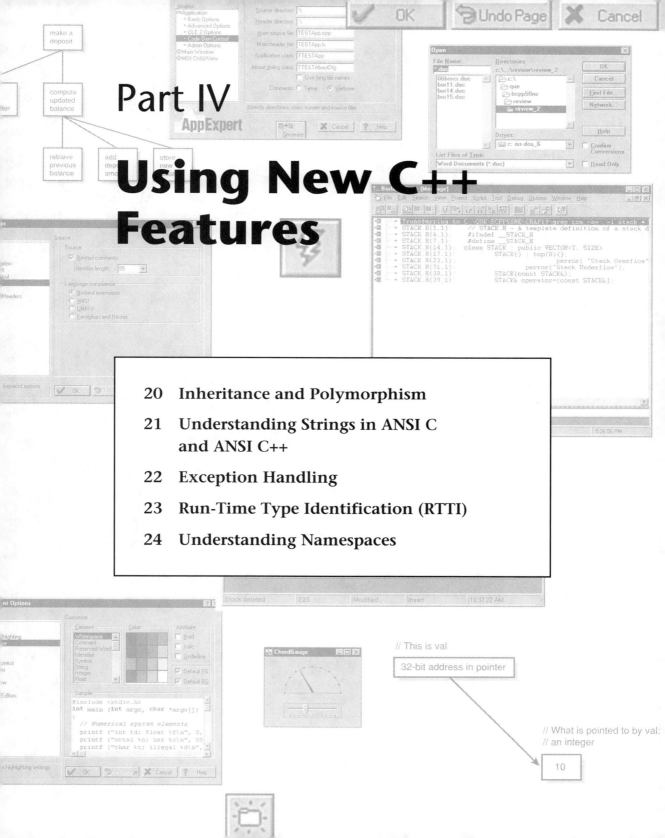

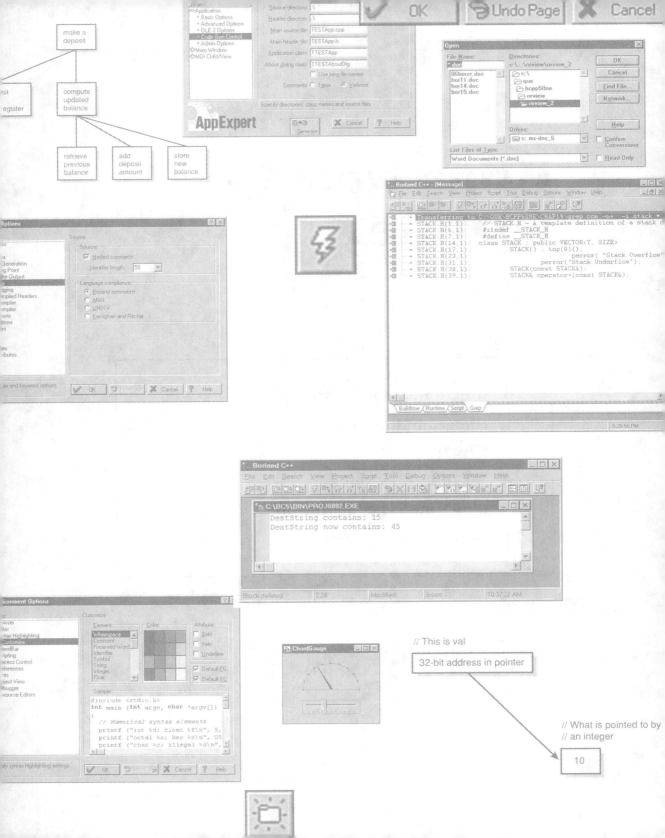

CHAPTER 20

Inheritance and Polymorphism

In chapter 3, "Object-Oriented Analysis and Design," we discussed several of the underlying design issues that together make up the foundation for object-oriented programming in C++ and other languages. One of the most important concepts we discussed was that of "hierarchy"—simply put, a manner of ordering abstract classes so that the relationships among and between classes of objects become more apparent, simplifying our understanding and implementation of solutions in a problem domain.

If you missed or skipped chapter 3, that last sentence may have gone right over your head. Don't worry—we'll review the concept of hierarchy again in this chapter, as well as the two starring concepts of this chapter—inheritance and polymorphism. In addition, we will discuss

- The role of inheritance in application frameworks such as Borland's Object Window Library
- How to exploit inheritance to derive your own classes quickly and efficiently from existing source code
- What makes polymorphism so special and how we incorporate it into C++ code

Understanding Hierarchy, Inheritance, and Polymorphism

The majority of you are most likely on familiar terms with the concept of hierarchy; it's something we deal with—and in—on a daily basis. If you happen to be an employee in a large corporation, you are probably part of a hierarchy that branches out into an almost unmanageable tree of presidents, vice-presidents, departments, managers and every imaginable variation on employee—from the janitorial staff to the sales force to accountants to human resource personnel, and so on. If you're a student, you're probably more familiar with academic departments, majors, graduate students, undergraduate students, graduation classes, etc. If you don't work and you're not in school, you still can't escape hierarchy—you are most likely in a family, be it a mother, father, husband, wife, child, brother, sister, grandparent, what have you. The point is: We all play a part in at least one hierarchy; our roles—who we are, what we are—are all defined to some extent by where we fit into a hierarchy.

Let's consider four employees in an engineering firm for a moment: a janitor, an engineer, an engineering department manager and a vice-president of operations. If I asked you to sketch the approximate hierarchy of these four individuals within the engineering firm, you would probably produce a diagram similar to the one in figure 20.1.

Fig. 20.1

A preliminary hierarchy of four employees within an engineering firm.

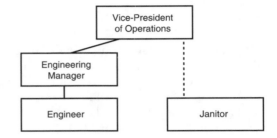

You would surely recognize that an engineer reports to the engineering department manager and the manager in turn reports to the vice-president of operations. As the janitor doesn't report to the engineering department manager, he or she would probably exist underneath the vice-president in a line of management that is not given in this example. This is one type of hierarchy—it is the organization chart of management within some companies; to climb the corporate ladder, you would start at the bottom and work your way up to the top.

However, in object-oriented programming we're interested in a different hierarchical structure. Let's now consider what shared roles exist among these four individuals and which roles distinguish one individual from another

First of all, what role do all four individuals share within the engineering firm? We would all certainly agree that each of these four individuals is considered an employee of the engineering firm. Each receives compensation for work performed on behalf of the company. There may be other shared roles as well—all four individuals may belong to a certain division of the firm; but for the purposes of this example we are most interested in the role of employee.

If we next consider the engineer and the janitor, both employees, what are some things that might separate the engineer from the janitor, aside from the fact that they may report to different managers? Well, for one thing, the engineer may be a salaried employee as opposed to an hourly employee. If we draw a diagram of the roles or relationships mentioned thus far, it resembles figure 20.2.

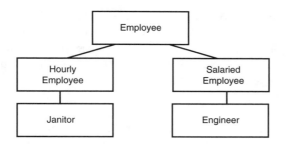

Fig. 20.2

A hierarchy of roles within the engineering firm.

I think you can see where we're headed now. Let's try to place our engineering manager and vice-president into the diagram. We would concur that the engineering manager, in the majority of instances, is a salaried employee; whether or not the engineering manager is also a working engineer within the company would differ from company to company. Let's assume that he or she still holds some engineering responsibilities within the company, but, in addition, has the added responsibilities of a manager within the firm—more of a working manager or team leader. Let's assume, on the other hand, that our vice-president of operations has solely managerial responsibilities within the company. Our resulting hierarchy is shown in figure 20.3.

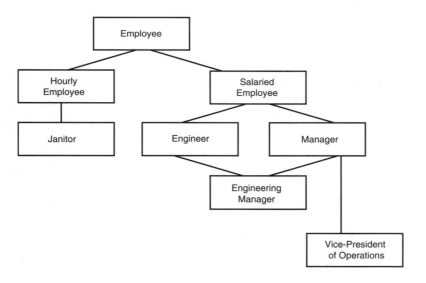

Fig. 20.3

The completed hierarchy of roles and relationships within the engineering firm.

Having isolated some of the hierarchical roles and relationships within the engineering firm, we can understand a great deal about each individual with the aid of this hierarchy. For instance, if employees have a social security number and a person to contact in case of emergency, then this applies to all four individuals—the janitor, the engineer, the engineering manager and the vice-president of operations. Likewise, if a salaried employee is subject to a salary range based on merit, then the engineer, the manager and the vice-president all have some set salary range. In a sense, we see that individuals within the engineering firm "inherit" certain characteristics and roles based on their position within the hierarchy, which leads us to our next topic, the concept of inheritance in object-oriented programming.

Inheritance

You might be asking yourself how all this talk of hierarchy contributes to programming in C++. Let's consider for a moment that we are modeling a portion of our previous hierarchy—namely the salaried employee branch—with C++ classes (say we're developing a personnel system). If, as we said, each employee within the engineering firm has a social security number, we might declare an Employee class as follows:

```
class Employee
{
public:
      Employee();
      virtual ~Employee();

      void SetSocialSecurityNumber(long);
      long GetSocialSecurityNumber();

private:
      long socialSecurityNumber;
};
```

which, of course, has a constructor and a destructor, along with two member functions for accessing the private data item socialSecurityNumber: SetSocialSecurityNumber and GetSocialSecurityNumber. Admittedly, a social security number is not much on which to build a class, but it will do for the purposes of this example.

Now consider the task of creating a class named SalariedEmployee—which includes a social security number in addition to an upper and lower salary range—without inheriting any information or functionality from class Employee. Such a task forces the programmer to reinvent the wheel—the Employee class and the SalariedEmployee class would both need to include a data item named socialSecurityNumber, along with some member functions to access that data if it remains private. Such duplication of development efforts is wasteful, both in terms of time and space, not to mention counterintuitive, given the hierarchy of the engineering firm that we established earlier.

Inheritance allows us to take advantage of existing logical relationships between classes of objects to share structure and behavior among our C++ classes. In the case of the class SalariedEmployee, we can inherit the social security number structure and member function behavior by deriving a new class from the existing base class,

Employee:

```
class SalariedEmployee : public Employee
{
public:
    SalariedEmployee();
    virtual ~SalariedEmployee();

    void SetLowerSalaryRange(float);
    float GetLowerSalaryRange();
    void SetUpperSalaryRange(float);
    float GetUpperSalaryRange();

private:
    float lowerSalaryRange;
    float upperSalaryRange;
};
```

Note

If it is the intent of our object-oriented design for class `SalariedEmployee` to access the data item `socialSecurityNumber` of class `Employee` directly (i.e., without calling `SetSocialSecurityNumber` or `GetSocialSecurityNumber`), we would need to declare `socialSecurityNumber` protected, as opposed to private, in our `Employee` base class.

It's easy to confuse the different combinations of inheritance and access specifiers, i.e., `public`, `protected` and `private`. Here it is in a nutshell: There are three access specifiers for base classes—public, protected and private. In the `public` case:

```
class B : public A
{

};
```

the `public` members of base class A are `public` members of derived class B; likewise, the `protected` members of class A are protected in B as well (`private` members of class A are, naturally, inaccessible unless given friend declarations).

In the `protected` case:

```
class B : protected A
{

};
```

the `public` and `protected` members of base class A are `protected` members of derived class B (the same comments apply regarding private members and friend declarations).

In the `private` case:

```
class B : private A
{

};
```

the `public` and `protected` members of base class A are `private` members of derived class B (the same comments apply regarding private members and friend declarations).

As such, we create a specialized `SalariedEmployee` class from the more general `Employee` class. Note that nowhere in class `SalariedEmployee` do we declare data or member functions for dealing with the salaried employee's social security number; we have inherited it from class `Employee`. So at any time, we can just as easily call `SetSocialSecurityNumber` or `GetSocialSecurityNumber` on instances of an `Employee` or a `SalariedEmployee`:

```
Employee firstEmployee;
SalariedEmployee secondEmployee;

firstEmployee.SetSocialSecurityNumber(394772386);
secondEmployee.SetSocialSecurityNumber(399814325);
```

To get some terminology out of the way, the inheritance relationship between the `SalariedEmployee` class and the `Employee` class is one of single inheritance, i.e., `SalariedEmployee` shares the structure and behavior of one base class, namely `Employee`. Likewise, it is possible to have instances of multiple inheritance.

Which of the "classes" in our engineering firm displays multiple inheritance, then? The engineering manager, inheriting from two base classes—that of the engineer and that of the manager—is an obvious choice. It is just as simple to inherit, or derive, the structure and behavior of several base classes as it is to inherit from one. Assuming that we have created an `Engineer` class and a `Manager` class, we could define an `EngineeringManager` class as follows:

```
class EngineeringManager : public Engineer, public Manager
{
public:
    EngineeringManager();
    ~virtual EngineeringManager();

    void SetDepartmentNumber(long);
    long GetDepartmentNumber();

private:
    long departmentNumber;
};
```

In effect, we have united the structures and functionality of both the `Engineer` and the `Manager` classes into the `EngineeringManager` class, while specializing the `EngineeringManager` class to include the department number managed by the engineering manager.

Our example classes thus far have been fairly trivial. We have designed a hierarchy within our fictional personnel system from scratch, allowing us to take advantage of the shared structure and behavior mentioned above. However, we've still written all the code. Admittedly, it is perhaps less code than we would have written without inheritance, but we still needed to undertake a considerable amount of work. Where inheritance truly pays off is when you have the opportunity to derive new classes from existing classes, which, of course, is software reuse.

So, where do you find these existing classes? You're probably familiar with some of them already, if you've used Borland C++ to any extent. What about all the classes that make up the Object Windows Library (OWL)? Here is an entire library of classes that encompasses most of the Windows API. It includes classes for windows, dialog boxes, buttons, scroll bars, everything you need to create your next killer Windows application. But, what if you don't like the buttons supplied by OWL? Simply derive your own class, specializing it for your needs! The same applies for all C++ classes. If you use Microsoft Foundation Classes (MFC), or if you purchase a third-party C++ library and need to specialize it to fit your needs, simply derive a new class from an existing one, adding or overriding the needed functionality. In a moment, we'll do an example using the Object Windows Library, after a short discussion of polymorphism.

Polymorphism

Polymorphism is a fairly easy-to-understand concept that plays a powerful role in object-oriented programming. Literally, of course, polymorphism means having many forms. An object in your code—an instance of some class—can actually be taken to represent many different classes if they are related by some common base class. Take, for instance, our engineering firm hierarchy as an example. An instance of the EngineeringManager class can be considered not only an EngineeringManager, but also an Engineer, a Manager, a SalariedEmployee or an Employee. This polymorphism is, of course, the direct result of inheritance.

So, what good does it do us if our EngineeringManager can be considered either an EngineeringManager, an Engineer, a Manager, a SalariedEmployee or an Employee? Consider what would happen if we defined a customized function for outputting information about each class in our engineering firm hierarchy. For instance, what if we added a virtual function entitled PrintData to our Employee base class? Well, declaring a function virtual in C++ forces the runtime system to locate the correct derived class's implementation of the virtual function, and to invoke it. Let's look at a few of our example classes again.

If we add the virtual function PrintData to our Employee class, as follows:

```
class Employee
{
public:
     Employee();
     virtual ~Employee();

     void SetSocialSecurityNumber(long);
     long GetSocialSecurityNumber();

     virtual void PrintData();

private:
     long socialSecurityNumber;
};
```

and declare the PrintData function:

```
void Employee::PrintData()
{
    cout << "Social Security Number:  " << socialSecurityNumber << endl;
}
```

we could, of course, have an instance of the `Employee` class and call `PrintData`, which would result in the output of the employee's social security number (which is already, in itself, an example of polymorphism: the operator `<<` outputs our long integer differently than it would a character string or a floating-point value):

```
Employee firstEmployee;

firstEmployee.SetSocialSecurityNumber(394772386);
firstEmployee.PrintData();
```

We could also define `PrintData` for our `SalariedEmployee`, as shown in listing 20.1.

Listing 20.1   Salaried.cpp—Defining *PrintData* for the Derived Class *SalariedEmployee*

```
class SalariedEmployee : public Employee
{
public:
    SalariedEmployee();
    virtual ~SalariedEmployee();

    void SetLowerSalaryRange(float);
    float GetLowerSalaryRange();
    void SetUpperSalaryRange(float);
    float GetUpperSalaryRange();

    void PrintData();

private:
    float lowerSalaryRange;
    float upperSalaryRange;
};

void SalariedEmployee::PrintData()
{
    cout << "Lower limit = " << lowerSalaryRange << ", upper limit = " <<
        upperSalaryRange << endl;
};
```

We could then continue on for all the remaining classes: `Engineer`, `Manager` and so on. Assuming `PrintData` is defined for all our classes, and that there is a global array of employees entitled `companyEmployee` and a global `numberOfEmployees` variable, what happens if we have the following piece of code:

```
extern Employee *companyEmployee[];
extern int numberOfEmployees;
```

```
void printAllEmployees()
{
    for (int count = 0; count < numberOfEmployees; count++)
    {
        companyEmployee[count]->PrintData();
    }
}
```

Because we're calling `PrintData` on `Employee` instances, you may assume that for each employee in the company, his or her social security number is displayed (this is how `PrintData` was implemented for class `Employee`). But what really happens is that the `PrintData` member function is located in each derived class. If `companyEmployee[0]` is a `Manager`, the method `Manager::PrintData` is invoked. If `companyEmployee[53]` is an Engineer, the method `Engineer::PrintData` is invoked. We have one variable `companyEmployee[count]`, on which we are calling `PrintData`, which actually can behave as an `Employee` variable or any derived class thereof. This is what polymorphism is all about.

What if we didn't have the luxury of this polymorphism? How would we call `PrintData` in a language like C, for instance, which for the most part lacks object-oriented programming constructs? We could declare a flag for each type of employee, and then check that flag in a large switch statement, calling functions accordingly:

```
switch(employeeType)
{
    case EMPLOYEE:

        // Call print function for employee.

    break;

    case HOURLY_EMPLOYEE:

        // Call print function for hourly employee.

    break;

    case SALARIED_EMPLOYEE:

        // Call print function for salaried employee.

    break;

        // and so on...
}
```

Such a strategy is, of course, time-consuming, somewhat difficult to maintain and simply too long. Putting polymorphism to use in your code can help you avoid such constructs. We'll see an example later.

> **Note**
>
> There is a more concise way of implementing polymorphism in C, and if you have ever done object-oriented programming in C (it is possible, just a little difficult), you're probably objecting right now. Instead of using flags and a large switch statement, we could have a union of all our different employee types, defining a function pointer in each structure. For instance, in the case of `Employee`:
>
> ```
> struct Employee
> {
>     long socialSecurityNumber;
>     void (*PrintData)();
> };
> ```
>
> Simply storing the address of a unique function for printing employee data in each employee structure, we could then call `PrintData` on each structure in our array. But this, too, is somewhat difficult to maintain and can become confusing. If you can, use the polymorphism of C++.

"Inheriting" Source Code

As mentioned earlier in our discussion of inheritance, there is a great deal of existing C++ source code that you can reuse in your own programming simply by deriving new classes from existing ones, tailoring functionality to meet your own programming objectives. In Borland C++ alone, there are countless classes in the class library, in examples, in the Object Windows Library, and so on. If you do a lot of Windows programming, this is a resource you must not ignore.

As C++ has gained popularity, so too have so-called application frameworks that provide easy-to-understand, hierarchical class interfaces to developing applications, especially in a graphical user-interface (GUI) environment like Windows. Most major compilers also ship with an application framework; Borland's Object Window Library (OWL) is a prime example. As discussed earlier, these application frameworks take full advantage of inheritance and polymorphism in C++. As most of today's graphical user-interfaces were originally written in C or PASCAL, mastering C++ and then being constrained to use a C interface can be somewhat of a let-down. Today this is no longer a problem.

> **Tip**
>
> To avoid long waits when building OWL applications, always make sure the precompiled headers option is enabled in your project options. The first time you compile your project, you'll still need to wait for the precompiled header to be built, but from then on, the precompiled header will simply be loaded from disk into your project.
>
> **1.** From the Option menu, choose Project.
>
> **2.** In the Topics list, double-click on Compiler.

3. Click on the Precompiled Headers subtopic.

4. In the Precompiled Header options on the right side of the Project Options dialog, click on Generate, and check the box to use precompiled headers.

5. Under Precompiled Header Name, select a name for your precompiled header (my project name is Chordg.ide, so the name defaults to Chordg.csm), as shown in figure 20.4.

6. If you wish to specify the last header file to include in the precompiled header, you can do so under Stop precompiling after header file.

7. Click OK to save your changes.

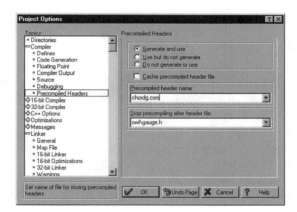

Fig. 20.4

Enabling precompiled headers for the Chordg project.

If you've had the opportunity to use OWL before, you may be familiar with the example applications that ship with Borland C++ which allow you to test out the various controls included in OWL—buttons, check boxes, combo boxes, sliders and so on. For example, in \Bc5\Examples\Owl\Classes\Gauge you can find a project entitled Gauge.ide which, when built, demonstrates the standard gauges provided in the Object Windows Library. If you build this project, be prepared for a bit of a wait; OWL, like all application frameworks, pulls a great deal of header files into even the smallest of projects. If you run Gauge.exe, you see something resembling figure 20.5.

Moving the slider bar at the bottom of the window updates the two horizontal gauges above it accordingly. Both gauges are instances of TGauge, a class supplied by the Object Windows Library (note that the gauges can also be instantiated so that they are drawn in a vertical fashion). You're probably very familiar with these gauges; they appear frequently in Windows programs when the duration and progress of a task— such as installing files—needs to be indicated. Borland recommends the solid bar for long durations and the broken bar for shorter tasks, but we're going off on a tangent now. The point is that horizontal and vertical gauges are great, but what happens when we need to incorporate a different type of gauge into an application?

Fig. 20.5

Running an example of the OWL gauge control.

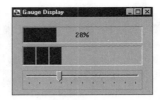

Let's assume we need a gauge that resembles the gas gauge or speedometer in your car, which is usually a semicircle with a hand that sweeps across the gauge. How does this type of gauge really differ from the gauges in figure 20.5? For the sake of comparison, figure 20.6 offers a sneak peak at the gauge we're developing.

Fig. 20.6

A sneak peak at the TChordGauge *control.*

Our gauge still has a starting and ending point (or range), and it still has only one value at any given time, which is indicated by the hand on the gauge. The only difference really is the appearance of the new gauge. Our desired gauge is, in geometrical terms, a chord (the region bounded by the intersection of an ellipse and a line segment) with a hand, as opposed to a rectangular gauge with a bar. The functionality, however, is identical.

If you're a C++ programmer and you find yourself in the position where a class exists that would certainly suit your needs with a few changes or additions, you're facing a prime opportunity to put inheritance to work in your code—don't pass it up!

The class TGauge, mentioned above, is derived from another class in the Object Windows Library, called TControl. TControl serves as the base class for all controls in the Object Windows Library, including text fields, buttons, check boxes, sliders, scroll bars, etc. Controls are, of course, added to windows and dialog boxes in order for the end user to communicate with an application. If we were to create a new control from scratch, we would need to derive a class from TControl, and implement all of the necessary data items and member functions that make up a control. For someone who's not experienced in using the Object Windows Library, this would imply some careful study and a considerable amount of effort. Luckily, we're not in that situation—being well-informed of the benefits of inheritance in C++, we are going to derive a new class from TGauge called TChordGauge, thus inheriting all the structure and behavior of the gauges demonstrated in this section.

In listing 20.2, you see exactly what the TGauge class has to offer. Let's take a look at a somewhat abbreviated version of its class definition in gauge.h (which is located in \Bc5\Include\Owl):

Listing 20.2   gauge.h—The Interface for the OWL Class *TGauge*

```
class _OWLCLASS TGauge : public TControl {
  public:
    TGauge(TWindow*        parent,
           const char far* title,
           int             id,
           int x, int y, int w, int h = 0,
           bool            isHorizontal = true,
           int             margin = 1,
           TModule*        module = 0);

    // Getting & setting gauge properties
    //
    void        GetRange(int& min, int& max) const;
    int         GetStep() const;
    int         GetValue() const;

    void        SetRange(int min, int max);
    void        SetStep(int step);
    void        SetValue(int value);  //!CQ SetPos/GetPos alias?
    void        DeltaValue(int delta);
    void        StepIt();
    void operator ++(int);

    // Set the LED style & sizing as well as the indicator color
    // Ignored by CommonControl impl.
    //
    void        SetLed(int spacing, int thickPercent = 90);
    void        SetColor(const TColor& color);

    static void SetNativeUse(TNativeUse nu);

  protected:

    // Override TWindow virtual member functions
    //
    char far*   GetClassName();
    void        Paint(TDC& dc, bool erase, TRect& rect);
    void        SetupWindow();

    // Self sent by method Paint(). override this if you want to
    // implement a border style that isn't supported
    //
    virtual void  PaintBorder(TDC& dc);

    // Message response functions
    //
    bool        EvEraseBkgnd(HDC);

  protected_data:
    int         Min;        // Minimum value
    int         Max;        // Maximum value
    int         Value;      // Current value (position)
    int         Step;       // Step factor
    int         Margin;     // margin between bevel & graphic
```

(continues)

IV

Using New C++ Features

Listing 20.2 Continued

```
    int         IsHorizontal;
    int         LedSpacing; // Spacing of leds in value units
    int         LedThick;   // Thickness of leds in percent of spacing
    TColor      BarColor;   // Bar or LED color, defaults to blue
    static TNativeUse ClassNativeUse;  // Default use of native control impl

  private:
    // Hidden to prevent accidental copying or assignment
    //
    TGauge(const TGauge&);
    TGauge& operator=(const TGauge&);

  DECLARE_RESPONSE_TABLE(TGauge);
};
```

As we mentioned earlier, the TGauge class already contains all the functionality for our TChordGauge class. If you look at some of the member functions defined here, there is handling for setting the range and value of the gauge that our class can use as-is, functions for indicating by how much the value should be incremented or decremented, and so on. Some functions, however, will remain particular to OWL's TGauge—SetLed, for instance, which controls the spacing of the broken bar we saw in the demonstration above (this doesn't really apply to our type of gauge). We can also find references to the types of functions that we will need to change to implement our TChordGauge class; those would be PaintBorder and Paint, which are responsible for actually drawing our gauge on the screen. For the purposes of this example, these are the two member functions that we need to concentrate on: PaintBorder, which draws the border of the control, and Paint, which draws the entire control, border and all.

How, then, would we go about deriving our TChordGauge class from TGauge? As we did in the employee examples above, we simply begin our class as follows (the _OWLCLASS indicates that the TChordGauge is defined as an Object Windows Library class):

```
class _OWLCLASS TChordGauge : public TGauge
{

};
```

Now we have all the structure and behavior of the TGauge class in our own TChordGauge class, right? Well, not quite. Right now there's no way to do the following, is there?

```
TChordGauge *ChordGauge = new TChordGauge(...);
```

We can't construct a TChordGauge yet; you cannot inherit a constructor in your C++ code. If we wanted to duplicate the TGauge constructor in our TChordGauge class, we could simply call a TChordGauge constructor with the same arguments that TGauge requires:

```
class _OWLCLASS TChordGauge : public TGauge
{
    TChordGauge(TWindow* parent, const char far* title, int id, int x, int y,
```

```
            int w, int h = 0, bool isHorizontal = true, int margin = 1,
            TModule* module = 0) :
        TGauge(parent, title, id, x, y, w, h, isHorizontal, margin, module) {
    }
};
```

Here we've defined the TChordGauge constructor exactly as it is in class TGauge, then passed all of the arguments directly to TGauge for processing. This is a perfectly valid way to proceed, but we can simplify our constructor because we won't make use of all the arguments to TChordGauge—we will have no title (although it's still available for future development), isHorizontal really doesn't apply to our gauge, and so on. In addition, what if we wanted to add something to our constructor that is unique to class TChordGauge? For instance, we'll see in a moment that our TChordGauge class can draw optional measuring "ticks" at equal distances around the gauge (it will draw none if "ticks" is equal to zero), much like the ruler of the slider in figure 20.5. The parameter ticks would be unique to our constructor. So, basically, we can customize our constructor as needed, as long as we remember that because we're using almost all of TGauge's functionality, we'll need to pass the TGauge constructor the information it needs to construct itself. Here's the constructor as defined in Chordg.cpp. (A complete listing can be found in file Chordg.cpp on the accompanying CD-ROM):

```
class _OWLCLASS TChordGauge : public TGauge
{
public:
    TChordGauge(TWindow* parent, int x, int y, int w, int h = 0, int ticks = 0) :
        TGauge(parent, 0, IDC_SOLIDGAUGE, x, y, w, h)
    {
        this->ticks = ticks;
    }

private:
    int ticks;
};
```

Notice that we have only five parameters in common with the TGauge constructor: parent (which is the window to which our control belongs), x and y (the upper-left corner of our bounding client rectangle), and w and h (the width and height of the bounding rectangle). We have simplified the interface to our class somewhat in that regard. Notice also that we have added our own unique parameter, ticks, which indicates how many equal sections our gauge should be divided into (dots will be placed between adjoining sections and at the beginning and the end of the gauge). We store this value in a private data item called ticks, which is all our constructor does; the rest is up to TGauge. We invoke TGauge's constructor with parent, we send 0 or NULL for title (because we're currently not using it), IDC_SOLIDGAUGE for ID (which is an OWL resource constant indicating that a TGauge with a solid bar should be constructed), then the dimensions of our bounding rectangle. Now if we instantiated our TChordGauge class, we would have the exact same functionality as class TGauge; we would have added only an assignment for our ticks. Our class has inherited all the functionality of TGauge in a line or two of code.

Our instantiation of TChordGauge would have a slight problem when drawn on-screen, though, wouldn't it? It would look an awful lot like a gauge with a solid bar (refer to fig. 20.5); in fact, it would look exactly like the gauge with a solid bar—we do indeed inherit all of TGauge's functionality. What we need to do now is to specialize our TChordGauge class to draw itself as in figure 20.3, effectively overriding some of TGauge's functionality.

To override the Paint and PaintBorder methods in class TGauge, we simply add them to our class definition:

```
class _OWLCLASS TChordGauge : public TGauge
{
public:
    TChordGauge(TWindow* parent, int x, int y, int w, int h = 0, int ticks = 0) :
        TGauge(parent, 0, IDC_SOLIDGAUGE, x, y, w, h)
    {
        this->ticks = ticks;
    }

protected:
    void Paint(TDC& dc, bool, TRect&);
    void PaintBorder(TDC& dc);

private:
    int ticks;
};
```

Paint and PaintBorder are both called with device contexts, which are necessary for most graphics functions in the Windows API. Paint also accepts additional parameters, but we won't make use of these (TGauge doesn't either, for that matter). That's all there is to our class definition for TChordGauge. We have our constructor, and we've defined Paint and PaintBorder; all that remains is to write some code to draw our gauge.

Whether or not you enjoy graphics programming will determine whether or not you even need to look at our implementation of Paint and PaintBorder that follows. The important point to remember here is that already at this point—in a few lines of code—we have taken a prepackaged class, and inherited and specialized its functionality for our purposes. Inheritance is not only a powerful concept—or a catchy buzzword, depending on your point of view—it is also a powerful tool. Let it work for you, and you will save yourself time and development efforts.

If you're not interested in the implementation of Paint or PaintBorder (or the thought of a little basic trigonometry causes terrible high school flashbacks), check out source file Chordg.cpp on the accompanying CD-ROM, then read how we put some polymorphism to work in our example. For those of you who aren't faint of heart, let's start with PaintBorder.

In `PaintBorder`, all we really need to do is draw the background of our `TChordGauge` control. This involves filling the rectangle that bounds our control with some content. In our case, we erase the client rectangle with the default system color for the face of an object, draw the actual chord and if necessary, draw ticks equally spaced around the chord. Listing 20.3 shows the function. I've left the comments in, so that the function is a little easier to follow.

Listing 20.3   Chordg.cpp—Drawing the Border of the *TChordGauge* Control

```cpp
// PaintBorder is responsible for drawing the border of our gauge; i.e., the
// chord and any ticks.
void TChordGauge::PaintBorder(TDC& dc)
{
    // Get the ClientRect which sets the bounds of our chord gauge.
    TRect cr(GetClientRect());

    // We need to blank out this rectangle with the system face color, then
    // decrease our ClientRect slightly in case we need to display ticks
    // see below).
    TBrush faceBrush(TColor::Sys3dFace);
    dc.SelectObject(faceBrush);

    dc.PatBlt(cr.left, cr.top, cr.right, cr.bottom);
    cr.Inflate(-2, -2);

    // We draw the outline of our chord gauge in the system shadow color.
    TPen shadowPen(TColor::Sys3dShadow);
    dc.SelectObject(shadowPen);

    // To draw our chord (an arc intersected by a line segment) to fill our
    // ClientRect, we need a rectangle twice as tall as our actual
    // ClientRect.
    TRect virtualRect(cr.left, cr.top, cr.right, cr.bottom + cr.Height());
    TPoint start(cr.right, cr.bottom);
    TPoint end(cr.left, cr.bottom);
    dc.Chord(virtualRect, start, end);

    // If we need to display ticks (i.e., if our gauge is broken into
    // sections), we need to calculate their position and draw them as
    // filled ellipses.
    if (ticks > 0)
    {
        // We fill ticks with the color of the bar, or hand, of our gauge.
        TBrush tickBrush(BarColor);
        dc.SelectObject(tickBrush);

        // We use simple trigonometry to break our 180-degree chord into
        // equal angles, drawing filled ellipses at each (cos(angle),
```

(continues)

Listing 20.3 Continued

```
        // sin(angle))point around the chord.
        int halfWidth = cr.Width() / 2;
        for (int count = 0; count <= ticks; count++)
        {
            double angleInDegrees = 180 - (count * (180.0 / ticks));
            double angleInRadians = angleInDegrees * (3.141592654 / 180);

            double x = cr.left + halfWidth + (cos(angleInRadians) *
            ➥halfWidth);
            double y = cr.bottom - (sin(angleInRadians) * cr.Height());

            dc.Ellipse(x - 2, y - 2, x + 2, y + 2);
        }
    }
}
```

Very briefly, as it gets away from the topic of inheritance, in `PaintBorder` we obtain our bounding rectangle. As already stated, we fill this rectangle with the `Sys3dFace` color, effectively erasing our control to some color. We then decrease our bounding rectangle by two pixels all the way around, in order to fit the top-most tick on our gauge, should we need to display ticks. We select the system background color pen, and draw our chord; notice that in order for our chord to fill the entire rectangle, we actually need to create another rectangle that is twice the height of the client rectangle (this forces the center of the ellipse to be at the bottom of our client rectangle, as opposed to its center). Finally, if we need to display ticks, we space them equidistantly around the chord, using trigonometric functions to calculate the (x, y) pairs; the ticks are drawn in the same color that the gauge's hand will be drawn in member function `Paint`. Remember that our base class `TGauge` provided a member function for changing this `BarColor`; simply call `SetColor` and the color of the ticks, and the hand will change.

Now that you've seen `PaintBorder`, `Paint` is very similar; you can glance at it in the source file Chordg.cpp on the accompanying CD-ROM. We use almost identical calculations for computing the (x, y) position of where the hand points to. We actually draw five lines, using the color specified in `BarColor` to fatten the hand a bit. Of note also are the `Max`, `Min` and `Value` variables, which were protected members of `TGauge`. `Max` and `Min` are set by `SetRange` and indicate the starting and ending value of the gauge, and `Value` is set by `SetValue`, which, of course, indicates the current value. You'll also notice the additional code in the source file Chordg.cpp required to create the test application that drives our gauge; this code is typical of applications in \Bc5\Examples\Owl\classes. Figure 20.7 shows what you get when you run Chordg.exe with 10 ticks indicated in the `TChordGauge` constructor.

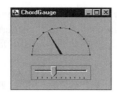

Fig. 20.7

Running an example of the TChordGauge *control with* 10 *"ticks."*

Putting Polymorphism to Work

In our engineering firm example, we demonstrated polymorphism by declaring a virtual function entitled `PrintData` in our `Employee` base class. We then were able to specialize `PrintData` for various derived classes, such as `SalariedEmployee`, `Manager` and so on. This allowed us basically to iterate through an array of `Employee` pointers, declared somewhat like the following:

```
Employee *employeeArray[maxNumberOfEmployees];
```

calling `PrintData` on those `Employees`:

```
for (int count = 0; count < numberOfEmployees; count++)
{
      employeeArray[count]->PrintData();
}
```

But, as we learned, we were not simply calling `Employee::PrintData` each time through the `for` loop. Our `Employee` pointer variable was actually able to act as if it were any derived class, or subclass, of `Employee` (in addition to being an actual `Employee` instance, of course). Again, if the current employee were a `Manager`, `Manager::PrintData` would be called, and so on. A name in a program (like a variable) behaving differently for any number of derived classes of a base class is said to be polymorphic, having many forms. Polymorphism in object-oriented programming allows the programmer great freedom in dealing with objects that benefit from inheritance. For instance, if you recall our engineering firm hierarchy, we had one class in our hierarchy entitled `EngineeringManager`. But this class was in no way the only way to refer to an `EngineeringManager`. An instance of an `EngineeringManager` class could just as well be considered an `Engineer` or a `Manager` or a `SalariedEmployee` or an `Employee`. When you put inheritance to work in your C++ code, there is a very powerful and flexible, almost common sense, logical structure to your designs and implementation, and polymorphism is one result of that logic.

Each demo application we have discussed consists of two or more controls: sliders, gauges, and "chord gauges." What happens when the screen needs to be updated and all the controls in a window need to be redrawn? Given that all controls in the Object Windows Library are derived from class `TControl`, do you think there is some giant switch statement in OWL that calls the slider's `Paint` function, the gauge's `Paint` function and so on? Of course not. How could it even guess at what the heck a `TChordGauge` is? We've only just made it up! Just as in our engineering firm example, polymorphism is at work in the Object Windows Library as well. Because all controls are derived from TControl, functions defined as virtual in TControl (or even a base class of TControl) will result in member functions being invoked for derived classes of TControl.

How might we put polymorphism to work in our TChordGauge example? Granted, right now we have only two "objects" that make up our control: a border (the chord and the ticks) and a face (the hand); but there could be more in the future. Basically, instead of having our Paint function call PaintBorder and painting itself, we would like to have a loop that iterates over an array of some class (let's call the class TChordGaugePart), putting polymorphism to use to call a member function (let's call it DrawPart) on each array member. Listing 20.4 shows the new Paint member function for TChordGauge.

Listing 20.4 Chordg2.cpp—The Paint Member Function for the
TChordGauge **Class**

```
void TChordGauge::Paint(TDC& dc, bool, TRect&)
{
    // We, of course, would need some new data members in our TGauge class
    // to represent the array of TChordGaugeParts (call it gaugePart) and an
    // integer indicating how many parts currently make up the gauge control
    // (call it numberOfParts).

    for (int count = 0; count < numberOfParts; count++)
    {
        // gaugePart is an array of TChordGaugePart *.
        gaugePart[count]->DrawPart(dc);
    }
}
```

Now, regardless of how many parts we add to our TChordGauge control, our Paint function would remain the same (and we can do away with the PaintBorder function, because it would become a derived class of TChordGaugePart). How might we go about declaring this TChordGaugePart class? It would need a virtual function called DrawPart:

```
class TChordGaugePart
{
public:
    TChordGaugePart();

    virtual void DrawPart(TDC &dc) = 0;
};
```

Here we've defined DrawPart to accept a device context, which again is required for most graphics functions in the Windows API. But why have we set DrawPart equal to zero? By doing this we have made DrawPart a so-called pure virtual function, which means it is up to derived classes of `TChordGaugePart` to implement `DrawPart`. Why do this at all? Well, consider a generic `TChordGaugePart` for a moment. What would it actually look like? Nothing really, it's too generic. In our `TChordGauge` example, we have a border and a face, which would end up being derived classes of `TChordGaugePart`. In those derived classes, we would actually define `DrawPart`, and the code would look almost identical to the code of `Paint` and `PaintBorder` earlier. Any class that contains one or more virtual functions is called an *abstract class*, and, in fact, an instantiation of an abstract class is not allowed. So you could not do the following:

```
TChordGaugePart myPart; // This is an error.
```

Abstract classes serve purely as base classes for other classes. They're very useful for defining interfaces at the base of a chain of derived classes.

So, given our abstract base class, `TChordGaugePart`, we could go on to declare two derived classes, `TChordGaugeBorderPart` and `TChordGaugeFacePart`, in the following manner:

```
class TChordGaugeBorderPart : public TChordGaugePart
{
public:
    TChordGaugeBorderPart();

    void DrawPart(TDC &dc);
};

class TChordGaugeFacePart : public TChordGaugePart
{
public:
    TChordGaugeFacePart();

    void DrawPart(TDC &dc);
};
```

As mentioned earlier, the actual implementation of `DrawPart` in each case would correspond to the code for `PaintBorder` and `Paint` in the source file Chordg.cpp, with one exception. Can you guess what it is? What about some of the variables used in the functions `PaintBorder` and `Paint`—Max, Min, Value, ticks—where did they come from? They, of course, come from either the `TChordGauge` class or the `TGauge` class; our classes derived from `TChordGaugePart`, however, have no access to those variables. These classes would need to use member functions like `GetRange` and `GetValue` (from `TGauge`) and `GetTicks` (from `TChordGauge`, which we would have to define) to access those values. This would require us to make one minor change to the three classes we have just developed; they would need a data member that stored the pointer of the `TChordGauge` to which they belong (called parent, for example), on which these accessor functions could be invoked.

> **Note**
>
> You may be asking yourself why we couldn't create a friend relationship between class
> `TChordGauge` and `TChordGaugePart`, so that we could access these variables. Unfortunately,
> friendship in C++ can't be inherited, and isn't transitive; for example, if `TChordGaugePart` were
> a friend of `TChordGauge`, it doesn't mean derived classes of `TChordGaugePart`—such as
> `TChordGaugeBorderPart`—would be friends (`TChordGauge` wouldn't be a friend of
> `TChordGauge`'s base class, `TGauge`, either).

Making these few changes, our `TChordGauge::Paint` member function would put polymorphism to good use. No matter how many—or how many different—parts we
added to a `TChordGauge`, it could handle them all in the same manner. Try making a
copy of Chordg.cpp and implementing these changes as we've developed them here.

> **Tip**
>
> Check out the listing of CHORDG2.CPP on the accompanying CD-ROM if you need some
> ideas.

Good luck inheriting!

From Here...

Polymorphism and inheritance are two of the strongest selling points of C++ and
object-oriented programming languages in general. As C++ continues to grow in
popularity and widespread commercial acceptance, you as a programmer will be confronted with countless opportunities to inherit functionality from existing class libraries and frameworks, just like you did in our Object Windows Library examples. Make
the best of these opportunities and you'll save yourself development efforts that can
be better spent on other aspects of your projects.

- Chapter 3, "Object-Oriented Analysis and Design," introduces design issues—
  including inheritance and polymorphism—related to object-oriented programming and C++ classes.

- Chapter 24, "Understanding Namespaces," introduces a new C++ language feature that ensures class and function names don't "collide" when multiple classes
  in a project contain similar names.

- Chapter 25, "Using the Graphics Device Interface," covers more examples of
  Windows graphics programming interfaces.

CHAPTER 21

Understanding Strings in ANSI C and ANSI C++

In the past few years, the paradigm shift from procedural languages to object-oriented languages like C++ has reached full swing. C++ stands out from other object-oriented languages, though, in that it still has the procedural C language at its core (C is a sub-set of C++). As such, all C functions are still available to the C++ programmer.

A particularly strong point of the C library is its functions for handling null-terminated arrays of characters—in other words, strings. In C++, a staggering array of string classes has sprung up from a variety of sources—compiler vendors, shareware authors, in-house programmers, among others—to take the place of the C library. Which one to choose? It's a difficult choice (find a C++ programmer who deals with strings to any great extent, and you'll probably find some code peppered with ANSI C functions like `strlen`, `strcat`, and `strcpy`).

The ANSI C++ string class strives to provide a standard string class with a great deal of functionality to any compiler that provides ANSI libraries. (ANSI is the American National Standards Institute, the United States's representative to ISO, the International Standards Organization.) For instance, I can use the string class in my Macintosh projects, my DOS projects and my Windows projects, and expect it to behave the same on all three platforms. And while Borland's implementation of the ANSI C++ string class remains essentially unchanged from Borland C++ 4.5 to 5.0 (a `#pragma` or two has been added to the cstring.h header file for 32-bit compatibility), it still merits examination for the simple fact that a lot of C++ programmers still hang on to ANSI C string functions, even though the ANSI C++ string class is easy to learn and use, while preventing perennial problems that plague C programs dealing with strings. These include wasted storage in anticipating the worst-case length of a string, incessant allocating and deallocating of memory when copying strings, misplacing or forgetting null termination, and so on—all of which cause even the best of us occasional debug-ging headaches.

Note

The most recent draft of the ANSI C++ string library, as of this writing, introduces templates to string handling; i.e., the string class can handle types `char`, `wchar_t` (wide characters—greater than one byte) or any type defined in C++. While the member functions remain essentially unchanged—what you learn in this chapter should serve you well—the notation is often difficult to read, in the style of STL (Standard Template Library), another ANSI C++ library. Look for it soon, as more and more compilers on all platforms provide template and STL implementations.

In this chapter, you'll learn how to:

- Find the header file for the ANSI C++ string class in Borland's directory hierarchy. We'll also look at how to get help on the string class from Borland's Class Library Reference.
- Create instances of the ANSI C++ string class in your own programs using a number of different constructors.
- Integrate Borland's implementation of the string class with Windows-platform-dependent resources like string tables.
- Take full advantage of the member functions provided by the string class, including those for concatenation, comparison, insertion, removal, searching, and substrings.
- Compare the string class member functions with C favorites, such as `strlen`, `strcat`, and `strcpy`. We'll also look at how to continue using old standbys from the C language, while still taking advantage of the ANSI C++ string class.
- Catch exceptions raised by the string class.
- Be aware and make use of—or avoid, in a cross-platform project—Borland's implementation-specific member functions.

Creating a Project from within the IDE

Before we can begin our examination of the ANSI C++ string class, we'll need to create our first project, entitled Welcome. To create our project from within the IDE, follow these steps:

1. In the File menu, choose New, then Project (or simply click on the New Project icon). You will see a dialog box similar to figure 21.1.
2. In the Project Path and Name text box, enter your path name and the project name, welcome.ide. Target Name will be updated automatically.
3. Select a Target Type of Application [.exe].
4. For Platform, select Win32 from the pop-up menu.

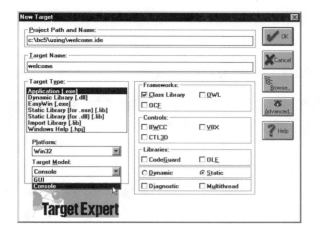

Fig. 21.1

Creating the Welcome.ide project.

5. Most importantly for this chapter, be sure to select Console from the Target Model, as we will simply be outputting strings to the console as we work with the string class.

6. Finally, under Libraries choose Static.

String Class Constructors

The first step in using a new C++ class is familiarizing yourself with its constructors—if you don't know how to instantiate a class, you won't get very far with its member functions. Where can we find such information? There are two sources in Borland C++: the actual header file for the string class included in your code, and Borland's online Help. Let's briefly examine where to find the constructors before getting into some examples.

Examining the Header File cstring.h. The header file for the ANSI C++ string class can be found in the \Bc5\Include directory. From the File menu, choose Open (or click on the Open a File icon) and maneuver yourself to the \Bc5\Include directory.

> **Note**
>
> If you installed Borland C++ 5 in a different location from \BC5, substitute the correct directory name.

Be sure to set Files of Type to either Source, Headers or All Files so that you will see files ending in .h. If you open cstring.h and scroll down a bit in the file, you will come to the roughly 15 constructors for class string. These are strictly function prototypes for the constructors, and do not offer much in the way of advice on how to use them. Less experienced users should probably consult Borland's Class Library Reference on-line Help.

Class Library Reference. To find descriptions of the string class constructors, follow these steps:

1. From the <u>H</u>elp menu, choose <u>C</u>ontents (see fig. 21.2).
2. From the topics at the top of the screen, select Class <u>R</u>ef.

Fig. 21.2

Locating Borland's Class Library Reference.

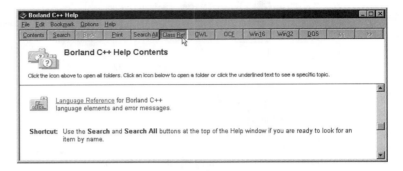

Tip

In general, if you refer to Help a lot, define a bookmark (in this case, for the string class). Simply choose <u>D</u>efine from the <u>B</u>ookmark menu, and give your bookmark a name. Later you can jump directly to your bookmark by choosing it from the <u>B</u>ookmark menu.

---

3. Then simply follow the hyperlinks Service Classes, string classes and string class. You're there, finally.
4. Under constructors, follow the hyperlink string::string (see fig. 21.3).

Fig. 21.3

Descriptions of some string class constructors.

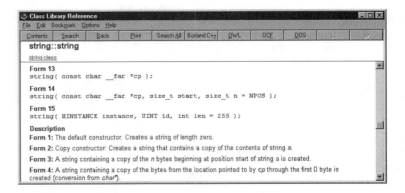

In browsing through the function prototypes and descriptions, you'll notice that a lot of the constructors are very similar in nature. This is referred to as a "fat" interface and is fairly typical of ANSI C++ libraries. The intent is to allow arguments of different types to the "same" function call—i.e., overloading. In the string class, you'll usually find yourself able to pass a char or unsigned char, a pointer to a null-terminated string, or another string instance.

Running Your Example Project. Now that we've found the string class constructors and descriptions of how to use them, let's try some out in the empty Welcome.cpp file included in our Welcome project (see fig. 21.4). If it is not open already, double-click on its name in the Project window.

Fig. 21.4

Opening the source file, Welcome.cpp.

Note

You may sometimes find in Borland C++—especially when switching back and forth between projects—that you can't find your Project window. When you attempt to reopen the project, the window may not appear in the file browser because it is already open. Choosing View, Project enables you to see your Project window.

In the Welcome.cpp text edit window, enter the code from listing 21.1 or refer to the accompanying CD-ROM. Do not forget #define STRICT, which is a requirement for Borland's string class.

Listing 21.1 Salaried.cpp—Source Code for Welcome.cpp Demonstrates Various String Class Constructors

```
#define STRICT
#include <iostream.h>
#include <iomanip.h>
#include <cstring.h>

void main(void)
{
    char exitKey; // key to exit program

    // here are our constructors:
    string emptyString;
    string nullTerminatedString("Welcome to the construction site!");
    string fromCharacterToCharacterString   (nullTerminatedString, 0, 7);
    string singleCharacterString('Z');
    string repeatedCharacterString('Z', 3);

    // let's see what they give us
    cout << endl;

    cout << setw(40) << "Here's an empty string:   "
        << emptyString << endl;
    cout << setw(40) << "Its length is:   "
        << emptyString.length() << endl << endl;
```

(continues)

Listing 21.1   Continued

```
    cout << setw(40) << "Here's our welcome string:   "
        << nullTerminatedString << endl << endl;

    cout << setw(40) << "Here's the word welcome:   "
        << fromCharacterToCharacterString << endl << endl;

    cout << setw(40) << "Here's a single character:   "
        << singleCharacterString << endl << endl;

    cout << setw(40) << "Here it is repeated:   "
        << repeatedCharacterString << endl << endl;

    emptyString = "Don't fall asleep on me yet!";

    cout << emptyString << endl << endl;

    cout << "Hit any key to continue..." << endl;

    cin.get(exitKey);
}
```

Once you have entered the code, you'll have to make one more change to your project before the Welcome project will compile correctly. If you look at the Project window again, you'll notice two files, Welcome.def and Welcome.rc. If you were to double-click on Windows.def, you would see that the file is empty. Since we are building a Windows project, we'll need a Windows definition file. For small projects like Welcome, we can usually rely on the default definition file provided by Borland. It is located in \Bc5\Lib and is called Default.def. To remove Welcome.def and replace it with Default.def:

1. Click on Welcome.def in the Project window and press Del.
2. Confirm that you would like to delete Welcome.def from the project.
3. Click on Welcome.exe in the Project window and press Insert.
4. In the file browser, move to \BC5\LIB and make sure that Files of Type is set to Definition [.def].
5. The definition file default.def should be the only one listed (see fig. 21.5). Double-click on it to add it to your project.

Fig. 21.5

Adding Default.def to your project.

Now we can run the project. Simply click on the Run icon and the Welcome project should compile and run. See figure 21.6 for the result.

Fig. 21.6

Output from the Welcome project.

If you referred to the constructor descriptions in the Class Library Reference earlier, you probably anticipated this output. In defining emptyString, we called the constructor string(), which creates a string of length zero (notice the string class member function length(), which is an equivalent for the strlen function in ANSI C). With nullTerminatedString, we made use of the constructor string(const char *). The string fromCharacterToCharacterString demonstrates the constructor (const string &s, size_t start, size_t n), which allows us to create a string instance from a substring of another string (if you leave off the last argument to this constructor, the string created will range from the first character indicated to the last character in the input string). So if we were to make the following change:

```
string fromCharacterToCharacterString(nullTerminatedString, 8);
```

The output of fromCharacterToCharacterString would be:

```
to the construction site!
```

Note also that we could have just as easily created fromCharacterToCharacterString by doing the following:

```
string fromCharacterToCharacterString("Welcome to the construction site!", 0, 7);
```

This is an example of the "fat" interface we spoke of earlier—the string instance nullTerminatedString we passed to the constructor in Welcome.cpp is easily replaced by a const char * argument.

Caution

Be very careful in reading the descriptions of constructors. While the following two constructors yield equivalent results:

(continues)

(continued)

```
string fromCharacterToCharacterString1(nullTerminatedString, 0, 7);

string fromCharacterToCharacterString2("Welcome to the construction site!",
➥0, 7);
```

the following two constructors do not:

```
string fromCharacterToCharacterString3(nullTerminatedString, 8);

string fromCharacterToCharacterString4("Welcome to the construction site!", 8);
```

If we output fromCharacterToCharacterString3, it would look like:

```
to the construction site!
```

fromCharacterToCharacterString4, on the other hand, yields the following output:

```
Welcome
```

This is due to the fact that when a const char * argument is passed to a string class constructor with a single size_t argument, the string constructed starts at byte zero of the const char * argument and continues on for size_t bytes.

Finally, the string constructors also take char arguments as demonstrated by singleCharacterString and repeatedCharacterString. Calling the constructor string(char) creates an instance of a string with one character; calling the constructor string(char, size_t) allows us to repeat a single character.

Combining the ANSI C++ String Class with Windows STRINGTABLEs. Borland, in its implementation of the ANSI C++ string class, has not forgotten Windows developers. STRINGTABLE resources are allowed as inputs to the ANSI constructors. The constructor, as listed in the Class Library Reference, is:

```
string( HINSTANCE instance, UINT id, int len = 255 );
```

If you deal directly with the Windows API, you can use this constructor much as you would the Windows LoadString call:

```
int LoadString(HINSTANCE hinst, UINT idResource, LPSTR lpszBuffer, int
➥cbBuffer);
```

The only difference in the string class constructors is that no lpszBuffer argument needs to be supplied—the buffer will be contained in the string instance returned by the structure. Once your string resource is contained in an instance of an ANSI C++ string, you can make use of all of the string class member functions discussed in the following section.

Exploring the Member Functions

Now that we're able to call the various string class constructors, we can get to the real functionality of the class: its member functions. I've chosen to break up the member functions into those that alter strings, those that compare them, those offering search capabilities, those providing input/output routines and those making up various miscellaneous routines. All of the following codes can be found in file Members.cpp. If you do not wish to create a new project or type in the following code, simply replace Welcome.cpp from the Welcome project with Members.cpp.

As we examine the various member functions, try to anticipate what the output will be from each of the function calls. Most of the functionality of the string class is fairly intuitive. Also be aware that we cannot exhaustively cover all possible permutations of arguments to the member functions—this is the hallmark of a "fat" interface. Try to take away as much as you can from the examples, and feel free to experiment!

Altering Strings

There are a great many ways to alter strings in any programming language and, as such, there are a number of associated operators and member functions that deal exclusively with altering strings in the ANSI string class. Assignment operators allow the C++ programmer to give a string instance a new value without resorting to C calls like strcpy—assigning string values is finally as painless as assigning integer values! Member functions for concatenating—or joining—strings together provide easy interfaces for adding a string to the beginning or end of an existing string. The string class also provides mechanisms for inserting strings into existing strings, as well as for removing—or deleting—portions of strings. In addition, the replace function allows the programmer to change any substring within an existing string. And, finally—as C character arrays still lie at the heart of the string class—you, the programmer, still can access each character of a string, including that terminating null character, should the mood strike you. Let's start by looking at the assignment operators.

Assignment Operators. The most obvious way to alter a string is to change its value; to do this, you need assignment operators. There is, of course, the = operator:

```
string firstAlterString = "This string will be altered."
```

A more verbose form of the = operator is the assign function:

```
string secondAlterString;
secondAlterString.assign("This string will also be altered.");
```

Another assignment operator that we sometimes forget is actually a constructor, the copy constructor. The following constructs copyString, assigning it the value of firstAlterString:

```
string copyString(firstAlterString);
```

One last way to assign a value to a string is to assign it the substring of a second string:

```
string subString = firstAlterString.substr(5, 6);
```

Assuming firstAlterString still holds the data "This string will be altered," the value of subString in this case would be "string." We took the substring from character position five (count from zero) of firstAlterString, for a length of six characters.

> **Note**
>
> Remember that calling the member function `substr` on an instance of the string class does not change the value of the string in question. It returns another string entirely. This is in contrast to other member functions we'll see later, such as `insert`, `remove`, and `replace`.

Concatenation in the String Library. There are two types of *concatenation*—joining one or more strings together—in the string library, appending and prepending. *Appending* means joining one string to the end of an existing string; *prepending*, on the other hand, simply implies joining one string to the beginning of an existing string. A number of different operators and functions produce the same results, as with the assignment operators.

The simplest way to append a string onto an existing string is to use the += operator:

```
string firstAlterString("This string will be altered.");
firstAlterString += "  Whether it likes it or not."
```

If we output `firstAlterString` after the += operator has been applied:

```
cout << firstAlterString << endl;
```

We have the following output:

```
This string will be altered. Whether it likes it or not.
```

The more verbose form of the += operator is the append function. The following is equivalent to the previous example:

```
string thirdString("  Whether it likes it or not."
firstAlterString.append(thirdString);
```

Two strings can also be concatenated to produce a third string:

```
string addedString = thirdString + thirdString;
```

Notice that the strings being concatenated can indeed be the same string

```
cout << addedString << endl;
```

generating the output:

```
Whether it likes it or not. Whether it likes it or not.
```

As previously stated, we can also prepend a string onto another string. Instead of concatenating the string onto the end of the existing string, we prepend it to the beginning of the string:

```
firstAlterString.prepend("1. ");
cout << firstAlterString << endl;
```

which generated the following output:

```
1. This string will be altered. Whether it likes it or not.
```

Insertion. If we insert one string at the beginning of another string we actually have prepending:

IV

```
string secondAlterString("This string will also be altered.");
secondAlterString.insert(0, "2. ");
```

Here we have inserted the string "2. " at character position zero in secondAlterString. We could just as easily have inserted "2. " anywhere else in the string by adjusting the first argument to insert. Since "2. " doesn't make much sense in the middle of our string, let's insert the word "new ":

```
string secondAlterString("This string will also be altered.");
secondAlterString.insert(5, "new ");
cout << secondAlterString << endl;
```

Outputting our new string verifies that we have inserted the word "new " at position 5 in our original string (the "s" in string):

```
This new string will also be altered.
```

Removal. Our firstAlterString is now equal to

```
1. This string will be altered. Whether it likes it or not.
```

We can easily remove the second sentence by calling remove:

```
firstAlterString.remove(32);
cout << firstAlterString << endl;
```

which results in this output:

```
1. This string will be altered.
```

Caution

Just as in the C language, you are still dealing, indirectly, with a character array when using the ANSI C++ string class. Don't forget that all indexing starts at zero, not one. If you start counting at one with functions like remove, you'll leave an extra character behind.

You do not necessarily have to remove the rest of the string. When passing two arguments to remove, you specify a starting position and a number of characters to remove:

```
string secondAlterString = "2. This string will also be altered. Whether it
➥likes it or not."
secondAlterString.remove(8, 7);
cout << secondAlterString << endl;
```

The output is

```
2. This will also be altered. Whether it likes it or not.
```

Here we have effectively removed seven characters—the word string—from secondAlterString, starting at character 8 (actually the ninth character, the "s" in string).

Replacement. The same type of indexing is used in replacing a portion of a string instance. Consider the next example:

```
string firstAlterString("1. This string will be altered.");
string tempString("replaced");
firstAlterString.replace(23, 7, tempString);
cout << firstAlterString << endl;
```

The output is:

```
1. This string will be replaced.
```

Here we've replaced the word `altered` with `replaced`. Note that `replaced` is one character longer than `altered`, and the period was not replaced. We replaced the seven characters in `firstAlterString` starting at character 23 with `tempString`, which is eight characters long. This is not a problem; if `tempString` had been 100 characters long we still would not have overwritten the period.

Indexing. Not only can we replace series of characters within a string, we can replace individual characters, using the indexing functions of the string class. The following is a simple way to change one character:

```
firstAlterString[1] = ':';
cout << firstAlterString << endl;
firstAlterString(1) = ':';
cout << firstAlterString;
```

The output is:

```
1: This string will be replaced.
```

```
1. This string will be replaced.
```

Note that both [ ] and ( ) operators are provided by Borland when using the string class. A more verbose method to do exactly the same thing is to use the put_at function, as in:

```
firstAlterString.put_at(1, ':');
```

If you would like to examine a single character within a string, use either [ ], ( ) or the get_at function:

```
cout << firstAlterString.get_at(1) << endl;
```

The output is:

```
:
```

Comparing Strings

In addition to being able to alter strings, a string class must provide an easy way to compare strings. Comparison is essential for—among other things—sorting and, in my opinion, strings are sorted more often than numbers—just check out the phone book!

The ANSI C++ string class supports all of the comparison operators: ==, !=, <, >, <= and >=. For the following examples, we'll continue with the two strings leftover from the previous section:

```
string firstAlterString("1. This string will be replaced.");
string secondAlterString("2. This will also be altered. Whether it likes it
➥or not.");
```

See if you can anticipate the output of the following statements:

```
cout << (firstAlterString == secondAlterString) << endl;
cout << (firstAlterString < secondAlterString) << endl;
cout << (firstAlterString.compare(secondAlterString)) << endl;

firstAlterString.remove(0, 3);
cout << (firstAlterString.compare(secondAlterString, 3, 4)) << endl;
```

The first comparison checks whether firstAlterString and secondAlterString are identical. They are obviously not; a zero would be output, indicating false.

In the second statement, we check whether firstAlterString is less than secondAlterString. It is indeed, already on the first character because 1 is less than 2 (the output would be 1, indicating true). If both strings had started out with 1, firstAlterString would still evaluate to less than secondAlterString. Where? The "s" in string is less than the "w" in will.

The third comparison uses a slightly different method of comparison, the compare function. The function compare, like ANSI C's strcmp, returns an integer less than zero if the first string is less than the second, zero if both strings are identical, and an integer greater than zero if the second string is greater than the first. Bearing this in mind, we would expect a negative value, as we've already determined firstAlterString is less than secondAlterString. The actual value output would be -1, because 1–2 equals -1. This is really only useful in some specialized routines, but if the difference between the differing characters had been greater, we would receive an integer less than -1 as the return value.

Finally, we mix in a remove and a compare. Removing three characters from firstAlterString, starting at character zero, leaves "This string will be replaced.". Comparing this new string, then, with the four characters in secondAlterString, beginning at character 3—take your time—leaves us with a result of zero, equality. How? Start at character 3 in secondAlterString and count off four characters ("This"). What are the first four characters of firstAlterString? "This."

Searching with the String Class

An essential function of any string class is searching—it ranks right up there with comparison. There are two types of searching provided by the string class. The first is very straightforward, using the functions find (searching from the beginning of a string) and rfind (searching from the end of a string; i.e., reverse).

If we have the following two strings:

```
string targetString("This is our target for searches and more searches.");
string searchString("target");
```

Try to predict the output of the following statements:

```
cout << targetString.find(searchString) << endl;
cout << targetString.find(searchString, 19) << endl;
cout << targetString.find("searches") << endl;
cout << targetString.rfind("searches") << endl;
```

In the first statement, we're looking for searchString ("target") in our targetString, starting at the beginning of targetString. "target" is indeed in targetString, starting at character 12. The value returned by find is 12.

In the second example, we're looking for target again, but we're starting from character 19, which corresponds to the "f" in "for." What do you expect the result to be? Zero? No, that would mean "target" was found at character zero. We agree that "target" does not occur after character 19 of targetString, correct? The actual return value turns out to be 4,294,967,295. How can this be? If you've been programming for a while, and dealing with hexadecimal notation on some level, you might recognize this decimal value masquerading as the hexadecimal value 0xFFFFFFFF. Depending on whether you look at this number as positive or negative, you'll get a very different decimal value.

Note

As an unsigned value, 0xFFFFFFFF is equal to 4,294,967,295; as a signed value it is -1. Think back to when you looked at the Class Library Reference for string class constructors. In quite a few of them, one of the arguments was listed as size_t n = NPOS. NPOS is used by the library as a sentry value; for example, when you want to remove some characters from a string starting at character position 3, and you leave off the number of characters you'd like to remove, NPOS comes into play. NPOS is the greatest unsigned value that will fit into a size_t argument; it allows the library to remove characters from position 3 to the end of the string. When we output the value NPOS using the iostream operator<< we see the value 4,924,967,295; it was defined, however, as size_t(-1). What gives? size_t is an unsigned integer. If you want to check if a search has failed using the string class, be sure to compare the return value to NPOS instead of -1. You could compare the value to -1 if you're sure to cast its value to type size_t, but you'll forget once or twice—I guarantee you. Compare the value to NPOS.

Tip

If they are available, always compare return values to symbolic values like NPOS. If not, the difference between a signed and an unsigned value can go unnoticed for a long time in a debugging session. Be careful!

The third and fourth examples illustrate the difference between a find and an rfind. Using find, we're searching for the word "searches" from the beginning of the targetString. It can be found at position 23. Using rfind, we search in reverse from the end of targetString. In this case, "searches" can be found at position 41.

Earlier I mentioned a second type of searching. The string class member functions `find_first_of`, `find_first_not_of`, `find_last_of` and `find_last_not_of` implement a type of search where the character sequence argument to the function is considered a set of characters. Perhaps an example is in order:

```
string targetString("This is our target for searches and more searches.");
cout << targetString.find_first_of("st") << endl;
```

Here we are looking for the first occurrence of an 's' or a 't' in `targetString`. The result is, of course, 3, as the first 's' occurs in character position 3 of `targetString`.

In relation to this, `find_first_not_of` looks for the first character in `targetString` that does not occur in the argument to the function, so

```
cout << targetString.find_first_not_of("This") << endl;
```

results in 4. The ' ' at position 4 in `targetString` is the first character not in the set {T, h, i, s} (remember, we're not looking for the word "This").

As you would expect, `find_last_of` and `find_last_not_of` start at the end of the string, and work in reverse order. Note that adding arguments to the function call restricts the search space.

```
cout << targetString.find_last_of("abcd", 19) << endl;
```

This example results in 13. Why? We're beginning our search at character position 19 in `targetString`, the "f" in "for," and working backwards. The last occurrence of an a, b, c, or d in `targetString` starting here is indeed the "a" in "target."

Wrapping up searching, consider the `find_last_not_of`:

```
cout << targetString.find_last_not_of("abcd", 19) << endl;
```

The return value is 19; i.e., the last occurrence of a letter not in the set {a, b, c, d} beginning at character position 19 in `targetString` and working backwards is character 19, the "f" in "for."

Input/Output of ANSI Strings with << and >>

Throughout our examples, you have seen how to output string class instances. Simply use the overloaded << operator. Input occurs in a similar fashion; use the >> operator:

```
string s;
cin >> s;
```

Also available is the function `getline` as defined in iostream.h.

```
string s;
cin.getline(s);
```

Miscellaneous String Class Functions

The remaining functions don't quite fit into the previous categories; they are, nevertheless, very useful. We're already familiar with one:

```
string lengthString("What is the length of this string?");
cout << lengthString.length() << endl;
```

This results in a return value of 34, the length of `lengthString`.

Another function that is not as intuitive is `reserve`:

```
cout << lengthString.reserve() << endl;
```

The return value here is 63 and indicates the actual space reserved for `lengthString`. This value is library-implementation-dependent and you'll see later that it is administerable in Borland's implementation.

The final two miscellaneous functions offer complete compatibility with ANSI C string libraries: copy and c_str. The member copy will copy a string instance to a character buffer:

```
char charBuffer[64];
lengthString.copy(charBuffer, 22);
cout << charBuffer << endl;
```

Our example results in:

```
What is the length of SDM.DLL (?)
```

We're back in the world of C—don't forget to terminate your string with a null. We have the 22 characters "`What is the length of`" followed by random characters. To correct this, add the following:

```
charBuffer[22] = 0;
```

> **Note**
>
> This is a great example of one of the problems with C libraries that the ANSI C++ string class prevents.

Finally, c_str

```
const char *charPointer = lengthString.c_str();
cout << charPointer << endl;
```

results in:

```
What is the length of this string?
```

c_str returns a const reference to a null-terminated character array (the data contained in the string instance). You should never write to this string or assume the pointer is valid after any changes to the string instance. If you would like to make use of the value, be sure to use an ANSI C string function like strcpy or the string class's copy function.

About String Class Exceptions

Borland's implementation of the ANSI C++ string class can raise a number of exceptions on various conditions. If you would like to use them, you need to #define

USE_THROW_SPECIFIERS before including cstring.h in your source code (see cstring.h for more information). If you do turn on the exceptions, the three main exceptions raised by Borland's string class library are xalloc (in constructors—this is not an error condition), string::outofrange (an error condition where you have overstepped the bounds of a string; for example, s[64] when s is only eight characters long) and string::lengtherror (an invalid length is specified; for example, in a constructor you've repeated the character "Z" too many times and there is not enough storage available).

If you would like to handle these exceptions, simply catch them and try to remedy the error situation, or report an error message to user. A prime example is checking that there's enough memory available for allocating a new string. To accomplish this, we can place our string class constructor in a try block and catch the string::lengtherror exception—should we run out of memory—alerting the user with an "out of memory" message:

```
try
{
        // This is a long string of Z's (8K worth) that could fail
        // in a low memory situation.
        string longString('Z', 8192);
}
catch (string::lengtherror)
{
        // Alert the user to our predicament.
        cout << "Sorry, out of memory!" << endl;
}
```

Now should our call to the string constructor for longString ever fail due to lack of memory, our user will be alerted to the fact—and we can start debugging (we should never run out of memory)!

Discussing Borland's ANSI String Class Implementation

If you did browse through the header file cstring.h at the beginning of this chapter, you've probably noticed there is some functionality in the header file (and described in the Class Library Reference) that I've skipped over. I have done this intentionally. As this chapter is entitled "Understanding Strings in ANSI C and ANSI C+," I have attempted to concentrate on functionality defined by the draft ANSI C++ standard. In the draft standard, the ANSI C++ string class is defined in header <string>, which includes header cstring (actually, the standard C library string functions). Borland C++ 5 does not yet provide the standard ANSI C++ header files. Look for them, perhaps, in the future.

Borland's implementation does extend the ANSI-defined functionality in a number of ways that we'll examine shortly. As a developer who needs to produce projects for Macintosh, DOS/Windows and UNIX operating systems, I personally avoid as many nonstandard extensions to the ANSI libraries as possible on any one of these platforms. If you are not in a similar situation, read on for a brief discussion of Borland's extensions.

When we looked at the string class earlier, you may remember the following statement taken from Borland's Class Library Reference: "This class uses a technique called "'copy-on-write.'" Multiple instances of a string can refer to the same piece of data so long as it is in a "read-only" situation. If a string writes to the data, then a copy is automatically made if more than one string is referring to it.

Borland's implementation of the string class locates your strings in memory based on a hashing algorithm. If you have two strings with the data "Welcome," there is only one copy of it in memory as long as you do not make any changes to it. When you change one copy of the string "Welcome," it creates another copy in memory. To locate a string quickly, the hashing algorithm is applied to the "Welcome" data, which returns a memory location. As with all hashing algorithms, collisions are possible (two or more strings being mapped to the same memory location). To prevent this, use Borland's member function `set_paranoid_check` to force a `strcmp` to ensure that your data is correct. This is one implementation-specific feature of Borland's string class library.

Other interesting extensions include being able to administer the default initial capacity of a string (the default is a length of 63). Try playing with the `initial_capacity` member function for performance better suited to your needs. You may want to have an initial capacity that is less than 63 if you anticipate mostly short strings.

Other useful Borland extensions include `to_upper` and `to_lower` (which change the case of a string instance), `set_case_sensitive` (for turning case-sensitivity on and off in searches), and `strip` (which strips a certain character from a string).

If you can make use of these extensions, read more about them in the Borland Help file, Class Library Reference. If you'd prefer to stick to the ANSI standard, try to concentrate on the functions outlined in this chapter. Remember that libraries serve your purposes—tailor them to your needs as much as possible!

From Here...

I hope that you have a much better picture of what the ANSI C++ string class has to offer in terms of functionality. You've also seen how string class instances can be seamlessly intermixed with C functions, using either the `copy` or `c_str` member functions. Only you can be the judge of which functions provide you with a better solution for your programming needs. For future reference, the following table provides a quick guide as to similar functionality in the ANSI C string library—which you may already be familiar with—and the ANSI C++ string class—which may be new to you.

ANSI C String Library	ANSI C++ String Class
`strcpy, strncpy`	`=, assign, copy constructor, substr`
`strcat, strncat`	`+, +=, append, prepend`
`strcmp, strncmp`	`==, !=, <, >, <=, >=, compare`
`strpbrk, strchr, strrchr`	`find, find_first_of`
`strlen`	`length`

Check out other ANSI C++ support in Borland C++ 5:

- Chapter 13, "Exploring iostreams," will guide you through the `cins` and `couts` (pun intended) of input/output handling in C++.

- Chapter 22, "Exception Handling," introduces you to throwing and catching exceptions in C++, a dynamic error-handling technique removed from the main thread of your code.

- Chapter 23, "Run-Time Type Identification (RTTI)," gives you an introduction to type checking and casting at runtime.

IV

Using New C++ Features

CHAPTER 22

Exception Handling

Exception handling provides a structured and formalized service for dealing with exceptional events. Typically, the term *exception handling* refers to handling error conditions; however, you can also use exception handling for a variety of other tasks. As you will see later in this chapter, traditional methods of error handling are flawed in several profound ways. Exception handling solves most of these problems.

C++ exceptions help programmers deal with several common programming headaches that typically require developers to write large amounts of tedious code that gets executed very infrequently. Specifically, exceptions help programs by doing the following:

- Providing a standardized error-handling mechanism
- Dealing with anticipated problems
- Dealing with problems that were completely unanticipated when the program was built
- Enabling programmers to recognize, track down, and fix bugs

This chapter begins by looking at some of the ways that programs currently handle error conditions. You learn about the following:

- How exception handling accomplishes the same results
- Why exceptions are a superior method for getting these results
- How to use and deploy exception handling throughout your Borland C++ programs
- How to modify a larger program to take full advantage of C++ exceptions

This chapter also looks at how exception handling accomplishes the same results. You see why exceptions are a superior method for getting these results. Then you see how to use and deploy exception handling throughout your Borland C++ programs. The chapter concludes with an example of how to modify a larger program to take full advantage of C++ exceptions.

Realize that exception handling is not a cure-all. If you choose to use exceptions, you must put a significant amount of work into using them. And, as with any powerful tool, exceptions can be improperly used or abused.

Understanding Exception Handling

Borland C++ 5 supports many of the powerful extensions that will be appearing in the final ANSI C++ standard. Borland C++ 4.*x* already supported templates (robust enough to support the Standard Template Library), exception handling, and run-time type identification. To these extensions the new version has added namespaces and a host of minor enhancements, most in the standard C++ library. All of these features are crucial for the development of sophisticated and reliable C++ programs.

Exploring Software Development in an Imperfect World

Suppose a fellow programmer claims to have developed a large C++ program that was totally bug-free after the first successful compile, and can deal with any error condition, any abnormal event, and anything that could conceivably go wrong. How would you react?

Your first reaction would probably be to have your poor, deluded friend immediately institutionalized. Such a boast is not only difficult to believe, it's actually funny! After all, computer programmers are only human, and human beings are notoriously error-prone. Even if the person making this outrageous claim were a truly exceptional programmer, writing a program that can deal with every single conceivable problem is impossible. Such a program would be gigantic, and most of its code would be dedicated to coping with situations that might never arise.

This premise is somewhat unsettling. If programmers resign themselves to writing imperfect programs that can't deal with a wide range of potential problems, is computer software inherently unreliable? Maybe so.

Many industry insiders have talked at great length about the *software crisis*. Despite exciting new paradigms (for example, object-oriented programming) and productive new development environments (for example, Borland C++ 5, Delphi), the cost of developing software is increasing, but the reliability of software is not increasing at a corresponding rate.

This is due to several unique factors that have conspired to make life miserable for programmers. The marketplace has forced software up a steep evolutionary path that has resulted in contemporary products that make the programs of 10 years ago look Cro-Magnon by comparison. The sophisticated users of today demand attractive, graphical applications that work together and provide immediate and tangible productivity benefits. When you consider that users want all this without their applications becoming completely overwhelming, today's programmers clearly have their work cut out for them.

All these market-induced pressures lead to a single fundamental problem: complexity. Today's programs are so complex that it's no wonder they're less reliable. They are, after all, doing much more. With increased complexity, things are much more likely to go wrong. And as Murphy's Law correctly asserts, "If something can go wrong, it will."

The problem is that you can't simply print Murphy's Law on the front of a software box or in a warranty disclaimer. You can't explain to an irate customer over a support line that he lost a week's worth of work because we live in an imperfect world (actually, you can try, but I wouldn't advise it). Instead, a concentrated effort must be made to ensure that new software is becoming more reliable.

Exception Handling: A Flagstone on the Road to Reliability

Several things can be done to alleviate the software crisis, and only a few of them have a direct relationship with Borland C++. Some strategies, such as teaching specific techniques for writing solid code, are simply extensions of the normal education process. Other strategies, such as using object-oriented programming to facilitate code reuse, require a profound change in the way that developers have traditionally built programs.

The use of C++ exception handling falls into this latter category. Exception handling is a relatively new approach to an old problem: what a program should do when something unexpected happens. The underlying mechanisms might surprise you (to the uninitiated, exception handling smells an awful lot like the dreaded goto), but don't be fooled. Exceptions are an elegant and effective way to combat complexity and ensure that your programs run more reliably.

Coping with Error in C

Before jumping into the details of the exception-handling syntax, it's beneficial to take a look at some of more traditional ways that C programs (and preexception handling C++ programs) have dealt with error conditions. (Exception handling is useful for more than simply trapping error conditions. However, because trapping errors is the context in which programmers most often use exception handling, this chapter focuses on that purpose.)

A program that cannot handle exceptions still has several ways in which to trap and process error conditions. Although the following overview is not an exhaustive list of strategies, it covers the most commonly used ones.

Returning Error Values Using Return Codes. By far the most common way to signal an error within a function or object method is simply to return a value that indicates whether something went wrong. All programmers have used these types of functions; after all, most C library functions use such functions to communicate error conditions. The class in listing 22.1, for example, has a single method that calculates a signed value that can theoretically be useful when used inside a program.

Listing 22.1 Using a Direct Return Value to Report an Error

```
// Our theoretically useful class
class AUsefulClass {
public:
    long CalcAUsefulValue()
    {
        Do some processing and return the value
    }
};

// Now use the class
AUsefulClass MyVar;
long lAUsefulValue = MyVar.CalcAUsefulValue();
if (lAUsefulValue != 0)
    cout << "The value is " << lAUsefulValue << "\n";
else
    cout << "An error occurred!\n";
```

In this case, the program could return a calculated number as appropriate, or return a value of zero if an error occurred. This code snippet checks the return value and flags an error if the returned value is zero.

This technique works fine, unless zero is a potentially valid return value. If the method can legitimately return zero, there's no way to differentiate between a calculated value of zero and an error.

You can often use a constant value or range of values as returnable error codes. In the preceding example, if zero were a valid return value, you can perhaps use –1 to signal an error instead. Still, this will not always be the case.

This method of reporting errors has three problems. First, for a program to check for an error condition, the programmer must remember what these "magic" error codes are. This strategy is quite error-prone. (Does –1 mean "Out of memory" or "Out of range?" Or are you thinking about a colleague's error codes for a SuperDooHicky class?) Forcing people to remember "magic" numbers is a remarkably effective way to introduce bugs into your programs.

Second, as alluded to previously, occasions will arise when it is very difficult (or even impossible) for the programmer to find a free value that an application can return as an error. Take the following function prototype, which simply adds two unsigned shorts:

```
unsigned short Add(unsigned short addend1, unsigned short addend2);
```

It is possible to pass two numbers into this function that, when added, will overflow the returned unsigned short value. Clearly, this would be an error condition and should be reported as such. But what error value could you possibly return? Zero doesn't work because that's a perfectly valid answer if both addends are zero. In fact, any unsigned short value is a valid answer in this example. There simply aren't any free numbers that you can use as error codes. This problem is not completely insurmountable, however, as you will see in the next section.

You cannot say the same about the third problem, however. A program must go through the effort of checking the return value to determine that an error has occurred. If a programmer is lazy or simply forgets to check the return value, serious errors can slip by unnoticed. If you think that this seems unlikely, ask yourself when was the last time that you checked the return value of a call to `strcpy()` or `printf()`.

Clearly, although it is the most frequently used mechanism for reporting errors, simply returning an error code has some problems associated with it.

Returning Error Values in Function Arguments. This error-reporting strategy is a simple improvement on the previous strategy. Instead of reporting errors with return codes, programs can pass in a variable whose sole purpose is to be assigned an error code if something goes wrong. Using this strategy, the `Add()` function from the preceding section might use the following prototype. Notice that this prototype uses a reference to a `short` (it could also use a pointer to a `short`) because the `ErrorCode` variable must be modifiable.

```
unsigned short Add(unsigned short addend1,
                   unsigned short addend2,
                   short& ErrorCode);
```

Alternatively, you could have a variable return the addition's result and have the function return an error code. Clearly, this is just a variation on the same theme:

```
short Add(unsigned short addend1,
          unsigned short addend2,
          unsigned short& Result);
```

This strategy solves the problem of having to search for freely available error values. Still, the programmer must remember the potential error values and remember to check the returned error variable's contents.

A Global Error Variable. Instead of passing an error variable into a method, the programmer can simply rely on a global error variable. This technique saves the function's user from having to pass an extra argument into a method call; however, it's hard to view this savings as a huge productivity win. Listing 22.2 demonstrates how a programmer might use this error-reporting technique.

Listing 22.2   Global.cpp—Using a Global Variable to Report an Error

```cpp
// Get needed include files
#include <limits.h>
#include <iostream.h>

// Global error variable declaration
short ErrorCode;

unsigned short Add(unsigned short addend1, unsigned short addend2)
{
    unsigned long sum = addend1 + addend2;
    if (sum > USHRT_MAX)
        ErrorCode = -1;
    return (unsigned short) sum;
}

void main()
{
    unsigned short Result = Add(12345, 54321);
    if (ErrorCode == -1)
        cout << "Overflow error!\n";
    else
        cout << "The answer is " << Result << "\n";
}
```

This technique is a valid mechanism for reporting errors, but has several serious problems as well. As in the previous two methods, the programmer calling the function still must remember the specific error codes for which to check. Also, the programmer still must remember to check the error variable after the call.

In addition, this strategy suffers from the simple fact that it relies on global data. Subsequent calls to other functions could change the error variable without the programmer realizing it. The problem is exacerbated under operating systems, such as Windows 95 and NT, that support multiple threads of execution. Under these operating systems, the error variable might change even before the program has a chance to check the value initially.

Using global variables for error codes has a long tradition, going back to the early days of programming in C under the UNIX operating system. The use of the errno variable continues to this day, although most compiler vendors support errno more for the sake of compatibility than as a serious error-reporting mechanism.

Using *goto* or *setjmp/longjmp*. Both goto and setjmp/longjmp interrupt the normal flow of execution, so an error-handling strategy based on one of these approaches cannot be ignored. This behavior is very valuable because potentially serious errors cannot slip by unnoticed. On the other hand, both of these techniques suffer from some serious problems when used with C++ objects.

Take a quick look at goto first. Listing 22.3 demonstrates how you might rely on goto to trap errors.

Listing 22.3   Using *goto* To Help Report an Error

```
unsigned long sum = addend1 + addend2;
if (sum > USHRT_MAX)
    goto OverflowError;
cout << "The sum is " << sum << "\n";

More relevant processing

OverflowError:
    cout << "An overflow occurred!\n";
```

In this example, if the code encounters an overflow condition, the programmer clearly is going to know about it. Unfortunately, goto has a serious limitation: You can use it only within a single function or method. Although you might be tempted to write such code in listing 22.4, you simply can't.

Listing 22.4   Badgoto.cpp—An Illegal Use of *goto* to Help Report an Error

```
// Get needed include files
#include <limits.h>
#include <iostream.h>

unsigned short Add(unsigned short addend1, unsigned short addend2)
{
    unsigned long sum = addend1 + addend2;
    if (sum > USHRT_MAX)
        goto OverflowError; // Illegal can't leave Add()
    return (unsigned short) sum;
}

void main()
{
    unsigned short Result = Add(12345, 54321);
    cout << "The answer is " << Result << "\n";
    return;

    // Error-handling section but you'll never get here using
    // this program
    OverflowError:
        cout << "Overflow error!\n";
        return;
}
```

On the other hand, setjmp/longjmp—which is essentially a goto on steroids—can help you with this problem. Listing 22.5 shows a version of the same program that at least works.

Listing 22.5 Jump.cpp—Using *setjmp/longjmp* to Help Report an Error

```cpp
// Get needed include files
#include <limits.h>
#include <iostream.h>
#include <setjmp.h>

jmp_buf jmp_info;

unsigned short Add(unsigned short addend1, unsigned short addend2)
{
    unsigned long sum = addend1 + addend2;
    if (sum > USHRT_MAX)
        longjmp(jmp_info, -1);
    return (unsigned short) sum;
}

void main()
{
    int ErrorCode = setjmp(jmp_info);
    if (ErrorCode == 0) {
        unsigned short Result = Add(12345, 54321);
        cout << "The answer is " << Result << "\n";
        return;
    }

    // Error-handling section
    else {
        cout << "Overflow error!\n";
    }
}
```

This strategy is better. It enables the programmer to design an error-handling infra-structure that cannot be ignored or forgotten. This increases reliability because the programmer must handle errors whether or not he or she wants to. There's still the problem of remembering error codes; however, because the error processing will be centralized (theoretically) into error-handling blocks, the programmer at least has the option of installing generic error handling that doesn't have to use specific error codes.

Unfortunately, the setjmp/longjmp strategy suffers from a fatal flaw: It doesn't know C++. This shortcoming might not seem like such a big deal, but think about what would happen in the pseudocode snippet in listing 22.6.

Listing 22.6 Creating a Memory Leak with *longjmp*

```cpp
void MyUsefulFunc()
{
    MyMemoryHogClass   Hog;

    ... Some processing ...
```

```
        if (Some error condition)
            longjmp(jmp_info, -1);

        ... Continue with more processing ...
    }
```

Assume that `MyMemoryHogClass` dynamically allocates a substantial amount of memory from the heap and releases that memory when its destructor is called. If an error occurs and the `longjmp` executes, a memory leak occurs because the `Hog` object instance is never destructed.

You need an error-processing strategy that contains elements of the `setjmp/longjmp` approach but is responsive to the needs of C++ programs when it comes to destructing object instances that move out of scope because of an error. Enter C++ exception handling, which does all of this and more.

A Better Way with Exceptions

At first glance, handling exceptions seems much like using `setjmp/longjmp`, but it quickly becomes apparent that exceptions are much more robust. For the most part, exception handling addresses many of the deficiencies of the error-processing strategies mentioned in previous sections while adding significant flexibility and additional functionality.

When using exception handling, programs have no choice but to respond to errors. As mentioned during the discussion of `setjmp/longjmp`, this increases reliability because errors cannot slip between the cracks and cause unanticipated problems later.

Exception handling enables programs to use any C++ object or built-in type to represent information about an error. Therefore, you need not rely on numeric error codes (unless you want to). Instead, you can create hierarchies of specialized classes dedicated to communicating information about abnormal events.

Finally, exception handling is inherently bound to the C++ language. If throwing an exception forces local object instances out of scope, you are assured that the appropriate destructors will be called.

Exception-Handling Fundamentals: Throwing, Catching, and Trying

Now that you have an understanding of the problems that exception handling addresses, it's time to see how to use Borland C++ exceptions. The easiest way to learn about exceptions is to see them in action, so take a close look at listing 22.7, which presents a trivial exception-handling example.

Listing 22.7 Simple.cpp—A Trivial Example of Exception Handling

```cpp
// Get needed include files
#include <limits.h>
#include <iostream.h>

unsigned short Add(unsigned short addend1, unsigned short addend2)
{
    unsigned long sum = addend1 + addend2;
    if (sum > USHRT_MAX)
        throw 1;
    return (unsigned short) sum;
}

void main()
{
    try {
        unsigned short Result = Add(12345, 54321);
        cout << "The answer is " << Result << "\n";
    }
    catch (int ErrorCode) {
        cout << "An overflow occurred! ErrorCode = "
            << ErrorCode << "\n";
    }
}
```

The example in listing 22.7 has three interesting elements. Notice that the call to the Add() function is enclosed within a scope preceded by the try keyword. This try block indicates to the compiler that the program is interested in exceptions that might occur within this block. For this reason, code enclosed within a try block is sometimes said to be *guarded*.

Immediately following the try block is the catch block (more commonly referred to as the *exception handler*). Program execution jumps to this block if an exception occurs. Although this simple example has only a single handler, programs might have many different handlers that can process a multitude of different exception types.

The last element of the exception-handling process is the throw statement, found within Add(). The throw statement actually signals an exceptional event. The metaphor is simple and elegant: Program code *throws* exception objects that are *caught* by handlers. This process is sometimes called *raising an exception*. In this simple example, the exception that the code is throwing is in the form of a simple integer (the ErrorCode); however, as you will see later, programs can throw virtually any type of exception.

Listing 22.8 demonstrates a slight modification to the example. See if you can guess this program's output.

Listing 22.8   Unwind.cpp—A Demonstration of Unwinding the Stack

```
Same #include Files as 22.7

class MyMemoryHogClass {
public:
    ~MyMemoryHogClass()
        { cout << "In the MyMemoryHogClass destructor.\n"; }
};

unsigned short Add(unsigned short addend1, unsigned short addend2)
{
    MyMemoryHogClass Hog;
    unsigned long sum = addend1 + addend2;
    if (sum > USHRT_MAX)
        throw 1;
    return (unsigned short) sum;
}

main() same as listing 22.7
```

If you type this example and run it, you get something like the following:

```
In the MyMemoryHogClass destructor.
An overflow occurred! ErrorCode = 1
```

As you can see, the program calls the Hog object instance's destructor when the exception forces execution from Add(). This is an absolutely crucial aspect of C++ exceptions that other error-handling techniques simply cannot emulate. The process of calling the destructors of local objects as exceptions to move them out of scope is often referred to as *unwinding the stack*.

Examining *try* Blocks

Take a closer look at what a try block is. The following is the official syntax of the try block:

```
try-block :
    try compound-statement handler-list
```

This syntax makes two important points. You must follow the try keyword with a compound statement (a block of code separated from the current scope by braces). Single-line try blocks are not supported in a manner similar to that allowed by the if, while, and for statements. Listing 22.9 makes this distinction clear.

Listing 22.9   Examples of Legal and Illegal *try* BLOCKS

```
// Legal -- "if" doesn't require compound statement
if (a > b)
    cout << "a is greater than b.\n";
```

(continues)

Listing 22.9   Continued

```
// Legal --_ "for" doesn't require compound statement
for (loop = 0; loop < numberOfElements; loop++)
    ProcessElement();

// Illegal -- try block needs a compound statement
try
    ProcessElement();

// Legal_-- try block uses a compound statement(enclosing a single line)
try {
    ProcessElement();
}

// Legal
try {
    ProcessFirstElements();
    ProcessSecondElements();
}
```

The second important thing that the official syntax tells you is that you must follow a try block immediately with at least one handler. This makes sense. After all, what would it mean if you told the compiler that you wanted to catch exceptions for a particular block of code, but you didn't tell the compiler where you wanted to route the exceptions? Listing 22.10 shows both legal and illegal examples demonstrating this rule.

Listing 22.10   Examples of Legal and Illegal Handler Placement

```
// Illegal -- No handler at all
try {
    ProcessElements();
}

// Illegal -- the catch handler doesn't immediately follow the try block
try {
    ProcessElements();
}
ProcessMoreElements();
catch (int ErrorCode) {
    ProcessException(ErrorCode);
}

// Legal
try {
    ProcessElements();
}
catch (int ErrorCode) {
    ProcessException(ErrorCode);
}
```

```
// Legal
try {
    ProcessElements();
}
catch (int ErrorCode) {
    ProcessException(ErrorCode);
}
catch (char * ErrorString) {
    cout << "Exception (" << ErrorString << ")\n";
}
```

You can place any code that you want into a try block, including calls to other local functions, functions in a DLL, or object methods. Any code in a try block, at any level of nesting, can throw exceptions.

You can nest try blocks inside of each other as appropriate. Examine listing 22.11, which shows one try block used within another.

Listing 22.11   Nested.cpp—An Example of Nested *try* Blocks

```
// Get needed include files
#include <stdlib.h>
#include <iostream.h>

// Constants
const int MIN_FLAG_VALUE = 0;
const int MAX_FLAG_VALUE = 10;
const int FLAG_OUT_OF_BOUNDS = 0xFF;

// Processing
void DoSomethingElse()
{
    cout << "Inside DoSomethingElse.\n";
}

void DoSomethingUseful(int Flag)
{
    cout << "Inside DoSomethingUseful.\n";

    // Is our flag too big or too small?
    if (Flag < MIN_FLAG_VALUE || Flag > MAX_FLAG_VALUE)
        throw FLAG_OUT_OF_BOUNDS;

    // Do some processing
    try {
        if (Flag == 0) {
            cout << "The flag was set to zero.\n";
            DoSomethingElse();
        }
        else
            throw "Flag is non-zero.";
```

(continues)

Listing 22.11   Continued

```
    }
    catch (char *ErrorString) {
        cout << ErrorString << "\n";
    }
}

void main(int argc, char *argv[ ])
{
    // If no command-line arguments, set the flag to zero
    int UseFlag = (argc == 1 ? 0 : atoi(argv[1]));

    // Do some processing
    try {
        DoSomethingUseful(UseFlag);
    }
    catch (int ErrorCode) {
        cout << "Caught an exception (" << ErrorCode << ")\n";
    }
}
```

Although this example looks deceptively simple, it has a couple of levels of subtlety. Table 22.1 shows the output of listing 22.11 depending on the command-line argument passed into it.

Table 22.1   Different Output Examples from Listing 22.11 (Nested.cpp)

Command-Line Argument	Program Output
No arguments	Inside DoSomethingUseful. The flag was set to zero. Inside DoSomethingElse.
Flag equal to 0	Inside DoSomethingUseful. The flag was set to zero. Inside DoSomethingElse.
Flag < 0 or flag > 10	Inside DoSomethingUseful. Caught an exception (255).
Flag between 1 and 10	Inside DoSomethingUseful. Flag is nonzero.

In the first and second case, the try block sets the flag to zero, calls DoSomethingUseful(), and checks to ensure that the flag value is within the allowed range. Because the value is within the range, the following if statement checks whether the flag is zero. Because the flag is zero, the block prints a message and calls DoSomethingElse(). These cases do not throw any exceptions and the program executes normally.

In the third case, when the flag is greater than 10 or less than 0, the block calls DoSomethingUseful() and the flag fails the "within valid range" check. This failure throws an exception (FLAG_OUT_OF_BOUNDS). This integer exception is caught by the handler that follows the try block in main(), which dutifully prints the exception value.

In the last case, the flag is passed in and passes through DoSomethingUseful()'s bounds check. However, it fails the if statement check for a zero value, and throws a string exception. This string exception is caught by the handler within DoSomethingUseful(), which simply prints the string.

In the next section, you see how the Borland compiler determines which handler to call under various circumstances. As you might imagine, things can get complex quickly unless you plan adequately beforehand. (And complexity is exactly what you want to avoid!)

Catching Exceptions

Exception handlers are tremendously important because they are responsible for determining the next course of action after catching an exception. Properly delegating responsibility to handlers is an important part of your program's design.

Handlers 101. The official syntax for a handler is the following:

```
handler-list :
    handler handler-list (opt)
handler :
    catch ( exception-declaration ) compound-statement
```

This syntax tells you several important things. A compound statement follows the handler, so you must enclose the handlers within braces just like try blocks. The syntax also shows that a handler list follows try blocks. This means that you can assign many different exception handlers to catch exceptions from a single try block. The only general limitation on this rule is that the exception type processed by each handler must be unique.

Take a quick look at listing 22.12. This listing shows some examples of both legal and illegal exception handlers.

Listing 22.12   Examples of Legal and Illegal Handlers

```
// Illegal -- the handler needs to be within a compound statement
try {
    ProcessStuff();
}
catch(int ErrorCode)
    ProcessError(ErrorCode);

// Legal
try {
```

(continues)

Listing 22.12 Continued

```
        ProcessStuff();
}
catch(int ErrorCode) {
    ProcessError(ErrorCode);
}

// Illegal --_ both catch blocks handle the same exception type (int)
try {
    ProcessStuff();
}
catch(int CommError) {
    ProcessError(CommError);
}
catch(int ErrorCode) {
    ProcessError(ErrorCode);
}

// Illegal -- CommErrorType is still just an int
typedef int CommErrorType;
try {
    ProcessStuff();
}
catch(CommErrorType CommError) {
    ProcessError(CommError);
}
catch(int ErrorCode) {
    ProcessError(ErrorCode);
}

// Legal --_CommErrorType is now a separate exception type
class CommErrorType {
public:
    int CommError;
};

try {
    ProcessStuff();
}
catch(CommErrorType CommError) {
    // Assuming ProcessError() is overloaded to handle CommErrorTypes
    ProcessError(CommError);
}
catch(int ErrorCode) {
    ProcessError(ErrorCode);
}
```

You can create a handler that specifies only the exception type and does not declare an exception object. Such a handler might be all that your program needs to process error conditions adequately. In fact, if you declare an exception object name, but don't reference it, the Borland C++ compiler complains that the local variable is unused. Listing 22.13 shows this behavior in action.

Listing 22.13   Specifying Only the Exception Type in a Handler Declaration

```
try {
    ProcessElements();
}
catch (int) {
    cout << "An error occurred in ProcessElements()!\n";
}
```

Programs use different exception types to distinguish among different kinds of error conditions. Each type must have a corresponding handler, because if the C++ run-time component cannot find an appropriate handler to which to route an exception, it terminates the program. (As you will see later, there are exceptions to this behavior—no pun intended!)

The Catch-All Handler. You can use a general-purpose handler that will match any type of exception. This handler, which is referred to simply as the *ellipsis handler,* is declared (appropriately enough) with an ellipsis for its exception argument. Listing 22.14 demonstrates this handler.

Listing 22.14   Ellipsis.cpp—Using the Ellipsis Catch-All Exception Handler

```cpp
// Get needed include files
#include <limits.h>
#include <iostream.h>

unsigned short Add(unsigned short addend1, unsigned short addend2)
{
    unsigned long sum = addend1 + addend2;
    if (sum > USHRT_MAX)
        throw 1;
    return (unsigned short) sum;
}

unsigned short Divide(unsigned short dividend, unsigned short divisor)
{
    if (divisor == 0)
        throw "Divide by zero";
    return (unsigned short)(dividend / divisor);
}

void main()
{
    try {
        unsigned short Result = Add(12345, 12345);
        cout << "The first answer is " << Result << "\n";
        Result = Divide(55, 0);
        cout << "The second answer is " << Result << "\n";
    }
    catch (int) {
        cout << "An addition overflow occurred!\n";
    }
    catch (...) {
```

(continues)

Listing 22.14 Continued

```
        cout << "Something else bad happened.\n";
    }
}
```

In this example, the call to Add() completes normally because the arguments to the function do not cause an overflow condition. The following call to Divide(), however, fails because a zero value passes in as the function's divisor argument. This raises a string exception that contains the words "Divide by zero". No exception handler is explicitly designed to deal with string exceptions. There is, however, an ellipsis handler, and the string exception is routed there.

The ellipsis handler must catch an exception, so you must make this handler the last handler in the handler list. At compile time, the code in listing 22.15 is flagged as an error.

Listing 22.15 Illegal Placement of the Ellipsis Handler

```
type {
    ProcessElements();
}
catch (...) {
    cout << "Some unidentifiable exception was raised.\n"
}
catch (int) {
    cout << "An integer exception was raised.\n";
}
```

The final thing to note about the ellipsis handler is fairly obvious—because the ellipsis handler is a catch-all handler that can accept any type of exception, there is no way to actually get at the thrown exception object. Even if there was some way to get at the object reference, you would have no way to determine the object's type. Unless you know an exception's type, framing the processing of the exception into any sort of useful context is difficult. For this reason, ellipsis handlers are typically used to catch unanticipated exceptions and deal with them in a generic fashion.

The Great Handler Search. Depending on the circumstances, searching for the right handler might not be quite as straightforward as the contrived examples in this chapter might have led you to believe. In fact, it is very important that you carefully order handler lists and that you sufficiently consider the precise type that they handle.

The C++ run-time code follows several key rules when dispatching an exception. These rules can become confusing, so read them carefully.

- *Rule 1*   Exception handler lists are searched from the beginning of the list to the end. The exception is dispatched to the first capable handler. Therefore, if—because of one of the following rules—more than one handler can potentially handle an exception, the first handle in the list gets the exception.

- *Rule 2*   As discussed in the previous section, the ellipsis handler can handle any exception.

- *Rule 3*   Code can dispatch an exception to a handler for the appropriate exception type or to a handler for a reference to that type. Therefore, both the `catch (MyClass&)` and `catch (MyClass)` handlers can accept an exception of type `MyClass`. You can use the `const` and `volatile` modifiers, but they are not factored into the matching process. After an exception is caught, however, any `const` or `volatile` modifiers remain in full force.

  The Borland compiler does not let you provide a handler list that contains both a handler for a type and a handler for a reference to that type because the first handler in the list will always win. The later section "The Subtleties of Throwing" explains in detail why you would provide one over the other.

- *Rule 4*   Code can dispatch an exception to a handler designed to catch a base class object of that exception. Therefore, if class B derives from class A, a class A handler can accept a class B exception.

  The Borland 5 compiler allows you to provide a handler list that contains a handler for a base type before a handler for a derived type, but it does warn you that the derived type handler is hidden by the base type handler. It is important that you pay attention to these warnings, because without correction the base type handler would always process the exceptions meant for the derived type handler.

- *Rule 5*   In accordance with rule 3, you can route an exception to a handler that can accept a *reference* to an object whose type is a base class of the exception. Therefore, if class B derives from class A, a class A reference handler can accept a class B (or class B reference) exception.

  As in the previous examples, the Borland compiler tries to prevent you from shooting yourself in the foot. It warns you whenever you provide a handler list that contains a handler for a reference to an exception's base class before a handler for the exception's type (or a reference to that type). Like rule 4, heed this warning, otherwise; the first handler in the list will always process the exception.

- *Rule 6*   You can route an exception to a handler that accepts a pointer to which you can convert a thrown pointer by using standard pointer conversion rules.

- *Rule 7*   If the program cannot find in the current handler list a handler for an exception, search for another handler list in an enclosing level of scope. If the search for a handler progresses all the way to the first level of scope (`main()`) without success, the C++ run-time system terminates the program abnormally. You can modify this by using the `set_terminate()` function described in the section "Installing Your Own *terminate()* Handler," later in this chapter.

To illustrate some of these rules, I present a few examples. Listing 22.16 shows a program with nested `try` blocks. Try to predict the output of this code.

Listing 22.16   Rule7.cpp—A Demonstration of Rule 7

```cpp
// Get needed include files
#include <iostream.h>

void Func1(int flag)
{
    try {
        cout << "In Func1.\n";
        if (flag)
            throw "String exception";
    }
    catch (int) {
        cout << "Caught an integer exception.\n";
    }
}

void main()
{
    try {
        Func1(1);
    }
    catch (char *str) {
        cout << "Caught a string exception: " << str << "\n";
    }
    catch (...) {
        cout << "Caught an unrecognized exception.\n";
    }
}
```

Passing in a nonzero value for `Func1()`'s flag variable causes the program to raise a string exception. However, there is no handler for string exceptions in `Func1()`'s `try` block, so the C++ run-time code drops to the next level of scope and searches the handler list in `main()`. That list does include a string exception handler, so this code dispatches the exception accordingly.

The next example, listing 22.17, demonstrates some of the implications of rules 1, 4, and 5.

Listing 22.17   Rules145.cpp—A Demonstration of Rules 1, 4, and 5 Using Multiple Inheritance

```cpp
// Get needed include files
#include <iostream.h>

class First1 { };
class First2 { };
class Last : public First1, public First2 { };

Last MyLast;
```

```
void Func1(int flag)
{
    cout << "In Func1.\n";
    if (flag)
        throw MyLast;
}

void main()
{
    try {
        Func1(1);
    }
    catch (First1&) {
        cout << "Caught a First1 exception.\n";
    }
    catch (First2&) {
        cout << "Caught a First2 exception.\n";
    }
    catch (...) {
        cout << "Caught an unrecognized exception.\n";
    }
}
```

This code contains a multiple inheritance hierarchy, with the Last class inheriting from both First1 and First2. When Func1() raises the MyLast exception, the program searches the handler list in main() for a match. The first handler checked is catch (First1&). The exception thrown is of type Last, so there is clearly no exact match with this handler. However, because Last derives from First1, this handler qualifies as an acceptable handler as stipulated by rule 4. Note also that even though the handler is designed to accept *references* to type First1, this handler is acceptable because of rule 5.

Suppose that you order this list with the First2& handler appearing before the First1& handler, as in the following example:

```
    catch (First2&) {
        cout << "Caught a First2 exception.\n";
    }
    catch (First1&) {
        cout << "Caught a First1 exception.\n";
    }
    catch (...) {
        cout << "Caught an unrecognized exception.\n";
    }
```

In this case, the First2& handler receives the exception because of rule 1.

As a final example, look at listing 22.18, which demonstrates how rule 6 affects the matching process. In this program, the exception being thrown is a pointer type. Because of rule 6, pointer-based exceptions are a little more adaptable than normal exceptions.

Listing 22.18   Rules16.cpp—A Demonstration of Rules 1 and 6

```cpp
// Get needed include files
#include <iostream.h>

class Base { };
class Derived : public Base { };

void Func1(int flag)
{
    cout << "In Func1.\n";
    if (flag)
        throw new Derived;
}

void main()
{
    try {
        Func1(1);
    }
    catch (Derived*) {
        cout << "Caught a Derived* exception.\n";
    }
    catch (Base*) {
        cout << "Caught a Base* exception.\n";
    }
    catch (void*) {
        cout << "Caught a void* exception.\n";
    }
    catch (...) {
        cout << "Caught an unrecognized exception.\n";
    }
}
```

The exception that this program is throwing—a Derived pointer—can be caught by any of the four handlers supplied. This is because you can legitimately cast a Derived pointer to either a Base pointer or a void pointer. Notice that you can cast down anything to a void pointer, so a void pointer handler catches any type of pointer exception.

What Exactly Are You Throwing, Anyway?

Several times this chapter has noted that even though most of the examples so far have concentrated on simple integer or string exceptions, an exception can actually be of any type. Your first reaction on hearing this might have been to ask, "Why?"

Maybe an appropriate (albeit somewhat coy) response to that question is, why not? Clearly a C++ object offers a much richer palette of functionality than a simple integral type. Class-based objects can present an interface to programs that imply a wide range of error-processing options, whereas a simple integer or string can only communicate a basic state or describe an error condition in a minimalist fashion.

Organizing exceptions into class hierarchies also gives programs the option of dealing with errors at several different levels of granularity. Take, for example, the simple exception hierarchy shown in figure 22.1.

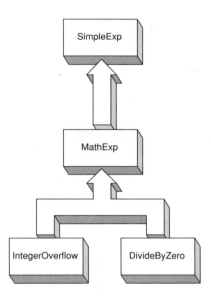

Fig. 22.1

A sample exception class hierarchy.

In this hierarchy, the topmost exception class is named SimpleExp. MathExp derives from SimpleExp, which, in turn, has children exception classes IntegerOverflow and DivideByZero. A program that uses this class hierarchy throws a wide variety of very specific exception objects such as IntegerOverflow and DivideByZero. However, when it comes to actually catching these exceptions, the program has the option of treating the exceptions generically (as SimpleExps), somewhat generically but within a math context (as MathExps), or as the specific exceptions that they really are.

The Subtleties of Throwing. You already know that you dispatch exceptions to handlers by using the throw keyword, but this chapter still hasn't discussed two subtleties associated with throw. Both of these subtleties are related to things that happen when a program throws an exception. The first is related to the concept of unwinding the stack. Remember that unwinding the stack refers to the process of calling the destructors of local class objects that the exception dispatch will move out of scope. This concept is pretty straightforward to understand and crucial to using exception handling effectively within C++ programs. Unwinding the stack, however, does *not* imply that objects created dynamically off the heap using the new operator will be destructed. For example, the MyLocalGuy object will get destructed in the following case:

```
void Func1()
{
    LocalGuy MyLocalGuy;
    throw 1;
}
```

However, the following case does not destruct the object:

```
void Func1()
{
    LocalGuy *MyLocalGuy = new LocalGuy;
    throw 1;
}
```

Caution

Your program must explicitly release dynamic allocations before raising the exception. Otherwise, your program could develop memory leaks. A program with memory leaks can use up some of the system's free memory and thus harm the system's performance.

The second subtlety relates to how you catch an exception after it is thrown. Remember that an exception can be caught by a handler designed to accept objects of the appropriate type or references to objects of the appropriate type.

When your program throws an exception by value or by reference, Borland C++ makes a copy of the object instance being thrown. This copy is stored in a temporary variable whose existence is hidden from your program. If the compiler didn't do this and you threw an object that was declared locally, by the time your handler was called the thrown object would be out of scope and would no longer exist. Your handler receives this mysterious "behind the scenes" copy—and not the instance that was originally thrown—as the exception argument.

The biggest implication here is that if you are throwing your exceptions by value or by reference, your classes must know how to copy themselves. If your class is complex and requires special copying behaviors, you must equip the class appropriately with a copy constructor that knows about these special requirements.

Contrast this to when you catch and throw an exception using a pointer. In this scenario, the run-time code directly passes the pointer into the handler, bypassing the copying that occurs when you throw by value or reference. Since the compiler does not make a copy, you are responsible for ensuring that the object is in a stable and completely constructed state.

Unfortunately, there are additional pitfalls associated with throwing exceptions using pointers. If you throw a pointer that refers to a local object, that object will no longer exist by the time your handler is called and the pointer will be invalid. If, on the other hand, you create a new object off the heap using the new operator, you must remember to delete the pointer in your handler or you will introduce a memory leak.

Yet another technique has your program throwing a temporary object.

```
void Func1()
{
    throw MyClass();
}
```

Borland C++ is smart enough to realize that you are throwing and catching using a temporary, and does not go through the unnecessary step of creating a clandestine copy (and triggering an invocation of your copy constructor). As one would expect, however, the temporary does need to be created, so its constructor is called.

Re-Throwing Exceptions. In the course of integrating exception handling into your programs, you might encounter a situation in which you want to field an exception in one try block, do some processing, and then pass the exception back up to another try block for additional processing. To do this, you use the throw keyword with no arguments. When the C++ run-time code encounters this syntax, it re-dispatches the current exception to the next matching exception handler. Listing 22.19 shows an example of how you might code this passing of exceptions.

Listing 22.19 Rethrow.cpp—An Example of Passing Exceptions

```
// Get needed include files
#include <iostream.h>

void Func1()
{
    try {
        throw "Something went wrong!";
    }
    catch (char *) {
        cout << "Doing some initial processing...\n";
        throw;
    }
}

void main()
{
    try {
        Func1();
    }
    catch (char*) {
        cout << "Doing some secondary processing.\n";
    }
}
```

When run, this program displays the following:

```
Doing some initial processing...
Doing some secondary processing.
```

The program re-dispatches the exception to the next enveloping `try` block. The run-time code does not look for new handler matches that might exist farther down in the current handler list.

Caution

Make sure when you re-dispatch an exception using the `throw;` syntax, that you only do so from within the scope of a catch handler. If you simply call `throw;` and there is no current exception being processed, the `terminate` handler gets called. Unless you have installed your own `terminate` function using `set_terminate()`, the invocation of `throw` results in the immediate termination of your program (see the later section "Installing Your Own *terminate()* Handler" for more details on `terminate`).

Throwing Exceptions from Inside Constructors. Before exception handling came along, one of C++'s great deficiencies was the lack of a simple way to signal errors from within object constructors. If, for example, a memory allocation within a constructor failed, programs typically had to rely on such hokey mechanisms as passed-in error variables (sound familiar?) and internal object state variables. For this reason, many C++ gurus have preached the virtues of not allocating resources within constructors at all.

All of that changes with the availability of exception handling. Exceptions can be thrown from within constructors just like anywhere else. When such an exception is thrown, the object construction process is aborted in a way that cannot be overlooked by the program initiating the creation of the new object. If any base classes are successfully constructed before the exception is raised, those classes' destructors are called in reverse order. If any objects are local to the constructor, those objects' destructors are guaranteed to be called.

To demonstrate these concepts, listing 22.19 shows a program with a `Base` class and `Derived` class that abort the construction of a `Derived` object in the constructor.

Listing 22.20 Cnstruct.cpp—An Example of Raising Exceptions from within a Constructor

```
// Get needed include files
#include <iostream.h>

class LocalGuy
{
public:
    LocalGuy() { cout << "In the LocalGuy constructor.\n"; }
    ~LocalGuy() { cout << "In the LocalGuy destructor.\n"; }
};

class Base
{
public:
```

```
    Base() { cout << "In the Base constructor.\n"; }
    ~Base() { cout << "In the Base destructor.\n"; }
};

class Derived: public Base
{
public:
    Derived(int flag)
    {
        LocalGuy MyLocalGuy;
        cout << "In the Derived constructor.\n";
        if (flag)
            throw -1;
    }
    ~Derived() { cout << "In the Derived destructor.\n"; }
};

void main()
{
    try {
        Derived(1);
    }
    catch (int) {
        cout << "Caught the Derived class exception.\n";
    }
}
```

When run, the program displays the following output:

```
In the Base constructor.
In the LocalGuy constructor.
In the Derived constructor.
In the LocalGuy destructor.
In the Base destructor.
Caught the Derived class exception.
```

As you can see, the program successfully constructs the Base class (remember that constructors are called in the order of Base to Derived). Execution then proceeds into the Derived constructor, which raises an exception. The program destructs the Base class and dispatches the exception to the appropriate handler. The LocalGuy instance confirms that the program destructs local class objects appropriately.

Note that the program does not call the destructor for Derived before dispatching the exception, which makes sense. Because the Derived object's construction has not completed, it is inappropriate to call a destructor that has been designed to destruct a completely constructed object. However, it is equally important to note that by the time execution of the Derived constructor begins, we know that the Base portion—the "subobject"—of the Derived instance has been fully constructed, so the Base destructor *does* get called.

Finally, remember that dynamically allocated resources are not automatically destructed when the program raises an exception. If a constructor allocates memory from the heap by using the new operator and you want to dispatch an exception from within the constructor, you must delete the allocated memory before dispatching the exception. If your class doesn't do this, you have no way to regain the pointer to the newly allocated memory, and your class introduces a memory leak.

Installing Your Own *terminate()* Handler

If your program throws an exception and the C++ run-time code returns all the way back to main() without finding a matching handler, your program is terminated by default. The run-time code stops program execution and display the on-screen message, Abnormal program termination.

If this behavior is too extreme for your taste, changing it is simple. The program calls the terminate() function when it cannot find an appropriate handler. You can install your own terminate() function by using set_terminate(). Listing 22.21 shows this procedure.

Listing 22.21   Term.cpp—Providing Your Own *terminate()* Function

```
// Get needed include files
#include <stdlib.h>
#include <iostream.h>
#include <except.h>

void MyTerminate()
{
    cout << "I regret to inform you that the exception could "
        <<_"not be dispatched.\n";
    cout << "I'm going away now...\n";
    exit(-1);
}

void main()
{
    set_terminate(MyTerminate);
    try {
        throw "Won't somebody catch me?";
    }
    catch (int) { }
}
```

Caution

You need to include the except.h header file in order to get access to the prototype for set_terminate().

set_terminate() takes as its single parameter a pointer to your new termination handler. The function's return value is a pointer to the new previous handler.

Using Exception Specifications

One of the potential dangers of using templates is that a programmer may not have a complete knowledge of what exceptions can possibly be thrown from a given try block. If you aren't aware that a particular exception type can be thrown out of a try block, there's no way for you to write a type-safe handler. Sure, you can ensure that your code always uses an ellipsis handler, but such a handler catches everything and will not allow you to catch exceptions in a particularly useful manner.

This problem is compounded once you start using code that you didn't write. If you are working in tandem with another developer, perhaps you can synchronize your exception hierarchies (you'd certainly hope so!), but what if you were using a third-party class library? Or what if the original developer of the classes you are using is long gone and his code exists only in the form of a library and some header files? When an exception is allowed to percolate back to main() and is not handled, the result is a call to terminate()—a fatal proposition indeed.

The C++ language has a solution to these problems in the form of a feature called *exception specifications*. In essence, exception specifications allow the programmer to note within a declaration what exceptions may be thrown by the function or method. As you can see in listing 22.22, the syntax involves the throw keyword, followed by a list of exception candidates.

Listing 22.22   Specs1.cpp—Using an Exception Specification

```
#include <iostream.h>

class SimpleException
{ };

class Pet
{ };

class Dog : public Pet
{ };

class Cat : public Pet
{ };

// Here's where we put our exception specification
void TestFunction(bool boolFlag) throw(Pet)
{
    // If the flag set?
    if (boolFlag)
        throw Cat();

    //Nope!
    throw SimpleException();
}
```

(continues)

Listing 22.22   Continued

```
void main()
{
    // First example -- Catch a Pet
    try {
        TestFunction(true);
    }
    catch(SimpleException&) {
        cout << "Caught a SimpleException!" << endl;
    }
    catch(Pet&) {
        cout << "Caught a Pet!" << endl;
    }

    // Second example -- Catch a SimpleException(??)
    try {
        TestFunction(false);
    }
    catch(SimpleException&) {
        cout << "Caught a SimpleException!" << endl;
    }
    catch(Pet&) {
        cout << "Caught a Pet!" << endl;
    }
}
```

In this example, `TestFunction()` has an exception specification that assures the programmer that only `Pet` exceptions—or exceptions derived from `Pet`—can be thrown from this function. There are a couple of things to note in this brief example. The Borland compiler is *not* obligated to analyze your source code and ensure that there is no logic path that allows non-`Pet` exceptions to be thrown, flagging such behavior as a compile-time error. Clearly, when the `boolFlag` variable is set to `false`, this example will throw an exception that does not appear in the exception specification (and yes, this example does compile and link correctly).

So what happens when a function violates its own exception specification? If you run the program created by listing 22.22, you'll find that it displays the `"Caught a Pet!"` message and then abnormally terminates. This termination behavior is caused by a function called the *unexpected* handler. When a function or method throws an exception that is not allowed by an exception specification, the unexpected handler is executed. With Borland C++ 5, the default unexpected handler simply displays a termination message and stops your program dead in its tracks. The next section, "Expecting the Unexpected," details how you can install your own unexpected handler.

So as you can see, exception specifications do help solve some of the problems mentioned at the beginning of this section. They do provide a programmer with a roadmap describing the twists and turns hidden within the source code. However, there are some serious pitfalls associated with the exception specification approach.

The fact of the matter is that exception specification-enabled programs suffer from many of the same problems as code that doesn't use specifications. This is because a programmer is now responsible for keeping track of all of the potential exceptions that can be thrown by a class or module, and this information needs to be tracked and managed down to the individual function and method level. In practice, this often turns out to be a tremendous hardship and is seldom worth the effort. This is especially true if you are using C++ code that you don't have the source code for. If you have some old libraries lying around, and the exception hierarchy isn't documented somewhere, you're out of luck. You can be pretty sure that most exception throws that originate inside that library will end up inside unexpected(). At least code without specifications can depend on the ellipsis handler to catch unexpected exceptions with less drastic results and more flexible constraints.

Expecting the Unexpected

As mentioned in the preceding section, the unexpected handler is called at runtime whenever your program throws an exception that violates an exception specification. Like the terminate handler, which simply gives your program the opportunity to perform an action before it dies, the unexpected handler is not allowed to return. If you allow execution to reach the end of your unexpected handler, your program will be immediately terminated. However, unlike the terminate handler, your unexpected handler is allowed to throw exceptions. This gives your program a second chance at life; hopefully the second time around, your unexpected handler will be able to throw an exception that does not violate the current exception specification.

You install your own unexpected handler in much the same way that you a install a new terminate handler. The only tangible difference is that the function you use is named set_unexpected(). Listing 22.23 shows a modified version of the program presented in listing 22.22 that installs a new unexpected handler and then puts it into action.

Listing 22.23 Specs2.cpp—Catching Unexpected Exceptions Using a Custom Handler

```cpp
#include <iostream.h>
#include <except.h>

class SimpleException
{ };

class Pet
{ };

class Dog : public Pet
{ };

class Cat : public Pet
{ };
```

(continues)

Listing 22.23   Continued

```cpp
// Here's the custom unexpected handler
void MyUnexpected()
{
    throw Dog();
}

// Here's where we put our exception specification
void TestFunction(bool boolFlag) throw(Pet)
{
    // If the flag set?
    if (boolFlag)
        throw Cat();

    //Nope!
    throw SimpleException();
}

void main()
{
    // Install our unexpected handler
    set_unexpected(MyUnexpected);

    // First example -- Catch a Pet
    try {
        TestFunction(true);
    }
    catch(SimpleException&) {
        cout << "Caught a SimpleException!" << endl;
    }
    catch(Pet&) {
        cout << "Caught a Pet!" << endl;
    }

    // Second example -- Catch a SimpleException(??)
    try {
        TestFunction(false);
    }
    catch(SimpleException&) {
        cout << "Caught a SimpleException!" << endl;
    }
    catch(Pet&) {
        cout << "Caught a Pet!" << endl;
    }
}
```

Let's take a quick look at what's going on here. The heart of this example is identical to listing 22.22; the test function is called twice, with the second call triggering an exception that violates the exception specification. In this version of the program, however, we have installed a new unexpected handler that always throws a Dog exception. Since Dog is derived from Pet, the exception specification is met, and the new Dog exception is successfully dispatched and caught.

Portable Exceptions

Both the Windows NT and Windows 95 operating systems support an error-handling infrastructure called *structured exception handling*. Note that although structured exception handling is compatible with Borland C++'s language-based exceptions, they are *not* the same thing. Languages other than C++ (most notably C) can use structured exception handling; C++ exception handling is obviously a language-dependent feature.

If you want to write more portable code, do not use structured exception handling in a C++ program. Occasionally, however, you might want to mix C and C++ source code and thus need some facility for handling both kinds of exceptions. Because a structured exception handler has no concept of objects or typed exceptions, it cannot handle exceptions that C++ code throws; however, C++ catch handlers can handle C exceptions. Therefore, the C compiler does not accept C++ exception-handling syntax (try, throw, and catch), but the C++ compiler does support structured exception-handling syntax (__try, __except, and __finally).

The structured exception-handling constructs that Borland C++ provides are interesting and beneficial for those non-C++ programs that must ensure that they deliver the most secure and robust performance possible. The vast majority of C++ programmers, however, should avoid structured exception handling.

Exploring a Hypothetical Application

So far, this chapter has concentrated on presenting the semantics of exception handling using trivial examples. This is all fine and good, but without taking a look at a more substantial example, it's still difficult to get a feel for how profoundly the use of exception handling affects the entire program.

The rest of this chapter explores a hypothetical application called ExpSum. This application is quite small, but still sizable enough to demonstrate some techniques that you might want to use when integrating exceptions into your standard programming practices.

An Introduction to the ExpSum Application

The function of the ExpSum program is to take a text file that contains expense voucher information and display the file's contents on-screen in a report format. During the processing of the file, the program is responsible for doing some (very limited) analysis of the file's expense information to ensure that it is valid. Listing 22.24 is the output of the ExpSum application using a sample voucher file.

Listing 22.24 An Example of the ExpSum Application's Output

```
+==================================================================+
|                      EXPENSE FILE PROCESSOR                       |
+==================================================================+


Employee #9264
Ben E. Eye
123 Liberty Bell South Dr.
Birmingham, AL 35244

Expenses

_____
8/1/94      New security badge              4.00
8/1/94      Phone calls                    47.89
8/13/94     Rental car                     87.99
===================================================================
Employee Total:                           139.88


Employee #8394
Jason R. Jordan
40 Hurt Ln.
Arlington, VA 22201

Expenses

_____
7/12/94     Beverages                     227.58
7/12/94     Taxi                           11.95
===================================================================
Employee Total:                           239.53

Employee #9520
Chris K. Corry
123 Car of Kings Blvd.
Arlington, VA 22204

Expenses

_____
8/4/94      Room rate                      77.00
8/4/94      Lodging tax                     6.16
8/6/94      In-room movies                104.97
===================================================================
Employee Total:                           188.13


+================================================================+
| EXPENSE FILE TOTAL:                              567.54 |
+================================================================+
```

Actually, this discussion presents two programs. The first, ExpSum1, shows the ExpSum application as it might be written by a programmer who was either unfamiliar with the use of exception handling or did not have the language extension at his disposal. The application relies on a variety of error-handling techniques that are all based on the traditional strategies discussed earlier in this chapter. For this reason, the program suffers from many of the maladies of contemporary C++ code; despite its small size, the program can be difficult to follow. There is no centralization of error-handling logic, and the error-handling logic that does exist is cumbersome and distracting.

The second example, ExpSum2, depicts ExpSum after the programmer overhauls it to take advantage of C++ exceptions. ExpSum2 is shorter (although that is not necessarily one of the goals of exception handling), the program's error-handling facilities are consolidated into a single location, and the entire program benefits from the simplification of the error-reporting code.

The ExpSum Application Structure

At the heart of ExpSum are two simple classes: `Employee` and `Expense`. The program primarily uses these classes in a relatively unsophisticated context: as containers for data pertaining to employees and expense reports. Although the two classes are rather unremarkable, they can either dump themselves out to a standard C++ output stream and load themselves in from a standard C++ input stream. Therefore, the ExpSum application can easily save and retrieve relevant information to the file system.

Listing 22.25 is the header file that contains the class definition for the `Employee` class.

Listing 22.25 employee.h—The Definition of the *Employee* Class

```
#ifndef EMPLOYEE_H
#define EMPLOYEE_H

// Get needed include files
#include <iostream.h>
#include <cstring.h>

class Employee {
public:
    Employee();

    void SetID(unsigned NewID)
        { EmployeeID = NewID; }
    void SetFirstName(const string& strNewName)
        { strFirstName = strNewName; }
    void SetMiddleInitial(char NewInitial)
        { MiddleInitial = NewInitial; }
    void SetLastName(const string& strNewName)
        { strLastName = strNewName; }
    void SetAddress(const string& strNewAddress)
        { strAddress = strNewAddress; }
    void SetCity(const string& strNewCity)
        { strCity = strNewCity; }
    void SetState(const string& strNewState)
        { strState = strNewState; }
```

(continues)

Listing 22.25   Continued

```
    void SetZip(unsigned long NewZip)
        { Zip = NewZip; }
    void SetNumExpenses(unsigned NewNumExpenses)
        { NumExpenses = NewNumExpenses; }

    unsigned     GetID() const { return EmployeeID; }
    string       GetFirstName() const { return strFirstName; }
    char         GetMiddleInitial() const { return MiddleInitial; }
    string       GetLastName() const { return strLastName; }
    string       GetAddress() const { return strAddress; }
    string       GetCity() const { return strCity; }
    string       GetState() const { return strState; }
    unsigned long GetZip() const { return Zip; }
    unsigned     GetNumExpenses() const { return NumExpenses; }

private:
    unsigned     EmployeeID;
    string       strFirstName;
    char         MiddleInitial;
    string       strLastName;
    string       strAddress;
    string       strCity;
    string       strState;
    unsigned long Zip;
    unsigned     NumExpenses;
};

ostream& operator<<(ostream& ostr, const Employee& employee);
istream& operator>>(istream& istr, Employee& employee);

#endif
```

Although these header files contain most of the class implementations, the C++ source files Employee.cpp and Expense.cpp (listings 22.26 and listing 22.27, respectively) contain the class operators.

Listing 22.26   Employee.cpp—The Implementation of the *Employee* Class

```
// Get needed include files
#include <employee.h>

Employee::Employee() :
    EmployeeID(0),
    MiddleInitial('\0'),
    Zip(0UL),
    NumExpenses(0)
{ }

ostream& operator<<(ostream& ostr, const Employee& employee)
{
```

```
        ostr << employee.GetID();
        ostr << employee.GetFirstName() << " ";
        ostr << employee.GetLastName() << " ";
        ostr << employee.GetMiddleInitial();
        ostr << employee.GetAddress() << "\n";
        ostr << employee.GetCity() << " ";
        ostr << employee.GetState() << " ";
        ostr << employee.GetZip() << " ";
        ostr << employee.GetNumExpenses() << " ";
        return ostr;
}

istream& operator>>(istream& istr, Employee& employee)
{
        char TempBuffer[256], TempChar;
        unsigned long TempUnsignedLong;
        unsigned TempUnsigned;

        istr >> TempUnsigned;
        employee.SetID(TempUnsigned);
        istr >> TempBuffer;
        employee.SetFirstName(TempBuffer);
        istr >> TempBuffer;
        employee.SetLastName(TempBuffer);
        istr >> TempChar;
        employee.SetMiddleInitial(TempChar);
        istr.getline(TempBuffer, 256);
        employee.SetAddress(TempBuffer);
        istr >> TempBuffer;
        employee.SetCity(TempBuffer);
        istr >> TempBuffer;
        employee.SetState(TempBuffer);
        istr >> TempUnsignedLong;
        employee.SetZip(TempUnsignedLong);
        istr >> TempUnsigned;
        employee.SetNumExpenses(TempUnsigned);

        return istr;
}
```

Listing 22.27 is the header file that contains the class definition for the Expense class.

Listing 22.27   expense.h—The Definition of the *Expense* Class

```
#ifndef EXPENSE_H
#define EXPENSE_H

// Get needed include files
#include <iostream.h>
#include <cstring.h>

class Expense {
public:
```

(continues)

Listing 22.27   Continued

```
    Expense();

    void SetDate(const string& strNewDate)
        { strDate = strNewDate; }
    void SetDescription(const string& strNewDescription)
        { strDescription = strNewDescription; }
    void SetExpenseAmount(float NewExpenseAmount)
        { ExpenseAmount = NewExpenseAmount; }

    string  GetDate() const { return strDate; }
    string  GetDescription() const { return strDescription; }
    float   GetExpenseAmount() const { return ExpenseAmount; }

private:
    string  strDate;
    string  strDescription;
    float   ExpenseAmount;
};

ostream& operator<<(ostream& ostr, const Expense& employee);
istream& operator>>(istream& istr, Expense& employee);

#endif
```

Listing 22.28 shows Expense.cpp, the C++ source file that implements the Expense class.

Listing 22.28   Expense.cpp—The Implementation of the *Expense* Class

```
// Get needed include files
#include <expense.h>

Expense::Expense() :
    ExpenseAmount(0.0F)
{ }

ostream& operator<<(ostream& ostr, const Expense& expense)
{
    ostr << expense.GetDate() << " ";
    ostr << expense.GetDescription() << "\n";
    ostr << expense.GetExpenseAmount() << " ";
    return ostr;
}

istream& operator>>(istream& istr, Expense& expense)
{
    char TempBuffer[256];
    float TempFloat;

    istr >> TempBuffer;
    expense.SetDate(TempBuffer);
```

```
        istr.getline(TempBuffer, 256);
        expense.SetDescription(TempBuffer);
        istr >> TempFloat;
        expense.SetExpenseAmount(TempFloat);

        return istr;
}
```

As you can see, the two classes do little more than manage access to their data members. If you are unfamiliar with the ANSI string class found within the Standard Library, you might want to skip ahead briefly to chapter 21, "Understanding Strings in ANSI C and ANSI C++," to learn more details about this class.

Three separate programs use these two classes. As already discussed, ExpSum1 is the version of the application that uses traditional error handling, whereas ExpSum2 is the version of the application that relies on C++ exception handling. The third program, ExpMaker, is the program responsible for creating the voucher files in the first place. ExpMaker is not a terribly exciting program, but it is obviously a necessary one. Because ExpMaker is not really relevant to the topics that this chapter discusses, this chapter doesn't analyze the program's design aspects; however, for the sake of completeness, listing 22.29 presents the program. After all, without ExpMaker (and the code needed to build it), the two ExpSum programs would have no expense files to process.

Listing 22.29 Expmaker.cpp—The Expense File Generator Program

```
// Get our needed include files
#include <fstream.h>
#include <iomanip.h>
#include <employee.h>
#include <expense.h>

void GetNewExpenseItem(ofstream& outfile, const unsigned itemnum)
{
    Expense NewExpense;
    float   ExpenseAmount;
    char    TempBuffer[256], ChompNewline;

    // User friendly stuff
    cout << "\nExpense #" << (itemnum+1) << "\n";

    // Fill in the basics
    cout << "Expense date   : ";
    cin.get(TempBuffer, 256);
    cin.get(ChompNewline);
    NewExpense.SetDate(TempBuffer);
    cout << "Description    : ";
    cin.get(TempBuffer, 256);
    cin.get(ChompNewline);
    NewExpense.SetDescription(TempBuffer);
    cout << "Expense amount : ";
```

(continues)

Listing 22.29   Continued

```
        cin >> ExpenseAmount;
        cin.get(ChompNewline);
        NewExpense.SetExpenseAmount(ExpenseAmount);

        // Write the expense record to the file
        outfile << NewExpense;
}

void GetNewEmployee(ofstream& outfile)
{
        Employee        NewEmployee;
        unsigned long   NewZip;
        unsigned        loop, NewID, NewNumExpenses;
        char            TempBuffer[256], ChompNewline, NewInitial;

        // User friendly stuff
        cout << "\nNew employee record\n";
        cout << "===================\n";

        // Fill in the basics
        cout << "Employee ID    : ";
        cin >> NewID;
        cin.get(ChompNewline);
        NewEmployee.SetID(NewID);
        cout << "First name     : ";
        cin.get(TempBuffer, 256);
        cin.get(ChompNewline);
        NewEmployee.SetFirstName(TempBuffer);
        cout << "Middle initial : ";
        cin >> NewInitial;
        cin.get(ChompNewline);
        NewEmployee.SetMiddleInitial(NewInitial);
        cout << "Last name      : ";
        cin.get(TempBuffer, 256);
        cin.get(ChompNewline);
        NewEmployee.SetLastName(TempBuffer);
        cout << "Address        : ";
        cin.get(TempBuffer, 256);
        cin.get(ChompNewline);
        NewEmployee.SetAddress(TempBuffer);
        cout << "City           : ";
        cin.get(TempBuffer, 256);
        cin.get(ChompNewline);
        NewEmployee.SetCity(TempBuffer);
        cout << "State          : ";
        cin.get(TempBuffer, 256);
        cin.get(ChompNewline);
        NewEmployee.SetState(TempBuffer);
        cout << "ZIP code       : ";
        cin >> NewZip;
        cin.get(ChompNewline);
        NewEmployee.SetZip(NewZip);
        cout << "\nNumber of expense items for this employee? ";
        cin >> NewNumExpenses;
```

```
        cin.get(ChompNewline);
        NewEmployee.SetNumExpenses(NewNumExpenses);

        // Write the employee record to the file
        outfile << NewEmployee;

        // Now get the expense records
        for (loop = 0; loop < NewEmployee.GetNumExpenses(); loop++)
            GetNewExpenseItem(outfile, loop);
}

void main(int argc, char *argv[])
{
    // Check for right number of command-line arguments
    if (argc != 2) {
        cout << "USAGE: expmaker <outfile name>\n\n";
        return;
    }

    // Open the outfile
    ofstream outfile(argv[1]);

    // Place our dummy employee count
    unsigned EmployeeCount = 0;
    outfile << setw(5) << EmployeeCount << setw(0) << " ";

    // Main employee loop
    char Again;
    do {
        char ChompNewline;
        EmployeeCount++;
        GetNewEmployee(outfile);
        cout << "\nEnter another employee (Y/N)? ";
        cin >> Again;
        cin.get(ChompNewline);
    } while (Again == 'y' || Again == 'Y');


    // Go to the beginning of the file and fill in the
    // real employee count
    outfile.seekp(0, ios::beg);
    outfile << setw(5) << EmployeeCount;

    // Close the outfile _ we're done!
    outfile.close();
}
```

You can build the ExpMaker program and then use it to generate a variety of different expense report files, including files that contain contextual errors (expenses that are too large or too small to be claimed, an invalid number of employees or expense reports, and so on). ExpMaker allows you to build incorrect expense report files so that the error-handling muscle of the two ExpSum applications can be tested. If ExpMaker ensured that it created valid expense files, determining whether this flashy exception-handling logic is working would be quite difficult.

ExpSum1: The Model T of Expense Reporting

Take a look at the first of these applications, ExpSum1. This program, presented in listing 22.30, consists of three sections: ProcessExpenseItem(), ProcessEmployee(), and main(). As you read the source code, pay special attention to how it reports errors and passes them through each of these sections.

Listing 22.30   Expsum1.cpp—the ExpSum Application Using Traditional Error Handling

```cpp
// Get our needed include files
#include <fstream.h>
#include <iomanip.h>
#include <employee.h>
#include <expense.h>

// Definitions
const int   MIN_ALLOWABLE_EMPLOYEES = 1;
const int   MAX_ALLOWABLE_EMPLOYEES = 20;
const int   MIN_NUM_EXPENSES = 1;
const int   MAX_NUM_EXPENSES = 10;
const float MIN_ALLOWABLE_EXPENSE = 1.0F;
const float MAX_ALLOWABLE_EXPENSE = 1000.0F;
const float MAX_ALLOWABLE_REIMBURSEMENT = 5000.0F;

// Error codes
typedef enum {
    EXP_NO_ERROR,
    EXP_ERR_EXPENSE_TOO_SMALL,
    EXP_ERR_EXPENSE_TOO_LARGE,
    EXP_ERR_NO_EXPENSE_ITEMS,
    EXP_ERR_TOO_MANY_EXPENSE_ITEMS,
    EXP_ERR_TOTAL_EXPENSE_TOO_LARGE
} ErrorCode;

float ProcessExpenseItem(ifstream& infile, ErrorCode& rc)
{
    Expense NewExpense;

    // Init the return code
    rc = EXP_NO_ERROR;

    // Read in the expense record from the file
    infile >> NewExpense;

    // Check for problems
    if (NewExpense.GetExpenseAmount() < MIN_ALLOWABLE_EXPENSE) {
        cout << "Error! Expense item under the minimum amount "
            << "eligible for reimbursement.\n\n";
        rc = EXP_ERR_EXPENSE_TOO_SMALL;
        return 0.0F;
    }
    if (NewExpense.GetExpenseAmount() > MAX_ALLOWABLE_EXPENSE) {
        cout << "Error! Expense item greater than maximum amount "
            << "eligible for reimbursement.\n\n";
```

```
            rc = EXP_ERR_EXPENSE_TOO_LARGE;
            return 0.0F;
    }

    // Display the expense
    cout << "      " << setw(10) << NewExpense.GetDate();
    cout << setw(35) << NewExpense.GetDescription();
    cout.unsetf(ios::left);
    cout << setw(12)<<NewExpense.GetExpenseAmount()<< "\n"<< setw(0);
    cout.setf(ios::left);

    return NewExpense.GetExpenseAmount();
}

float ProcessEmployee(ifstream& infile, ErrorCode& rc)
{
    Employee NewEmployee;
    float    EmployeeTotal = 0.0F;
    unsigned loop;

    // Init the return code
    rc = EXP_NO_ERROR;

    // Read in the employee record from the file
    infile >> NewEmployee;

    // Check for problems
    if (NewEmployee.GetNumExpenses() < MIN_NUM_EXPENSES) {
        cout << "Error! No expense items for this employee.\n\n";
        rc = EXP_ERR_NO_EXPENSE_ITEMS;
        return 0.0F;
    }
    if (NewEmployee.GetNumExpenses() > MAX_NUM_EXPENSES) {
        cout << "Error! Too many expense items for this employee.\n\n";
        rc = EXP_ERR_TOO_MANY_EXPENSE_ITEMS;
        return 0.0F;
    }

    // Display the employee record
    cout << "Employee #" << NewEmployee.GetID() << "\n";
    cout << NewEmployee.GetFirstName() << " ";
    cout << NewEmployee.GetMiddleInitial() << ". ";
    cout << NewEmployee.GetLastName() << "\n";
    cout << NewEmployee.GetAddress() << "\n";
    cout << NewEmployee.GetCity() << ", ";
    cout << NewEmployee.GetState() << " ";
    cout << NewEmployee.GetZip() << "\n\n";

    // Now get the expense records
    cout << "      Expenses\n";
    cout << "      --------------------\n";
    for (loop = 0; loop < NewEmployee.GetNumExpenses(); loop++) {
        EmployeeTotal += ProcessExpenseItem(infile, rc);
        if (rc != EXP_NO_ERROR)
            return 0.0F;
    }
```

(continues)

Listing 22.30 Continued

```cpp
    // Check for problems
    if (EmployeeTotal > MAX_ALLOWABLE_REIMBURSEMENT) {
        cout << "Error! Expense total greater than maximum "
            << "amount eligible for reimbursement.\n\n";
        rc = EXP_ERR_TOTAL_EXPENSE_TOO_LARGE;
        return 0.0F;
    }

    // Display the employee total
    cout << "      =========================="
        << "===============================\n";
    cout << "        Employee Total:";
    cout.unsetf(ios::left);
    cout << setw(42) << EmployeeTotal << "\n\n\n";
    cout.setf(ios::left);

    return EmployeeTotal;
}

void main(int argc, char *argv[])
{
    // Check for right number of command-line arguments
    if (argc != 2) {
        cout << "USAGE: expsum1 <infile name>\n\n";
        return;
    }

    // Open the infile
    ifstream infile(argv[1], ios::nocreate);
    if (!infile) {
        cout << "Expense file \"" << argv[1]
            << "\" not found.\n\n";
        return;
    }

    // Read in our number of employees
    unsigned EmployeeCount;
    float    FileTotal = 0.0F;
    infile >> EmployeeCount;
    if (EmployeeCount < MIN_ALLOWABLE_EMPLOYEES ||
        EmployeeCount > MAX_ALLOWABLE_EMPLOYEES) {
        cout << "Invalid number of employees specified in "
            << "expense file.\n\n";
        infile.close();
    }

    // Set the stream display flags
    cout.setf(ios::left | ios::showpoint | ios::fixed);
    cout.precision(2);
```

```
    // Display our main heading
    cout << "+================================="
         << "=================================+\n";
    cout << "¦                          EXPENSE "
         << "FILE PROCESSOR                        ¦\n";
    cout << "+================================="
         << "=================================+\n\n\n";

    // Main employee loop
    ErrorCode rc;
    do {
        FileTotal += ProcessEmployee(infile, rc);
        if (rc != EXP_NO_ERROR) {
            infile.close();
            return;
        }
    } while (--EmployeeCount);

    // Display the file total
    cout << "+================================="
         << "=================================+\n";
    cout << "¦ EXPENSE FILE TOTAL: ";
    cout.unsetf(ios::left);
    cout << setw(43) << FileTotal << " ¦\n";
    cout.setf(ios::left);
    cout << "+================================="
         << "=================================+\n";

    // Close the infile _ we're done!
    infile.close();
}
```

The ExpSum1 program takes a single command-line argument indicating the expense file's name. The program opens this file, displays it in a formatted manner, and then closes it. If the program identifies any errors in the file during processing, an appropriate error message appears and the program terminates.

A Quick Overview of How ExpSum Works. The ExpSum application's execution strategy is quite simple. The program obtains the expense filename from the command line, opens the file, and reads an initial value that indicates how many employee records the file contains. The program proceeds into a loop that calls the ProcessEmployee() function for the appropriate number of times.

Inside ProcessEmployee(), the program reads in the next employee record from the file and displays the initial employee information (employee number, name, address, and so on). One of the pieces of information that the Employee class knows about is the number of expense items that a particular employee has outstanding. ProcessEmployee() proceeds to call ProcessExpenseItem() the appropriate number of times for each employee.

`ProcessExpenseItem()` works similarly to `ProcessEmployee()`. The function reads in the next expense item from the file and displays it on-screen. After moving through the file, the program displays some final totals and closes the input file.

ExpSum1's Error Handling. ExpSum relies on the error-reporting strategy explained previously in the section "Returning Error Values in Function Arguments." As calls are made to `ProcessEmployee()` and `ProcessExpenseItem()`, an error code variable is passed along with the function arguments. When problems occur, the program displays a message and modifies the contents of the error variable. The calling functions check the error variable when they regain control. If an error occurs, the functions return to their caller. This process continues until control reverts to `main()`, where execution stops.

Although this program works the way that it's supposed to, ExpSum could do better. In ExpSum, error values are forced back through the calling chain like a large truck that has driven into a dead-end alley. This propagation code results in situations where the program initially catches and processes errors but then must reprocess them at every point in the calling sequence. This bloats the program and makes it significantly more difficult to follow. Code that's hard to read is hard to maintain, and that means that bugs will be harder to track down.

The error handling hard-wired into ExpSum1 is also inflexible. Suppose, for example, you later decide to have the employee ID return to `main()` when a particular error condition occurs. To implement this behavior, you would have to retrofit the program severely, and as you did so, you would leave your application susceptible to the introduction of new bugs. In turn, you would spend more time debugging when you could be adding functionality.

Fortunately, the ExpSum2 application resolves all these concerns.

ExpSum2: The Ferrari of Expense Reporting

Perhaps it's a jump to call ExpSum2 an expense reporting Ferrari, but the application certainly is a big improvement over ExpSum1. The use of exceptions enables the program to consolidate error handling into a single place without sacrificing readability or flexibility.

ExpSum2's Exception Class Hierarchy. Listing 22.31 shows the contents of Expex.h. This new header file contains definitions for the exception types used by ExpSum2's new error-handling infrastructure.

Listing 22.31   expex.h—The Definitions for ExpSum2's Exceptions

```
#ifndef EXPEX_H
#define EXPEX_H

// Get needed include files
#include <cstring.h>
```

```cpp
// Error codes
typedef enum {
    EXP_NO_ERROR,
    EXP_GENERIC_ERROR,
    EXP_ERR_EXPENSE_TOO_SMALL,
    EXP_ERR_EXPENSE_TOO_LARGE,
    EXP_ERR_NO_EXPENSE_ITEMS,
    EXP_ERR_TOO_MANY_EXPENSE_ITEMS,
    EXP_ERR_TOTAL_EXPENSE_TOO_LARGE
} ErrorCode;

// Our base exception class
class ExpException {
public:
    ExpException(ErrorCode NewErrorCode,
                const char* NewReason = NULL) :
        TheError(NewErrorCode),
        strTheReason(NewReason)
    { }

    void SetErrorCode(ErrorCode NewErrorCode)
        { TheError = NewErrorCode; }
    void SetReason(const string& strNewReason)
        { strTheReason = strNewReason; }

    string   Why() const { return strTheReason; }
    ErrorCode GetErrorCode() const { return TheError; }

private:
    ErrorCode TheError;
    string    strTheReason;
};

// Specific exception classes
class ExpenseTooSmall : public ExpException
{
public:
    ExpenseTooSmall() :
        ExpException(EXP_ERR_EXPENSE_TOO_SMALL,
                    "Expense item under the minimum amount eligible "
                    "for reimbursement.")
    { }
};

class ExpenseTooLarge : public ExpException
{
public:
    ExpenseTooLarge() :
        ExpException(EXP_ERR_EXPENSE_TOO_LARGE,
                    "Expense item greater than the maximum amount "
                    "eligible for reimbursement.")
    { }
};
```

(continues)

```cpp
class EmployeeException : public ExpException
{
public:
    EmployeeException(ErrorCode NewErrorCode,
                      unsigned NewEmployeeID,
                      const char* NewReason = NULL) :
        ExpException(NewErrorCode, NewReason),
        EmployeeID(NewEmployeeID)
    { }
    unsigned GetEmployeeID() const { return EmployeeID; }
private:
    unsigned EmployeeID;
};

class NoExpenseItems : public EmployeeException
{
public:
    NoExpenseItems(unsigned NewEmployeeID) :
        EmployeeException(EXP_ERR_NO_EXPENSE_ITEMS,
                          NewEmployeeID,
                          "No expense items for this employee")
    { }
};

class TooManyExpenseItems : public EmployeeException
{
public:
    TooManyExpenseItems(unsigned NewEmployeeID) :
        EmployeeException(EXP_ERR_TOO_MANY_EXPENSE_ITEMS,
                          NewEmployeeID,
                          "Too many expense items for this employee")
    { }
};

class ExpenseTotalTooLarge : public ExpException
{
public:
    ExpenseTotalTooLarge() :
        ExpException(EXP_ERR_TOTAL_EXPENSE_TOO_LARGE,
                     "Expense total greater than maximum amount "
                     "eligible for reimbursement.")
    { }
};

#endif
```

The exception hierarchy used by ExpSum2 is pretty elaborate for a program of this size. For applications that are only a couple of pages long, the number of exception types used is generally quite small, but the exaggerated hierarchy found in listing 22.31 demonstrates some of the functionality that programs significantly larger than ExpSum2 would probably need. Figure 22.2 presents a graphical overview of the exception hierarchy.

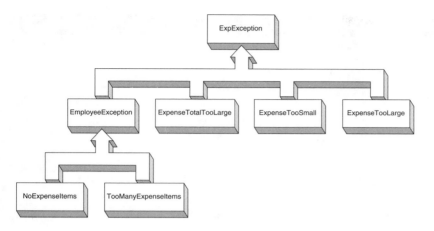

Fig. 22.2

ExpSum2's exception class hierarchy.

The topmost exception class is `ExpException`. This generic exception class provides the simplest of error-reporting services. When throwing an exception, the thrower can specify an error code and an optional description of the error, but there are no provisions for passing on any other contextual information. Still, with the `ExpException` class alone, the ExpSum2 application exhibits more error-processing functionality than ExpSum1 because of the addition of the error-description string.

New exception classes derive from `ExpException` as appropriate. This class hierarchy uses two different strategies. Classes deriving from `ExpException` serve to narrow the scope of a particular error. Although `ExpException` could represent virtually any error, classes such as `ExpenseTooSmall` leave little room for speculation about what went wrong. Given a class hierarchy with this level of granularity, an application has the option of interacting with errors in the abstract (treating all exceptions as `ExpExceptions`) or in the specific (treating exceptions as their actual type).

The second strategy used by classes within this hierarchy is to provide additional information. Recall the previous example about how difficult it is to return an employee ID through the calling chain. With exception handling, such a request becomes almost trivial and ExpSum2 does exactly this. The `EmployeeException` class provides the capability to throw an employee ID, and both the `NoExpenseItems` and `TooManyExpenseItems` classes take advantage of this service.

ExpSum2's Main Function. Instead of presenting ExpSum2 all at once and in its entirety, this section breaks the program into its component parts and discusses each with regard to its integration into the exception-handling framework. Listing 22.32 shows how `main()` changes between ExpSum1 and ExpSum2.

Listing 22.32   Expsum2.cpp—ExpSum2's *main()* Function

```cpp
// Get the needed include files
#include <fstream.h>
#include <iomanip.h>
#include <employee.h>
#include <expense.h>
#include <expex.h>

// Definitions
const int MIN_ALLOWABLE_EMPLOYEES = 1;
const int MAX_ALLOWABLE_EMPLOYEES = 20;
const int MIN_NUM_EXPENSES = 1;
const int MAX_NUM_EXPENSES = 10;
const float MIN_ALLOWABLE_EXPENSE = 1.0F;
const float MAX_ALLOWABLE_EXPENSE = 1000.0F;
const float MAX_ALLOWABLE_REIMBURSEMENT = 5000.0F;

void main(int argc, char *argv[])
{
    // Check for right number of command-line arguments
    if (argc != 2) {
        cout << "USAGE: expsum2 <infile name>\n\n";
        return;
    }

    // Open the infile
    ifstream infile(argv[1], ios::nocreate);
    if (!infile) {
        cout << "Expense file \"" << argv[1]
            << "\" not found.\n\n";
        return;
    }

    // Main try block
    try {

        // Read in our number of employees
        unsigned EmployeeCount;
        float     FileTotal = 0.0F;
        infile >> EmployeeCount;
        if (EmployeeCount < MIN_ALLOWABLE_EMPLOYEES ||
            EmployeeCount > MAX_ALLOWABLE_EMPLOYEES)
            throw ExpException(EXP_GENERIC_ERROR,
                                "Invalid number of employees specified "
                                "in expense file.");

        // Set the stream display flags
        cout.setf(ios::left | ios::showpoint | ios::fixed);
        cout.precision(2);

        // Display our main heading
        cout << "+===================================="
            << "====================================+\n";
        cout << "|                         EXPENSE FILE "
            << "PROCESSOR                          |\n";
        cout << "+===================================="
            << "====================================+\n\n\n";
```

```
        // Main employee loop
        do {
            FileTotal += ProcessEmployee(infile);
        } while (-EmployeeCount);

        // Display the file total
        cout <<"+================================="
             << "=================================+\n";
        cout << "¦ EXPENSE FILE TOTAL: ";
        cout.unsetf(ios::left);
        cout << setw(43) << FileTotal << " ¦\n";
        cout.setf(ios::left);
        cout <<"+================================="
             << "=================================+\n";
    }

    // Handlers
    catch (EmployeeException& EmpExp) {
        cout << "\nError! ";
        cout << EmpExp.Why() << " (Employee "
             << EmpExp.GetEmployeeID() << ")\n";
    }
    catch (ExpException& Exp) {
        cout << "\nError! " << Exp.Why() << "\n";
    }
    catch (...) {
        cout << "Caught an unrecognized exception.\n";
    }

    // Close the infile --  _ we're done!
    infile.close();
}
```

Start by looking at what hasn't changed. The program still processes the command-line argument the same way, and, at least from main()'s perspective, the general processing algorithm doesn't seem to have been modified. The formatting and display of banners and text-based frills have not been altered.

Now you can sink your teeth into what's different. The most obvious change is that the program now encloses most of the function within a single try block—the only try block in the program. This change enables you to consolidate all the application's error handling into a single handler list.

This try block has three handlers. None of them explicitly accepts any of the detailed exception types found in expex.h. Instead, ExpSum2 relies primarily on two general-purpose handlers that catch EmployeeException first and other instances of ExpException second. This handler list also has an ellipsis handler to ensure that no other exceptions slip by unnoticed. (Actually, they wouldn't go unnoticed at all; unhandled exceptions would end execution and ExpSum2 wouldn't have a clue of what hit it!) These handlers display the description of what went wrong. In the case of the EmployeeException, the program also displays the employee ID that was at fault.

Note that none of these handlers actually stops program execution. Although severe errors often require that a program stop, ExpSum2 has a good reason for not stopping execution. Note the last line of the program:

```
// Close the infile - we're done!
infile.close();
```

Although C++ streams know that they must close themselves if they are still open when destructed, you should still explicitly ensure that the program takes that responsibility. In this case, you can easily do so. More importantly, to close the file, you need not use the error-processing code that was previously scattered throughout the program. Notice, for example, the sections of main() that must close the file in ExpSum1:

```
do {
    FileTotal += ProcessEmployee(infile, rc);
    if (rc != EXP_NO_ERROR) {
        infile.close();
        return;
    }
} while (_EmployeeCount);
```

These sections need not worry about this task in ExpSum2:

```
do {
    FileTotal += ProcessEmployee(infile);
} while (_EmployeeCount);
```

Nor does the ExpSum2 code have to deal with returned error codes in any context. The code is free to concentrate on solving the problem instead of worrying about what to do if something goes wrong.

Processing Employees. Now focus your attention on ProcessEmployee(). Listing 22.33 contains the ExpSum2 code for this function.

Listing 22.33 Expsum2.cpp—ExpSum2's *ProcessEmployee()* Function

```
float ProcessEmployee(ifstream& infile)
{
    Employee NewEmployee;
    float    EmployeeTotal = 0.0F;
    unsigned loop;

    // Read in the employee record from the file
    infile >> NewEmployee;

    // Check for problems
    if (NewEmployee.GetNumExpenses() < MIN_NUM_EXPENSES)
        throw NoExpenseItems(NewEmployee.GetID());
    if (NewEmployee.GetNumExpenses() > MAX_NUM_EXPENSES)
        throw TooManyExpenseItems(NewEmployee.GetID());

    // Display the employee record
    cout << "Employee #" << NewEmployee.GetID() << "\n";
    cout << NewEmployee.GetFirstName() << " ";
    cout << NewEmployee.GetMiddleInitial() << ". ";
```

```
        cout << NewEmployee.GetLastName() << "\n";
        cout << NewEmployee.GetAddress() << "\n";
        cout << NewEmployee.GetCity() << ", ";
        cout << NewEmployee.GetState() << " ";
        cout << NewEmployee.GetZip() << "\n\n";

        // Now get the expense records
        cout << "        Expenses\n";
        cout << "        -------------------\n";
        for (loop = 0; loop < NewEmployee.GetNumExpenses(); loop++)
            EmployeeTotal += ProcessExpenseItem(infile);

        // Check for problems
        if (EmployeeTotal > MAX_ALLOWABLE_REIMBURSEMENT)
            throw ExpenseTotalTooLarge();

        // Display the employee total
        cout << "        ================================"
             << "==========================\n";
        cout << "        Employee Total:";
        cout.unsetf(ios::left);
        cout << setw(42) << EmployeeTotal << "\n\n\n";
        cout.setf(ios::left);

        return EmployeeTotal;
    }
```

This function has really been cleaned up. Most of the ExpSum1 error checking has been replaced with exception-handling equivalents. `ProcessEmployee()` checks for various conditions. If something is not right, the function throws an exception. `ProcessEmployee()` doesn't have to worry about displaying error messages or setting return codes. These tasks are now either unnecessary or handled by `main()`'s handler list.

Notice also that `ProcessEmployee()` does not check for errors on the call to `ProcessExpenseItem()` because if anything goes wrong in that function, an exception is thrown back to `main()`. Still, apart from its error-processing aspects, this function is the same as the one in ExpSum1.

Processing Expense Items. The last part of the ExpSum application is the `ProcessExpenseItem()` function shown in listing 22.34.

Listing 22.34   Expsum2.cpp—ExpSum2's *ProcessExpenseItem()* Function

```
    float ProcessExpenseItem(ifstream& infile)
    {
        Expense NewExpense;

        // Read in the expense record from the file
        infile >> NewExpense;
```

(continues)

Listing 22.34   Continued

```
// Check for problems
if (NewExpense.GetExpenseAmount() < MIN_ALLOWABLE_EXPENSE)
    throw ExpenseTooSmall();
if (NewExpense.GetExpenseAmount() > MAX_ALLOWABLE_EXPENSE)
    throw ExpenseTooLarge();

// Display the expense
cout << "     " << setw(10) << NewExpense.GetDate();
cout << setw(35) << NewExpense.GetDescription();
cout.unsetf(ios::left);
cout <<setw(12)<< NewExpense.GetExpenseAmount()
     << "\n"<< setw(0);
cout.setf(ios::left);

return NewExpense.GetExpenseAmount();
}
```

By now, you shouldn't be surprised that the same sort of things that were done to slim down error processing in ProcessEmployee() have been done in ProcessExpenseItem(). This function pares down the error checking on the expense amount range checking to the throwing of a simple exception. Everything else is the same as in ExpSum1.

Wrapping Up the ExpSum Application

The ExpSum example shows some of the techniques that you can use in your own programs. At the same time, you will quickly learn that using exception handling effectively is somewhat an acquired skill. For example, depending on your application's size and complexity, you might have to do multiphase error checking, in which nested try blocks partially process error conditions and then pass exceptions for processing by surrounding try blocks. Other applications might be better served by very simple exception hierarchies that utilize only one or two handlers. With experience, you will come to recognize the signs that favor one approach over another.

Regardless of ExpSum's ultimate applicability to larger programs, it is important to understand the fundamental lessons that the example alludes to. Exception handling increases a program's robustness and reliability by making it easier for the programmer to concentrate on the task at hand, whether that task is error handling or developing application logic.

Enabling and Disabling Borland C++ Exception Handling

Most of this chapter's discussion of exception handling is oriented toward C++ exceptions in general. To use exceptions in your programs, however, you must understand the compiler settings that Borland C++ makes available for modifying exception-handling behaviors.

If you are accustomed to using the Integrated Development Environment (IDE), the setting for exception handling is in the Project Options dialog box (shown in fig. 22.3). From the command-line compiler, you can turn exception handling on and off using the -x flag.

Fig. 22.3

The Project Options dialog box, containing the Exception Handling/RTTI entry.

Why would you want to turn off exception handling? Probably the biggest drawback of using exceptions is that the compiler must perform much trickery to pull off the functionality that exception handling provides. This translates into additional "hidden" code embedded in your executables, which in turn means that your program sizes will be larger and your programs will run a little slower. These are both faults that make programmers cringe. If you cannot accept the additional overhead that exception handling imposes on your programs, you might want to turn off the feature.

From Here...

As you've seen, buying into exception handling may mean learning a few new tricks, but the new lessons to be learned are fairly simple and straightforward. Remember that exception handling remedies many of the flaws of traditional error-handling strategies. Exceptions allow you to consolidate your error handling without worrying about whether or not C++ objects will be correctly destructed when something goes wrong. Your old programs can often be retrofitted to accommodate these new error-handling tactics with a relatively small amount of effort.

There are several other chapters in this book that address new and advanced issues in C++ programming. Be sure to check out the following chapters:

■ Chapter 19, "Using Template Classes," introduces you to templates, which are powerful language extensions that allow you to create "families" of classes that are all related through common functionality in ways that cannot be easily obtained with simple inheritance. This chapter shows how to effectively leverage templates by explaining both basic and advanced template implementations.

■ Chapter 23, "Run-Time Type Identification," covers run-time type identification (RTTI), which is a relative newcomer to the C++ feature set. RTTI allows programmers to query objects and determine the type of objects at runtime. While this is outwardly an esoteric sounding feature, this chapter explains why this capability can be so valuable.

Run-Time Type Identification (RTTI)

The Borland C++ 5 compiler provides full support for a recently adopted ANSI/ISO extension called run-time type identification (RTTI). Although not widely used today, RTTI provides a variety of important services that can help make your code more robust and portable.

Programs can use the features of RTTI for several different purposes. Specifically, using RTTI enables your programs to do the following:

- Determine the precise type of an object instance, even if the pointer used to perform the query is of a type higher up in the class hierarchy.
- Safely cast a pointer up and down an inheritance hierarchy. This includes casting pointers to virtual base classes down to derived classes (a practice that has been illegal until now).
- Utilize object instance types in expressions.

At first glance, these features appear to be fairly uninspired; but, as you will see throughout the rest of this chapter, these simple and somewhat pedestrian language features, when correctly applied, can actually provide some important capabilities. In this chapter, you do the following:

- Investigate the different components of RTTI
- Walk through the steps required to integrate RTTI features into your programs
- Learn that the most important aspects of RTTI involve the `dynamic_cast` and `typeid` operators and the `typeinfo` class

Understanding Portability and Compatibility Concerns

In March of 1993, the standards committee accepted run-time type identification into the working draft of the X3J16 ANSI standard. To date, however, few compiler vendors have supported the RTTI extensions (particularly on Intel-based operating systems). You, however, won't have to wait any longer. Being the proud owner of a shiny new copy of Borland C++ 5 places you into the select group of programmers using a compiler with a full-fledged implementation of RTTI.

Unfortunately, the rest of the world appears to be approaching RTTI more conservatively. Although Borland and Microsoft have full RTTI implementations, second-tier players like Symantec and Watcom are close behind. Many other compiler venders are still struggling to provide full RTTI support in their development products. The implications, at least for the time being, are pretty obvious. If you use RTTI features in your code, your programs might not compile on other operating systems or with other compilers. If portability is not of immediate concern to you, use these RTTI features with reckless abandon (well, maybe not *reckless* abandon). After all, they are destined to be part of the final ANSI C++ specification anyway, and ultimately all C++ compiler vendors will have to support these features.

On the other hand, if portability is important to you, don't feel guilty about skipping the rest of this chapter. Although RTTI provides useful services, its features are not absolutely essential. You are better off waiting until all of your compilers support these capabilities.

Dealing with C++ Objects

C++ enables programmers to abstract complex problems and break them into descriptions about the relationships among different object classes. This arrangement is fine, but the C++ object model breaks down somewhat when compared to the tangible interaction that takes place between humans and objects on a day-to-day basis.

When you pick up an apple, you are relatively certain that you are holding an apple, not a kiwi fruit. Most human beings have a range of experiences that tell them what an apple looks and feels like, and there is little chance that they will confuse it with another fruit.

Things can get a little trickier when dealing with C++ objects. Generally, C++ programs have a pretty good idea of what object types they are dealing with at any given time. If your code does its job right, an initialized pointer to an `Apple` object actually points to an `Apple` object, and that object behaves as expected.

Assuming, however, that your `Apple` class derives from a generic `Fruit` class, and a program is given a pointer to a `Fruit`, there is no easy way to determine whether the pointer refers to an `Apple`, a `KiwiFruit`, or any other class derived from `Fruit`. To make matters worse, if `Fruit` derives from a top-level `GenericObject` class (as is typical in many SmallTalk-like class libraries) and you give your code a pointer to a `GenericObject`, your code might be working with an `Apple`, a `KiwiFruit`, or a `Boeing747`. If you have ever tried to peel a 747, you know how undesirable such confusion can be.

Casting a `GenericObject` pointer to an `Apple` and then calling its `Peel()` method can have disastrous results if the pointer is actually pointing to a `Boeing747` object. Clearly

C++ classes could benefit greatly from some mechanism that enables programs to identify the precise type of an object pointer. Unfortunately, knowing your fruit in C++ is not as straightforward as it is in real life.

There *isA()* Way

To a large degree, C++ programmers solved the problem of type identification back when the language was in its infancy. The most common solution is to declare a virtual function—sometimes named isA() at the highest level of the class hierarchy that is responsible for returning the unique name of the class. As the class hierarchy evolves, each derived class is responsible for overloading isA(), so that it returns the name of the new class. This structure makes possible code similar to that in listing 23.1.

Listing 23.1   Using *isA()* to Perform Class-Specific Actions

```
void MakeSalad(GenericObject* pObject)
{
    switch(pObject->isA()) {

        case OBJ_APPLE:
        case OBJ_ORANGE:
        case OBJ_BANANA:
            pObject->Peel();
            break;

        case OBJ_LETTUCE:
            pObject->Chop();
            break;

        case OBJ_BOEING747:
            cout << "Very funny, wiseguy!\n";
            break;
    }
}
```

In this example, the code declares the isA() function so that it returns a numerical value that a switch statement can check. Each object class presumably has been assigned a unique class ID that corresponds to the appropriate OBJ_* constant or enumeration member.

Unfortunately, implementing isA() in this way can result in several problems. Returning a number implies that all classes can coordinate in such a way that doesn't duplicate any class IDs. Using numerical constants for class ID constants is easily accomplished for smaller class libraries, in which the developer possesses all the library source code. In some cases, however, the programmer might not have access to all the library sources. This lack of access, at the very least, precludes using an enumeration to store the class ID constants.

Using constant numerical values can be quite useful, but it can quickly become a maintenance and managerial nightmare. For that reason, programmers often prototype their isA() methods to return a character string representation of the class name. The code to check whether a GenericObject is an Apple, for example, is similar to the following:

```
// Is this pointer referencing an Apple?
if (!strcmp(pObject->isA(), "Apple")) {
    // Yes it is, do Apple stuff
    ...
}
else {
    // Nope, do otherwise
    ...
}
```

This code is a bit messier than it would be if isA() simply returned an integer, but it provides a little more flexibility. With isA() coded this way, the chance that two different class designers will inadvertently implement overlapping isA() return values is considerably less likely.

Problems with the isA() approach remain, however. What happens if a programmer forgets (or ignores) the requirement to provide an isA() method? An object instance of the new class will return the isA() value of its parent class, which is simply wrong. Even if the programmer implements the method, the possibility (albeit a slim one) remains that the programmer might return a value from isA() that is identical to a value already in use (talk about a hard bug to track down). Finally, what if you want to integrate one of your class libraries with another one, but that class library's type identification method is called IsA()? Or GetTypeID()? Or even worse, what if the other developer didn't even use and implement a type identification method?

Ultimately, the problem boils down to an issue of standard practices. *If* you always follow the rules, and *if* you're fortunate enough to avoid overlapping type IDs, and *if* you don't need to interface with third-party class libraries, then the isA() approach will probably work well for you. On the other hand, all these *ifs* should probably make you feel a little nervous. Writing code on a foundation of *ifs* is just asking for trouble.

Enter the *dynamic_cast*

The Borland compiler's run-time type identification system offers a better way for you to provide isA() type services (among other things) without worrying about politically charged development mandates or relying on error-prone programmatic devices built in to your class libraries.

dynamic_cast Basics

One way that RTTI provides improved isA() type services is through a new casting operator—the dynamic_cast. Essentially, a dynamic_cast is designed to cast a pointer safely up and down an inheritance hierarchy. The operative word here is *safely* because a normal C++ cast usually enables you to cast pointers up and down inheritance trees as well.

A dynamic_cast pointer uses the following syntax:

```
dynamic_cast<T*>(ptr)
```

T, as used here, refers to a valid C++ type, and *ptr* is the source pointer. The cast returns a pointer of type *T* if *ptr* points to an object of type *T*. If *ptr* doesn't point to a *T*, the dynamic_cast fails and returns NULL.

Keep these important caveats in mind when using dynamic_cast; however, dynamic_cast (and other RTTI constructs) are designed to be used only with polymorphic classes. A *polymorphic class* is a class that contains at least one virtual (or purevirtual) function. Further, classes that inherit virtual functions from a superclass also qualify to use RTTI.

Note

Because integral types are not polymorphic, the compiler does not support RTTI operations and manipulations on these types. Only user-defined classes and structures are eligible for RTTI use. Notice that this rule does *not* exclude classes that are part of the C++ Standard Library (for example, the string class or the xalloc exception class).

Using the *dynamic_cast*

Listing 23.2 shows the dynamic_cast in action (your use of this language feature is certain to be more profound than this frivolous example). The program simulates the preparation of salad ingredients and, obviously, is not designed to be particularly useful. Take special note of the dynamic_cast used in the ProcessIngredient() function.

Listing 23.2   Salad1.cpp—Using the *dynamic_cast* to Discern an Object Instance Type

```cpp
#include <iostream.h>

// Some miscellaneous definitions we will need
typedef enum {
    WHOLE,
    SHREDDED,
    GRATED,
    SLICED,
    CHOPPED
} FoodState;

// The top of the inheritance tree
class Food {
public:
```

(continues)

Listing 23.2 Continued

```
    // Constructor
    Food(const FoodState = WHOLE);
    // Virtual methods - all food
    // must be able to set and return
    // its state. These functions also
    // ensure that Food is polymorphic
    // and can use RTTI.
    virtual FoodState GetState() const;
    virtual void SetState(const FoodState);

private:
    // Private member data
    FoodState theFoodState;
};

// Food constructor
Food::Food(const FoodState newState)
{
    SetState(newState);
}

// Getter and setter virtual methods
FoodState Food::GetState() const
{
    return theFoodState;
}

void Food::SetState(const FoodState newState)
{
    theFoodState = newState;
}

// Overload << so we can display our state
ostream& operator<<(ostream& outstrm,
    Food&    theFood)
{
    switch(theFood.GetState()) {
        case WHOLE:     outstrm << "Whole";
                        break;
        case SHREDDED:  outstrm << "Shredded";
                        break;
        case GRATED:    outstrm << "Grated";
                        break;
        case SLICED:    outstrm << "Sliced";
                        break;
        case CHOPPED:   outstrm << "Chopped";
                        break;
        default:
            outstrm << "Bad state!";
    }
    return outstrm;
}
```

```
// Individual food types
class Apple : public Food {
public:
    void Chop() { SetState(CHOPPED); }
    void Slice() { SetState(SLICED); }
};

class Cheese : public Food {
public:
    void Grate() { SetState(GRATED); }
};

class Lettuce : public Food {
public:
    void Shred() { SetState(SHREDDED); }
};


// Process a single ingredient
void ProcessIngredient(Food* pIngredient)
{
    // Is this an Apple?
    Apple* pApple =
                dynamic_cast<Apple*>(pIngredient);
    if (pApple) {
        pApple->Chop();
        return;
    }
    // Is this a head of Lettuce?
    Lettuce* pLettuce =
                dynamic_cast<Lettuce*>(pIngredient);
    if (pLettuce) {
        pLettuce->Shred();
        return;
    }

    // Is this a piece of Cheese?
    Cheese* pCheese =
                dynamic_cast<Cheese*>(pIngredient);
    if (pCheese)
        pCheese->Grate();
    return;
}

// Let's prepare a salad
void main()
{
    Lettuce     MyLettuce;
    Apple       MyApple;
    Cheese      MyCheese;
    // Process the vegetables
    ProcessIngredient(&MyLettuce);
    ProcessIngredient(&MyApple);
    ProcessIngredient(&MyCheese);

    // Show what we've done
```

(continues)

```
Listing 23.2   Continued
    cout << "The lettuce is ";
    cout << MyLettuce << "\n";
    cout << "The apple is ";
    cout << MyApple << "\n";
    cout << "The cheese is ";
    cout << MyCheese << "\n";
}
```

This program defines a high-level Food class that knows only that food always exists in a certain state. The Food class enables you to set, query, and display the food's state, but is generally uninteresting. In fact, within a class hierarchy of any appreciable complexity and size, the Food class would probably have several pure virtual methods returning more detailed information about the specific type of food—an arrangement that is not part of this particular program.

Several specific food classes derive from Food. Each of these classes makes methods available that correspond to different ways that these foods might be processed. No rocket science going on here!

The most interesting part of the program is the ProcessIngredient() function. This function accepts a pointer to an object of type Food; after all, you don't want to limit your programs to just using fruits and vegetables. Maybe you like cheese on your salads, and maybe someone else likes croutons or peanut butter (there's no accounting for taste!). The point is, ProcessIngredient() should not limit the types of objects that can be processed, except to insist that they be foods and not wide-bodied aircraft (or something equally unappetizing).

ProcessIngredient() takes this Food pointer and proceeds to attempt casts to various object pointer types. Because a dynamic_cast is safe and returns NULL if the requested cast is inappropriate, each of these casting attempts fails until the correct cast succeeds. Once a dynamic_cast succeeds, the function knows the type of Food to which the pointer refers and can process the object accordingly.

dynamic_cast versus Virtual Functions

Just because you can use dynamic_cast to determine the identity of an ambiguous pointer doesn't mean that you should. The dynamic_cast can be tremendously useful for ensuring that your pointers are referencing what you think they are and for providing a generalized mechanism for determining object types. On the other hand, dynamic_cast isn't intended to be used as a crutch when a design can accomplish the same thing through virtual functions.

In the previous salad-making example, assume that the classes in that example are more concerned with making salad than they are with providing a generic Food class hierarchy. In this case, you can write the program better using virtual functions. Listing 23.3 shows how this program might look.

Listing 23.3 Salad2.cpp—Using Virtual Functions to Create a Better Salad

```cpp
#include <iostream.h>

// Some miscellaneous definitions we will need
typedef enum {
    WHOLE,
    SHREDDED,
    GRATED,
    SLICED,
    CHOPPED
} FoodState;

// The top of the inheritance tree
class Food {
public:
    // Constructor
    Food(const FoodState = WHOLE);
    // Virtual methods -- all food
    // must be able to set and return
    // its state. These functions also
    // ensure that Food is polymorphic
    // and can use RTTI.
    virtual FoodState GetState() const;
    virtual void SetState(const FoodState);

private:
    // Private member data
    FoodState theFoodState;
};

// Food constructor
Food::Food(const FoodState newState)
{
    SetState(newState);
}

// Getter and setter virtual methods
FoodState Food::GetState() const
{
    return theFoodState;
}

void Food::SetState(const FoodState newState)
{
    theFoodState = newState;
}

// Overload << so we can display our state
ostream& operator<<(ostream& outstrm,
           Food&    theFood)
{
    switch(theFood.GetState()) {
        case WHOLE:     outstrm  << "Whole";
                        break;
```

(continues)

Listing 23.3 Continued

```
            case SHREDDED:   outstrm << "Shredded";
                             break;
            case GRATED:     outstrm << "Grated";
                             break;
            case SLICED:     outstrm << "Sliced";
                             break;
            case CHOPPED:    outstrm << "Chopped";
                             break;
    default:
                outstrm << "Bad state!";
        }
        return outstrm;
}


// Intermediate class grouping
class SaladIngredient : public Food {
public:
    // Pure virtual function which any
    // salad ingredient class must
    // provide
    virtual void ProcessIngredient() = 0;
};


// Individual food types
class Apple : public SaladIngredient {
public:
    void ProcessIngredient() { SetState(CHOPPED); }
};

class Cheese : public Food {
public:
    void ProcessIngredient() { SetState(GRATED); }
};

class Lettuce : public Food {
public:
    void ProcessIngredient() { SetState(SHREDDED); }
};


// Let's prepare a salad
void main()
{
    Lettuce     MyLettuce;
    Apple       MyApple;
    Cheese      MyCheese;

    // Process the vegetables
    MyLettuce.ProcessIngredient();
    MyApple.ProcessIngredient();
    MyCheese.ProcessIngredient();
```

```
      // Show what we've done
      cout << "The lettuce is ";
      cout << MyLettuce << "\n";
      cout << "The apple is ";
      cout << MyApple << "\n";
      cout << "The cheese is ";
      cout << MyCheese << "\n";
   }
```

As you can see, this salad-making variant completely removes RTTI use. This is because the `ProcessIngredient()` virtual function that is forced on any class derived from `SaladIngredient` assumes the responsibility for changing the object's state as appropriate. Using virtual functions in this case is much cleaner than having to rely on the cascading `if` statements and `dynamic_cast` in the listing 23.2 `ProcessIngredient()` function.

> **Tip**
>
> Any time that you are tempted to use a `dynamic_cast` to determine a pointer's type (as opposed to simply providing a safe cast), ask yourself whether there is a way to accomplish the same thing using virtual functions. Leveraging polymorphism is superior to using the brute force capabilities of RTTI's `dynamic_cast`.

Of course, the program might want to use some of the specific food classes in a context different than simply making salads. The class hierarchy, for example, can have a `PizzaIngredient` class. The `Cheese` class then can use multiple inheritance and derive from both `SaladIngredient` and `PizzaIngredient`. Be careful, though; if a program adopts this approach, it must ensure that the `Food` class is a virtual base class. Additionally, the program must change the `ProcessIngredient()` method names in `SaladIngredient` and `PizzaIngredient` to avoid any naming conflict. In some cases, you might decide to use the RTTI approach of listing 23.2 because it alleviates the need for multiple inheritance and its messy problems.

dynamic_cast and References

You also can use the `dynamic_cast` operator to create a reference to a particular type. The syntax for this operation is as follows:

```
      dynamic_cast<T&>(ref)
```

T, as used in this syntax, refers to a valid C++ type, and *ref* is the source reference. The cast returns a reference of type *T* only if *ref* refers to an object of type *T*. Because a NULL reference is not possible, you have no way to compare the result of a dynamic reference cast to determine whether it has failed. In the case of an invalid dynamic reference cast, a `Bad_cast` exception is thrown. (For a thorough discussion of exception handling, see chapter 22, "Exception Handling.") The following code snippets demonstrate the differences in checking for invalid dynamic pointer casts and invalid dynamic reference casts:

```
// Checking for errors with dynamic pointer cast
Derived* pDerived = dynamic_cast<Derived*>(pBase);
if (!pDerived) {
    // Whoops! This was an invalid cast
    ...
}

// Checking for errors with dynamic reference casts
try {
    Derived& MyDerived = dynamic_cast<Derived&>(MyBase);
}
catch (bad_cast) {
    // Whoops! This was an invalid cast
    ...
}
```

In every other way, using the dynamic reference is just like using the dynamic pointer cast, except that the former obviously returns a reference rather than a pointer.

Boring Classes Need Not Apply (Usually)

The "polymorphic class only" RTTI limitation is not exactly a hard and fast rule. There is an important exception: casting from a derived class object pointer up to a base class pointer. Examine the code sample in listing 23.4.

Listing 23.4   Dyncast1.cpp—Using the *dynamic_cast()* with Nonpolymorphic Classes

```
#include <iostream.h>

class Base {
    // Do nothing (not a polymorphic class)
};

class Derived : public Base {
    // Do nothing (not a polymorphic class)
};

void main()
{
    Derived  MyDerived;
    Derived* pMyDerived = &MyDerived;
    // Successful upcast
    Base* pBaseTest = dynamic_cast<Base*>(pMyDerived);
    cout << "pMyDerived ";
    cout << (pBaseTest ? "is" : "is not");
    cout << " a Base*.\n";
}
```

This code compiles and runs as expected. As it turns out, the Borland compiler enables you to dynamic_cast *up* a class hierarchy (for example, from a derived class to a base class) even if the classes involved are not polymorphic. Listing 23.5, however, shows a change to this code that breaks the program.

Listing 23.5 Dyncast2.cpp—Incorrect Use of the *dynamic_cast* for Downcasting

```
#include <iostream.h>

class Base {
    // Do nothing (not a polymorphic class)
};

class Derived : public Base {
    // Do nothing (not a polymorphic class)
};

void main()
{
    Derived  MyDerived;
    Derived* pMyDerived = &MyDerived;
    // Successful upcast
    Base* pBaseTest = dynamic_cast<Base*>(pMyDerived);
    cout << "pMyDerived ";
    cout << (pBaseTest ? "is" : "is not");
    cout << " a Base*.\n";

    // Successful(??) downcast
    if (pBaseTest) {
        Derived* pDerivedTest =
                    dynamic_cast<Derived*>(pBaseTest);
        cout << "pBaseTest ";
        cout << (pDerivedTest ? "is" : "is not");
        cout << " a Derived*.\n";
    }
}
```

This program cannot even compile because the second use of dynamic_cast attempts to cast a base pointer down to a derived pointer, and neither class is polymorphic. The Borland compiler complains that *Type 'Base' is not a defined class with virtual functions*, just as you would expect.

You can fix listing 23.5 by adding a single line to the definition of Base, as shown in listing 23.6.

Listing 23.6 Dyncast3.cpp—Description of Code

```
class Base {
    // Do nothing
    void virtual Nothing() { } // Now polymorphic
};
```

This change rids you of the troublesome compiler error and enables the program to compile, link, and run as expected.

Using RTTI and Multiple Inheritance

Before RTTI, programmers often were frustrated in their attempts to construct a piece of code to cast a pointer down a class hierarchy that incorporated a virtual base class. C++ simply does not support this sort of coding with the normal casting syntax.

Listing 23.7 shows a very simple class hierarchy consisting of a Base class, two Middle classes deriving from the base class, and then a main Derived class deriving through multiple inheritance from both of the middle classes. The program itself simply tries to take a pointer to a Derived class instance, cast the pointer down to the Base level, and then cast the pointer back up to the Derived level.

Listing 23.7   Vrtbase1.cpp—A Simple Multiple Inheritance Hierarchy

```
#include <iostream.h>

class Base {
public:
    // Do nothing (not a polymorphic class)
    void BaseFunc() { cout << "In Base.\n"; }
};

class Middle1 : public Base {
public:
    // Do nothing (not a polymorphic class)
    void Middle1Func() { cout << "In Middle1.\n"; }
};

class Middle2 : public Base {
public:
    // Do nothing (not a polymorphic class)
    void Middle2Func() { cout << "In Middle2.\n"; }
};

class Derived : public Middle1, public Middle2 {
public:
    // Do nothing (not a polymorphic class)
    void DerivedFunc() { cout << "In Derived.\n"; }
};

void main()
{
    Derived  MyDerived;
    Base*    pBase = (Base*) &MyDerived;
    pBase->BaseFunc();
    Derived* pDerived = (Derived*) pBase;
    pDerived->DerivedFunc();
}
```

This program does not compile. The compiler gives you the following two error messages: Cannot cast from 'Derived *' to 'Base *' and Cannot cast from 'Base *' to 'Derived *'.

You easily can fix this first error message. Because `Derived` indirectly inherits from `Base` twice, you have the classic multiple-instance problem that often plagues users of multiple inheritance. Clearly, you must make `Base` a virtual base class. Listing 23.8 shows the changes to the `Middle1` and `Middle2` classes that accomplish this task.

Listing 23.8 Vrtbase2.cpp—Changes to Make Base a Virtual Base Class

```cpp
#include <iostream.h>

class Base {
public:
    // Do nothing (not a polymorphic class)
    void BaseFunc() { cout << "In Base.\n"; }
};

class Middle1 : virtual public Base {
public:
    // Do nothing (not a polymorphic class)
    void Middle1Func() { cout << "In Middle1.\n"; }
};

class Middle2 : virtual public Base {
public:
    // Do nothing (not a polymorphic class)
    void Middle2Func() { cout << "In Middle2.\n"; }
};

class Derived : public Middle1, public Middle2 {
public:
    // Do nothing (not a polymorphic class)
    void DerivedFunc() { cout << "In Derived.\n"; }
};

void main()
{
    Derived  MyDerived;
    Base*    pBase = (Base*) &MyDerived;
    pBase->BaseFunc();
    Derived* pDerived = (Derived*) pBase;
    pDerived->DerivedFunc();
}
```

The solution shown in listing 23.8 works—almost. The program still doesn't compile. Instead, you now get the remaining error: `Cannot cast from 'Base *' to 'Derived *'`. The fact that you can't perform a simple cast from a virtual base class down to a derived class is simply a limitation of C++, and without RTTI there isn't an easy or type-safe way to get around this problem.

Of course, because the Borland compiler supports the `dynamic_cast`, you have a simple and safe solution to this problem. Listing 23.9 shows the changes that you must make to the program to get it to work properly.

Listing 23.9 Vrtbase3.cpp—Changes Needed to Incorporate RTTI and Make the Program Finally Work

```cpp
#include <iostream.h>

class Base {
public:
    // Do nothing
    void BaseFunc() { cout << "In Base.\n"; }
    // Now polymorphic so we can use RTTI
    virtual void Nothing() { }
};

class Middle1 : virtual public Base {
public:
    // Do nothing (not a polymorphic class)
    void Middle1Func() { cout << "In Middle1.\n"; }
};

class Middle2 : virtual public Base {
public:
    // Do nothing (not a polymorphic class)
    void Middle2Func() { cout << "In Middle2.\n"; }
};

class Derived : public Middle1, public Middle2 {
public:
    // Do nothing (not a polymorphic class)
    void DerivedFunc() { cout << "In Derived.\n"; }
};

void main()
{
    Derived  MyDerived;
    Base*    pBase = dynamic_cast<Base*>(&MyDerived);
    pBase->BaseFunc();
    Derived* pDerived = dynamic_cast<Derived*>(pBase);
    pDerived->DerivedFunc();
}
```

This version of the program not only compiles, but runs as expected. Although you might find that you rarely need to perform an operation as relatively esoteric as this one, you certainly will appreciate dynamic_cast on those occasions when you do need this sort of casting manipulation.

As a final note on using the dynamic_cast operator with inheritance trees that utilize multiple inheritance, understand that RTTI enables programs to cast pointers and references *across* inheritance trees. Conceptually, this action is like casting a base pointer down to the lowest class in the inheritance tree and then casting the same pointer back up the tree, but through a different inheritance path. Listing 23.10 shows how you can change the Vrtbase3.cpp example to demonstrate this lateral casting capability.

Listing 23.10   Vrtbase4.cpp—Hopping across a Multiple Inheritance Hierarchy

```
// All class declarations and definitions the same as
// vrtbase3.cpp

1 void main()
2 {
3     Derived  MyDerived;
4     Middle1* pMiddle1 = dynamic_cast<Middle1*>(&MyDerived);
5     pMiddle1->Middle1Func();
6     Middle2* pMiddle2 = dynamic_cast<Middle2*>(pMiddle1);
7     pMiddle2->Middle2Func();
8 }
```

In this example, you set the pMiddle1 pointer to point to a class in the middle of the inheritance tree (line 4). On line 6, the program uses the dynamic_cast operator to move across the inheritance tree to another class located between Base and Derived. Notice that the syntax makes absolutely no reference to Derived and that the compiler is responsible for finding a path from one class in the tree to another.

Using Declarations inside Conditions

The ANSI C++ standards committee has adopted a language change that allows for the declaration of variables inside conditional statements (for example, if, while, and switch). These declarations can be used in conjunction with the dynamic_cast. Borland is one of the first compiler venders to support this feature.

Briefly, conditional declarations refer to the fact that standard C++ enables a variable declaration to return a value and that this value is usable inside an expression evaluation. Take, for example, the following C++ declaration:

```
MyClass* pMyClass = new MyClass;
```

With conditional declarations, this syntax now yields a value that indicates whether or not pMyClass has been correctly initialized. A programmer could rewrite the declaration so that it was evaluated within an expression designed to trap memory allocation errors.

```
if (MyClass* pMyClass = new MyClass) {
    // Do something
}
else {
    // The call to new failed
}
```

A full-fledged discussion of the implications of using valued declarations is beyond the scope of this chapter, but it is important that you can at least recognize the feature's use. Other compilers support conditional declarations sooner rather than later, and the feature's use appears in code snippets that you may run into in books, magazines, and other users' code.

The most important use of valued declarations, at least with respect to RTTI and the dynamic_cast, is in conditionally creating variable instances with limited scope. Look closely at the following code snippet:

```
1 void DoNothing(Base* pBase)
2 {
3     Derived* pDerived = dynamic_cast<Derived*>(pBase);
4     if (pDerived) {
5         // Do something with the object
6         cout << "It's a Derived!\n";
7     }
8     // pDerived is still in scope and is accessible
9 }
```

On line 8, you can see that the variable pDerived is still in scope and is fully accessible to the rest of the function, even though pDerived has clearly been declared simply for the purpose of determining whether or not pBase is also a Derived instance.

This semantic problem can be solved by creating explicitly a new level of scope, in this way:

```
1   void DoNothing(Base* pBase)
2   {
3       { // Start of new scope
4           Derived* pDerived = dynamic_cast<Derived*>(pBase);
5           if (pDerived) {
6               // Do something with the object
7               cout << "It's a Derived!\n";
8           }
9       } // End of new scope
10      // pDerived is not in scope and is inaccessible
11  }
```

Lines 10 and on do not have access to pDerived, so technically this code does solve the problem—but it's not pretty. You can use conditional declarations to solve the problem more elegantly:

```
void DoNothing(Base* pBase)
{
    if (Derived* pDerived =
                        dynamic_cast<Derived*>(pBase)) {
        // Do something with the object
        cout << "It's a Derived!\n";
    }
    // pDerived is not in scope and is unaccessible
}
```

As you can see, with conditional declarations you can combine the declaration of pDerived, its initialization, and the evaluation of the result into a single unit. This combination helps to avoid errors that often result from using variables before they have been validated. This approach also resolves those ugly scoping problems and makes the resulting function smaller and easier to understand.

Conditional declarations will soon be a widely used feature. Although the feature is hardly earth shattering, it is so convenient that programmers are sure to latch onto it and use it often. Be prepared.

Exploring *typeinfo*s and the *typeid* Operators

Obviously the capability to determine whether a pointer or reference is of a particular type can be quite useful. Occasionally, however, you want even more information about a particular class than you can obtain through the dynamic_cast operator.

The standard C++ implementation of RTTI includes a specification for a typeinfo class that you can use to describe various attributes of a particular type. Figure 23.1 shows the specific structure of Borland's typeinfo class.

```
class typeinfo
{
public:
    // Public ctors and dtors
    virtual ~typeinfo();

    // Comparison operators
    int operator==(const typeinfo&) const;
    int operator!=(const typeinfo&) const;

    // Misc. public methods
    int before(const typeinfo&) const;
    const char name() const;

private:
    // Can't copy these guys!
    typeinfo(const typeinfo&);
    typeinfo& operator=(const typeinfo&);
};
```

Fig. 23.1

The typeinfo *class.*

> **Note**
>
> For a Borland C++ 5 program to utilize typeinfo and the typeid operators, it must include the typeinfo.h header file.

Now take a brief look at some of things that you can do with typeinfo. As evidenced by the overloaded equality and inequality operators, typeinfos can be compared to each other. Using the name method, a program can retrieve the name of a type in the form of a character string. Finally, a program can determine the lexical order of two types (based on their name) by using the before method.

Note

Because both the copy constructor and the assignment operator are declared as private, you cannot copy typeinfos.

Caution

Borland C++ 5 conforms to early drafts of the ANSI C++ draft standard that specified certain RTTI type names should have mixed-case names (specifically Bad_cast, Bad_typeid, and Type_info). In the September 1995 draft (the most current version at the time of this writing) these names were changed to lowercase equivalents. Ironically, the Borland compiler is somewhat schizophrenic with regard to Type_info; the C++ 5 compiler will accept either Type_info *or* the correct typeinfo form. Borland's noncompliance with the draft might cause you problems when porting code originally developed with compilers that support the new naming conventions. Symantec's C++ 7.2 is not a problem because it also uses the older names. On the other hand, RTTI-aware code developed with the Visual C++ 4 compiler is probably the most pervasive culprit in this regard, since the Microsoft compiler uses the new names.

How does a program create or otherwise access these typeinfo instances? RTTI provides an operator called typeid that is designed expressly to return typeinfos. typeid takes a single argument that can be either a simple type name or an expression. The operator returns to the program a typeinfo reference that corresponds to the requested type, or a typeinfo reference that corresponds to the type of the supplied expression.

The typeid operator does not require that you feed it exclusively polymorphic types. Consider, for example, the following code snippet:

```
// Show some integral type names
cout << typeid(int).name() << "\n";
cout << typeid(unsigned long).name() << "\n";
cout << typeid(char*).name() << "\n";
```

As you might expect, these three lines of code output int, unsigned long, and char *, respectively.

Because the typeid operator can accept expressions, you can pass variable names to the operator and manipulate the resulting typeinfo reference. As expected, the following code displays class Apple:

```
// Define our class
class Apple {
    // Do nothing
};

// Create an instance
Apple MyApple;

// Display the instance's name
cout << typeid(MyApple).name() << "\n";
```

In cases where the expression being evaluated is an instance of a polymorphic type, the `typeid` operator checks the actual object and returns an appropriate `typeinfo` object. The following code displays `class Derived`:

```cpp
// Define our classes
class Base {
    // Do nothing
    // We have to make this class polymorphic
    // for this example to work correctly
    virtual void Nothing() { }
};

class Derived : public Base {
    // Do nothing
};

// Create an object instance
Derived  MyDerived;
Base*    pBase = dynamic_cast<Base*>(&MyDerived);

// Now show the "true" type of pBase
cout << typeid(*pBase).name() << "\n";
```

In this example notice that the classes must be polymorphic to get the correct behaviors. If you omit the stub definition of the `Nothing` method in the class `Base`, this code snippet reports that the type name is `class Base`.

Caution

If RTTI features are disabled, the `typeid` operator still functions, but might not return the results that your program expects. If RTTI is off and a program passes a polymorphic pointer or reference into `typeid`, `typeid` returns a reference to a `typeinfo` instance that represents the declared type of the argument and not the `typeinfo` for the actual object to which the pointer or reference is pointing.

Salad-Making Revisited

You can use `typeinfo`s in many of the same ways that you use the `dynamic_cast` operator. Recall that in the Salad1.cpp program (see listing 23.2) you used the `dynamic_cast` operator to query the type of a provided base pointer. If the base pointer was not of the correct type, `dynamic_cast` returned a `NULL`, and you could determine that you needed to process the pointer differently. Listing 23.11 shows how you can use the `typeid` operator to make the same sort of determination.

Listing 23.11 Salad3.cpp—Using *typeid* to Determine an Object's Type

```cpp
#include <iostream.h>
#include <typeinfo.h>

// The definitions of FoodState, Food, Apple, Cheese,
```

(continues)

Listing 23.11   Continued

```
// and Lettuce are the same as in salad1.cpp

// Process a single ingredient
void ProcessIngredient(Food* pIngredient)
{
    // Is this an Apple?
    if (typeid(*pIngredient) == typeid(Apple)) {
        ((Apple*) pIngredient)->Chop();
        return;
    }

    // Is this a head of Lettuce?
    if (typeid(*pIngredient) == typeid(Lettuce)) {
        ((Lettuce*) pIngredient)->Shred();
return;
    }

    // Is this a piece of Cheese?
    if (typeid(*pIngredient) == typeid(Cheese))
        ((Cheese*) pIngredient)->Grate();

    return;
}

// Let's prepare a salad
void main()
{
    Lettuce MyLettuce;
    Apple   MyApple;
    Cheese  MyCheese;

    // Process the vegetables
    ProcessIngredient(&MyLettuce);
    ProcessIngredient(&MyApple);
    ProcessIngredient(&MyCheese);

    // Show what we've done
    cout << "The ";
    cout << typeid(MyLettuce).name() << " is ";
    cout << MyLettuce << "\n";
    cout << "The ";
    cout << typeid(MyApple).name() << " is ";
    cout << MyApple << "\n";
    cout << "The ";
    cout << typeid(MyCheese).name() << " is ";
    cout << MyCheese << "\n";
}
```

As you can see, Salad3.cpp explicitly checks the typeinfo of the passed-in ingredient pointer with the typeinfo of each of the possible food types. Because all the classes are polymorphic, the typeinfo returned by typeid(*pIngredient) refers to the actual object, which makes this comparison possible.

So which way should you write this program? It's a toss up. Using the `typeinfo` method is a little easier to read and looks more obvious. However, the `typeinfo` method also relies on dangerous and unprotected C-style typecasts rather than the safer `dynamic_cast`. Because `dynamic_cast` essentially performs two jobs simultaneously—checking for the correct pointer type and then safely performing the cast—you probably are safer using the `dynamic_cast` solution rather than the `typeid` solution in this case.

The *typeinfo before( )* Enigma

Recall that the `typeinfo` class contains a method called `before()` that is a mechanism to help collate a class hierarchy. Unfortunately, `before()` is actually of limited use (to say the least). Take a close look at listing 23.12.

Listing 23.12   Before.cpp—Using the typeinfo *before()* Method

```
#include <iostream.h>
#include <typeinfo.h>

// Define our classes
class Base {
    // Do nothing
    // Force polymorphism
    virtual void Nothing() { }
};

class Middle : public Base {
    // Do nothing
};

class Derived : public Middle {
    // Do nothing
};

// Show before relationship
void ShowBefore(const typeinfo& info1,
 const typeinfo& info2)
{
    cout << info1.name();
    cout << (info1.before(info2) ? " is " : " is not ");
    cout << "before " << info2.name() << "\n";
}

void main()
{
    // Show the relationships
    ShowBefore(typeid(Base),    typeid(Middle));
    ShowBefore(typeid(Base),    typeid(Derived));
    ShowBefore(typeid(Middle),  typeid(Base));
    ShowBefore(typeid(Middle),  typeid(Derived));
    ShowBefore(typeid(Derived), typeid(Base));
    ShowBefore(typeid(Derived), typeid(Middle));
}
```

The most useful implementation of before() enables you to tell whether one class derives from another (for example, Base is before Derived). Using that definition, listing 23.12 would output the following:

```
Base is before Middle.
Base is before Derived.
Middle is not before Base.
Middle is before Derived.
Derived is not before Base.
Derived is not before Middle.
```

This output, however, is not what Borland C++ returns. Instead, the Borland product outputs what appears at first glance to be almost random-ordering information:

```
Base is before Middle.
Base is before Derived.
Middle is not before Base.
Middle is not before Derived.
Derived is not before Base.
Derived is before Middle.
```

According to the compiler, the ordering of this class hierarchy is Base, Derived, then Middle. This ordering certainly does not describe the inheritance relationship. What's going on here?

When the names of the classes change from Base, Middle, and Derived to A, B, and C, the compiler returns the following results:

```
A is before B.
A is before C.
B is not before A.
B is before C.
C is not before A.
C is not before B.
```

By now, you undoubtedly have realized that the compiler is just sorting the names of the classes alphabetically. If you don't understand the advantage of this order, don't worry—neither does anyone else. Ultimately, Borland's implementation of the before() method appears to have limited utility. If you can find a good use for it, more power to you.

> **Tip**
>
> Even though the before() method probably doesn't strike you as being particularly interesting or useful, you still can use the dynamic_cast operator to provide the information that before() doesn't.

Setting the Borland C++ RTTI Compiler Switch

The Borland C++ compiler has only one command-line compiler switch that relates to run-time type identification. The -RT switch, which is on by default in both the IDE and the command-line compiler, controls whether RTTI information is created and stored for polymorphic classes. You can effectively deactivate RTTI by placing -RT- on your compiler command line or by un-checking the IDE's Enable Run-time Type Information check box in the Project Options dialog box (see fig. 23.2). You can display this dialog box by choosing Option, Project.

Fig. 23.2

Turning on RTTI.

From Here...

Run-time type identification is a relative newcomer to the C++ feature set. RTTI allows programmers to query objects and determine the type of objects at runtime. While this is outwardly an esoteric sounding feature, this chapter has explained why this capability can be valuable. You also might want to investigate some of the other chapters in this book that discuss advanced C++ language extensions:

■ Refer to chapter 19, "Using Template Classes" for more information on templates, which are probably the most frequently used C++ extension. Templates enable programs to build class families that function similarly, but perform operations on a wide variety of different data types.

■ For more information on exception handling, refer to chapter 22, "Exception Handling." This chapter shows you how exception handling enables programmers to localize error-processing logic and logically structure the way their programs deal with abnormal execution events.

CHAPTER 24

Understanding Namespaces

Namespaces are a relatively recent addition to the C++ language feature set, having been added to the ANSI C++ draft standard in July 1993. Borland C++ 5 is one of the very first development systems to support this new language feature. To many programmers, namespaces are a mysterious feature, designed to be used on only the largest and most complex of programming projects.

Unfortunately, this is a rather short-sighted view. Namespaces are an important part of the language and are essential to the development and maintenance of large C++ code bases over an extended period of time. Additionally, the entire C++ Standard Library is broken into namespaces, so an appreciation and working knowledge of the feature is a must for virtually any serious programmer. Finally, you can expect to see most commercial C++ class libraries embrace the namespace feature. Programs that want to use these products will almost certainly need to use namespace syntax to leverage these product's capabilities.

This chapter endeavors to give you an introduction to the capabilities of C++ namespaces in addition to some insights on why the feature was added to the draft standard. In particular, this chapter covers

- Naming collisions and what happens when the Borland compiler encounters them.
- How basic namespaces are constructed, and strategies for namespace nesting and extension.
- The concepts of aliases and how code placed into namespaces can be hoisted into the current scope.
- Practical advice on how best to integrate with third-party products using the namespace features.

What's in a Name?

Imagine that you've been asked by your boss to plan the department's annual holiday party. There are almost 50 people invited and you are determined to make a good impression by ensuring that everything goes smoothly. The day before the party, however, your boss slips you a piece of paper. "This is the seating chart for tomorrow night's party," he confides. "Make sure that you follow it to the letter. It is imperative that certain people don't sit next to each other; some individuals simply don't get along, while others tend to get tipsy and might prematurely disclose some details of our department's pending reorganization. I'm depending on you."

That night, as you help to set up the tables you pull out the seating chart and begin to lay out the guests' name cards. To your horror, you realize that your boss has only specified first names on his seating chart. Your department has four Jim's, three Mary's, two John's, and a gaggle of Chris's.

You try your best to sort out the mess, but invariably you make mistakes. In the middle of the party a drunk and indignant Jim pours champagne on a pouting John's head. Your boss is simultaneously confronted by a dozen mainframe programmers, demanding to know why they are about to be placed in cubicles and forced to learn how to program OLE. And a Chris is reduced to sobs when a Mary inadvertently reveals that he is being transferred to the Siberia office to program grain elevators.

You arrive at work the next morning to find your belongings in a cardboard box, a pink slip taped to the front.

Obviously, there are many situations where using the correct name is of critical importance. This is especially true of C++ programs, where objects of various types rely on a known and distinct set of names for everything from types to variables to methods. When two separate program constructs are given the same name, this is called a name clash (or alternatively, a symbol clash). As you will see, name clashes can cause some pretty vexing problems that are solved by the namespace language extension.

When Names Collide

If the above story seems far removed from a realistic grounding in programming with C++, think again. It is not rare to encounter situations where you may want to use classes but can't because of name clashes, or even worse, end up using different classes than you think you are. Before the C++ namespace language extension was born, name clashes could cause a programmer to abandon class libraries or simply resort to "rolling their own" code.

The crux of the problem is that non-namespaced C++ relies on a single, global level of scope for the vast majority of a typical program's declarations. Note that while the single global scope problem does affect the declarations of global variables, the fundamental issues run much deeper (see Listing 24.1).

Listing 24.1   Clash.cpp—A Simple Program with Duplicate Class Declarations

```
#include <iostream.h>
#include <cstring.h>
```

```
class Dog
{
public:
    string Bark() const
    {
        cout << "Woof! Woof!";
    }
};

class Dog
{
public:
    string Bark() const
    {
        cout << "Bow Wow!";
    }
};

void main()
{
    Dog    Rover;
    Rover.Bark();
}
```

Clearly, any compiler worth its salt will immediately complain about the duplicate definition of the Dog class. And any programmer worth his salt would never write code like this anyway. So this is a silly and contrived example, right?

Don't be so sure. Suppose you were working on a development team and one of the other programmers also needed a Dog class. Unless the two of you got together and carefully planned your strategy, there is a very good chance that you would both end up writing a definition for Dog. In itself this is not such a big deal; the first time you tried to mix your coworker's code with your own, the Borland compiler would signal a duplicate symbol error, and the two of you could work out your differences.

But what if the clashing class wasn't written by a coworker, but instead resided inside a class library that you had purchased? Assuming that the class library did not include source code and was only delivered in the form of a library with header files, you would be in a real bind. In truth, this is exactly the same problem you ran into planning that cursed holiday party!

There are a variety of solutions for this problem that don't require namespaces. You could, for example, ensure that all of your definitions are prefixed with a unique set of characters that are relevant to your program, such as your initials or company name. It seems pretty unlikely that you'll run into naming collisions if you name your class ErnieFinklebaumDog, or even EFDog. Still, this feels rather inelegant and begs for a solution that doesn't seem quite so arbitrary.

When Names Collide Part II: Hiding

In C++, every symbol exists within a clearly defined level of *scope*. The scope defines what code has access to a given set of symbols. Code that can't see into a particular scope isn't allowed to reference symbols in that scope. To do so is a compile-time error.

Scopes are created in a variety of different ways—creating a new class, inheritance, calling a function or method, and so on. For the purpose of illustration, however, the easiest way to create a scope is to use a new set of matching braces. Take a look at listing 24.2. Look closely at what happens to the Dog variable. Can you predict the output of this code?

Listing 24.2 Hide.cpp—Creating Different Areas of Overlapping Scope

```cpp
#include <iostream.h>

void main()
{
    long   Dog = 123;

    // These braces create a new scope
    // We'll call it Scope A
    {
        long   Cat = 456;
        cout << "\nInside first scope:\n";
        cout << "Dog is " << Dog << "\n";
        cout << "Cat is " << Cat << "\n";
    }

    // Cat is now out of scope. The below line is
    // illegal.
    // cout << "Cat is " << Cat << "\n";

    // These braces create yet another scope
    // We'll call it Scope B
    {
        long   Dog = 987;    // Hmmmm... what's this?
        long   Lizard = 789;
        cout << "\nInside second scope:\n";
        cout << "Dog is " << Dog << "\n";
        cout << "Lizard is " << Lizard << "\n";

     // Note that Cat is not accessible in here
    }

    // Both Cat and Lizard are out of scope here.
    cout << "\nInside main() scope:\n";
    cout << "Dog is " << Dog << endl;
}
```

In this program there are three scopes: the scope created by the main() function, and then two enclosed scopes created by slipping in a pair of braces. We'll call these inner scopes A and B, as noted by the comments in the program.

Since `main()` envelopes scope A, anything found in `main()` is accessible by scope A. Indeed, the first part of our program outputs the expected values for `Dog` and `Cat`. Note, however, that the `Cat` variable defined within scope A is not accessible by `main()`.

You might expect exactly the same behaviors to apply to the relationship between `main()` and scope B. In fact, there is little difference. Since `main()` also envelopes scope B, anything found in `main()` is accessible by scope A. Like the `Cat` variable, `Lizard` is not accessible by `main()`.

However—and here's the catch—scope B defines its own `Dog` variable. And this program compiles and runs fine. When it comes time to display the value of `Dog` within scope B, the version of `Dog` that is local to the scope (for example, the version with a value of 987) takes precedence and is used over `main()`'s version. In essence, the scope B local `Dog` hides the `main()` version.

Now we have a problem that is considerably more insidious than a simple name clash. Normally, these hiding characteristics of C++ are a benefit. Variables within the innermost level of scope take precedence over variables in outer scopes, a convention that facilitates encapsulation. All the same, it doesn't take much to imagine a case where a programmer thinks he is using one variable (or class definition, or enumeration, and so on) when, in fact, he's using something completely different.

For the sake of clarity, this example has been kept simple, and for most readers it will be review anyway. However, you don't have to be a very experienced C++ programmer to imagine how a multitude of definitions, nested within each other and stacked on top of each other using class inheritance, can lead to situations where symbols get inadvertently hidden and ultimately misused. What we really need is some mechanism that allows us the flexibility to fully qualify our use of symbols so that our programs are unambiguous.

When Is a Name Clash Not a Name Clash?

Up to this point, we've been talking about naming collisions as if they were the most troublesome thing that could ever afflict a program. While there is a healthy amount of hyperbole at work here, there are actually cases where symbol clashes are legal and extremely useful. The experienced C++ programmer will immediately recognize this useful exception as *overloading*.

In C++, a function or method may have more than one definition as long as the arguments to each of the different versions differ. Take a look at listing 24.3. This example shows the code for two forms of an `Add()` function, both coexisting within the same program.

Listing 24.3   Add.cpp—Function Overloading

```
#include <iostream.h>
#include <cstring.h>
```

(continues)

Listing 24.3   Continued

```
long Add(const long addend1, const long addend2)
{
     return addend1 + addend2;
}

string Add(const string& str1, const string& str2)
{
     return str1 + str2;
}

void main()
{
     cout << "-11 + 67 = " << Add(-11, 67) << "\n";
     cout << "\"Root \" + \"beer\" = \""
<< Add("Root ", "beer") << "\"\n";
}
```

In listing 24.3, the Add() function is said to be overloaded. This means that even though there are two definitions of the Add() function, the program will compile and link. Depending on how the function is called—that is to say, depending on what arguments are being passed in to a given invocation of Add()—the compiler ensures that the correct version is used.

Overloading is a useful and important language feature of C++. Since the compiler knows how to discern the difference between different forms based on parameter signatures, the name clash is allowed. Indeed, this name clash can provide a useful service. In the above example, both versions of Add() perform essentially the same operation on two fundamentally different types. Why should you have to write an AddLong() function and an AddString() function when you can write one and be done with it?

Note

It's probably worth mentioning that the above example is better written as a template, instead of using function overloading. For a detailed discussion of templates, refer to chapter 19, "Using Template Classes."

A Simple Namespace Example

Namespaces solve some of the problems discussed in the preceding section by allowing a complex system to be broken into manageable units, each composed of a collection of named scopes. A namespace is really little more than a named grouping of definitions, all appearing at the same level of scope.

There are at least two steps you need to perform in order to use a namespace. You must first declare what resides in the namespace, and then you must qualify your use of the namespaced items within your program code.

Declaring the namespace is easy, and very similar to the procedure we used to create a new scope in listing 24.2. To declare a namespace, simply use the keyword `namespace` with an optional name and follow it with a new scope delimited by braces. In general, you can describe this form as follows:

```
namespace [optional name]
{
    Your declarations and definitions here
}
```

Each namespace you declare can be given a name. All namespaces within a particular program need to be given unique names in order for them to work as intended. (But be sure to check out the section "Extending Namespaces" later in this chapter). There may not exist any other symbols (classes, variables, and so on) that share the same name as a namespace. Of course, these rules present their own possibilities for name clashes, but nothing's perfect.

You can place anything into a namespace that you would normally place into a level of scope. This includes just about everything: declarations and definitions of types, classes, structures, variables, and pretty much anything else you can think of. Listing 24.4 shows the declaration for a simple namespace.

Listing 24.4   A Simple Namespace Declaration

```
namespace Simple
{
    // How about some typedefs?
    typedef enum { Red, Green, Blue } Color;

    // Take care of our function declarations
    Color MyFunc();

    // And a class...
    class Dog
    {
    public:
        void Bark();
    };

    void Dog::Bark() { cout << "Woof!\n"; }

    // Can't forget the definition of the MyFunc
    // function we declared!
    Color MyFunc() { return Red; }
}
```

By placing the above declaration into your program, you have defined a set of declarations and definitions that all belong to the `Simple` namespace.

Now that we have declared our namespace, we are in a position to actually use it. Remember that a namespace is a new level of scope and is effectively invisible to program code that does not explicitly indicate that it wants to use the namespace.

Listing 24.5, for the sake of example, tries to use definitions that appear within the Simple namespace without explicitly referring to the fact that the definitions reside within a namespace.

Listing 24.5 Illegal Use of the Simple Namespace (Lacks Qualification)

```
void main()
{
    // Use the class
    Dog    MyDog;
    MyDog.Bark();

    // And now some of the other stuff
    Color MyColor = MyFunc();
    cout << "The color is ";
    switch (MyColor) {
        case Red:
            cout << "Red";
            break;
        case Green:
            cout << "Green";
            break;
        case Blue:
            cout << "Blue";
            break;
    }
    cout << "\n";
}
```

While you may be tempted to try to use the namespace in this manner, the Borland compiler complains with a host of undefined symbol errors. Because all of those items that appear in the Simple namespace are essentially invisible to main(), this is not surprising.

Definitions that reside within a namespace are accessed using the good old scope resolution operator (::) that you're probably used to using when working with C++ classes. The namespace name is coupled with the name of the definition being referenced. See listing 24.6 for the corrected version of the program that compiles, links, and runs as expected.

Listing 24.6 Simple.cpp—The Correct Use of the Simple Namespace

```
void main()
{
    // Use the class
    Simple::Dog  MyDog;
    MyDog.Bark();

    // And now some of the other stuff
    Simple::Color MyColor = Simple::MyFunc();
    cout << "The color is ";
    switch (MyColor) {
```

```
            case Simple::Red:
                cout << "Red";
                break;
            case Simple::Green:
                cout << "Green";
                break;
            case Simple::Blue:
                cout << "Blue";
                break;
    }
    cout << "\n";
}
```

As you can see, this is exactly the same program as depicted in listing 24.5, except the use of every Simple namespace declaration is prefixed with Simple::.

Nesting Namespaces

Namespaces are essentially global entities. They cannot be declared within the body of functions, templates, classes, or the like. They can, however, be nested within other namespaces. A nested namespace follows the normal C++ scoping rules; a child namespace that is contained within a parent namespace has access to all of the parent's definitions. The parent, on the other hand, does not have access to the child's definitions. The code fragment shown in listing 24.7 demonstrates some of these principles.

Listing 24.7   Nest.cpp—Nesting a Namespace

```
#include <iostream.h>

namespace Outer
{
    long Dog = 123;
    long Cat = 456;

    namespace Inner
    {
        long Lizard = Dog;
        // Or alternatively...
        // long Cat = Outer::Dog;

        // Hide Outer's Cat
        long Cat = 789;

        // Now sort them all out
        void AFunc()
        {
            cout << "Cat: " << Cat << "\n"; // Uses Inner:Cat
            cout << "Inner Cat: " << Inner::Cat << "\n";
            cout << "Outer Cat: " << Outer::Cat << "\n";
        }
```

(continues)

Listing 24.7   Continued

```
    }
}

void main()
{
    // Illegal - AFunc() not known to Outer
    // Outer::AFunc();

    // Illegal - Inner not known to main()
    // Inner::AFunc();

    // The right way
    Outer::Inner::AFunc();
}
```

In this code fragment, we see an example of namespace nesting. There are a couple of important things worth noting here. First of all, notice the similarity between this code and the code found in listing 24.2. In that example we created two sub-scopes. Each of the sub-scopes was nested within the main() scope.

Exactly the same dynamics are at work here, for better and for worse. The Inner namespace has unfettered access to the Outer namespace's Dog variable. At the same time, the Inner namespace has hidden its parent's definition for the Cat variable by providing its own.

At first glance, it would appear that namespaces still suffer from the same name hiding feature of listing 24.2. While this is true for the most part, take a close look at the definition for AFunc() in the above program.

```
    // Now sort them all out
    void AFunc()
    {
        cout << "Cat: " << Cat << "\n"; // Uses Inner:Cat
        cout << "Inner Cat: " << Inner::Cat << "\n";
        cout << "Outer Cat: " << Outer::Cat << "\n";
    }
```

It's true that a programmer who elects to simply use Cat without qualification gets the Inner version, which does indeed hide the version defined by Outer. Perhaps this is the intended behavior (or perhaps not!). An experienced programmer working with a simple scenario, like the one depicted here, may feel confident enough to not qualify the variable's use.

On the other hand, because we are using namespaces, we now have the option of fully qualifying our use of the Cat variable. In AFunc() we do just that, printing out the values of both the Inner and Outer versions of Cat. As a rule, you can always sidestep the definition hiding issue by always using fully qualified namespace names. It may take a few extra seconds to type in, but that's nothing compared to the time you can spend hunting down elusive bugs that arise from inadvertently using the wrong version of a definition.

Qualifying the use of nested namespaces is straightforward. Remember that your code must reference every intervening namespace level between the current scope and the definition it wants to use. The following `main()` function from listing 24.7 does just that:

```
void main()
{
    // Illegal - AFunc() not known to Outer
    // Outer::AFunc();

    // Illegal - Inner not known to main()
    // Inner::AFunc();

    // The right way
    Outer::Inner::AFunc();
}
```

The first attempted use, `Outer::AFunc()`, is illegal because `AFunc()` is not known to the `Outer` namespace. Recall that although the `Inner` namespace has access to definitions in the `Outer` namespace, `Outer` knows nothing of what is contained within `Inner`.

The second attempted use, `Inner::AFunc()`, suffers from a similar problem. Although `Inner::AFunc()` does exist, it is not immediately accessible from `main()`. Because `Inner` is nested inside `Outer`, code that wants to use things from `Inner` must first contend with the intervening level of scope imposed by `Outer`. Note, however, that `Inner::AFunc()` is the right form to use if `AFunc()` was being called from code that resided within the `Outer` namespace.

The correct way for the `main()` function to call `AFunc()` is to move through the entire nesting chain, starting with the outermost namespace and moving inward until the desired level of scope is reached.

Note

Although the declaration of a namespace may look similar to a class declaration, they are very different constructions that serve completely disparate purposes. One important difference worth noting is that namespaces have no provisions for access control. Because namespaces cannot have portions of their declaration defined as private or protected, anyone who knows a given namespace's name can access the definitions contained within.

Extending Namespaces

Namespaces have a number of interesting and unusual attributes, not the least of which is that namespace declarations are cumulative. That means that a program can declare a namespace containing an initial set of definitions and then extend it later in the code. Let's start our investigation of this capability by looking at listing 24.8.

Listing 24.8   Extend1.cpp—Extending a Namespace

```cpp
#include <iostream.h>

// Here's the initial declaration of the namespace
namespace Test
{
    void JustAFunc() { cout << "Ho there!\n"; }
}

// This function does NOT belong to the namespace
void InterestingFunc()
{
    cout << "Not really that interesting...\n";
}

// And here we extend the namespace
namespace Test
{
    void JustAnotherFunc() { cout << "Hi there!\n"; }
}

void main()
{
    Test::JustAnotherFunc();
    Test::JustAFunc();
    InterestingFunc();
}
```

You might assume that this program would not compile because of the duplicate namespace declaration for Test. This is not, however, the case. Although there are clearly two declarations of the Test namespace used by this example, they are one and the same. Don't believe it? In the above program, try to change the extension of the Test namespace to the following:

```cpp
// And here we extend the namespace
namespace Test
{
    void JustAFunc() { cout << "Not what you think...\n"; }
    void JustAnotherFunc() { cout << "Hi there!\n"; }
}
```

The Borland compiler gives you the following error message when you try to compile this version:

```
Body has already been defined for function 'Test::JustAFunc().
```

This demonstration does bring up an interesting string of questions. If a namespace can be split apart across multiple declarations like this, is function and method overloading still supported? The answer, and one that should hardly be unexpected, is a resounding "Yes, of course!" Listing 24.9 modifies the previous program slightly to demonstrate this capability by overloading the JustAFunc() function.

Listing 24.9   Extend2.cpp—Extending a Namespace While Overloading a Function

```cpp
#include <iostream.h>

// Here's the initial declaration of the namespace
namespace Test
{
    void JustAFunc() { cout << "Ho there!\n"; }
}

// This function does NOT belong to the namespace
void InterestingFunc()
{
    cout << "Not really that interesting...\n";
}

// And here we extend the namespace
namespace Test
{
    void JustAnotherFunc() { cout << "Hi there!\n"; }

    // And here's our overloaded version of JustAFunc
    void JustAFunc(bool) { cout << "I'm overloaded!\n"; }
}

void main()
{
    // Calls the first version
    Test::JustAFunc();

    // Calls the second version
    Test::JustAFunc(true);
}
```

You may be wondering why a special case is being made of function overloading. So fine, a namespace can be split across multiple definitions. Why belabor the point? Why go through the hassle of pointing out that yes, as any reasonable programmer might expect, function and method overloading works as advertised? Well, it just so happens that some unusual things *can* happen when you mix extended namespaces that use overloading. Take a very close look at listing 24.10, a slightly modified version of listing 24.9 that also uses overloading.

Listing 24.10   Extend3.cpp—A Namespace/Overloading Gotcha

```cpp
#include <iostream.h>

// Here's the initial declaration of the namespace
namespace Test
{
    void JustAFunc(int AnInt)
    {
        cout << "Nice int! (Value = " << AnInt << ")\n";
```

(continues)

Listing 24.10 Continued

```
        }
}

// This function does NOT belong to the namespace
// Notice the call to JustAFunc()
void InterestingFunc()
{
    cout << "Calling JustAFunc()...\n";
    Test::JustAFunc(24.7);
}

// And here we extend the namespace
namespace Test
{
    // And here's our overloaded version of JustAFunc
    void JustAFunc(float AFloat)
    {
        cout << "Nice float! (Value = " << AFloat << ")\n";
    }
}

void main()
{
    InterestingFunc();
}
```

The programmer who wrote this was expecting to see the "Nice float..." message, but instead was given the "Nice int..." message and a truncated value. Can you tell what happened here?

A very important point to keep in mind is that the Borland compiler does not compile all of the declarations for a given namespace before looking at the rest of the code. Namespaces are processed just like the rest of your program: left-to-right, top-to-bottom. That means that code that rests between two declarations for the same namespace can only use items declared within the first namespace declaration. When you stop to think about it, this makes perfect sense. If the compiler didn't follow this strategy, it would have to have some way of knowing that it had to go back once it was finished processing the two namespace declarations. That's asking a lot of today's compiler technology!

Normally, a program that breaks this rule is relatively safe. If the code between the two namespace declarations tries to use items that are declared later on, the compiler will emit an error complaining that it can't find the referenced declarations. The programmer looks at the error, a light bulb goes off in her head, and the problem is fixed. However, when function overloading is involved, the situation can be a little more complex.

Let's go back to listing 24.10. The first declaration of the Test namespace contains a version of JustAFunc() that accepts an integer as its single argument.

```
    // Here's the initial declaration of the namespace
    namespace Test
    {
        void JustAFunc(int AnInt)
        {
            cout << "Nice int! (Value = " << AnInt << ")\n";
        }
    }
```

The definition of the InterestingFunc() function sits between the two Test
namespace declarations, and this is where the trouble starts. The programmer who
wrote this function knew that JustAFunc() was overloaded to accept a float argument, and this is the version of the function that she was trying to call.

```
    Test::JustAFunc(24.7);
```

Unfortunately for us, the only version that the compiler knows about at this point is
the integer version. In C++, floats can be promoted to integers during a function call.
This is exactly what happens; the integer version of JustAFunc() is called with an
integer argument of 24. That's certainly not an easy bug to track down!

The moral of this example is to be very careful when splitting up your namespaces,
especially when overloading is involved. Because the vast majority of programmers
keep all of the different versions for overloaded functions and methods together,
problems like the one described above are quite rare occurrences. Still, there's no
substitute for being forewarned.

The Unnamed Namespace

You may have been a little confused to learn that the name of a namespace is optional. What exactly does it mean for a namespace, which is little more than a named
level of scope, to not have a name?

For one thing, all unnamed namespaces (also called anonymous namespaces) that are
not nested within another namespace are all shared. Because this namespace has no
name with which to qualify access, this namespace has global scope. Take a quick
look at listing 24.11.

Listing 24.11 Unnamed1.cpp—An Unnamed Namespace that Is Not Nested

```
#include <iostream.h>

namespace {
    int i = 10;
    int z = 5;
}

int i = 1;

void main()
{
```

(continues)

Listing 24.11 Continued

```
        z++;
        cout << z << endl;
}
```

In this example, we have two definitions of i that are at global scope. It is very important to note that these are two different definitions of i; as strange as it may appear, they do not both refer to the same variable. As a consequence, the compiler does not flag this as a duplicate symbol error. However, if you modify main() to use an unqualified i, you get into trouble.

```
void main()
{
    i++;
    cout << i << endl;
    z++;
    cout << z << endl;
}
```

When you try to compile this version of the program, the Borland compiler complains about "Ambiguity between 'i' and '<unnamedNS>::i'". There doesn't seem to be much point in letting a program declare these variables if it's going to flag an error when the code actually tries to use them. While this is true, the variable i in the above example can be used, as long as it's qualified.

Whoa, wait a minute! Clearly you can't qualify the use of i with the name of the namespace; the anonymous namespace doesn't have a name! However, the global scope does have a name, in a sense. Remember that one of the more arcane rules of C++ states that you can always access definitions that exist in the global scope (not the unnamed namespace) using an unqualified scope resolution operation. Therefore, ::i will refer to the global version of i and not the version that resides within the anonymous namespace. Look at the revised version of the program that appears in listing 24.12.

Listing 24.12 Unnamed2.cpp—Using the Global Version of *i*

```
#include <iostream.h>

namespace {
    int i = 10;
    int z = 5;
}

int i = 1;

void main()
{
    ::i++;
    cout << ::i << endl;
    z++;
    cout << z << endl;
}
```

This program outputs the numbers 2 and 6. Clearly the global, non-namespaced version of i is being used. Of course, this still leaves us with the problem of how to access the namespaced version of i. To that question there is a very simple answer—you can't, at least not without nesting the anonymous namespace inside another namespace.

To quickly summarize, a non-nested anonymous namespace acts as if its contents are global, but is separate and distinct from other truly global definitions. Name clashes are allowed, but only the "true" global definitions can be accessed, and even then, only by using the unqualified scope resolution operator.

Now let's move into a discussion of what happens when an anonymous namespace is nested. Listing 24.13 depicts just such a situation.

Listing 24.13   Unnamed3.cpp—An Unnamed Namespace that Is Nested

```cpp
#include <iostream.h>

namespace Outer
{
    // Anonymous namespace
    namespace
    {
        int i = 8;
    }

    namespace Inner
    {
        int i = 10;

        void AFunc()
        {
            cout << "Inner::AFunc\n";
            cout << i << "\n";
            cout << Inner::i << "\n";
        }
    }

    void AFunc()
    {
        cout << "Outer::AFunc\n";
        cout << i << "\n";
        cout << Inner::i << "\n";

        // Illegal - There is no Outer::i
        // cout << Outer::i << "\n";
    }
}

void main()
{
    Outer::Inner::AFunc();
    Outer::AFunc();
}
```

Take a quick walk through the sample program. You have two functions that appear within two separate namespaces. (Note how both functions are named AFunc(), but we use nested namespaces to differentiate between the two). The Outer namespace includes an anonymous namespace in addition to the nested Inner namespace.

In this example, the anonymous namespace sits at the same level of scope as Outer. Therefore, unqualified references to items appearing within the unnamed namespace, but not in Outer, resolve to the anonymous namespace version. That is exactly what happens in Outer::AFunc().

```
void AFunc()
{
    cout << "Outer::AFunc\n";
    cout << i << "\n";
    cout << Inner::i << "\n";

    // Illegal - There is no Outer::i
    // cout << Outer::i << "\n";
}
```

Notice that the unqualified reference to i resolves to the version that lives inside the anonymous namespace. The qualified use of Inner::i, however, correctly finds the version of i found within the Inner namespace. Additionally, trying to access Outer::i will not resolve to the version of i in the anonymous namespace. Outer does not have its own version of i, so the compiler would complain about an "Undefined symbol Outer::i."

When you come right down to it, anonymous namespaces have limited usefulness and are seldom used. Because non-nested anonymous namespaces resolve to global scope, they are useful for storing global variables without having to use the static keyword. Apart from that, though, you may decide that they are more trouble than they are worth.

Using Aliases

By this point, you may be feeling a little disillusioned by namespaces. Although they certainly lend order and organization to mid- and large-sized programs, typing in all of those namespace qualifications is nothing short of painful. The situation is further exacerbated if your company has a policy of giving your namespaces long and descriptive names. Is it really worth it when you have to type in AmalgamatedWoodchuckFeedCorp::Bark, instead of plain old Bark?

On one hand, the irritable cynic would probably retort, "Don't give your namespaces such long names!" On the other hand, we are looking for a solution with a certain degree of elegance and simplicity. A partial solution is to use *aliases*.

An alias allows you to give several different names to the same namespace. This means you can satisfy your boss by placing your code into an AmalgamatedWoodchuckFeedCorp namespace, but have your code actually use a namespace named ChuckFood or AWFC.

The syntax for creating an alias is simple:

```
namespace alias = namespace;
```

To use our woodchuck example, we can create a more approachable alias as follows:

```
namespace AmalgamatedWoodchuckFeedCorp
{
    Definitions go here
}
namespace AWFC = AmalgamatedWoodchuckFeedCorp;
```

In listing 24.14, you can see a variety of techniques for using aliases. This program creates a rather wretched namespace hierarchy and then radically simplifies it using some much shorter aliases.

Listing 24.14   Alias.cpp—Using Aliases to Make Namespace Use Easier

```cpp
#include <iostream.h>

// Our namespace mess from hell
namespace CrazySusansCustomRecipePlanner
{
    void Func1() { cout << "In Func1\n"; }

    namespace UserInterfaceWidgets
    {
        void Func2() { cout << "In Func2\n"; }

        namespace WindowControls
        {
            void Func3() { cout << "In Func3\n"; }

            class Window
            {
            public:
                void ShowYourself()
                    { cout << "Don't want to!\n"; }
            };
        }
    }
}

// And now the aliases
namespace RecipePlanner = CrazySusansCustomRecipePlanner;
namespace RP = RecipePlanner;
namespace Widgets = RP::UserInterfaceWidgets;
namespace Win = Widgets::WindowControls;

void main()
{
    // Different ways to call Func1()
    CrazySusansCustomRecipePlanner::Func1();
    RecipePlanner::Func1();
    RP::Func1();
```

Listing 24.14   Continued

```
    // Different ways to call Func2()
    RecipePlanner::UserInterfaceWidgets::Func2();
    Widgets::Func2();

    // Different ways to call Func3()
    CrazySusansCustomRecipePlanner::UserInterfaceWidgets::WindowControls::Func3();
    ➡Win::Func3();

    // Using the Window class
    Win::Window MyWindow;
    MyWindow.ShowYourself();
}
```

There are two things worth pointing out in this example. Notice that an alias can refer to a namespace that is at an arbitrary level of nesting. This can really help to cut down on the size of your qualifications (just take a look at the invocation of Func3() in the above listing). However, use this feature with a certain degree of caution. The whole point of using namespaces is to enforce a structured mechanism for definition access. Using aliases for nested namespaces somewhat circumvents these controls, so use them sparingly.

The last thing worth pointing out is that aliases can readily access the definitions of previous aliases. That way, aliases can build upon each other, making the declaration of later aliases easier.

The *using* Keyword

But you're still not satisfied. Yes, aliases help out a little, but there's still no hiding the fact that every use of a namespaced definition has to be fully qualified. In the best of cases, this is a hassle, aliases or no aliases. At worst, it is impractical to retrofit large amounts of code that have already been written.

Don't worry, there is a solution. The answer lies in a new C++ keyword: using. The using keyword allows you to indicate that an entire namespace (or alternatively, a specific definition inside a namespace) be elevated into the same level of scope. This procedure is sometimes referred to as *hoisting* because the definitions are being hoisted out of the specified namespace into the current scope.

Once a namespace has been hoisted, there is no need to qualify your use of namespace entities. Of course, you run the danger of running into name clashes again, but the compiler allows you to hoist definitions that collide with global definitions. In fact, you can hoist to your heart's content and rack up as many name collisions and duplicate definitions as you want. In the event of a collision with a global, the compiler will flag an error and force you to decide which one should be used. In the event of collisions with local definitions or other namespaces, the compiler will not flag an error unless you actually try to use the definitions in question.

There are actually two forms of the using statement. The first is the using declaration, which simply pulls in a specific definition from a namespace. Its form is

```
using namespace::definition;
```

The second form is referred to as the using directive. The using directive hoists an entire namespace into the current scope. The using directive form is

```
using namespace name;
```

Looks pretty easy doesn't it? Let's take a look at some examples, shown in listing 24.15.

Listing 24.15   Using1.cpp—Hoisting Out of a Namespace

```cpp
#include <iostream.h>

namespace Functions
{
    void Func1() { cout << "In Func1()\n"; }
    void Bark()  { cout << "Bow wow!\n";   }
}

namespace Data
{
    int   i = 56;
    long  z = 12L;
}

// Global Bark() function
void Bark()
{
    cout << "Whoof!\n";
}

namespace Dog
{
    void Bark()  { cout << "Yip yip!\n";   }
}

void main()
{
    // A using declaration
    using Data::z;

    // Outputs Data::z
    cout << z << "\n";

    // Outputs Data::z
    cout << Data::z << "\n";

    // Illegal - i hasn't been hoisted
    // cout << i << "\n";

    // Outputs Data::i
    cout << Data::i << "\n";
```

(continues)

```
Listing 24.15   Continued
        // A using directive
        using namespace Functions;

        // Calls Functions::Func1()
        Func1();

        // Illegal - Functions::Bark() and global Bark() collide
        // Bark();

        // Calls global Bark()
        ::Bark();

        // Another using directive
        using namespace Dog;

        // Illegal - Functions::Bark(), Dog::Bark(), and global Bark() collide
        // Bark();
    }
```

In listing 24.15 we have three namespaces. The first, Functions, contains only the functions Func1() and Bark(). The second, Data, contains the definitions for two variables, i and z. The final namespace, Dog, contains only the definition of its own Bark() function.

In function main() you find an example of a using declaration and two using directives. The declaration hoists only the z variable into the current scope; Data::i remains in the namespace and can only be accessed with a full qualification. This is demonstrated in the code immediately following the using declaration. Trying to display the value of an unqualified i results in an undefined symbol error.

The second part of main() hoists the entire Functions namespace into the current scope. Func1() now operates as if it were a function in scope. Note that there appears to be a name clash here involving the Bark() function. Namespace Functions has a version of Bark(), but there is a Bark() also declared globally. The compiler allows this collision only because there is not code that tries to call Bark() without qualification. As demonstrated, the program can always call the global version using the ::Bark() syntax.

The last part of main() hoists the entire Dog namespace locally, which includes yet another Bark() function. Now there is a three-way naming collision between the global Bark(), Functions::Bark(), and Dog::Bark(). When the compiler sees a call to Bark() after the Dog namespace has been hoisted, there is no way to discern which of the two hoisted Bark () functions should be called—or whether the program really means to use the global bark—and an error is flagged. It is not an error, though, if the function is never called.

The using directive is transitive, which means that code that hoists a namespace that in turn hoists other namespaces will get the sum total of all the namespace definitions pulled into the local scope. Listing 24.16 shows a quick example of this capability in action.

Listing 24.16 Using2.cpp—Transitive *Using* Directives

```cpp
#include <iostream.h>
#include <cstring.h>

namespace A
{
    int a = 123;
}

namespace B
{
    long b = 456L;
}

namespace C
{
    string c = "Hello world!";
    using namespace A;
    using namespace B;
}

void main()
{
    using namespace C;

    cout << a << "\n";
    cout << b << "\n";
    cout << c << "\n";
}
```

Integrating with Other Code Using Namespaces

One of the aforementioned benefits of using namespaces is to allow you to use other people's code without concern for duplicate definitions. More often than not, these situations manifest themselves in the form of third-party class libraries and development tools.

Try to imagine the following situation: You're assigned to develop an exciting multi-media application that requires an extensive amount of graphics expertise; expertise that you don't have. However, just as you are about to sink into the depths of despair, your boss knocks on your office door. Because he understands your predicament, he has purchased a class library from MegaKlutz that will make the task at hand considerably easier. (Your new boss sounds pretty cool. Maybe getting fired from your previous job wasn't such a bad thing after all.) "This project is of the highest importance," he says. "I'm depending on you."

You rip open the package, prepared to save the day and prove your skills as a programming guru. However, no sooner have you cracked the reference manual than a strangled cry breaks from your lips. The MegaKlutz class library makes widespread use of a class named Error. Unfortunately, your development team already uses a typedef that maps your own Error type onto an unsigned long. You don't have the source code for the MegaKlutz libraries, and it is politically unfeasible to ask your team to modify all of your preexisting code to use a different type for their error codes. You slump back into your chair, fighting off images of grain elevators in Siberia.

Then it hits you. You can simply place the MegaKlutz definitions into its own namespace and selectively use the definitions that will allow you to finish your program. The biggest headache will involve going through the MegaKlutz header files and wrapping them all in namespace declarations. Thank goodness namespace declarations don't have to be contiguous.

There's an even better way to create the MegaKlutz namespace that doesn't involve changing any of the third-party header files. Listing 24.17 shows the intermediate header file that you create to define the MegaKlutz namespace.

Listing 24.17   3rdparty.h—A Header File that Declares the MegaKlutz Namespace

```
#ifndef 3RDPARTY_H
#define 3RDPARTY_H

// Here's the declaration of the MegaKlutz namespace
namespace MegaKlutz
{
    #include <megaklutz.h>
    #include <animate.h>
    #include <3Dgraph.h>
    #include <doitall.h>
}

// Our alias
namespace MK = MegaKlutz;

#endif
```

As you can see, your program can #include right into a namespace and everything in the include file becomes members of the namespace, requiring qualification before they can be used. Listing 24.18 shows an excerpt of some code that you might write that uses your definition of the Error type and the version that ships with the MegaKlutz class library.

Listing 24.18   A Source File that Uses the MegaKlutz Class Library

```
#include <3rdparty.h>

// Your team's version of Error
typedef unsigned long Error;

/*
    This function places a digitized image on the
    screen and morphs it into the company logo
    of Amalgamated Woodchuck Feed Corporation.
*/

Error MorphToWoodchuck(long xaxis, long yaxis)
{
    // Let the MegaKlutz class library do all
    // the work for me
    MK::Error Result;
    Result = MK::MorphImage(x, y, ...);

    // Now translate a MegaKlutz error into
    // one of ours
    return (Error) Result.GetErrorCode();
}
```

Even though this example is a little trite, you should be able to see that namespaces provide an elegant and effective way for integrating external code sources with your own. While there is still a certain amount of additional leg work associated with resolving name clashes, namespaces bring these tasks into the realm of feasibility.

From Here...

Namespaces will probably not be used extensively by everyone. After all, name collisions and definition hiding are relatively rare and usually occur only in larger programs. Still, when you need the feature, you really need it. The ability to coordinate the activities of class libraries that were developed with little or no regard for each other becomes of critical importance in the construction of large and complex C++ programming systems. Some of you will be forced to use namespaces because the third-party products that you buy will leverage them.

There are several other chapters in this book that address new and advanced issues in C++ programming. Be sure to check out the following chapters:

■ Refer to chapter 19, "Using Template Classes," for more information on templates, which are probably the most frequently used C++ extension. Templates enable programs to build class families that function similarly, but perform operations on a wide variety of different data types.

- For information on another C++ extension, refer to chapter 22, "Exception Handling." This chapter shows you how exception handling enables programmers to localize error-processing logic and logically structure the way their programs deal with abnormal execution events.

- Chapter 23, "Run-Time Type Identification (RTTI)," covers run-time type identification (RTTI), which is another relative newcomer to the C++ feature set. RTTI allows programmers to query objects and determine the type of objects at run-time. While this is outwardly an esoteric sounding feature, this chapter explains why this capability can be so valuable.

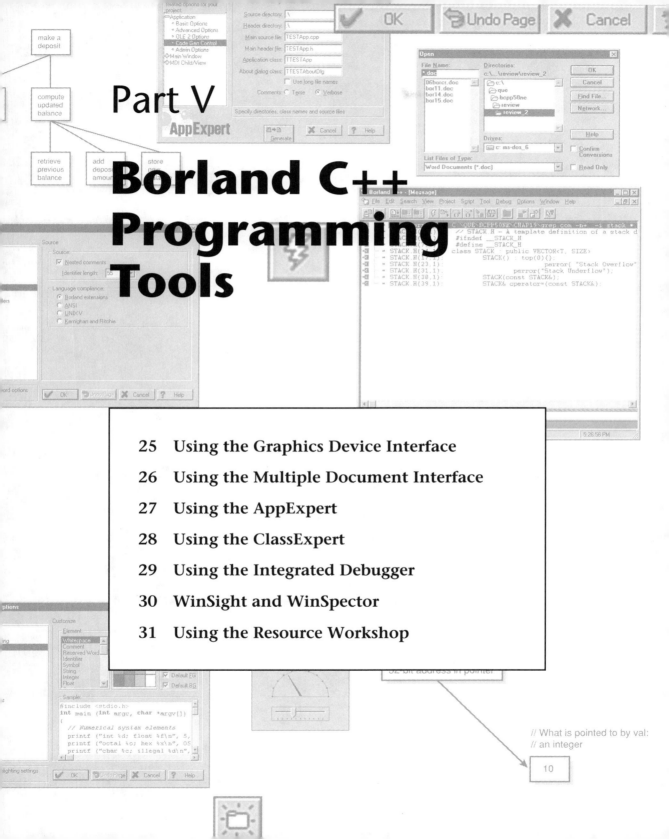

Part V

Borland C++ Programming Tools

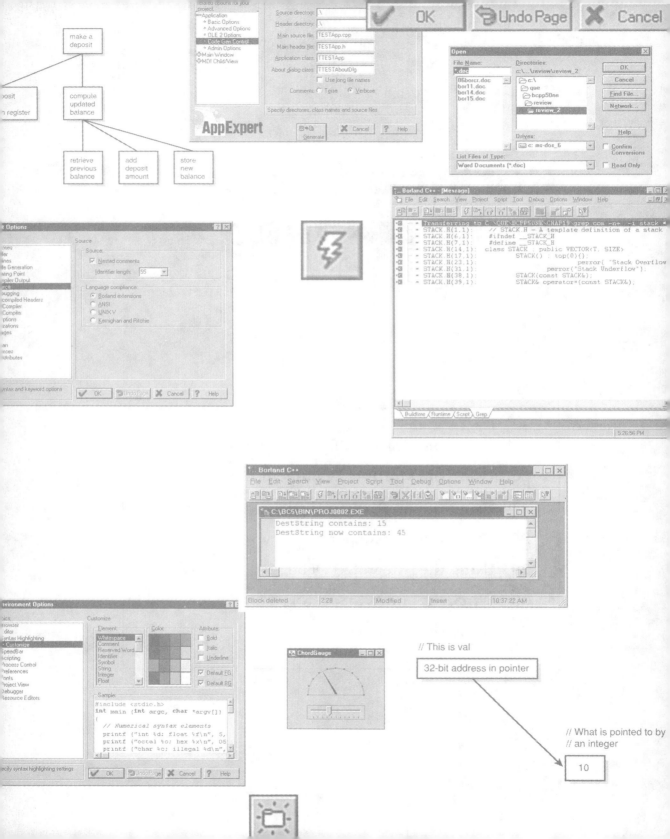

CHAPTER 25

Using the Graphics Device Interface

Graphics Device Interface is the rather uninspired name for the subsystem that Windows uses to manipulate graphical images. The Graphics Device Interface—more affectionately known by the acronym GDI—is directly responsible for expressing the graphical nature of Windows. Everything that you see on your monitor, everything that is spit out by your printer, everything that inputs and outputs graphical information, uses the GDI. When you're talking about graphics under Windows, you're usually talking about the GDI.

At the system level, the GDI is fairly complex and is comprised of approximately 200 functions. Borland has incorporated GDI support into the proprietary class libraries that ship with Borland C++ 5, the Object Windows Libraries (OWL). The GDI support provided within OWL is comprehensive, but considerably more approachable and easier to use than writing directly to the Win32 APIs.

In this chapter, you learn about

- OWL-based GDI fundamentals
- The importance that OWL places on device context objects and how device contexts interact with other GDI objects like pens and brushes
- The drawing functionality that OWL has placed into the TDC class
- Borland's GDI support in action by seeing a simple but fully functional sample program

Why You Need the GDI

The GDI has a large audience, but no user of the GDI is as important as Windows 95 itself. Windows uses the GDI to display windows, dialog boxes, controls, and pretty much everything that appears on-screen. This implies that virtually every Windows program written in Borland C++ is going to use the GDI whether it wants to or not.

It is very possible, however, to write a program that never has to resort to making explicit GDI function calls or to using the OWL classes that provide direct access to GDI functionality. If your program simply creates a few windows and interacts with the user through simple dialog boxes, you may never have to worry about what a TDC is and why you might want to pass it a TBrush. On the other hand, there is a lot that you miss out on by forsaking the GDI.

What Is the GDI?

The purvey of the GDI is vast and diverse. If you want your application to perform virtually any graphical operation, you will need to make GDI calls. That includes using any of the following services:

- Graphics primitives (shapes, paths, fills, patterns, etc.)
- Text output and font management
- Palettes and color management
- Bitmaps (including device-independent bitmaps, icons, and cursors)
- Printing
- Graphical device interaction
- Metafiles
- Viewports and scaling

Clearly a program that doesn't use the GDI is destined to be a pretty boring application. This chapter dwells primarily on GDI graphics primitives, so there is plenty of room for further exploration. For example, mapping modes and user-defined logical units are not covered in this chapter. The code fragments and sample programs that you will see all run with Windows and OWL defaults, which means that measurements are provided in pixels. However, advanced programmers may choose to modify their coordinate systems so that they can provide measurements in common units like fractions of an inch or fractions of a millimeter. The GDI is a large and exciting place and there is a lot to learn.

What the GDI Isn't

Despite the pervasive use of the GDI, you may be surprised to learn that the GDI is not the only way to display graphics in a 32-bit Windows program. Microsoft is supplying, or will supply in the near future, a number of alternatives to the GDI.

The GDI Is Not OpenGL. OpenGL is a standard for displaying three-dimensional graphics. Although the technology underlying OpenGL was initially developed by Silicon Graphics, it has since been placed under the control of an independent standards group that includes the likes of IBM, Intel, Silicon Graphics, and—of course—Microsoft. While OpenGL is currently the preeminent choice for 3-D graphics on high-end UNIX workstations, Microsoft has jumped onto the bandwagon by building the graphics subsystem into Windows NT. Unfortunately, Windows 95 did not initially ship with OpenGL support (although Microsoft has publicly stated that OpenGL support is forthcoming). For now, Windows-based OpenGL applications are inherently tied to Windows NT.

Borland C++ 5 supports OpenGL but only at the API level. Since OpenGL support is not built directly into ObjectWindows it is much harder to program than OWL, and mixing the two together becomes even more problematic. If, however, you are still interested in using OpenGL, rest assured that you can still use the Borland compiler to do so.

Note

If you want to learn how to program in OpenGL, you'll probably want to obtain the official documentation for the library. The official reference document for OpenGL is the *OpenGL Reference Manual* (Addison-Wesley) by the OpenGL Architecture Review Board. The official guide to learning OpenGL is the *OpenGL Programming Guide* (Addison-Wesley) by Jackie Neider, Tom Davis, and Mason Woo. Que also offers a book on OpenGL programming, *3D Graphics Programming with OpenGL* by Clayton Walnum.

The GDI Is Not WinG or DirectDraw. Microsoft has started courting developers of computer games by promising them extensions to Windows 95 and NT that offer superior performance. Initially Microsoft's efforts centered around a high-performance graphics subsystem called WinG. WinG bypasses the GDI and allows programs to copy graphical bitmap images from a program memory buffer directly into your video card memory. Using WinG, programmers can develop games and multimedia programs that run almost as fast as their DOS-based counterparts. Under OWL 3.0, Borland supports WinG through the TWinGLibrary and TWinG classes.

Of course game developers—being the performance-obsessed bunch that they are—insisted that they needed something even faster than WinG. Microsoft has responded with the DirectDraw set of APIs. Unlike WinG, which facilitates the *copying* of bitmaps into video memory, DirectDraw lets developers directly access video memory without requiring an intervening copy operation. The distinction is admittedly subtle but quite important when display performance is critical. Unlike WinG, DirectDraw is *not* supported by OWL classes.

When it comes to speed, both WinG and DirectDraw make the GDI look positively lazy. At the same time the GDI and Borland's wrapping of the API within the OWL class libraries provide a variety of abstractions that make the generation of complex displays considerably easier.

Using GDI Objects and Device Contexts

Understanding OWL's support of the GDI requires a familiarity with two basic concepts: graphics contexts and GDI objects. Figure 25.1 shows an OWL inheritance hierarchy with a base class named TGDIBase. Most of the OWL GDI support is shored up in classes derived from TGDIBase.

Fig. 25.1

The TGDIBase *inheritance hierarchy.*

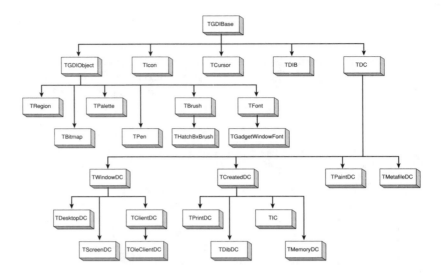

There is one interesting thing about this class hierarchy that should immediately jump out at you. The standard OWL window classes that you are probably most familiar with are not part of this inheritance tree. But aren't windows and toolbars graphical entities?

The answer, of course, is a resounding "Yes," but it is important to realize that the GDI is a graphics library that is primarily concerned with low-level infrastructure services. The GDI is blissfully unaware of user-interface issues like how wide a title bar should be or what's the correct color for the shaded bevel on a button. Windows knows the answers to these sorts of questions and the operating system, in turn, uses the GDI to actually place the graphical elements onto your screen.

As you can see in figure 25.1, the TGDIBase inheritance tree has three distinct parts: those classes beneath TDC, those classes beneath TGDIObject, and a few straggler classes that don't seem to fit into either of the two previous sub-trees. TDC, as you may have guessed, is the base device context class. Even though they are ultimately derived from TGDIBase, the device context classes are functionally segregated into their own inheritance tree and are really completely different animals than those classes derived from TGDIObject.

Device Contexts

So fine, a device context is not a GDI object. If it's not a GDI object, what is it? Device contexts represent the connection between your program code and your drawing area. Think of a device context as a (somewhat) intelligent assistant that takes drawing commands from your program and translates those commands into a form that the display device understands. If your program tells a device context to draw a red square at coordinates (10,10), the device context will communicate the request to the video driver, which will in turn make the appropriate modifications to a memory area used by your display adapter card. All of this, however, is hidden from you. All you need to be concerned with is how your program talks to the device contexts.

Device Independence. Device contexts also conspire to hide details about hardware characteristics from your application. If you haven't made any assumptions in your drawing code, your program can be readily moved from one computer to another without having to be modified. In fact, device contexts can also insulate your applications from the *type* of output device that is being used. This means that the procedures for sending output to a printer are often the same procedures that you would use to send output to the screen.

Of course, if you want to take advantage of a particular feature of your hardware, then device contexts will usually allow you to do so. Just because device contexts typically allow your programs to act as if all video cards were created equal doesn't mean that you are guaranteed to write device-independent code. One such example would be a program that assumes that it's running on a display device with 1024×768 pixel resolution. If you execute this program on a computer equipped with a lowly VGA card, the device context will happily sit back accepting display commands that refer to areas off the screen. A better way is to ask the device context how big the screen is up front, before making assumptions. If the device context indicates that the screen is smaller (or larger), your application has the opportunity to tailor its drawing behaviors accordingly. The device context also allows you to use coordinates other than pixels (centimeters, for example).

Types of Device Contexts. The granddaddy of the device context classes is TDC. This class presents OWL's view of the GDI library to client applications; as you might imagine, this is a *large* class. The key to understanding TDC (and its subclasses) is to bite off small pieces and tackle them one at a time.

Most of the Win32 GDI functions have at least one counterpart method inside the TDC class. Many GDI operations have several different ways that they can be called, depending on what information you currently have at hand. For example, all of the following calls to the Rectangle() method are valid *and equivalent*.

> **Note**
>
> Virtually all of the short code fragments in this chapter assume the existence of a device context instance named dc.

```
// a la the normal Windows API
dc.Rectangle(10, 10, 150, 150);

// Using two points
TPoint p1(10, 10), p2(150, 150);
dc.Rectangle(p1, p2);

// Using a point and a size
TPoint pnt(10, 10);
```

```
TSize sz(140, 140);
dc.Rectangle(pnt, sz);

// Using a rect
TRect rect(10, 10, 150, 150);
dc.Rectangle(rect);
```

Tip

Here's a little rule of thumb that you can often (although not always) apply if you are familiar with the Windows C-based API. Most Windows GDI functions have a corresponding device context method that accepts the same arguments. In the OWL class-based version, however, there's no need to pass a handle to a Windows device context (i.e., HDC) because the class instance *is* the HDC. You might want to try using overloaded methods that use the OWL convenience classes like TRect, TPoint, and TSize. They are often easier to read, understand, and program.

Since your programs will often be using a device context handed to you by OWL (in an event handler, for example), you will often be interacting with what appears to be an instance of TDC. However, you are almost always being given a device context of a derived type.

For example, printing the contents of a window requires a specialized context named, appropriately enough, TPrintDC. Since a program's printing code is often very similar (if not outright identical) to its window painting code, printing will usually involve OWL sending your program a simple Paint message. In this scenario, however, the TDC that gets passed into your Paint handler is actually a TPrintDC. Conversely, the device context which usually gets passed into your Paint handler because it responded to a normal screen painting request, is actually an instance of TPaintDC.

Clearly, when it comes to contexts, things are not always what they seem! The beauty of OWL is that your program usually doesn't care. Treat everything like a simple generic TDC and you can't go wrong. Table 25.1 enumerates the different device contexts that OWL supports. Remember that many of these classes will not be used directly by your programs; some may be instantiated by OWL and given to you in the guise of a regular old TDC.

Table 25.1 Types of OWL Device Contexts

Context Type	Description
TDC	Basic device context class. Since a TDC is constructed using normal Windows context handles, TDC's (and their derived brethren) are most often created by OWL and passed into application event and command handlers.
TWindowDC	A device context that is associated with drawing into a specific window and it permits full access to the entire window area.

Context Type	Description
TDesktopDC	This device context is associated with the desktop window (i.e., the screen behind all other windows). This specialized context provides access needed by programs like wallpaper/background animators.
TScreenDC	The TScreenDC gives an application direct access to the bitmap representing the entire screen. Items drawn into this context will appear on top of all other windows. This specialized context provides access needed by programs like screen-capture utilities.
TClientDC	A device context that is associated with drawing into the client portion of a specific window. Unlike the more generic TWindowDC, this device context permits access to the client area only.
TOleClientDC	Used by an OLE server to help with the potential translation of coordinates between different windows. This class handles generic scaling, scrolling, and translation behaviors required by any but the most trivial of OLE servers.
TPaintDC	TPaintDC wraps and hides the begin/end GDI calls (i.e., BeginPaint() and EndPaint()) used during Paint message processing.
TCreatedDC	An abstract class that cannot be directly instantiated, TCreatedDC is the base class of other device contexts that need to be explicitly created and deleted by the programmer.
TDibDC	A device context used to draw into a device-independent bitmap (DIB). Note that OWL provides an abstraction for the DIB itself in the form of the TDib class.
PrintDC	The TPrintDC is used when the output device is a printer. Most OWL applications create and interact with an instance of TPrinter, which in turn provides access to a TPrintDC as appropriate.
TIC	A TIC provides an interface for programs to explicitly bind the context to a specific driver or device.
TMemoryDC	Used to allow direct-to-memory GDI operations.
TMetafileDC	A device context used to draw into a window's metafile. A metafile provides a way to capture GDI commands into a sort of API macro. Playing back a metafile causes the commands to be reissued. The result of a metafile is encapsulated into the OWL class, TMetaFilePict.

Now that you have a somewhat basic understanding of what a context is, let's move on and investigate some of the things you can actually do with a TDC class. Since the TDC class is so large, I'll only address a few of the high points in the upcoming sections.

The Basics: *MoveTo* and *LineTo*. A given device context always has a current position associated with it. This current position represents an invisible point within the drawing area of the TDC. Think of this current position as the tip of a computerized pencil.

V

Programming Tools

You can pick up the pencil tip and put it down somewhere else or you can move the pencil tip to another point on the page without lifting it up, creating a line.

You can simulate the same actions with a device context using the `MoveTo()` and `LineTo()` methods. The `MoveTo()` method "picks up" the current position and moves it to another point without drawing a line. Similarly, `LineTo()` moves the current position but joins the two points with a line.

Moving the current position can take one of three forms, all of them pretty trivial. The first form takes two explicit horizontal and vertical coordinates while the second form simply takes a reference to a destination `TPoint` object.

```
// Move to coordinates (10, 20)
dc.MoveTo(10, 20);

// Move to the coordinate represented by pnt
TPoint pnt(10, 20);
dc.MoveTo(pnt);
```

The third form of `MoveTo()` allows you move the current position while saving the preceding position. The following code fragment—albeit a rather silly and useless example—demonstrates how you might bounce the current position back and forth a dozen times between a distant point.

```
// Bounce back and forth a dozen times
TPoint pnt1, pnt2(500, 200);
for (int loop = 0; loop < 12; loop++)
{
 dc.MoveTo(pnt2, pnt1);
 pnt2 = pnt1;
}
```

In this example, the current position is saved off into the pnt1 variable and then moved to the point indicated by the pnt2 variable.

The `LineTo()` methods are similar except there is no function analogous to `MoveTo`'s third form demonstrated in the last example.

```
// Assuming the current position is (10, 10), draw a
// short horizontal line
dc.LineTo(50, 10);

// And now draw a vertical line
dc.LineTo(50, 50);
```

Tip

If you want to know the device context's current position, you probably won't be surprised to learn that you can call the method `GetCurrentPosition()`. This method fills in a single `TPoint` object instance with the appropriate horizontal and vertical coordinates.

The Rectangle Family. In a previous section you saw the multiple forms of the Rect-
angle() method. There are, however, a variety of other commands that you can use
to draw rectangles. RoundRect(), for example, draws a rectangle into the device context
with rounded corners. This method has a couple different forms; the code fragment
below depicts one that uses the TPoint and TSize helper classes.

```
// Draw a rectangle with rounded corners
TPoint pntUpperLeft(50, 50), pntRadius(100, 100);
TSize Size(210, 210);
dc.RoundRect(pntUpperLeft, Size, pntRadius);
```

The radius argument to RoundRect() bears a little closer scrutiny. Examine figure 25.2,
which depicts the annotated output of the above code scrap.

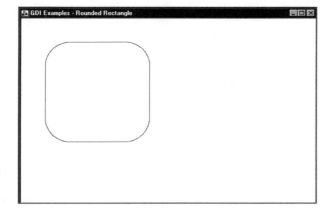

Fig. 25.2

A rounded rectangle.

The radius argument controls how rounded the rectangle's corners will be. The degree
of curvature in each corner is equivalent to that of the intersecting arc of an ellipse
with a horizontal radius equal to pntRadius.x and a vertical radius equal to
pntRadius.y. Yes, that sounds pretty scary, but if you look closely at figure 25.2 you'll
see that it's actually quite straightforward.

Unlike Rectangle() and RoundRect() methods, the FillRect() method creates (surprise!) filled rectangles. The rectangle is filled with a color and, optionally, a pattern as
described by the supplied brush. Don't worry—pens and brushes are very important
and will be fully discussed in the upcoming sections on GDI objects.

```
// Create a Red filled-in rectangle
TBrush brush(TColor::LtRed);
TRect rect(10, 10, 150, 150);
dc.FillRect(rect, brush);
```

Note

Note that when using the FillRect() method, the filled part of the rectangle includes the left
and top borders, but not the right and bottom boundaries.

V

Programming Tools

The `InvertRect()` method takes a rectangular region and changes its color. If your program is running on a black and white (i.e., monochrome) display, then pixels that were white become black, and pixels that were black become white. The behavior on color displays is a little less predictable and will depend on the specific characteristics of your video card, and the current palette your program is using. Typically, however, the effect is not unlike that of creating a photographic negative. This method is usually used by applications to indicate that a screen object is in a selected or highlighted state. For example, a drawing program may call this method when the user clicks to select a rectangle object that they drew previously.

```
// Invert the colors in a rectangular region
TRect rect(10, 10, 150, 150);
dc.InvertRect(rect);

// Return the region back to its original state
dc.InvertRect(rect);
```

Note that calling `InvertRect()` an even number of times results in a restoration of the original color state.

Getting the Run-Around: Circles and Related Exotica. Since there are so many different ways to draw rectangles into a device context, it should come as no surprise to hear that TDC has methods for drawing circles. The TDC also has a number of more elaborate methods for drawing various graphical figures related to circles.

Note

Watch out, high school geometry flashback ahead! You'll recall that an ellipse is a closed curve that describes how you would move a point around two fixed points (remember the foci?) in such a way that the sum of the distances between the floating point and the foci are constant. A circle is just a specialized case of a ellipse where the two foci are both located at the same point.

The first method in this group, and the easiest to understand, is `ellipse()`. This method creates a ellipse that is bounded by the rectangle described by passed-in arguments. Take, for example, the shape drawn by the following code fragment:

```
// Draw a big ellipse
TRect rect(100, 30, 300, 330);
dc.Ellipse(rect);
```

Figure 25.3 depicts the ellipse drawn by this code and shows the relationship between the ellipse and the provided rectangular coordinates.

Most of the other device context methods that are related to circles employ the bounding rectangle concept in their required input parameters (no foci here!). The arguments passed into the `Arc()` method, for example, describe a rectangle that defines an ellipse. The arc drawn is that part of the ellipse that falls between the angle formed from the center of the ellipse and two provided points. Whew! That's quite a mouthful to describe, but it's really not as complicated as it sounds. Figure 25.4 shows the arc created by the following code fragment. It also depicts the arc's bounding rectangle and its relationship to the two points that control the arc's size.

```
// Show the bounding rectangle
TRect rect(100, 30, 300, 330);
dc.Rectangle(rect);

// Create the arc defined by the topmost portion of an ellipse
TPoint pnt1(350, 45), pnt2(50, 45);
dc.Arc(rect, pt1, pt2);
```

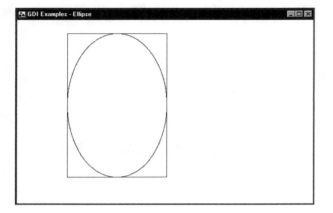

Fig. 25.3

An ellipse and its bounding rectangle.

Note that the arc angle is defined as sweeping counterclockwise around the path of the ellipse.

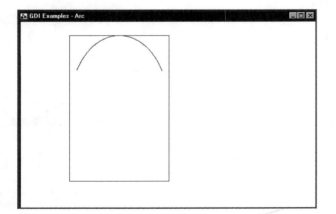

Fig. 25.4

An arc and its control points.

The Chord() and Pie() methods take the same parameters as Arc(), and the arguments have the same meanings as described earlier. A chord is simply a closed figure defined by an arc with its two endpoints joined. A pie is a closed figure defined by an arc and two line segments that join the arc endpoints with the ellipse center. Figure 25.5 and 25.6 illustrate `Chord()` and `Pie()` figures respectively.

Fig. 25.5

A TDC-drawn chord.

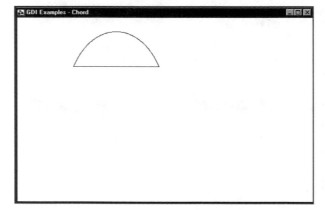

Fig. 25.6

A TDC-drawn pie.

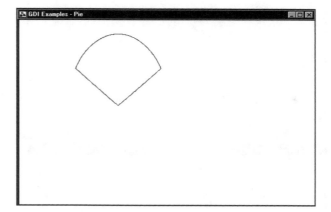

Displaying Text. Outputting text to an OWL window can be a real enigma. Although font management and precise text formatting is a challenging and often frustrating exercise, OWL also makes it very easy to output text in a quick-and-dirty fashion. In many cases, the methods discussed in this section will be more than adequate for your text display requirements.

OWL provides a host of TDC methods for querying and setting font information. Methods like `EnumFontFamilies()`, `GetOutlineTextMetrics()`, `GetTextFace()`, and others are all used to coordinate the intricacies of typeface management. These procedures can get quite involved and are not covered in this chapter.

On the other hand, OWL's device contexts also provide a number of methods that make outputting text a fairly straightforward process. Take, for example, the good old TextOut() function. This method outputs a string at the requested point.

```
// Show our string
TPoint pt(100, 100);
dc.TextOut(pt, "Using Borland C++ 5, New Edition");
```

Of course, one of the problems with this mechanism is that you'll usually want to know how much space in the window the string will take up before actually displaying it. This ensures that you're not overwriting any part of the screen that you know you shouldn't be. The GetTextExtent() method does just this, returning the height and width required to output the supplied string in a TSize instance. The below function, for example, displays a string with a box around it.

```
void BoxString(TDC& dc, const TPoint pnt, const char* szText)
{
 TRect rect;
 TSize size = dc.GetTextExtent(szText, strlen(szText));
 rect.left = pnt.x - 10;
 rect.top = pnt.y - 10;
 rect.right = pnt.x + size.cx + 10;
 rect.bottom = pnt.y + size.cy + 10;
 dc.Rectangle(rect);
 dc.TextOut(pnt, szText);
}
```

Figure 25.7 depicts the BoxString function in action.

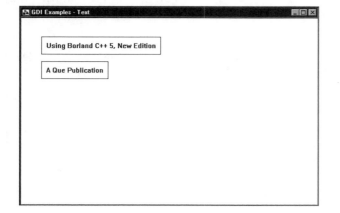

Fig. 25.7

Outputting text with TDC's TextOut *method.*

There are several other device context methods that allow you to display text. You might want to continue your explorations in this area by checking out the DrawText(), ExtTextOut(), TabbedTextOut(), and GrayString() methods. These methods elaborate on the simple services provided by TextOut() by supporting text justification, tab stops, and the like.

Fills. Fills allow you to specify an area of the screen that you want filled in with a particular color. Since Windows is smart enough to determine the boundaries of the area, you aren't restricted to filling in only those shapes that OWL knows how to draw. Examine the following code fragment. This code uses the `Ellipse()` method to draw a simple circle that is bisected by a line.

```
// Draw the circle
TRect rect(10, 10, 210, 210);
dc.Ellipse(rect);

// Draw the bisecting line
dc.MoveTo(110, 10);
dc.LineTo(110, 210);
```

You can use the device context `ExtFloodFill()` method to paint one of this circle's halves with the device context's current background color. `ExtFloodFill()` takes three arguments: a point lying within the region you want to be filled, the color of the boundary or border of the region to be filled, and an argument that describes the fill type requested. This last argument may be specified as `FLOODFILLBORDER` or `FLOODFILLSURFACE`. If you indicate the `FLOODFILLBORDER`, the region filled is defined by the border color passed in as the second argument. The following call, therefore, would start filling at the specified point and fill outwards until it encountered red lines that indicated a border.

```
dc.ExtFloodFill(pnt, TColor::LtRed, FLOODFILLBORDER);
```

If, however, you specify `FLOODFILLSURFACE`, the fill is defined by the contiguous region beneath the given point that is of the given color. Look at the following call to `ExtFloodFill()`.

```
dc.ExtFloodFill(pnt, TColor::LtRed, FLOODFILLSURFACE);
```

Assuming that pnt refers to a point within a circle and assuming that the circle's background is already red, this call will fill the circle with the current background color.

Returning to our original example, filling in the right half of the circle is now a simple matter of calling `ExtFloodFill()` with a type of `FLOODFILLBORDER`.

```
// Fill the right half of the circle
TPoint pnt(160, 160);
dc.ExtFloodFill(pnt, TColor::Black, FLOODFILLBORDER);
```

Figure 25.8 shows what the circle looks like after being filled.

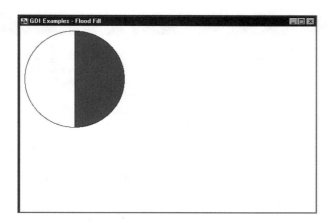

Fig. 25.8

Filling a bisected circle using ExtFloodFill.

V

Programming Tools

> **Note**
>
> You might be wondering why the designers at Borland decided to call this method
> ExtFloodFill() instead of simply FloodFill(). The truth of the matter is that there already is
> a FloodFill(). The FloodFill() method is very similar to ExtFloodFill() except it does not
> accept a fill style parameter. Instead, all fills performed by FloodFill() are assumed to be of
> type FLOODFILLBORDER. Borland recommends that new 32-bit C++ programs use the
> ExtFloodFill() method instead of the older FloodFill(). However, not all display adapters
> support this method, so you will need to call dc.GetDeviceCaps() first with an index of
> RASTERCAPS. You may use the ExtFloodFill() operation only if the return value has the
> RC_FLOODFILL bit set.

Other GDI Objects

As important as OWL's device context classes are, there are a variety of other GDI-related classes that collaborate with contexts to perform various functions. Upcoming sections describe two of the most important, TBrush and TPen. Table 25.2 gives brief descriptions of those other GDI classes that are used less frequently.

Table 25.2   Other Types of OWL GDI Objects

GDI Class	Description
TIcon	Abstracts interactions with icons. Provides an easy mechanism for reading in icons from an application's private resources, or from an external resource file. This object can be used with any Windows API that requires a handle to an icon (HICON).
TCursor	Abstracts interactions with cursors. This object can be used with any Windows API that requires a handle to a cursor (HCURSOR).
TDib	Abstracts interactions with device-independent bitmaps (DIBs). Working with DIBs can get a little tricky and the TDib class helps to reduce some of this complexity.

(continues)

Table 25.2 Continued	
GDI Class	**Description**
TGDIObject	Although technically not a true abstract class, TGDIObject should be treated as such. It serves as the parent class for many handle-based GDI classes. This class encapsulates logic for handling the deletion of GDI objects and reference counting.
TRegion	Describes a rectangular, elliptical, or polygonal region within a device context. Various operations within the TDC class are available for manipulating TRegions (e.g., FillRgn(), PaintRgn(), InvertRgn()). This class is a subclass of TGDIObject.
Bitmap	Abstracts interactions with bitmaps. Unlike the TDib class, the bitmaps represented by TBitmap are device-dependent. This class is a subclass of TGDIObject.
TFont	Abstracts interactions with fonts. Device contexts have a large number of methods that deal with font management and manipulation (e.g., EnumFontFamilies(), EnumFonts(), GetTextFace()). TFont is used in conjunction with these methods. (This class is a subclass of TGDIObject and is selectable.)
TPalette	Abstracts various aspects of color management. A palette represents a table of color values. They can be used in conjunction with a device context and are also useful when working with instances of TDib. This class is a subclass of TGDIObject and is selectable (selectable classes are discussed later in this section).

Some of the classes listed in table 25.2 are said to be selectable into a device context. A *selectable* class means that device contexts always have an instance of one of these classes set as an attribute. For example, a particular instance of TDC may have its font set to Times Roman, 12-point. This attribute is easily changed by selecting a new TFont object into the device context. In addition to the TBrush and TPen classes described later, TFont and TPalette are device context-selectable.

Selecting a new object is as easy as calling the device context method SelectObject(). The previously selected attribute is saved and can be restored with a call to RestoreObjects(). Individual attributes can also be restored with a call to their corresponding restoration method (RestoreFont(), RestorePalette(), etc.). The following code fragment shows how this might be done. In the interest of keeping things simple, constructor arguments have been omitted.

```
// Instantiate our GDI objects
TFont NewFont1(...), NewFont2(...);
TPalette NewPalette(...);

// Select the objects into the context
dc.SelectObject(NewFont1);
dc.SelectObject(NewPalette);

// Restore the old font
dc.RestoreFont();
```

```
// Select the third font
dc.SelectObject(NewFont2);

// Reset the whole context back
dc.RestoreObjects();
```

Selecting GDI objects into a device context is a very common activity. Most of the time, however, your programs will be selecting instances of the two most common GDI objects—pens and brushes.

Caution

Most of the time your code will create GDI objects on the stack and they will be deconstructed and discarded when the flow of execution causes them to go out of scope. However, if you create GDI objects off the heap (i.e., using the new() operator), it is very important that you remember to delete them when you are finished. Normally OWL takes care of this task for you, but if you allocate GDI resources off the heap and don't release them, you can cause a system-wide resource leak. Since resources like fonts, palettes, pens, and brushes are entities that are all allocated from the same, limited memory pool, it is very important that you remember to return them to the pool when you are finished with them. If your program terminates without releasing them, Windows 95 has no way of getting them back!

Pens. In real life, the pen that you use dictates the color and width of the lines that you draw. Using the TPen class under Windows 95 is similar but with some important differences. In addition to color and width, Windows pens also allow you to set the style of line: normal, dotted, dashed, etc. You can change any of these attributes at any time and then re-select the pen into your device context for further drawing. Try doing that with your trusty ballpoint!

The TPen class is a selectable class. As you've already learned, this means that a device context has a pen attribute that it refers to when drawing all of its lines. By changing the pen, you can change the colors, line widths, and styles of any of your shape's borders.

TPen has no fewer than six different constructors taking a variety of different arguments. The most commonly used form, however, is one of the simplest and straightforward:

```
TPen(TColor color, int width=1, int style=PS_SOLID);
```

The first parameter is an instance of a TColor object that represents a particular color. The second argument represents the width of the pen and the last argument represents the style. Table 25.3 lists the various styles available to pen objects and shows what each style looks like.

Table 25.3 *TPen* Line Styles	
Style	**Appearance**
PS_SOLID	————————————————
PS_DASH	· — — — — — — — — — —
PS_DOT	··························
PS_DASHDOT	— · — · — · — · — ·
PS_DASHDOTDOT	· — ·· — ·· — ·· — ··
PS_NULL	(none)
PS_INSIDEFRAME	————————————————

Two of the style options are worthy of additional comment. The PS_NULL style effectively turns the pen off. Regardless of its other settings, a PS_NULL-styled pen will not draw anything. The PS_INSIDEFRAME style is a little less straightforward.

Since the borders of GDI shapes are drawn with the currently selected pen, it is possible to create figures with borders greater than a single pixel (i.e., the width argument passed into the TPen constructor is greater than one). By default, borders thicker than one pixel extend beyond the figure being drawn. The following line of code draws a simple rectangle:

```
dc.Rectangle(10, 10, 20, 20);
```

The upper-left corner of this shape lies at (10, 10) and the lower-right corner is at (20, 20). If, however, the width of the border were extended by five pixels, the rectangle's upper-left corner would actually be located at (6, 6). The lower-right corner would be at (24,24). Specifying a line style of PS_INSIDEFRAME indicates that the lines will be drawn in a manner that guarantees no edge extends beyond the boundaries of the shape.

You can now coordinate your use of pens with other device context methods to add color and variety to your graphics output. The follow code fragment draws two overlapping ellipses. The first ellipse is yellow with a three-pixel-wide border and the second ellipse is blue with a single-pixel-wide, dashed border.

```
// Select the first pen into the device context
dc.SelectObject(TPen(TColor::LtYellow, 5));

// Draw the first circle
TRect rect(10, 10, 110, 110);
dc.Ellipse(rect);

// Select the second pen into the device context
dc.SelectObject(TPen(TColor::LtBlue, 1, PS_DASH));

// Draw the second circle
rect += TSize(70, 0);
dc.Ellipse(rect);
```

You can see the output of this fragment in figure 25.9.

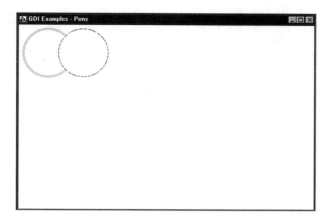

Fig. 25.9

Drawing ellipses with different pens.

Brushes. Although the names are similar, brushes are actually quite different from pens. Whereas a pen is used by OWL to specify the colors and styles of lines and borders, brushes are used to indicate the colors and styles of backgrounds and fills. Select a red brush into a device context and any rectangles that you draw will have red backgrounds. Select a new brush and your FloodFill can turn green.

Although you can construct brushes that paint backgrounds with bitmaps and patterns, the most commonly used forms are the simple brush and the hatched brush.

```
// Create a simple brush
TBrush(TColor color);

// Create a hatched brush
TBrush(TColor color, int style);
```

Both of these constructor forms take an initial argument describing the color of the background fill. In the first case, the brush will simply fill in shapes with the indicated color. In the case of a hatched brush, the device context will fill backgrounds with hatching pattern of the indicated color. A "hatch" is really just a simple pattern composed of line segments; table 25.4 shows what the various hatching patterns look like.

Table 25.4 *TBrush* **Hatch Styles**

Style	Appearance
HS_BDIAGONAL	
HS_CROSS	
HS_DIAGCROSS	

(continues)

Table 25.4 Continued	
Style	**Appearance**
HS_FDIAGONAL	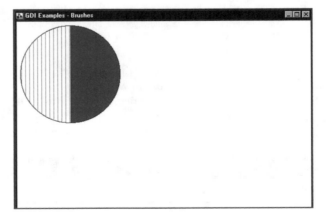
HS_HORIZONTAL	
HS_VERTICAL	

Going back to our half-filled circle example, you can modify the code so that the background of the circle is comprised of green, vertical hatching.

```
// Select the second pen into the device context
dc.SelectObject(TBrush(TColor::LtGreen, HS_VERTICAL));

// Draw the circle
TRect rect(10, 10, 210, 210);
dc.Ellipse(rect);

// Draw the bisecting line
dc.MoveTo(110, 10);
dc.LineTo(110, 210);

// Fill the right half of the circle
TPoint pnt(160, 160);
dc.ExtFloodFill(pnt, TColor::Black, FLOODFILLBORDER);
```

You can see the output of this fragment in figure 25.10.

Fig. 25.10

Filling an area with a different brush.

Putting It All Together

Okay. You've seen how it's all supposed to fit together—in theory. Now let's take a look at a complete program that puts into practice some of the techniques discussed in previous sections. Although our sample program won't do anything particularly useful, you will get a good feeling for how you might integrate OWL device contexts and GDI objects into your own programs.

The program depicted in figure 25.11 shows a screen shot of the program that will be discussed (and dissected) during the rest of this chapter.

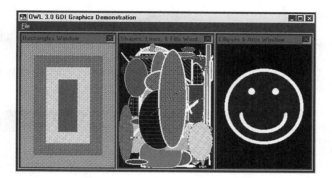

Fig. 25.11

The OWL 3.0 GDI demonstration program, Picdemo.exe.

Picdemo creates three central windows that each continuously cycle through a separate and distinct demonstration. The first window displays a series of rectangles drawn inside one another. Every second the color of the rectangles changes. Although this may not appear to be a particularly difficult feat, you might be surprised to learn that the code required for this window's Paint() routine is only six lines long. This fact is due in no small part to the elegant but logical abstractions that OWL supplies for programming the GDI.

The second window demonstrates a lot of different GDI drawing behaviors. Every 50 milliseconds a new GDI element is blasted into the client window area, with various operating parameters being randomly generated. Depending on what values are generated, you can be treated to a wide variety of different lines, ellipses, and rectangles (with sharp and rounded corners). The styles and colors of the pens and brushes are also randomly generated so depending on the luck of the draw (and your personal tastes) the window may appear chaotically vibrant or hideously garish.

The last window is perhaps the most endearing (if a graphics demonstration could ever be called endearing!). Window three displays a smiley face locked in a continuous cycle of shrinkage and growth. Of the three demonstrations, Smiley is actually the most sophisticated, for reasons that will soon become apparent.

Basic Program Structure

Before you can start to investigate the code that is responsible for actually drawing the various displays, it will help to have an understanding of how the program is structured. Although there is nothing unusual about the layout of the program and its classes, the addition of a timer has several implications.

Tip

The structure of the timing mechanism used in Picdemo is adopted from the GDIDemo sample program that ships with Borland C++ 5. GDIDemo is another good resource for examining some of the intricacies of GDI programming under OWL. It can be found in the \Bc5\Examples\Owl\Owlapps\Gdidemo directory.

Listing 25.1 shows the Picdemo program's main header file. Two classes are defined here, `DemoMDIWindow` and `GraphicsApp`. These classes are predominately responsible for initialization of the graphical demo windows, and for managing the interactions with the Multiple Document Interface (MDI) classes.

Listing 25.1   demo.h—The Main Application Header File

```
#ifndef DEMO_H
#define DEMO_H

// OWL constants
const int MenuId = 100;
const int IconId = 100;

// Message Ids
const int ShowChildrenId   =  205;

IMPLEMENT_CASTABLE1(BaseWindow, TWindow);

// Main MDI client window class
class DemoMDIWindow : public TMDIClient {

  public:
  // Constructor
  DemoMDIWindow() : TMDIClient() { }

  protected:
  // Various message and event handlers
  void SetupWindow();
  void CmShowChildren();
  void EvTimer(UINT TimerId);
  void EvSize(uint Type, TSize& NewSize);
  void EvDestroy();

  private:
  // Array of pointers to the actual demo windows
  TMDIChild *Children[4];

  DECLARE_RESPONSE_TABLE(DemoMDIWindow);
};


// Main application window class
class GraphicsApp : public TApplication {
```

```
public:
// Constructor
GraphicsApp() : TApplication() {}

// Message handlers
void InitMainWindow();
};

#endif
```

The really interesting aspects of the DemoMDIWindow and GraphicsApp classes are found in the implementation source file, Demo.cpp. It's in this file—displayed in listing 25.2—that you will find the creation of the timer and the child windows.

Listing 25.2   demo.h—The Main Application Source File

```
// Get needed include files
#include <owl\mdi.h>
#include "demo.h"
#include "rects.h"
#include "smiley.h"
#include "fills.h"

IMPLEMENT_CASTABLE1(BaseWindow, TWindow);

DEFINE_RESPONSE_TABLE1(DemoMDIWindow, TMDIClient)
  EV_COMMAND(ShowChildrenId, CmShowChildren),
  EV_WM_TIMER,
  EV_WM_SIZE,
  EV_WM_DESTROY,
END_RESPONSE_TABLE;

// ===================== Demo MDI Window =========================

// Initialize the children windows and create the timer
void DemoMDIWindow::SetupWindow()
{
  // Give our parent class a chance to initialize first
  TMDIClient::SetupWindow();

  // Create the timer
  if (!SetTimer(0, 50, 0)) {
  MessageBox("Could not Create Timer",
      "OWL 3.0 GDI Demonstration", MB_OK);
  PostQuitMessage(0);
  return;
  }

  // Create our children windows
  Children[0] = new TMDIChild(*this, "Rectangles Window",
    new RectsWindow);
  Children[1] = new TMDIChild(*this, "Shapes, Lines, & Fills Window",
    new ShapesAndFillsWindow);
```

(continues)

Listing 25.2 Continued

```
    Children[2] = new TMDIChild(*this, "Ellipses & Arcs Window",
      new SmileyWindow);

    // Set the styles so the children windows are hidden, disabled,
    // and without title-bar controls. Then create the windows.
    for (int iLoop = 0; iLoop < 3; iLoop++) {
     Children[iLoop]->Attr.Style &= ~(WS_VISIBLE      |
             WS_SYSMENU      |
             WS_MINIMIZEBOX  |
             WS_MAXIMIZEBOX);
     Children[iLoop]->Attr.Style |= WS_DISABLED;
     Children[iLoop]->Create();
    }

    // Post the message that will tell us to show and tile the
    // children windows
    PostMessage(WM_COMMAND, ShowChildrenId);
}

// The app is up and on its feet. Show the children and then
// tile them.
void DemoMDIWindow::CmShowChildren()
{
    for (int iLoop = 0; iLoop < 3; iLoop++) {
     Children[iLoop]->Show(true);
    }
    TileChildren();
}

// Typecast the child window to a window class that has the
// TimerTick() method (i.e., a class derived from BaseWindow).
// Follow the casting sequence of TWindow -> TFrameWindow (the
// child MDI frame window) -> BaseWindow (frame client).
void ChildTimers(TWindow* Child, void*)
{
    TFrameWindow* Frame = TYPESAFE_DOWNCAST(Child, TFrameWindow);
    CHECK(Frame);
    BaseWindow* DemoWin = TYPESAFE_DOWNCAST(Frame->GetClientWindow(),
            BaseWindow);
    CHECK(DemoWin);
    DemoWin->TimerTick();
}

// Call each of the TimerTick() methods
void DemoMDIWindow::EvTimer(UINT)
{
    ForEach(ChildTimers, 0);
}

// Anytime the window is resized we need to retile our
// children windows
void DemoMDIWindow::EvSize(uint sizeType, TSize& size)
{
```

```
   TMDIClient::EvSize(sizeType, size);
   TileChildren();
}

// Make sure that we destroy our timer
void DemoMDIWindow::EvDestroy()
{
  KillTimer(0);
  TMDIClient::EvDestroy();
}

// ===================== Main App Class ===========================

void GraphicsApp::InitMainWindow()
{
  MainWindow = new TMDIFrame("OWL 3.0 GDI Graphics Demonstration",
          MenuId, *new DemoMDIWindow);
  MainWindow->SetIcon(this, IconId);
}

int OwlMain(int, char*[])
{
  // Seed the random number generator
  randomize();

  // Kick off the demo
  return GraphicsApp().Run();
}
```

There are a couple of things in this source file that are worthy of note. Demo.cpp will look familiar to anyone with experience writing simple OWL programs. The ubiquitous `OwlMain` function simply initializes the random number generator and "runs" an instance of the `GraphicsApp` class. A main frame window of class `DemoMDIWindow` is created in `GraphicApp`'s `InitMainWindow()` method.

Things start to get interesting inside `DemoMDIWindow`. `DemoMDIWindow` is derived from `TMDIClient`, an OWL class that is responsible for managing child windows in a manner consistent with the Multiple Document Interface. If you aren't familiar with OWL's support for MDI (or MDI in general), don't worry. The use of MDI is virtually transparent in Picdemo so you don't have to be an MDI expert to follow what's going on. On the other hand, if you want to become an MDI expert, chapter 26, "Using the Multiple Document Interface," will do a good job of starting you on your way.

`DemoMDIWindow`'s `SetupWindow()` method is the first message callback to get executed once the main window handle becomes valid. In this method two main tasks are performed: A timer is created and the child demo windows are created. The following snippet shows the code that is responsible for starting the timer:

```
    // Create the timer
    if (!SetTimer(0, 50)) {
     MessageBox("Could not Create Timer",
           "OWL 3.0 GDI Demonstration", MB_OK);
```

```
        PostQuitMessage(0);
        return;
    }
```

The `SetTimer()` method creates a timer that sends a message to the application every 50 milliseconds. When one of these timer messages is received, OWL intercepts the notification and routes it to the `EvTimer()` handler for the `DemoMDIWindow`.

Each of the graphical demo window classes are derived from a common base class called `BaseWindow`. The `BaseWindow` class is fully defined in the base.h header file (don't look for a .cpp file; there isn't one). Since the class really provides nothing at all except the formalization of an interface, the header file is not presented here. Classes derived from `BaseWindow` are expected to override the `TimerTick()` method that will get called every time the application receives a timer notification.

So how does the message notification get from the `EvTimer()` handler to each of the `TimerTick()` methods? Easy. The following line of code is found in `EvTimer()`:

```
    ForEach(ChildTimers, 0);
```

This method call tells OWL to iterate across all of the child windows and call the method `ChildTimers()` for each one. `ChildTimers()`, in turn, safely typecasts the provided child window pointer to a `BaseWindow` and then calls that window's `TimerTick()` method.

That takes care of the timer but now the children windows still need to be created. Right after the timer is constructed in `SetupWindow()`, `DemoGDIWindow` creates a new instance of each of the three demo window classes (i.e., `RectsWindow`, `ShapesAndFillsWindow`, and `SmileyWindow`). Pointers to these windows are stored in an array so the program can easily manipulate the windows in an identical fashion. After constructing the new window instances the following code is applied to each of the window instances:

```
    for (int iLoop = 0; iLoop < 3; iLoop++) {
        Children[iLoop]->Attr.Style &= ~(WS_VISIBLE     |
                    WS_SYSMENU      |
                    WS_MINIMIZEBOX  |
                    WS_MAXIMIZEBOX);
        Children[iLoop]->Attr.Style |= WS_DISABLED;
        Children[iLoop]->Create();
    }
```

The program modifies the style bits so that the demo windows are initially created invisible, disabled, and without the standard window controls. The windows are created invisible because the application will be tiling the three windows within the client area of `DemoMDIWindow`, but that operation cannot be accomplished immediately. If the windows were created as visible and then tiled, there would be a perceptible flash as the windows were resized and repositioned. Hiding the windows until right before they are ready to be titled minimizes (but doesn't completely alleviate) this flash.

`SetupWindow()` finishes up by posting a message "reminding" itself to tile the children windows. This needs to be done because the `DemoMDIWindow` instance needs to be fully initialized before it can successfully process a `TileChildren()` request. By the time `CmShowChildren()` is called, the application knows that the `DemoMDIWindow` is alive and well; the children windows are unhidden and then tiled so that each will get equal exposure (this is, after all, a democratic demo).

Now that you have a feel for the way the program hangs together, it's on to the good stuff—using the GDI.

The Rectangles Window

Listing 25.3 shows the header file for the `RectsWindow` class. Like the other graphical demo window classes, this class does little except react to timer and `Paint()` messages. This is reflected in its rather minimalist definition.

Listing 25.3   rects.h—The *RectsWindow* Header File

```
#ifndef RECTS_H
#define RECTS_H

// Get needed include files
#include "base.h"

// Here's our class definition
class RectsWindow : public BaseWindow {

  public:
    // Constructor
    RectsWindow();

    // Message handlers
    void TimerTick();
    void Paint(TDC& dc, BOOL, TRect&);

  protected:
    // WM_SIZE message handler
    void EvSize(UINT, TSize& Size);

  private:
    // Tick count tracking variable
    unsigned short usTickCount;

    DECLARE_CASTABLE;
    DECLARE_RESPONSE_TABLE(RectsWindow);
};

#endif
```

Of course, the real action is contained in the actual source code (see listing 25.4). This is where you find the actual code for the window painting routine.

V

Programming Tools

Listing 25.4   Rects.cpp—The *RectsWindow* Source File

```cpp
// Get needed include files
#include "rects.h"

// The size of our rectangle "bands"
static const int BAND_SIZE = 25;

// Here's the response table for the Rectangles window class
DEFINE_RESPONSE_TABLE1(RectsWindow, BaseWindow)
  EV_WM_SIZE,
END_RESPONSE_TABLE;

// Make sure we can do typesafe casts
IMPLEMENT_CASTABLE1(RectsWindow, BaseWindow);

// Constructor
RectsWindow::RectsWindow() : BaseWindow(),
           usTickCount(0)
{ }

// In response to a size message, we simply repaint ourself
void RectsWindow::EvSize(UINT Type, TSize& NewSize)
{
  BaseWindow::EvSize(Type, NewSize);
  Invalidate();
}

// Callback for timer ticks
void RectsWindow::TimerTick()
{
  // Repaint every second (i.e., every 20 ticks)
  if (++usTickCount == 20) {
    Invalidate(false);
    usTickCount = 0;
  }
}

// Draw our rectangles
void RectsWindow::Paint(TDC& dc, BOOL, TRect&)
{
  TRect rect = GetClientRect();
  int iSize = min(rect.right, rect.bottom);

  // Loop until our rectangles get too small
  do {
    // Create a filled rectangle with a randomly colored brush
    dc.FillRect(rect, TBrush(RGB(random(255),
                 random(255),
                 random(255))));

    // Shrink our rectangle
    rect.Inflate(-BAND_SIZE, -BAND_SIZE);

  } while ((iSize -= 2*BAND_SIZE) > BAND_SIZE);
}
```

Let's start with an examination of what happens when the window receives a timer message. The following code is executed inside the `TimerTick()` method every 50 milliseconds:

```
if (++usTickCount == 20) {
    Invalidate(false);
    usTickCount = 0;
}
```

Although the `RectsWindow` class could have been coded to redraw and cycle the color of the rectangles every time it received a timer notification, that would have cause a psychedelic explosion that wouldn't give the viewer enough time to absorb a given set of rectangles. On the other hand, perhaps you are the sort of individual who is partial to psychedelic explosions; if so, you might want to remove the checking of the `usTickCount` variable in the above code.

Each time a timer message is received, the `usTickCount` variable is incremented and a check is made to see if the number is evenly divisible by twenty. If this is the case, then approximately a full second has elapsed (i.e., 20 messages sent every .050 seconds) and a repaint is forced by invalidating the client window. Note the "false" parameter passed into the `Invalidate()` method call. This signals to OWL and Windows 95 that the background should not be erased before sending the window a `Paint()` message. Since our painting algorithm covers the entire window area, any work that Windows 95 performed erasing the background would be completely wasted.

That brings us to our paltry six line `Paint()` handler.

```
TRect rect = GetClientRect();
int iSize = min(rect.right, rect.bottom);
do {
  dc.FillRect(rect, TBrush(RGB(random(255),
              random(255),
                random(255))));
  rect.Inflate(-BAND_SIZE, -BAND_SIZE);
} while ((iSize -= 2*BAND_SIZE) > BAND_SIZE);
```

This painting algorithm works by getting the size of the window and then drawing consecutively smaller rectangles until the center of the window is reached. The rectangles are filled using a brush whose color is randomly generated. As you can see, OWL makes it easy to get simple but visually interesting results in a very small amount of code.

The Shapes, Lines, and Fills Window

Since the definition for the `ShapesAndFillsWindow` class is virtually identical to that of the `RectsWindow` class discussed above, I'll skip the inclusion of the header file and jump right to the source code. Listing 25.5 shows the file.

Listing 25.5   Fills.cpp—The *ShapesAndFillsWindow* Source File

```cpp
// Get needed include files
#include "fills.h"

// Enumeration for various GDI operations
typedef enum { Lines, Ellipses, Rectangles, Fills } GDIDrawType;

// Here's the response table for the Rectangles window class
DEFINE_RESPONSE_TABLE1(ShapesAndFillsWindow, BaseWindow)
  EV_WM_SIZE,
END_RESPONSE_TABLE;

// Make sure we can do typesafe casts
IMPLEMENT_CASTABLE1(ShapesAndFillsWindow, BaseWindow);

// Constructor
ShapesAndFillsWindow::ShapesAndFillsWindow() : BaseWindow(),
            usTickCount(0)
{ }

// In response to a size message, we simply repaint ourself
void ShapesAndFillsWindow::EvSize(UINT Type, TSize& NewSize)
{
  BaseWindow::EvSize(Type, NewSize);
  Invalidate();
}

// Callback for timer ticks
void ShapesAndFillsWindow::TimerTick()
{
  // Paint the window. Clear the screen every 10 seconds
  // (i.e., every 200 ticks)
  if (++usTickCount == 200) {
    Invalidate();
    usTickCount = 0;
  }
  else
    Invalidate(false);
}

// Draw our shapes
void ShapesAndFillsWindow::Paint(TDC& dc, BOOL, TRect&)
{
  // Get the dimensions of the client window
  TRect rect = GetClientRect();

  // Create a random pen and brush
  dc.SelectObject(TPen(TColor::Black, random(5), random(7)));
  if (!random(5))
    // Hatched brush
    dc.SelectObject(TBrush(RGB(random(255),
            random(255),
            random(255)), random(5)));
  else
```

```
            // Non-hatched brush
        dc.SelectObject(TBrush(RGB(random(255),
                random(255),
              random(255))));

    // Now draw a random shape
    TPoint pnt;
    TSize size;
    switch(random(4))
    {
      // Line
      case Lines:
          dc.MoveTo(random(rect.right), random(rect.bottom));
          dc.LineTo(random(rect.right), random(rect.bottom));
          break;

      // Ellipse
      case Ellipses:
        pnt.x = random(rect.right);
        pnt.y = random(rect.bottom);
          dc.Ellipse(pnt,
                TSize(random(rect.right - pnt.x) + 1,
                  random(rect.bottom - pnt.y) + 1));
          break;

      // Rectangle
      case Rectangles:
          pnt.x = random(rect.right);
          pnt.y = random(rect.bottom);
          size.cx = random(rect.right - pnt.x) + 1;
          size.cy = random(rect.bottom - pnt.y) + 1;
          if (!random(2))
              // Normal rectangle
              dc.Rectangle(pnt, size);
          else
              // Rounded corner rectangle
              dc.RoundRect(pnt, size,
                TPoint(pnt.x + random(5),
                  pnt.y + random(5)));
      break;

    // Fill
    case Fills:
      // Only fill if the tick-count is divisible by 10.
      // (a fill is slow and distracting to the eye)
      if (!(usTickCount % 10)) {
       pnt.x = random(rect.right);
       pnt.y = random(rect.bottom);
       dc.ExtFloodFill(pnt, TColor::Black, FLOODFILLBORDER);
    }
      break;
    }
}
```

As you read through this file, the first thing you'll probably notice is that the
ShapesAndFillsWindow class lives a little more rebelliously and kicks off a Paint()
notification for each timer message that it receives. This means that the output to this
demo window is considerably more accelerated compared to RectsWindow. Since it's
easy for this class to create a window display that is just plain ugly, the TimerTick()
method has been mercifully supplied with the code needed to clear the window and
start with a clean slate every ten seconds.

Once again, the most interesting code is found in the Paint() method. The class begins
by creating a new pen and brush with random attributes. One brush out of five is of the
"hatched" variety, which means that the inside area of shapes drawn with this brush is
filled with a hatching pattern instead of a solid color.

The class proceeds to select a GDI operation at random and draw the appropriate shape
into a random area of the window. Although most of this code is very simple, the case
where a fill is selected is worthy of additional comment. In the following code, fills are
not performed with the same reckless abandon that are employed when drawing other
shapes:

```
// Fill
case Fills:
  // Only fill if the tick-count is divisible by 10.
  // (a fill is slow and distracting to the eye)
  if (!(usTickCount % 10)) {
  pnt.x = random(rect.right);
  pnt.y = random(rect.bottom);
  dc.ExtFloodFill(pnt, TColor::Black, FLOODFILLBORDER);
  }
  break;
```

Note that when the FloodFill() method is called, OWL tells Windows 95 to look for a
region that is delineated by black lines. If you pop back up a dozen lines or so, you'll
see that even though some attributes of the TPen that is selected into the device context are randomly generated, the pen color is always hardcoded to be black. This is to
ensure that when a fill is requested, Windows will have a halfway decent chance of
finding an area that is bordered. If these steps weren't taken (i.e., the FloodFill
method looked for a random color) then virtually every fill would completely blot out
the entire window, and you'd never get to see any of the other shapes being drawn
into the window.

While there is only a one in four chance of a given timer tick causing the fill logic to
get selected, the chances of a fill actually occurring are far less than 25 percent. This is
because a fill is performed only if the usTickCount happens to be divisible by ten. The
ShapesAndFillsWindow class goes to such extreme lengths to limit the number of fills
for a couple of reasons. If you are a shape fan, you probably think the fills in this
program are fundamentally annoying because they often cause shapes to be blotted
out and overdrawn. However, if you are a fill fan you probably don't care; you want to
see wide expanses of brilliantly colored backgrounds. Picdemo, on the other hand, is
not partisan. The ShapesAndFillsWindow class restricts the number of fills for a very

simple reason: they're slow. Even on a very fast machine you can often notice the entire display seize up as a long fill is executed.

The Ellipses and Arcs Window

The last two demos have concentrated on some rather contrived operations. It seems unlikely that you'll ever be called upon to write code that randomly colors in rectangles. However, drawing smiley faces is a different matter altogether. Draw a better smiley face and the world will beat a path to your door.

The only problem is, drawing a smile is not nearly as simple as you might think. You can hardcode coordinates and have your windows smiling in no time, but that's a DOS programmer's mentality. Under Windows 95 the name of the game is device independence, and a hardcoded smiley face that looks fine at VGA resolutions will look positively tiny on a 1024×768 Super VGA display.

The `SmileyWindow` class implements resolution-independent smiley face drawing. It demonstrates the effectiveness of its approach by continuously growing and shrinking. Although you may find the pulsating face a little disconcerting, the `Paint()` method demonstrates some of the techniques that you might want to employ when divining your own drawing code.

Before you look at the code for `SmileyWindow` implementation, examine listing 25.6 and take note of the floating-point scaling variables and private `ScaleRect()` method.

Listing 25.6   smiley.h—The *SmileyWindow* Header File

```
#ifndef SMILEY_H
#define SMILEY_H

// Get needed include files
#include "base.h"

// Here's our class definition
class SmileyWindow : public BaseWindow {

  public:
  // Constructor
  SmileyWindow();

  // Message handlers
  void TimerTick();
  void Paint(TDC& dc, BOOL, TRect&);

  protected:
  // WM_SIZE message handler
  void EvSize(UINT, TSize& Size);

  private:
  // Private variable
  float fCurrScaling, fScalingFactor;
```

(continues)

```
        // Method for scaling the smiley-face bounding rectangle
    void ScaleRect(TRect& InRect);

    DECLARE_CASTABLE;
    DECLARE_RESPONSE_TABLE(SmileyWindow);
};

#endif
```

It's also worth noting that the SmileyWindow class doesn't keep track of elapsed timer
ticks in a usTickCount variable. Since the drawing of the smiley face is more complex
and CPU-intensive, Picdemo doesn't run into the problem of running too fast (in fact,
it could benefit from some performance optimizations). Listing 25.7 shows the code
used to implement the SmileyWindow class.

```
// Get needed include files
#include "smiley.h"

// Initial values for our scaling and scaling factor
const float INITIAL_SCALING = 1.00;
const float INITIAL_SCALE_FACTOR = 0.08;

// Here's the response table for the Smiley-face window class
DEFINE_RESPONSE_TABLE1(SmileyWindow, BaseWindow)
  EV_WM_SIZE,
END_RESPONSE_TABLE;

// Make sure we can do typesafe casts
IMPLEMENT_CASTABLE1(SmileyWindow, BaseWindow);

// Constructor
SmileyWindow::SmileyWindow() :
     BaseWindow(),
     fCurrScaling(INITIAL_SCALING),
     fScalingFactor(INITIAL_SCALE_FACTOR)
{ }

// In response to a size message, we simply repaint ourself
void SmileyWindow::EvSize(UINT Type, TSize& NewSize)
{
  BaseWindow::EvSize(Type, NewSize);
  Invalidate();
}

// Callback for timer ticks
void SmileyWindow::TimerTick()
{
  // Repaint our window
  Invalidate();
}
```

```
// Put on a happy face
void SmileyWindow::Paint(TDC& dc, BOOL, TRect&)
{
  // THE MAIN FACE

  // Calculate the initial bounding rectangle for the face
  TRect FaceRect, ClientRect = GetClientRect();
  int iDiameter = min(ClientRect.right, ClientRect.bottom);
  FaceRect.left = (ClientRect.right - iDiameter)/ 2;
  FaceRect.top = (ClientRect.bottom - iDiameter)/ 2;
  FaceRect.right = FaceRect.left + iDiameter;
  FaceRect.bottom = FaceRect.top + iDiameter;

  // Scale the rectangle. Recalculate the face's diameter (it's
  // used in later portions of the code).
  ScaleRect(FaceRect);
  iDiameter = min(FaceRect.right - FaceRect.left,
    FaceRect.bottom - FaceRect.top);

  // Based on the size of the face, set the line thickness. This
  // prevents us from having huge lips and eyes when the face gets
  // small (or tiny lips and eyes when the face gets big). The
  // line thickness is defined to be 1/2 of a percent of the
  // facial diameter. Also set a yellow brush.
  int iLineWidth = iDiameter * .05;
  if (iLineWidth < 1)
  iLineWidth = 1;
  dc.SelectObject(TPen(TColor::Black, iLineWidth, PS_INSIDEFRAME));
  dc.SelectObject(TBrush(TColor::LtYellow));

  // Draw the main face
  dc.Ellipse(FaceRect);


  // THE SMILE

  // Calculate the bounding rectangle for the smile. The arc will
  // be defined as the lower half of the ellipses that fits into
  // this rectangle.
  TRect SmileRect = FaceRect;
  SmileRect.Inflate(-(iDiameter * .20), -(iDiameter * .25));
  SmileRect += TSize(0, iDiameter * .10);
  int iMidPoint = SmileRect.top +
     (SmileRect.bottom - SmileRect.top) / 2;
  dc.Arc(SmileRect,
   TPoint(SmileRect.left, iMidPoint),
   TPoint(SmileRect.right, iMidPoint));


  // THE EYES

  // Set our pen and brush; we don't really need a pen so we use
  // PS_NULL, the brush uses a simple black fill.
  dc.SelectObject(TPen(0, 0, PS_NULL));
  dc.SelectObject(TBrush(TColor::Black));
```

(continues)

Programming Tools

V

> **Listing 25.7   Continued**
>
> ```
> // Calculate the size of the eyes (10% of the diameter of
> // the face).
> int iEyeDiameter = iDiameter * .10;
> TSize EyeSize(iEyeDiameter, iEyeDiameter);
>
> // Draw the left eye first...
> TPoint UpperLeft(ClientRect.right / 2,
>     FaceRect.top +
>     ((FaceRect.bottom - FaceRect.top) * .3));
> int iOffset = ((UpperLeft.x - SmileRect.left -
>   iEyeDiameter) / 2);
> UpperLeft.x = SmileRect.left + iOffset;
> UpperLeft.y -= iEyeDiameter / 2;
> dc.Ellipse(UpperLeft, EyeSize);
>
> // And then the right one.
> UpperLeft.x = (ClientRect.right / 2) + iOffset;
> dc.Ellipse(UpperLeft, EyeSize);
> }
>
>
> // Scale the smiley-face bounding rectangle, based on the
> // fScalingFactor member variable.
> void SmileyWindow::ScaleRect(TRect& InRect)
> {
>   // If we are at the end of the scaling cycle (i.e., 100%
>   // going up or 10% going down), reverse the direction of the
>   // scaling. Recalculate the scaling value.
>   if ((fCurrScaling >= 1.00 && fScalingFactor > 0.0) ¦¦
>       (fCurrScaling <= .10 && fScalingFactor < 0.0))
>  fScalingFactor = -fScalingFactor;
>   fCurrScaling += fScalingFactor;
>
>   // Calculate new widths based on the current scaling value.
>   float fWidth = InRect.right - InRect.left;
>   float fWidthDiff = (fWidth - (fWidth * fCurrScaling)) / 2;
>   float fHeight = InRect.bottom - InRect.top;
>   float fHeightDiff = (fHeight - (fHeight * fCurrScaling)) / 2;
>
>   // Modify the x & y axis rect values as appropriate.
>   InRect.Inflate(-fWidthDiff, -fHeightDiff);
> }
> ```

Since the `TimerTick()` method doesn't do anything except force a background erase and a repaint, you can jump right in and start exploring the `Paint()` method. The routine starts out innocuously enough by getting the size of the window and calculating the largest, centered square that will fit inside of it.

```
TRect FaceRect, ClientRect = GetClientRect();
int iDiameter = min(ClientRect.right, ClientRect.bottom);
FaceRect.left = (ClientRect.right - iDiameter)/ 2;
FaceRect.top = (ClientRect.bottom - iDiameter)/ 2;
```

```
FaceRect.right = FaceRect.left + iDiameter;
FaceRect.bottom = FaceRect.top + iDiameter;
```

If you were simply looking for a way to draw a smiley face that was scaled to fit the entire window, the first part of your job would be complete. However, in order to make the face grow and shrink, you need to be able to arbitrarily scale the `FaceRect` object. This task is accomplished by a call to the `ScaleRect()` method.

`ScaleRect()` performs three distinct tasks. It begins by checking to see if the current scaling factor is at a boundary condition. That is to say, is the current scaling factory greater than or equal to 100 percent? Is it less than or equal to 10 percent? After all, you don't want your face expanding beyond the limits of the window, or shrinking so small that it can't be seen. If the current scaling factor is at a boundary condition, then the base scaling factor's sign is reversed and the current scaling factor is recalculated.

```
// If we are at the end of the scaling cycle (i.e., 100%
// going up or 10% going down), reverse the direction of the
// scaling. Recalculate the scaling value.
if ((fCurrScaling >= 1.00 && fScalingFactor > 0.0) ||
    (fCurrScaling <= .10 && fScalingFactor < 0.0))
    fScalingFactor = -fScalingFactor;
fCurrScaling += fScalingFactor;
```

The next task to be performed inside `ScaleRect()` is to take the current scaling factor and calculate exactly how much the x-axis and y-axis extents of the rectangle need to be reduced (or increased if the face if growing).

```
// Calculate new widths based on the current scaling value.
float fWidth = InRect.right - InRect.left;
float fWidthDiff = (fWidth - (fWidth * fCurrScaling)) / 2;
float fHeight = InRect.bottom - InRect.top;
float fHeightDiff = (fHeight - (fHeight * fCurrScaling)) / 2;
```

Finally, `ScaleRect()` actually modifies the rectangle to reflect the current scaling factor. The end result is a square that is still perfectly centered within the client window but is appropriately scaled.

```
// Modify the x & y axis rect values as appropriate.
InRect.Inflate(-fWidthDiff, -fHeightDiff);
```

At this point, the `FaceRect` has been scaled to the appropriate dimensions. In order for the rest of the routine to work correctly, it is crucial that the following pieces of code base their calculations on the dimensions of `FaceRect` and not `ClientRect`.

Back in the `Paint()` routine, the face diameter is now updated to reflect the diameter of the scaled face, and the device context pen and brush are modified. Notice that special attention needs to be given to setting the width of the pen.

```
int iLineWidth = iDiameter * .05;
if (iLineWidth < 1)
iLineWidth = 1;
dc.SelectObject(TPen(TColor::Black, iLineWidth, PS_INSIDEFRAME));
```

V

Programming Tools

If you hardcoded the width of the pen to some arbitrary value, you'd be virtually assured of running into a situation where at some point during the scaling cycle the smiley face is very large but has thin lips and facial boundaries or, alternatively, is very small but has proportionally enormous lips and facial boundaries. By defining the line width to be a certain percentage of the size of the face (in this case PICDEMO uses one half of the diameter), you ensure that Smiley always looks right regardless of the dimensions of FaceRect.

Drawing the smile and the two eyes is now simply a matter of doing the math and coming up with the right percentages and ratios. This last step involves a certain amount of experimentation; for example, it's not immediately obvious that the best smiley face has eyes that are 10 percent as wide as the faces diameter, or that the eyes should be placed 30 percent of the diameter down into the forehead. Some things simply require a little bit of trial-and-error.

> **Tip**
>
> Depending on the speed of your computer (and even if your machine is very fast) you'll probably notice a significant amount of screen flicker in Smiley's window. One partial solution to this problem can be found in the Lines/MoveTo portion of the GDIDemo program that comes with Borland C++ 5. Instead of drawing directly into the window, the program first draws the Spirograph-like pattern into a memory-based device context that it creates on-the-fly. Then the program makes a call to the window's device context method BitBlt(). The method allows Windows 95 to blast a bitmap onto the screen very quickly and efficiently, and this technique does a good job of cutting down on screen flicker.

The end result is hardly spectacular (what do you want from a half-page of code?) but it gets the job done right. You may not be able to cut-and-paste much of this code into your future programs, but hopefully you have an understanding of why you need to take the steps required to make your graphics device independent and arbitrarily scalable.

From Here...

Although this chapter is only a primer on GDI programming with OWL, you now have the basic skills needed to start dressing up your OWL programs with interesting and informative graphics. However, there's still a lot more to learn about Borland C++ 5. Check out these chapters for more inside information on getting the most out of OWL.

- Part V: "Borland C++ Programming Tools" concerns teaching you how to incorporate sophisticated, professional features into your OWL applications. Master the concepts in Part V and you will be well on your way to guru-hood.

CHAPTER 26

Using the Multiple Document Interface

A wide variety of situations arise where it is useful to have multiple windows open and accessible in a single application. Users often want to have many documents open when performing word processing. Selecting an image is easier if many images are displayed on the screen simultaneously. While it is possible to accomplish the above by running multiple instances of each program, a more elegant solution is to create an application that can open multiple documents, files, or images while using only one instance. The Multiple Document Interface (MDI) is the basis for such applications.

Prior to the development of Windows class libraries like OWL, MDI programming was an arduous feat. The ability to do MDI programming was sometimes regarded as the mark of a true Windows expert. Some of this mystique still surrounds MDI programming, but there's little reason for this. Developing an MDI application in OWL is quite straightforward, as you're about to see.

In this chapter, you learn:

- What basic behavior is expected in an MDI application
- Types of applications where MDI is advantageous
- OWL MDI class structure
- OWL MDI event and command handling
- How to incorporate specific application capability into MDI child windows

What Is MDI?

The Multiple Document Interface (MDI) is a framework for managing multiple child windows within the main window client region (application workspace) of an application. Examples of MDI are widespread in Windows. The Borland C++ IDE is one example. Most major word processors are also MDI applications.

In its simplest incarnation, MDI is used to manage multiple windows of a single type. The Windows 3.1 File Manager is a good example. In File Manager, you can pretty much have as many disk windows open as you like, but a disk window is the only type of window you can have.

A similar, but slightly more complicated, variation of MDI manages documents that all have the same basic characteristics, but may have different file extensions.

At the other extreme are MDI applications that manage multiple windows of two or more different types. The Borland C++ IDE offers a good example of this. You can readily have several different code windows open for editing source or header files. You can also open module definition files (.def), windows help project files (.hpj), etc., as regular text windows. You may at first think these are all the same type because they use text. Notice however that syntax highlighting only occurs in source windows, header windows, or resource script windows. The IDE also maintains separate window types for the project, for messages, and for debug output, but only a single instance of these latter types is permitted.

MDI offers a number of advantages to the application developer and user alike:

- Consistent user interface features that ensure the user knows what to expect when dealing with multiple child windows.
- Capability to view one or more child windows in several different ways.
- Ability to have many child windows present and quickly accessible via icons.
- A highly efficient vehicle for drag-and-drop file handling.
- Relatively straightforward programming—particularly using Windows class libraries such as OWL.
- Capability to be extended to provide more specialized handling and to display of multiple child windows.

Understanding Basic MDI Behavior

The SimpleMDI example application (Simplmdi.exe) on the accompanying disk is a good way to demonstrate the fundamental characteristics of an MDI application. Later in this chapter we will also examine the coding in the SimpleMDI project as an example of OWL MDI construction.

The Application Workspace

Figure 26.1 shows what SimpleMDI looks like when it first opens. Notice that when an MDI application opens without any child windows, you see the application workspace as the window background. This is the first major difference between an MDI application and a Single Document Interface (SDI) application. The application workspace is the staging area for most of what MDI does with child windows.

Fig. 26.1

The SimpleMDI application when it first opens.

Adding Child Windows

You can add a child window in the SimpleMDI application with the File, New command. Figure 26.2 shows the appearance of SimpleMDI after opening a single child window. In MDI applications, when the first child window is opened, it typically only partially overlaps the application workspace. Notice that the child window has its own title. New child windows are always given an enumerated default title, as for example in figure 26.2. Whenever a child window is opened from a file, the title is usually the filename.

In SimpleMDI, the File, New command provides the only way to add a child window, because child windows in this simple example aren't associated with a file or other storage. Most MDI applications also offer File, Open as a mechanism for adding a child window. There are, however, applications that use an MDI interface to manage child windows, but offer no procedure for adding child windows. The Windows System Configuration Editor (Sysedit.exe) is one such application.

Tip

The Windows System Configuration Editor (located in the Windows\System directory) is a useful, but little-documented utility for editing Autoexec.bat, Config.sys, System.ini, Win.ini, and several other Windows .ini files. The use of .ini files is slowly being superseded by the System Registry, which can be viewed using the Regedit.exe program.

V

Programming Tools

Fig. 26.2

An open child window in the SimpleMDI application.

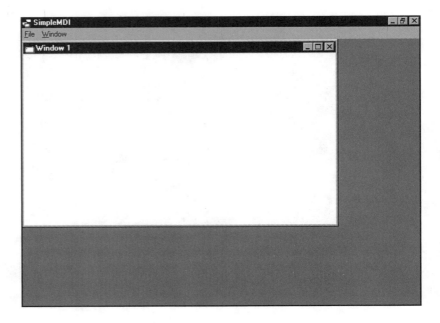

Viewing Child Windows

MDI child windows can exist in three different states—maximized, minimized, or overlapped on the application workspace. We've already seen one example of a window in the overlapped state.

The maximized state allows a child window to take over the entire application workspace. Naturally this state makes it easiest to view or otherwise work on a particular child window. Figure 26.3 shows an example of a maximized MDI child window in SimpleMDI. Whenever an MDI child is maximized, its title is appended to the main application title. Also, its icon joins the left side of the application menu bar, and its Minimize, Restore, and Close buttons appear at the right side of the menu bar. (In Windows 3.1, the system button appears instead of the window icon, and there is no exit button.) The Restore button allows the user to return the window to an overlapped state. The Minimize button allows the user to directly reduce the window to an icon at the bottom of the application workspace.

In figure 26.4, you see four different child windows minimized at the bottom of the application workspace in SimpleMDI. There is also one overlapped window. This points up the advantage of the minimized state in an MDI application. Minimized windows take up relatively little real estate on the application workspace, but they can easily be restored. Usually you restore a minimized window by double-clicking with the mouse, but you can also open the system menu for a minimized window with a single click of the mouse. From the system menu, you can then restore, maximize, or close the window.

Fig. 26.3

An example of a maximized MDI child window in the SimpleMDI application.

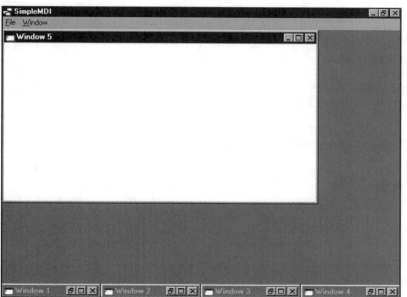

Fig. 26.4

The SimpleMDI application showing four minimized child windows at the bottom of the application workspace.

V

Programming Tools

> **Caution**
>
> MDI windows have some occasional idiosyncracies. You might think from the preceding discussion that restoring a minimized window makes it overlapped. That happens to be true if it was in the overlapped state before it was minimized. However, if it was originally in the maximized state, then restoring the window makes it maximized again. Features like this make sense at a certain level, and they can sometimes be an advantage. They can also lead to some confusing situations—the kinds that developers have to worry about. This is just one more reason to make sure you thoroughly test every application you create to make sure it really does what you want and not what you assume.

Organizing Multiple Windows

In many MDI applications, the most prominent MDI advantage is ease in comparing or switching between different related child windows. You can readily move child windows around on the application workspace how ever you desire. And because MDI child windows have a thick-frame style, you can also adjust the size and shape of open windows to anything you want. MDI provides several other mechanisms for organizing multiple child windows. These are available from the Window menu, which is always present on the menu bar of an MDI application.

Cascading. The MDI Window, Cascade command positions open windows in an overlapped fashion as shown in figure 26.5. Cascaded windows always show a sizeable portion of the topmost child window. As long as there aren't too many windows open, other open windows are immediately accessible with a single click of the primary mouse button. This is true even if you select one of the bottom windows in the cascade. Cascading does have its limits. Eventually the application runs out of space to cascade new windows and starts over at the top.

A cascade is also the default presentation for child windows as they're first opened— as long as a child window isn't already maximized.

Tiling. Another useful method for displaying multiple open child windows is tiling. Figure 26.6 shows two windows tiled side-by-side in SimpleMDI. Figure 26.6 is an example of vertical tiling. The command for vertical tiling is usually either Tile or Tile Vertical on the Window Menu.

Many MDI applications also support horizontal tiling, as demonstrated in figure 26.7. Tile Horizontal is normally the Window menu command to produce horizontal tiling.

Vertical tiling is the default style for tiling. The differences between vertical and horizontal tiling are only apparent with two or three open windows.

Tiling can sometimes be useful with more than three windows. Figure 26.8 shows an example of five tiled windows. This figure also demonstrates the effect of tiling when one or more icons is present on the application workspace.

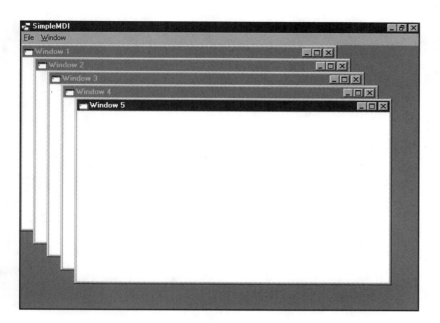

Fig. 26.5

The SimpleMDI application with five cascaded child windows.

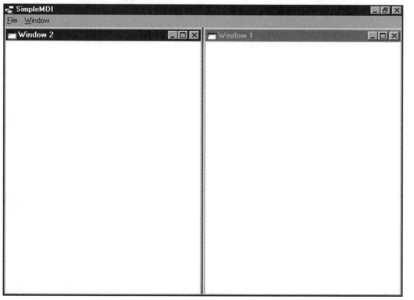

Fig. 26.6

The SimpleMDI application showing two vertically tiled child windows.

As you can probably guess, tiling of more than a few windows is usually only helpful when there is specialized scaling of the window contents. Such specialized scaling is provided by some MDI applications that present graphical images.

Fig. 26.7

An example of horizontal MDI tiling in the SimpleMDI application.

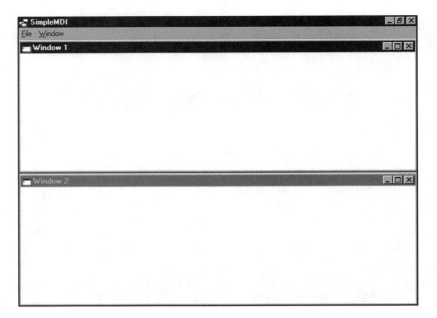

Fig. 26.8

Complex tiling in the SimpleMDI application.

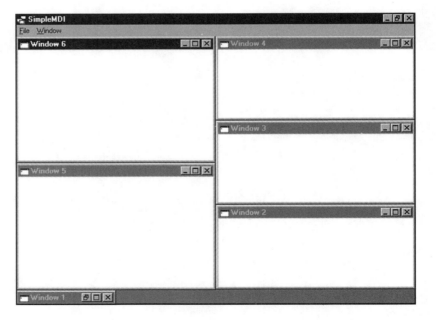

Arranging Icons. MDI applications permit an arbitrarily large number of child windows. Usually this is only manageable if most of the child windows are minimized. Icons for minimized child windows can be moved around at will on the application workspace. If you do so, sooner or later you will need to reorganize the icons. The

Arrange Icons command on the Window menu does this automatically. Figure 26.9 shows eleven minimized child windows in the SimpleMDI application after invoking the Arrange Icons command.

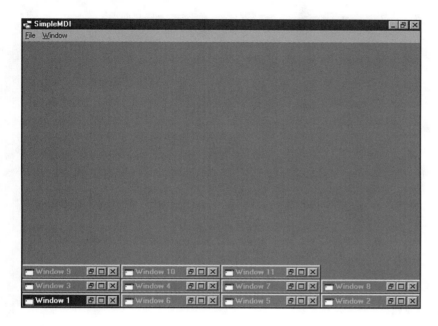

Fig. 26.9

The SimpleMDI applica-tion after arranging minimized child windows.

The Window List

MDI applications maintain a running list of current child windows. This list is found at the bottom of the Window menu, as shown in figure 26.10. You can select any child window (open or minimized) from this list. If the window you select is initially minimized, the application restores it.

Closing Child Windows

There is some diversity in the methods different MDI applications support for closing child windows. In most applications, you can close individual windows by double-clicking on the system button or by selecting Close from the window's system menu. Some applications also provide a Close command under either the File menu or Window menu. This command always affects the currently selected child window in the application.

Many, but not all, applications also implement a Window, Close All command. This can be a convenient feature. However, an application may not offer this command if closing all windows is either inappropriate or likely to get the user into trouble.

V

Programming Tools

Fig. 26.10

The Window menu in SimpleMDI.

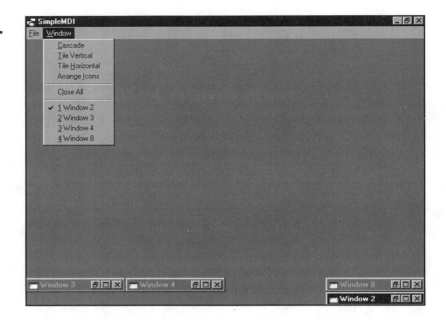

Coding a Basic MDI Application with OWL

Coding a simple OWL MDI program actually requires only slightly more work than coding a simple OWL application that doesn't use MDI. Listing 26.1 shows the C++ code for the SimpleMDI example application we've been using. This code is part of the simplmdi.ide project on your accompanying disk. To build the project, you also need the resource script file Smdiapp.rc found on the disk.

Listing 26.1   Smdiapp.cpp—The C++ Source Code for the SimpleMDI Application

```
/////////////////////////////////////////////////////////////////
// PROJECT:     SIMPLMDI.EXE Application
// FILE:        SMDIAPP.CPP
// AUTHOR:      Bruce R. Copeland
//
// SimpleMDI application source
/////////////////////////////////////////////////////////////////

#include <owl\mdi.h>
#include <owl\applicat.h>
#include <owl\mdi.h>

// Resource IDs
#define IDI_MDIAPPLICATION      1001   // Application icon
#define IDI_DOC                 1002   // MDI child window icon
```

```
#define MDI_MENU                100    // Application Menu
#define CM_MDIFILENEW           24331 // File new command
#define CM_FILECLOSE            24339 // File close command


// Definition of SimpleMDIApp class
class SimpleMDIApp : public TApplication
{
  public:
    SimpleMDIApp() : TApplication("SimpleMDI") {};
    virtual ~SimpleMDIApp() {};
    virtual void InitMainWindow();
};


// Definition of SimpleMDIClient class
class SimpleMDIClient : public TMDIClient
{
  public:
    int   ChildCount; // Number of child windows created

  public:
    SimpleMDIClient(TModule* module = 0);
    virtual ~SimpleMDIClient() {};
  protected:
    void CmFileNew();
    void CmFileClose();
    void CeFileClose(TCommandEnabler& tce);
  DECLARE_RESPONSE_TABLE(SimpleMDIClient);
};


/////////////////////////////////////////////////////////////////
// SimpleMDIApp::InitMainWindow()
//
// Create and initialize the main frame window
void SimpleMDIApp::InitMainWindow()
{
  // Construct a TMDIFrame instance
  TMDIFrame* frame = new TMDIFrame(Name, MDI_MENU,
                     *(new SimpleMDIClient), false);

  // Set icon & menu for the frame
  frame->SetIcon(this, IDI_MDIAPPLICATION);
  frame->AssignMenu(MDI_MENU);

  // Make frame the application main window
  SetMainWindow(frame);
}


// Definition of the event response table for commands handled
// by the client class
DEFINE_RESPONSE_TABLE1(SimpleMDIClient, TMDIClient)
  EV_COMMAND(CM_MDIFILENEW, CmFileNew),
  EV_COMMAND(CM_FILECLOSE, CmFileClose),
```

(continues)

Listing 26.1 Continued

```
  EV_COMMAND_ENABLE(CM_FILECLOSE, CeFileClose),
END_RESPONSE_TABLE;


////////////////////////////////////////////////////////////////
// SimpleMDIClient::SimpleMDIClient()
//
// Client class constructor
SimpleMDIClient::SimpleMDIClient(TModule* module)
 : TMDIClient (module)
{
  // Initialize the number of children created
  ChildCount = 0;
}

////////////////////////////////////////////////////////////////
// SimpleMDIClient::CmFileNew()
//
// Handler for CM_MDIFILENEW command
void SimpleMDIClient::CmFileNew()
{
  // Make a child window title based on child number
  char    title[255];
  wsprintf(title, "Window %d", ++ChildCount);

  // Instantiate a new TMDIChild
  TMDIChild* child = new TMDIChild(*this, title, 0);

  // Set icon for the child
  child->SetIcon(GetApplication(), IDI_DOC);

  // Open new child maximized if current child is maximized
  TMDIChild *curChild = GetActiveMDIChild();
  if (curChild && (curChild->GetWindowLong(GWL_STYLE)
      & WS_MAXIMIZE))
    child->Attr.Style |= WS_MAXIMIZE;

  // Create the window interface for the new child
  child->Create();
}


////////////////////////////////////////////////////////////////
// SimpleMDIClient::CmFileClose()
//
// Handler for CM_FILECLOSE command
void SimpleMDIClient::CmFileClose()
{
  // Current active MDI child is the one to close
  TMDIChild* child = GetActiveMDIChild();

  // Destroy the child interface and delete the object instance
  child->Destroy();
  delete child;
}
```

```
///////////////////////////////////////////////////////////////
// SimpleMDIClient::CeFileClose()
//
// Enabler for CM_FILECLOSE command
void SimpleMDIClient::CeFileClose(TCommandEnabler& tce)
{
  // Only enable if there's an active MDI child
  tce.Enable(GetActiveMDIChild() != NULL);
}


///////////////////////////////////////////////////////////////
// OwlMain()
//
// Everything begins and ends here
int OwlMain (int , char* [])
{
  SimpleMDIApp    app;
  return app.Run();
}
```

Class Structure in an MDI Application

In order to ensure consistent MDI behavior, Windows requires an MDI application to use three special kinds of windows. These are the MDI frame window, the MDI client window, and the MDI child window. Each of these kinds of windows must be organized and registered in a particular fashion. OWL provides special window classes that accomplish all this. These classes are called, naturally enough, TMDIFrame, TMDIClient, and TMDIChild. To enforce application safety, OWL requires that you use these classes or classes derived from them whenever you produce OWL MDI applications.

The SimpleMDI application uses four classes, which are summarized in table 26.1. Three of these classes serve the functions described above. The fourth is an application class—required in any OWL application. The application class SimpleMDIApp is derived from the standard TApplication class, and the SimpleMDIClient class is derived from TMDIClient. The TMDIFrame and TMDIChild classes are used without derivation in the SimpleMDI application.

Table 26.1   Classes in the SimpleMDI Example Application

Class Name	Application Role
SimpleMDIApp	Application class
TMDIFrame	MDI frame window serving as application main window
SimpleMDIClient	MDI client window to manage MDI children in the main window client region
TMDIChild	MDI child window (frame and client)

The following SimpleMDIApp class differs from its base TApplication only in the InitMainWindow() function:

```
void SimpleMDIApp::InitMainWindow()
{
  // Construct a TMDIFrame instance
  TMDIFrame* frame = new TMDIFrame(Name, MDI_MENU,
                       *(new SimpleMDIClient), false);

  // Set icon & menu for the frame
  frame->SetIcon(this, IDI_MDIAPPLICATION);
  frame->AssignMenu(MDI_MENU);

  // Make frame the application main window
  SetMainWindow(frame);
}
```

The `InitMainWindow()` begins by constructing a frame window as an instance of
`TMDIFrame`. The `TMDIFrame` constructor differs from other non-MDI frame window
constructors in one interesting way. Other frame constructors take a pointer to a client window as a parameter. That allows you to avoid using a client window in simple
cases by passing `NULL` as the parameter. However, the rules for MDI applications require an MDI client window. The `TMDIFrame` constructor enforces this by taking a
reference to a `TMDIClient` object rather than a pointer. `InitMainWindow()` constructs a
new `SimpleMDIClient` object as the MDI client window parameter for the `TMDIFrame`
constructor.

> **Note**
>
> You may be concerned about the use of dynamic memory allocation in the construction of the
> `SimpleMDIClient` object for the `TMDIFrame` constructor in `InitMainWindow()`. In fact,
> some of you may have noted that this object is not explicitly deleted anywhere in SimpleMDI.
> OWL classes often take pointers to other objects in their classes. In such cases, the convention is
> that the class "owns" and therefore has responsibility for cleanup of any such objects. `TMDI`
> `Frame` is a special case in which the class takes a reference to a `TMDIClient` object, but expects
> to own the object. `TMDIFrame` does not make a copy of the `TMDIClient` object. So if you at-
> tempt to construct `TMDIFrame` by using a temporary `TMDIClient` object, you get incorrect
> behavior because the temporary object soon goes out of scope and is automatically deleted.

The remaining lines in `InitMainWindow()` simply carry out activities that are standard
for most OWL applications.

Basic MDI Command Handling

The following code from listing 26.1 declares one event response table:

```
DEFINE_RESPONSE_TABLE1(SimpleMDIClient, TMDIClient)
  EV_COMMAND(CM_MDIFILENEW, CmFileNew),
  EV_COMMAND(CM_FILECLOSE, CmFileClose),
  EV_COMMAND_ENABLE(CM_FILECLOSE, CeFileClose),
END_RESPONSE_TABLE;
```

In this table, the application sets up command handling for the File, New and File,
Close menu commands. The handler functions for these commands are the

CmFileNew() and CmFileClose() member functions of the SimpleMDIClient class. The table also provides enabling for the File, Close command via the SimpleMDIClient function CeFileClose().

Opening a New MDI Child Window. The SimpleMDIClient member function CmFileNew() takes care of creating and initializing new MDI child windows for the SimpleMDI application. This function looks like

```
void SimpleMDIClient::CmFileNew()
{
  // Make a child window title based on child number
  char    title[255];
  wsprintf(title, "Window %d", ++ChildCount);

  // Instantiate a new TMDIChild
  TMDIChild* child = new TMDIChild(*this, title, 0);

  // Set icon for the child
  child->SetIcon(GetApplication(), IDI_DOC);

  // Open new child maximized if current child is maximized
  TMDIChild *curChild = GetActiveMDIChild();
  if (curChild && (curChild->GetWindowLong(GWL_STYLE)
      & WS_MAXIMIZE))
    child->Attr.Style |= WS_MAXIMIZE;

  // Create the window interface for the new child
  child->Create();
}
```

CmFileNew() begins by preparing a title for a new child window. The title consists of the string "Window " followed by the value of the incremented ChildCount member variable. This title is then used in constructing an instance of the TMDIChild class as a new child.

In the next step, CmFileNew() associates the IDI_DOC icon with the new child. This child icon is what appears whenever an MDI child window is minimized. It differs from the IDI_MDIAPPLICATION icon established as the application icon in SimpleMDIApp::InitMainWindow().

When an MDI application opens a new child window while an existing child window is maximized, the new window is supposed to open in the maximized state. To make certain that this happens, the CmFileNew() function first obtains a pointer to the currently active MDI child window through a call to GetActiveMDIChild() (a member of the base TMDIClient class). CmFileNew() then gets the style for this current window by calling the current child's GetWindowLong() function using GWS_STYLE as the argument. If the currently active MDI child is maximized, its style will contain the WS_MAXIMIZED bit. In that case, CmFileNew() sets the WS_MAXIMIZED bit for the new child's Attr.Style member.

When all this is done, CmFileNew() finally calls the new child's Create() function to create the new child window interface element.

Closing an MDI Child Window. Compared to opening a new MDI child window, closing a child window is simple. `SimpleMDIClient::CmFileClose()` does this in response to a File, Close menu command. The code for `CmFileClose()` is shown below:

```
void SimpleMDIClient::CmFileClose()
{
  // Current active MDI child is the one to close
  TMDIChild* child = GetActiveMDIChild();

  // Destroy the child interface and delete the object instance
  child->Destroy();
  delete child;
}
```

Because a File, Close command always applies only to the active child, the `CmFileClose()` function first gets a pointer to the active child by calling the `GetActiveMDIChild()` function. The function then uses that pointer to close the active child.

The last two lines of `CmFileClose()` show the proper way to close a child window. The first step is to call the child window object's `Destroy()` function. `Destroy()` eliminates the window interface element—somewhat in analogy to the way the `Create()` function creates it. Once the interface element is destroyed, it is then appropriate to explicitly delete the object (assuming it was created originally by dynamic memory allocation).

It is poor form to have a menu option like File, Close enabled if there are no child windows. In fact, executing the `CmFileClose()` function under such circumstances would probably produce a general protection fault. To avoid this possibility, the `SimpleMDIClient` class uses a command enabler for the File, Close command. The enabler function `CeFileClose()` looks like this:

```
void SimpleMDIClient::CeFileClose(TCommandEnabler& tce)
{
  // Only enable if there's an active MDI child
  tce.Enable(GetActiveMDIChild() != NULL);
}
```

This simple function enables the command only if a call to `GetActiveMDIChild()` doesn't return `NULL`.

Behind-the-Scenes Command Handling

We're finished looking at the MDI code in listing 26.1 for the SimpleMDI example. But you probably wonder where all the code is located for the various Window menu commands demonstrated earlier? This situation is typical of many OWL applications—MDI or not. A lot of important functions are buried behind the scenes in the standard OWL classes.

OWL *TMDIClient* Class Command Handling. The TMDIClient class provides default handlers for most standard MDI <u>W</u>indow menu commands. Table 26.2 summarizes the options available on the SimpleMDI <u>W</u>indow menu along with their command identifiers and the names of the TMDIClient functions used to handle these commands.

Table 26.2 MDI Window Menu Commands for the SimpleMDI Application		
Menu Option	**Command Identifier**	***TMDIClient* Handler**
<u>C</u>ascade	CM_CASCADECHILDREN	CmCascadeChildren()
<u>T</u>ile Vertical	CM_TILECHILDREN	CmTileChildren()
Tile <u>H</u>orizontal	CM_TILECHILDRENHORIZ	CmTileChildrenHoriz()
Arrange <u>I</u>cons	CM_ARRANGEICONS	CmArrangeIcons()
C<u>l</u>ose All	CM_CLOSECHILDREN	CmCloseChildren()

As long as an MDI application uses these TMDIClient handler functions, the command identifiers are only needed in the resource file for the application. There are two ways to incorporate these identifiers into a resource file. One way is to include the OWL Mdi.rh resource header file. Another way is to simply define these identifiers to have the same values used by TMDIClient. The necessary values are summarized in table 26.3. This is the method used in the SimpleMDI example.

Table 26.3 Window Menu Command Identifiers and Their Associated Values	
Command Identifier	**Identifier Value**
CM_CASCADECHILDREN	24361
CM_TILECHILDREN	24362
CM_TILECHILDRENHORIZ	24363
CM_ARRANGEICONS	24364
CM_CLOSECHILDREN	24365

MDI Message Handling. Like most things in Windows, MDI applications are ultimately implemented through certain Windows messages. Table 26.4 shows the principal Windows MDI messages and their roles in MDI.

V

Programming Tools

Table 26.4   Windows MDI Messages

MDI Message	Role
WM_MDIACTIVATE	Sent to an MDI client to activate a particular child
WM_MDICASCADE	Sent to an MDI client to cascade its children
WM_MDICREATE	Sent to an MDI client to create a child
WM_MDIDESTROY	Sent to an MDI client to destroy a child
WM_MDIGETACTIVE	Sent to an MDI client to find the active child
WM_MDIICONARRANGE	Sent to an MDI client to arrange its child icons
WM_MDIMAXIMIZE	Sent to an MDI client to maximize a child
WM_MDINEXT	Sent to an MDI client to activate the child in back of the currently active child
WM_MDIRESTORE	Sent to an MDI client to restore a particular MDI child that's maximized or minimized
WM_MDITILE	Sent to an MDI client to tile its children

Several of these messages carry additional information in their lParam and wParam values. (See the Win16 or Win32 online Help for a more thorough description of individual messages.) Not all these messages are necessarily used either.

To get consistent MDI behavior, many of these messages are really designed to be handled through default processing (i.e., by Windows on behalf of the particular window). The TMDIClient class takes advantage of this. It does not explicitly handle most of these messages. However, several TMDIClient functions, in effect, send these messages to the class as a way to get the proper default processing. An example is the CascadeChildren() function (which is called by CmCascadeChildren()). This function has the form

```
void TMDIClient::CascadeChildren()
{
  HandleMessage(WM_MDICASCADE);
}
```

Here, HandleMessage() is just a shortcut way for the class instance to send the message to itself. But TMDIClient doesn't process WM_MDICASCADE; it lets Windows do it by default processing.

Tip

Borland C++ comes complete with source code. This means you can examine the source code for any of the Borland class or function libraries.

SimpleMDI does a good job of demonstrating MDI application behavior. But like so many simple examples, the application itself doesn't really do anything useful. It's time to move on to an MDI application with some real function. To do so, we need to put some muscle into the MDI children.

Exploring MDI Child Window Functionality

There are several approaches for providing specific application functionality in an MDI child window. Probably the best strategy is to put application function into a window class that serves as a client window for the MDI child class. In this scenario, the MDI child class is really an MDI child frame. This in fact is why `TMDIChild` is derived from `TFrameWindow`. This strategy requires more classes in an application. You also have to get comfortable with the concept that you have an MDI client window to manage the main window client region and then MDI child client windows that provide application function in the MDI child windows. However, once you get comfortable with this concept, this approach proves to be quite clean and modular.

The ResourceText application (Resrctxt.exe) on the accompanying disk is an MDI application that uses this strategy. ResourceText, shown in figure 26.11 is a utility that allows you to edit multiple resource scripts and dialog files as text. Even though Borland's Resource Workshop provides a convenient graphical environment for routine resource development, most developers find there are times when it is much more straightforward to edit resource scripts as text. Resource Workshop and the Borland C++ IDE do provide some capabilities along these lines, but they have a number of drawbacks. ResourceText is designed to fill the void.

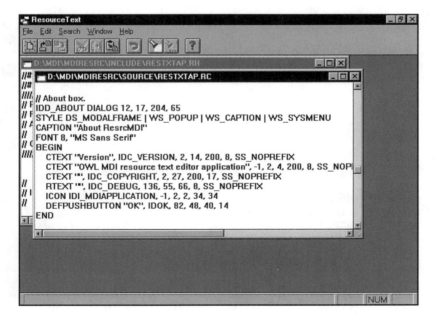

Fig. 26.11

The ResourceText application for text editing of multiple resource scripts.

V

Programming Tools

The Resrctxt.ide file, on your accompanying disk, is the project file for the ResourceText application. This project uses three of its own classes and a number of different source and header files. Only the source and header files for the main application and the MDI client class are discussed here.

The ResourceText application class, ResTextApp, is defined in listing 26.2. This class is considerably more extensive than the application class for the earlier SimpleMDI example. However, most of the extra data and function members are used to support either context-sensitive Help or drag-and-drop file handling. We'll look briefly at drag- and-drop file handling, but our primary interest is the MDI characteristics of ResTextApp.

Listing 26.2   restxtap.h—The Main Application Header for the ResourceText Application

```
#if !defined(__restxtap_h)// Use file only if not already included
#define __restxtap_h

//////////////////////////////////////////////////////////////////
// PROJECT:      RESRCTXT.EXE Application
// FILE:         RESTXTAP.H
// AUTHOR:       Bruce R. Copeland
//
// Class definition for ResTextApp
//////////////////////////////////////////////////////////////////

#include <owl\owlpch.h>
#pragma hdrstop

#include <classlib\bags.h>


// Class to keep info about a dropped file, its name, where it was
// dropped, and whether or not it was in the client area
class TFileDrop
{
  public:
    char*    FileName;
    TPoint   Point;
    bool     InClientArea;

  public:
    TFileDrop(char*, TPoint&, bool, TModule*);
    ~TFileDrop();
    LPCSTR WhoAmI() {return FileName;};
    operator==(const TFileDrop& other) const
      {return this == &other;};
  private: // hidden to prevent accidental copying or assignment
    TFileDrop(const TFileDrop&);
    TFileDrop& operator= (const TFileDrop&);
};

typedef TIBagAsVector<TFileDrop> TFileList;
typedef TIBagAsVectorIterator<TFileDrop> TFileListIter;
```

```
class ResTextApp : public TApplication
{
  private:
    bool     HelpState;    // Has the Help engine been used?
    bool     ContextHelp;  // Context-sensitive Help state
    HCURSOR  HelpCursor;   // Context-sensitive Help cursor
  public:
    TOpenSaveDialog::TData  FileData; // Open/saveas dialog.

  public:
    ResTextApp();
    virtual ~ResTextApp() {};
    virtual void InitMainWindow();
    virtual void InitInstance();
    virtual bool CanClose();
    virtual bool ProcessAppMsg(MSG& msg);
  protected:
    void CmHelpContents();
    void CmHelpUsing();
    void CmHelpAbout();
    void EvDropFiles(TDropInfo drop);
  private:
    void SetupToolbar(TDecoratedMDIFrame *frame);
    void AddFiles(TFileList* files);
  DECLARE_RESPONSE_TABLE(ResTextApp);
};

#endif // __restxtap_h sentry.
```

> **Note**
>
> On the CD-ROM that accompanies this book, refer to Restxtap.cpp to see how the ResTextApp class is implemented.

The MDI characteristics in ResTextApp prove to be remarkably similar to the application class in the SimpleMDI example earlier. The ResTextApp constructor is shown below:

```
ResTextApp::ResTextApp() : TApplication("ResourceText")
{
  // Initialize flags and help cursor
  HelpState = false;
  ContextHelp = false;
  HelpCursor = 0;
}
```

It serves mainly to initialize two flags and the cursor associated with online Help.

The InitMainWindow() function is where most of the interesting application initialization occurs. This function has the following form:

```
void ResTextApp::InitMainWindow()
{
```

```
// Construct the MDI frame (and MDI client)
TDecoratedMDIFrame* frame = new TDecoratedMDIFrame(Name,
                        MDI_MENU, *(new ResMDIClient), true);

// Assign icon, menu, and accel. table for application
frame->SetIcon(this, IDI_MDIAPPLICATION);
frame->AssignMenu(MDI_MENU);
frame->Attr.AccelTable = MDI_MENU;

// Set up the toolbar
SetupToolbar(frame);

// Set up the status bar
TStatusBar *sb = new TStatusBar(frame, TGadget::Recessed,
                    TStatusBar::CapsLock    ¦
                    TStatusBar::NumLock      ¦
                    TStatusBar::Overtype);
frame->Insert(*sb, TDecoratedFrame::Bottom);

// Make frame the application main window
SetMainWindow(frame);

// Set up common file dialog flags, filters, & extension
FileData.Flags = OFN_FILEMUSTEXIST ¦ OFN_HIDEREADONLY
               ¦ OFN_OVERWRITEPROMPT;
FileData.DefExt = "RC";
FileData.SetFilter("Resource Scripts (*.RC)¦*.rc¦\
Dialog Resources (*.DLG)¦*.dlg¦Resource Headers (*.RH)¦*.rh¦");
}
```

The construction of the MDI frame here is quite similar to what we saw earlier. The frame class TDecoratedMDIFrame is used in this case to allow for a status bar and toolbar. A new ResMDIClient class object is passed as the MDI client in the TDecoratedMDIFrame constructor.

Once the frame is constructed, InitMainWindow() assigns the menu, main application icon, and accelerator table for the frame. It then proceeds with construction of the toolbar and status bar, before assigning frame as the application main window. On your own, you may want to examine the SetToolbar() function and the code for inserting a status bar in greater detail, but these are standard methods used in many OWL applications for establishing a toolbar and status bar.

The last several lines of InitMainWindow() serve an important role by assigning flags, filters, and default extension for a common file dialog data structure. This data structure is ultimately used every time the user opens or saves an MDI child resource file.

MDI and Drag and Drop

The ResourceText application implements drag and drop as a way to make it easier to compare and edit different resources files. It is precisely such editing that is so cumbersome with Resource Workshop.

While not strictly an MDI feature, drag-and-drop file handling is quite appropriate in MDI applications. Drag and drop offers the capability to select and move multiple files from a file directory into an application. This capability fits nicely with the MDI capability to quickly open and organize a number of different file windows.

The `ResTextApp` class enables drag and drop with the line

```
GetMainWindow()->DragAcceptFiles(true);
```

at the end of the `InitInstance()` function. Two other `ResTextApp` member functions also help implement drag and drop. These are the `EvDropFiles()` function and the `AddFiles()` function.

`EvDropFiles()` is the handler for the `WM_DROPFILES` message. Whenever `ResTextApp::EvDropFile()` responds to a `WM_DROPFILES` message, it calls the class member function `AddFiles()` to open any dropped files. You may want to examine Restxtap.cpp on the accompanying CD in greater detail to see exactly how these functions work.

The remaining functions in `ResTextApp` are involved with online Help. Online Help is provided in ResourceText to make it a full-fledged Windows utility. However, a thorough discussion of the implementation of Help in ResourceText is out of the realm of this chapter.

The MDI Client Class and MDI Child Functionality

`ResMDIClient` is the MDI client class for ResourceText. This class is substantially similar to the `SimpleMDIClient` class used in the earlier example. However, this class has been augmented to provide file handling for the MDI children. This turns out to be a key ingredient that allows the MDI children to have application-specific functionality with minimum coding. Listings 26.3 and 26.4 show the `ResMDIClient` definition and implementation.

Listing 26.3   rmdicln.h—The ResMDIClient Class Definition for the ResourceText Application

```
#if !defined(__rmdicln_h) // Use only if not already included
#define __rmdicln_h

/////////////////////////////////////////////////////////////////
// PROJECT:      RESRCTXT.EXE Application
// FILE:         RMDICLN.H
// AUTHOR:       Bruce R. Copeland
//
// Class definition for ResMDIClient
/////////////////////////////////////////////////////////////////

#include <owl\owlpch.h>
#pragma hdrstop


class ResMDIClient : public TMDIClient
{
```

(continues)

Listing 26.3   Continued

```
public:
  int   ChildCount; // Number of child window created

public:
  ResMDIClient(TModule* module = 0);
  virtual ~ResMDIClient () {};
  void OpenFile(LPCSTR fileName = 0);
protected:
  void CmFileNew();
  void CmFileOpen();
  void CmFileClose();
  void CeFileClose(TCommandEnabler& tce);
  DECLARE_RESPONSE_TABLE(ResMDIClient);
};

#endif // __rmdicln_h sentry
```

Listing 26.4   Rmdicln.cpp—The ResMDIClient Implementation for the ResourceText Application

```
//////////////////////////////////////////////////////////////////
// PROJECT:      RESRCTXT.EXE Application
// FILE:         RMDICLN.CPP
// AUTHOR:       Bruce R. Copeland
//
// Implementation of ResMDIClient (TMDIClient)
//////////////////////////////////////////////////////////////////

#include <owl\owlpch.h>
#pragma hdrstop

#include <dir.h>
#include <owl\mdichild.h>
#include <owl\editfile.h>
#include "rmdicln.h"
#include "restxtap.h"
#include "restxtap.rh"


// Response table for messages/commands handled by ResMDIClient
DEFINE_RESPONSE_TABLE1(ResMDIClient, TMDIClient)
  EV_COMMAND(CM_MDIFILENEW, CmFileNew),
  EV_COMMAND(CM_MDIFILEOPEN, CmFileOpen),
  EV_COMMAND(CM_FILECLOSE, CmFileClose),
  EV_COMMAND_ENABLE(CM_FILECLOSE, CeFileClose),
END_RESPONSE_TABLE;


//////////////////////////////////////////////////////////////////
  // ResMDIClient::ResMDIClient()
  //
```

```
// Class constructor
ResMDIClient::ResMDIClient(TModule* module)
 : TMDIClient (module)
{
  // Give the client window scrollbars
  Attr.Style |= WS_VSCROLL | WS_HSCROLL;

  // Initialize the child count
  ChildCount = 0;
}

//////////////////////////////////////////////////////////////////
// ResMDIClient::CmFileNew()
//
// File, New (CM_MDIFILENEW) handler
void ResMDIClient::CmFileNew()
{
  char  title[255];

  // Increment Childcount & Generate title for MDI child window
  wsprintf(title, "Resource %d", ++ChildCount);

  // Construct a new MDI child with empty TEditFile as client
  TEditFile* childClient = new TEditFile(0, 0, 0);
  TMDIChild* child = new TMDIChild(*this, title, childClient);

  // Associate document icon with the child window
  child->SetIcon(GetApplication(), IDI_DOC);

  // Maximize new child if current child is maximized
  TMDIChild *curChild = GetActiveMDIChild();
  if (curChild && (curChild->GetWindowLong(GWL_STYLE)
      & WS_MAXIMIZE))
    child->Attr.Style |= WS_MAXIMIZE;

  // Create window interface element for new child
  child->Create();

  // Override inappropriate default new window titling
  child->SetCaption(title);

  // Give the child client correct file filters
  ResTextApp *theApp = TYPESAFE_DOWNCAST(GetApplication(),
          ResTextApp);
  childClient->FileData = theApp->FileData;
}

//////////////////////////////////////////////////////////////////
// ResMDIClient::OpenFile()
//
// Does the work opening new child from a file
void ResMDIClient::OpenFile(const char *fileName)
{
  ResTextApp *theApp = TYPESAFE_DOWNCAST(GetApplication(),
          ResTextApp);
```

(continues)

V

Programming Tools

Listing 26.4 Continued

```
  if (fileName)
    strcpy(theApp->FileData.FileName, fileName);

  // Construct a new MDI child with TEditFile as client
  TEditFile *childClient = new TEditFile(0, 0, 0, 0, 0, 0, 0,
                            theApp->FileData.FileName);
  TMDIChild* child = new TMDIChild(*this, "", childClient);

  // Associate document icon with the child window
  child->SetIcon(GetApplication(), IDI_DOC);

  // Maximize new child if current child is maximized
  TMDIChild *curChild = GetActiveMDIChild();
  if (curChild && (curChild->GetWindowLong(GWL_STYLE)
      & WS_MAXIMIZE))
    child->Attr.Style |= WS_MAXIMIZE;

  // Create window interface element for new child
  child->Create();

  // Give the child client correct file filters
  childClient->FileData = theApp->FileData;
}

//////////////////////////////////////////////////////////////////
// ResMDIClient::CmFileOpen()
//
// File, Open (CM_MDIFILEOPEN) handler
void ResMDIClient::CmFileOpen()
{
  ResTextApp *theApp = TYPESAFE_DOWNCAST(GetApplication(),
          ResTextApp);

  // Display standard Open dialog box to select a file name.
  *(theApp->FileData.FileName) = 0; // Initialize FileName
  if (TFileOpenDialog(this, theApp->FileData).Execute() == IDOK)
    OpenFile();
}

//////////////////////////////////////////////////////////////////
// ResMDIClient::CmFileClose()
//
// File, Close (CM_FILECLOSE) handler
void ResMDIClient::CmFileClose()
{
  // Current active MDI child is the one to close
  TMDIChild* child = GetActiveMDIChild();

  // Bail out if not OK to close
  if (!child->CanClose())
    return;

  // Destroy the child interface and delete the object instance
  child->Destroy();
```

```
      delete child;
    }

    ///////////////////////////////////////////////////////////////////
    // ResMDIClient::CeFileClose()
    //
    // Enabler for CM_FILECLOSE command
    void ResMDIClient::CeFileClose(TCommandEnabler& tce)
    {
      // Only enable if there's an active MDI child
      tce.Enable(GetActiveMDIChild() != NULL);
    }
```

To see how `ResMDIClient` provides file handling for the MDI children, let's look first at the `CmFileNew()` function. This function has the following form:

```
    void ResMDIClient::CmFileNew()
    {
      char   title[255];

      // Increment Childcount & Generate title for MDI child window
      wsprintf(title, "Resource %d", ++ChildCount);

      // Construct a new MDI child with empty TEditFile as client
      TEditFile* childClient = new TEditFile(0, 0, 0);
      TMDIChild* child = new TMDIChild(*this, title, childClient);

      // Associate document icon with the child window
      child->SetIcon(GetApplication(), IDI_DOC);

      // Maximize new child if current child is maximized
      TMDIChild *curChild = GetActiveMDIChild();
      if (curChild && (curChild->GetWindowLong(GWL_STYLE)
          & WS_MAXIMIZE))
        child->Attr.Style |= WS_MAXIMIZE;

      // Create window interface element for new child
      child->Create();

      // Override inappropriate default new window titling
      child->SetCaption(title);

      // Give the child client correct file filters
      ResTextApp *theApp = TYPESAFE_DOWNCAST(GetApplication(),
              ResTextApp);
      childClient->FileData = theApp->FileData;
    }
```

This function prepares a title and uses it in constructing an instance of `TMDIChild` much as did the `SimpleMDIClient` `CmFileNew()` function. An important difference is that `ResMDIClient::CmFileNew()` constructs an instance of the OWL `TEditFile` class as a child client. It then passes a pointer to this object as the client window parameter for the `TMDIChild` constructor. This small, but significant change gives the ResourceText application text-handling capability in its child windows.

There's only one other new ingredient in the `CmFileNew()` function. The last few lines of the function obtain an application pointer and use it to set the child client's `FileData` member equal to the application's `FileData` member. This ensures that the child client `FileData` member always has the correct file filters, flags and default extension.

The `ResMDIClient` class introduces two functions that together provide the capability to open a file. The `CmFileOpen()` function is the handler for the `CM_MDIFILEOPEN` command message. This function looks like:

```
void ResMDIClient::CmFileOpen()
{
  ResTextApp *theApp = TYPESAFE_DOWNCAST(GetApplication(),
          ResTextApp);

  // Display standard Open dialog box to select a file name.
  *(theApp->FileData.FileName) = 0; // Initialize FileName
  if (TFileOpenDialog(this, theApp->FileData).Execute() == IDOK)
    OpenFile();
}
```

As you can see, this function executes a common file open dialog box. If the user exits the common file open dialog with OK, then `CmFileOpen()` calls the `OpenFile()` function.

The `OpenFile()` function does most of the work in opening a file. If you examine the `OpenFile()` function in listing 26.4, you see that it is quite similar to the `CmFileNew()` function above. The one really important difference is that `OpenFile()` constructs the `TEditFile` child client as follows:

```
TEditFile *childClient = new TEditFile(0, 0, 0, 0, 0, 0, 0,
                    theApp->FileData.FileName);
```

Here, `theApp->FileData.FileName` is the filename selected by the user in the common file open dialog box. By constructing, the MDI child window client this way, the contents of the file is used to fill the MDI child window client.

There is only one other noteworthy feature in `ResMDIClient`. The `CmFileClose()` function contains the lines

```
if (!child->CanClose())
    return;
```

preceding the code to close the child. These lines ensure that a child window doesn't close before the user has a chance to save the contents. The `CanClose()` function for `child` calls the `CanClose()` function for the child client window to verify that any changes in the document have been saved. If not, the function prompts the user to save the changes. `CanClose()` returns true only if the file is up-to-date or the user elects not to save any changes.

MDI Child Client Capability

The above description largely completes our coverage of MDI child application function. But "Wait," you say. "Where is all the code to provide the text handling in

ResourceText?" Well that's sort of the point of this example. It's all contained in the standard OWL `TEditFile` class. By using a client window to add this capability to the MDI children, we avoid ever having to do anything except create object instances of the existing `TEditFile` class.

Naturally, in many of your own specialized applications, you are going to have to write some code for the MDI child client class. But if you're careful organizing that class, it will be easy to merge it into the MDI application. In addition, you'll probably have a class that can be used with a minimum of effort for other purposes besides an MDI application. That's the kind of thing that C++ is all about!

Using Advanced and Specialized MDI

The examples in this chapter have demonstrated the basics of developing an OWL MDI application. That's all many of you will ever need, but some of you will want more.

MDI applications with more than one type of child are fairly common. There is a straightforward way to create them in OWL using document/view.

Earlier, I mentioned MDI applications that provide specialized scaling for child windows. When there's a need to compare more than two or three tiled windows in an MDI application, it's often useful to scale the contents of all the child windows by some constant amount to make them completely visible. Usually this scaling is only done when the windows are tiled, and not when they are cascaded or maximized.

This isn't too difficult to accomplish. You can keep track of the necessary scaling information in the MDI client class. You then override the MDI client `CmTileChildren()` and `CmCascadeChildren()` handler functions to notify the children about the correct scaling every time there's a change. Dealing with the maximized window state is a little more difficult. You have to do some careful handling of the `WM_SYSCOMMAND` message in the MDI child window class. Still, all in all, this is pretty straightforward stuff using C++ and OWL.

From Here...

As you've now seen, MDI application development isn't really very difficult using OWL. It does, however, require you to use all your skills as a C++ OWL programmer. At this point, you may want to look at some related material elsewhere:

- Chapter 14, "Basic Class Concepts," gives you a good understanding of classes.
- Chapter 15, "Function Overloading," helps you get up to speed on derived classes and the behavior of their functions.
- Chapter 22, "Exception Handling," gives advice and examples on how to handle errors that have been trapped by your program.
- The creation of classes and their linkage into code are covered in Chapter 28, "Using the Class Expert."

CHAPTER 27

Using the AppExpert

Borland C++ provides a very easy method for defining and creating all the pieces needed to create a project. Borland provides the AppExpert as part of the IDE. The AppExpert guides you through the process of defining the target platform you are creating an application for, and all the parameters that will simplify the creation and maintenance of programs.

In this chapter, you will learn how to

- Start the AppExpert
- Customize the application features of a project
- Customize the main window features of a project
- Customize the MDI client/view features of a project
- Generate an application template

Starting the AppExpert

Borland has provided a powerful tool that will allow you to define the characteristics of your projects. These include what types of windows you will have, their colors, where you will store your code, whether help is available, and quite a few others.

Creating this project shell manually can be tedious. Borland has made creating this shell as easy as point and shoot. To start the AppExpert, Choose File, New, AppExpert from the IDE menu, as shown in figure 27.1.

Once you launch the AppExpert, you will be presented with a dialog box, as shown in figure 27.2. This dialog box allows you to navigate through your directory structure and place your new project where you want it. You also have to provide a name for the project. This will be the default name of the executable that will be created from your project.

Fig. 27.1

Starting the AppExpert from the IDE.

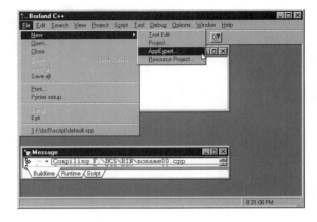

Fig. 27.2

The New AppExpert Project dialog box.

Once you have decided on a location and filename for your project, click on the Open button to define your project using the AppExpert. You will be creating a program shell, complete with all the components linked together, ready for you to add your code to. You will see the AppExpert's main window, as shown in figure 27.3.

Fig. 27.3

The AppExpert main window.

Using the AppExpert features is described in the following sections.

Customizing the Application

The AppExpert is broken down into two main sections. The list box on the left shows the topics that can be configured using the AppExpert, while the right side of the window shows the features available for each topic.

If you refer to figure 27.3, you will notice that there are three main topics available for customization within the AppExpert. Each of these has a plus sign to the left of the topic. Click the mouse button on the plus sign next to the Application topic. You will see all the possible subtopics available under Application, as shown in figure 27.4.

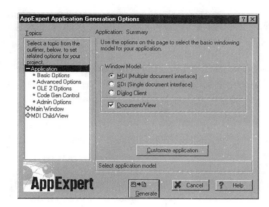

Fig. 27.4

The subtopics available under Application.

The Application has several choices that you must make before defining any of the subtopics. These are the Window Model that you want your application to have, and whether or not you want your project to be a Document/View model.

You can choose from an SDI Client, MDI Client, or a Dialog client for the Window Model. Once you have chosen the type of application you want to create, click on the Basic Options topic under Application.

Basic Options

The Basic Options topic for Application definition allows you to define the basic options you want for your application. You can see these options in figure 27.5.

The first option that you can change is the name and location of the target executable to be created. In figure 27.5, the name of the file to be created will be Test.exe, and the location is in f:\Bc5\Bin.

Fig. 27.5

The Basic Options available under Application.

The next set of options allows you to define the type of main window you want your application to have. You can include a toolbar, status line, mail support, registry support and several other options.

The last set of basic options lets you specify if you are going to include Help file support, and if so, what the name of the Help file is.

Advanced Options

The Advanced Options allow you to specify the startup state of your application, whether that is normal, minimized, or maximized. You can also choose which style of controls you want your application to have. These include Standard Windows controls, Borland BWCC, or MS Control 3D. Figure 27.6 shows the advanced options available.

Fig. 27.6

The Advanced Options available under Application.

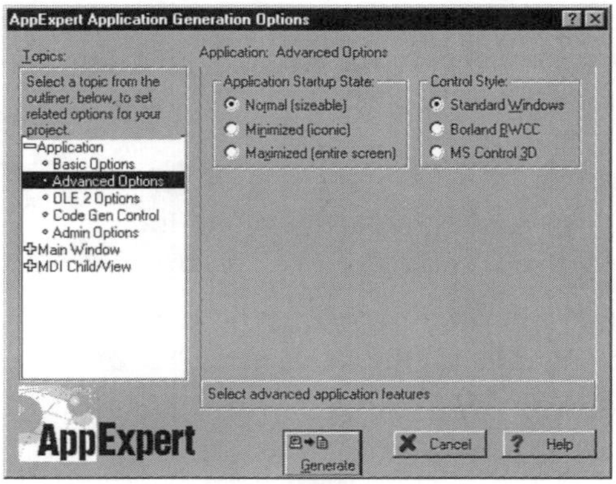

OLE 2 Options

Borland C++ supports the creation of OLE 2 containers and servers. The OLE 2 options topic allows you to specify whether you want to create applications that are OLE-enabled. The OLE 2 options are shown in figure 27.7.

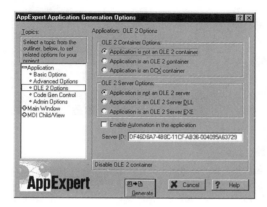

Fig. 27.7

The OLE 2 Options available under Application.

You can choose to make your application an OLE 2 container, not an OLE 2 container, or an OCX container under the group titled OLE 2 Container Options.

If you want to make your application an OLE 2 server, then you can choose to create an OLE Server DLL or an EXE. These options are available in the OLE 2 Server Options group.

You can also choose to enable OLE automation by selecting the check box at the bottom of the dialog box.

Code Generation Options

The options available for code generation allow you to choose directories for your source and header files. You can also define the names of the main source (.cpp) and header (.h or .hpp) files. The other options available are the application base class and the dialog base class. You can customize these options to suit the needs for your project.

Another option available for code generation is the use of long filenames. While long filenames can make the contents of the files easier to understand, the use of this option can limit your ability to move your projects across platforms that do not support the longer filenames. You can also have the compiler generate Terse of Verbose comments in the header file. Figure 27.8 shows the options available on the Code Generation Options page.

Fig. 27.8

The Code Generation Options available under Application.

Administrative Options

The administrative options allow you to embed version and copyright information within the compiled executable. You can type in a description for the project, the author and the company, if applicable. These options are shown in figure 27.9.

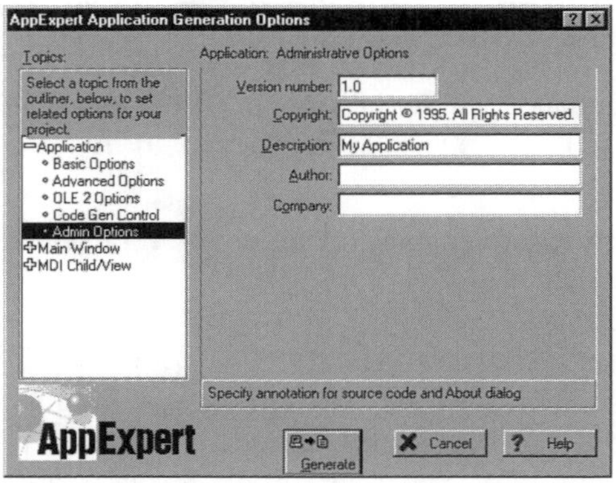

Fig. 27.9

The Administrative Options available under Application.

Customizing the Main Window

By selecting the options within the Main Window topics, you can customize the look and feel of your main application window. The options available for the Main Window topic are shown in figure 27.10.

You can select what text you want to appear in the title bar of your main window. The other option available is the color that you want your main window to be. You can choose from the default color or one of the predefined system color constants, or you can use a specific color if you so choose.

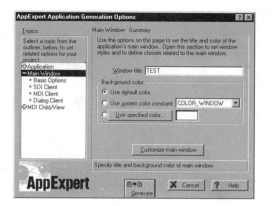

Fig. 27.10

The Main Window options.

Keep in mind that your users may not want an application that comes up with a purple window. Many users want all their applications to have the same colors; choosing the default color allows your application to be the same default color as the rest of your users' programs, regardless of what color scheme they have chosen.

Basic Options

The Basic Options for the main window allow you to specify what types of controls you want your main window to have. These options are shown in figure 27.11.

Fig. 27.11

The Basic Options available under Main Window.

The options include the general options available for most Windows applications. You can choose to include Min and Max buttons, a border, a caption, the system menu, and other features.

SDI Client

The SDI option allows you to specify the options you want for an application that is an SDI (Single Document Interface) application. These options are shown in figure 27.12.

Fig. 27.12

The SDI options available under Main Window.

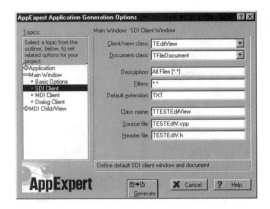

The SDI options allow you to select a Client/View base class and a Document base class. You can also choose the description, filters, and extensions for any document to be used in your SDI. The last options are the class name, source, and header files for your document class.

MDI Client

If you are creating an application that is a MDI client, this topic allows you to choose the Client class, source, and header files for your MDI client class. The options are shown in figure 27.13.

Fig. 27.13

The MDI options available under Main Window.

Dialog Client

The Dialog Client options are very similar to the MDI Client options. These options allow you to choose the client class and source and header files for your Dialog client class. The options are shown in figure 27.14.

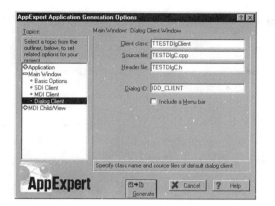

Fig. 27.14

The Dialog Client options available under Main Window.

Customizing the MDI Child/View

The final main topic available for creating your application is the MDI Child/View. The options in this topic allow you to choose the client class and source and header files for your MDI Child class. The options are shown in figure 27.15. These options apply only to MDI applications.

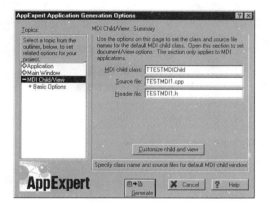

Fig. 27.15

The MDI Child/View options.

The Basic Options allow you to specify the options you want for your MDI Child class. These options are shown in figure 27.16.

The SDI Options allow you to select an MDI client/View base class and a Document base class. You can also choose the description, filters, and extensions for any document to be used in your child class. The last options are the class name and source and header files for your document class.

V

Programming Tools

Fig. 27.16

*The Basic Options
available under MDI
Child/View.*

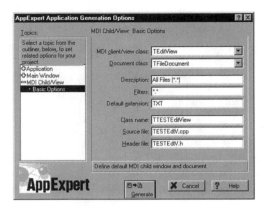

Generating the Application Template

Once you have chosen all your options for your project and application, all you have
to do to generate your application shell is to click the Generate button (refer to fig.
27.16). You will be asked to confirm your choice to generate the application. Select
the Yes button to generate your application.

If you had retained all the default selections, then you would be returned to the IDE
with the new project loaded. The Project window of the IDE would look similar to
figure 27.17.

Fig. 27.17

*The Project window of a
newly created project.*

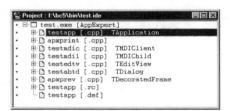

From Here...

The Application Expert can help take a lot of the tedium out of creating the skeleton
and links of an application. You can use the AppExpert to create your projects, and
then pull up these pieces in the IDE and fill in the blanks with the code and functionality that your applications need.

- In chapter 28, "Using the Class Expert," you learn about using this feature to
  help you tailor and create your own classes.

- In chapter 31, "Using the Resource Workshop," you learn about how to use and
  exploit the power of the Resource Workshop to create your own application
  resources, including menus, dialog boxes and other application components
  that will speed up your application development time.

CHAPTER 28

Using the ClassExpert

At the heart of every object-oriented program are its classes. Classes are the DNA of every instantiated object in the system that you are writing. Just as the DNA in a cell tells the cell how it should look and act, the class definition tells the object created from that class how it should look and act.

As computer systems become more complex, the programmers normally create more and more classes. As a programmer, your job is to be wise and to create classes that match closely the problem being solved. In the course of creating simple examples, the creation of classes is not very difficult. Difficulties arise, however, whenever the complexity of a system exceeds a dozen classes with five or six member functions each. Borland has created a tool called ClassExpert to manage classes, their associated state variables, and their member functions.

In this chapter, you will:

- Learn basic class design
- Create a sample application using AppExpert
- Examine that application using ClassExpert
- Examine, add, and change virtual functions with ClassExpert
- Examine, add, and change command notifications with ClassExpert
- Examine, add, and change Windows message handlers with ClassExpert

Creating Classes

Classes are the fundamental unit of an object-oriented program. Their development occurred as a part of the natural evolution of programming languages. Early languages, such as Assembler and Fortran IV, used variables to manage their programs and hold data. In later languages, such as Pascal and C, the concept of a record data type or structure allowed individual variables to be grouped together into user-defined data types. This innovation allowed the programmer to group variables logically within her programs in order to make it easier to maintain and enhance.

The next logical progression in the evolution of programming languages was to allow code to be added to these structures. This innovation allowed the programmer to encapsulate not only the data into a logical unit, but also the code that acts upon that data. These new structures were called classes to distinguish them from simpler structures.

Classes have been widely accepted by the programming community as a superior way of creating functionality. The reason for this is the human need to manage complexity in order to avoid confusion. Properly designed classes create objects that fit our intuitive notions of what an object should be. When we see a ball, we know that it is really a complex object at the molecular level. Ball manufacturers study material properties, performance characteristics, longevity, and so on, and write tomes on the manufacture, care, and feeding of balls. The players know that the information is available somewhere, but they are not often interested in it. Their interface with a basketball is simply to dribble, pass, and shoot. In other words, they treat it like an object.

For a class to be good, it must allow the creation of objects that fit this same description. The objects may be very complex and sophisticated to the engineer who creates and maintains the classes, but they must be simple to use. A window class should contain all of the code to maintain the behavioral integrity of window objects, while at the same time being easy to use for the programmer. You don't need to understand how televisions work in order to watch a show, and you shouldn't have to understand how a window repaints itself when moved in order to move it.

Creating an Application

As you learned in chapter 27, "Using AppExpert," a Windows application can be created very easily in Borland C++ 5. To create an application for use in this chapter, follow this procedure:

1. Open the Borland C++ 5 integrated development environment (IDE) by double-clicking on the icon.

2. Choose New from the File menu and specify AppExpert when the secondary menu appears to the side. This will display the dialog box shown in figure 28.1.

   This dialog box allows you to give your project a base name. The base name will be used to name all of the components that will make up the application. AppExpert appends certain suffixes to this name to create filenames.

> **Tip**
>
> When creating a new project using AppExpert, choose a name that will be unique enough to recognize the naming approach used by Borland C++ 5. Avoid names that resemble too closely names that are used by the system, such as driver, window, app, class, and so on. This will flatten the learning curve associated with the AppExpert and ClassExpert.

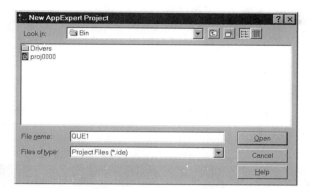

Fig. 28.1

The AppExpert guides you through the process of creating a sample application.

For this project, name it QUE1. Click on the Open button and a dialog box like figure 28.2 appears.

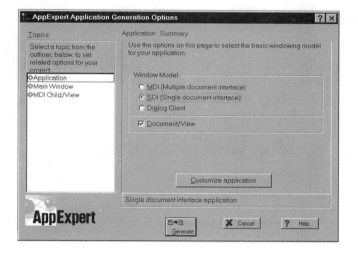

Fig. 28.2

The AppExpert Application Generation Options dialog box allows you to specify what kind of application you have built.

V

Programming Tools

3. Select SDI (Single Document Interface) for the window model. All that you need for this chapter is a simple application. Choose the Document/View check box. This will build code to perform print and print preview activities. At this point, click on the Generate button and watch the messages as they appear on the screen.

4. When the generation completes, a child window in the IDE will appear. It will have the name of the project file, Que1.ide, in the title bar. The rest of the window will contain about 15 filenames in a list, as shown in figure 28.3.

    The top of the list box shows "que1.exe," which is the target. The rest of the files contain the classes created to provide the functionality of the application. On the right, you will see the base classes for each of these files. This will help you determine where each of the classes resides.

Fig. 28.3

The files that make up the project are shown as dependencies in the Project window.

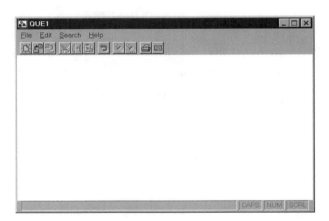

```
Project : c:\bc5\bin\que1.ide
⊟·☐ que1.exe [AppExpert]
  ⊟·☐ queapp [.cpp]    TApplication, TDecoratedFrame
  │  └─☐ queapp [.h]    TApplication, TDecoratedFrame
  ⊟·☐ apxprint [.cpp]
  │  └─☐ apxprint [.h]
  ⊟·☐ queledtv [.cpp]   TEditView
  │  └─☐ queledtv [.h]   TEditView
  ⊟·☐ quelabtd [.cpp]   TDialog
  │  └─☐ quelabtd [.h]   TDialog
  ⊟·☐ apxprev [.cpp]    TDecoratedFrame
  │  └─☐ apxprev [.h]    TDecoratedFrame
  ⊟·☐ queapp [.rc]
     └─☐ queapp [.rh]
     └─☐ queapp [.def]
```

> **Tip**
>
> Many programmers who grew up creating all of their own code are very uncomfortable with AppExpert and ClassExpert. This is natural. Try to avoid a hasty judgment on the value of these until you have had time to become accustomed to this new approach. While debugging generated code is not fun, it is rare to find a generated bug. Most of the bugs will be in code that you add.

5. Choose <u>M</u>ake All from the <u>P</u>roject menu (or press F9) to compile and link the application. Even though you have added no code, an application created by AppExpert already exists.

6. Click on <u>R</u>un from the <u>D</u>ebug menu. This will cause the application to pop up a window like the one shown in figure 28.4.

Fig. 28.4

A functional application is created without a single line of code added by the programmer.

7. To gain an appreciation of the depth of the application that was created, place your mouse cursor over the printer icon on the toolbar. A ToolTip for that icon will appear after the mouse cursor has been still for about one second, as shown in figure 28.5.

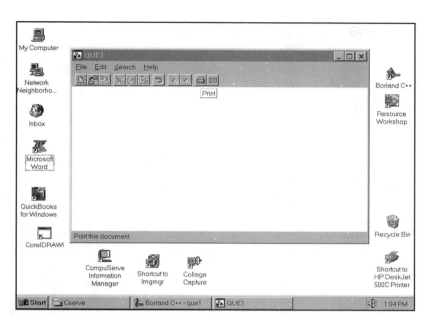

Fig. 28.5

ToolTips are created automatically when the toolbar is added to the project.

8. A complete menuing system has also been added, with many of the menu picks backed by the appropriate code to implement the functionality. Click on the word File in the menu bar. Figure 28.6 shows the File menu after it has been pulled down.

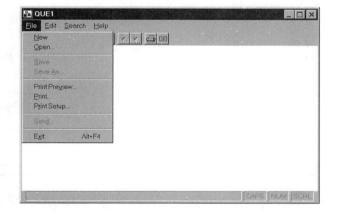

Fig. 28.6

The File menu was created complete with working New and Open commands.

9. Choose Open on the File menu. You will probably be surprised to find that an Open dialog box pops up, as shown in figure 28.7. This is logical if you think about it. The idea behind C++ is to inherit as much functionality as possible. The base class TEditView provides this functionality.

Fig. 28.7

The Open dialog box behavior is inherited from the TEditView base class.

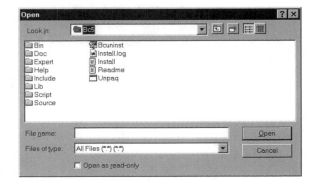

10. Perhaps even more surprising is what happens if you use the Open dialog box to find a real file on your system. Look around until you locate the Autoexec.bat file on your system. Click the Open button and an edit window opens with that file in it, as shown in figure 28.8.

Fig. 28.8

The QUE1 application can be used to edit files on your system.

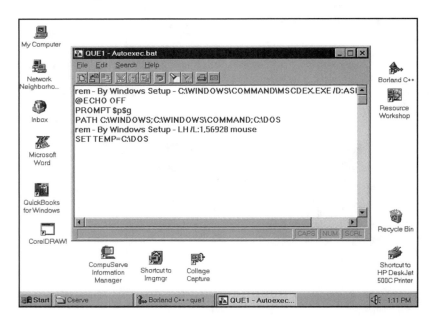

11. With the Autoexec.bat file open, choose Print Preview from the File menu. This functionality is also provided by the base class TEditView. This command will cause a full sheet display of what the Autoexec.bat file would look like if printed, as shown in figure 28.9. In an earlier tip, you were asked to reserve judgment on these Experts until you could experience the benefits as well. This Print Preview function is a great time-saver. If you chose to code this functionality yourself, you would have to invest considerably more time than you have invested here.

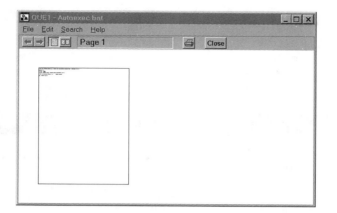

Fig. 28.9

The Print Preview functionality is immediately available once the application is generated.

12. Another automatically generated feature that you will examine later is the About box. Choose <u>A</u>bout from the <u>H</u>elp menu to display a dialog box that looks like the one in figure 28.10.

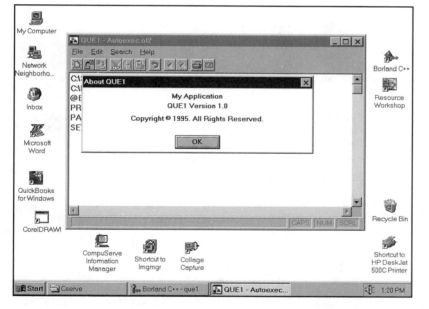

Fig. 28.10

The About dialog box is a generated feature of the application.

V

Programming Tools

13. Close the application by choosing E<u>x</u>it from the File menu. This will put you back in the IDE. Now that you have a fully operational application, you can use the features of Borland C++ 5's IDE to discover how the application was built.

Learning about the Classes

The first step in understanding the application that has been built is to identify the names and roles of all of the functions that were created. By choosing Project from the View menu, you can open the child window shown earlier in figure 28.3. Table 28.1 summarizes these files.

Table 28.1	The Files and Classes Created
File	**Description**
Que1.exe	Executable for the application.
Que1app.cpp	Contains source code for TQUE1App, the application class that contains all of the other objects. This class controls the appearance of the screen and the message map that controls the behavior of objects. This file also contains the OwlMain() function that serves as the entry point for this entire application.
que1app.h	Contains class definition for TQUE1App, the application class that contains all of the other objects.
Apxprint.cpp	Contains source code for the implementation of class TAPXPrintout, which adds printing to this application.
apxprint.h	Contains the class definition for TAPXPrintout.
Que1edtv.cpp	Contains source code for TQUE1EditView. This class is derived from TEditView, which provides a view wrapper for the ObjectWindows text edit class (TEdit). This streamable class includes event-handling functions that pass messages between a document and its views.
que1edtv.h	Contains the class definition for TQUE1EditView.
Que1abtd.cpp	Contains the source code that implements the TQUE1AboutDlg class. This class is derived from TDialog class, which implements all dialog boxes.
que1abtd.h	Contains the class definition for TQUE1AboutDlg.
Apxprev.cpp	Contains the source code that implements the PreviewWindow class. This class provides the member functions used to manage the Print Preview menu command.
apxprev.h	Contains the class definition for PreviewWindow class.
Que1app.rc	Contains all of the resources used in the application.
que1app.rh	Contains all of the IDs used in the application.
Que1app.def	Contains the module definition data for the application, such as the memory-management parameters.

Learning the Ancestry of Classes

Knowing the names of all the files helps us to know where to go when editing, but tells us little about the ancestry of the classes. One of the strengths of C++ and object-oriented programming is *inheritance*. Inheritance allows two classes to share part of their functionality without forcing them into an artificial similarity. By declaring another class to be the base class, your new class can obtain a number of member functions for "free" and simply add more functions as needed. This leads to considerable improvement in productivity when used correctly.

A class lower in the hierarchy is known as a *derived class*. One higher is called a *base class*. A derived class automatically inherits the characteristics of its base classes. It automatically receives all of the data members and member functions from every base. It can add its own data members and member functions, even so far as overriding the member functions of the base. It is this feature that gives you an increase in productivity by allowing you to change a standard class into one that suits your needs.

If you stop to consider it, the AppExpert and ClassExpert allow you to do similar things. They create the basic functionality that allows you to add your own features and override those of the base classes until they meet your needs.

Understanding what classes are derived from is a challenge. Borland C++ 5 has provided a tool to browse the class structure of an application. It is invoked by choosing Classes from the View menu of the IDE. Click on this menu pick for the QUE1 application to have Borland C++ create a map of your classes and display it on the screen. Do not despair if you see no action on the computer screen for a minute or perhaps two. The processing required to create this map is substantial and does not normally access the hard drive during processing. It may look as if your machine has hung, but it will eventually come back and display a map like the one shown in figure 28.11.

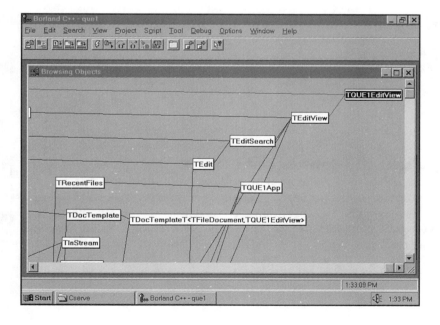

Fig. 28.11

The browser allows you to see the relationships between the classes in your application.

V

Programming Tools

The base classes are on the left and the derived classes are on the right. Looking at figure 28.11, you can see that class TQUE1EditView is highlighted and that it is derived from TEditView, which was derived from TEditSearch, which was derived from TEdit. By double-clicking on the TQUE1EditView class, you can drill down and see the member functions of the class, including the member functions of its base classes, which it inherits because of the relationships shown in figure 28.12.

Fig. 28.12

Drilling down is a good way to find out which member functions are available to an object via its class hierarchy.

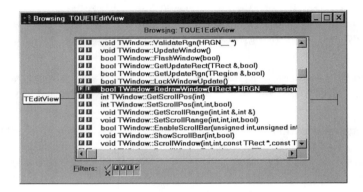

Notice also that the lines running between a class, its base classes, and its derived classes turn red when highlighted. This helps you decipher a graphic that may have lines that are too close together to be easily viewed. Drilling down another level will bring up a window with only one member function in it. In some cases, this window can be easier to read than it was in the dialog box beside all of the other member functions, as shown in figure 28.13.

Fig. 28.13

Drilling is allowed down two levels in the class browser.

Learning about the Contents of Classes

Now that you are well trained in the art of finding out the pedigree of a class, you are ready to learn how to examine the internals of a class. ClassExpert is Borland C++'s way of aiding the programmer in the formidable task of creating and modifying the contents of a class. The importance of this task cannot be overstated. To illustrate this point, the entire main program loop for the QUE1 application has been listed in listing 28.1.

Listing 28.1   The *OwlMain()* Section of an AppExpert-Created Program Is Very Small

```
int OwlMain(int , char* [])
{
  TQUE1App    app;
  return app.Run();
}
```

As you will quickly observe, this main loop does very little. An object called "app" is created of type TQUE1App. Its Run() member function is called, and the return value assigned the return value of the OwlMain() function. This is all there is. Everything else is handled by member functions in the classes. This means that to take the application to the next level, you will need to go in and edit classes that were written by the code generator. Given this scenario, most of you will welcome your new best friend, ClassExpert.

You invoke the services of ClassExpert by choosing the ClassExpert command on the View menu. This will bring up the ClassExpert window, as shown in figure 28.14.

Class section

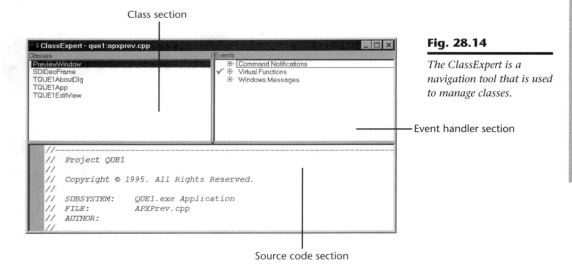

Fig. 28.14

The ClassExpert is a navigation tool that is used to manage classes.

Event handler section

Source code section

In the upper-left quadrant of the ClassExpert window is the Class section. On the upper-right is the Event Handler section, and at the bottom is the Source Code section. Each of these panels will be explained in detail in the following sections.

Examining the Virtual Functions for a Class

As the class is the fundamental unit of work in C++ and in all of object-oriented programming, it is fitting that a special facility has been created for viewing and modifying classes. As we saw in listing 28.1, nearly none of the work required to write a C++ program is performed in the main() function. So, in order to modify and enhance a program, you need to locate the appropriate function and edit the code. The following process does just that:

1. With the ClassExpert screen open, select the PreviewWindow class by clicking on it. This will load the information for this class into the Event Handler section. Notice in figure 28.14 that a check mark is beside the "Virtual Functions" entry in the Event Handler section. This indicates that a virtual function has been overridden in your application.

2. Your goal is to locate the overridden function, so you click on the "+" sign next to the "Virtual Function" entry. This will expand the list of virtual functions, as shown in figure 28.15.

Fig. 28.15

The expanded Virtual Functions entry will display a listing of all the virtual functions of the base classes.

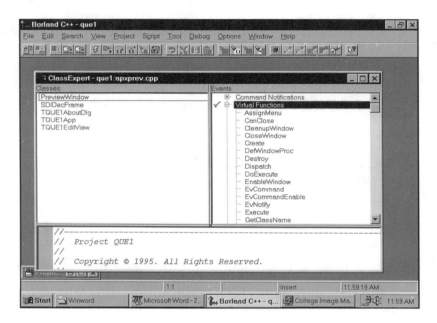

3. Highlight the function called SetupWindow() in the list in the Event Handler section. Then click on the class name to load the code for this function into the Source code window. The code for this function is shown in listing 28.2.

Listing 28.2 The Source Code for a Virtual Function Can Be Edited by Clicking on the Name of the Class and the Name of the Virtual Function

```
void PreviewWindow::SetupWindow()
{
  TDecoratedFrame::SetupWindow();

  TPrintDialog::TData& data = Printer->GetSetup();
  Page1 = new TPreviewPage(Client, *Printout, *PrnDC, *PrintExtent, 1);
  Page1->SetPageNumber(1);
  data.MaxPage = 1;
```

```
Page2 = 0;

TLayoutMetrics metrics1;

metrics1.X.Set(lmLeft, lmRightOf, lmParent, lmLeft, 15);
metrics1.Y.Set(lmTop, lmBelow, lmParent, lmTop, 15);

// Determine major axis of preview page, have that follow parent size.
// Make minor axis a percentage (aspect ratio) of the page's major axis
//
TRect r = Client->GetClientRect();
long ratio;

if (PrintExtent->cx > PrintExtent->cy)
  ratio = ((long)PrintExtent->cy * 100) / PrintExtent->cx;
else
  ratio = ((long)PrintExtent->cx * 100) / PrintExtent->cy;

bool xMajor = ((r.Width() * ratio) / 100) > r.Height();
if (xMajor){
  metrics1.Height.Set(lmBottom, lmAbove, lmParent, lmBottom, 15);
  metrics1.Width.PercentOf(Page1, (int)((long)PrintExtent->cx * 95 /
  ➥PrintExtent->cy), lmHeight);
}
else {
  metrics1.Height.PercentOf(Page1, (int)((long)PrintExtent->cy * 95 /
  ➥PrintExtent->cx), lmWidth);
  metrics1.Width.Set(lmRight, lmLeftOf, lmParent, lmRight, 15);
}

Page1->Create();

Client->SetChildLayoutMetrics(*Page1, metrics1);
Client->Layout();
}
```

The code for this section deals mainly with the appearance of the window that will be created to display the previewed page. The first line

```
TDecoratedFrame::SetupWindow();
```

calls the same function that you are overriding here. This means that you don't want to change what that function does; you merely want to add to it.

Just below that, the statement

```
Page1 = new TPreviewPage(Client, *Printout, *PrnDC, *PrintExtent, 1);
```

appears actually to create the page. The page, Page1, is created in dynamic memory using the new operator. It is an instance of the class TPreviewPage(). This class already provides much of the functionality for the preview page.

Near the end of the listing is the following line:

```
Page1->Create();
```

This member function creates the pages according to the values in the member variables of the Page1 object.

4. At this point you would change the code in this function to fit your requirements, and choose <u>M</u>ake All from the project window.

Examining and Creating the Command Notifications for a Class

Some of the classes will have a menu that controls much of the behavior of the application. The implementation of some of the menu picks, such as <u>F</u>ile Print Pre<u>v</u>iew, are created by AppExpert, while others, such as <u>F</u>ile <u>N</u>ew, are created as stubs only. It will be up to you to finish adding the code for these functions. To learn how to do this, follow these steps:

1. Select the class TQUE1App from the Class section.

2. Notice that all three categories in the Event Handler section have a check mark beside them in this class. Click on the Command Notifications entry to expand the list of commands, as shown in figure 28.16.

Fig. 28.16

The Command Notification entry is used to add code that will respond to the user menu commands.

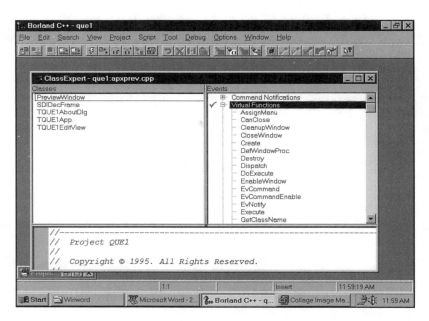

3. Click on the + next to the CM_FILEPRINT entry to expand it one more level. Select the Command entry and click on the class name to bring the code into the Source Code section. The name of the member function of the TQUE1App class is CmFilePrint(), and is in listing 28.3.

```
void TQUE1App::CmFilePrint()
{
  // Create Printer object if not already created.
  //
  if (!Printer)
    Printer = new TPrinter(this);

  TDocument* currentDoc = GetDocManager()->GetCurrentDoc();

  char docName[_MAX_PATH];

  if (currentDoc->GetTitle())
    strcpy(docName, currentDoc->GetTitle());
  else
    strcpy(docName, "Document");

  // Create Printout window and set characteristics.
  //
  TAPXPrintout printout(Printer, docName, GetMainWindow()-
  ➥>GetClientWindow());
  printout.SetBanding(true);

  Printing++;

  // Bring up the Print dialog and print the document.
  //
  Printer->Print(GetWindowPtr(GetActiveWindow()), printout, true);

  Printing--;
}
```

This code is fairly straightforward. The line

```
    Printer = new Tprinter(this);
```

creates a `Printer` object from the class `Tprinter` if necessary. Then the sentence

```
    TDocument* currentDoc = GetDocManager()->GetCurrentDoc();
```

uses the Document manager to determine which document object is the current document and assigns its address to a pointer called `currentDoc`. After some determination about the title and name of the document, the line

```
    Printer->Print(GetWindowPtr(GetActiveWindow()), printout, true);
```

fires up the Print dialog box and sends the document to the `Printer` object, which sends it to the printer.

   4. At this point, you would change the code in this function to fit your requirements, and choose Make All from the Project window.

You might want to alter the way printing is handled in your applications, but it is certain that you will want to write code to fill in all of the menu picks that are not implemented. The following procedure shows how to accomplish this.

1. With TQUE1App still selected in the class section, click on the + beside the CM_EXIT entry. This will expand the list to include the Command and Command Enable list entries. These are the two types of command handlers that you can create.

2. Highlight the entry for Command and click the right mouse button to bring up the floating menu, as shown in figure 28.17.

Fig. 28.17

The right mouse button brings up a menu to allow you to add a command handler.

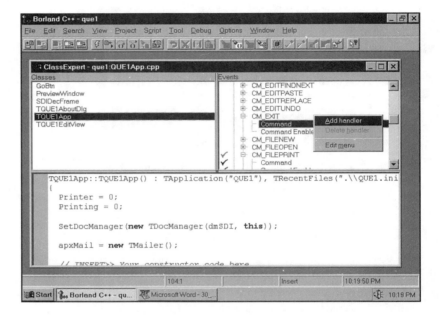

3. Click on <u>A</u>dd Handler to bring up the dialog box shown in figure 28.18.

4. Either choose a name to your own liking or accept the default of CmExit(). This will cause a new member function to be created that will be called whenever the <u>F</u>ile, E<u>x</u>it menu command is selected.

```
void TQUE1App::CmExit()

{

   // INSERT>> Your code here.

}
```

5. Insert code in place of the comment to satisfy the requirements of your system, then choose <u>M</u>ake All from the project window.

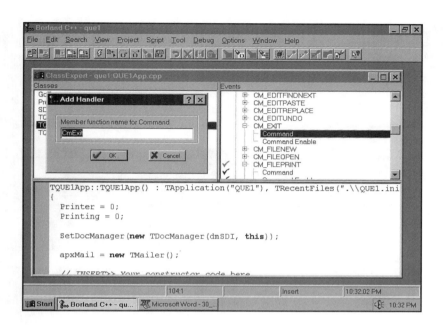

Fig. 28.18

The name of the command handler function is suggested but can be overridden by the programmer.

Examining and Creating the Windows Message Handlers

Another category of event handlers are the Windows message handlers. Unless you want your class to ignore all Windows messages, you will need to add code for all messages that you want to handle. The following procedure will show you how to examine the contents of a Windows message handler that was created by AppExpert:

1. Choose the TQUE1EditView class from the Classes section in ClassExpert.

2. Click on the + next to Windows Messages entry to expand the list of messages.

3. Notice that the Other Messages entry contains the check mark. This means that a handler exists for this Windows message category. Click on the + beside Other Messages to expand it further, as shown in figure 28.19.

Click on the WM_GETMINMAXINFO entry to display the event handler in the Source Code section. The code that the AppExpert has created is listed in listing 28.4.

Listing 28.4   The *EvGetMinMaxInfo()* Member Function Was Created by the AppExpert

```
void TQUE1EditView::EvGetMinMaxInfo(MINMAXINFO far& minmaxinfo)
{
  TQUE1App* theApp = TYPESAFE_DOWNCAST(GetApplication(), TQUE1App);
  if (theApp) {
    if (theApp->Printing) {
      minmaxinfo.ptMaxSize = TPoint(32000, 32000);
```

(continues)

V

Programming Tools

Listing 28.4 Continued

```
        minmaxinfo.ptMaxTrackSize = TPoint(32000, 32000);
        return;
      }
    }
    TEditView::EvGetMinMaxInfo(minmaxinfo);
}
```

Fig. 28.19

The Windows messages are trapped if a handler is created to respond to them.

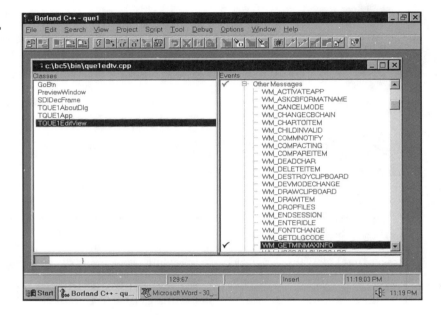

4. At this point you would change the code in this function to fit your requirements, and choose Make All from the Project window.

A different case would require that you add a new event handler to your application.
To do this, follow this procedure:

1. Select the message that you want to handle from the Event Handler section of
the ClassExpert.

2. Click on the right mouse button to open the menu.

3. Click on Add Handler. This will create the code in listing 28.5.

Listing 28.5 ClassExpert Adds Code to Receive the Windows Events

```
void TQUE1EditView::EvActivateApp(bool active, HTASK hTask)
{
    TEditView::EvActivateApp(active, hTask);
    // INSERT>> Your code here.
}
```

4. Replace the code in the function in place of the comments. Notice that the application will call the `EvActivateApp()` event handler function for the base class before executing your code. Be careful if you change this behavior, as it may cause interesting malfunctions.

From Here...

ClassExpert is a positive step in the direction of lean software production. Although it takes time to learn any tool, the time spent learning ClassExpert will be quickly offset by the time saved in modifying the class definitions of your Windows programs.

As you've now seen, ClassExpert is a very useful tool. At this point you may want to look at some related material elsewhere:

- Chapter 3, "Object-Oriented Analysis and Design," offers an introduction to design issues—including inheritance and polymorphism—related to object-oriented programming and C++ classes.

- Chapter 25, "Using the Graphics Device Interface," examines more examples of Windows graphics programming interfaces.

- Chapter 29, "Using the Integrated Debugger," demonstrates how to use the Integrated Debugger of Borland C++ 5 in your quest to track down and fix errors and problems within programs.

Using the Integrated Debugger

In this chapter you will learn how to use the Borland C++ Integrated Debugger. The Integrated Debugger is one of the most useful features of the Integrated Development Environment (IDE). The IDE provides you with a multitude of powerful tools to design, create and run your programs. All of these features are nice, but without the ability to track down and fix errors, you could spend countless hours trying to find and correct these bugs by hand.

In this chapter, you will learn

- What debugging is
- About the debugging options available
- How to step through your programs
- How to trace into functions
- What breakpoints are and how to use them
- Methods available to view program variables
- What the call stack is and how to view it

Understanding Debugging

Debugging refers to fixing a problem within a program. There can be as many types of bugs as there are styles of programming. Every one of us will, at some point, make errors. In fact, even the simplest programs usually go through a few corrections in order to work properly. This is no reflection on the programmer, by any means. The best programmers I have had the pleasure of working with have all told the same tale. No program will compile on the first attempt, and every program has bugs (even those you think are fine).

Having a program not compile for you means that you have made a syntax error of some type. The compiler did not understand what you typed. These errors are usually easy to find and correct, since the compiler will tell you what line and what function or variable caused the problem. Most of these errors can be attributed to mistyping a variable or function name, a missed semicolon to terminate a statement, or too many or too few braces to enclose a code block or a function. You have probably already seen several of these as you worked through the preceding chapters (I know that I did when writing them).

Debugging does not really refer to syntax errors. Your program will not compile, much less link and run, when there are syntax errors. Finding and correcting logical errors is where the Integrated Debugger will come in very handy. In the days before development suites and GUI tools, debugging was mainly done by inserting `printf()` statements into your code to print out the values of variables at certain points during execution. Beeping the speaker was another quick-and-dirty method for determining if program flow was making it to a certain point before the bug caused the problems. By using these two methods, you could isolate the offending section of code and then locate and repair the problem. Although this method did work, using these techniques on a very large application could take a very long time just to determine which source file the problem resided in.

Using the Integrated Debugger you can view, inspect, and modify variables and structures, insert breakpoints to stop execution at suspect points, and even evaluate expressions to determine their result.

The Integrated Debugger is an integral part of the Borland IDE. Even if you don't want or need to use it, you can't remove it; it's part of the package. When you have run any of your programs from earlier chapters, you have chosen Run from the Debug menu option of the IDE. This menu is shown in figure 29.1.

The Debug menu provides a lot more than just the ability to run your programs. The features of the debugger are discussed in the following section.

The following sections will show you how to become as productive at debugging your programs as you are at writing them. Remember, there can be a fine line between writing and debugging skills. Both are needed to be a successful programmer.

Fig. 29.1

The Debug menu of the IDE.

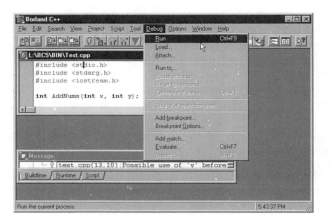

Understanding Debugger Functions

The Debugger can be used to find problems quickly and easily in your code. You can step through your program one line at a time, inspecting values along the way, until you find the problem. You can even edit the code when you find a problem. Be mindful, though, that if you edit your program while it is running, the Debugger will ask you if you want to recompile. While there may be a reason to say no to the recompilation, I can think of only a few cases where you might not want to do this. If you do not recompile the code, you will see the new code while the old code is actually running. This can be very confusing. To be safe, always recompile any changes that you make prior to further execution of the program.

Using Single-Stepping

Single-stepping through a program is one of the benefits that the Debugger provides. What is single-stepping, though? *Single-stepping* is a way for you to have each line of code execute and then suspend itself. It is this ability to suspend the program that provides you with the ability to view the values of variables or to check the return value from a function.

In order to understand how single-stepping works, let's take a look at a simple program that will illustrate how to do this. Type (or go to the CD-ROM that accompanies this book and use cut and paste) in the example shown in listing 29.1.

Listing 29.1   Debug01.cpp—Single-Stepping through a Program

```cpp
#include <stdio.h>
#include <stdarg.h>
#include <iostream.h>

int AddNums(int x, int y);

void main()
{
    int Result;
    int x = 5;
    int y;

    Result = AddNums(x, y);

    cout << "The returned value from AddNums is: " << Result << endl;

}

int AddNums(int x, int y)
{
    return (x + y);
}
```

In order to single-step through this program, you will need to choose Run To from the Debug menu. This selection acts very much like the Run command. If your program needs to be compiled prior to running, it will be. The main difference is that the program will not automatically execute. When you select Run To, you will see a screen similar to that shown in figure 29.2.

Fig. 29.2

Choosing Run To from the Debug menu.

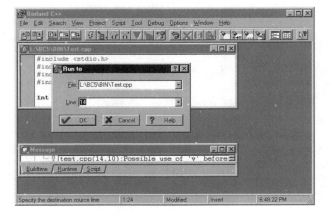

When you choose Run To, you are prompted for the line of the program to begin execution at. By default, the line shown is the first executable line in the main function (refer to fig. 29.2). Click OK to accept the default line number. You can continue stepping through the program until you reach the end, or you can stop at any point and inspect the state of the various parts of the program. To continue stepping through the program, you can either press F8, or you can display the context menu by right-clicking the mouse button anywhere in the code window. This menu is shown in figure 29.3. From the context menu, choose Statement Step Over to advance one line at a time through the program.

The Statement Step Over option is called that for a simple reason. Whenever a function call is encountered, the Debugger will step over the call. This means that the code in the function is executed and the results are returned, but you will not see the execution. The highlighting bar will simply move to the line of code following the function call.

To illustrate this, step over the call to the AddNums() function. You may have noticed that the step took a fraction longer when stepping over the function. This is caused by the overhead of calling the function, executing the code in the function, and returning before the Debugger can position the highlight bar on the next executable line of code and pause to await your next instruction. What if you want to be able to step into a function and see the logic flow or variable value inside the function? The Statement Step Into option on the Debug menu can be used for that purpose. Choose the Terminate Program option to end this application. The next section will show you how to trace into the AddNums() function.

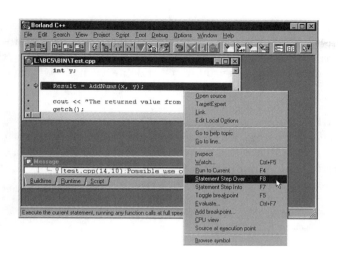

Fig. 29.3

Single-stepping over a function call.

Tracing into a Program

Tracing into a program is almost identical to stepping over a program, with one subtle difference. If the line of code to be executed is traced into and contains a function, the Debugger will branch to that function and wait patiently for your next command. Take the example shown in listing 29.1 and choose $\underline{S}$tatement Step Over. You will see the results shown in figure 29.2. Continue to step over the code until you have the call to the AddNums() function highlighted. Instead of choosing the $\underline{S}$tatement Step Over command from the context menu, choose $\underline{S}$tatement Step Into. You will see that the Debugger has moved you into the AddNums() function and is waiting for your next command. This is shown in figure 29.4.

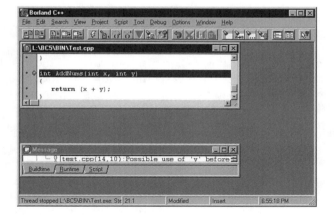

Fig. 29.4

Tracing into a function.

As you can see from figure 29.4, you can now step through the function just as you could through the main() function. The Debugger would be fairly worthless if you could step through only one function. Both the $\underline{S}$tatement Step Over and $\underline{S}$tatement

Step Into commands are ones that you will find yourself using quite often, although it can be quite tiresome to have to single-step through a very large program one line at a time. Most of the time you will want your program to run to a certain point and then stop and wait for you to decide what you want to see or do next. That is what breakpoints are for.

Setting Breakpoints

Breakpoints, combined with stepping over and tracing into your programs, provide you with a powerful set of tools that will allow you to let your program run to a certain location, and then stop and wait for you to determine if the program is acting as you expect. Enter the program shown in listing 29.2, but don't run it yet.

Listing 29.2 Debug02.cpp—Using Breakpoints

```
#include <iostream.h>

void main(void)
{
int LoopCtr = 0;
int NumArray[5];

    do {
        NumArray[LoopCtr] = LoopCtr+5;
        LoopCtr ++;
    } while ( LoopCtr < 5 );

LoopCtr = 0;
    do {
        cout << "NumArray[" << LoopCtr << "] holds the number " <<
            NumArray[LoopCtr] << endl;
        LoopCtr ++;
    } while ( LoopCtr < 5 );

}
```

After you have entered the program in listing 29.2, move your cursor to the line that sets the LoopCtr variable to 0. Choose the Add Breakpoint option from the Debug menu. You will be presented with a dialog box that allows you to set the properties of your breakpoint (see fig. 29.5).

The Add Breakpoint dialog box lets you define to the Debugger how you want this breakpoint to act. You can have an unconditional breakpoint that will cause the program to break every time it encounters the breakpoint. This is the default. You can also make a breakpoint conditional. This can be useful if you want the program to stop only if a variable is True, or if, for example, a loop counter reaches a certain number. These features are available by clicking the Advance button on the Add Breakpoint dialog box. For this breakpoint, just click the OK button to make this an unconditional breakpoint.

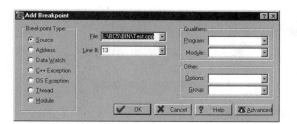

Fig. 29.5

The Add Breakpoint dialog box.

You will now see that your code window has a highlighted bar on the line you chose for your breakpoint. If you did not customize the color scheme of Borland C++, your breakpoint will be red, the default. Your screen should be similar to that shown in figure 29.6.

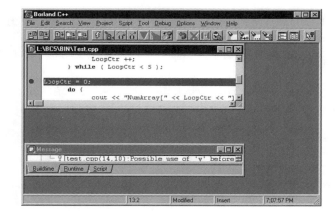

Fig. 29.6

A breakpoint shown in the code window.

Now that you have a breakpoint set, how do you use it? You could either step or trace your way to it, but that would defeat the purpose of the breakpoint. You should choose Run from the Debug menu. When you run the program, execution will stop at the breakpoint, just as if you were stepping or tracing through the program. This will allow your program to run through any code that you know is working, do any initialization, or gather input from the user without having to step through each line. Then when the program has reached the point that you want to debug, it will stop and wait for you to tell it what to do next. You can see this in figure 29.7. You can either step through the rest of the program or choose the Terminate Program option from the Debug menu.

The Debug menu offers another way to set a breakpoint. You can toggle a breakpoint on the line where your cursor is located. This will set or clear an unconditional breakpoint on that line. There will be no properties dialog box; the breakpoint will be just turned on or off. The hot key for this option is F5. Experimenting with this toggle will show you how easy it is to use.

Fig. 29.7

Execution of a program stopped on a breakpoint.

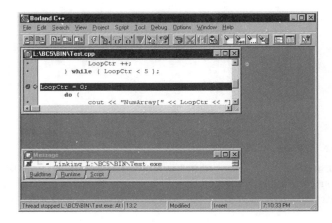

Now we will set a conditional breakpoint in the same program. First, toggle off the breakpoint that already exists. Next, move your cursor to the line inside the do...while loop that increments the LoopCtr variable. Choose Add Breakpoint from the Debug menu.

When the Add Breakpoint dialog box appears, click the Advanced button. Fill in the Expr. True text box as shown in figure 29.8. This instructs the Debugger to break at this line only when, and if, LoopCtr is equal to 3.

Fig. 29.8

Setting a conditional breakpoint.

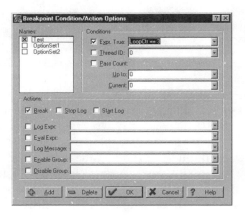

Run the program again. It will appear to have done nothing more than to have stopped on the breakpoint. So how do you know that the value of LoopCtr is really 3? One way is to trust the Debugger. It wouldn't have stopped there if LoopCtr hadn't been a 3, would it? The answer is no, it wouldn't have, but I always like to be able to see these things for myself.

You can take a quick peek at the data, just to be sure. To check the value of the LoopCtr variable, use the mouse to right-click on the variable, in this case, LoopCtr. You will see a pop-up menu similar to that shown in figure 29.9. Choose Inspect from the menu. You will see the value shown in a window, as seen in figure 29.10.

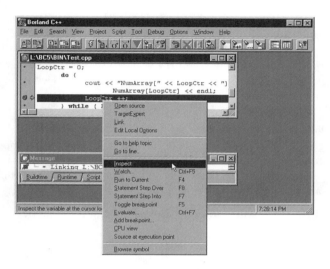

Fig. 29.9

The context menu for variables.

Fig. 29.10

The value of the variable LoopCtr *at the breakpoint.*

As you can see, without the ability to view the data that is contained within your program as you are debugging them, you would not really be able to know what the status of the program variables and execution is. The next section of this chapter will explore the different ways that you can view the data contained within your program through the features of the Debugger.

Viewing Data

The ability to view your program's data is perhaps the most valuable feature offered by the Integrated Debugger. When you are trying to determine why a loop is not executing properly, or why a value of a structure variable is not what you expect, you can use the capabilities of the Debugger for viewing this data. Your program has to be running in order to see the values of the data. With this in mind, you can see that you will need to use a combination of ways to suspend the program execution and the data-viewing capabilities. You have already seen how you can suspend the program's execution; this section will show you the different ways the Integrated Debugger offers for viewing your program's data.

Watches Windows

Perhaps the simplest method for seeing the value of a variable is the *Watches window*. This window will remain active on your screen, with the value of the variable(s) that you have chosen visible. This can be very handy if you want to see the changes in several variables as you are stepping through your program.

The example shown in listing 29.3 will be used to illustrate using the Watches window to view various types of variables.

Listing 29.3 Debug03.cpp—Using the Watches Window

```cpp
#include <iostream.h>
#include <ctype.h>

void main(void)
{
typedef struct _MyStruct
{
    int  iVar;
} MYSTRUCT;


MYSTRUCT NewStruct;
MYSTRUCT *pNewStruct = &NewStruct;

int LoopCtr = 0;
int NumArray[5];

    do {
        NumArray[LoopCtr] = LoopCtr+5;
        NewStruct.iVar = LoopCtr ++;
    } while ( LoopCtr < 5 );

LoopCtr = 0;
    do {
        cout << "NumArray[" << LoopCtr << "] holds the number " <<
            NumArray[LoopCtr] << endl;
        LoopCtr ++;
    } while ( LoopCtr < 5 );
```

```
        cout << "pNewStruct->iVar = " << pNewStruct->iVar << endl;

}
```

Type in the example shown in listing 29.3. You will need to set a breakpoint on the line that sets the `LoopCtr` variable to 0 (line number 23). You can do this by moving your cursor to this line and choosing <u>D</u>ebug, <u>A</u>dd Breakpoint or by pressing the F5 key. Choose <u>D</u>ebug, <u>R</u>un from the menu. The program will stop execution at the breakpoint.

Now you will need to choose which variables you want to view in the Watches window. This is done in one of two ways. You can move your cursor to the variable you are interested in viewing. Move your cursor to the variable `NumArray` on line 19. Then choose <u>D</u>ebug, Add <u>W</u>atch. You will see a dialog box like the one shown in figure 29.11.

Fig. 29.11

The Add Watch dialog box.

The dialog box shown in figure 29.11 allows you to define how you want to view the variable, array, or structure. For most purposes, choosing the default, as shown in the figure, will suffice. Click OK and you will see the Watches window as shown in figure 29.12.

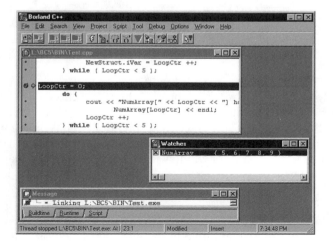

Fig. 29.12

The Watches window.

As you can see from figure 29.12, the array `NumArray` is shown. The values of the array can be easily viewed. You can add many watches to your Watches window. Each one will allow you to determine just what is happening within your program. The Watches window shown in figure 29.13 shows the various variables in the program being watched.

If you notice the last entry in the Watches window list, you will see that the value of `NumArray[LoopCtr]` is 4225533. This certainly does not seem to fit in with what you might expect the array to contain. In the code, you loaded the values 5 through 9 into the array. So why is the value not a 9? The answer is simple if you look at the value of `LoopCtr`. All C/C++ arrays begin with a zero-based index. That means that the valid array entries are 0 through 4. The value of `LoopCtr` is a 5. This shows you the area of memory just outside the `NumArray` variable. If you were to attempt to use this value, unpredictable results would occur. You will undoubtedly use the Watches window quite often. Experiment with trying to view different variables in your programs until you feel comfortable with what you can do with them.

Fig. 29.13

Assorted variables in the Watches window.

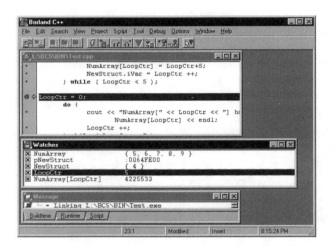

Inspector Windows

Inspector windows allow you to view a particular object. "Object," in this context, refers to any variable, structure, class, or pointer contained within your programs. Inspector windows are similar, in that they allow you to see the content of various program components. An Inspector window will allow you to view only one variable at a time. The information contained in the Inspector window is more comprehensive than that shown in a Watches window.

Using the program shown in listing 29.3, set a breakpoint on the line that sets the `LoopCtr` variable to 0. This is line 23.

1. Run the program. When the program stops at the breakpoint, you can choose different variables to inspect.

2. Choose the `LoopCtr` variable. This is done in the same manner as choosing a variable to watch. You can either highlight the variable, or place the cursor under it, and choose Inspect from the context menu to choose a variable for inspection. You will be shown the dialog box shown in figure 29.14, which allows you to confirm that the Debugger understood what variable you were interested in inspecting.

3. If the variable is not correct, you can either manually type in the correct variable, or choose Cancel, highlight the variable you want, and try again.

4. If you click OK, you will see the Inspector window containing that variable.

Figure 29.15 shows the Inspector window for the `LoopCtr` variable.

Fig. 29.14

The Inspect dialog box.

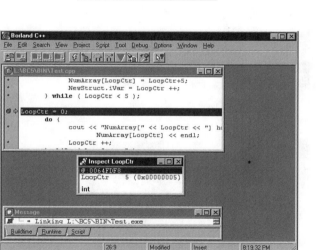

Fig. 29.15

The `Loop Ctr` *variable in the Inspector.*

Using the Inspector is especially helpful for viewing arrays and structures. Figures 29.16 and 29.17 show the `NumArray` and `NewStruct` variables, respectively.

If you look at the Inspector window shown in figure 29.15, you will see that the array is shown in its entirety. The subscripts are shown in the leftmost column, with their values shown on the right. Viewing a structure as shown in figure 29.16 shows you the member names, their data type, and their values in decimal and in hex. Both the Watches window and the Inspector window allow you to view variables. If you want to see what an expression will evaluate to, you can use the Evaluate option for that purpose.

Fig. 29.16

The NumArray variable in the Inspector.

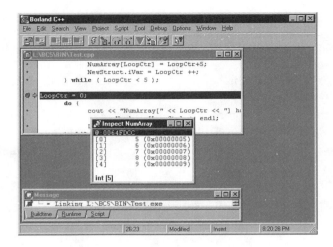

Fig. 29.17

The NewStruct variable in the Inspector.

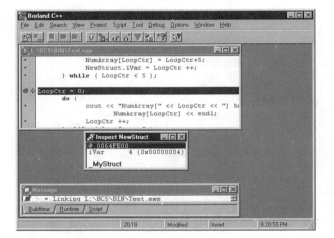

Evaluating Program Variables

Occasionally you will want to know what an expression will evaluate to. This is possible by choosing the Evaluate option on the context menu. Using the example shown in listing 29.3, set a breakpoint on the line that sets the value of LoopCtr to 0. Run the program.

Highlight the expression LoopCtr < 5, as shown in figure 29.18. Choose Evaluate from the context menu. You will see a dialog box as shown in figure 29.19.

If you select the f(x) Eval button you will see the result of the evaluation appear in the New Value entry field. Choose Eval for this expression. The result is false. Why? If you look at the value of LoopCtr, either in the Watches window or by using the Inspector, you will see that the LoopCtr variable is a 5, which is not less than 5.

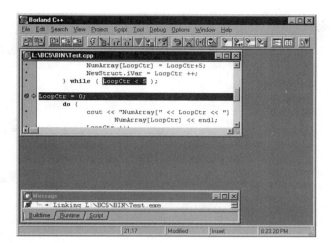

Fig. 29.18

Highlight an expression.

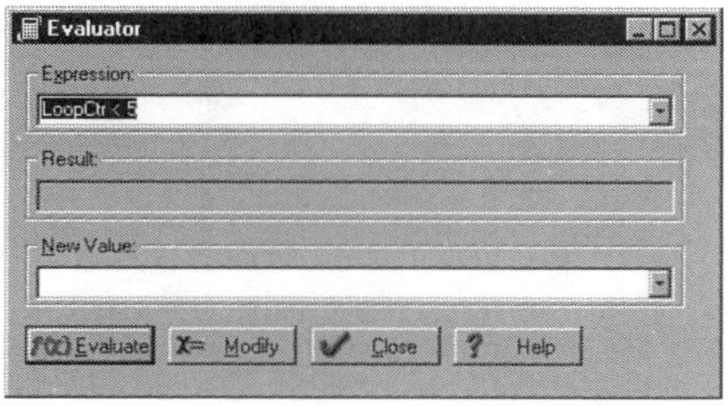

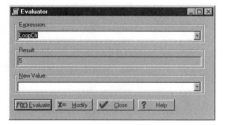

Fig. 29.19

The Evaluator dialog box.

V

Programming Tools

Fig. 29.20

Evaluating the LoopCtr variable.

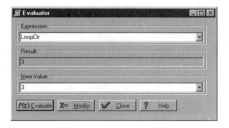

Fig. 29.21

Modifying the LoopCtr variable.

The Evaluate option can also be used to view and/or change the value of a variable. To illustrate, select the LoopCtr variable. Then select the Evaluate option on the context menu. Click OK on the Evaluator dialog box. Click Eval on the Evaluator, and you will see that the value is a 5, as shown in figure 29.20. Type in a **3** value and click the Modify button. The new value is displayed as shown in figure 29.21.

By using a combination of the Watches, Inspector, and Evaluator options, you can view and change the data in your programs. This will allow you to locate and correct any logical problems that may exist in your applications.

Viewing the Call Stack

There will be times when you will want to see the order in which functions have been called to make certain that your program is behaving as expected. This can be done by viewing the *Call Stack*. This View window allows you to see what functions have been called and in what order. By using the example shown in listing 29.4, you can see how the Call Stack works.

Listing 29.4   Debug04.cpp—Viewing the Call Stack

```cpp
#include <iostream.h>

void Func1(void);
void Func2(void);
void Func3(void);

void main(void)
{

    Func1();
    Func3();

}

void Func1(void)
{
    cout << "Inside of Func1" << endl;
    Func3();

}

void Func2(void)
{
    cout << "Inside of Func2" << endl;
}

void Func3(void)
{
    cout << "Inside of Func3" << endl;
    Func2();
}
```

Enter the code shown in listing 29.4. Set a breakpoint on the cout line inside the Func2() function. Run the program. When the program execution suspends, choose the <u>V</u>iew, Call <u>S</u>tack option shown in figure 29.22.

When you choose to view the Call <u>S</u>tack, you will see a dialog box similar to that shown in figure 29.23. This shows you the order of execution that your program has currently taken. The most recent function is shown at the top. In this case, it will be the Func2() function, since that is where the execution was suspended. The first function called, main(), is shown at the bottom of the list.

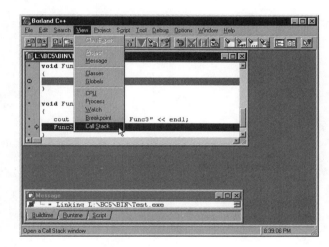

Fig. 29.22

The <u>V</u>iew, Call <u>S</u>tack menu option.

Fig. 29.23

Viewing the call stack.

From Here...

In this chapter, you learned about the fundamentals of debugging your programs. Any time you spend practicing and learning about the different features of the Borland C++ Debugger will pay off tenfold when you are writing your own applications.

- In chapter 2, "Using the Integrated Development Environment," you will learn about the different tools available from the IDE to help you create and customize your applications.

- In chapter 30, "WinSight and WinSpector," you will learn how to use these two powerful tools to monitor window messages and view applications while they run.

WinSight and WinSpector

This chapter examines two tools available with Borland C++ that allow you to perform debugging operations on your applications, as well as spy on the operation of other Windows applications. The WinSight application, included with Borland C++, provides you with the capability to examine Windows messages passed to and from Windows applications. These messages provide information to applications in order to execute operations within Windows.

The WinSpector application, also provided with Borland C++, provides a means of examining log files generated when an application crashes. The notorious *beep of death*, otherwise known as a UAE or Unrecoverable Application Error, causes grief for many programmers because trace information is never left by Windows. WinSpector allows log files to be generated when an application crashes so that you may know the state of an application when the crash occurred. WinSpector also allows you to examine the log files and better debug the errant application.

In this chapter, we review the following topics:

- What is WinSight?
- Tracing messages with WinSight
- Using WinSpector
- WinSpector reports

What Is WinSight?

WinSight is a Windows application that provides a means of monitoring Windows messages passed to and from Windows-based applications. Windows messages are used by applications to notify an application that a certain event has occurred. If the application is programmed to process the message, then the application accepts the message to perform certain operations.

WinSight captures these messages and displays them in a hierarchical view of the system's windows. The messages that WinSight tracks include mouse, window, input, system, initialization, clipboard, DDE, non-client, controls, and multimedia, as well as any user messages that are generated for a Windows application.

When viewing the Windows messages, WinSight can display a class list view, a window tree view, and a message trace view (see fig. 30.1). The class list view displays all the currently registered window classes in the operating system. These classes are those that are standard Windows classes, as well as those registered by user applications with the `RegisterClass()` function of the Windows API.

Fig. 30.1

WinSight displays information about windows, window classes, and messages being received and sent by Windows applications.

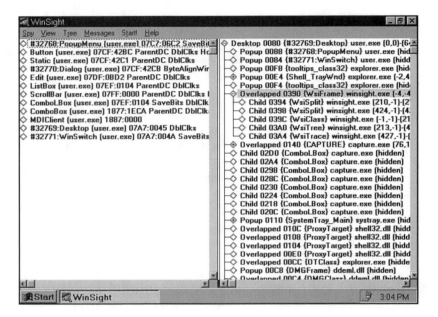

The window tree view displays the windows hierarchy for Windows. In this view you can determine what windows are actually present by visually determining the windows available within the hierarchy. You can also see the status of a window, including those windows that are currently hidden. Through status markers in WinSight, you can see which windows are receiving messages and select which of those windows you want to visually trace.

The message trace view displays detailed information about messages received by a particular window or by a selected class of windows. In this view, you see the actual information sent between applications as well as to and from any Windows application.

Using Windows Messages

Windows messages are an input method to an application. Each message represents events generated by Windows to which the application can respond. The message passed between applications is a structure that contains a message identifier and message parameters on which the application operates on.

Each message passed to a window contains several parameters that are used in both routing the message and passing information to a window (see listing 30.1). The hwnd parameter contains the handle to the window that is to receive the message. The message parameter is the message identifier to send to a window. Such messages include WM_COMMAND and WM_PAINT.

Listing 30.1   The Windows Message Structure Passes Event Information to Windows-Based Applications

```
typedef struct tagMSG
{
        HWND hwnd;
        UINT message;
        WPARAM wParam;
        LPARAM lParam;
        DWORD time;
        POINT pt;
} MSG;
```

The wParam and lParam parameters of a message contain additional information associated with the message parameter. For instance, if you are sending a message to a list box to add a string, you use LB_ADDSTRING as the message, wParam is equal to 0, and lParam contains a pointer to the string to be added to the list box. The values for lParam and wParam vary depending on the message value and can contain information for painting a window as well as DDE messages destined for other applications.

Tip

The handles all message-passing paradigms, but it is still a good idea to know what happens at the lower levels of a Windows application.

The time parameter specifies the system time when the message was posted. This time is used to determine when the message was placed into a queue and for managing double-clicks with the mouse. For instance, when you click the mouse on a window enabled to receive double-clicks, the window monitors the queue for a second click within a given period of time. If received, a double-click message is sent to the application queue (for example, WM_RBUTTONDBLCLK or WM_LBUTTONDBLCLK).

The pt parameter contains the X and Y coordinates of the cursor when a given message is posted. For instance, when the right mouse button is clicked over a window, the WM_RBUTTONDOWN message is sent to the window. In this instance, the pt parameter contains the X and Y screen coordinates of the mouse cursor when that click occurred.

> **Note**
>
> The cursor position of a message is returned in coordinates relative to the device or screen. To convert the device-relative coordinates to window-relative coordinates, you should use the DPtoLP() function of the Windows API.

Generating and Processing Messages

The Windows operating system generates a message for each event that occurs for a given Windows application. Such events include when the user moves the mouse or presses a key on the keyboard, when an application window is resized or moved, or when a control is selected in an application window.

As these message are generated, Windows places them in a kernel, or systemwide, message queue (see fig. 30.2). The Windows kernel then retrieves each message and passes them to an application message queue associated with the window handle, hwnd, located within the message.

A good analogy is that of sending letters to a friend. You address the letter, place it in the mailbox, and the postman picks it up and delivers it to your friend's mailbox, where it waits until he retrieves it. The kernel manages the systemwide message queue, which is the postman carrying letters in his sack. Once the kernel places the message in the application queue, it's the same as the letter waiting in your friend's mailbox.

Application message queues are first-in, first-out (FIFO) queues in which Windows places messages that belong to a specific application. The application reads each message each time the GetMessage() function is called within a message loop. The message is then dispatched to the appropriate window procedure with a call to the DispatchMessage() function.

> **Note**
>
> The two exceptions to the FIFO rule of Windows queues are WM_TIMER and WM_PAINT messages. These messages reside in an application's message queue until the application has completed all other messages.

Some Windows messages bypass the application queue and are passed directly to a window's callback function. These types of messages are appropriately named *unqueued messages,* since they are not queued up to the application message queue. For example, the CreateWindow() function sends the WM_CREATE message directly to the window procedure of an application and waits until the window procedure has processed the message. In this example there is no window available, as of yet, to which a message can be sent, so the only course of action is to send the message directly to the callback function.

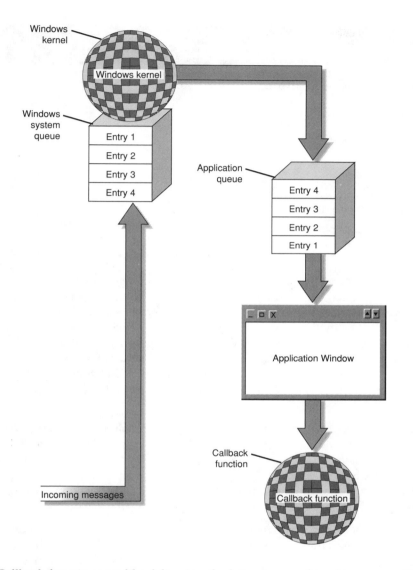

Callback functions are like delivering the letter to your friend in person. You don't bother with the mailman or wait for it to be delivered. Your friend takes the letter, reads it, and responds to you immediately.

Applications remove messages from an application queue by calling the `GetMessage()` function in a loop within its `WinMain()`. The *main message loop* (see listing 30.2), using the `GetMessage()` function, searches through an application's message queue and returns the top message in the queue. If the message queue is empty, the `GetMessage()` function relinquishes control to Windows, allowing other applications to process their own messages, and waits for a message to be placed in the application queue.

Listing 30.2   Retrieving Messages from the Application's Message Queue and Dispatching Them to the Appropriate Window

```
int PASCAL WinMain(HINSTANCE hinstCurrent, HINSTANCE hinstPrevious,
    LPSTR lpszCmdLine, int nCmdShow)
{
    MSG msg;

        .
        .
        .

    while (GetMessage(&msg, NULL, 0, 0)) {
        TranslateMessage(&msg);
        DispatchMessage(&msg);
    }
    return (int) msg.wParam;
}
```

When an application's GetMessage() function retrieves a message from the application's message queue, it dispatches the message to a window procedure with a call to the DispatchMessage() function. This function informs Windows that it should call the callback function of the window associated with the message (hwnd). During this call, Windows passes the message as the arguments to the callback function. The callback function then processes the message and performs any operations required by the message's contents. Upon a return from the callback function, control is returned to the main message loop so that it may then retrieve the next message from the queue.

This is very similar to what we do each day when we get our mail: first we go through the stack one by one, separating the bills and important items from the junk mail. Sometimes it seems that most mail is coupons, sales brochures, and catalogs for things we don't want. Likewise, Windows sends applications messages for every little thing that happens, like the mouse moving across the screen or the user changing the system colors. Most of these messages we probably don't want to worry about.

Going through the stack of incoming mail corresponds to the GetMessage() function. Dispatching the message is the process of putting it in our stack to examine. The DispatchMessage() function sends the message information to the callback function, where all the junk mail gets sorted out from what we want. Typically, the callback function has a huge switch statement that lists each message we want to respond to with some programming. Most of Windows programming is responding to these messages. Instead of calling functions to control the computer, a programmer is more likely to wait until certain things happen and then respond to them. That explains the popular saying, "This is Windows programming. Don't call us, we'll call you."

Examining Messages

Applications can also look at a message queue without actually removing them from the queue, as does the `GetMessage()` function. The `PeekMessage()` function allows an application to examine its message queue for specific messages without removing them from the queue. If a particular message being searched for by `PeekMessage()` exists in the application queue, the function returns a nonzero value and allows the application to retrieve the message and process it outside the application's main message loop.

Applications usually use `PeekMessage()` to check periodically for certain messages when the application is performing operations that do not relinquish control for a long period of time (for instance, processing input and output). For example, if an application is perfoming a repetitive operation that is ended by a message from the user, the application can use `PeekMessage()` to check when the terminating message arrives on the queue.

`GetMessage()` is like your friend getting the mail from his mailbox. `PeekMessage()` is more like him opening the box to see if a certain letter has arrived, without taking any of his mail out.

Sending Messages

The `SendMessage()` and `PostMessage()` Windows API functions provide a means of posting messages to windows of the current application as well as windows of other applications. The `SendMessage()` function informs Windows to send a message directly to a window's callback function, thus bypassing the application's message queue. Control is not returned to the caller until the called callback function processes the message or returns control by a call to the `ReplyMessage()` function.

The `PostMessage()` function informs Windows to place, or post, a message in an application's message queue. The `PostMessage()` function returns control to the caller immediately, and all subsequent processing is performed asynchronously.

Exploring the Elements of WinSight

Now that you have an understanding of the underlying messaging of Windows, let's examine the features of WinSight used to trace and examine the messages exchanged by Windows-based applications.

To start WinSight, simply double-click its icon within the Borland C++ program folder. Once WinSight is started you see a window in which you can view a window tree, window classes, and window messages (see fig. 30.3). Each of the different views can be selected from the <u>V</u>iew menu selection of the WinSight window.

V

Programming Tools

Fig. 30.3

WinSight allows you to view the window classes and a window tree, as well as window messages.

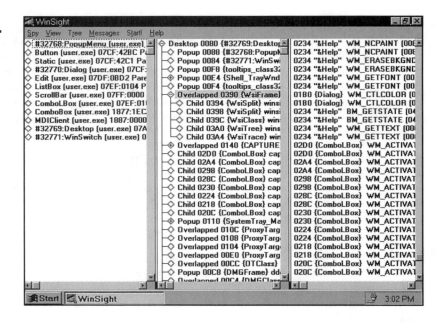

Window Tree View

To view the window tree, choose View, Window Tree. This selection loads the window tree window, as shown in figure 30.4, to show you all of the top-level windows in the system.

Fig. 30.4

The window tree view contains a hierarchical view of the windows currently active in the system.

The format for each entry in the tree contains information about the top-level windows in the following format:

```
Tree Handle {Class} Module Position "Title"
```

The `Tree` of the windows contains lines and diamonds representing the hierarchy of the windows. Some of the diamonds contain plus signs, representing the fact that the top-level window presented contains children.

- To view the siblings simply click the diamond with the mouse, press the + key on the keyboard, or choose Tree, Expand One Level. When expanded, the plus sign changes to a minus, meaning that the branch can be collapsed back to the single entry for the parent.

- To collapse a branch, click the diamond with the mouse, select the – key on the keyboard, or choose Tree, Collapse Branch.

- To expand all branches, choose Tree, Expand All or press Ctrl+*.

- To expand one entire branch, as opposed to one level of the branch, choose Tree, Expand Branch or press the * key on the keyboard.

The `Handle` parameter of a window branch is the handle to the window created by the `CreateWindow()` function called by the application. This handle is used by Windows to know which window callback function is to receive a message based on the `hwnd` parameter of the message.

The `Class` parameter is the name of the window class from which the repsective window tree entry was created. Some default window classes have numeric values and are therefore displayed with the numeric value and a name. User-defined classes have only names and are displayed with that name in the window hierarchy.

The `Module` name is the name of the application associated with the window in the window tree.

The `Position` parameter is the position of the window in the user desktop. If the window is a hidden window, the text (`hidden`) appears; otherwise, the X and Y position of the window appears. For top-level windows, the X and Y coordinates are relative to the screen as (`xBegin, yBegin`)-(`xEnd, yEnd`). All children provide coordinates relative to the parent window.

The `"Title"` is the text title returned by `GetWindowText()` or a `WM_GETTEXT` message sent to the window. If the title of the window is nonexistent, or `NULL`, the quotation marks are omitted, and no text appears for the title in the window tree view.

By double-clicking, pressing the Enter key on any of the window items in the window tree view, or choosing Spy, Open Detail, you can access a detail window containing additional information about a given window (see fig. 30.5). The detail window displays the class name and executable module, as well as information inherited from the class associated with the selected window.

V

Programming Tools

Fig. 30.5

The detail window provides additional information about the window selected from the window tree view.

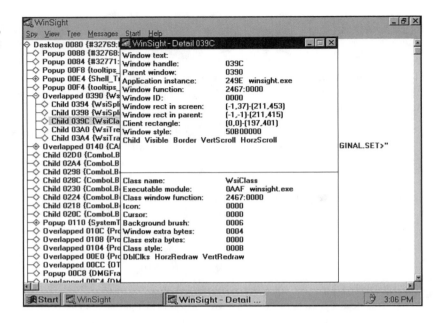

Periodically you will notice that the diamonds for the window tree items fill with black. This color change represents the fact that a message had been passed to the window associated with the flashing diamond. Later in this chapter, we will discuss the actual messages that are detected by WinSight whenever the diamond flashes.

Window Class View

Accessed by choosing View, Class List, this allows you to view all of the window classes available in the system. These classes are used by applications with the CreateWindow() function to create a window with characteristics of a selected class (see fig. 30.6).

The format for each entry in the class list contains information about the classes in the following format:

```
Class (Module) Function Styles
```

The Class parameter contains the same class names listed in the window tree view. Some default classes have numeric values and, therefore, appear with the numeric value and a name. User-defined classes have only names and appear with that name in the window hierarchy.

The Module parameter is the name of the application or dynamic link library that registered the class.

The Function parameter is the address, or name, of the callback function of the associated class. Each window class registered with the RegisterClass() function uses the WNDCLASS structure for storage of class-specific information. The lpfnWndProc member of the structure contains a pointer to the callback function which is used for this parameter of the class list display.

Fig. 30.6

The class view contains a list of the window classes available under Windows for use by applications to create class-specific windows.

The Styles parameter contains a list of styles associated with the window class. These styles determine how windows derived from a class appear and function in the Windows environment.

By double-clicking, pressing the Enter key on any of the window items in the window tree view, or choosing Spy, Open Detail, you can access a detail window containing additional information about a given class (see fig. 30.7). The detail window displays the class name and executable module, as well as information contained in the WNDCLASS structure used to register the class with the RegisterClass() function.

Fig. 30.7

The detail window for a class displays detailed information about a selected window class.

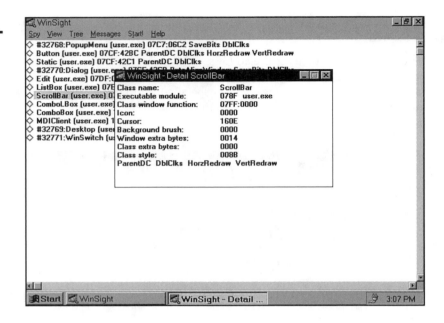

Message Trace View

Using the window or class views of WinSight allows you to monitor messages being passed between applications and Windows. The message trace view, accessed by choosing View, Message Trace, displays information about messages received by selected windows or windows classes (see fig. 30.8).

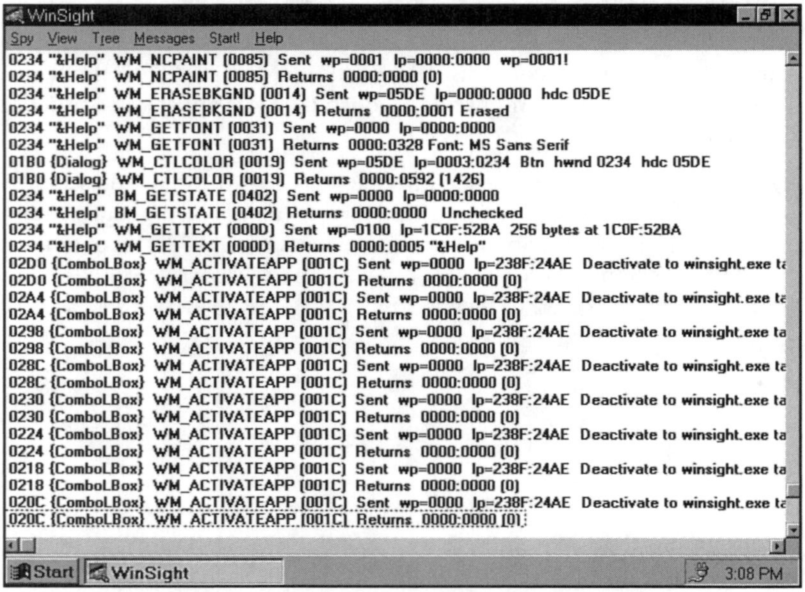

Fig. 30.8

The message trace view contains a list of the messages intercepted by WinSight for a given window or window class.

The format for each entry in the message list contains information about the messages in the following format:

```
Handle "Title"-or-{Class} Message Status
```

The `Handle` parameter is the destination window handle for a message. This handle is used by Windows to determine the appropriate callback function to call in order to process the message.

The `"Title"` or `Class` parameter represents the window title or the window class receiving the message. The parameter can be one or the other depending on the type of tracing you are doing. If tracing messages for a particular class, then the class name is listed; otherwise, the window title is visible.

The `Message` parameter is the actual message passed to the application. This message is the identifier stored in the `message` member of the message structure (refer to listing 30.1) passed between applications.

The `Status` parameter can be one of three possible items. The first, `Dispatched`, means that the message was sent via `DispatchMessage()`. The second, `Returns X`, is a return message sent from an application as a response to a call to the `SendMessage()` function. The `X` represents the actual value returned from the application that received the message sent by `SendMessage()`. The third, `Sent [from XXXX]`, means that the message was sent by a call to `SendMessage()`. If sent from another window, the `from XXXX` contains the handle of the window that sent the message. If the message was sent from the same application that received it, this parameter reads `Sent from self`. If the message was sent from Windows itself, the entire `from` phrase is omitted.

Messages sent by `SendMessage()` are shown twice in the message view. The first occurrence is when messages are sent to an application, and the second is when the application sends a return to the originating application. Messages sent by `DispatchMessage()` are shown only once since their return value is meaningless.

To filter messages that you want to monitor during a message trace, choose Messages, Options. This selection opens the Message Trace Options dialog box shown in figure 30.9.

Selecting the All Messages checkbox, the default mode, enables WinSight to capture every message that is passed in the Windows environment. You also have the option of selecting one of several groups of messages by selecting the respective checkbox of the group.

To monitor one or more specific messages, you can deselect the All Messages checkbox and use the list at the right of the dialog box (see fig. 30.10). You can use the mouse and scroll through the list, selecting the desired messages by clicking them with your mouse.

V

Programming Tools

Fig. 30.9

The Message Trace Options dialog box allows you to filter all or only those messages that you want to trace.

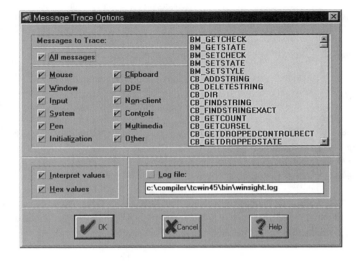

Fig. 30.10

From the Message Trace Options dialog box you can select specific messages that you want to trace.

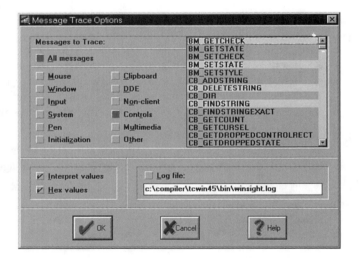

The Interpret Values checkbox enables WinSight to interpret all messages that are intercepted. This interpretation reads the information stored in the message and converts them into a readable form. The Hex Values checkbox enables the display of information stored in intercepted messages as hexadecimal values.

Selecting the Log File checkbox enables WinSight to save information collected from intercepted messages into the file named in the text box. In figure 30.10, the file in which messages would be logged if the checkbox were selected is Winsight.log.

Tracing Messages with WinSight

Monitoring the activity of windows or classes sending and receiving messages allows you to trace the patterns of these messages. Tracing messages with WinSight involves each of the views that we have just discussed. The window tree and class views are used to select windows and classes for which messages are traced, while the message trace view displays these messages.

To begin a trace session, you must first select the messages you want to trace. This is accomplished in the Message Trace Options dialog box (refer to fig. 30.10). By selecting which groups or which specific messages you want to monitor, you are filtering out a lot of messages that might otherwise get in the way of an effective trace session.

You may select to monitor messages for a particular class or group of classes, messages for a window or group of windows, or messages for all windows.

1. To select classes to monitor, you must first select the class view from the menu by choosing View, Class List.

2. Once the class view is selected, you can select the classes you want to monitor from the class window by holding down the Shift key and selecting the classes with your mouse.

   Holding the Shift key allows you to select more than one class of window to monitor.

Once the classes are selected, choose Messages, Selected Classes from the WinSight menu. WinSight begins tracing the messages and displays any events that occur in any window derived from the selected class in the message view (see fig. 30.11). For example, you may want to monitor all the messages sent to list boxes, or perhaps you have created your own custom control and want to see how it responds to messages.

To monitor messages for one or more windows, you must select the window tree view by choosing View, Window Tree. In the window tree view, you can select the windows you want to monitor by holding down the Shift key and selecting the windows with your mouse. Holding the Shift key allows you to select more than one window to monitor.

To monitor the selected windows, you must choose Message, Selected Windows. This selection allows monitoring of messages with destination window handles of those windows selected in the window view (see fig. 30.12).

To monitor all windows for messages, choose Messages, All Windows. WinSight starts tracing all messages selected in the Message Trace Options dialog box (see fig. 30.13).

Fig. 30.11

WinSight allows you to monitor messages destined for windows of a particular class.

Fig. 30.12

Choosing the Selected Windows menu selection begins the trace for the windows selected in the window tree view.

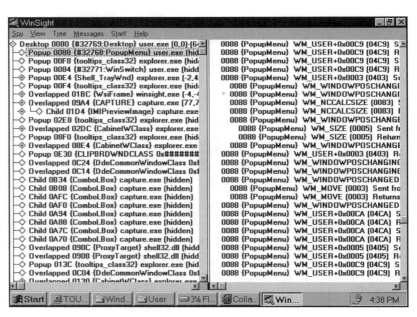

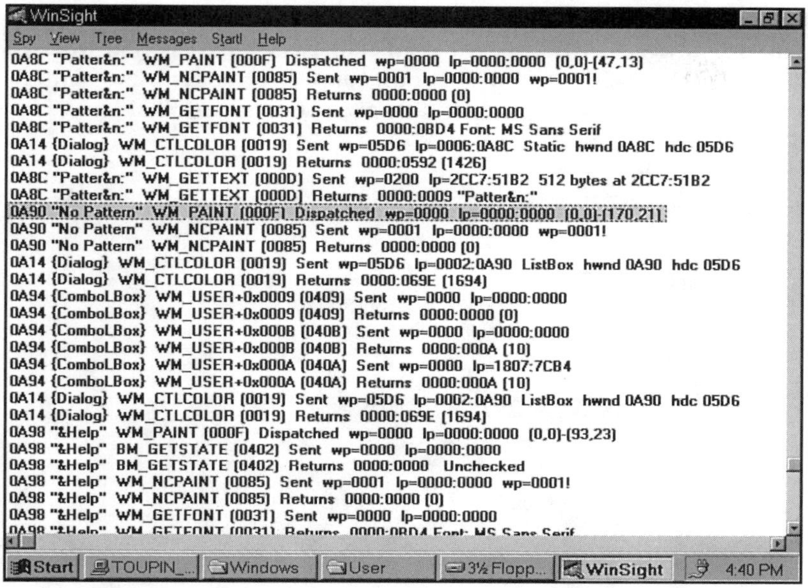

Fig. 30.13

WinSight also allows you to monitor messages destined for all windows currently available in the operating system.

There are three important selections available that start and stop tracing of messages by WinSight: Messages, Trace Off; Start!; and Stop! Choosing Messages, Trace Off turns off all tracing of messages. This selection is mutually exclusive with the All Windows, Selected Classes, and Selected Windows menu selections.

Selecting the Stop! command also stops tracing; however, this selection additionally stops WinSight from performing real-time updates of its user interface. In this instance, WinSight waits idly until you select the Start! menu option. To trace, you must also have selected the Start! menu option; otherwise, no updates to WinSight occur.

> **Tip**
>
> The Start! and Stop! menu selections in WinSight are actually the same menu selection. Selecting Start! toggles the menu selection to Stop! During a trace operation, selecting Stop! toggles the menu selection back to Start!

Using the WinSpector Application

The WinSpector application and its utilities allow you to perform postmortem examination of information generated by applications that experience Unrecoverable Application Errors (UAE) or General Protection Errors (also General Protection Exceptions).

V

Programming Tools

UAEs and GPEs occur whenever the application performs an operation from which the application cannot recover (see fig. 30.14). For instance, such errors occur whenever you *step on* memory that is being used by another application or another part of the current application. The following block of code generates an error that is capturable by WinSpector:

```
#include <string.h>

void main()
{
        char *tempchar;
        strcpy(tempchar,"This will give us a GPE");
}
```

Fig. 30.14

When a General Protection Error occurs, Windows displays an Unhandled Exception dialog box.

The variable `tempchar` is declared as a pointer to a `char` data type, but it is never allocated for storage. The line `strcpy(tempchar,"This will give us a GPE")` copies a string into the unallocated variable. The reason that the application crashes is that a 24-character string, including the terminator, is being copied into a block of memory reserved for a pointer (four bytes). When copied, the string overwrites any information that resides in the adjoining memory, causing the GPE.

When a Windows Unrecoverable Application Error box or General Protection Error box is displayed, click the OK or Close button to close the error window. At that point, a WinSpector dialog box containing a brief exception report appears. To read the log file generated by WinSpector, simply click OK.

The log file contains information that can help you find the cause of an exception. WinSpector provides for you the call stack, function names in the call stack at the time of the crash, registers of the CPU, a disassembly listing of the instructions current at the time of the crash, and Windows information at the time of the crash.

Configuring and Starting WinSpector

Before using WinSpector, make sure that the Toolhelp.dll library is available in your system's path. To ensure proper operation of WinSpector, make sure that no other other exception debugging tools are running concurrent with WinSpector.

Start WinSpector by double-clicking the WinSpector icon located in the Borland C++ program folder. Once started, WinSpector appears as an icon in the Windows 95 taskbar (see fig. 30.15).

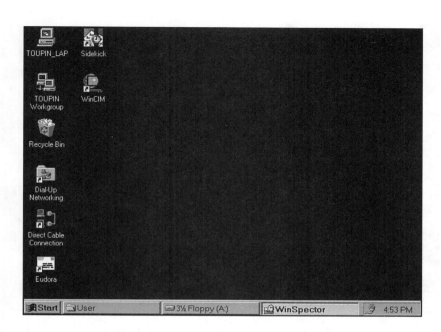

Fig. 30.15

On startup, WinSpector appears in the Windows 95 taskbar.

Clicking the taskbar icon for WinSpector displays a dialog box informing you of the status of WinSpector as well as providing access to the configuration portion of WinSpector (see fig. 30.16).

Fig. 30.16

The WinSpector dialog box provides access to error information as well as the configuration dialog box.

To configure WinSpector, click the Set Prefs button. When selected, the main dialog box disappears, and the WinSpector Preferences dialog box appears to allow you to select configuration information (see fig. 30.17).

The Directory text box of the dialog box allows you to select where the log file is generated. The Viewer text box allows you to select the text editor that you want to use to view the log file. Append New Reports (Alt+A) and Overwrite Previous Reports are mutually exclusive and determine how the log files are generated. If Append New Reports is selected, each new log file generated is appended to any existing WinSpector logs for the selected Directory. Selecting Overwrite Previous Reports causes WinSpector to delete any previous log files and create a new log file for each error.

Programming Tools

Fig. 30.17

The WinSpector Prefer-
ences dialog box allows
you to configure
WinSpector to handle
logging operations for
errors.

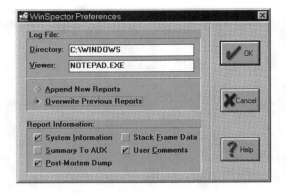

The Report Information checkboxes allow you to tailor the generation of log files for errors captured by WinSpector. Selecting the System Information checkbox lets you add the Task List, Module List, and information about the USER and GDI heaps to the log file. The Summary to AUX checkbox lets WinSpector write a summary version of the report to the standard DOS file AUX (referenced as STDAUX in the C library) in addition to writing the log file to the directory.

The Post-Mortem Dump checkbox generates a Winspctr.bin file. The DFA utility takes a Winspctr.bin file and Turbo Debugger information (.tds files) and translates the raw binary data into a readable format. It generates a file that contains a stack trace similar to the one in the log file but with function names and line numbers, as well as local and global variables.

The Stack Frame Data checkbox adds a verbose stack trace display to the log file. For each stack frame that does not exceed 256 bytes, a hex dump is performed, starting at the SS:BP for that frame. If there are more than 256 bytes between two successive stack frames, the memory display is omitted for that frame. This data can be used to get the values of parameters that were passed to the function.

The User Comments checkbox allows you to add information about what happened at the time the error occurred. To allow you to enter your comments, a dialog box appears for your comment entry immediately after the exception log is written (see fig. 30.18). All of your comments are appended to the end of the log file.

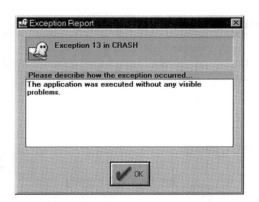

Fig. 30.18

WinSpector allows you to enter comments for each error.

Using the DFA Utility

The DFA Utility processes information for Turbo Debugger gathered by WinSpector at the time an exception occurs. If configuration information is set to collect a post-mortem dump, WinSpector writes a Winspctr.bin file that can be used by the DFA Utility to create a file containing useful information.

Since only one Winspctr.bin file is written for each Windows session, make sure you run DFA immediately after a UAE has occurred. For example, if three UAEs occur in succession, WinSpector writes three reports to the log file, but binary data exists for only the first report. For this reason it is suggessted that DFA be executed immediately after receiving the first UAE.

The following command line demonstrates how you execute the DFA Utility:

```
DFA [option] <WINSPCTR.LOG> [WINSPCTR.BIN]
```

Command-line options for DFA:

/0[outputfile]	(DFA.OUT default)
/D	(DFA writes out a hex dump of the saved data segments)

When using the DFA Utility, the Winspctr.log generated by WinSpector at the time of a error is required. With Winspctr.log, you get source file and line numbers, while with the Winspctr.bin file you get variable information.

If the utility is used with the Winspctr.log file alone, DFA generates minimal stack trace information, including addresses. Source file names and line numbers are added to the report when Turbo Debugger information in a .tds is present, either in the executable file or in a separate file.

When used with the Winspctr.bin file, DFA generates additional information. Such information includes stack-based variables, including structures and arrays, as well as variable types, values, and addresses.

V

Programming Tools

Understanding the WinSpector Log File

WinSpector creates a report file (Winspctr.log) when a UAE or GPE occurs. The log file can be helpful in finding out what caused the exception. The latest log file can be viewed directly from the Latest UAE dialog box.

To view the report, load WinSpector from the taskbar by clicking WinSpector's icon. Notice that the text within the dialog box has changed to state that a UAE has occurred, as well as the time at which it occurred (see fig. 30.19). To view the log file, click the View Log button on the dialog box.

Fig. 30.19

When a UAE occurs, the text in the WinSpector dialog box shows that a UAE occurred, as well as the time at which the error occurred.

The log file in listing 30.3 was generated when the application that generated the UAE shown in figure 30.14 crashed. The first line of the log file contains the date and time that the error occurred as well as the title of the exception report. The second line of the log file lists the type of exception that occurred, the errant module name, the logical and physical addresses at which the error occurred, and the currently running task at the time of the exception.

Listing 30.3   The Top of the WinSpector Log File Contains Information about the Exception Report for the Most Recent Exception

```
========
WinSpector failure report - 4/10/1995  12:51:51
Exception 13 at CRASH 0002:0034 (351F:0034)  (TASK=CRASH)

Disassembly:
351F:0034  POP     DS
351F:0035  POP     BP
351F:0036  DEC     BP
351F:0037  RETF
351F:0038  ADD     BYTE PTR [BX+SI],AL

Stack Trace:
0   CRASH      <no info>
    CS:IP 0002:0034 (351F:0034)   SS:BP 347F:2DB2
    C:\COMPILER\TCWIN45\WORK\CRASH.EXE
```

The Disassembly section contains the assembly language version of the instruction that caused the exception. This information is followed by subsequent commands that are listed to provide a point of reference for locating the task that caused the exception.

The first line of the Stack Trace section identifies the function or procedure that was executing at the time of the exception. The Stack Trace information includes the frame number, errant module name, the name of the function immediately preceding the address of the one that caused the exception, plus a number indicating the distance from that function. This information allows you to locate rapidly the code in which the error occurred.

The Stack Trace information also contains the logical and physical address for the stack frame, as well as the location the program returns to after the call.

Listing 30.4 contains the Registers and Message Queue sections of the log file. The Registers section contains the values that are in the standard registers at the time of the exception. The Message Queue section contains the last message actually received in the middle of processing. Also appearing is a list of any messages that were waiting in the queue at the time of the exception. When the exception for listing 30.4 occurred, no messages were in the queue; therefore, the message No messages in queue is shown in the log file.

Programming Tools

V

Listing 30.4 The *Registers* Section of the Log File Contains Information about the Values Stored in the System Registers at the Time of the Crash

```
Registers:
AX    0010
BX    FFF0
CX    0000
DX    0000
SI    0C1C
DI    0C46
SP    2DB0
BP    2DB2
IP    0034
FL    0206
CS    351F Limit: 003F  execute/read
DS    347F Limit: 3DDF  read/write
ES    347F Limit: 3DDF  read/write
SS    347F Limit: 3DDF  read/write

Message Queue:
No messages in queue
```

The sections shown in listing 30.5 show the Tasks and Modules section of the log file. The Tasks section lists all programs running in the system at the time of the exception. Information given with the exception includes the complete path to the application, the name of the module, the handle to the module, a handle to the task, and the data segment, or instance handle, value for the task.

Similar to the Tasks section, the Modules section contains information about the modules currently loaded in the system at the time of the exception. Information given in the `Modules` section includes the path to the module, the date of creation and file size of the module, the module's handle, and the reference count of the module.

Note

A reference count is the number of times the module is accessed by other applications.

Listing 30.5   The *Tasks* and *Modules* Sections of the Log File Display Information about the Tasks that Were Currently Running at the Time of the Exception

```
Tasks:
C:\WINDOWS\SYSTEM\SYSTRAY.EXE
     Module: Systray    hModule: 1D3F   hTask: 1E9E   hInstance: 1E9E
C:\WINDOWS\EXPLORER.EXE
     Module: Explorer   hModule: 1ED7   hTask: 1EDE   hInstance: 1EDE
C:\WINDOWS\SYSTEM\MPREXE.EXE
     Module: Mprexe     hModule: 1FF7   hTask: 2016   hInstance: 2016
C:\WINDOWS\SYSTEM\MSGSRV32.EXE
     Module: MSGSRV32   hModule: 1517   hTask: 1506   hInstance: 14E6
C:\COMPILER\TCWIN45\BIN\WINSPCTR.EXE
     Module: WINSPCTR   hModule: 1F3F   hTask: 1C76   hInstance: 1C66
C:\WINDOWS\SYSTEM\KRNL386.EXE
     Module: KERNEL32   hModule: 010F   hTask: 0097   hInstance: 0097
C:\COMPILER\TCWIN45\BIN\TCW.EXE
     Module: TCW        hModule: 06F7   hTask: 1F16   hInstance: 2826
C:\COMPILER\TCWIN45\WORK\CRASH.EXE
     Module: CRASH      hModule: 348F   hTask: 3436   hInstance: 347E

Modules:
C:\WINDOWS\SYSTEM\KRNL386.EXE          Date: 03/02/1995  Size: 120832
     Module: KERNEL     hModule: 010F  reference count: 63
C:\WINDOWS\SYSTEM\system.drv           Date: 03/02/1995  Size: 2160
     Module: SYSTEM     hModule: 01DF  reference count: 42
C:\COMPILER\TCWIN45\BIN\TCWDBV16.DLL  Date: 01/26/1995  Size: 380416
     Module: TCWDBV16   hModule: 296F  reference count: 1
C:\COMPILER\TCWIN45\BIN\TCWS16.DLL     Date: 01/26/1995  Size: 820629
     Module: TCWS16     hModule: 2967  reference count: 2
C:\COMPILER\TCWIN45\BIN\TCWDBK16.DLL  Date: 01/26/1995  Size: 243200
     Module: TCWDBK16   hModule: 3677  reference count: 1
C:\COMPILER\TCWIN45\WORK\crash.exe     Date: 04/10/1995  Size: 66642
     Module: CRASH      hModule: 348F  reference count: 1
(Many other module listings follow here)
```

The sections in listing 30.6 contain system information at the time of the exception. The USER and GDI information section contains the percentage of both the USER and GDI heap available at the time of the exception.

> **Tip**
>
> Since Windows 3.1 maintains only 64K of heap space for applications to share, it is a good idea to keep track of used space if you're developing for this platform. Even in Windows 95, memory usage is an important consideration. If the USER and GDI percentages are low, representative of the application taking up a lot of heap space, make sure that you have deallocated resources not in use.

The System info section of the log file contains the mode and Windows version under which your program was operating. Other such information includes CPU information, the largest free memory block, total linear memory space, free linear memory space, and swap file pages.

The final section at the end of the log file contains the user comments entered at the time of the exception. These comments are primarily used to understand the operational circumstances, as observed by the user, in which the error occurred.

Listing 30.6   The Last Section of the Log File Contains System Information as well as the User Comments Entered by the User when the Exception Occurred

```
USER  Free  93%
GDI   Free  91%

System info:
Running in enhanced mode under Windows 3.95 retail version
CPU: 80486
Largest free memory block: 15548416 bytes
Total linear memory space: 58480 K
Free linear memory space : 15184 K
Swap file Pages: 31b2 (50888 K)


- - - - - - - - - - - - - - - - - - - - - -
The application was executed without any visible problems.
```

Listing 30.7 contains an abbreviated listing of the detailed report generated by the DFA Utility. This file is generated when the Winspctr.log and Winspctr.bin files are used with the DFA Utility.

The first section of the output contains the source file, line number, local variables, and parameters of any calls. Section two of the listing contains the module name for the task with the fault, file names associated with the fault, segments and selectors, and whether the contents are data or code.

The third section of the report contains information such as global variables, static variables, and values at the time of the exception. The final section is a hexadecimal dump of the application as it appeared when the exception occurred.

V

Programming Tools

Listing 30.7   Running DFA on the Winspctr.log and Winspctr.bin File Generates a Detailed Listing of the Post-Mortem Dump as a Result of the Exception

```
==========

0   CRASH       _strcpy +001A
    CS:IP 0001:04BE (34E7:04BE)   SS:BP 3407:2D06
    C:\COMPILER\TCWIN45\WORK\CRASH.EXE


==========

1   CRASH       _main +001C
    CS:IP 0002:001C (33FF:001C)   SS:BP 3407:2D1A
    C:\COMPILER\TCWIN45\WORK\CRASH.EXE
    CRASH.CPP line: 7

SS:2D14 tempchar
char far *  446F:33EF

==========

2   CRASH       WINMAIN +001B
    CS:IP 0001:5503 (34E7:5503)   SS:BP 3407:2D3C
    C:\COMPILER\TCWIN45\WORK\CRASH.EXE


==========

Module:   CRASH
Filename: C:\COMPILER\TCWIN45\WORK\crash.exe

Segments:
  Segment 01  Selector: 34E7  Length 58A0  CODE
  Segment 02  Selector: 33FF  Length 0040  CODE
  Segment 03  Selector: 33EF  Length 36E0  CODE
  Segment 04  Selector: 34F7  Length 0C40  CODE
  Segment 05  Selector: 3407  Length 3D40  DATA

Data Dumps:

Segment: 05  Selector: 3407  Length 3D40  Offset: 01A0

0000: 00 00 00 00 00 00 50 2D  00 00 D4 0D 3E 2D 3E 2D  ......P-....>->-
0010: 02 00 00 00 FF FF A4 02  07 34 ED FE 00 00 00 00  .........4......
0020: 00 00 00 00 00 00 00 00  00 00 00 00 00 00 00 00  ................
0030: 00 00 08 00 04 00 01 00  4F 34 06 34 00 00 80 00  ........O4.4....
0040: 01 00 07 00 00 00 00 01  00 00 00 42 6F 72 6C 61  ...........Borla
0050: 6E 64 20 43 2B 2B 20 2D  20 43 6F 70 79 72 69 67  nd C++ - Copyrig
0060: 68 74 20 31 39 39 34 20  42 6F 72 6C 61 6E 64 20  ht 1994 Borland
0070: 49 6E 74 6C 2E 00 54 68  69 73 20 77 69 6C 6C 20  Intl..This will
0080: 67 69 76 65 20 75 73 20  61 20 47 50 45 00 00 80  give us a GPE...
0090: 00 80 00 80 00 80 50 00  19 00 50 00 90 01 00 00  ......P...P.....
00A0: 00 00 00 00 00 00 01 00  AE 01 07 34 01 00 01 00  ...........4....
00B0: 01 00 00 00 00 00 03 00  A7 27 E7 34 00 00 00 00  .........'.4....
```

```
00C0:  06 34 67 16 0E 16 8E 05    00 00 00 00 BC 01 07 34    .4g..........4
00D0:  00 00 00 00 00 00 00 00    00 00 00 00 00 00 00 00    ...............
00E0:  00 00 00 00 00 00 00 00    00 00 00 00 00 00 00 00    ...............
00F0:  25 00 00 00 00 01 00 27    00 01 01 00 01 00 24 00    %......'......$.
0100:  06 00 00 01 00 23 00 07    00 00 01 00 26 01 00 01    .....#......&...
0110:  00 00 00 28 01 01 01 00    01 00 21 01 02 01 00 00    ...(......!.....
0120:  00 22 01 03 01 00 00 00    25 00 00 00 00 27 00 00    ."......%....'..
0130:  00 01 25 01 00 00 02 27    01 00 00 03 24 00 00 00    ..%....'....$...
0140:  06 23 00 00 00 07 26 27    00 01 00 28 00 00 01 01    .#....&....(....
0150:  21 00 00 01 02 22 00 00    01 03 24 01 00 01 06 23    !...."....$....#
0160:  01 00 01 07 C6 01 07 34    10 00 00 00 CC 01 07 34    .......4.......4
0170:  00 00 C8 00 D2 01 07 34    01 00 C9 00 DE 01 07 34    .......4.......4
0180:  00 00 CA 00 E5 01 07 34    00 00 CB 00 F1 01 07 34    .......4.......4
0190:  00 00 CC 00 64 01 07 34    8C 01 07 34 00 00 00 00    ....d..4...4....
```

From Here...

In this chapter, you learned about the WinSight and WinSpector applications and how these applications can assist you in debugging problems that may occur with your applications. WinSight allows you to view messages passed between applications so that you can make sure that appropriate messages are being passed and processed by the applications. WinSpector allows you to extract system information that was present when a UAE or GPE occurred.

- To read about using the Borland C++ Integrated Development Environment refer to chapter 2, "Using the Integrated Development Environment."

- To examine the Borland C++ Library functions refer to chapter 12, "Using Borland C++ Library Functions."

- For information on using the Turbo Debugger refer to chapter 29, "Using the Integrated Debugger."

V

Programming Tools

CHAPTER 31

Using the Resource Workshop

The Resource Workshop is now integrated into the Borland C++ 5 IDE. This chapter demonstrates how to create and use resources such as icons, cursors, and bitmaps with the new integrated Workshop. I have also included example code that will show you how to manipulate reusable resources whether you are using the Windows API interface or the Borland ObjectWindows Library (OWL) classes.

The integrated Workshop provides you with the capability to create and modify reusable Windows resources seamlessly without ever leaving the IDE. Topics in this chapter provide specific examples of creating and using resources.

In this chapter, you learn about

- Using the new integrated Resource Workshop
- Changing cursors
- Displaying icons
- Associating icons with Windows
- Displaying bitmaps

Using the New Integrated Resource Workshop

Resources are parts of programs that can be created and stored independently of an individual program, and used over and over. In addition to writing header files and module files, programmers writing Windows applications can create resource (.rc) files that can describe some of the visual or reusable aspects of each program. The Resource Workshop is used for this purpose.

In the Workshop you can create and modify resources such as bitmapped images, cursors, icons, and dialog boxes. These items are then stored and "compiled" into a resource file (.res), and can be used as many times as you want. In the following subsections, let's take a look at how the integrated Workshop fits into the Windows 95 IDE, and how we can use this tool to enhance the graphical appeal of Windows programs.

Starting the Resource Workshop

The Resource Workshop can still be executed as a stand-alone application from the Windows 95 Start button (see fig. 31.1). The integrated Workshop does not run a shelled version of the stand-alone application; rather, the view you'll see from the IDE is seamless and fully integrated.

Fig. 31.1

You may still run the Resource Workshop as a stand-alone application without ever starting the IDE.

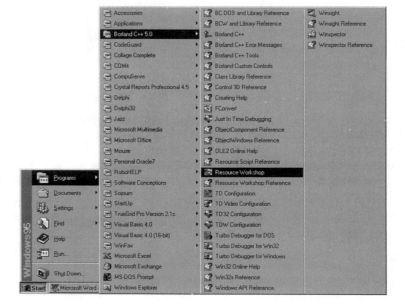

The Resource Workshop is started from the File, New, Resource Project menu (see fig. 31.2). A second way to invoke the Resource Workshop is to double-click on the .rc file in the Project window (see fig. 31.3). It is simply a matter of convenience which route you choose to take.

If you invoked the Resource Workshop from the File, New menu, you may select between specific resource types—icons, cursors, or bitmaps—or you may start a new resource project, which is what you get when you click on the .rc file in the Project window.

Once you have chosen to create a new resource project, a Resource menu appears in the IDE menu and a Resource Identifiers dialog box opens. Using the Resource menu, you may add, create, and modify a variety of resource types. The following sections demonstrate how to create some of the most common resource types and incorporate these into your Windows applications. Let's proceed by looking at a couple of different ways to use existing cursors, and then we'll design and incorporate a custom cursor with the Workshop.

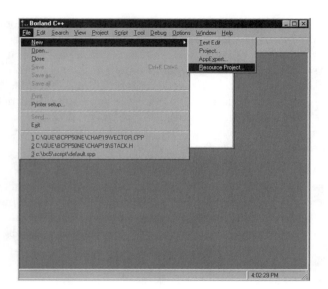

Fig. 31.2

A new resource project can be executed from the Resource Project command, which invokes the Resource Workshop.

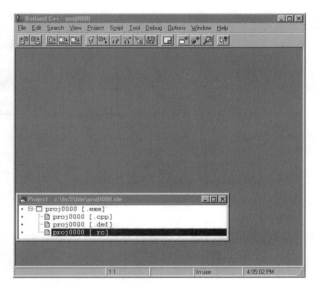

Fig. 31.3

Double-clicking on the .rc file in the Project window invokes the Workshop, just as in Borland C++ 4.5.

V

Programming Tools

Changing Cursors

Give a moment's consideration to your favorite Windows programs and you can probably picture a half dozen or so different cursors; you might even be able to imagine the scenarios where specific cursors are used. This probably has something to do with the adage "a picture is worth a thousand words."

The word processor I am using displays a vertical bar (similar to the pipe symbol) while typing. If I move the mouse toward the menus, as it passes over a pull-down list it becomes an I-beam, and quickly converts to the standard mouse pointer as it reaches the menu. And, of course, there is the infamous hourglass when a selection is processing. Windows 95 displays a pointer/hourglass combination pointer. Most of us now recognize that we have to wait as long as the hourglass appears. Interestingly, you have probably developed a sixth sense about just how long that hourglass will stay displayed. The hourglass doesn't really do anything, but it does help provide you with a chronometer of sorts.

Some applications, like my word processor, should probably not deviate too much from some of these expected pointer icons referred to as cursors. Maybe a game would be a good place to get creative with cursors. One that I like is SWAT, an example program provided with the Borland suite. The SWAT game provides a nonstandard use of a cursor shaped liked a hammer. I will come back to custom cursors, but let's begin by looking at how we use the predefined cursors.

Using System Cursors

The Windows API provides quite a few standard cursor types. These define the common cursors you have seen in standard software applications, like word processor, spreadsheet, and database programs. Table 31.1 displays a list of cursor constants found in the Help system when I clicked on the Search button in Help, Windows API.

Table 31.1   Windows API Cursor Constants

Constant	Displays
IDC_ARROW	The standard arrow cursor
IDC_CROSS	A crosshair cursor
IDC_IBEAM	The text I-beam cursor
IDC_ICON	An empty icon
IDC_SIZE	Two offset squares
IDC_SIZENEW	Crossed arrows pointing northeast and southwest
IDC_SIZENS	Crossed arrows pointing north and south
IDC_SIZENWSE	Crossed arrows pointing southeast and northwest
IDC_SIZEWE	Crossed arrows pointing west and east
IDC_UPARROW	Vertical arrow
IDC_WAIT	The hourglass

I followed this search with a search for the same function from the Help, OWL API menu. The result was the ObjectWindows Library function LoadCursor. The OWL LoadCursor function takes a TResId argument and returns an HCURSOR object.

The `TResId` type is declared in the geometry.h file. The contructors for `TResId` are an integer constant and a `char*` (`filename`). Which form of the `LoadCursor` function you use will probably depend on your experience and comfort level with the implementations of either. However, there might be more important considerations when choosing between two similar tasks: one provided by the OWL API and the other by the Windows API.

A topic of discussion that doesn't seem to have hit the mainstream yet is "resource acquisition is initialization." The idea is that most resources are not used in a void. Usually the resource needs to be initialized and released. The two ideas coincide with constructors and destructors. Barring a careful investigation, I would be inclined to believe that the Windows API provides a C-like interface, and the OWL is object-oriented. The implication is that the ObjectWindows Library is more likely to take advantage of resource acquisition and initialization. Therefore, if asked, I would probably defer to `LoadCursor` implementation in the Borland OWL. I referred to the Borland *User's Guide*, and in this case the lines of code used were in favor, with a 3 to 1 ratio, of using the OWL method. Keeping this in mind, let's take a look at how we can use either of these two methods to use the cursors mentioned in this section earlier.

> **Note**
>
> The heart of the idea, "resource acquisition is initialization," is that some resources, such as files, are not used without initializing them in some way. A constructor can take care of the initialization and the destructor can release the resource. The constructor could open the file, the destructor could close the file, and an operator function could provide access to the file pointer. The user does not need to remember to close the file because the destructor would do it when the object goes out of scope.

Changing the Cursor Using the Windows API. The Windows API provides a C-style implementation that allows you to change the active cursor. The code required amounts to little more than specifying which cursor value you want to display. The following code will set the active cursor:

```
HCURSOR hCursor;
hCursor = LoadCursor(hInst, IDC_ARROW);
SetCursor(hCursor);
```

The first line defines an `HCURSOR` variable, the second calls the API `LoadCursor` function, and the last calls the API `SetCursor` function with the handle returned from `LoadCursor`. The `hInst` is a handle to the application and `IDC_ARROW` is a macro that is replaced by the preprocessor with `MAKEINTRESOURCE(constant)`. The end result is that the arrow becomes the active cursor.

> **Tip**
>
> The notation characterized by the "h" prefix may be unfamiliar to you. This style of notation is commonly referred to as Hungarian notation. The prefix provides a hint as to the data type of the variable. The hCursor has an "h" prefix. The "h" indicates that this is a handle type, which is usually an integral type. It is not necessary to conform to this style, but it does represent the style of code you will see most frequently in the API Library. Whatever style you use, be consistent.

The following section shows a smaller code fragment that does the same thing. The fragment uses the OWL functions and employs a more object-oriented approach. Where semantically similar constructs exist in the Borland OWL, I will defer to using those functions in the future.

Changing the Cursor Using the Borland OWL. Where similar constructs exist in both the Windows API and the Borland OWL, it's a good bet that the OWL builds off the API. While the API presents the code in a C-style, the OWL uses object-oriented techniques. This provides you with objects that initialized upon acquisition and, generally, require smaller code. Look at:

```
GetMainWindow()->SetCursor(this, IDC_ARROW);
```

The GetMainWindow function returns a pointer of Window-type and uses the *this* pointer in place of the hInst value. Here it is unnecessary to acquire the cursor handle with LoadCursor.

Using a Custom Cursor

The Resource Workshop provides you with the tools for creating a header file and a resource file to add cursors (and other graphics items) to your Windows programs. All you need to do is provide the types and names of the graphics files and the Resource Workshop creates the header (.h) file and the resource (.rc) file for you.

Whenever you update the resource file, the IDE or makefile will call the resource compiler (Rc.exe) program and compile the .res file for you. Let me demonstrate how easy it is to use the Resource Workshop to add a custom cursor to your Windows programs.

For demonstration purposes, I have created a demo that uses the OWL and incorporates a custom cursor added to the project. The instructions begin with a new project. To create the new project, choose File, New, Project from the IDE. Type in a project name in the New Target dialog box (see fig. 31.4).

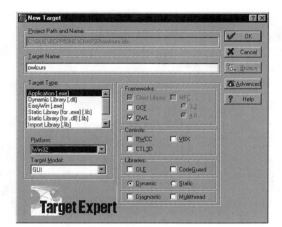

Fig. 31.4

*Select the Project command
to create a new project.*

Next modify the empty .def file. This file contains information about how the compiled program will operate and the system resource that will be allocated to it. Double-click on the *filename*.def file in the IDE window and add the following lines to the file:

```
EXETYPE        WINDOWS
CODE           PRELOAD MOVEABLE DISCARDABLE
DATA           PRELOAD MOVEABLE
HEAPSIZE       65536
STACKSIZE      65536
```

Close the file by clicking on the Close button in the upper-right corner of the Edit dialog box. You will be prompted to save the changes. Press Y to indicate that you want the changes saved.

Double-clicking on the .rc file in the IDE window will execute the integrated Resource Workshop, opening the .rc project file. You can add a header file to the project via the right-click speed menu. To add a header file where the resource identifiers are stored, follow these steps:

1. Place the mouse cursor over the Resource dialog box.

2. Click the right mouse button.

3. From the speed menu, choose Add to Project.

4. Select the header file, if it exists, to store your resource names. If you enter a file that doesn't exist, you will be prompted to create the file. (Figure 31.5 shows the Windows 95 Add to Project dialog box.)

V

Programming Tools

Fig. 31.5

Select the header file in which you wish to store the resource identifiers.

The resource project has been created. You have added a header file that will be used by the Workshop to store identifiers; you'll need these to refer to specific resources within your applications. Having completed the groundwork, you can easily add the custom cursor to the application. Follow these steps to add the cursor to the resource file:

1. With the cursor over the Resource dialog box, click the right mouse button.

2. Choose Add to Project from the speed menu.

3. In the List Files of Type combo box, select the cursor file mask *.cur.

4. Use the Windows 95 Add to Project dialog box to select the cursor (*.cur) file to add. (For our application, I used the Handflat.cur that I found in my Dephi 2.0 directories, included on the CD-ROM. You may use any *.cur file to complete the demonstration.)

5. Click OK.

Listing 31.1 uses the TApplication class defined as part of the ObjectWindows Library to tie it all together.

Listing 31.1   Owlcurs.cpp—Demonstrates Using the ObjectWindows Classes to Add a Custom Cursor

```
1.  // OWLCURS.CPP - Using a custom cursor.
2.  // Borland OWL Headers
3.  #include <owl\applicat.h>
4.  #include <owl\framewin.h>
5.  // Non-Borland Headers
6.  #include "owlcurs.h"
7.  class TApp : public TApplication{
8.  public:
9.      TApp() : TApplication() {};
10.     void InitMainWindow(){
11.         MainWindow = new TFrameWindow( 0, "OWL Cursor" );
12.         MainWindow->SetCursor( this, CURSOR_1 );}
13.     };
14. int OwlMain(int /*argc*/, char* /*argv*/[]){
15.     return TApp().Run();
16. }
```

First, I included the framewin.h, applicat.h, and owlcurs.h files in my program. The first two contain the `TFrameWindow` class and the `TApplication` class respectively, and the last one contains the resource identifiers created with the Resource Workshop. Next, I created a `TApp` class that inherits from `TApplication`. I redefined the *virtual* `InitMainWindow` function defined in `TApplication`, allocated a new `TFrameWindow` object on the heap and used the `SetCursor` function defined in `TFrameWindow` to set my custom cursor. The OWL `SetCursor` function is declared like

```
SetCursor( TModule*, TResID );
```

requiring a pointer to a `TModule` object and a `TResID` object. The `TFrameWindow` class is derived from a `TModule`, so I used the *this* pointer, and a `TResID` object can be constructed from a resource identifier, allowing me to use the macro `CURSOR_1` defined in the owlcurs.h file. The program is finished by defining an `OwlMain` function and calling the inherited `Run()` function from a `TApp` object. The unusual cursor is shown in the program output in figure 31.6.

Fig. 31.6

This output was generated from Owlcurs.exe, a Windows demo program that demonstrates how to use custom cursors with the Borland OWL.

In summary, the steps required to add a custom cursor to your application are

1. Open the target project.
2. Open the IDE window and double-click on the resource (.rc) project file, starting the integrated Resource Workshop.
3. Choose a header file in which to store the cursor resource identifier.
4. Add the cursor file (Filename.cur) to the resource project.
5. Close the Resource dialog box. This causes the resource file to be saved and compiled.
6. When using the cursor resource, refer to it by the identifier stored in the header file.

Each control, such as windows, frames, and dialog boxes, has a cursor associated with it. When adding custom controls to your Windows applications, specify the cursor in a similar manner; when a specific control has the focus, its cursor becomes the active one.

Displaying Icons

Icons are small bitmaps used for a wide variety of purposes. There are icons used to indicate OLE attachments, program items within the Windows environment itself, icons representing minimized applications, and in fact, Windows 95 uses program icons displayed on buttons on the Windows 95 taskbar (as illustrated in fig. 31.7).

Fig. 31.7

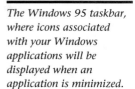

The Windows 95 taskbar, where icons associated with your Windows applications will be displayed when an application is minimized.

Icons are used in many operating systems with a graphical user interface—not just Windows. Icons can represent in a single small picture a concept that may be difficult to represent with several words; this can be very important given the limited physical screen space available. This section demonstrates the code necessary to add icons to a Windows program.

If it were not for direct Windows API support and the Borland OWL, displaying icons would be quite a chore. Manually displaying icons requires knowledge of compression algorithms, manipulating bits, and detailed information about video hardware and video modes. There are entire books devoted to displaying bitmaps and compression algorithms, but the ObjectWindows Library and the Windows API simplify the task greatly.

The code for displaying an icon is syntactically very similar to that for displaying cursors. The Windows API code requires a cursor handle, a call to LoadCursor to get the resource, and a function call to SetIcon:

```
HICON hIcon;
hIcon = LoadIcon(hInst, MAKEINTRESOURCE(ICON_RESOURCE));
// hIcon = LoadIcon(hInst, /*LPCSTR */ szIconName );
SetIcon( hIcon );
```

The ObjectWindows Library simplifies the code required to load a cursor.

```
GetMainWindow()->SetIcon(this, ICON_RESOURCE_ID );
```

The following declaration of the SetIcon function in the TFrameWindow class provides insight into how this function works:

```
bool SetIcon(TModule* iconModule, TResId iconResId);
```

The *iconModule variable is a pointer to the base class TModule. Since the TApp is indirectly derived from the TModule class, the this pointer suffices for the TModule* (the inheritance lattice is shown in fig. 31.8). The TResId type is a class that loads a resource given a resource ID.

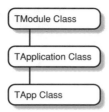

Fig. 31.8

The inheritance lattice of the TApp *class.*

Icons, like cursors, seldom exist or are displayed in a void. They usually have an implied meaning or an attached "value." Icons may be displayed on buttons, and the picture represents the operation performed when the button is pressed. An iconic stop sign may be displayed in a dialog box to indicate to the user that careful consideration may be required before proceeding. Because a considerable amount of meaning can be represented by simple symbols, icons have a richly diverse opportunity for reuse. The first icons any Windows user sees are the icons representing programs available for execution in the Windows 95 environment.

Associating Icons with Windows

Icons provide a pictorial means of communicating a great deal of information in a very small space. The physical space of your monitor certainly qualifies. Icons seldom float alone on the screen representing nothing. Icons can represent the availability of options, imply significance of messages, or be used for decorative purposes like displaying your logo.

In Windows 95, icons associated with programs are in great abundance. While the underlying significance of icons has not taken on more or less importance, they appear more frequently. In previous versions, the user usually had to find his or her way back to the Program Manager, click on the Program Group icon, find the item icon and double-click on that icon to execute the program. Windows 95 provides a modified approach to executing programs.

Windows 95 displays the associated icon at the top-left corner of the running application, in the menus accessed by the Start button on the taskbar, and on buttons placed on the taskbar that are currently executing. A benefit of this to software developers is that there is a constant association between the application and the icon; everywhere the application can be accessed, its icon appears. The icons are displayed in a sufficient variety of ways to make them easy to remember. Because of this, icons will become even more important as the popularity of the new operating system grows. The implication is to find meaningful icons because they will be seen more often.

Associating Icons with Windows Using OWL

The ObjectWindows Library provides a very simple method of attaching icons to your Windows programs—easy enough, in fact, that the whole thing can be accomplished with a handful of lines of code. Applying the simple code displayed in the last section, listing 31.2 accomplishes the task.

Listing 31.2   Owlicon.cpp—Demonstrates How to Incorporate Custom Icons Using ObjectWindows

```
 1. // OWLICON.CPP - Demonstrates setting cursors and icons.
 2. #include <owl\applicat.h>
 3. #include <owl\framewin.h>
 4. class TApp : public TApplication{
 5. public:
 6.         TApp() : TApplication() {};
 7.         void InitMainWindow(){
 8.             MainWindow = new TFrameWindow( 0,
 9.                 "Example Program" );
10.             MainWindow->SetIcon( this, "EARTH");
11.             MainWindow->SetCursor( this, "HANDFLAT" );
12.         }
13.     };
14. int OwlMain(int /*argc*/, char* /*argv*/[]){
15.   return TApp().Run();
16. }
```

This little bit of code represents a complete, working Windows application—although it doesn't do much, it does attach the selected icon to the program—line 10 does the whole job. The icon highlighted in figure 31.9 is as it appears in the Browse dialog box when running the program from the Start menu.

Fig. 31.9

The icon assigned to the main window in the resource file becomes the file associated by Windows 95 with this executable file.

The only code that has been modified in this program is line 10. (See the earlier section "Using a Custom Cursor" for an explanation of the entire program.) Line 10 calls the SetIcon function passing TApp's this pointer as the TModule* argument. This simple code associates the icon with the program. The ObjectWindows Library TApplication class allows you to write Windows programs very simply. The underlying code is a derivative of C-style code provided in the Windows API.

Associating Icons with Windows Using the API

The program in the previous section uses the Borland ObjectWindows Library. This object-oriented code uses functionality provided by the Windows API. The shell program presented in this section produces a working Windows program shell. Either the program in the previous section or this program can be used to build complete working applications; if you are using the Borland OWL, use the program shell in the prior section; otherwise, you can use the C-style API style shell.

As an alternative to using ObjectWindows, listing 31.3 demonstrates using custom cursors and icons with basic Window code.

Listing 31.3   Cursor.cpp—A Basic Windows Shell Program

```
1.  // CURSOR.CPP - Example program displays cursors and icons
2.  #include <windows.h>
3.  #include <string.h>
4.  LONG FAR PASCAL WndProc(HWND, UINT, WPARAM, LPARAM);
5.  static char szProgram[] = "cursor";
6.  static char szIconName[] = "ICON_1";
7.  #pragma argsused
8.  int PASCAL WinMain( HINSTANCE hInst, HINSTANCE hPrevInst, LPSTR
    ➥lpszCmdLine, int nCmdShow)
9:  {
10.   HWND hWindow;
11.       MSG lpMsg;
12.       WNDCLASS wcApplication;
13.       if( !hPrevInst ){
14.       wcApplication.lpszClassName = szProgram;
15.       wcApplication.hInstance = hInst;
16.       wcApplication.lpfnWndProc = WndProc;
17.       wcApplication.hCursor = LoadCursor(NULL, IDC_ARROW);
18.       wcApplication.hIcon = LoadIcon(NULL, szIconName);
19.       wcApplication.lpszMenuName = NULL;
20.       wcApplication.hbrBackground = GetStockObject(WHITE_BRUSH);
21.       wcApplication.style = CS_HREDRAW¦CS_VREDRAW;
22.       wcApplication.cbClsExtra = 0;
23.       if( !RegisterClass( &wcApplication ))
24.           return FALSE;
25.       }
26.       hWindow = CreateWindow(szProgram, "Cursor Example",
27.           WS_OVERLAPPEDWINDOW, CW_USEDEFAULT,
28.             CW_USEDEFAULT, CW_USEDEFAULT,
29.             CW_USEDEFAULT, (HWND)NULL, (HMENU)NULL,
30.                 (HANDLE)hInst, (LPSTR)NULL);
31.       ShowWindow(hWindow, nCmdShow);
32.       UpdateWindow(hWindow);
33.       while( GetMessage(&lpMsg, NULL, NULL, NULL)){
34.           TranslateMessage(&lpMsg);
35.           DispatchMessage(&lpMsg); }
36.           return(lpMsg.wParam); }
37.     LONG FAR PASCAL WndProc(HWND hWnd, UINT message,
38.       WPARAM wParam, LPARAM lParam){
39.       PAINTSTRUCT ps;
40.       HDC hdc;
```

(continues)

V

Programming Tools

Listing 31.3   Continued

```
41.       switch(message){
42:       case WM_PAINT:
43:             hdc=BeginPaint(hWnd, &ps);
44:             ValidateRect(hWnd,NULL);
45:             EndPaint(hWnd, &ps);
46:             break;
47:       case WM_DESTROY:
48:             PostQuitMessage(0);
49:             break;
50:       default:
51:             return (DefWindowProc(hWnd,
52:                 message, wParam, lParam));
53:       }
54:        return (0L);
55:  }
```

Line 17 does all of the work with regard to icons. The WNDCLASS has an HICON variable hIcon. All you have to do is call the LoadIcon function with the string name of your resource icon name. Remember that the LoadCursor function requires a null string. You can create the null string by enclosing the name of the resource in quotes or passing it as an argument to the MAKEINTRESOURCE macro, which will create the string for you. This code loads the cursor for the wcApplication object.

Displaying Bitmaps

Bitmaps are used in a wide variety of application areas. Included in the set of bitmaps are icons and cursors. For our purposes here, when I refer to bitmaps, I am excluding icons and cursors and am referring to files with .bmp extensions (see fig. 31.10).

Fig. 31.10

Bitmap images are widely available on bulletin boards. Some are shipped with Windows 95 and they can easily be created or scanned with commercial applications.

The Windows 95 API and the Borland ObjectWindows Library provide functions for displaying, editing, and saving bitmapped images. In this section, I will demonstrate how to display both 16- and 256-color bitmaps. Bitmaps require a bit more code to use but considerably less than if you had to supply the compression and decompression algorithms, too.

16-Color Bitmaps

The 16-color bitmaps are capable of providing a high-resolution image with a good variety of colors. These bitmaps can be drawn quickly in Windows, and usually require fewer resources in terms of disk space and runtime memory. The demo program in this section displays a bitmap, created with Paintbrush, based on a popular comic strip.

In preparation for using the example program, open your .ide project file from within the Borland environment. Run the Resource Workshop and open the resource project file. Add the bitmap that you want to use to the resource by choosing File, Add to Project or Resource, New and creating a bitmap. You can choose Edit, Rename to rename the resource, or simply make note of the default resource name for your bitmap, save the project, and exit the Resource Workshop.

You now have a header (.h) file containing a reference to the resource, a resource file with the bitmap in it, and an empty .cpp file for your program code. While you may want to display an image on a variety of backgrounds, listing 31.4 provides you with the basic concepts of displaying bitmaps within an application (refer to fig. 31.10 for the output).

Listing 31.4 Owlbmp.cpp—Inherits a *FrameWindow* to Create a Bitmap Window that Displays a Custom Bitmap

```
1.  // OWLBMP.CPP - Sample program displays a 16-color bitmap
2.  // Borland Header Files
3.  #include <owl\applicat.h>
4.  #include <owl\framewin.h>
5.  #include <owl\owlpch.h>
6.  #include <owl\dc.h>
7.  // Non-Borland Header Files
8.  #include "owlbmp.h"
9.  class TBitmapWindow : public TFrameWindow{
10. public:
11. TBitmapWindow( const char *title );
12. ~TBitmapWindow();
13. protected:
14. void Paint( TDC&, BOOL, TRect& );
15. private:
16. TBitmap *mooBitmap;
17. TPoint center;
18. };
19. // Bitmap Window Constructor
```

(continues)

Listing 31.4 Continued

```
20. TBitmapWindow::TBitmapWindow( const char *title)
21. : TFrameWindow(0, title, 0 ), TWindow( 0, title ){
22.       mooBitmap = new  TBitmap(*GetModule(), BITMAP_2);
23.       // Adjust the window size to the image size
24.       // plus the border sizes
25.       Attr.W = mooBitmap->Width() +
26.             2*GetSystemMetrics(SM_CXBORDER);
27.       Attr.H = mooBitmap->Height() +
28.             GetSystemMetrics(SM_CYBORDER) +
29.             GetSystemMetrics(SM_CYCAPTION) +
30.             GetSystemMetrics(SM_CYMENU);
31.       Attr.Style &= ~(WS_THICKFRAME ¦ WS_MAXIMIZEBOX);
32.       center.x = mooBitmap->Width() / 2;
33.       center.y = mooBitmap->Height() / 2; }
34.    TBitmapWindow::~TBitmapWindow(){
35.       delete mooBitmap; }
36.    void TBitmapWindow::Paint( TDC& dc, BOOL, TRect& ){
37. TMemoryDC memDC(dc);
38. memDC.SelectObject(*mooBitmap);
39.       dc.BitBlt( 0,0, mooBitmap->Width(),
40.       mooBitmap->Height(), memDC, 0, 0, SRCCOPY);}
41. class TApp : public TApplication{
42. public:
43. TApp() : TApplication(){};
44.       void InitMainWindow(){
45.          MainWindow = new TBitmapWindow(
46.             "Using Bitmaps with OWL");}
47. };
48. int OwlMain( int, char* [] ){
49.  return TApp().Run();}
```

Much of this program you have seen before in earlier sections of this chapter. If you have forgotten it, take a moment to review earlier sections so the whole program makes sense. Unless you have skipped to this section, you have already seen the code in lines 1–8 and lines 41–49, so I will not review those here. The code that has changed significantly lies between lines 9 and 40.

Tip

If you have forgotten what some of the common threads of this program are responsible for, take a moment to review earlier sections. Because this shell code is reusable, it might be helpful to get a good understanding of this code.

The gist of what this additional code does is to provide a new type—TBitmapWindow—derived from the TFrameWindow. By deriving the new type, you will gain intimate access to the window handle, the device context variables, and other data pertinent to drawing a bitmap in the client window. Lines 9 through 18 consist of the `TBitmapWindow` class declaration, including the constructor, destructor, a `Paint` function, a pointer to a `TBitmap`, and a point object. The rest of the functionality exists in the parent classes. The important work is done in the constructor and the `Paint` function.

The *TBitmapWindow* Constructor. The constructor allocates a TBitmap object on the heap, which in turn will load the bitmap. Next, some adjustments are made to the window, taking into account the additional space required for the borders, and the window style is set with

```
Attr.Style &= ~(WS_THICKFRAME | WS_MAXIMIZEBOX);
```

This esoteric bit of code ensures that the window will have whatever the normal default attributes are, except for a thick frame and maximize capabilities. Finally, the relative image center is calculated. Now when Windows sends a WM_PAINT message to the program, the image is ready to be displayed.

The *TBitmapWindow* *Paint* Function. The TWindow base class provides a virtual Paint function. Because the program needs to perform some bitmap-specific task, a specific `Paint` function was defined for the TBitmapWindow class. When Windows sends a WM_PAINT message to our application, this function will be called and the image will be displayed. The Paint function is straightforward: It creates a memory device context object for the window and uses the BitBlitter (or BitBlaster) function to display the image in the client area of the window. As a matter of fact, the same program can display 256-color bitmaps, which is the topic of the next section.

256-Color Palette-Based Bitmaps

The 256-color palette-based bitmaps provide for a much greater image selection. These images are actually capable of displaying 256 colors from a single palette at one time, but can choose from 1,024 different palettes. This diversity allows for an amazing variety of colors; the end result is usually really nice graphics. Most display monitors produced today are capable of displaying 256-color images.

The program in the previous section (on 16-color bitmaps) will actually display 256-color images. To run that application with a 256-color image, just add the image to the resource, and use it as an argument to the `TBitmap` constructor call in line 22.

You probably want the static images to display the image as it appeared when scanned or created. But if you are creating or editing images at runtime, you may want to modify the palette information for the image. The palette table information can be modified by manipulating `TPalette` objects associated with the image.

V

Programming Tools

From Here...

When you see specific code in writing you must remember that the code represents a particular implementation. All such implementations are highly subjective, and there may be many ways to perform similar tasks. This very notion represents one of the true complexities and, paradoxically, the joy of programming.

Those with more or different experiences from your own can show what is believed to be the safest or easiest ways to perform particular tasks. This chapter demonstrated a couple of ways to perform tasks related to reusable system resources. These do not represent the best or only ways to perform these kinds of tasks. They are examples that are intended to be easy enough to get you started.

C++ programming and Windows programming are two different things. There are many ways to write Windows programs, as well as many other operating systems that will execute code written in C++. Successes or failures in either endeavor can be looked upon as learning experiences.

- For an introduction to the new and powerful features of Borland C++ 5, see chapter 1, "What's New."
- To learn about the different interface elements of the IDE as well as how to configure the IDE, see chapter 2, "Using the Integrated Development Environment."
- For more information on OWL-based GDI fundamentals, refer to chapter 25, "Using the Graphics Device Interface."

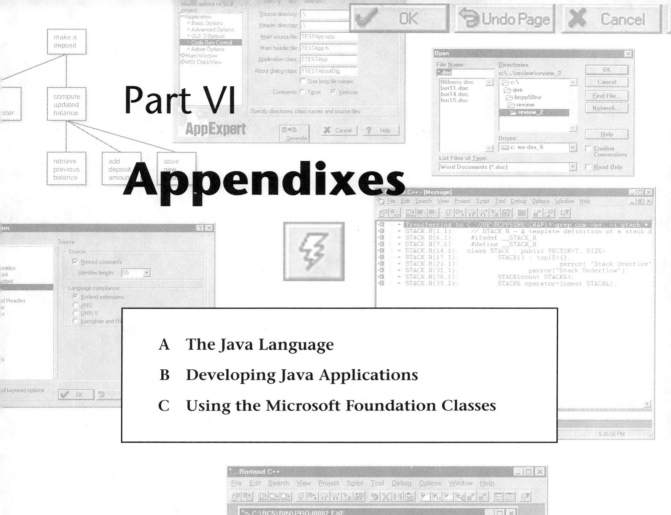

Part VI

Appendixes

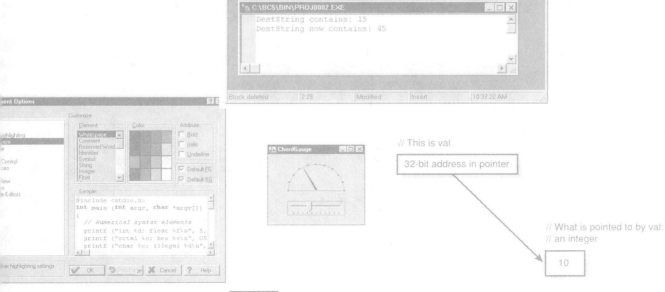

APPENDIX A

The Java Language

In this appendix, you will get an overview of the Java language. Java is a new language that is revolutionizing software development and is poised to make a large impact on the industry in the years to come. With the Internet gaining popularity and Java near to becoming the de facto standard for Internet application development, Borland has provided support for Java classes in the Borland C++ 5 product. This enables developers to develop Java applications with the Borland C++ development environment. It also allows for C++ to be combined with Java more easily. This unification of technologies makes Borland C++ 5 the ideal tool for developing Internet-aware applications.

In this appendix, you learn to

- Understand Java fundamentals
- Familiarize yourself with the Java Runtime System
- Write a simple Java applet
- Interface Java with C

The Internet and the World Wide Web

The Internet is a network of computers that spans the globe, making it the world's largest wide area network (WAN). Unlike private LANs and WANs, where access is restricted by the institutions that own them, no one person or group owns the Internet, and any individual or organization can get connected to the Internet through dial-up or dedicated lines.

The Internet offers several services, such as e-mail, news, Gopher, WAIS, FTP, and telnet, with which you can gain access to vast resources of information and exchange messages with other users of the Internet. One of the most common services is the World Wide Web (WWW).

The architecture of the WWW is straightforward, with Web browsers acting as clients requesting information and Web servers servicing these requests. Web browsers, in addition to requesting information, can send commands to the Web server, which takes appropriate actions to process the commands. Web servers and Web browsers use the *HTTP* protocol for communication. HTTP is an application-level protocol built on top of the TCP/IP protocol. Web browsers render the information sent back by Web servers using the *Hypertext Markup Language* (HTML), which is derived from *Standard Generalized Markup Language* (SGML).

WWW application development is in its infancy and many architectures have emerged in the past year. Traditionally, applications have tended to reside on the server. To invoke an application, you go to a Web page using your Web browser, click a link that triggers the Web server, which calls the application residing on the server. The Web server and the application communicate using the *Common Gateway Interface* (CGI). Once the application is finished processing, it returns the results to the Web server, which relays it to your Web browser as seen in figure A.1. The applications themselves have been written in languages such as Perl, C, Tcl, Visual Basic, and others.

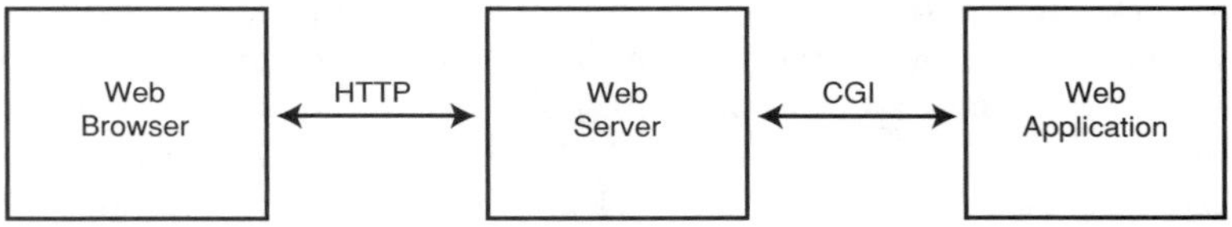

Fig. A.1

Web applications using Common Gateway Interface.

This application architecture has its limitations in that all code resides on the server and there is little partitioning of code. Java provides an alternative architecture for developing Web applications.

Understanding Java

Java was conceived by engineers at Sun Microsystems and has been in development since 1991. It was originally intended as a programming language for consumer electronics such as cable-TV set top boxes.

Java is an object-oriented language that is easy to use and robust while boasting features such as multithreading, support for Internet protocols, garbage collection, and cross-platform support. Although Java has its roots in C and C++, it has eliminated much of the complexity of its predecessors and instead has a smaller, more elegant syntax without compromising on functionality.

Java is an interpreted language and each Java program is compiled for a hypothetical machine called the Java Virtual Machine. The output of compiling a Java program is *Java bytecodes*. For Java to run on any *real* operating system, such as Windows 95 or NT or Solaris, it has to have a *Java Runtime System* that interprets the Java bytecodes into native machine code.

Java Runtime System

The Java Runtime System has the responsibility of interpreting Java bytecodes and converting them into the native machine code. This is a process that occurs in multiple stages as seen in figure A.2.

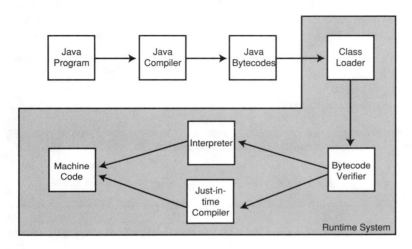

First, the Java bytecodes are loaded into the runtime system by a *class loader*. The class loader ensures that all the classes necessary for the application to run are loaded. Next, the code is checked by the *Bytecode Verifier* to ensure that it does not perform any illegal operations that would compromise the security of the host machine or cause it to crash. After the code is verified as being safe, it is executed on your machine.

Java also provides garbage collection for memory that is dynamically allocated. This relieves the developer from having explicitly free memory, which has been identified as the major cause of memory leaks in C and C++ programs. By performing automatic garbage collection, Java improves the robustness and stability of applications.

Methods of Deploying Java Applications

Java can be used for developing any application, either as stand-alone programs or as applets for the Internet. At present, Java only runs on Windows 95 or NT and Sun Solaris, although support for other platforms is imminent. Stand-alone applications are compiled for your local machine, and you can use Java to write any application that you may have chosen to write in C, C++, Basic, and so on. Although Java's database support is untried, many vendors have pledged support with products shipping over the next several months.

Java's main claim to fame is its popularity as a language for Internet application development. This is because Java has built-in support for several Internet protocols and languages including telnet, FTP, NNTP, HTTP, and HTML. In addition, Java enables Internet applications to be partitioned in such a way as to leverage the processing power of client machines.

As discussed earlier, CGI applications on the Web lead to server-centric architectures. With Java, the client machines run at least part of the Web application. Imagine for a moment that you are on a Web page and click a link to invoke a Java application. The Java application that resides on the server is downloaded onto your machine and then starts running locally. For your machine to be able to run the Java application locally, you need a Web browser capable of interpreting Java, such as Netscape Navigator or Sun's HotJava. These Web browsers have the Java Runtime System built-in.

Applets. With Java applets, you can create dynamic content for your Web pages. Java applets can be embedded in your Web page by using the <applet> and </applet> tags. The information contained within these tags identifies a Java applet, its location and its runtime parameters as shown in listing A.1.

Listing A.1   LstA_01.txt—The *<applet>* Tag Definition

```
<applet attributes>
parameters
alternate-content
</applet>
```

For example, you can load a TicTacToe applet on your HTML page as shown in listing A.2.

Listing A.2   LstA_02.txt—A Tag for Loading and Running TicTacToe

```
<applet
    code=TicTacToe.class
    width=120
    height=120>
</applet>
```

The first line of the <applet> tag contains important information about the tag, including the associated .class file and the applet's width and height. The last line completes the applet declaration.

Optional Attributes for Applets. There are several optional attributes you can use with the <applet> tag. The first is codebase, which specifies the applet's base folder or Uniform Resource Locator (URL). This folder or URL is used in combination with the file specified in the code attribute to find the applet's code. In the case of a folder, the codebase attribute is relative to the location of the HTML document containing the applet's tag. In listing A.2, because the codebase attribute is missing, the Web browser looks for the applet's files in the same folder as the HTML document. The <applet> tag in listing A.2 looks like listing A.3 when using the codebase attribute.

Listing A.3   Lsta_03.txt—Using the *codebase* Attribute

```
<applet
    codebase=tictactoe
    code=TicTacToe.class
    width=120
    height=120>
</applet>
```

The previous tag tells the browser that the Tictactoe.class file is located in a folder called Tictactoe. This folder must be on the same level in the directory tree as the HTML file. That is, if the HTML file is in the folder Java\Demo, then the path for the .class file is Java\Demo\Tictactoe\Tictactoe.class. You can also use an URL, such as

http://www.provider.com/my_pages/tictactoe

for the codebase attribute. This loads the applet from the specified site.

Other optional attributes you can use with the <applet> tag are alt, align, name, hspace, and vspace. The alt attribute enables you to specify text that is displayed by text-only browsers, whereas the name attribute gives the applet a symbolic name that's used to reference the applet.

The align, hspace, and vspace attributes all work together to position the applet within the text flow of the HTML document. These attributes work exactly as they do with the <img> tag that's used to display images in Web pages. The align attribute can be one of these values: left, right, middle, absmiddle, bottom, absbottom, baseline, top, or texttop. The hspace and vspace attributes control the amount of white space around the applet when align is set to left or right.

Listing A.4   Lsta_04.txt—A Simple HTML Document Using the *<applet>* Tag

```
<title>TicTacToe</title>
<hr>
This is a bunch of text whose sole purpose is to demonstrate
the placement
<applet
    codebase=TicTacToe
    code=TicTacToe.class
    width=120
    height=120
    alt="This is the TicTacToe applet."
    name=TicTacToe
    align=middle>
</applet>
of the TicTacToe applet within the text flow of an HTML document.
<hr>
```

Listing A.4 shows the script for a simple Web page using the <applet> tag. Figure A.3 shows Netscape Navigator 2.0 displaying the page.

VI

Appendixes

Fig. A.3

*This is the Web page
created by listing A.4.*

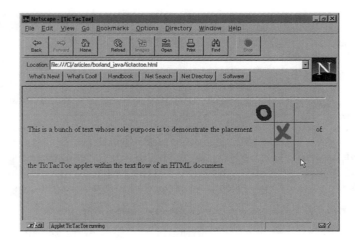

Local versus Remote Applets. The codebase attribute of the `<applet>` tag indicates whether an applet is local or remote. If an applet is local, then the `codebase` tag can be omitted or can contain the path where the applet is stored. This path is relative to the directory where the HTML document is stored. Listing A.3 shows a local applet.

Remote applets are stored at an external site and the `codebase` attribute reflects this by containing a URL to remote location. Listing A.5 shows how to write an HTML reference to a remote applet.

Listing A.5   Lsta_6.txt—Specifying a Remote Applet

```
<applet
    codebase="http://www.myconnect.com/applets/"
    code="TicTacToe.class"
    width=120
    height=120>
</applet>
```

Applet Parameters. As you know, many Java applets are configurable, meaning that the applet user can specify certain values that the applet uses when it starts.

When you need to specify parameters for an applet, you use the `<param>` tag. The `<param>` tags, one for each parameter you want to set, are placed after the starting `<applet>` tag and before the ending `</applet>` tag. For example, listing A.6 shows parameters being set for the `BarChart` applet. Figure A.4 shows the resultant bar chart. As you can see from the listing, each parameter has two parts, the parameter name and the value to which it should be set.

Listing A.6   Lsta_7.txt—Using Parameters with Applets

```
<title>Bar Chart</title>
<hr>
<applet
    code="Chart.class"
    width=251
    height=125>
<param name=title value="Sales">
<param name=orientation value="vertical">
<param name=scale value="5">
<param name=columns value="3">
<param name=c1_style value="solid">
<param name=c1 value="10">
<param name=c1_color value="blue">
<param name=c1_label value="Jan">
<param name=c2_style value="solid">
<param name=c2 value="12">
<param name=c2_color value="green">
<param name=c2_label value="Feb">
<param name=c3_style value="solid">
<param name=c3 value="15">
<param name=c3_color value="red">
<param name=c3_label value="Mar">
</applet>
<hr>
```

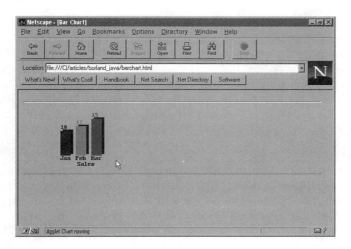

Fig. A.4

This is the bar chart created by the parameters in listing A.6.

Java Development Environment

The Java Development Environment consists of a set of tools. Provided by Sun Microsystems when you download their Java Development Kit (JDK) these are tools that assist in various phases of developing a Java application. They are non-graphical in nature, are not part of an IDE, and are driven from the command-line.

- The Appletviewer Tool—This serves as a good testing tool and allows you to run applets outside of the context of a Web browser.

- HotJava Browser—This is a browser that was developed by Sun Microsystems using Java. This is one of two browsers (Netscape being the other) that support Java applets.

- Java Interpreter (java)—This tool executes Java bytecodes.

- Java Compiler (javac)—This tool compiles Java source code in .java files into Java bytecodes stored in .class files.

- Java C Header/Stubs Generator (javah)—When you interface Java with C, you need to generate a C header file and a stub file. These files enable Java and C to communicate properly.

- Java Disassembler (javap)—This is a useful tool that disassembles a Java class and returns information about its public variables and methods.

- Java Profiler (javaprof)—When the Java interpreter is run with the `-prof` option, it creates a profile file. This tool takes that profile file and extracts useful information from it. For example, it can indicate the number of times each method was called.

The Borland IDE integrates the functionality of several of these tools by making them part of the Borland IDE, which greatly simplifies the task of building Java applications. In appendix B, "Developing Java Applications," you will see some examples of using these tools within the Borland C++ environment.

Interfacing Java with C

There are circumstances under which you may want to mix your C and Java code. Because C has been around for a long time, there are many tried and true programs and routines that you may not want to rewrite in Java and instead opt to call those routines from Java.

Before doing so, realize that this compromises some of Java's benefits, such as portability, security, and robustness. However, outside of legacy code, C is executed very quickly and may take advantage of the existing hardware. Java, on the other hand, is interpreted to bytecodes and is architecturally neutral; that is, it is not optimized for specific hardware platforms. Instead, one of its primary design goals is to run on any machine without recompilation. As a result, C programs optimized for, say, Windows 32-bit environments, may actually run faster than Java.

The steps for interfacing Java with C are as follows:

1. Write Java methods corresponding to C routines.
2. Create C header files using javah.
3. Create the stub files using javah.
4. Write C routines.

5. Compile C code into a DLL, including the stub file generated in step 3.

6. Link the C code into the Java source code using the dynamic linker class called Linker found in the Java.util package.

Summary

Java is a new language designed from the "ground-up" and aims to improve on its predecessors, such as C, C++, Ada, SmallTalk, Lisp, and Pascal, by incorporating some of the best features found in these languages. It is relatively easy to learn and may be the first of a new wave of programming languages that are Internet-aware and have advanced multimedia features such as support for animation and sound built-in. Clearly Java has claimed its spot in this new era of Internet application development. It remains to be seen how aggressively it is adopted in enterprises to build industrial-strength, mission-critical applications.

Developing Java Applications

Borland C++ 5 has included support for Java application development using the Borland C++ *Add-On Environment for Java* (BCAJ). Using BCAJ, you can write, compile, view, and debug Java applications and applets from within the Borland IDE.

BCAJ includes the following components that speed up Java applications:

- AppExpert
- AppAccelerator
- Debugger
- Project Manager
- Integrated Bytecode compiler

This appendix focuses on building Java applications using the Borland IDE and is not intended to be a Java language tutorial. Readers interested in learning more about the syntax and architecture of the language can refer to *Java by Example* from Que Corporation.

In this appendix, you will

- Understand how to use the Borland IDE to build Java applications
- Familiarize yourself with the Java Debugger
- Write a simple Java application using AppExpert

> **Note**
>
> The sample programs written in this appendix were tested under Windows NT and Windows 95.

Installing Borland C++ Add-On Environment for Java

The BCAJ can be installed from the initial setup window by clicking the BCAJ check box. If you have already installed Borland C++ 5 and need to install BCAJ, perform the following steps:

1. Go the \Bc5\Bin directory using either File Manager or Explorer.

2. Run Addonreg.exe. Select New Entry, choose the Bcwjava.dll, and click OK. This makes an entry for BCAJ in the registry.

3. Run the self-extracting executable, Bc5\Java\Src.zip. This installs the required Java class libraries, sample applications, and tools.

4. Add the environment variable `Classpath=C:\Bc5\Java\Classes`. In Windows NT, you can change the environment variables by double-clicking the System icon in the Control Panel. In Windows 95, you can change the environment variables by modifying the Autoexec.bat file.

5. Reboot your machine to reinitialize the environment variables.

6. Start Borland C++ to load all of the components that make up the BCAJ.

The Borland IDE

When it was first released by Sun Microsystems, Java was a set of tools without an integrated development environment. Although Java is a relatively easy-to-use language, it was cumbersome to construct large applications and keep track of projects. With the Borland IDE, the tasks of managing projects, compiling, and debugging become much easier because of the graphical user interface that allows developers to focus on the project at hand.

Before starting your first Java project, you may want to set up your Borland IDE so that it is more suitable for Java development. Choose Options, Environment. The Environment Options dialog box appears. In the Topics list box, choose SpeedBar, Customize. Next, from the Available Buttons list box, select Syntax Highlight Java Files and move it to the Active Buttons list box by clicking the right arrow, as seen in figure B.1.

This enables the Borland IDE to highlight the Java syntax when editing .java files. You will notice an additional button on your toolbar.

If you have already added the C++ syntax checking option, then you can switch between Java syntax checking and C++ syntax checking by clicking the appropriate toolbar button.

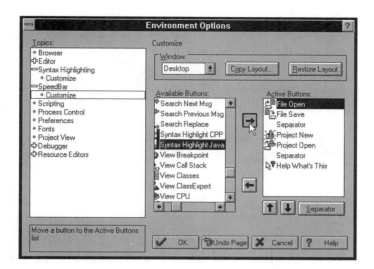

One of the main uses of Java is for developing Internet applications. This requires Java programs to be coded as Java applets and embedded in HTML files. To test Java applets, it is recommended that a Web browser be associated with the Borland IDE. For example, if you want to associate the Netscape Navigator Web browser, choose Options, Tools. In the Tools dialog box, click the New button (see fig. B.2). The Tool Options dialog box appears (see fig. B.3).

Fig. B.2

Associating Netscape with the Borland IDE.

VI

Appendixes

> **Note**
>
> The Command Line text box has a suffix, file:///, that may vary from browser to browser. For example, in the HotJava browser the suffix is docs:///. The variable EDNAME is an internal Borland variable that is set to the name of the currently active file in a project.

Fig. B.3

Associating HTML files with Netscape in the Borland IDE.

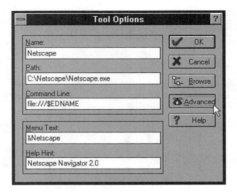

Click the <u>A</u>dvanced button to set up advanced configuration options for the Netscape browser.

Figure B.4 shows the Tool Advanced Options dialog box with advanced configuration options for setting up the Netscape browser.

Fig. B.4

Advanced configuration options for Netscape.

Notice that the <u>V</u>iewer option is set to .html:, which indicates that Netscape is now one of the viewers capable of handling HTML files. The <u>D</u>efault For text box indicates the files types for which Netscape is the default viewer or editor. I have left it blank so that the default viewer for .html files is a text editor. This means that you can use the Netscape Web browser in addition to the text editor to view or edit .html files.

Now with Netscape setup, you can select Netscape as a viewer for .html files where appropriate. We cover this later in the section "Running a Java Applet."

> **Note**
>
> Windows 95 and NT support long filenames as well as .html extensions. You can set up the
> Viewer option for .htm files in the same way.

Creating a Java Project

Now you are ready to embark on your first Java project! To create a project, choose
File, New, Project, and the New Target dialog box appears. Select Java [class] as your
Target Type and set the Project Path and Name as shown in figure B.5.

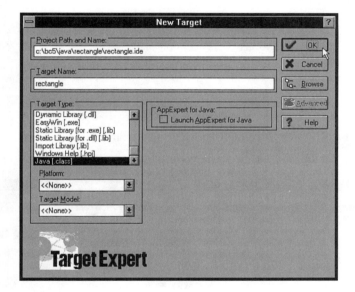

Fig. B.5

Creating a Java Project.

Notice that the Launch AppExpert for Java checkbox is unselected. This has been
done intentionally because you first explore the steps in creating a Java program without the AppExpert. You tackle the AppExpert later in the "Using AppExpert" section.
Click the OK button to create the project.

Once the project is created, the Borland IDE creates three files (or nodes) as shown in
figure B.6.

In our first project, we write a simple Java program that draws a rectangle between
two Cartesian coordinates, (x1,y1) and (x2,y2). The rectangle is drawn with a blue
frame and filled with yellow using the Java Graphics library.

Fig. B.6

Nodes created by the Borland IDE.

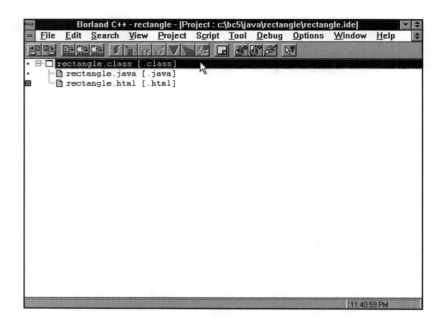

To enter the code for the project, double-click the Rectangle.java node or right-click and choose the View, Text Edit (see fig. B.7).

Fig. B.7

Editing a Java program.

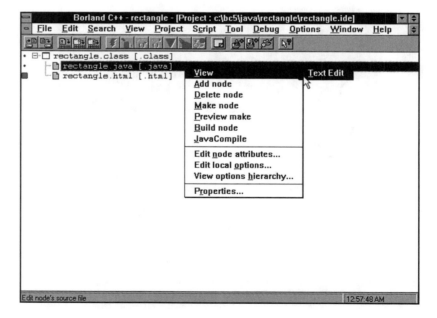

Listing B.1 shows the code for the Rectangle application.

```
// Author: Rahi Racharla
// Creates color filled rectangle for every two mouse clicks.
// calculates the height, width of the rectangle using Math class

1.   import java.applet.*;
2.   import java.awt.*;
3.   public class rectangle extends Applet
4.   {
5.     int x1, y1, x2,y2,flag;
6.     public void paint(Graphics g)
7.     {
8.       int a,b,c,d;
9.       a = Math.min(x1,x2);
10.      b = Math.min(y1,y2);
11.      c = Math.abs(x1-x2);
12.      d = Math.abs(y1-y2);
13.      g.setColor(Color.blue);
14.      g.drawRect(a,b,c,d);
15.      g.setColor(Color.yellow);
16.      g.fillRect(a+2,b+2,c-2,d-2);
17.    }
18.    public boolean mouseUp (Event evt, int x, int y)
19.    {
20.      if (flag==0)
21.      {
22.        x1 = x;
23.        y1 = y;
24.        flag = 1;
25.      } else {
26.        x2 = x;
27.        y2 = y;
28.        flag = 0;
29.        repaint();
30.      }
31.      return true;
32.    }
33. }
```

In the Rectangle application, the init function overrides the init function of the Applet class and creates a canvas for the Java applet, which has a size of 300×500. Next, it stores the coordinates for the rectangle using the coordinates of the mouse when the user clicks the mouse. When two consecutive mouse clicks are recorded, the repaint function is called. The repaint function causes the rectangle to be drawn and filled. Prior to drawing the rectangle, we use the Math class supplied by the BCAJ and utilize its abs and min functions to correctly determine the top-left coordinate and the width and height for the rectangle.

Setting Up Runtime, Compiler, and Debugger Options

Before compiling your rectangle application, you need to set up the Project options. Choose Options, Project to open the Project Options dialog box (see fig. B.8). Highlight the Java topic and observe the entries to the right of the dialog box.

The CLASSPATH text box is important. Note that we entered a CLASSPATH environment variable back when we were installing the BCAJ, which set up the default path for all system-wide Java classes. Now, if we had additional user-defined Java classes, we can specify them here.

The Output Class Base Directory text box is where the resulting compiled Java bytecodes are stored. The output files have a .class extension.

The Class Runtime Arguments text box can contain any options mentioned in table B.1. Finally, the AppAccelerator for Java Enabled checkbox is marked by default. The AppAccelerator is Borland's just-in-time compiler for Java that enables applications to run ten times faster when compared with the interpreted-mode Java.

Fig. B.8

Setting the Java project options.

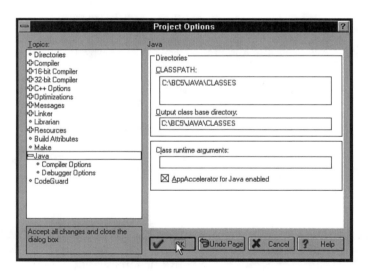

Java Runtime options are listed in table B.1.

Table B.1 Java Runtime Options	
Runtime Option	**Description**
-cs	Checks the source if it is up to date before running. If the source is out of date, it recompiles the class.
-ms x	Sets the memory allocation pool to *x* bytes. Default 3 MB, minimum is 1K.

Runtime Option	Description
-noasyncgc	Switches off asynchronous garbage collection.
-noverify	Switches off bytecode verification.
-oss x	Sets the maximum stack size for a Java thread to x bytes.
-prof	Creates a profile file for use with Java Profiler.
-ss x	Sets the maximum stack size for a 'C' thread to x bytes. Minimum is 1K.
-v	Displays a message on Stdout whenever a class is loaded.
-verbosegc	Prints a message when garbage collector frees memory
-verify	Switches on bytecode verification.
-verifyremote	Switches on bytecode verification for remote classes loaded using Class Loader.

You can set various compiler options with BCAJ in the Project Options dialog box under the Java topic as seen in figure B.9. The compiler options are listed in table B.2.

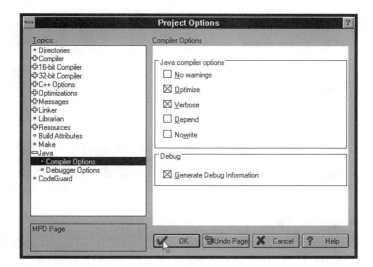

Fig. B.9

Setting Java compiler options.

Table B.2 Java Compiler Options

Compiler Option	Description
No Warnings	Suppresses compiler warnings.
Optimize	Optimizes the compiled code by inlining static, private, and final methods.
Verbose	Displays messages about source files being compiled and classes being loaded.

(continues)

Table B.2 Continued	
Compiler Option	**Description**
Depend	Compiles all dependencies of the file as well as the selected file.
Nowrite	Reads and compiles source, but writes no class files. This is useful if you want to check for compile-time errors.
Generate Debug Info	Switches on/off creation of debugging information for use by Java Debugger.

You can also set up Debugger options used with BCAJ in the Project Options dialog box under the Java topic as seen in figure B.10. You would fill the Source Path text box with the path to the Java classes that you want to debug.

Fig. B.10

Setting Java Debugger options.

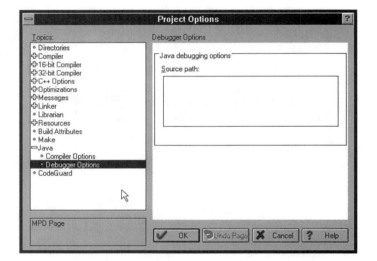

Compiling a Project

Now that you have set up the various Java runtime, compiler, and debugger options, you are ready to compile the program. To compile a single Java file, highlight the Java file, right-click, and choose JavaCompile (see fig. B.11).

If your project consists of more than one Java file, select the Build All option from the Project menu.

After compilation, a status window appears and indicates if the compilation ran successfully, as shown in figure B.12.

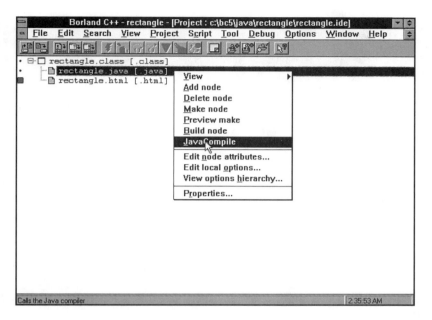

To intentionally generate a few errors, I have introduced a small typographical error from our code listed in listing B.1. I removed the semicolon at the end of line 14. These error messages can be viewed by choosing View, Message (see fig. B.13). Although the error is a simple typographical one, notice that it generates several other error messages.

Fig. B.13

The Message window showing compilation errors.

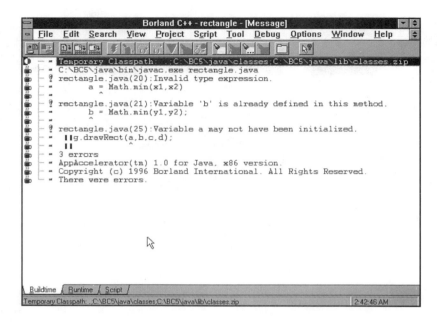

An exclamation mark "!" in the left margin indicates an error message; the line immediately following the exclamation point is the line of code that contains the error.

Debugging a Project

After having successfully compiled the Java program, you can run your Java program. However, to appreciate the Java debugger, a logical error is introduced in line 10 of listing B.1, which now reads b = min(x1,x2);.

This code passes through the compiler successfully but does not provide the desired effect of drawing the rectangle properly between the first and second Cartesian coordinates.

Note

To run the Java Debugger, you must set the compiler options to Generate Debug Information. Once debugging is complete, it is recommended that the program be recompiled with the Generate Debug Information checkbox turned off because it creates additional overhead.

To invoke the Java Debugger, select the class file, and right-click. Next, choose View, Debug Java Code option (see fig. B.14).

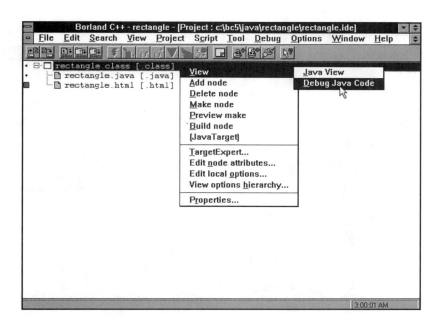

The Java Debugger has five panels (see fig. B.15):

Panel	Description
Code	Contains the source code.
Message	Displays messages about the state of your applet as you run and debug it.
Stack	Shows the methods yet to be run when you come to a breakpoint.
Current Context	Displays information about objects and their attributes when debugging a more complex applet.
Watch	Shows the values of variables that you have selected to keep track of.

To set a breakpoint, go to the appropriate line in the Code panel and click the left margin of a line with executable code. For example, you cannot set a breakpoint on a comment line.

Breakpoints are indicated by small red dots appearing on the left margin of the lines where the breakpoints are set. You can clear a breakpoint by clicking the left margin.

To watch variables, the Current Context panel displays variables that are in scope. So if you want to watch specific values, select the variables from the Current Context panel, which is organized as a hierarchical series of folders. After highlighting the variable in question, you can add it to the Watch panel by choosing Debug, Add Watch.

Fig. B.15

Setting a breakpoint.

Stack panel

Code panel

Current Context panel

Message panel

Watch panel

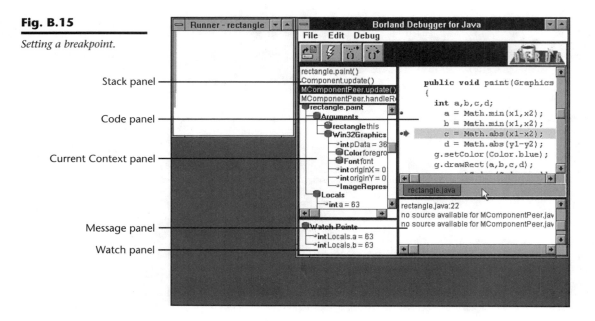

Conversely, you can remove a variable from the Watch panel by highlighting it and choosing Debug, Remove Watch.

Select Debug, Run to execute the code. Execution pauses when it hits a breakpoint. At this stage, you have three options:

- Step Into (F7)—Step into the lines of code by selecting Debug, Step Into, which executes each line of code. The active thread of execution is highlighted by a red arrow in the Code panel (refer to fig. B.15).

- Step Over (F9)—This is different from the Step Into option in that it does not trace through the details of each and every executable line. Instead, it focuses on executing the next statement at the layer at which the initial breakpoint was set. Stepping over code is achieved by selecting the Debug, Step Over.

- Jump to Next Breakpoint—To jump to the next breakpoint, select Debug, Run (or press Ctrl+F9). If there isn't any other breakpoint, execution continues.

When a running a Java program that takes parameters, the parameter values appear in the Current Context panel. You view them just like any other variable.

Running a Java Program

To run a Java program you can either run it as a standalone application using the Java View in the Borland IDE, or as an applet by creating a HTML page and invoking a Java-enabled Web Browser.

Running a Stand-Alone Java Program

To run a stand-alone Java program, you select the .class file in the project and select View, Java View from the speed menu (see fig. B.16). This invokes a viewer program called Java View, which provides an environment to execute the program.

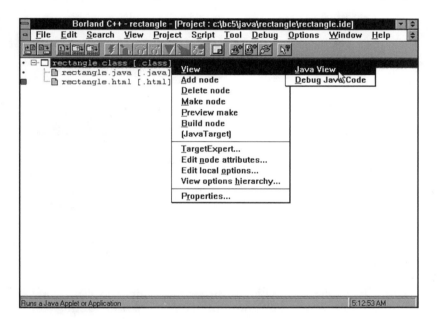

Fig. B.16

Invoking Java View.

The output of the Hello World application can be seen by choosing View, Message. In figure B.17, you will notice the output Hello World! is displayed along with other system output messages. The Message window acts as a console and displays any output directed to the standard output.

Fig. B.17

Running a stand-alone Java program.

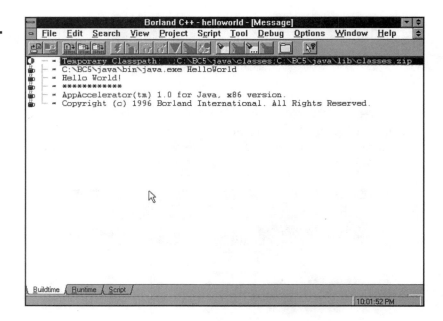

Running a Java Applet

To run a Java applet in a browser, you need to create an HTML document that has references made to the applet in question. You use the <applet> and </applet> tags to accomplish this.

The HTML document can be created in a number of ways. One method is to select the HTML file within the project and select View, Text Edit from the speed menu. This puts you into a blank file where you enter the code in the listing B.2, which shows an HTML document with an embedded call to the Rectangle applet. The Rectangle applet, Rectangle.class, must reside in the same directory as your HTML for the following example to work.

> **Note**
>
> Borland C++ 5 automatically places the compiled Java programs into the C:\Bc5\Java\Classes directory. If you do not have the codebase attribute specified in your <applet> tag (see appendix A), then you must copy the Java applets from the C:\Bc5\Java\Classes directory to the directory where your HTML source documents are stored.

Listing B.2   Lstb_2.html—HTML Document-Calling Rectangle Applet

```
<title>The Rectangle Applet</title>
<hr>
<applet code=rectangle.class width=300 height=500>
</applet>
<hr>
```

After having saved the HTML document, then you can invoke the Web browser (for example, Netscape), you configured earlier to work with your HTML files.

Figure B.18 shows the Java applet running on the Netscape Navigator 2.0 Web browser.

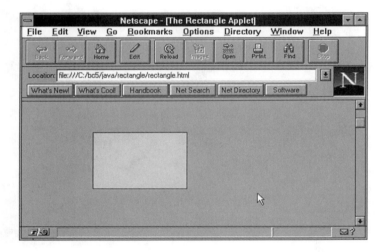

Fig. B.18

Running a Java applet in a Web browser.

Using AppExpert

What we have done thus far is to create a Java application by hand. BCAJ comes with an AppExpert tool that simplifies some of the steps in creating a Java application. AppExpert generates skeleton code depending on options you select.

When you create a new Java project, ensure that the Launch AppExpert for Java checkbox is checked as seen in figure B.19.

AppExpert generates three nodes as seen earlier in figure B.5. Borland AppExpert for Java is launched at this time (see fig. B.20).

Fig. B.19

Generating AppExpert skeleton code.

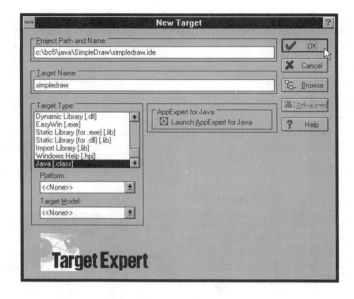

Fig. B.20

The Borland AppExpert for Java window.

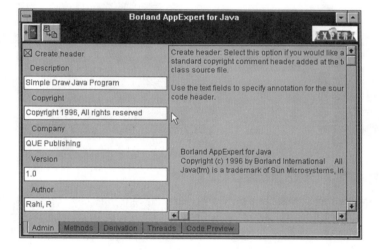

The AppExpert wizard allows you to develop Java applications quickly by providing a few user-configurable settings. These settings can be configured via a tab folder control with options such as:

- Admin—This contains header information such as the author's name, copyright information, version number, and so on.
- Methods—Creates event handlers for paint and mouse methods.

- Derivation—Indicates the class libraries to import and whether the application is run as a stand-alone program or as an applet.
- Threads—Creates stub methods for Thread support.

Once these user configurable values are entered, AppExpert generates skeleton code (see fig. B.21) that can be viewed by selecting the Code Preview tab (refer to fig. B.20).

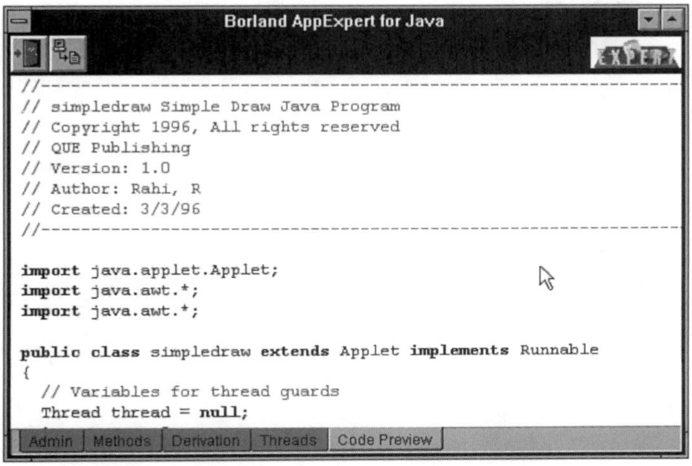

Fig. B.21

Code preview in the Borland AppExpert for Java window.

> **Caution**
>
> To save the code generated by AppExpert, do not forget to click the Save button on the AppExpert toolbar.

Listing B.3 shows the source code generated by AppExpert.

Listing B.3   LstB_3.java—Code Generated by AppExpert

```
//------------------------------------------------------------------------
----
// simpledraw Simple Draw Java Program
// Copyright 1996, All rights reserved
// QUE Publishing
// Version: 1.0
// Author: Rahi, R
// Created: 3/3/96
//------------------------------------------------------------------------
----

import java.applet.Applet;
import java.awt.*;
```

(continues)

VI

Appendixes

```java
import java.awt.*;

public class simpledraw extends Applet implements Runnable
{
  // Variables for thread guards
  Thread thread = null;
  int count = 0;


  // Class initialization code
  public void init()
  {
    startThread();

  }

  void startThread()
  {
    if (thread == null)
    {
      // Start another thread on this object);
      thread = new Thread(this);
      // Will ultimately cause a separate thread to call the run method
      thread.start();
    }
  }

  void stopThread()
  {
    if (thread != null)
    {
      thread.stop();
      thread = null;
    }
  }

  // Mouse button pressed handling code
  public boolean mouseDown(Event event, int x, int y)
  {
    // Insert your mouse code here;

    return false; // because we didn't handle the event
  }

  // This routine handles the painting
  public void paint(Graphics graphic)
  {
    // Insert your paint code here;
  }

  // Implements Runnable Interface
  public void run()
  {
    // This method is called when a new thread is started (care of Runnable
    // interface)
```

```
      // This is a waste of CPU resources
      while (true)
      {
        try
          Thread.sleep(1000);
        catch (InterruptedException e)
          ;
        repaint();
      }
    }

    // For running standalone
    public static void main(String[] argv)
    {
      // Create the frame and launch simpledraw
      Frame f = new Frame("simpledrawFrame");
      f.reshape(100, 100, 200, 100);
      f.show();

      simpledraw x = new simpledraw();
      f.add("Center", x);
      x.init();
      x.start();
    }

    // Constructor
    public  simpledraw()
    {
    }

  } // end class simpledraw
```

Using this code framework as a starting point, you can build feature-rich Java applications.

Summary

Borland has put forth a commendable effort in integrating Java into its C++ toolset and surrounding it with a usable set of tools that will invariably enhance developer productivity. Borland C++ is known for its top-notch class library, OWL, and now with Java integration, the product has made a leap toward building custom Internet-aware applications.

It will be interesting to see if future versions of Borland C++ will use Java to include support for developing visual applications that incorporate forms, dialog boxes, and controls, such as checkboxes and radio buttons. It will be intriguing how Java classes, and OWL or MFC will be made to interact with one another. Finally, many in the industry are looking for database integration for Java with popular back-ends such as Sybase, Oracle, and ODBC data sources with Borland C++ playing an integral part.

VI

Appendixes

Using the Microsoft Foundation Classes

Reusable classes provide more examples to learn from and teach from; they provide more classes to extend your toolbox and ease the burden of reimplementing. Therefore, the more reusable classes you have to draw from, the better. Reusability does require a short-term expenditure of considerable disk space. The Borland C++ 5 development suite is for serious C++ developers and requires about 175 megabytes (MB). Additionally, while building the compatible versions of the MFC classes, you will need to install Visual C++ (which you can remove after you perform the steps in this appendix). Finally, add at least 100 MB for the debug version of the recompiled MFC classes, and you are going to need about 600 MB of free disk space. Certainly no trifle, but it demonstrates that the flexibility of a wide variety of compiled classes has a substantial price.

Borland provides easy to follow steps that enable you to rebuild the Microsoft Foundation Classes (MFC) and use them with the Borland C++ 5 compiler. By the time you finish the steps outlined in this appendix, you'll have added an additional library of tools to the already expansive Borland classes. If there is some trifle you want (and happen to know exists in the MFC library), you have come to the right place.

In this appendix, we will discuss

- Installing Visual C++, Borland C++, and Tasm32
- Verifying the version of MFC to rebuild
- Executing the automated patch program and what it does
- Rebuilding the MFC libraries and dynamic link libraries
- Copying the rebuilt libraries
- Potential problems and where to look for more help

Not including the time it takes you to read this appendix, converting the MFC classes will take about two hours on a Pentium 75 (most of this is compile-time) and about an hour on a Pentium 100. The whole process, which includes installing the version of Visual C++ that contains the MFC class version you desire, installing Borland C++ 5, and patching and rebuilding, might take as much as four hours depending on your computer. Luckily, almost all of this time is moderated by the computer during installation and compiling, requiring little or no human interaction.

I assume that you have installed both Visual C++—I used version 4—and Borland C++ 5 in their respective default directories, that is, C:\Msdev for Visual C++ and C:\Bc5 for Borland C++. (You'll need to install Visual C++, which includes installing MFC libraries, to simplify the rebuilding process.) If you select different base directories for either of the C++ languages, you'll need to make the substitution when performing the conversion steps outlined in this appendix.

I suggest that you install Visual C++, not just the MFC classes. Some header files were missing and the rebuilds failed when I installed just the Microsoft Foundation Classes and not the entire product. (Of course, you can delete Visual C++ when you are finished rebuilding the libraries.) You'll need to install Borland C++ 5 and 32-bit Turbo Assembler, which comes with the Borland 5 suite.

> **Tip**
>
> After deleting the Microsoft compiler, you can still access the Microsoft MFC sample programs from the CD by looking in the \Msdev\Samples\Mfc directory.

Most of the conversion process is automated, and by using the default settings, the process works almost flawlessly the first time. (Refer to the section "Solving Common Problems.")

Whether you are actually going to use MFC version 3.2 or version 4 hardly matters. The steps are almost identical. The biggest differences will be the ultimate name of the libraries and DLLs and whether to select the MFC 3.2 or MFC 4.0 radio button in the Borland TargetExpert dialog box.

Finally, if you just want to patch and recompile the MFC libraries, the "Quick Start Reference" section at the end of the appendix has the steps summarized and you can skip right to that section of the appendix now.

Installing Microsoft Visual C++ 4

Figure C.1 shows the Visual C++ 4 Setup utility main menu. To avoid problems when rebuilding the MFC classes, use the Typical Installation and install Visual C++ 4 (which includes the MFC classes and source code).

You will need about 120 MB of hard disk space to perform a complete installation. However, when you have completed the library rebuild, you can delete most of the Visual C++ stuff. If you intend on building debug versions and tracing the MFC source code, you will need to keep the source files. (You can also copy these from the Visual C++ CD-ROM anytime.)

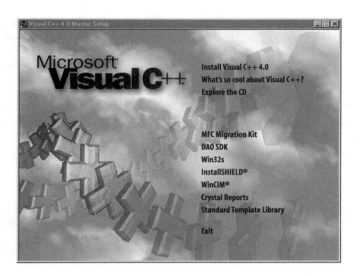

Fig. C.1

The Visual C++ 4 Setup utility.

Visual C++ 4 comes with an uninstaller. When you rebuild the MFC libraries and copy them to their final resting place (refer to the section "Building the Borland-Compatible MFC Libraries"), you can uninstall Visual C++ 4 in Windows 95. To uninstall Visual C++, from the Windows 95 Start button, choose Settings, Control Panel and run the Add/Remove Programs utility.

Installing Borland C++ 5

I performed the typical installation of Borland C++ 5 (see fig. C.2) to verify the steps described in this appendix. The full installation requires about 175 MB and installs everything you need to rebuild the MFC classes except the Setup utility (described in the next section "Running the Borland Setup Program").

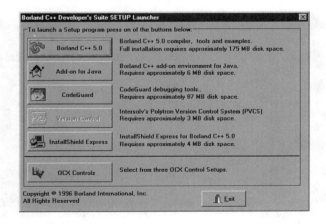

Fig. C.2

The Borland C++ Developer's Suite SETUP Launcher.

VI

Appendixes

One thing you definitely need in order to recompile the MFC libraries is the 32-bit version of Turbo Assembler (Td32.exe). The Typical Borland C++ 5 installation process also installs Turbo Assembler, which is used to compile some of the MFC source code.

Running the Borland Setup Program

You are just about ready to rebuild the MFC libraries. There are several setup programs on your Borland C++ 5 CD-ROM. The setup program you'll be using is in the \Setup\Mfc32 or \Setup\Mfc40 directory, depending on your version of MFC. (For this example, we are using MFC 4.0.)

From here on, I am describing the steps necessary to convert the MFC libraries, assuming that you are using MFC 4.0 and Visual C++ is installed in the default directory of C:\Msdev. Further, I am assuming you used the default directory for Borland C++ 5 (C:\Bc5). Before you run the Setup utility, verify the following:

- Tasm32.exe has been installed in the C:\Bc5\Bin directory
- The file C:\Msdev\Mfc\Include\Afxver_.h, line 17, has the macro definition and comment:

```
#define _MFC_VER 0x0400 // Microsoft Foundation Classes version 4.00
```

You are now ready to execute the Setup utility. Locate the correct version of the setup utility on the Borland C++ 5 CD. Depending on which version of MFC you are using, look on the Borland C++ 5 CD in D:\Setup\Mfc32 or D:\Setup\Mfc40 (where D: is the drive letter of your CD-ROM drive), and execute the program Setup.exe (see fig. C.3).

Fig. C.3

The Setup utility performs the most important steps prior to recompiling the MFC libraries.

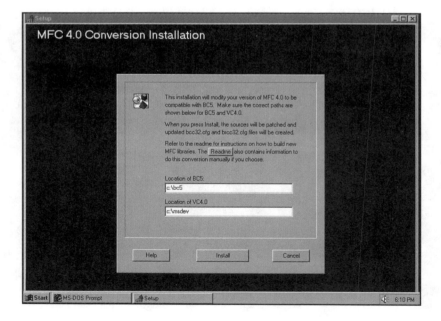

Ensure that the paths for Borland C++ and Visual C++ point to the directories containing those two products. Click the Install button. The program only takes a few seconds to execute. The Setup utility performs the following steps automatically (so you don't have to):

- Executes the Patch.exe utility, modifying several files (see the Readme.txt file in the same directory as the Setup utility for more details).

- Creates the file C:\Msdev\Mfc\Src\Bcc32.cfg, which is used by the makefiles (Borland.mak) that you will use to rebuild the MFC libraries.

- Creates the file C:\Msdev\Mfc\Src\Brcc32.cfg.

Double-check that the two configuration files in the second and third steps were created. Listing C.1 shows the Bcc32.cfg file.

> **Listing C.1 Bcc32.cfg—File Automatically Created When You Run the Setup Utility**

```
-I..\include;c:\bc5\include;c:\msdev\include
-Ic:\bc5\include
-Ic:\msdev\include
-Lc:\bc5\lib
-D_MSC_VER=900
-D_WINDOWS
-D_WCHAR_T_DEFINED
-D_AFX_PORTABLE
-D_AFX_NOFORCE_LIBS
-D_CRT_PORTABLE
-D_AFX_NO_DEBUG_CRT
-DDllMain=DllEntryPoint
```

The file Brcc32.cfg contains one line of text:

```
/i..\include;c:\bc5\include;c:\msdev\include
```

If either of these files were not created, you can use a text editor to manually create them. This part of the process seems to work flawlessly, so you shouldn't have any problems. You do want to ensure that lines 2, 3, and 4 of the file Bcc32.cfg (in listing C.1) and line 1 above of the file Brcc32.cfg do contain the correct directories for Visual C++ 4 and Borland C++ 5.

Building the Borland-Compatible MFC Libraries

Now you are ready to build the *.lib files. The non-debug versions of these files are Bfc40.lib, Nafxcw.lib, and Bfcs40.lib; these files are placed in the directory C:\Msdev\Mfc\Lib\Borland when they are finished compiling. The non-debug version requires about 5 MB of disk space, but the debug versions of these libraries—which have a d-suffix, so the debug version of Bfc40.lib is Bfc40d.lib—require a whopping 87 MB of disk space.

To build the three library files, make the current directory C:\Msdev\Mfc\Src, where C:\Msdev is the actual location where you install Visual C++ 4. Assuming that the path C:\Bc5\Bin is in your system path—it should be if you properly installed Borland C++ 5—execute the following command from DOS:

```
make -fborland.mak DEBUG=0
```

to build the non-debug libraries

Execute

```
make -fborland.mak
```

to build the libraries with debug code.

> **Note**
>
> There is no space between the -f switch and the makefile name, borland.mak.

If you encounter any errors while building the .lib files, see the section "Solving Common Problems."

Now that you have successfully built the library files, you need to copy them to the C:\Bc5\Lib directory. Type in the following command at the DOS prompt:

```
move c:\msdev\mfc\lib\borland\*.lib c:\bc5\lib
```

Next, you'll build the dynamic link libraries and move those to the C:\Windows\System directory, and then you'll be ready to try some example programs.

Building the Borland-Compatible MFC DLLs

This section describes how to build both the debug and non-debug versions of the Bfc40.dll. According to the Readme.txt file (included on the Borland C++ 5 CD and used as the resource for this appendix), building the non-debug .dll actually builds one .dll, Bfc40.dll. But, if you want the debug .dll, the .dlls are split into separate files.

Building the "monolithic," single .dll, run make from the DOS prompt with the following syntax:

```
make -fbfcdll.mak DEBUG=0 LIBNAME=BFC40
```

If you want the debug code included in the .dlls, you'll have to run make for several makefiles. Here is the list of commands to run at the DOS prompt:

```
make -fbfcdll.mak LIBNAME=BFC40D

make -fbfcole.mak LIBNAME=BFCO40
```

```
make -fbfcdb.mak LIBNAME=BFCD40

make -fbfcnet.mak LIBNAME=BFCN40
```

> **Note**
>
> By the way, even though you are running make from the DOS command line, you are using the new 32-bit Borland compiler.

The output from these makefiles—the library .dll names specified after LIBNAME—will be written to the C:\Msdev\Mfc\Src directory. Move them from there to the C:\Windows\System directory. You are now ready to try an example.

Working through an MFC Example Program

Using the MFC tools is as easy as loading an example program in the Borland C++ 5 IDE and executing it.

If the sample MFC files were not installed, you can copy them manually from the Visual C++ CD to the directory in step 3 below. The following steps create a project and build Hello.exe:

1. Run the Borland IDE.

2. Choose File, New, Project.

3. Select the file C:\Msdev\Samples\Mfc\General\Hello.cpp and name the project Hello.ide (as show in fig. C.4). The MFC samples will not contain Borland project (*.ide) files.

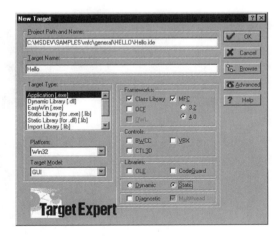

Fig. C.4

The figure shows the correct settings to execute the Hello.ide MFC project.

VI

Appendixes

4. In the TargetExpert dialog box, deselect OWL, select MFC, and select the version number (3.2 or 4).

5. Select the Static radio button.

6. Click OK.

7. Delete the *.def file in the Project window.

8. Choose Options, Project and then make sure the Directories topic is highlighted (see fig. C.5) and add **C:\Msdev\Include;C:\MsDev\Mfc\Include** to the Include path statement.

9. Click OK.

10. Choose Project, Build All and the program is ready to run.

Fig. C.5

Don't forget to add the Visual C++ include directories to the Include path in the IDE (as shown).

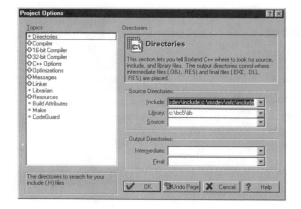

The output from the Hello.exe sample program is shown in figure C.6. (I'm sure MFC classes will be a welcome addition for many programmers.)

Fig. C.6

This is the output from the Hello.exe program, which is a variation of the classic "Hello, World!" program.

The next section discusses potential problems you may have encountered while rebuilding the MFC libraries.

Solving Common Problems

This section contains some problems you may have encountered (and work-arounds) when trying to rebuild the MFC libraries. Refer to table C.1 for problems and solutions.

Table C.1   Problems and Work-Arounds

Problem	Solution
Compile error file Eh.h not found.	The surest solution is to completely install Visual C++ before rebuilding the libraries.
File Afxwin.h file not found. C:\Msdev	Modify the Options, Project, Directories Include path to include the C:\Msdev\Include and directories, where C:\Msdev\Mfc\Include is the directory where you installed Visual C++.
Warnings received during library builds.	Contact Borland technical support.
Can't find example MFC programs.	Look on the Visual C++ CD in \Msdev\Samples\Mfc. (If they were not installed you can simply copy them to your hard drive.)
Can't find the correct readme files.	Check the Borland C++ 5 CD in the directories \Setup\Mfc32 or \Setup\Mfc40, depending on the version of Visual C++ you installed.
Can't find the patch program.	The program Patch.exe and Setup.exe are located on the Borland C++ 5 CD in both \Setup\Mfc32 and \Setup\Mfc40 directories. (Use the one appropriate for your version of Visual C++.)

The Microsoft Foundation Classes are classes, like any others, written in C++. If you have mastered the techniques described in this book and have tried some example programs too, all that's left is to learn the names of the classes in MFC and the interface functions (those in the public and protected sections of the classes). You can then use these classes as easily as any others.

Most of the information in this appendix was derived from the \Setup\Mfc32\ Readme.txt files and \Setup\Mfc40\Readme.txt located on the Borland C++ 5 CD. The files are almost identical and contain very little information that is not found here. If you are having problems, these files will offer an alternate perspective.

VI

Appendixes

Summary

This appendix was designed for and describes all of the steps necessary to rebuild (Borland calls it patching) the MFC libraries so you can easily use them with the Borland 5 compiler.

To recap, here is a down-and-dirty list of steps that will build the non-debug version of the MFC 4.0 libraries:

1. Install Borland C++ 5.

2. Install Visual C++ 4 (not just the MFC classes).

3. Make sure Tasm32.exe is in the \Bc5\Bin directory.

4. On the Borland C++ 5 CD, execute the \Setup\Mfc40\Setup.exe program. (Use \Setup\Mfc32\Setup.exe for Visual C++ 3.2.)

5. In the directory C:\MsDev\Mfc\Src, at the DOS prompt, type `make -fborland.mak DEBUG=0`.

6. Copy all of the library files (from step 5) from C:\Msdev\Mfc\Lib\Borland*.Lib to C:\Bc5\Lib.

7. In the directory C:\Msdev\Mfc\Src, at the DOS prompt, run `make -fbfcdll.mak DEBUG=0 LIBNAME=BFC40`.

8. Copy the .dll C:\Msdev\Mfc\SrcBfc40.dll to the C:\Windows\System directory.

9. Load a sample MFC program (included with Visual C++) into a new project. In the TargetExpert dialog box, select the following: the MFC check box, the radio button 4.0 and Static. Click OK.

10. Modify the Include path (by choosing Options, Project, Directories) to include C:\Msdev\Include and C:\Msdev\Mfc\Include, and then compile.

These steps provide a complete overview of what's necessary to use MFC and exactly what's discussed in this appendix.

Index

A V I A C O M   S E R V I C - E

The Information SuperLibrary™

Bookstore   **Search**   **What's New**   **Reference**   **Software**   **Newsletter**   **Company Overviews**

Yellow Pages   **Internet Starter Kit**   **HTML Workshop**   **Win a Free T-Shirt!**   **Macmillan Computer Publishing**   **Site Map**   **Talk to Us**

CHECK OUT THE BOOKS IN THIS LIBRARY.

You'll find thousands of shareware files and over 1600 computer books designed for both technowizards and technophobes. You can browse through 700 sample chapters, get the latest news on the Net, and find just about anything using our massive search directories.

All Macmillan Computer Publishing books are available at your local bookstore.

We're open 24-hours a day, 365 days a year.

You don't need a card.

We don't charge fines.

And you can be as **LOUD** as you want.

The Information SuperLibrary

http://www.mcp.com/mcp/   ftp.mcp.com

Complete and Return this Card for a *FREE* Computer Book Catalog

Thank you for purchasing this book! You have purchased a superior computer book written expressly for your needs. To continue to provide the kind of up-to-date, pertinent coverage you've come to expect from us, we need to hear from you. Please take a minute to complete and return this self-addressed, postage-paid form. In return, we'll send you a free catalog of all our computer books on topics ranging from word processing to programming and the internet.

Mr. ☐   Mrs. ☐   Ms. ☐   Dr. ☐

Name (first) ☐☐☐☐☐☐☐☐☐☐☐   (M.I.) ☐   (last) ☐☐☐☐☐☐☐☐☐☐☐☐☐☐☐☐☐

Address ☐☐☐☐☐☐☐☐☐☐☐☐☐☐☐☐☐☐☐☐☐☐☐☐☐☐☐☐☐☐☐

☐☐☐☐☐☐☐☐☐☐☐☐☐☐☐☐☐☐☐☐☐☐☐☐☐☐☐☐☐☐☐

City ☐☐☐☐☐☐☐☐☐☐☐☐☐☐☐☐☐☐   State ☐☐   Zip ☐☐☐☐☐ ☐☐☐☐

Phone ☐☐☐ ☐☐☐ ☐☐☐☐   Fax ☐☐☐ ☐☐☐ ☐☐☐☐

Company Name ☐☐☐☐☐☐☐☐☐☐☐☐☐☐☐☐☐☐☐☐☐☐☐☐☐☐☐

E-mail address ☐☐☐☐☐☐☐☐☐☐☐☐☐☐☐☐☐☐☐☐☐☐☐☐☐☐☐

1. Please check at least (3) influencing factors for purchasing this book.

Front or back cover information on book .... ☐
Special approach to the content .... ☐
Completeness of content .... ☐
Author's reputation .... ☐
Publisher's reputation .... ☐
Book cover design or layout .... ☐
Index or table of contents of book .... ☐
Price of book .... ☐
Special effects, graphics, illustrations .... ☐
Other (Please specify): _____ ☐

2. How did you first learn about this book?

Saw in Macmillan Computer Publishing catalog .... ☐
Recommended by store personnel .... ☐
Saw the book on bookshelf at store .... ☐
Recommended by a friend .... ☐
Received advertisement in the mail .... ☐
Saw an advertisement in: _____ ☐
Read book review in: _____ ☐
Other (Please specify): _____ ☐

3. How many computer books have you purchased in the last six months?

This book only .... ☐   3 to 5 books .... ☐
2 books .... ☐   More than 5 .... ☐

4. Where did you purchase this book?

Bookstore .... ☐
Computer Store .... ☐
Consumer Electronics Store .... ☐
Department Store .... ☐
Office Club .... ☐
Warehouse Club .... ☐
Mail Order .... ☐
Direct from Publisher .... ☐
Internet site .... ☐
Other (Please specify): _____ ☐

5. How long have you been using a computer?

☐ Less than 6 months   ☐ 6 months to a year
☐ 1 to 3 years   ☐ More than 3 years

6. What is your level of experience with personal computers and with the subject of this book?

	With PCs	With subject of book
New	☐	☐
Casual	☐	☐
Accomplished	☐	☐
Expert	☐	☐

Source Code ISBN: 0-7897-0284-3

7. Which of the following best describes your job title?

Administrative Assistant ☐
Coordinator ☐
Manager/Supervisor ☐
Director ☐
Vice President ☐
President/CEO/COO ☐
Lawyer/Doctor/Medical Professional ☐
Teacher/Educator/Trainer ☐
Engineer/Technician ☐
Consultant ☐
Not employed/Student/Retired ☐
Other (Please specify): _____ ☐

8. Which of the following best describes the area of the company your job title falls under?

Accounting ☐
Engineering ☐
Manufacturing ☐
Operations ☐
Marketing ☐
Sales ☐
Other (Please specify): _____ ☐

9. What is your age?

Under 20 ☐
21-29 ☐
30-39 ☐
40-49 ☐
50-59 ☐
60-over ☐

10. Are you:

Male ☐
Female ☐

11. Which computer publications do you read regularly? (Please list)

_____
_____
_____
_____
_____
_____
_____
_____
_____

Comments: _____
_____
_____

Fold here and scotch-tape to mail.

FIRST-CLASS MAIL PERMIT NO. 9918 INDIANAPOLIS IN

POSTAGE WILL BE PAID BY THE ADDRESSEE

ATTN MARKETING
MACMILLAN COMPUTER PUBLISHING
MACMILLAN PUBLISHING USA
201 W 103RD ST
INDIANAPOLIS IN 46290-9042

NO POSTAGE
NECESSARY
IF MAILED
IN THE
UNITED STATES

Licensing Agreement

The patch, \Patch\Bc50p1.zip, is to be used by licensed Borland C++ users, and, as such, the user is subject to the terms of the license agreement for Borland C++. This patch makes a number of modifications to your Borland C++ 5.0 installation. For details on the specific problems it solves, refer to the file B50p1.txt included in this archive. Install this patch using Patch.exe version 3.10, available on this book's CD-ROM in the \Patch directory or on your Borland C++ 5.0 CD-ROM in the \Setup\Mfc32 directory.